Under the Editorship of
EDWARD MCCHESNEY SAIT
POMONA COLLEGE

FROM
Luther to Hitler

THE HISTORY OF FASCIST-NAZI
POLITICAL PHILOSOPHY

William Montgomery McGovern

PROFESSOR OF POLITICAL SCIENCE
NORTHWESTERN UNIVERSITY

VISITING LECTURER ON GOVERNMENT
HARVARD UNIVERSITY

HOUGHTON MIFFLIN COMPANY

𝕿𝖍𝖊 𝕽𝖎𝖛𝖊𝖗𝖘𝖎𝖉𝖊 𝕻𝖗𝖊𝖘𝖘 𝕮𝖆𝖒𝖇𝖗𝖎𝖉𝖌𝖊

The Riverside Press

CAMBRIDGE · MASSACHUSETTS

PRINTED IN THE U.S.A.

EDITOR'S INTRODUCTION

IDEAS, as well as men, may have a life that is worth telling about. Professor McGovern gives us here a unique biographical study. Through a period of four centuries he has traced the growth of certain doctrines which, according to official apologists, provide a foundation for the Fascist and Nazi regimes. Such a biography of ideas possesses great value as showing persistent continuity, in spite of all lapses and modifications; it also makes a more dramatic appeal because of its bearing upon the political phenomena of today.

The relation between philosophical doctrines and human conduct will, of course, always be debatable. Does theory determine practice, or does practice determine theory? Has some pre-existing theory been seized upon to justify a course of action and then erroneously assumed to be the reason for such action — *post hoc, ergo propter hoc?* Whatever view we take, Doctor McGovern's contribution has great significance. It is significant, first of all, because Fascists and Nazis alike profess to have a philosophical basis for their political systems; and, secondly, because the fate of democracy elsewhere may be involved. Not long ago men spoke of democracy as permanent and as destined to encompass the whole world. Its onward march was "irresistible"; to discuss the comparative merits of other forms of government would be a waste of time; once having acquired control, the people would never relinquish it. This was the language commonly employed twenty years ago and even more recently. Then came the shock — the recurrence of despotism, the establishment of the so-called dictatorships. Whether or not the explanation of this *débâcle* lies in the domain of theory, what Professor McGovern tells us about the Italian and German ideologies and their genetic background has wider implications. Democracy appears to be on the defensive; and, in combating the enemy, it should know something about the philosophical weapons that are being used against it.

In addition to its timeliness, this book has several other claims to distinction. Professor McGovern has the gift of making obscure and recondite philosophers, like Hegel and Green, comprehensible to the layman; and his scholarly equipment will save him from the accusation of being clear at the expense of accuracy. He does not write with the pedantry that so often afflicts the academic mind when it enters the region of philosophy. His exposition is never labored or abstruse. Instead of contenting himself with dull abstracts and sticking them away in appropriate pigeonholes, he constantly illuminates one point of view by means of contrast with or analogy to another. By this method the reader is enabled to get hold of nice shades and fine distinctions. He cannot but feel grateful to an expositor who, being an expert, can shed so clear a light on murky places.

Doctor McGovern is a man of varied accomplishments. In some quarters he may be best known as an anthropologist and explorer. His interest in these fields would be suggested by the content of his numerous books and by the legend of the shako and worm-eaten sheepskin coat (tailored in Tibet) which he is supposed to wear when the snow flies in Chicago. But he has not turned from anthropology for the moment to dabble as an amateur in political thought. He ranks as an authority in this field. He studied philosophy at Oxford (Ph.D., 1922), Berlin, and the Sorbonne; and he teaches political theory at Northwestern regularly, sometimes at Harvard. It is his familiarity with the philosophers that enables him to deal with them so freely and cogently.

There is unity in the theme. We encounter a succession of philosophers from the Reformation down. But the materials are not heterogeneous, not a mere potpourri of disconnected doctrines. The author is laying before us the development of certain ideas that do form parts of a common design. Far from confusing us in a maze of incongruous subtleties, he is making plain some aspects of current practical politics. Nevertheless, he has not confined himself narrowly to the specific theme — the background of Fascist and Nazi ideologies. Strict adherence to the straight line would have made the book less useful and less interesting. About any theorist the student will be curious to know something besides his attitude toward authoritarianism and toward what Doctor McGovern calls etatism (the subordination of the individual to the state). A tendency to include other phases of thought that are not altogether apposite to the main purpose gives the book additional value; for it is advisable to present the contribution of each theorist as a whole, without distorting it by overemphasis upon a single point. But what of the liberals, the opponents of authoritarianism and etatism? They have not been ignored. John Locke, for example, looms large in this discussion; for, in the growth of the absolutist tradition, his powerful arguments against it could not be ignored.

Professor McGovern's text does not follow the conventional pattern. He covers a long period, but concentrates upon tracing one stream of thought to its culmination in the political systems of Mussolini and

Hitler. He describes the course of the stream mainly in his own language, but he adds vividness by giving many excerpts from the original sources, as an explorer in central Africa or the basin of the Amazon would have recourse to maps and photographs. The book is admirably suited to form the basis of a half-year course either in philosophy or in government; and, because it is so intimately related to contemporary problems, both teachers and students will be glad to use it as a substitute for traditional courses. Indeed, its appeal extends beyond college gates. At the present time eyes are focused upon Rome and Berlin, curious to discover what lies behind the vagaries of the Axis powers. Professor McGovern himself has such clear vision that he makes others see what would escape their attention otherwise. The general reader, the man who has never opened a philosophical treatise or heard a lecture on philosophy, will find this book much to his taste; for so lucidly are the thinkers interpreted that it can be understood easily without any previous training.

EDWARD McCHESNEY SAIT

ACKNOWLEDGMENTS

IN WRITING and in revising this book I have been greatly aided by the advice and assistance of many persons. I owe an especial debt of gratitude to the following persons: Professor E. M. Sait of Pomona College; Professors A. R. Hatton, K. W. Colegrove, E. Schaub, D. T. Howard, and H. Simon of Northwestern University; Professors A. N. Holcombe, H. Bruening, C. H. McIlwain, and Crane Brinton, and Doctor George Pettee of Harvard University. Each of these persons has read through one or more sections of the book. I am also deeply grateful to Mr. H. G. Sonthoff for many valuable suggestions and for his work in preparing the index. I have profited greatly by the criticisms made by these and other persons; it should be noted, however, that I alone am responsible for the opinions expressed.

WILLIAM M. McGOVERN

CAMBRIDGE, MASSACHUSETTS

CONTENTS

Introduction

THE LIBERAL AND THE FASCIST TRADITIONS
A STUDY IN CONTRASTS

CHAPTER I

The Liberal and the Fascist Tradition: A Study in Contrasts

To THE average Englishman, Frenchman, or American who was alive and interested in politics about the year 1912 the world seemed comparatively simple. He was not only convinced that such things as democracy, majority rule, and representative government were excellent institutions; he was also firm in the belief that sooner or later these institutions were bound to prevail all over the world.

Such a person was aware that such things as dictatorship, despotism, or even absolute monarchy continued to prevail in "backward countries," but it seemed clear that it was only a matter of time and of increasing civilization for these "relics of the dark ages" to be swept away. The tendency towards democracy and all the things which go with democracy was held to be inevitable. It was believed that England, France, and America were the most democratic merely because they were the most advanced countries. It was thought that such countries as Germany or Japan were politically somewhat retarded, but even in these regions there were strong democratic movements, and experts were willing to prophesy that within a few years the vestiges of despotic power which still prevailed would disappear.

Elsewhere, in the very homelands of conservatism and of autocracy there seemed to be portents of a better day. In 1905 the Russian Czar had been forced to grant his subjects a popularly elected Duma. In 1906 a revolution forced the Shah of Persia to bestow upon the Persians a written constitution, a document which curbed many of his former absolute powers. In 1908 a similar revolution took place in Turkey as a result of which effective rulership was transferred from the Sultan to the Committee of Union and Progress, which was regarded as the agent of the Turkish people. It was generally admitted that many of the so-called republics in Latin America were merely veiled dictatorships, but even in this area there seemed to be portents that the dawn of true democracy was not far away. The Mexican Revolution of 1910 and the subsequent overthrow of the Dictator Diaz were widely hailed as the first step in the Spanish-American march towards political liberalism. In 1911 the age-old monarchy in China was overthrown, and in its place there was established a republic modeled, on paper, after the most approved European and American patterns. The Englishmen, Frenchmen, and Americans of that generation read about these events in their newspapers and smiled approvingly and hopefully. Surely if Persia and Turkey and China were going democratic there was no final hope for despotism in any corner of the world.

The World War of 1914–1918 came as a great shock to many persons who had looked forward to the peaceful progress and spread of democratic ideals, but before long most Englishmen and Frenchmen came to look upon this conflict as a sort of necessary crusade of the forward-looking democratic powers against the backward-looking despotic powers. Even in America the war came to be regarded, not as a mere battle between England or France and Germany, but as a battle between democracy, liberalism, and freedom on the one side, and absolutism, tyranny, and divine right of kings on the other. It was largely because of this belief that America eventually entered the war herself. Was it not her duty, as a democratic power, to aid in "Making the World Safe for Democracy"? It was widely felt that if the "Kaiserism" of Germany were once overthrown, there would be and could be no further barriers to the peaceful and world-wide development of democratic institutions to the end of time.

How charming and attractive were all these beliefs and hopes and aspirations — and yet how childish do they appear in the light of subsequent events. The democratic powers after much tribulation were indeed triumphant in battle. Not only was Germany defeated, but the German monarchy with its autocratic traditions was overthrown, and a democratically organized republic took its place. The era of despotism appeared to be over and yet — the millennium of liberalism failed to arrive. Even before the war was over, the Czarist regime in Russia was overthrown, but in its place, after a few months of turmoil, there arose, not a liberal republic for which so many democratically inclined persons had hoped, but a new type of dictatorship, a dictatorship of the proletariate in theory, a dictatorship of a small group of radical politicians in fact. In 1922 liberalism received another blow. Italy had for many decades most of the advantages and all the disadvantages of representative and parliamentary government. But in the economic and political chaos which followed the World War the machinery of government practically collapsed, and with surprisingly little effort Mussolini was able to impose the Fascist type of dictatorship upon the Italian kingdom. Not long afterwards a tendency towards dictatorial rule appeared in a number of other countries. In Turkey the ancient Sultanate was, to be sure, overthrown, but in its place there arose the strong one-man rule of Mustafa Kemal Ataturk who, under the title of President, exercised as rigid and autocratic control as any of the Khalifs in former times. In 1925 a similar transformation took place in Persia. The old dynasty was deposed, but its place was taken by a new dynasty, and the new Shah, Riza Pahlavi, has as absolute power over his Iranian subjects as has Mussolini over the Italians. In China the attempt to establish a republic along American lines failed miserably, and in the period 1926–1928 supreme power over the Chinese state fell into the hands of a single political party, the Kuomintang, and more especially into the hands of one or two men, such as Chiang Kai-shek, who controlled this party. In 1931 the democratic movement, which had long played an important part in Japanese politics, began to subside. As time went on, the military leaders, men violently opposed to all forms of parliamentary government, were able to secure ever more effective control over the organs of the state, and today the Japanese system of government differs from the European dictatorships only in that in Japan supreme power rests, not with a single individual, but with a small group of persons, most of them high ranking officers of the armed forces.

In 1933 the cause of liberalism received another staggering blow when for all practical purposes the German Republic ceased to exist, its place taken by the Hitler *Reich*. To many liberals the defection of Germany from the liberal movement seemed more serious than any of the earlier developments elsewhere. After all, such persons argued, Turkey and Persia, even China, Japan, and Italy were from the political and economic point of view relatively backward countries. Perhaps their progress towards democracy had been too rapid. Perhaps they needed a brief breathing spell, a despotic interlude, before again trying to march to the ultimate liberal goal. But when Germany, one of the most modern and progressive countries, turned its back on the liberal tradition and embraced National Socialism, it seemed as if something must be wrong with the whole theory of the inevitable tendency towards democratic government.

If the newly arisen dictators had been content to crush liberalism within the borders of their own countries it would have been bad enough. But this was not all. Before long these same dictators began to manifest a passionate desire to conquer and destroy their neighbors, more especially those neighbors which "were weak and effete" enough to re-tain democratic regimes. The Japanese aggression in Manchuria and China, the Italian conquest of Ethiopia and Albania, were shocking enough to the liberal world which had gradually come to adopt a rather rigid code of international morality, but at least neither Ethiopia nor Albania was democratic, and Japan could make use of the excuse that Manchuria was bandit-infested and suffered from chronic misgovern-ment. Far more startling was the forcible annexation of Austria and the crushing of Czechoslovakia, the latter especially being a country genu-inely devoted to liberal ideals. Then came the blood and slaughter of World War II. Germany set about crushing, in rapid succession, Po-land, Denmark, Norway, Holland, and Belgium, and was able to make France pathetically impotent. The devotion of Poland to the liberal cause is open to question, but there can be no doubt that the govern-ments of the other countries were genuinely democratic in character. Nor can there be any doubt that, if Germany prevails, these countries will be forced to adopt some form of dictatorial regime.

Such being the situation, it is obvious that the open-minded student of present-day politics, especially if he happens to be an Englishman or an American, is forced to adopt a very different attitude towards politi-cal problems and political tendencies from that of his predecessor three or four decades ago. He must face the fact that at present there is no in-evitable and world-wide tendency towards the liberalizing of govern-mental institutions. He must face the fact that if existing liberal sys-tems of government are to be preserved it is necessary that the believers in liberalism be prepared to struggle and, if need be, to fight for their preservation. The battle for liberalism is far from being lost, but for the moment liberalism is definitely on the defensive and is in urgent need of support from groups which formerly were content to let political problems alone or to drift aimlessly with the prevailing political tide.

In this connection it is well to stress the fact that neither Fascism nor National Socialism is new or casual or an ephemeral movement. Both are the products of a long, slowly developing but deep-rooted tradition. This fact is of major importance. Many persons have been foolish enough to imagine that Fascism and National Socialism are the acci-dental products of temporary economic upsets in Italy and Germany, and that if once these economic dislocations were adjusted it would be easy for both countries to re-establish liberal regimes. Other persons are apt to think that the establishment of the Fascist and Nazi dictator-ships was due merely to the power and prestige secured by such leaders as Mussolini and Hitler, and that were these leaders to be removed, it would be comparatively simple to restore liberal institutions. To the present writer it appears that both these ideas are completely fallacious. It is undoubtedly true that the rise of Fascism and National Socialism was greatly aided by the economic stress which existed in Italy in 1922 and in Germany in 1933, but it is also true that this economic stress would not have permitted the establishment on a permanent basis of the Fascist and Nazi regimes if there had not existed a widespread and deep-rooted feeling in both countries that liberal institutions were essentially pernicious; and this feeling, in turn, can be traced back to a political tradition and to a political philosophy which had been slowly emerging and crystallizing throughout the nineteenth century and during the early years of the twentieth century.

It is obvious that the Fascist and Nazi movements owe much of their success to the fact that they were led by such outstanding personalities as Mussolini and Hitler, but it is equally true that the movements themselves are of even greater importance and significance than the individual leaders. Wherever there is widespread belief that dictatorship is the best form of government, it is not difficult to find persons to fill the office of dictator; and wherever there is a widespread dislike of dictatorship, it is difficult, if not impossible, for such persons as Mussolini or Hitler to seize the reins of power. In other words, the political philosophy which dominates the general public of a given country is the major factor which determines whether or not a would-be dictator is able to secure power. Mussolini and Hitler were successful only because of the gradual spread and wide acceptance of a political tradition which despised democracy and looked forward to dictatorial control. It is tragic but true that the removal of the present leaders would not result in the destruction of the Fascist and Nazi regimes as long as large numbers of the Italian and German peoples accept the basic tenets of the Fascist and Nazi ideologies. Many of the doctrines of both regimes were formulated and began to infiltrate into the populace long before Mussolini and Hitler were born. We must beware lest they persist and retain powerful support long after Mussolini and Hitler are dead.

The importance of what we may call the Fascist-Nazi tradition (we must use this name, although the tradition originated long before the establishment of Fascist and Nazi parties) becomes obvious when we realize that neither Mussolini nor Hitler is the creator of a new political philosophy Both men are merely the popularizers of doctrines which began four centuries ago, which slowly developed and were transformed during the subsequent period, and which received their final formulation during the opening years of the twentieth century. If we would seek to understand the true nature of Fascism and National Socialism, therefore, we cannot be content to study merely the speeches and writings of Mussolini or Hitler and their immediate followers, but must strive to understand the underlying political philosophy of which the Fascist and Nazi doctrines are concrete expressions. More especially is this important because of the fact that if the Fascist and Nazi movements persist and retain their political power, in all probability they will not only seek to carry out the official program formulated by their present leaders, but will also seek to apply many ideas which, though embodied in the general political tradition of which the Fascist and Nazi movements are merely constituent parts, have not as yet been expressly formulated by either the Fascist or Nazi leaders. A study of this tradition should not only, therefore, give us an insight into the past and present significance of the Fascist and Nazi regimes; it should also aid us in trying to discover the line of development which these regimes are likely to take in the future.

It seems obvious that there is now going on a great world conflict between the liberal movement on the one side and the movement which may be called Fascist-Nazi on the other. This conflict is of importance not only for the development of political institutions on the continent of Europe, but also for the political future of all other portions of the world. If Germany and Italy are successful in Europe, more especially as they are now openly allied with Japan, it seems certain that they can and will impose governmental systems similar to their own upon all portions of Europe and Asia. The repercussions of such an event upon the Western Hemisphere are bound to be enormous.

Quite apart from the possibility that the totalitarian powers may seek by economic, diplomatic, and military means to bring some, if not all, of the American countries within their orbit, a smashing Fascist-Nazi victory in Europe would necessarily be followed by the rise of powerful groups inside the Americas determined to overthrow the existing liberal institutions in this area and to substitute for them institutions modeled upon the Fascist or Nazi patterns. Political doctrines, like children's diseases, are remarkably contagious, especially when they are associated with an air of glory as the result of diplomatic and military success. Already we hear in England and in America a number of voices, especially among members of the younger generation, which murmur,

"Surely if the German regime has proved itself so efficient and so successful, we ought to adopt some of the essential features of this regime, so that we too can be efficient and successful." If the military triumph of Germany should prove permanent, it is certain that these voices will grow in number and in volume.

We are now acutely aware that the liberals of a generation or two ago were completely wrong when they supposed that there is an inevitable and constant trend towards liberal institutions. At the same time we must be careful not to adopt the equally fallacious doctrine that there is now a constant and inevitable trend towards anti-liberal institutions, and that sooner or later we must all, willy-nilly, accept a Fascist or semi-Fascist system of government. A study of the political history of the world from classical times to the present shows that at certain times and certain places there has existed for a considerable period a strong trend towards the establishment of free and democratic institutions. At other times and at other places there has existed an equally strong tendency to depart from or to suppress such institutions. But at no time has such a tendency been constant or even long-enduring, and in no case has such a tendency been inevitable or unavoidable. History shows that at any time a determined group of persons, dominated by a firm and zealous political faith, have been able to check and even reverse such a tendency. At a time when the world seemed to be dominated by liberal ideology, a comparatively small group of Fascists and Nazis were able to destroy the dominance of liberal ideas in their respective countries. What was true of the Fascists and the Nazis is equally true of the liberals today. At a time when Fascist ideology appears to be sweeping the world it is perfectly possible for a determined group of liberals to stem this tide, directly in their own country, and indirectly throughout the world.

In other words, it is up to the present-day Englishman and to the present-day American to decide whether England and America are to go Fascist or are to remain liberal. Upon his beliefs and upon his actions depend the political future of the Anglo-Saxon world. But in making this decision it is above all imperative that he have a clear understanding of just what liberalism stands for and just what Fascism and National Socialism stand for. This is a matter of really great importance. Only too often do we find that persons who claim to be passionately in favor of liberalism and violently opposed to Fascism and National Socialism have only the haziest notions as to the real meaning of these three movements. In like manner, we find that many persons who are eager to defend the actions of Mussolini and Hitler are extremely vague if asked to define just what basic principles their heroes advocate.

More especially is it essential that those who call themselves liberals make a serious study of this problem. In the Anglo-Saxon world there are numerous political parties and an even larger number of political ideologies. In America, for example, not only do we have the Republican and Democratic Parties, but also within each of these parties there are several different wings or sections, each with its own pet political doctrines and aspirations. Quite frequently there are sharp differences of opinion between the different parties and between the different sections of each party. From time to time these differences of opinion lead to feelings of bitter animosity. And yet both the Republican and the Democratic Parties are definitely included within the liberal tradition. In like manner, the liberal tradition, in the broader sense of the term, includes not only the so-called Liberal Party of England, but also the vast majority of the members of the Conservative Party and also the bulk of the Labor Party, except for those few Laborites who have renounced liberal principles in favor of communism. To the liberal there is certainly nothing wrong in the existence of the party system nor in the fact that keen rivalry exists between the different parties. But it is obvious that the different sections and parties within the liberal tradition must be willing, in times of peril, to cooperate very closely in common defense against the attacks launched against liberal institutions by groups of Fascists and Nazis. For this close cooperation to take place and be effective, it is imperative that the various branches of the liberal movement agree as to what constitutes the true essence of liberalism, which all are prepared to support and defend, however much they may disagree on all non-vital issues.

It is well to remember that there are many vague and uncertain definitions of liberalism; there are many other definitions which are not only inexact but which are completely erroneous. Let us take one concrete example. Largely because of the historic conflicts between the so-called Liberal and Conservative Parties in nineteenth century England, it is often supposed that liberalism must be identified with belief in change, "reform," or "progress," with a willingness to depart from traditional institutions and to make new political experiments. This definition is certainly false, for liberalism in the broader sense of the word is something far deeper and vaster than the program of the English Liberal Party or other similar political groups in other parts of the Anglo-Saxon world. In its essence, true liberalism is associated neither with

"progressivism" nor with "conservatism." When the existing regime
is dominated by autocracy or despotism the followers of liberalism are
ardent reformers and demand rapid and widespread political changes.
When, on the other hand, a country has a free and democratic government and this government seems threatened by a drift towards autocracy and despotism, the true liberal is a conservative, resisting all
efforts to overthrow the existing regime.   This is true at the present
time; it has also been true all through the historic past.   In eighteenth
century France, when absolutism was the rule, the French liberals were
advocates of change, of reform, even of revolution.   In sixteenth century France, on the other hand, there were still many traces of semi-
democratic or at least parliamentary rule, though there was a marked
trend towards absolutism.   At this time the French liberal writers were
clamorous in their insistence that France should abide by "the good old
ways" and refuse to embark upon political changes.[1]

If liberalism is thus, in its essence, neither reformism nor conservatism, what are its true and fundamental characteristics?   To the present
writer it seems clear that liberalism as a political creed is a compound
of two separate elements.   One of these elements is democracy, the
other is individualism.   Not infrequently these two elements are confused because of their long association inside the liberal tradition, but
it is well to keep the two doctrines clearly separate and distinct.

Democracy, of course, means the belief that ultimate political control
should rest with the citizens of the country concerned and more particularly with the numerical majority of such citizens, rather than be entrusted permanently to a single person or to any minority group.   There
are, of course, many different types and degrees of democracy.   In some
countries democracy means that the right of voting and of being elected
to office is open to all adults whether male or female.   In other cases
women are ruled out and democracy means universal manhood suffrage.
In still other cases the right to vote and hold office is limited by property
or literacy tests.   But even here the regime must be called democratic if
ultimate control over the machinery of government rests with the bulk
of the people rather than with a special minority.   Under this definition,
present-day England most certainly belongs to the group of democratic
states, for though she retains an hereditary monarch and an hereditary
House of Lords, all ultimate or final power rests with a popularly elected
House of Commons.

In some few cases, as in the smaller Swiss cantons and in some of the
New England townships, democracy is able to function directly, laws

being passed and taxes raised at meetings attended by all the citizens. In some cases, where it is impossible to hold such meetings, a large measure of this direct democratic control is exercised by means of such devices as the initiative, referendum, and recall. In still other cases no attempt is made to govern by the direct democratic process, the people ruling indirectly through elected agents and representatives; but as long as periodic elections make it possible for the people to control the machinery of government, the government must be considered democratic. In all countries which have democratic constitutions, we find that the whole basis of government rests upon certain fundamental assumptions, which have played a great part in the development of the liberal tradition. Among the more important of these fundamental assumptions is the idea that "all government must rest upon the consent of the governed." Another is the idea that "all rulers and magistrates derive their authority from the people." As a final bulwark against despotism, most democratic regimes have either tacitly or expressly adopted the doctrine of "the right of armed rebellion against a tyrannous government," or, in other words, the right to rebel in case a single person or a minority group attempts to seize or retain control over governmental institutions.

To be sharply distinguished from democracy is the doctrine of individualism, which implies the right of each person to control his own actions as long as he does not seriously interfere with the liberty or the actions of others. Individualism asserts the right of each person to "life, liberty, and the pursuit of happiness." Individualism is intimately associated with the concept of freedom: the freedom of each person to choose his own religion, absolute freedom of thought, freedom of speech and of writing within the widest possible range, and the freedom of each person to choose, without governmental interference, the occupation or profession which most appeals to him. Individualism implies belief in and respect for private property, the right of each person to control his own belongings as long as such control does not seriously interfere with the economic welfare of his fellow citizens.

Clearly, individualism is quite distinct from democracy, even though the two doctrines are not necessarily incompatible. It would be perfectly possible to have a regime which is completely democratic and yet which ignores all the doctrines and claims of individualism. Democracy, after all, is majority rule, and individualism asserts that even the majority has no right to claim complete domination over the actions of minority groups nor over the actions of a single individual. In a country which is overwhelmingly Catholic, a popularly elected assembly might well pass a law forcing all citizens to join the Catholic Church. Such a law would be thoroughly democratic, but it would be contrary to the tenets of individualism. In like manner, a country the vast majority of whose citizens were non-smokers might, through a popular referendum, pass a law prohibiting the use of tobacco by all persons. Such a law would be democratic, but here again it would be in direct opposition to the principles of individualism.

There are different types and degrees of individualism, just as there are different types and degrees of democracy. Some radical individualists, such as Thomas Jefferson, insisted that the government should not embark upon any program of "public improvement," such as the building of roads or bridges; but most later liberals believe that such activity on the part of the government does not seriously interfere with individual liberties. Some liberals have insisted that individualism implies the doctrine that the government shall not own or operate any economic enterprise. Other liberals, and they are in the majority, believe that the governmental ownership and operation of such institutions as the post office, of the parcel post, of postal savings banks, or even, as in England, of the telephone and telegraph systems, does not go contrary to the basic principles of individualism. Some liberals, such as the members of the Manchester school in England and of the Liberty League in America, have been convinced that individualism should be identified with *laissez faire*, the doctrine that the government should in no way interfere with the economic life of its citizens. Other liberals insist that true individualism not only permits but requires a certain amount of governmental regulation of economic and industrial life, on the ground that under the system of *laissez faire* the private individual becomes a slave to the great capitalistic trusts and hence ceases to have real freedom of action.

But though there is thus marked difference of opinion as to the exact meaning and scope of individualism, all persons who claim to be liberals are agreed as to their ultimate ideal, however much they disagree as to the means to secure this ideal. This ultimate ideal is the greatest possible real freedom for the individual citizen. Even the groups which insist upon governmental control in the economic sphere are zealous in their defense of freedom of thought, of speech, and of writing. Such persons argue that even as regards economic life their aim is the protection of the liberty of the average private citizen from the domination of minority groups. Above everything, all sections of liberal opinion in sist that the welfare of the individual citizens must be regarded as the goal of political activity rather than the welfare of the state of which these citizens form a part. To the liberals, in other words, the state must be regarded not as an end in itself but merely as a means to an end. In consequence, to the liberal it seems completely wrong for the individual to be subordinated to or sacrificed for the state. Rather must the state be patterned and run to make for the welfare of the individuals who compose it.

If liberalism is thus a combination of the two principles of democracy and individualism, we may likewise say that the Fascist tradition is an expression of the two opposing principles of autocracy or authoritarianism and of state worship or etatism. The principle of authoritarianism is the direct opposite of the principle of democracy. There have been and still are many different versions of the authoritarian creed, just as there are many different forms of democracy; but all forms of authoritarianism agree in rejecting majority rule and in substituting for it a strong, forceful government centered in a single person, a comparatively small group of persons, or, at the most, in a minority group or party. During the sixteenth and seventeenth centuries authoritarianism found its most notable expression in the doctrine of the divine right of kings, the idea that all ultimate authority rests not with the people but with God, and that God has delegated much of his temporal power to princes and kings, who must, therefore, be blindly followed and obeyed.

In modern times the doctrine of the divine right of kings has lost all its popular appeal, but in its place there have arisen several other forms of authoritarianism. Some of these forms stress the pragmatic or utilitarian virtues of dictatorship as contrasted with democratic control. The followers of this type of authoritarianism emphasize the idea that democracy is weak, vacillating, and corrupt as opposed to the strong and efficient government that follows from the rule of a single individual vested with complete control. Other authoritarians stress the natural inequality of men, the fact that some persons are inherently and innately more intelligent and generally worth-while than others, and argue that it is better for the state to be run by the wise and industrious few than by the stupid and indolent many. Not infrequently these two types of authoritarianism are combined, as in the writings of Carlyle, where the doctrine is emphasized that the stupid many should be led by the wise few, but that in addition, for the sake of efficiency, the wise few in turn should be controlled by one all-powerful leader.

If authoritarianism is the opposite of democracy, so is etatism the opposite of individualism. The word etatism comes, of course, from the French term *état*, meaning state, and the word etatism implies political emphasis upon and devotion to the state as opposed to the private individual. It would be perfectly possible to speak of statism instead of etatism except for the fact that the word state, especially in America, has been identified with certain self-governing local units as opposed to the Federal Union; as a result the term statism seems to be associated with the historic doctrine of "States' Rights" rather than with devotion to the all-inclusive political unit. Hence, in spite of many disadvantages, we must be content to use the term etatism when we wish to indicate the body of doctrines which stands in violent opposition to all forms of individualism. All etatists are agreed that the state is something higher and greater than the individual citizens who compose it. All etatists likewise agree that the state is not the means to an end (such as the welfare of its citizens) but an end in itself, and that to promote the welfare of the state all individual interests must be subordinated and if necessary sacrificed. To the etatists it seems clear that it is perfectly right and proper for the individual to be subordinated to the family; the family, in turn, to the local community; and the local community, finally, to the supreme unit, the national state.

Because of their emphasis upon the state and their rejection of individual rights, the etatists insist that the state not only may but should curb the speech and the actions and even the thoughts of its citizens, when such speech, action, or thought is contrary to the aims which the state sets for itself. To the etatist, not only should the state for its own benefit abolish all pretense at freedom of speech, freedom of the press, and the right of free association, but it should also set rigid limits to religious toleration lest devotion to the doctrines of a church interfere with devotion to the dictates of the state. Even the spread of philosophical or scientific doctrines must be closely watched and, if necessary, stopped if these doctrines appear inconsistent with the intellectual ideas which have been established by the state. The thoroughgoing etatists, and there are many such persons, go even further and insist that the state must exercise a rigid censorship over literary, artistic, and musical movements on the ground that widespread acceptance of certain literary, artistic. and musical ideals might injure the morale of the populace and thus indirectly injure the power and prestige of the state.

It goes without saying that the etatists are vociferous in their claim that the state must exercise strict supervision and control over the economic activity of its citizens. On this point it should be noted that there is a sharp difference between the etatists and those liberals who are willing to accept the regulation of commerce and industry by the government. The liberal has as his ultimate aim the welfare of the private individual and to assure this welfare he is willing to have the state curb the activity of trusts, monopolies, or other agents of organ· ized capital. The etatist, on the other hand, is concerned not with the individual but with the state, and believes that the state should set up and protect the economic organization which is most suited to its own needs. According to the etatist creed, if the state were to find that a socialistic regime (government ownership and operation of industry) were beneficial to its own interests, it should unhesitatingly adopt such a regime. It is only because the etatists are convinced that the state does not benefit from socialism that they reject the socialist creed. In like manner, the etatists argue that if the state would benefit by thoroughgoing *laissez faire*, it should hold to this system, no matter how much the individual citizens might suffer. But in point of fact most etatists are agreed that the state does best for itself when it combines the principles of private enterprise and state regulation, and this type of organization has become characteristic of etatist regimes.

There are, of course, many different types and degrees of etatism. There is the milk-and-water type advocated by certain nineteenth century philosophers, differing from certain types of liberalism only by the special reverence paid to the state, which would still grant to the individual a certain amount of responsibility and freedom. In the twentieth century, on the other hand, we have seen the rise of thoroughgoing or radical etatism, generally known as totalitarianism. The totalitarian creed is best expressed in a phrase of Mussolini's, "all is in the state and for the state; nothing outside the state, nothing against the state." This phrase is especially directed against the old liberal doctrine that political life is only one aspect, even though an important aspect, of human life and activity. To the liberal, economic activity, cultural activity, religious activity, and social activity are also important and at the same time separate and independent phases of human life. To the totalitarians such an idea is anathema. To them the state and its accompaniment, political activity, is the be-all and end-all of human existence. The state to them includes but transcends all lesser phases of human life, so that such things as economics, or philosophy, or art are only subordinate aspects of the attributes and functions of the state.

From the point of view of pure reason it would appear that there is no necessary connection between authoritarianism and etatism. It would be perfectly possible to have an authoritarian state (i.e., one controlled by a small aristocracy or by a single person) which allowed the private citizen a great deal of individual freedom.   Such in fact was the type of state dreamed of by the Italian philosopher, Vilfredo Pareto. In like manner it would be perfectly possible to have an etatist, even a totalitarian regime which was controlled by the bulk of the people and thus formed a democracy.   Such in fact is the type of state dreamed of by many socialists both in ancient and modern times.   It so happens, however, that just as liberalism grew up as a combination of the two doctrines of democracy and individualism, so has the Fascist tradition grown up as a combination of the two doctrines of authoritarianism and etatism.   Fascism and its cousin, National Socialism, can only be understood when this fact is kept clearly in mind.

The Fascist tradition, the principal object of our present study, is thus seen to be authoritarianism plus etatism, but if we would get beyond the mere matter of definition and seek to understand the real essence of the Fascist creed, we must transcend formal definition and seek to interpret many of its less open and obvious undertones.   This can only be done by an examination of the origin and slow development of the Fascist ideology.   Above all, if the liberals are to combat Fascism with any chance of success, they must be aware not only of what the Fascist creed is, but also of some of the arguments used by the Fascists to bolster up their creed.   If a democratic power is forced to enter into armed conflict with a totalitarian power, it is essential that the democratic power become fully informed of the type of cannon, tanks, and aeroplanes which may be used against it.   In like manner, in the ideological conflict between liberalism and Fascism (and such a conflict is already under way) it is essential that the defenders of liberalism become aware of the types of argument which are used by the Fascists to win converts to their cause.   If this is not done the liberal leaders may wake up one morning and find that because of enemy propaganda a large proportion of their following has gone over to the other camp.
        It is then with the aim of giving liberals an historical interpretation of the Fascist (or Fascist-Nazi) ideology, and of elucidating the main arguments which have been used by the Fascist philosophers in support of their cause, that the present work has been undertaken.

NOTE TO CHAPTER ONE

1. Consider such persons as François Hotman, the author of *Franco-Gallia*, written in 1573.

Part One

THE EARLY PRECURSORS OF FASCISM

CHAPTER II

The Effect of the Reformation upon Political Philosophy

THE LEGACY OF THE MIDDLE AGES

FASCISM in the broader sense of the term means, as we have seen, belief in hierarchic authority as opposed to democracy, combined with belief in the supremacy of the state as opposed to the supremacy of the individual. Such being the case it is not difficult to find for the Fascist tradition a long and distinguished genealogy. We find writers advocating these doctrines or similar doctrines throughout the Middle Ages, in the days of the Roman Empire, and even in the days of classic Greece. We have, in fact, in Plato's *Republic* one of the world's most brilliant expositions of the theory that the community should completely dominate the private citizen, coupled with the doctrine that control over the community should rest, not with the vulgar mob, but with a small specially gifted minority.

It is, however, more accurate to say that Fascism, certainly in the narrower sense of the word, started in the sixteenth century at the time of the Reformation, if only because Fascism is intimately associated with devotion to the idea of the *national state* (as opposed to other forms of community life) and the very notion of the national state emerged into public consciousness only after and largely as the result of the Reformation. In the period of classical antiquity, political thought was concerned either with the small city-state or with a world empire. The Middle Ages continued this tradition. In fact, during this period the idea of world empire was even more dominant than it had been during the classical period.

Europe was, to be sure, broken up into a vast number of small political units, but this very complexity served to make men strive after unity and base their speculation upon the notion that after all Christendom was but a single entity. During this period the very word *state* was unknown. The political unit was the *Respublica*, or the Commonwealth, and the "Christian Commonwealth" was held to include all the peoples of Western Europe.

For the idea of separate, completely independent states to command general attention, it was necessary to overthrow the three concepts which had dominated all political thought from the fifth to the fifteenth century.   One of these was the concept that the pope was and should be the supreme arbiter of all Christians, whatever their nationality. The second was that the "Emperor," the ruler of the "Holy Roman Empire," had a claim to overlordship of the lesser princes of Europe. The third was the concept underlying feudalism, the notion that inside each kingdom there existed many persons possessing certain inalienable political rights and privileges which could not legally be ignored by the ruler of the realm.

Since the days of St. Augustine in the fifth century A.D., the inhabit-ants of Western Europe had come to regard the commonwealth as a church-state, having as citizens all those who professed the Catholic faith.   The church was not merely the clergy or the ecclesiastical hierarchy, but the whole body of Christians in whatever country they might reside.   But though the church included both clergy and laity, it was to be governed by the clerical hierarchy, and more especially by the pope, the Bishop of Rome, who had ultimate jurisdiction over all ecclesiastical affairs.

Jurisdiction over ecclesiastical affairs meant, of course, among other things, control over church property wherever it might lie.   Normally all church property was exempt from regulation or even taxation by the secular rulers.   The amount of land thus withdrawn from secular jurisdiction varied from time to time and from country to country, but always included a considerable portion of the land in each king-dom.

Members of the clergy, moreover, were held to be beyond the juris-diction of the secular courts.   Whatever offense a priest had committed, he should be tried, it was believed, only by the ecclesiastical courts, all of which in the long run were subject to papal control.   All members of the clergy, therefore, enjoyed what would now be called extraterritorial privileges wherever they happened to reside.

The ecclesiastical courts, moreover, had jurisdiction not only over the persons of the clergy, but in all cases where a matter of canon law was involved.   This came to mean that even the laity were forced to bring their cases to the ecclesiastical courts in a great many instances, includ-ing all cases involving problems of marriage and testaments and many cases of what would now be called commercial law because of the church's claim to judge the crime of "usury."

The church, and thereby the pope, was considered the guardian not only of faith but also of morals; hence, the laws of any country which touched upon the moral life of any private citizen, to be valid had to be in accordance with "divine law" as interpreted by the papal decretals.

Last but not least, the pope was held to have ultimate control over the temporal rulers themselves. Many rulers, such as King John of England and the Kings of Aragon, held their thrones as immediate vassals of the pope. But even over other monarchs, in less direct sub-jection, the pope had far-reaching powers. In case of need the pope could not only excommunicate a refractory ruler, but he could also secure the deposition of this monarch by releasing the latter's subjects from their oath of allegiance. The Middle Ages are full of instances of proud and headstrong kings being forced to bow to papal orders lest they lose their thrones. In fact, as Figgis has pointed out,

> In the Middle Ages the Church was not a State, it was the State; the State or rather the Civil Authority (for a separate society was not recognised) was merely the police department of the Church. The latter took over from the Roman Empire its theory of the absolute and universal jurisdiction of the supreme authority and developed it into the doctrine of the *plenitudo potestatis* of the Pope, who was the supreme dispenser of law, the fountain of honor, including regal honor, and the sole legitimate earthly source of power.[1]

As a result of this doctrine it was believed that the state was not a separate organization in contrast with the church, and hence did not possess inherent rights of its own. Rather was it held that the church and the state formed but a single community, with two sets of officers, one secular, the other spiritual. Needless to say, the clergy held that ultimate control over this community rested with the spiritual officers.

Even with regard to the secular rulers it was generally believed that all the rulers of Christendom constituted, at least in theory, but one vast hierarchy, at the apex of which was the Holy Roman Emperor.

This belief was, of course, but little more than a relic of the prestige which had once been enjoyed by the Roman Empire of antiquity. At one time the whole of the western world had in fact been dominated by Rome and the Roman emperors. The downfall of the western branch of the Roman Empire, as the result of barbarian invasions, had, of course, brought this "universal" dominion to an end. But the Roman Empire as an ideal persisted for many centuries after it had ceased to exist in fact. The kings of the Goths, the Burgundians, and the Lombards insisted upon ruling their subjects as they saw fit, but most of them felt that in some way or other they and their kingdoms were still inside and a part of the Roman Empire.

Just as the belief in the empire was slowly fading from the western world it was revived by the rise to supremacy over Western Europe of Charlemagne, and his assumption (in 800 A.D.) of the title of emperor. For a brief period most of the peoples of the West were again reunited under the rulership of a single monarch who claimed to be the legitimate successor of the ancient Caesars.

Under the descendants of Charlemagne the newly reconstructed empire soon fell to pieces, and Europe was again broken up into a number of hostile kingdoms, but the tradition of the empire and its claim to universal dominion persisted. In 962, Otto, Duke of the Saxons, assumed the titles and dignities of emperor, and from that time until 1806 the Holy Roman Empire continued uninterruptedly to maintain a legal existence.

It is easy to say with Voltaire that this new Holy Roman Empire was neither holy, nor Roman, nor an empire. It is true that most of the emperors found it impossible to maintain order or exercise control even over the regions which acknowledged their supremacy. It is true that, at the best of times, the empire included within its actual boundaries only the Germans and Italians, and that neither Otto nor his successors were ever able to secure jurisdiction over the Spaniards, or the English, or even over the bulk of the French-speaking peoples.

Nevertheless, the legend that the emperor was superior to all other secular monarchs lasted for many centuries and dominated much of the literature of the Middle Ages. In the fourteenth century the empire was so weak that it was unable to control half the lands nominally subject to it, yet at this very time we find Dante composing a book (*De Monarchia*) in praise of the empire as a symbol of world dominion, giving peace and order to all men. The popes were frequently in violent conflict with the emperors on points of policy, yet Pope Boniface VIII, one of the most arrogant occupants of the papal throne, in rebuking the King of France for claiming to have no superior, reminds this monarch that legally the French are and ought to be subject to the emperor. The writings of the celebrated William of Occam are further evidence that it was frequently, though erroneously, held that the emperor had inalienable rights over the French monarchs.

England never formed part of the empire of Charlemagne, and its monarchs were naturally never willing to subject themselves to the later less powerful emperors. Nevertheless, "the fact that an ignorant writer in the fourteenth century [the author of the *Mirror of Justice*] can declare that a statute which he dislikes is invalid because it has received no confirmation from the Emperor is evidence, not of the truth of his statement, but of the existence in men's minds of some lingering belief . . . in the Imperial claims to sovereignty." [2]

If the claims of the individual state to complete independence were lessened by the counter claims of the popes and emperors from without, its assertion of complete jurisdiction was equally weakened from within by the hereditary rights and privileges of the feudal nobility.

We in the twentieth century tacitly assume that each state has complete jurisdiction over all persons within its boundaries — that the state has the power to make and enforce any laws it pleases; that it has the right to levy any taxes it pleases; that the execution of justice is its monopoly, and that all courts shall be state courts; that all armed forces are either directly or indirectly under its command.

In the Middle Ages each and every one of these propositions would have been considered absurd, both theoretically and practically. In each kingdom a certain amount of land remained "crown land," directly subject to the king. In this region, and in this region alone, the monarch might raise taxes, appoint administrative and judicial officials, raise an army, and exercise what we may call legislative rights.

The greater part of the territory in each state, however, was handed over as fiefs to one or another of the members of the nobility. Each one of these fiefs might be, and frequently was, further broken up into lesser fiefs which were handed on to members of the lesser nobility, and so on indefinitely. Each fief-holder was, of course, bound to do homage to his immediate superior, so that the king at the top of the pyramid nominally enjoyed suzerainty directly or indirectly over all his subjects. But in most cases this suzerainty was more theoretical than real, and even theoretically was hedged by many restrictions.

In most instances the relations between each vassal and his overlord were regulated by a specific contract, sometimes written, sometimes merely verbal or traditional, but equally valid. The fief-holder was bound to perform certain specific obligations, but these obligations were strictly limited, and the overlord could not ask for services other than those specified or implied in the contract. The contracts differed widely in individual instances, so that it was impossible for the monarch to make any general legislation for his subjects. Any law which he might make might be consonant with some contracts but not with others.

In nearly all cases it was considered the duty of the fief-holder to assemble his own subordinates as a military force when his overlord was endangered. At the same time, the fief-holder retained the right to lead the force thus assembled, so that the feudal levies remained private and semi-independent armies. Not infrequently the vassal could and would claim that his overlord had broken the contract binding them. On such occasions the military force at the command of the fief-holder would be used not in defense of but directly against the overlord.

In many of the countries dominated by the feudal principle, the jurisdiction of the king's courts was held to be confined to the territory immediately subject to the crown. In each of the larger and more important fiefs, the vassal meted out his own justice. In like manner, the king's administrative officials had no control over the feudal domains, each vassal having his own administrative hierarchy, as far as such an organization was needed.

Taxation in the modern sense of the term was impossible, for each fief was held on a basis of fixed rental. On accepting his fief, each vassal bound himself to render each year or on certain special occasions a specified payment, either in money or in goods. This return was usually very small, frequently almost nominal, yet the overlord had no right to demand a larger payment unless the vassal voluntarily consented.

It should be noted that feudal rights, which at first lay almost exclusively in the hands of the nobility, soon came to be shared by many towns and cities. Partly by purchase, partly by peaceful usurpation, partly by the use of armed force, many of the European municipalities freed themselves from the control of the neighboring feudal lord and became "free cities," possessing their own rights in judicial, administrative, and financial matters, and subject only to the supreme overlordship of the king or emperor.

In the period between the thirteenth and sixteenth centuries there was a slow but steady decline of feudalism. In the Holy Roman Empire the major vassals retained most of their rights, but in the other countries of Europe the power of the crown grew steadily in strength at the expense of the individual vassal.

Nonetheless the feudal nobility and the burghers of the free cities retained collectively many of the rights and privileges which they had lost individually. The nobles as a class and the burghers as a class fre-

quently enjoyed certain judicial and financial immunities. Some of
these immunities were to have important political consequences, one
of the most significant being the growth of representative assemblies —
the Cortes in Spain, the States-General in France, the Reichstag in
Germany, and Parliament in England.

In earlier days it had been held that the king could increase taxation
only by obtaining the consent of each of his vassals individually. It
now came to be believed that the action of the majority of the vassals
could bind the minority. Hence if the king were in financial straits he
would summon his principal vassals or their representatives and ask
for grants in aid. The voting of such grants was the principal function
of these early assemblies, but not infrequently the assemblies would
consent to an increase in taxation only on condition that the king
promised to make or revoke some particular law. As a result, as time
went on, the assemblies came to exercise considerable influence upon
legislation.

We must look upon these early assemblies as the germ of the democratic institutions of modern times. But it must not be forgotten that
in origin these assemblies were essentially aristocratic. They represented, not the people of each country, but the country's privileged
classes, intent upon preserving their own rights and immunities.

THE RESULTS OF THE REFORMATION

The political developments, theoretical and practical, of the sixteenth
century were to result in sweeping away most of the concepts, and in
radically modifying most of the institutions which had thus dominated
Europe during the Middle Ages.

The Reformation and its consequence — the splitting-up of Christendom into a number of rival, conflicting churches — destroyed the concept that all Europe formed but a single community. It destroyed the
concept that the pope was to be regarded as the supreme arbiter over
all the countries of Christendom. Indirectly it destroyed the concept
that the church was the ultimate master of human affairs. Before the
Reformation the state had been the handmaiden of the church; after the
Reformation most churches became the handmaidens of the state.

The Reformation, or at least the political consequences of the Reformation, likewise destroyed the old romantic ideas which had grown
around the title and office of emperor of the Holy Roman Empire
Though the pope and emperor had frequently fought desperately with

one another, the two offices were closely associated in mediaeval ideology.   One was the supreme spiritual ruler, the other, in theory at least,
the supreme temporal ruler of the Christian Commonwealth.   With
the break-up of this Christian Commonwealth into many different
states, the very notion of a supreme temporal ruler became ridiculous.

The fact that the Reformation began in Germany, the heart of the
old Holy Roman Empire, had enormous and disastrous consequences
to the position and powers of the emperor.   Had the emperor succeeded
in crushing the Reformation in Germany, or, on the other hand, had he
accepted Lutheranism and imposed it upon the whole of Germany, his
office would probably have maintained its ancient prestige.   But as the
result of innumerable conflicts it came to be accepted that each of the
German princes had the right to choose what religion he pleased and
the further right to impose this religion upon his own subjects.   In
consequence of this condition the claim of the emperor to exercise
jurisdiction over all Germany was manifestly absurd.   And if the
emperor were only a shadow figure in Germany, how could he possibly
be regarded as the supreme lord of the whole of Europe?

The Reformation thus had as one of its principal consequences the
freeing of the temporal ruler of each state from all superior international
controls.   Equally important among the political developments of this
period was the tendency to strengthen the control which each temporal
ruler undertook to exercise over all his subjects.   Those few feudal
privileges, shackles upon the supremacy of kings, which had survived
until the beginning of the sixteenth century, rapidly disappeared in the
following decades.   Even the rights and prerogatives of the nobility
and the burghers as a group tended to dwindle in importance, and those
prerogatives which were maintained came to be regarded, not as inalienable rights, but as grants of immunity given by the king, the source of
all power.

The right of the king to legislate for all his subjects; the right of the
royal courts to exercise jurisdiction over all citizens, irrespective of
rank; the right of the king to maintain administrative officials in all
portions of his realm; the right of the king to command all the armed
forces of the kingdom — all these rights were universally accepted.
In most European countries it was also believed that the king should
have the right to tax his subjects as he pleased.

Apart from England, which in many ways occupies a special position,
even the representative assemblies which had played such important
roles during the later Middle Ages continually dwindled in power.   In
several instances they entirely disappeared.

It is in Spain that we find the first traces of representative government in mediaeval times. There was a Cortes in Aragon and Castile many decades before there was a Parliament in England. Yet in the sixteenth century we find that the Cortes convened less and less often, and in the end its very existence was forgotten. The meeting of the States-General of France in 1614 was the last before the reconvening of this assembly on the eve of the French Revolution. The representative assembly of Denmark was abolished in 1660; that of Portugal in 1674. At about the same time the assemblies (Landtage) of most of the principalities inside Germany gradually ceased to function. In all these cases supreme legislative power was transferred from the assembly to the monarch.

What was the reason for this rather astonishing political transformation? It is clear that there were not one but many underlying causes. The Reformation had at least an indirect influence upon this development, for the reformers, if only to undermine the position of the papacy, had been forced to stress the majesty and importance of kings. It was partly due to the revival of Roman law throughout Western Europe, for Roman law as codified under Justinian presupposed the supremacy of the emperor over all his subjects, and accepted as a fundamental postulate, *quod princeps voluit legis vigorem habet*: "the will of the prince has the force of law."

Radical changes in economic conditions also tended to strengthen the kings and weaken the assemblies. In the Middle Ages the monarchs had been almost entirely dependent upon land taxes, and as we have seen, these taxes could normally be increased only with the consent of the estates of the realm, or the assembly. But with the discovery of America and the opening of the sea routes to Asia, the kings acquired many new sources of income, most of them independent of the will of the assemblies.

The collection of customs dues, the sale of commercial rights and monopolies, the tribute sent by colonies or outlying possessions, often became the major items in the national exchequer. In most cases the money from these sources flowed directly into the royal coffers and was not subject to parliamentary control. The silver from the mines of the Indies alone (or rather that portion paid to the crown as royalty) was sufficient to make the Spanish monarchs financially independent of the grants of their Cortes. With the passing of exclusive financial control, the assemblies slowly but surely lost all political control.

Last but not least, the growth of the royal power in the sixteenth and seventeenth centuries must be regarded as in large measure a popular, in fact, a democratic movement. The rights of the assemblies meant not the rights of the people as a whole, but rather the rights of certain privileged classes. The average man was inclined to believe that the yoke which would be laid upon him by the king would be less onerous than the yoke already laid upon him by the nobility or the closed corporations which controlled the cities. The increase of the royal powers meant a decrease in the rights of the local lord, who was frequently very cordially hated. In many cases of internal conflict, the issue was not between the king and his people, but between the king and the people on one side and the nobles and privileged burghers on the other.

It is in the light of these conditions that the political philosophy of the sixteenth and seventeenth centuries must be examined.

MARTIN LUTHER

The Reformation, as we have seen, had important and far-reaching effects upon the political institutions of Western Europe. It is therefore imperative that we examine some of the political ideas of the leaders of the Reformation movement. It is well known that the leaders in the Reform or Protestant movement differed radically among themselves regarding theological matters. It is of importance to note that they also differed regarding political matters, and that these differences finally led to the rise of separate and opposed political philosophies.

If our main task were to study the rise of the liberal tradition, we should have to devote some time to an analysis of the political ideas of John Calvin and of his disciples, the Huguenots of France, and the Presbyterians of Scotland. We should also have to deal at length with the political ideas which inspired the English Puritans. Though neither the Calvinists nor the Puritans were liberals in the modern sense of the word, the development of their political ideas eventually led to the establishment of the liberal tradition.

Since, however, our principal interest is a study of the early precursors of Fascist ideology, we must turn our attention to some of the other leaders in the Protestant movement, more especially to the political ideas formulated by Martin Luther and the Lutherans on the one hand, and those formulated by Henry VIII and the early Anglican divines on the other. Though the Lutherans and the Anglicans differed radically from one another in many essential respects in theology and in politics, both movements agreed in stressing the importance of the national state and the need for strong authoritarian government within this state.

Not dissimilar to the ideas put forth by the Lutherans and the Anglicans were the political theories of the leaders of the Gallican movement in France.   Though the Gallicans remained Catholics and hence theologically were in opposition both to the Lutherans and the Anglicans, in political philosophy they assumed a position closely analogous to that of Luther and Henry VIII, and this position led to the same political consequences.

In many ways the political philosophy of Martin Luther (1483–1546) must be regarded as an amazing paradox.   Luther started with a plea for reform in the concept of the church and ended with a reform in the concept of the state.   He started with a plea for individual liberty and for freedom of conscience; yet his doctrines led directly to a belief in the divine right of kings and to the belief that monarchs have a right to dictate religious dogmas to the private individual.   He started as an internationalist with a message to the peoples of all nations; he ended by formulating the doctrine of all-powerful national states in perpetual antagonism to one another.   He started with the doctrine of the basic equality of all men, and ended with the doctrine that all men should be subject to the iron will of their secular lord.

To the student of the Fascist tradition Luther is of importance largely because his doctrine led to the freeing of the state from all ecclesiastical control.   Prior to Luther the state was generally regarded as subordinate to the church; it was generally held that no state law was valid if it was contrary to canon or church law; it was generally held that temporal magistrates were inferior to the members of the ecclesiastical hierarchy and that temporal magistrates must obey the commands issued by the ecclesiastical hierarchy.   As long as such notions were common it was impossible for the state to be considered the all-important element in human activity.   In other words, it was impossible for etatism to flourish as a political philosophy.

Luther broke the power of the church over the state by his insistence upon the idea that the true church, the only church to which the pious Christian should pay any attention, is the church invisible, rather than the church visible.   To the mediaeval mind the church was a visible community, consisting of all professing Christians, ministered to by priests with certain special sacramental powers, and ruled over by an ecclesiastical hierarchy at the apex of which stood the pope. To Luther the real or true church was an invisible, intangible group of men who were under the direct rulership of God.   To Luther only a fraction of those persons who professed Christianity were members of this true church.   As the true church was the church invisible, it was obviously impossible for this church to be formally organized or for it to have any control over temporal affairs.

After the pope had excommunicated him from the visible church, Luther denied all power and jurisdiction to the Bishop of Rome and the whole church hierarchy.   Along with the rejection of the traditional powers of the organized church there went a complete denial of the validity of canon law and of the powers of the ecclesiastical courts which had enforced this law.   Logically enough there followed the denial of all intrinsic sacerdotal privilege.   No man had the right to claim any supernatural power.   Every true Christian was a priest — which meant that in the old sense of the word no man was a priest.

The direct political consequences of these views were far-reaching and, to Luther's contemporaries, startling.   No longer did the pope have the right to excommunicate or depose a secular ruler.   No longer need a secular ruler tremble before the decrees of a very visible organization which claimed the right to review and condemn the actions of all men who ruled merely with material power.   The clergy, who formerly had been subject only to the papal courts, were henceforth to be subject to the temporal rulers.   Ecclesiastical courts, which formerly had competed in jurisdiction with secular courts, were to be disbanded. Questions of marriage and of testaments, which had once been a matter of church law, were to be decided in accordance with the law of the land.

Of even greater significance was the fact that Luther decided that instead of letting the visible church control the state, it was the duty of the state to control the visible church.   To Luther the visible church was not, of course, the true church, but after all it was necessary to have some type of visible church, with church buildings and ecclesiastical ceremonies, in order to lead men to the invisible church.   Now the visible church was obviously concerned more with outward than with inward or spiritual things, and it was therefore only right and proper for the temporal authorities to exercise control over it.   In the old days the material phases of the church had been controlled by the ecclesiastical hierarchy, but Luther had destroyed this hierarchy as far as the evangelical churches went, and he had no intention of restoring it.   Among the followers of Calvin, control over the visible church was vested in synods, constituted on a semi-democratic basis, but Luther had an innate distrust of democratic institutions and would not permit this development to take place among his own followers.   As a result, ultimate control over ecclesiastical affairs came to be vested in the temporal ruler of each state which accepted the Lutheran doctrine. The prince of each state became the "supreme bishop" of all Lutheran communities within his realm, and direct control over the churches was vested in a consistory whose members were appointed by the prince. In most Lutheran countries the salary of the clergy was paid directly by the state, and the vast majority of the parochial clergy received their appointments by government nomination.

During the early portion of his career as a leader of the Protestant movement, Luther argued that faith and, through faith, membership in the Kingdom of God or the church invisible were personal matters that could not be inspired by secular action, but only by the secret action of God. As a result of this doctrine it was claimed that the extirpation of heresy and the promulgation of orthodoxy were no part of the function of the state. Later events were to change this attitude. The doctrinal extravagances of some of the lesser Protestant leaders, especially of the group known as Anabaptists, led to widespread social unrest, and this in turn forced Luther to adopt a far less tolerant attitude. If it was impossible for the state to insure right faith, it was at least possible for it to put down doctrines which were in open contradiction to right faith. It became the duty of the state to crush the Anabaptists on the one hand and to prevent the public performance of Catholic rites on the other. As time went on the doctrine that the state had supreme power in religious matters became more and more emphasized in Lutheran circles. It came to be believed that it was the duty of the state to enforce membership at least in the visible church amongst its citizens. Not only could the temporal ruler force his subjects to make public profession of the orthodox Lutheran creed, but after Luther's death it became more and more possible for the temporal ruler to lay down the law as to what did and what did not constitute orthodox Lutheranism.

The power of the secular authority, or in other words of the state, was greatly magnified by Luther's ideas regarding the nature and function of the church. In addition to this Luther had other doctrines which tended to elevate the power and prestige of the temporal authorities. In disagreement with Aristotle, Luther did not look upon the state as "natural," that is, as the result of the normal functioning of man. With St. Augustine he regarded the state, or at least the need of the state, as the result of sin. Before the Fall of Adam and Eve from the

Garden of Eden, man had no need of political organization, but because of the frailty and wickedness which prevailed after the Fall, it was necessary to provide man with a stern discipline, to place over him rulers who would punish him for his crimes and forcibly prevent him from committing further crimes. As the result of this attitude Luther tended to regard governments and rulers as necessary evils. At times he seemed to look upon princes as he might upon executioners and hangmen — disagreeable persons who fulfill a useful, in fact, an indispensable purpose. As jailers and hangmen are frequently undesirable persons socially, so Luther was prepared to admit that princes are not uncommonly "the biggest fools and the worst knaves in creation."

But in spite of this attitude Luther was convinced that temporal government is divine in origin, receiving its authority directly from God.   Government may be an evil, but it is necessary, and it is part of God's plan for crushing all other evils.   Princes may be fools and knaves, but they have been delegated by God to rule, and must be blindly obeyed.   The theory that temporal authority is derived directly from God is, of course, in marked contrast with the view that government is a mere human device and that the authority of governments rests upon the consent of the governed.   Luther mentions this latter view only to dismiss it with scorn.   According to Luther, the secular authority is of divine origin and must invariably be obeyed save where it commands something directly contrary to God's Word as revealed in the Scriptures.   Even in this case, the most that a man should do is offer passive resistance.   Though the ruler be wicked and tyrannical, rebellion is inexcusable.   The right to punish the wicked ruler rests with God.

During the early part of his career Luther considered that blind obedience was due *all* secular rulers from the emperor down to the lowest member of the governing hierarchy in mediaeval Germany.   The events of his later life forced Luther to change this point of view.   The emperor, it so happened, became the chief and most bitter opponent of the Lutheran cause, while Luther's chief support came from some of the subordinate princes.   For this reason Luther, towards the end of his life, found it reasonable to believe that because of the peculiar nature of the imperial post, the emperor might be resisted — but it remained unlawful to resist the subordinate princes, who were thus elevated into completely sovereign rulers.   The adoption of this view and the ultimate triumph of Lutheranism in most of Northern Germany meant the complete collapse of the old imperial ideal.   For many years the imperial power had been more nominal than real, but this power had been dormant, not dead. The triumph of Lutheranism completely destroyed any hope that this power might be revived. Though the Holy Roman Empire persisted in name until the nineteenth century, in reality it died in 1530 when the Lutheran princes took up arms to defend their faith against the imperial forces.

Effective sovereignty was transferred from the amorphous empire to the erstwhile feudal principalities, but there was no further devolution of authority. Inside his own realm the prince was to be supreme. Among the followers of other Protestant leaders, such as Calvin and Zwingli, there was a certain democratic tendency. This was completely lacking in Luther's philosophy of the state. Luther had a very poor opinion of the political abilities of the average man. The average man, to him, was full of wickedness and needed to be restrained by the strong arm of temporal authority. All human souls might be equal in the sight of God, but the temporal state must rest upon inequality. To Luther, it was the duty of every subject to know his place and keep it, fulfilling the law of God within his own sphere. When the peasants of Germany rose in rebellion against their lords, Luther was filled with wrath and commanded that the rebels be shown no mercy, that the insurrection be put down with fire and sword.

Luther believed that the monasteries should be suppressed, and this belief had political as well as religious significance. Luther was opposed to the monastic ideal not only from the religious point of view but also because he regarded with dislike the existence within the state of semi-independent corporations such as the monastic communities. The feudal idea of the state as a corporation of corporations was to be displaced by the state as a single corporation having direct control over all its subjects as individuals.

HENRY VIII AND THE ANGLICAN CHURCH

The influence of Henry VIII upon political theory in England was strikingly similar to the power which Luther exercised upon political thought in Germany. In many ways this fact is rather remarkable as in aims, in fundamental beliefs, and in character Henry VIII and Luther were poles apart. Luther was a religious zealot and a mystic. Henry VIII was neither. Though he professed a profound interest in theological matters, Henry was really concerned only with the affairs of this world. Luther rejected many of the essential features of Catholic

doctrine   Henry looked with horror at most of the doctrines put forward by the reformers.   A confirmed believer in transubstantiation and
the other features of Catholic dogma, he wrote a book attacking Luther's
ideas and received from the pope the title, Defender of the Faith.

Yet only a few years after having thus stepped forth as the champion
of Catholic orthodoxy, Henry VIII was forced, for domestic reasons,
to break with the papal hierarchy.   In consequence of this break, the
Church of England arose as a separate ecclesiastical organization.
From the very nature of things this new church adopted a theory of the
state to which it was required to hold fast, however much it might
change in matters purely doctrinal.   At one time the Church of England
might and did hold that transubstantiation was a true doctrine, acceptance of which was indispensable for salvation; at another that transubstantiation was a vain and wicked superstition.   But regarding the
supremacy of the state in all matters both spiritual and temporal it
was forced to be adamant lest its own existence be endangered.   It was
this theory of the supremacy of the state which brought Henry VIII
and his followers to a political philosophy very similar to that of Luther.

There was only one substantial difference between the Anglicans and
the Lutherans — the Anglicans could and did stress nationalism to a
degree which was impossible for Luther and his adherents.   Luther
himself was an incipient nationalist.   He addressed an appeal to the
German nobility with stress upon the word German.   He could and
did emphasize the idea that papal supremacy resulted in the economic
subjection of Germans to Italians.   But the very fact that only part
of Germany answered his appeal and that the emperor, the nominal
head of the German nation, was violent in his objection to the reformed
doctrines made it impossible for Luther to associate his church with
the cause of German nationalism.   In fact the success of Luther, or
rather the fact that he was only partially successful, stultified the
growth of the German national movement for over two centuries.

In England, on the other hand, Henry VIII's actions resulted in the
creation of a national church, to which in theory all Englishmen gave
allegiance and to which, for the moment, only Englishmen were eligible
for membership.   Luther believed that he was establishing, or at least
reforming, a universal church.   Henry's church laid no claim to universal dominion.   It merely claimed to have absolute, independent
jurisdiction over the souls of Englishmen.   In so doing it laid down the
principles of nationalism both in politics and in religion.

There was one further difference between the Lutheran and the

Anglican attitude towards the state. Though Luther, in practice, permitted the temporal rulers to have complete control over ecclesiastical organization and discipline, Luther never departed from the idea that church and state were really two separate things — the church an invisible organization concerned only with the things of the spirit and the state a visible organization in charge of all secular affairs.

The Anglican divines, on the other hand, started with the assumption that church and state were merely two different aspects of the same thing, that church and state were both phases of the national commonwealth. "I perceive," says Archbishop Whitgift, "no such distinction of the commonwealth and the church that they should be counted as if it were two several bodies governed by divers laws and divers magistrates." [3]

To understand this point of view it must be remembered that for the Anglicans the church was not the church invisible, but the church visible. Nor was the church merely the body of clergy. The church for them included the whole body of believers under the national jurisdiction. "The Church of England," says Gardiner, one of the most noted of the Anglican divines, "is nothing else but the congregation of men and women of the clergy and of the laity, united in Christ's profession." [4]

This conception is distinctly mediaeval, but the Anglican conception differed from that of the Middle Ages in two important respects: first, the Anglicans believed that Christendom was not a single entity, but was broken up into a number of different national communities or church-states; and second, the church-state was to be ultimately under the control of the secular authorities.

The Anglicans admitted the theoretical unity of all the orthodox churches of Christendom, but inside this spiritual unity there necessarily existed a number of national churches. There was an English church, a French church, and an Italian church. At any one time these churches might or might not admit the supremacy of the Bishop of Rome (the Church of England had done so in the past); but at any moment this recognition could be withdrawn without affecting the constitution of each such national church. To recognize but a single ruler for the whole of Christendom was as unnecessary as it was to recognize the emperor as the supreme secular ruler of Christendom. Inside each country, however, religious uniformity had to be maintained. To permit the existence of several churches within one state would overthrow the whole concept of the commonwealth as a church-state, and the

Anglicans at this period felt that the overthrow of this concept meant not only religious but also political anarchy.

In the Middle Ages there had been a sharp struggle between the ecclesiastical and secular hierarchies for the control of the church-state. In this struggle the ecclesiastical hierarchy had usually been successful, but as the result of Henry VIII's activity, not only did the Anglican Church withdraw its recognition of the pope as supreme ruler of Christendom, but it placed the whole ecclesiastical organization in subjection to the secular authorities. The Anglican Church possessed its own ecclesiastical hierarchy, its archbishops, its bishops, its Houses of Convocation; but the overthrow of the papal claims did not mean spiritual independence for the Archbishop of Canterbury and his clerical cohorts, for in 1534 an Act of Parliament, which the clergy were forced to accept, declared the king to be the supreme head of the Church of England.

To justify this position the Anglican writers were forced to discuss at some length the proper relations between the spiritual and secular authorities and to admit, at times rather grudgingly, that on all important points the spiritual was to be subject to the secular authority. Archbishop Whitgift declared, "The continual practice of Christian churches in the time of Christian magistrates, before the usurpation of the Bishop of Rome, hath been to give to Christian princes supreme authority in making ecclesiastical orders and laws, yea, and that which is more, in deciding matters of religion, even in the chief and principal points." In the Church Homilies it was officially stated that Christ had forbidden the clergy to assume any kind of worldly dominion and in particular had forbidden to all ecclesiastical ministers dominion over the Church of Christ.

With Luther, the Anglicans tacitly assumed that secular government was of divine origin. "When mankind increased and spread itself more largely over the world," say the Homilies, "He [God] by his holy word did constitute and ordain in cities and countries several and special governors and rulers." And again, "All kings, queens, and governors are especially appointed by the ordinance of God." ... "Such subjects as are disobedient or rebellious against their Princes disobey God and procure their own damnation."

The Anglicans, like the Lutherans, were agreed that rebellion or resistance against the monarch was a crime, for which there was no justification, or, to use the words of Cranmer, "Though the magistrates be evil and very tyrants, yet the subjects must obey in all worldly things."

In all cases the laws laid down by the magistrates had to be explicitly obeyed, however much the individual citizen might dislike them. There was only one exception. The citizen did not need to, nay must not obey a law which was directly contrary to a law of God. But even in this instance the citizen might practice only passive resistance. As Latimer puts it, "When laws are made against God and His word, then I ought to obey more God than man ... yet for all that I may not rise up against the magistrates nor make any uproar; for if I do so, I sin damnably. I must be content to suffer whatsoever God shall lay upon me."

GALLICANISM

As a result of the work of Luther and Henry VIII, the Protestant rulers of Northern Europe found their powers enormously enhanced. No longer were their thrones or their prerogatives menaced by the dictates of an international overlord such as the pope, and inside each state the once powerful ecclesiastical organization had become subject to the control of the secular ruler.

But what of the rulers of those countries which remained Catholic? It is hardly surprising to find that Catholic monarchs of the time, though perfectly content to remain within the bosom of Mother Church, were distinctly envious of the new importance and prestige which had been acquired by their Protestant brethren, and made efforts to secure some of these privileges for themselves.

In Spain, to be sure, it was scarcely necessary for the monarchs to lay special claim to independence of the papal authority, for during the greater part of the sixteenth century the Spanish kingdom had such a control over Italian affairs and such an influence over the papal court that at times it almost appeared as if the pope was but a puppet of the Spanish monarchy, and hence an increase of papal prestige over Europe as a whole was very advantageous to the Spanish interests.

In France conditions were very different. In previous centuries France had occupied a position with reference to papal affairs analogous to that now held by Spain. French monarchs had made and unmade popes. For seventy years the popes had been compelled to dwell at Avignon, within the shadow of the French throne, and during this period the papacy had been little more than a mouthpiece for French interests. But in the sixteenth century France had lost all control over papal affairs. Yet the kings of France, unlike the princes of Northern

Germany or the King of England, could not entirely reject the authority of the pope.   If therefore the French monarchs did not wish to sink into insignificance in comparison with the Protestant rulers, it was necessary for them to formulate a new conception of the relations which should exist between the church and the state.   This new conception is best expressed by the term Gallicanism.

There were two aspects to the Gallican movement: one general, which had reference to the powers of the papacy over all Christian communities; the other particular, which had reference to the special rights and privileges of the French branch of the Catholic Church.   In its general aspect the Gallican movement emphasized the idea that a General Council was above the pope; that in the absence of a General Council the pope was, indeed, permitted to take the initiative in laying down points of discipline and doctrine, but his judgments must be tacitly or expressly confirmed by the other bishops before they had the force of law.   Finally it was held that kings received their powers directly from God, and hence the temporal concerns of these rulers lay entirely outside the jurisdiction of the pope.

The particular aspect of Gallicanism was an application of these principles to the French Church in its relation to the French monarchy. In the works of the two French writers, Pithou and Servin, we find the logical development of the Gallican position.   Even in spiritual matters the pope's authority is bounded, as far as France is concerned, by such bulls, canons, and conciliar decrees as the French Church and the French crown choose to regard as valid.   In point of fact none of the papal bulls could be promulgated or published in France until permission had been obtained from the French government.   Already, by the concordat signed between Francis I and the papal court the nomination to all bishoprics and higher benefices lay with the French crown so that for all practical purposes the French ecclesiastical hierarchy consisted of royal appointees.   The Gallicans emphasized the usefulness and intrinsic merit of this arrangement, but went even further and declared that the royal courts should have immediate jurisdiction even over ecclesiastical affairs whenever the law of the land was supposed to have been broken.

Finally the Gallicans insisted that the pope had no power, not even an indirect power, to interfere with the temporal affairs of France.   As the King of France held his authority directly from God, only God could judge him.   Hence the pope had no right to depose or otherwise interfere with the secular authority of the French monarchs, even though these monarchs were guilty of heresy or other crimes.

During the sixteenth and seventeenth centuries the power of the Gallican movement was enormous, numbering among its adherents not merely monarchs and their lay advisers, but also most of the members of the French ecclesiastical hierarchy. Though there was always a minority which maintained the old doctrine of the supreme authority of the popes, including his right of deposition, the popes themselves were careful never to take advantage of the existence of this minority. Fearing no doubt that insistence upon their "rights" might lead the French monarchs to follow the example of Henry VIII and declare the French Church completely independent of papal control, they were extremely cautious in their attempts to exercise influence over the secular magistrates of France — in fact, not only of France but of the other countries of Europe.

Though there was no such organized body as the Gallicans in Italy or in Austria, the papal court seems to have felt that undue interference in secular affairs in these countries might cause an analogous movement to arise. When a dispute broke out between the Republic of Venice and the papacy, and the Venetians were successful in resisting the papal claims, it was realized that the old mediaeval doctrine of the pope as the overlord of all temporal rulers was gone forever, at least as an issue of practical politics.

GROTIUS AND THE RISE OF INTERNATIONAL LAW

The triumph of Protestantism in Northern Europe and the spread of Gallicanism and similar philosophies in Catholic countries heralded a new age in the sphere of international relations. It was necessary for the political theorists of the time to frame a new system for the regulation of the intercourse of states.

In the old days when the whole of Christendom had formed in theory but a single community, international relations in the modern sense of the word did not exist. During the period when the Holy Roman Empire was an effective force, the emperor was regarded as the overlord of all temporal sovereigns, and conflicts between the lesser monarchs could be regarded as merely conflicts between two subjects inside a single state. In theory at least, the emperor should serve as the arbiter and adjudicator of all such "internal disputes."

During the later Middle Ages when the claim to universal dominion by the emperors was seen to be an obvious anachronism, it could still be maintained that Christendom formed but a single community, and that the supreme arbiter and adjudicator of disputes between kings and princes was the pope. It was in connection with the papacy that the first notions regarding international law were developed.

Catholic theologians emphasized the idea that all men at all times were bound by law. But there were several different types of law. There was civil law, promulgated by the secular powers, and owing its validity to the command of the ruler. There was natural law, or the law of nature, a sort of abstract moral law, discovered by the use of reason and of conscience. Finally there was divine law, or the laws ordained directly by God, discoverable only by revelation.

The Catholic writers were unanimous in supposing that all civil or human laws had to be in accordance with natural law, that any human law which was contradictory to the principles of natural law was *ipso facto* invalid. As nature was but a creation of God, it necessarily followed that natural law in its turn was always in complete accord with divine law, and that any attempt to interpret natural law as being contrary to the laws of God as known to us through revelation was *ipso facto* illogical and blasphemous. Last but not least, it was unanimously asserted that the interpretation of divine law was in the hands of the church in general and of the pope in particular.

The effect of this philosophy upon the theory of international relations was obvious. Inside any one state men were bound by civil laws promulgated by the ruler of the state. For the intercourse between nations civil law could not apply because, since the decay of the empire, there was no supreme secular ruler to issue commands to the rulers of the separate principalities.

But the rulers of the separate states and the separate states themselves in their intercourse with one another were bound by the precepts of natural law. As natural law or moral law was intimately allied with divine law or the immediate commands of God as revealed through his church, it followed that the principles for the intercourse of states were the principles of Christian morality as interpreted by the church. Once this idea was accepted it was only logical to assert that the church and its mouthpiece the pope should be regarded as the supreme arbiter in international affairs. Not only should international intercourse be regulated by the decrees laid down by the pope, but it was also advisable that all international disputes be laid before the pope for settlement.

This conception of international relations was all very well when all Western Europe was Catholic in the strictest sense. But when, in the sixteenth century, half of the Catholic world was convinced that the pope had no right to interfere in temporal matters whatever the provo-cation, and when all the Protestant world refused to consider the pope supreme even in spiritual matters, it appeared as if a period of inter-national anarchy had set in.

If kings were subject neither to emperor nor pope, were they not free to do as they pleased with respect to their neighbors? Were they not free to make war when it pleased them, and to conduct warfare in what manner it pleased them? Though justice might prevail inside each state, as far as the relations of states were concerned, was not the only law the law of tooth and claw?

When the Dutch jurist Grotius (1583–1645) began writing (in the early part of the seventeenth century), he was deeply impressed with this problem, all the more so as secular rulers were obviously taking advantage of their newfound freedom from supernational control.

> I have had many and grave reasons [he states] why I should write a book on this subject. For I saw prevailing throughout the Christian world a license in making war, recourse being had to arms for slight reasons or for no reason, and when arms were taken up, all reverence for divine and human law was lost, just as if men were henceforth authorized to commit all crimes without restraint.

It was to obviate or at least check this situation that Grotius set about framing the system of what is now called international law.

Grotius starts with the fundamental assumption that the world is divided, and probably always will be divided, into a number of territorial states. Inside its own boundaries each state is supreme, subject to no higher authority, either secular or spiritual. From this it follows that, legally speaking, all states are to be considered equals, however dispro-portionate their size or their military importance. The power and extent of France or England may be enormous compared with Liechten-stein or San Marino, but from the point of view of international law all these states must be regarded as equals, as none of them admits being subject to a higher power.

The Grotian doctrine of juristic equality of independent states is of great importance in the development of political thought and has been adopted by all subsequent exponents of international law, even though political facts have frequently been in marked contrast to legal theory.

Grotius further assumes that in every state there is a person or a group of persons who have complete control over the state and can therefore adequately represent the state in its relations with other states. All legal relations between states require this assumption, as otherwise it would be impossible for any state to enter into binding treaty relations with another.

As Grotius was a native of the Netherlands, a country in which the republican tradition had been dominant for some time, he was well aware that a state could be governed by an aristocratic or a democratic assembly, but he made it quite clear that in his opinion the natural and normal form of government was monarchy — in fact, absolute monarchy.

Grotius did accept the social contract theory, according to which all political organizations are supposed to have originated in a contract freely entered into by men who had formerly been independent agents, living in a state of nature. But the acceptance of the social contract theory did not interfere with Grotius' advocacy of absolute monarchy. According to him, the social contract, once made, was irrevocable, and no man might free himself from the obligations which the contract implied.

In Roman or in Hebrew law a free man, oppressed by poverty, could and sometimes did sell himself into slavery, and once the sale had been completed, the man could not recover his liberty unless his master vol untarily manumitted him. In like manner once the people have voluntarily delegated supreme power to their monarch, it is wrong, legally and morally, for them to seek by forcible means to recover their independence. "We mistrust the opinion of those who say that sovereignty ... belongs to the people [where such a delegation has taken place], so that the people have authority to coerce and punish kings when they abuse their power."

Having postulated the existence of a number of completely independent states, most of which are normally ruled over by absolute monarchs, Grotius next turns to the crux of his problem — how are the relations of these states to be regulated? It is impossible for these relations to be regulated by any kind of civil law, for civil law is the command of a ruler enforced by sanctions. Civil law exists inside each state, but the very assumption of the independence of each state makes it illogical for them to accept the commands of a higher power.

In order to solve this difficulty, Grotius was forced to revive and reinterpret the old doctrine of natural law, or the law of nature. Law, says Grotius, may be of two types, one "volitional," and the other "rational." Volitional law is the command laid down by a ruler. Rational law is an impersonal, eternal system of right and wrong, laid down by no ruler, which may be known by the use of reason.

The Catholic writers of the Middle Ages had said that natural law is volitional law in that it was the command of the Supreme Ruler, namely God. Grotius did not deny that his natural law was of divine origin, but being a Protestant, he was suspicious of the idea that natural law was the direct command of God, for such an idea led to the notion that natural law could best be interpreted by the church, which claimed to be God's representative on earth.

As if determined to circumvent any attempt by the theologians to monopolize the interpretation of natural law or to grant dispensations from some of its dictates, Grotius declared that the law of nature is so immutable that it cannot be changed even by God Himself, any more than God can change the rule that two and two make four. In fact the dictates of natural law would still be valid, "even if we should grant, what we cannot without great wickedness, that there is no God, or that He bestows no regard upon human affairs."

Grotius insisted that natural law did not need any priestly interpretation, but could be known by all rational beings. The principles of this law are so patent that no one can deny them without doing violence to his own nature. If one has any doubt as to its dictates one has only to refer to the philosophers, the historians, even the poets of all ages. Has it not been the unanimous opinion of all thinkers that murder, theft, and breach of contract are wrong — inherently wrong?

It may be objected that the doctrine of natural law is all very well in theory, but that it is useless in practice, on the ground that law unsupported by force is destitute of all effect. Men refrain from murdering and stealing because they know that they will be punished for murdering and stealing, but how can nations be kept from defying the dictates of moral or natural law when they are aware that there is no higher power which will punish them for breaking this law?

Grotius is fully aware of this objection, but he is a convinced optimist, for he believes that normally men obey, to a greater or lesser extent, the dictates of their conscience. Justice or obedience to natural law brings ease of mind and injustice brings remorse.

Grotius refuses to believe that living beings are motivated entirely by self-interest. Even among the lower animals we find that the principle of self-interest is tempered by regard for their offspring and for others of their species. "The same thing is to be said of infants in whom, previous to all teaching, there is manifested a certain disposition to do good to others." This instinct is still stronger among grown men and women, for man possesses a marked social feeling, a desire to live in company with his fellow man, and he realizes the social life is possible only when there is general obedience to natural law.

Grotius believes that there is such a thing as public conscience, and argues that the mere formulation and exposition of a set of rules for international morality will go far towards forcing nations to keep within the bounds of these rules.

He further argues that even the principle of self-interest will eventually force all states to abide by the dictates of natural law. "Honesty is the best policy." Even in private life a firm noted for its shady practices, though it keep within the letter of the law, gradually acquires a bad reputation and loses customers. In like manner nations in the long run need the approbation of their neighbors if they are to survive. "A people which violates the law of nature . . . breaks down the bulwark of its own tranquillity for future time." . . . "Alliances are sought even by the most powerful peoples and kings; the force of such alliances is entirely destroyed by those who confine law within the boundaries of a state," that is, by those who do not abide by the dictates of natural law.

Having decided that in theory the intercourse of independent states *should* be regulated by natural law, Grotius proceeds to examine the actual intercourse of states and the principles which appear to underlie this intercourse. This leads him to revive and reinterpret another mediaeval doctrine, that of *Jus Gentium* or the law of nations.

The term *Jus Gentium* was originally applied in Roman law to a body of law consisting of those rules which were discovered to be common to the juristic practice of many different peoples. This system of law developed at a time when Rome ceased to be a city-state and became a world empire. At this period the old Roman civil law was applied only to the intercourse of Roman citizens, who constituted a small fraction of the total number of those subject to Roman rule. For the intercourse of Roman subjects who were not Roman citizens, it was found impossible to apply the laws of any one tribe or people, and the Roman jurists sought to give justice to all by applying those rules which seemed to be common to all or to most of the peoples with whom they came into contact. At this time, though *Jus Gentium* was a body of law common to different nations, it still applied to individuals and the relations between individuals.

In the sixteenth century, in large measure as the result of the influence of Grotius and his writings, the old notion of *Jus Gentium* was radically changed. *Jus Gentium* became a body of laws, or rather a set of customs and traditions, regulating the relations between nations. At this period it had already become customary to grant special privileges and immunities to the ambassadors of foreign powers; hence, Grotius could claim that diplomatic immunity formed part of the *Jus Gentium* or law of nations.

What is the relation between the law of nature and the law of nations? The former is the foundation on which the intercourse of nations *should* be based. The latter is the foundation upon which the intercourse of nations is actually based. Man being weak and sinful, the customary law of nations is not always in accord with the eternal moral maxims of the law of nature. It is perhaps impossible in this humdrum world for the pure law of nature ever to be directly applied to the intercourse of states. Nevertheless it is obvious from Grotius' fundamental principles that the law of nations must be based upon the law of nature and may not depart from it too radically.

The principal work of Grotius, his monumental *Law of War and Peace*, is in reality a study of the precedents which do govern and have governed the intercourse of nations and a criticism of these precedents from the point of view of the law of nature. Grotius therefore had a twofold object in writing his book. One was the codification of existing customs in such matters. The other was an attempt to rectify the injustices and inequalities of some of these customs from the standpoint of natural or moral law. On these points Grotius feels that the light of reason (in other words, Grotius' own arguments) will be sufficiently powerful to cause men to alter the old unjust customs.

The details of the system of international law (actual and ideal) worked out by Grotius do not concern us here. Most of his ideas have passed into the body of international law as recognized today. As is but natural, seeing how commonly the intercourse of states is of a martial character, a large part of Grotius' work deals with war and the rules which should regulate the conduct of war.

Grotius was in many ways an idealist, but he was enough of a realist to recognize that war was more or less inevitable, in fact in certain cases he believed it to be perfectly just. By natural law a man has the right to defend his own person, so by international law a nation has the duty to undertake a war when its boundaries or the lives of its citizens are endangered. Grotius thus distinguishes between "just" and "unjust" wars — a very valuable distinction in theory, but somewhat ridiculous in practice, as every nation persuades itself that every war upon which it embarks is a "just" war.

Even when a war is in progress, Grotius thinks that the rules of international law hold good.   Nations are not permitted to use poisons or
poisoned missiles.   In most cases, they may not confiscate or destroy
the private property of the subjects of the enemy, but in a war against
pirates or rebels any property seized belongs to the captors.

NOTES TO CHAPTER TWO

1. J. N. Figgis, *Political Thought from Gerson to Grotius*, p. 4.   By permission of
The Cambridge University Press and The Macmillan Company, publishers.
2. Figgis, *Divine Right of Kings*, p. 142.
3. Quoted in J. W. Allen, *History of Political Thought in the Sixteenth Century*, p. 174.
4. Quoted in *ibid.*, p. 163.

BIBLIOGRAPHY

C. Petrie, *Story of Government*.   Boston, 1929.

H. Sidgwick, *Development of European Polity*.   London, 1903.

F. J. C. Hearnshaw, ed., *Social and Political Ideas of Some Great Mediaeval
Thinkers*.   London, 1923.

R. W. and A. J. Carlyle, *History of Mediaeval Political Theory*.   London, 1903–
1936.

J. N. Figgis, *Political Thought from Gerson to Grotius*.   Second edition.   Cambridge, 1923.

J. N. Figgis, *Divine Right of Kings*.   Second edition.   Cambridge, 1922.

J. W. Allen, *History of Political Thought in the Sixteenth Century*.   New York, 1928

F. J. C. Hearnshaw, ed., *Social and Political Ideas of the Renaissance and Reformation*.   London, 1925.

F. J. C. Hearnshaw, *Social and Political Ideas of the Sixteenth and Seventeenth
Centuries*.   London, 1926.

R. H. Murray, *Political Consequences of the Reformation*.   London, 1926.

R. H. Tawney, *Religion and the Rise of Capitalism*.   New York, 1926.

E. Troeltsch, *Soziallehre der Christlichen Kirchen und Gruppen*.   Munich, 1912.

L. H. Waring, *The Political Theories of Martin Luther*.   New York, 1910.

R. G. Usher, *Reconstruction of the English Church*.   New York, 1910 (for Angli-
canism).

G. Weill, *Les Théories sur le pouvoir royal en France pendant les guerres de religion*.
Paris, 1892 (for Gallicanism).

H. Grotius, *De Jure Belli ac Pacis*, Latin text with an abbreviated English translation by W. Whewell, London, 1853; see also the English translation by F. W.
Kelsey, Oxford, 1925.

H. Vreeland, *Hugo Grotius*.   New York, 1917.

J. M. Littlejohn, *Political Theories of the Schoolmen and Grotius*.   College Springs,
1894.

CHAPTER III

The Defense of Absolute Monarchy

LARGELY as the result of the Reformation, the political thought of the sixteenth and seventeenth centuries recognized the complete independence of the various states into which Europe was divided.

Equally important was the stress most political philosophers of this period laid upon the need for unity within each state. This unity implied that the state should no longer be broken up into a number of semi-independent fiefs nor checked in its actions by the privileges and immunities of special groups and classes. Henceforth the state was to have direct and complete control over all its citizens.

In order to secure this internal unity, the majority of the political theorists of this era emphasized the supremacy and absolute power of the highest ruler of each state, who was normally an hereditary king. It was essentially this striving for unity, for internal peace and order, which resulted in the widespread acceptance of absolute monarchy as the best and wisest system of government.

Among the writers who achieved most prominence as advocates of monarchic government were the little group of French, Scottish, and English thinkers who championed the idea of "the divine right of kings." Of even greater importance were the complete political philosophies developed by Bodin and by Hobbes.

THE DIVINE RIGHT OF KINGS

The full collapse of the doctrine of the divine right of kings in the eighteenth and nineteenth centuries has left us with the idea that the whole conception was inherently ridiculous. It is difficult for us to believe that our forefathers could be and were perfectly sincere in their acceptance of this doctrine, yet it is clear that the belief in the divine right of kings was accepted by many of the subtlest and ablest minds of the age. In fact, working upon the assumptions which were universally accepted in the sixteenth century, we find the idea that kings rule by divine right was perfectly logical and consistent.

It should not be forgotten that the doctrine of the social contract which dominated men's minds in the seventeenth and eighteenth centuries was quite as absurd as the doctrine of the divine right of kings, which it tended to displace.   But just as we must retain a warm spot in our hearts for the doctrine of the social contract because of the magnificent results it achieved by preparing public opinion to accept the English Revolution of 1688 and the French and American Revolutions of the following century, so in like manner must we pay due reverence to the doctrine of the divine right of kings because of its political consequences.

It was really the belief in the divinity of the temporal ruler of each state which once and for all broke the mediaeval concept of the universal church-state, and permitted the emergence of the national state of today.   The work of Luther in Germany, of Henry VIII in England, of the Gallicans in France had been important, but it had been negative. It had rejected the belief that it was the function of the pope to interfere with the national affairs of Germany, England, and France, but this rejection had left a void in men's minds which it was necessary to fill before the work of the reformers and the Gallicans could be called complete.

The Protestant who denied all connection between God and the papacy felt forlorn in the absence of contacts with some divinely appointed institution, until he was told that he could find this contact in the monarch who ruled over him.   If his state and the ruler of his state owed their existence and their power to Divine Providence, he could be content even though all ties with other countries were cut.

The Catholic who wished to remain Catholic, but who desired to share in the thrill of nationalist emotion which was arising all over Europe, felt that he could do so if he accepted the doctrine that though the pope was ordained by God to rule over purely spiritual matters, his own ruler was no less directly ordained by God to rule over temporal affairs.

If the doctrine of the divine right of kings was of great importance in the transition from internationalism to nationalism, it was of equally great importance in tending to centralize all power within the state, minimizing feudal privileges, and abolishing municipalities to a semi-independent existence.

Most of the defenders of divine right believed that all authorities ultimately derived their power from God, but they were also unanimously of the opinion that the lower magistrates received the divine commission only indirectly, as a result of their appointment or recognition by the supreme temporal ruler in each state.   It was this supreme temporal ruler who governed by God's direct ordaining. The inferior magistrates, even dukes and earls, could and should be held accountable to other men and to courts of law, but the king, the supreme ruler was accountable for his actions only to God. How could feudal privileges and corporate rights survive after the acceptance of such a philosophy?

The germs of the doctrine of the divine right of kings go back to very ancient times. It is, moreover, expressed in one form or another by several writers in the Middle Ages, but the fully developed doctrine first appeared only in the sixteenth century. It is significant that most of the adherents of this belief at this time were Catholics, who were desirous of getting the political benefits of the Reformation without breaking with the historic Roman Church.

The immediate cause of the theory can be traced to the peculiar political situation which existed in France at this period. The House of Valois having died out, the legitimate heir to the throne was Henry of Navarre, later Henry IV. Now Henry was a Protestant and was because of this fact officially banned by the pope in 1585. How was a patriotic Frenchman to remain a good Catholic if he wished to see the legitimate heir ascend the throne?

Eventually Henry solved the problem by becoming converted to the Catholic faith; yet even before taking this step he had secured a great deal of support from the French Catholics because of the promulgation of the doctrine of the divine right of kings.

Belloy (1540–1609), who was the most important advocate of the theory at this period and who wrote shortly after Henry had been excommunicated, was insistent that Henry's right to the succession had in no way been affected by the papal ban. The crown comes to a particular man through the action of Divine Providence, and the right of God's chosen cannot be taken away by any human action, not even by the pope. Nor, when once on the throne, can the king ever be deposed, for he holds his crown immediately under God and by God's authority.

Belloy insists that a government must rest upon the obligation of its subjects to obey it. A people may grant a ruler a certain amount of actual power, but what they give, they can also take away. Hence the idea that a government rests upon popular consent leads to revolution and hence to anarchy. Real authority, the right to rule and to demand obedience, rests with God and God's deputies. God has deputed kings to act for him in temporal affairs. Therefore rebellion against a king is rebellion against God.

The doctrine of the divine right of kings was developed by Belloy and numerous other Frenchmen as an instrument of propaganda at a particular time and for a particular issue — to prove that Henry of Navarre had a divine right to the French throne. But the doctrine was soon broadened by other writers of many different nationalities to prove that all monarchs at all times rule by divine appointment. The persons most prominent in the spread of the divine right theory throughout Europe were two Scottish writers, William Barclay and King James VI (later James I of England).

There is something curiously contradictory about the career of Barclay (1546–1608). A learned and distinguished Scotsman, he was regarded with high favor by his royal master at home, yet was forced to spend all the latter part of his life in France because of his devout adherence to Catholicism. At the same time, Barclay stressed the doctrine that his religious overlord, the pope, had no control over temporal rulers. Had he been willing to forgo his Catholicism, Barclay would have risen to high office in Scotland; had he been willing to forgo his belief in the divine right of kings, he might have had a splendid career in the service of the Catholic Church. As it was, he was forced to eke out a precarious existence by serving as professor of civil law in various French academies.

Barclay has little new to add to the doctrine of the divine right of kings; he contents himself with developing and generalizing the ideas formulated by his predecessors. Nevertheless his works may be considered the best, the most complete, and the most logically consistent of those which seek to prove that monarchs rule by divine right.

By citing the behavior of insects and animals (bees, he claims, are governed by a king), Barclay tries to prove that monarchy is the natural form of government. By an appeal to history he attempts to prove that monarchy has shown itself to be the wisest and noblest form of government. By an appeal to Scripture, he seeks to prove that monarchy is the form of polity most in conformity with God's wishes and commands.

As with Belloy, the essential point of Barclay's political system is that all authority is ultimately derived from God. Authority itself can never be granted by the people. Even in the case of an elective monarchy, the electors merely choose which person shall enjoy this authority. The authority itself remains of divine origin. But though Barclay admits that an elective monarchy is a valid form of government, it is clear that he believes the ideal monarchy is one in which the throne passes from father to son, and in which no legitimate heir to the throne may be excluded for any reason whatsoever.

By monarchy Barclay means, of course, absolute monarchy. The king, being the true source of all legislation, is himself *legibus solutus*, not subject to law. Though the pope should have spiritual jurisdiction over all persons, he may never interfere with the action of a temporal monarch, as temporal monarchs receive their powers directly from God and are responsible to God alone. Though a monarch may find it useful to summon his subjects in parliaments, the fact that these assemblies meet when the monarch summons them and are prorogued or dissolved when he so commands shows that the power of these assemblies is entirely derivative. The powers they possess are conferred on them by monarchs, and these powers may be taken away when the monarch chooses.

King James (1566–1625) was almost as much of a paradox as Barclay. Henry VII, Henry VIII, and Elizabeth were in many ways far more absolute rulers than was James, yet none of these monarchs expressly claimed to rule by divine right. James by his pedantry, his miserliness, his love for unworthy minions, his tirades against tobacco, did much to make the person and the office of king ridiculous. We find many of his subjects praying for the welfare of their "silly king"; to others he was known as the "most learned fool in Christendom." No monarch did more to make kingship less inspiring, less glamorous, yet James was the only monarch who ever attempted by preaching and writing to prove that the rulership of kings was divine in origin — that all kings must not only be obeyed, they must also be regarded with reverent awe by their subjects. Other kings may have believed in these doctrines, but James was the only monarch openly to expound them.

King James' political philosophy may be summed up in his own words:

> The duties and alleagance of the people to their lawful king ... ought to be to him as to God's lieutenant in earth, obeying his commands in all things ... as the commands of God's minister, acknowledging him a Judge set by God over them, having power to judge them, but to be judged only by God, following and obeying his lawful commands, eschewing and flying his furie in his unlawful, without resistance, but by sobs and tears to God.[1]

In a speech before Parliament King James is even more emphatic in associating divinity with the office of king.

> Kings are justly called Gods for they exercise a manner or resemblance of divine power upon earth. For if you consider the attributes to God you will see how they agree in the person of a king. God hath power to create or

destroy, make or unmake at his pleasure, to give life or send death, to judge all and to be judged or accountable to none, to raise low things and make high things low at his pleasure, and to God are both soul and body due. And the like power have kings. They make and unmake their subjects: they have power of raising and casting down: of life and of death: judges over their subjects and in all causes and yet accountable to none but God only. They have power to exalt low things and abuse high things and make of their subjects like men at the chess.[2]

One of the most interesting and popular exponents of the divine right of kings was Sir Robert Filmer (?–1653). Unlike King James, Filmer was a rather obscure person. Though knighted by Charles I he was never a great state personage, nor did he even enjoy the intimacy or especial favor of the royal court. Nevertheless Filmer became the most noted of the defenders of absolute monarchy during the troublesome seventeenth century when the English engaged in civil war to solve the problem whether kings should or should not be allowed to exist at all.

Filmer differed and was forced to differ from the earlier advocates of the divine right theory. These earlier advocates had written when the movement towards a strong national monarchy was popular and seemed progressive. They could be content with a few simple assertions, knowing that they could be sure of a great measure of popular approval, however threadbare their arguments. Filmer, on the other hand, wrote his books and pamphlets when, in England at any rate, absolute monarchy was unpopular; when the people were lending a willing ear to the advocates of the anti-monarchic cause; when Parliament had already engaged in armed conflict with the king. Filmer was therefore on the defensive. His principal task was to answer the claims of those who asserted that kings derived their powers not from God but from the populace, and that powers granted by the people might be taken away by the people.

Filmer's predecessors had, for the most part, contented themselves with citing scriptural texts to prove that there was a divine sanction for kingship, and that in consequence anyone who revolted against kings was guilty of blasphemy. But it was soon seen that Scripture could be used to reach very different conclusions. If some texts seemed to preach the divinity of kings, other texts could be brought forward which described kings as tyrants lacking all authority from God. Though many scriptural passages might be quoted which taught complete submission to the higher magistrates, anti-royal advocates argued that obedience to Parliament was as important as obedience to the king, or even that the king in struggling to free himself from parliamentary control was himself guilty of disobedience to the fundamental laws and institutions of his country.

Filmer was obviously aware of this difficulty, and though he himself accepted the position of the older adherents of divine right, he felt it necessary to emphasize a different type of argument in favor of the divinity of kings: namely, that absolute monarchy is in accordance with nature and human nature, and as both nature and human nature were created by God, absolute monarchy is in accordance with divine law.

Many of Filmer's contemporaries were preaching that in a state of nature men are free and equal. Filmer argues, however, that equality and freedom are as absent there as in the most developed state, since in any state there are gross inequalities in the physical and mental capacities of individual men. To assert that in a natural state men are "free" is absurd. It is universally agreed that at all times parents have a natural right to control their children. Hence, far from coming into the world free, every man is born into a condition of natural subjection to his parents and to his tribal leaders.

Filmer is merciless to those of his contemporaries who taught that a government must be based upon the consent of the governed because government itself was first instituted as the result of a social contract between individuals. In the first place, says Filmer, the doctrine of the social contract leads straight to anarchy, for from this doctrine it logically follows that any man and any group of men have the right to withdraw from the social contract and resume their natural rights. And so, "any petty company hath a right to make a kingdom of itself, and not only every city but every village and every family; nay and every particular man a liberty to choose himself to be his own king if he please." [3]

In the second place, Filmer points out, the doctrine of the social contract is completely unhistorical. At what period in human history did the social contract take place? "It cannot be truly said that the whole people or the major part or indeed any considerable part of the whole people of any nation ever assembled to any such purpose." [4] Even if one part of the people had met for this purpose, how could the absent be in any way bound?

Filmer's opponents argued that the vote of the majority binds the whole people. But on the basis of the social contract it would have to be admitted that when the contract was made, it was unanimously agreed that in future the decision of the majority should bind everyone; and surely such an agreement was never made.

In contrast with the idea that the state is a mechanical organization created by contract, Filmer postulates the doctrine that the state is a natural and organic growth. In accordance with this doctrine, the first unit in political organization was the family ruled over by the *pater familias*. Gradually the family expanded into the tribe ruled over by the patriarch, who was only the *pater familias* on a large scale. Finally the tribe expanded into the nation or state in which the office of patriarch developed into that of king. As the father is the natural ruler of his family, as the patriarch is the natural ruler of his tribe, so the king is the natural ruler of his people. This rulership rests neither on force nor on the "consent of the governed," but on human nature as formed by God.

Led astray in his logic by the custom of family inheritance common to most countries in Western Europe, Filmer next postulates the idea that it is "natural" for the power of the father to descend to the eldest son. Once this postulate is granted, it follows that the power of the patriarch and of the king should also "naturally" descend to their eldest sons by indefeasible hereditary right, and that anyone who attempts to alter this line of succession or who rebels against the lawful heir is acting contrary to nature and to nature's God.

JEAN BODIN

The advocates of the divine right of kings were for the most part concerned only with one political problem, the nature and the power of the monarchy. In contrast with the narrow scope of these thinkers, we find that Bodin and Hobbes attempted to construct complete political philosophies, covering all phases of state and governmental activity.

Bodin (1530–1596) was the most vigorous and logical of the political theorists of the sixteenth century, and because of his scholarliness, his clear vision, and his rationality, deserves to be ranked with the great political philosophers of all times. Though a lawyer and therefore primarily interested in the problems of the state from a legal point of view, Bodin had an astonishingly wide range of interests. He pondered long on the philosophy of history and wrote what may be called the first book on the subject. He was profoundly interested in what would now be called sociology and economics. He even dabbled in the obscure fields of astrology and psychic research.

Two of the outstanding contributions of Bodin in the realm of general speculation were his idea of the progress of mankind and his notions of the influence of environment and climate upon human institutions.

Classical antiquity and the Middle Ages were both dominated by the idea of the fall or degeneration of mankind. The classical authors looked back with envy to a mythical "golden age" in remote antiquity. The pious thinkers of the Middle Ages felt sure that man's first parents had been blissful and serene in the Garden of Eden. Both the ancient and the mediaeval philosophers took it for granted that neither the world in general nor man in particular was getting any better as time went on. They were usually convinced that both were getting worse.

Bodin was the first to enunciate the doctrines, so dear to the optimists of the nineteenth and twentieth centuries, that man's lot is steadily improving, that the moderns are definitely superior to the ancients, and that there is no limit to man's potential progress. When men doubted the law of progress, Bodin pointed to gunpowder and printing as examples of the great superiority of the moderns to the ancients.

The consequences of this theory upon political speculation are of major importance. If progress be true, there is no need for us to base our political ideas or our political institutions upon those prevalent in ancient times. It might well be that modern Europe can surpass ancient Greece and Rome, not merely in mechanical inventions, but also in political and social organization.

The theory of the influence of environment upon mankind and his political and social institutions was no less significant. The mediaeval Christians, like the Greek Stoics and the Roman jurists, had been cosmopolitans at heart. A man possessed the same reasoning ability and the same emotions, at least potentially, whatever his race and whatever region of the earth's surface he might inhabit. As a result of this attitude, it was believed that political and social institutions were or should be universal in character — that there certainly could be no objection to transplanting the institutions of one country to another.

In contrast with this universalism Bodin was a particularist. He believed that both latitude and longitude have an effect upon men's character, and hence upon their economic, social, and political organization. The peoples of the colder zone have always been noted for their military ability, the inhabitants of hot regions for their craft and their skill in philosophy and diplomacy. The inhabitants of the temperate countries, in which France, Bodin's own motherland, was included, are especially adapted to legal and political life and are bound to assume leadership in these matters.

This environmentalism in Bodin's philosophy was destined to have an important effect upon later speculation.   Revived in the eighteenth century by Montesquieu, it led to the establishment of the sciences of anthropo-geography and geo-politics in the nineteenth and twentieth centuries.

To Bodin's own mind the doctrine of environmentalism was of significance because of its political implications.   It strengthened his disbelief in the possibility of a universal empire, an ideal for which the Middle Ages had struggled so long in vain.   It led to his acceptance of the idea that a multitude of states each with a somewhat different type of government is the normal condition of affairs.

While Bodin's doctrine of progress and his belief in the influence of climate are for us of especial interest and significance, to his contemporaries Bodin was chiefly known for his contributions to the theory of the origin and function of the state.

Bodin's theory of the origin of the state differed radically from those of most of his predecessors and contemporaries.   In contrast with those philosophers who claimed that the state was of divine institution and in contrast with those who believed that the state originated in a voluntary social contract between its individual members, Bodin attempted to show that the state originated by *force.*

He postulates a pre-social life of mankind when each man, or at least each *pater familias,* was "free" in the sense that he was not subject to any external restraints.   But this stage did not last long. The natural gregariousness of mankind gradually brought about a grouping of families around a few favored spots, thereby forming the rudiments of social organization.   Although the spontaneous working of human nature can thus account for the origin of *society,* it does not account for the origin of the state, as primitive society was completely lacking in political organization.   Even so, this social grouping lessened the liberty of each family, as all associations, even those voluntarily entered into, necessarily infringe upon the liberty of the individual.

Political, as opposed to social organization begins when a strong man or a group of strong men set out to dominate and conquer their neighbors.   The victor establishes permanent political control over the vanquished.

Bodin tries to prove this point, not only by quoting examples from ancient history, but also by citing cases taken from the primitive peoples of his own time.   We are told that the people of Gao in Africa had known nothing of political organization until a short time previously.

Then one of their numbers, inspired by the examples of the North African kingdoms, secured by brute force control over his fellow tribesmen. The son of this despot, Bodin tells us, assumed the title of king and, from motives of expediency (in order the better to preserve his rule against revolt), adopted the policy of equity and justice to disguise the brutal origin of the royal power. A similar development is assumed to have taken place in all politically organized states.

Bodin's theory of the origin of the state by force is of singular interest to us. Rejected or ignored by most of the writers of the sixteenth and seventeenth centuries, it was revived in the nineteenth and twentieth centuries by a group of sociologists and is today accepted by most social scientists.

In Bodin's own mind the value of his *force* theory was that it enabled him to annihilate those of his contemporaries who believed in the social contract theory or who otherwise argued that governmental authority was derived from or based upon the consent of the governed.

But though Bodin believed the state originated in force, he also held that human progress and the development of culture and civilization make it necessary, or at least advisable, that rulership be in accord with divine and moral law. Bodin looked askance at forceful usurpation of power in modern states. Most of his writings were inspired by his attachment to the cause of Henry IV, the legitimate claimant to the French throne, and Bodin naturally wished to see no high-handed military leader take Henry's place as the sovereign of France.

Bodin's theory of the origin of the state enables us to understand his insistence upon the doctrine of *sovereignty*. In fact the idea of sovereignty was Bodin's chief contribution to political philosophy. Though notions akin to this doctrine had not been entirely unknown to earlier writers, it was Bodin who first systematically dealt with the subject. It was Bodin, therefore, who may be considered as its originator.

Since Bodin's time the problem of sovereignty has played a major role in all political theorizing. It has been made the subject of an enormous literature. The vast majority of subsequent theorists have accepted, with some modifications, Bodin's concept, and it was only amongst the small group of political pluralists that the idea of sovereignty was definitely denied.

What was the theory of sovereignty which was thus introduced into political literature by Bodin? It may be summarized as the claim that *the state shall have sole ultimate control over all persons and corpora-*

tions within its territory, and, secondly, that *within every state a person or a group of persons possess potentially absolute power over the state and the legislative activities of the state.* As a necessary corollary of this last statement, Bodin holds that the sovereign shall not be subject to law.

The idea that the state should possess absolute power over all persons and corporations within its territory rules out, first of all, the theory that the state is in any way subject to external authority. Though Bodin was himself a Catholic, he thus denies all papal control over the secular affairs of France. He ignores the shadowy claims of the emperor as the overlord of all nations as not being worthy of serious discussion.

More important still (for freedom from external control had already been taught by Luther and Henry VIII), Bodin proclaimed the complete subjection to the state of all persons and all groups of persons within the state. As we have already had occasion to observe, the Middle Ages had been full of examples of great lords who lived in little more than nominal subjection to the king. The Dukes of Burgundy had only paid lip allegiance to the Kings of France. The feudal nobility as a class had secured for themselves many special privileges which it was impossible for the royal power to take away. Many of the cities and some of the guilds and corporations within the cities had secured charters granting them important and supposedly inalienable rights against aggression from the head of the state.

It was the existence of these conditions which had prevented the recognition of sovereignty in earlier times. But in the period in which Bodin wrote, the powers of the nobility and the corporations were definitely waning. Those powers which remained were regarded as survivals from evil and disorderly eras. "Progress" — and let it not be forgotten that Bodin was a great believer in progress — was all in the direction of unification and centralization of authority. In handing to the state complete control over all its citizens, Bodin was giving theoretical justification to a tendency which was already becoming dominant in all the countries of Western Europe.

Molière, the great French dramatist, tells us that M. Jourdain was happy to find that he had been talking prose all his life. Somewhat similarly the monarchs of the sixteenth century were delighted to have Bodin tell them that their endeavors to dominate all their subjects were merely attempts to exercise the inalienable rights of sovereignty which were inherent in every state.

In later times the doctrine of sovereignty was held to imply the equality of all citizens under the law. By some it was believed to be incompatible with the possession of special privileges by the nobility. Bodin himself did not go this far in his beliefs. He definitely scoffed at the idea of social equality and praised the existence of the privileged nobility as a very useful and praiseworthy institution. Or rather he taught that it was useful for the state to *grant* the nobles certain special rights, on the condition that they understood these rights might be withdrawn at will. Even the greatest of the nobles, indeed the nobility as a class, has no inalienable rights as opposed to the sovereign state.

He believed the same in regard to the numerous guilds and corporations within the state. Bodin recognized the value and importance of these guilds and devoted much space to a consideration of their function and purpose. He believed their existence necessary in a well-ordered state, but he was firmly convinced that their existence should be based upon their recognition and control by the state. To express this idea in modern phraseology, clubs, labor unions, religious organizations, all fulfill a useful function, but only as long as they admit the supremacy of the state.

Having postulated the sovereignty of the state itself, Bodin next turns to the proposition that supreme and absolute power must exist in the hands of one person or group of persons within each state. To Bodin's mind the truth of sovereignty in this sense is implied in the very nature of laws and lawmaking. A law to be valid is not merely a postulate of reason; it is also the command of a sovereign and is enforced by sanctions. Divine and natural laws owe their validity to the fact that they are the commands of God. Civil or human laws owe their validity to the fact that they are the commands of the supreme legislator or legislators within each state. According to Bodin, it is possible to see where sovereignty rests within any particular state by determining where the ultimate lawmaking power resides.

Following the age-old classification of Aristotle, Bodin asserts that this sovereign power may reside in the hands of a single person, in which case we have a monarchy; or in the hands of a limited number of persons, in which case we have an aristocracy; or, finally, it may rest in the hands of the people, or at least in the hands of a majority of the people, in which case we have a democracy. Several of the classical authors had spoken of the possibility, and even of the advisability, of a "mixed state," usually associated in their minds with the idea of check and balance. In other words, inside the same state we may find control divided among king, aristocracy, and democracy.

Bodin claims that sovereignty is indivisible and that a "mixed state" not only is ludicrous but is really impossible. In order to prove this assertion, Bodin is forced to distinguish between state and government — an important distinction which he was one of the first to point out, but which was later recognized by most other political philosophers. A government consists of the normal officers of administration. In a particular country we may have a king, a House of Lords, and a House of Commons; but ultimate control must rest with one and only one of these three organs of government, the other two possessing only derivative or delegated powers.

Thus Bodin asserted that the "Holy Roman Empire" of his day was really an aristocracy — since the real power was in the hands of the princes, in spite of the fact that these princes were nominally subject to an emperor. Sixteenth century England, according to Bodin, was really a monarchy as ultimate power was in the hands of the king, notwithstanding the existence of a House of Lords and a House of Commons. The present government of England would undoubtedly be classed by Bodin as a democracy, for, though the king continues to reign, supreme power has passed into the hands of the people.

Bodin would probably have pointed with delight to the United States as a clear example of a state possessing one "sovereign" (namely, the people taken as a whole), and yet maintaining an elaborate system of checks and balances upon the organs of government — the legislative, the executive, and the judicial branches being thus strictly limited in their functions.

After having declared that no matter how many organs of government a state may contain, sovereignty or supreme power must rest either in a monarchy, an aristocracy, or a democracy, Bodin next proceeds to weigh the merits and demerits of each one of these systems. He has much to say regarding the advantages and the disadvantages of each form of government. In the end he comes to the conclusion that for most countries and most peoples, and certainly for France, hereditary monarchy is by far the best form of the state — largely because it is in this system that the whole idea of sovereignty receives its clearest and simplest expression.

By the very definition of sovereignty, the monarch is to be the source of legislation, and is *legibus solutus*, not subject to law himself, as all laws are merely the expression of his command. Bodin admits the sanctity of contracts and includes among valid ones the solemn promise which a monarch makes that he will obey certain laws, but he is bound, however, merely by his promise and not by the law itself. Bodin strongly urges the king not to tie his hands by making rash promises to his subjects, but the matter does not appear to be very important, as the king is allowed in certain circumstances to break his promise. Just as a private person may be relieved of his obligation if he has been circumvented by fraud, error, or threat, so may a monarch be released from those promises which tend to impair his sovereignty and also where "his private and domestic affairs are imperiled."

In the absence of specific promises, the monarch may, Bodin insists, make, modify, and abrogate any law he pleases without the consent of his subjects. Bodin deals at some length with the national and provincial States-General, which in the sixteenth century were still the normal channels for enacting legislation in France. Bodin admitted that these assemblies have their value and believed that the wise monarch will consult the representatives of his subjects before enacting or rescinding legislation, but he was adamant in denying to the States-General absolute right to enact or to veto any law. The opinion of those who claim that the king is in any way bound by the desires of these assemblies is a "seditious doctrine and leads to disturbance in the state."

Bodin was also insistent that the monarch is not at all bound by custom or customary law, an idea which is recognized as important when we remember that all during the Middle Ages customary law held a paramount place in the legal systems of Western Europe. As late as the seventeenth century, many lawyers and judges in England held that the common law, based on custom, was supreme and could not be abrogated by statute law, even though the latter be enacted by both king and Parliament. Bodin indignantly denies any such doctrine. He admits the value of custom and customary law, but asserts that custom has compelling force only as long as the monarch sanctions and endorses it. And "what the monarch permits, he commands."

Such in a few words is Bodin's famous doctrine of sovereignty. At first glance it appears that by this doctrine the national monarch was given absolute power over his subjects. Such were the natural and logical implications of the doctrine, and such was the concept of sovereignty as expounded by later authors. Bodin himself, however, the first person formally to postulate the idea of sovereignty, was at times unaware of some of the conclusions to which his doctrine should naturally lead.

Later theorists when speaking of absolute sovereignty meant absolute sovereignty. With Bodin absolute sovereignty turns out to mean limited sovereignty, as he enumerates a number of very important checks upon the exercise of sovereign power. In the first place, Bodin states that though the monarch is not subject to civil or human law, he is necessarily subject to divine and natural laws, as these are the commands of God, who is the supreme sovereign of the universe. In actual practice this reservation was not of major importance, as it seems the monarch could place his own interpretation upon both types of laws. When, however, the monarch enacted a law which was manifestly contrary to divine or to moral law, the subordinate magistrates were not required to enforce it.

The doctrine of the superiority of divine and natural law, as the command of a real or supposed superior sovereign, was perfectly logical. Far less logical was Bodin's claim that the monarch might not act contrary to a few fundamental laws (*leges imperii*), the most important of which, as far as France was concerned, was the Salic law, by which the throne descended only by the principle of primogeniture, but with the exclusion of females. The absolute King of France, therefore, was unable to change the law of succession — though Bodin does not tell us who first enacted these fundamental laws and from whom they still derive their validity.

Even more astonishing was Bodin's claim that his "absolute sovereign" possessed no right to interfere with the sanctity of his subjects' family life, that is, had no right to take possession of his subjects' womenfolk. More important still was the statement that the monarch had no right to seize private property. "Without just cause the sovereign can neither seize nor give away the property of another." In other words the "absolute monarch" can take no man's property without the latter's consent. In consequence, the monarch in normal times has no right to levy direct taxation on his subjects without having first obtained their consent through the agency of the States-General. Unless this consent is forthcoming, the monarch is forced to rely upon the income from the crown lands (always a considerable item) or else have recourse to indirect taxes, which, according to Bodin, the monarch is free to impose upon his subjects without seeking their consent.

It seems difficult for us to reconcile the notion of an absolute monarch who can legislate as he pleases with the idea of a monarch who is strictly limited in his taxing power. But it appears that Bodin regarded the family and private property as the eternal and essential elements of any state, so that when the sovereign oversteps the bounds in either

of these two spheres, he is destroying the foundations of the state itself
and thereby interfering with the very purpose for which sovereignty
exists.

After having enunciated the fundamental principles of his philosophy
of the state, Bodin proceeds to give some sage counsel to the administration regarding certain matters of practical policy.   Many features of
this counsel show that Bodin possessed great sagacity.   In several instances he shows himself far in advance of his time.

At a time when religious persecution was rampant and open warfare
was being waged between Catholics and Protestants, Bodin preached
the doctrine of religious toleration.   The toleration of Bodin was not
without its limitations.   Atheists were not to be suffered, on the ground
that atheists would not make good citizens.   The state should seek to
prevent the rise of new sects and heresies, as these might lead to social
disturbances.   But where two or more religions already existed in a
state, as in France with its Catholic majority and large Huguenot
minority, it was useless and worse than useless for the state to seek to
impose religious uniformity.   To do so would merely lead to civil war
and thus weaken the state; and to Bodin the weakening of the state was
the greatest of all calamities.

Though Bodin's doctrine tended to make the citizens of a country
completely subservient to their monarch, Bodin was violently opposed to
slavery.   At one time slavery had been almost universal in Europe, bu·
for centuries this system had been on the wane, and Bodin revolted at the
revival of an "ancient barbarous custom" in the form of Negro slavery.

In like manner Bodin was opposed to too great social and economic
inequality.   Though he regarded the idea of absolute equality as dangerous and absurd, he was careful to point out that vast and insuperable
inequalities in a state tend to produce revolutions.   While the monarch
is not permitted to confiscate wealth already accumulated, he should
frame laws which will prevent the growth of unduly large fortunes.

Bodin was vociferous in pointing out some of the prevalent abuses of
the time.   He was opposed to the debasement of the currency, an early
form of inflation.   He was a "sound-money" man, largely because he
believed in the quantity theory of money.   He preached against the
widespread custom of farming out taxes and against the sale of magis-
tracies, especially of judicial offices.   The need of this preaching is
obvious when one remembers that both these customs remained commor.
in France down to the period of the Revolution.

Last but not least, Bodin warned the sovereign against too frequent and too drastic changes in the law.   The sovereign, to be sure, was legally omnipotent.   He could make and unmake laws at his pleasure, but the monarch was urged to make very sparing use of this legislative power lest he upset public opinion.   Bodin was convinced that too frequent tinkering with the laws leads to revolution.   Though he advocated the restoration of the old Roman office of public censor, an officer charged with, among other things, suppressing flagrant breaches of the moral law, Bodin was opposed to too many and too severe laws on the ground that it was impossible to enforce them.

All Bodin's suggestions regarding administrative problems are interesting.   Many of them are valuable.   But it is necessary to enumerate only a few of them, because apart from the advocacy of partial toleration, they had little influence upon contemporary thought.   Bodin's chief work, *The Six Books on the Republic*, went through edition after edition and was translated into all the principal languages of Europe. But this popularity was almost entirely due to the universal interest in the doctrine of sovereignty, and it is as the father of the idea of sovereignty that Bodin had best be remembered.

THOMAS HOBBES

The culminating genius of the school founded by Bodin was Thomas Hobbes (1588–1679), who was also one of the greatest English speculative and political philosophers.

The element of paradox has entered into the lives and thoughts of many political theorists, but with few has this contradictory element been as obvious and as amusing as with Hobbes.   Hobbes is concerned above all with the individual and the rights and privileges of the individual; yet this individualism leads him straight to thoroughgoing etatism, the belief that the state should have absolute control over all the actions of the individual.   Hobbes is more of an egalitarian than many of the later revolutionary thinkers, for he believes that all men are naturally equal, both physically and mentally; yet his reasoning on this matter leads him to the conclusion that one man should have complete dominion over the lives and fortunes of his fellow countrymen.

It is often stated that Hobbes believed in the divine right of kings yet the very words divine right imply some connection with the deity, and Hobbes' views on the deity were so vague and so radical that he was accused of being an atheist. In fact, though Hobbes believed in the absolute right of kings, he was in so little sympathy with the true devotees of the divine right theory that the latter persecuted and reviled him with ever increasing vigor.

Hobbes is undoubtedly the greatest, the clearest, and the most logical of all the advocates of absolute monarchy, although he lived at the time and the place where absolute monarchy was resisted and overcome. Absolute monarchy was to persist in most European countries until the end of the eighteenth century. It was only in England that democracy was able to secure public recognition in the seventeenth century. However, none of the countries in which royalism had undisputed sway produced a work in favor of royalism half as convincing as that of the English Hobbes who wrote one defense of monarchy when Charles, the English king, was a prisoner, and the other in 1651, two years after King Charles had been decapitated.

To many contemporary English observers, it seemed as if Hobbes, with his belief that kings should be allowed to rule as they see fit, was "behind the times," a relic of a bygone age. Hobbes' real glory and fame started a century after he was dead, in the nineteenth century, the era of democracy; and it was Bentham and his fellow utilitarians, the most radical advocates of democracy, who did the most to revive Hobbes' popularity.

The utilitarians, to be sure, disagreed with Hobbes' conclusions even though they adopted his methods. They were sure that these conclusions were entirely outmoded. Yet a century later, in our own generation, we find a revival of the principles which Hobbes defended and the utilitarians rejected. In fact we can best understand Hobbes if we regard him, not as a singer of the swan song of the Stuarts, but as the prophet of a system which was to be carried out nearly three centuries later by Mussolini and Hitler.

Hobbes, like Bodin, his spiritual ancestor, was a universal genius. Just as Bodin busied himself with problems affecting every sphere of human activity, so Hobbes studied and wrote upon mathematics, physics, biology, psychology, and metaphysics, as well as attempted to lay the foundations for a complete political philosophy. By very reason of this universality of interest, both philosophers occasionally made egregious mistakes. Just as Bodin became involved in witchcraft, necromancy, and astrology, so did Hobbes spend several useless years trying to prove that he had outdone all other mathematical geniuses and had succeeded in solving the problem of how to square the circle.   But with both Bodin and Hobbes these eccentricities are irrelevant matters.

In many ways Hobbes was more successful as a universal genius than was Bodin.   Bodin speculated upon almost everything in heaven and earth, sometimes very acutely; but it is only to the political theorist that he is of major importance.   Hobbes, on the other hand, in addition to being a classic in political speculation is also a major figure to all metaphysicians and psychologists.

It is unnecessary for us to delve into the details of the metaphysical and psychological systems established by Hobbes, but a word must be said regarding these systems as a whole because of the light they throw upon Hobbes' fundamental postulates in the realm of politics.

First and foremost, it is necessary to stress Hobbes' methodology or the means he used to arrive at what he considered truth.   An ex-secretary of Bacon, a contemporary and friend of Descartes, Hobbes was naturally a great advocate of the "new" philosophies based upon the discoveries of the natural sciences, as opposed to the transcendental metaphysics which had dominated Europe during the Middle Ages and from whose influence even Bodin had not been entirely free.

Bodin had insisted that he was "modern" and that his system was entirely rational, that is, based upon pure reason; but he was fond of citing the opinion of such ancient worthies as Cicero, Aristotle, or the Old Testament prophets in confirmation of many of his ideas.   Hobbes paid almost no attention to what these or any other ancient sages had to say.   He was proud that he based his doctrines upon immediate knowledge of facts rather than upon the opinions or the arguments of other men.   "If I had read as many books as other men, I should be as ignorant as they."

Hobbes was a firm believer in the doctrine that all knowledge comes through sense experience and resolutely rejected the notion of "innate ideas," or ideas implanted in the soul by God and known to be true without scientific experimentation.   Scholastic metaphysics he despised as being a vain juggling of words, completely out of keeping with the world of reality.   The only use of reason of which he thoroughly approved was either a logical or mathematical use and logic and mathematics are essentially one and the same thing.

Hobbes was in fact swept away by his enthusiasm for mathematics. To him knowledge and measurement were almost synonymous.   He was especially attracted by geometry and felt that the methods of geometry should be applied to all the other sciences.   The *Leviathan*, his great work on politics, has many analogies with a textbook on geometry.

Hobbes is the ancestor of all modern materialists. To him the whole universe is reducible to matter — homogeneous matter which appears diverse because of the separate motion of different material particles. Bodies appear to have color, taste, smell, not because of some inherent mysterious qualities, as was believed in the Middle Ages, but merely because the motions of these external bodies affect our senses in these particular ways.

Mind Hobbes regarded as "decaying matter," or as a kind of matter so refined as to escape the observation of the senses. Mind, like matter, is subject to the eternal laws of cause and effect, so that the belief in free will is ridiculous. Both animals and men are governed by irresistible impulses, the chief difference between brute creation and humanity being the faculty of speech.

All our complex emotional life can ultimately be reduced to attraction and repulsion. Man incessantly strives to gain those things which attract him and avoid those things towards which he feels repulsion. Happiness or "felicity" is continual success in getting those things to which he is attracted. There is nothing inherently good or bad, morally speaking, about these attractions and repulsions, as there is nothing good or bad about the motions of physical bodies. Morality and moral judgments are the products of civilization.

Upon the foundations of this philosophy, Hobbes proceeds to erect his outline of the nature and functions of the state. At the root of all Hobbes' political doctrines is his idea of man and human relations in the "state of nature," that is, the condition of mankind free from the bonds of political society. This state of nature exists not merely in the infancy of mankind, but continues to exist amongst barbarous peoples today. Hobbes believed that many of the American Indians of his day were in a state of nature and that, moreover, any of the civilized peoples of Europe were liable to revert to this state if the bonds of government were once loosened. It is the state to which man naturally reverts in the absence of artificial restraints.

Filmer, the great advocate of the divine right of kings, argued that in a state of nature man is neither free nor equal, because he felt that if man were naturally free and equal it would be difficult to defend the bonds of absolute monarchy. Hobbes did not share this feeling. He was perfectly willing to admit (with the liberals) that in a state of nature man possesses both freedom and equality. Man is free, because by definition there is a complete absence of political bonds. He further believes that an examination of human beings shows there is no great difference between them. "Nature hath made men so equal in the faculties of the body and mind; as that though there be found one man sometimes manifestly stronger in body or quicker mind than another, yet when all is reckoned together the difference between man and man is not considerable." [5]

But though man in the state of nature is both free and equal, Hobbes finds this state of nature to be far from agreeable. Man is essentially motivated by self-interest, so that in a natural state one man is perpetually at war with every other man. Aristotle and even Bodin had claimed that man is essentially a social animal. This Hobbes denies. "Men have no pleasure, but on the contrary a great deal of grief in keeping company, where there is no power able to overawe them all." [6]

Man in a state of nature is like the beasts in the jungle. Each takes what he can with impunity, robbing and murdering the weaker and fleeing in terror from the stronger. An examination of human nature shows that there are three instincts which cause mankind to engage in civil war when left to itself. One is the acquisitive instinct, as the result of which man uses violence to make himself master of other men's persons, wives, children, and cattle. The second is the natural corollary of the acquisitive instinct, namely, the possessive instinct as the result of which man endeavors to prevent his neighbors from securing those things which he himself possesses. The third is the love of glory, as the result of which each man seeks the praise and the envy of his fellows.

In a firmly established political society these instincts are repressed, or at least held in check, but they continue to exist underneath the surface of human society. This continuance is evident by the conduct of the respectable citizen even in a civilized state. "When taking a journey he arms himself and seeks to go well accompanied. When going to sleep he locks his door, even when in his house he locks the chests." [7] And this in spite of law and law-enforcing officers. From this we can see what our respectable citizen thinks of his fellow citizens, his servants, and his children.

If the existence of these lawless instincts renders life uncomfortable in a political society, it is obvious that in a state of nature, where positive law and law-enforcing officers are unknown, life is almost unbearable. In this state of nature there is and must be "continual fear and danger of violent death, and the life of man is solitary, poor, nasty, brutish, and short." [8]

Many of Hobbes' contemporaries, especially those with a liberal tinge in their political speculation, were perpetually talking about natural rights and natural laws. Generally, these two concepts were held to be identical. Hobbes was careful to distinguish between the two ideas, though he accepted the validity of both.

In a state of nature man has indeed natural rights. These rights allow him to do anything he pleases as long as he can "get away with it." He has a perfect right to murder or steal if he can do so successfully, for he is as yet bound by no law prohibiting these actions.

With Grotius and with Bodin, natural law is essentially moral law, which commands man to do good and avoid evil, even when man has no positive laws to regulate his conduct. Hobbes has a very different concept of the essence and functions of natural law. Like Bodin and many others, Hobbes claims that a law is the command of a sovereign, and as in the state of nature there is no sovereign, natural law is not law in the true sense of the word. With Grotius, Hobbes believes that the so-called natural laws are the precepts or dictates of reason. But by dictates of reason Hobbes means something far different from what Grotius means in using these words. Grotius, it will be remembered, believed that some actions are intrinsically good, others intrinsically bad, and that reason merely tells us which are good and which are bad. Hobbes, on the other hand, believes that reason merely tells us which actions tend towards self-preservation and which towards self-destruction. All natural laws, to him, are really only precepts which tend in the long run to self-preservation. The basis of judgment is expediency. In disobeying these laws man is not wicked; he is merely foolish.

What are some of the natural laws postulated by Hobbes? The first and most fundamental of these laws, the one from which all the others follow, is, "*Seek to obtain and preserve peace.*" [9] The state of nature is a state of war, but in this state of war everyone suffers. Even the strong and able man is never safe from the attack of his enemies. At any moment he is liable to be caught in a trap, or be slain by the artifice of a weaker man, just as Goliath, the strong, was slain by David, the weak. It is, therefore, to everyone's advantage to seek to emerge from the state of war to a state of peace.

The second law is, "In order to secure peace, *each man must be willing, when all other men are equally willing, to lay down his right to all things, and must be content with so much liberty against other men as he would* allow other men against himself." [10]   Peace is impossible as long as each man preserves his natural right to do and to take what he pleases. For a man to give up his natural rights, however, if all other men were to retain theirs, would be ridiculous.   It would be tantamount to committing suicide.   But if all men were willing to forgo the right to seize forcibly what they please, in the long run all would work out to the advantage of everyone.   As peace can only be secured by this universal renunciation of natural rights, it behooves everyone to be willing to make this sacrifice and to urge others to do so.

The third of the natural laws is, "*Every man should carry out his covenants and promises.*" [11]   The state of war can only give way to a state of peace when each man promises, and abides by this promise, to give up some of his own natural rights.   I give up my rights only on the strict understanding that you promise to give up yours.   If you carry out this promise, the peace between us continues.   If you do not, I shall naturally resume my rights and the state of war between us is recommenced.   The basis of all peaceful intercourse between men is faith that all men will keep their covenants and that those who break their covenants will be punished.   To break a covenant is unjust. In fact, to Hobbes, the very definition of injustice is the non-performance of solemn promises.

Hobbes believes that there are numerous other postulates of natural law, but all of these other postulates are merely supplements or corollaries of the three foregoing fundamental principles.   Gratitude, mercy, modesty, equity may be said to be in accord with natural law, but only because and in so far as they tend to preserve peace and hence carry out the first and second natural laws.

In short, all natural laws are maxims which aid man in escaping from the state of nature.

The state, according to Hobbes, arises from the observance of the three fundamental natural laws.   It is the means by which men escape from their natural condition of war to a condition of peace.

Hobbes' definition of the state is "regulated and established peace." Hence, in obedience to the first natural law everyone should strive for the foundation and maintenance of the state.   For peace to be preserved, each man must give up his natural rights (the second natural law).   This means that each man must transfer all his natural rights to the state.   All men must abide by their covenants (the third law). This means that no man may seek to regain from the state the rights the latter has secured, and that it is the duty of the state to punish any such attempt.

Bodin, it will be remembered, believed that the origin of the state was in *force*. Hobbes insists that the origin of each state is in a contract or covenant between the members of the state. He is willing to admit that sometimes the contract is entered into under duress. As the result of war the people may be forced to accept the overlordship of a conqueror. But even in this case Hobbes claims that the basis of government is contract, for the overlordship of the conqueror hinges upon the fact that the people, lest they lose their lives, contract either explicitly or implicitly with the victor to serve him as subjects. "It is not therefore the victory which giveth the right of dominion over the vanquished, but because of his own covenant." [12] A state created in this fashion, Hobbes calls *government by acquisition*.

In most cases, however, says Hobbes, the state originates, not by force, but as the result of the voluntary agreement of the inhabitants of a certain region to unite in the form of a state. These inhabitants, finding the state of nature too unbearable to be endured, come to the conclusion that it is to the advantage of all to form a political union. For such a union to be formed it is necessary for each and every person to agree to transfer his natural rights to a man or to an assembly of men, who thus constitute a neutral third party and who thereafter shall exercise sovereign rights over every member of the newly formed state. A state formed in this fashion, Hobbes calls a *government by institution*.

There are several features in this theory worthy of especial comment. In the first place, Hobbes claims that a minority has no right to object to the choice of a majority in the selection of the sovereign power (a point brought up by Filmer), for it can be argued that the minority tacitly agreed to abide by the will of the majority, or else, and this is the important point, it can be argued that the minority never agreed to become members of the social contract with its necessary obligations. In this case, the minority must still be considered to exist in the primeval state of war, and they may therefore be destroyed without injustice by the newly constituted state unless this minority submit to the decree of the majority.

In the second place, Hobbes is insistent that the members of the newly formed state have no right to withdraw their promises of obedience, whatever the provocation. By the third natural law, men are forced to stand by their covenants, lest they relapse into the horrible state of nature. Hence any attempt to rebel against or resist the commands of the sovereign is a violation of the third natural law and leads straight back to primeval anarchy.

Many of the advocates of the social contract theory argued that the contract is between the governor and the governed. The governed or subjects agree to do so and so, but only on condition that the governor or monarch fulfills his obligations and treats his subjects justly and fairly. In consequence of this theory it could be and was held that if the governor acts unjustly, his subjects can claim that the contract has been broken and are justified in rebelling.

Hobbes would have none of this theory. According to him the social contract is not between the governor and the governed, but between each and every member of the state — the sovereign, in fact, is not a party to this contract — (at least in governments by institution). By the terms of Hobbes' contract, each member of the community agrees to forgo his natural rights, or rather to transfer them to the neutral third party (the sovereign); hence whatever the sovereign may do must necessarily be in accord with this contract. By the first universal, irrevocable transfer of power to the sovereign, the action of the sovereign, whatever it be, becomes the action of every member of the state.

Finally, it should be noted that by the terms of the social contract the sovereign obtains absolute and complete control over all the citizens of the state. Bodin originated the doctrine of sovereignty, but, as we have seen, Bodin's sovereign was far from absolute. Bodin would not permit his sovereign to act contrary to the laws of God, the laws of nature, or fundamental constitutional laws. His sovereign could not interfere with family or property rights.

From what Hobbes says about the rights inherent in sovereignty, it is clear that all these restrictions are swept away.

First, the sovereign has the power to make and repeal all laws; of hearing and deciding all controversies which may arise concerning any law; and of either punishing or pardoning those who break these laws.

Second, the sovereign has the right to appoint and dismiss all officials and magistrates, both civil and military. No man can claim to have an inalienable or hereditary right to any office. In like manner, the sovereign must be the fountain of honor, with power to grant such ranks and titles as please him.

Third, the sovereign has the right to maintain peace or conduct war with neighboring states. This in turn means that the sovereign must have control over the armed forces of the state. This control is in contrast with the old feudal levies in which the bulk of the soldiers were led by their own lords and were only indirectly subject to the commands of the monarch.

Fourth, in contrast with Bodin, Hobbes insists that the sovereign must have full power to levy taxation in order to provide for the army and the civil magistrates. It is useless to grant the sovereign the right to raise an army and appoint magistrates unless he also has the right to levy money from his subjects so that these persons may be paid.

Fifth, not only has the sovereign the right to tax the private property of his subjects, but the very ownership of private property and the laws governing this ownership are derived from the will of the sovereign. Other advocates of the social contract theory claimed that private property was a natural right governed by natural law. But in Hobbes' scheme a man possesses property in a civil state only as the result of a grant on the part of the sovereign.

Finally, the sovereign has a right to censor and prevent the spread of all opinions which appear dangerous. Hobbes was frightened of the results which might arise from liberty of speech and liberty of the press. "The actions of men proceed from their opinions and in the well governing of opinions consisteth the well governing of men's actions." [13]

Bodin had claimed that the monarch could not change the laws of succession. Hobbes, on the other hand, claims that if sovereignty really be in the hands of one person, this person must have the right to choose as his heir anyone he pleases, though Hobbes was prepared to admit that normally the monarch would and should permit succession to the throne by hereditary rules.

What of Bodin's statement that the laws of the temporal sovereign might be contrary to the laws of nature and the laws of God? In Hobbes' system the conflict between civil and natural laws is rendered impossible. In the first place the chief purpose of the natural laws is to secure peace through the erection of an omnipotent state; hence the state in using these omnipotent rights in any way it pleases is merely following the dictates of natural law.

Against those stubborn persons who persisted in advocating the supremacy of natural over civil law, Hobbes made use of another argument. All laws, he states, have need of interpretation, including the law of nature. In fact, owing to passions and prejudices the law of nature has now become very obscure, and has the greatest need of

authoritative interpretation.   Now, it is not permissible for this interpretation to lie in the hands of private persons.   Rather must its
interpretation come from the judges appointed by the sovereign.   Indeed natural law, which is essentially a body of rational maxims, only
acquires the force of true law when it is interpreted and applied by the
sovereign and his judicial agents.

In view of the strong theological passion of the age, Hobbes could
not directly deny the dictum that the laws of the sovereign might be
contrary to the laws of God, but he was able to get around this maxim
in much the same manner as he circumvented the laws of nature.
How, he asks, are we to know which really are the commands of God?
There are many persons and groups of persons who claim to have received God's law by direct revelation, but these persons usually contradict one another even on fundamental points.   "How can man be
assured of the revelation of another without a revelation particularly to
himself?" and again, "If men were at liberty to take for God's commandments their own dreams and fancies, or the dreams and fancies of
private men, scarce two men would agree upon what is God's commandment... I conclude... therefore that... all subjects are bound
to obey that for divine law which is declared to be so by the laws of the
commonwealth."   In other words, men must indeed obey God's law,
but it is up to the state to decide what is and what is not God's law.[14]

From the above passages it is obvious that Hobbes dismisses as
absurd the claims of the Catholic and of all other churches to act as
infallible judges of divine revelation.   To him the only possible church is
a church established and controlled by the state, whose supreme
pastor is the sovereign.   From this it follows that any body of men
meeting for worship without the sovereign's command is no church, but
merely an unlawful assembly.

For Hobbes there is only one important limitation to the sovereign's
power.   The sovereign may kill a man (for treason or other causes)
and not act unjustly.   But the sovereign may not lawfully command a
man to kill himself nor not to resist those who assault him.   The reason
for this is not a horror of suicide, but merely a corollary to Hobbes'
view of the nature of the social contract.   Man enters into the contract
in order to preserve his own existence; hence the command to commit
suicide is a direct breach of this contract, and is the only act which can
be considered such a breach.   In the presence of such a command, a
man is freed from the obligations of the contract and goes back to the
original state of nature.

This idea brings up another phase of Hobbes' philosophy. Hobbes is insistent upon the absolute obligation of subjects to obey the commands of their sovereign, except under one condition. When the legitimate sovereign has lost all power to protect his subjects or to preserve them from injury, the duty of obedience ceases. The subject under the terms of the social contract must blindly obey the *de jure* monarch as long as the latter can maintain peace and order; but in the event of successful civil war, the *de jure* monarch loses his power, and the duty of obedience automatically ceases; the subject is then free to seek peace by serving under the new *de facto* ruler. It was by means of this doctrine that Hobbes, the pillar of royalism, justified his own actions in accepting the rule of Cromwell after the execution of Charles I.

Hobbes was perfectly willing to admit, as did Bodin, that sovereignty may be placed in the hands of more than one person. In dealing with this problem he adopts the old classification of monarchy, aristocracy, and democracy. Older writers from Aristotle on sought to distinguish between monarchy and tyranny, aristocracy and oligarchy, democracy and mob rule. Hobbes rejects this system of classification on the ground that such distinctions are subjective rather than objective. "They that are discontented under monarchy call it tyranny, they that are displeased with aristocracy call it oligarchy, so also they who find themselves grieved under a democracy call it anarchy." [15] The same government may well be considered a monarchy by some and a tyranny by others.

Having postulated the idea that there are three and only three forms of government, Hobbes proceeds to discuss the merits and demerits of each system. Considering his background, it is not surprising to find that for both theoretical and practical reasons, monarchy is ultimately declared to be the best.

Many of Hobbes' arguments are the same as those of his predecessors. Like them he points out the weakness and vacillation of democratic assemblies — how the common people are more likely to be swayed by passions than by reason. More interesting are the arguments which Hobbes bases upon his conception of human nature, the inevitable tendency of man to be dominated by self-interest.

All men are necessarily swayed more by private than by public interests.

> From whence it follows that where the public and private interest are most closely united, there is the public most advanced. Now in monarchy the

private interest is the same as the public.   The riches, power, honor, of a monarch arise only from the riches, strength and reputation of his subjects ... whereas in a democracy or aristocracy the public prosperity confers not so .nuch to the private fortune of one who is corrupt or ambitious as doth many time a perfidious advice, a treacherous action, or a civil war.[16]

Hobbes is willing to admit that a monarch may and probably will be selfish, granting special favors to his friends and flatterers.   But he believes that the members of a democratic assembly will pursue the same policy.   "And whereas the favorites of monarchs are few, and they have none to advance save their own kindred, the favorites of an assembly are many, and the kindred more numerous than of any monarch." [17]   In a monarchy, in other words, public money may be wasted on the king's mistresses, but the sums spent in this way are nothing compared with the "pork barrel" money and the soldiers' bonuses which will be voted by a democratic assembly in order to win favor with the mob.

In addition to formulating a general philosophy of the state, Hobbes also gives many specific pieces of advice to rulers on how best to govern their subjects.   Though interesting, most of this advice must be passed over in silence.

It is, however, of interest to observe that Hobbes insists upon the equality of all subjects before the law.   To counterbalance this notion, he also insists upon the idea that all subjects are equally liable to taxation.

He also argues in favor of the public care of those incapable of looking after themselves.

> Whereas many men by accident inevitably become unable to maintain themselves by their labor, they ought not to be left to the charity of private persons.   But if the unfortunates should be provided for, stern measures should be used against those who are destitute merely because they are lazy. For such as have strong bodies ... they are to be forced to work, and to avoid the excuse of not finding employment, there ought to be such laws as may encourage all manner of arts, such as navigation, agriculture, fishing, and all manner of manufacture which requires labor.   The multitude of poor and yet strong people yet increasing, they are to be transplanted into countries not sufficiently inhabited.[18]

The implications of this doctrine are of especial interest.   In contrast with the early followers of the liberal-democratic tradition who believed in the doctrine of *laissez faire*, that the government should interfere as little as possible in the private affairs of its subjects, and should let commerce and industry look after itself, Hobbes believed that it was the duty of the state to look after the welfare of its citizens by public relief on the one hand and by the promotion and regulation of industry on the other.

NOTES TO CHAPTER THREE

1. King James, *Political Works*, p. 61. Reprinted by permission of the President and Fellows of Harvard College. 2. *Ibid.*, p. 307.
3. Robert Filmer, *The Anarchy of a Limited or Mixed Government*, p. 9.
4. *Ibid.*, p. 10.
5. Thomas Hobbes, *Leviathan*, p. 63.
6. *Ibid.*, p. 64.   7. *Ibid.*, p. 65.   8. *Ibid.*   9. *Ibid.*, p. 67.   10. *Ibid.*
11. *Ibid.*, p. 74.   12. *Ibid.*, p. 106.   13. *Ibid.*, p. 93.   14. *Ibid.*, pp. 152–153.
15. *Ibid.*, p. 97.   16. *Ibid.*, p. 98.   17. *Ibid.*, p. 99.   18. *Ibid.*, pp. 184–185.

BIBLIOGRAPHY

For a general survey of absolutism during the sixteenth and seventeenth centuries, see J. N. Figgis, *Divine Right of Kings*, second edition, Cambridge, 1922. For the doctrines of Belloy and Barclay, see J. W. Allen, *History of Political Thought in the Sixteenth Century*, New York, 1928. For the doctrines of James I, see *Political Works of James I*, edited and with a valuable introduction by C. H. McIlwain, Cambridge, Massachusetts, 1918.

R. Filmer, *The Anarchy of a Limited or Mixed Government*. London, 1648.
R. Filmer, *Observations Concerning the Originall of Government*. London, 1652.
R. Filmer, *Patriarcha, or the Natural Power of Kings*. London, 1680. There is also a reprint of this work in Morley's edition of Locke's *Treatises on Civil Government*.
J. Bodin, *Les Six Livres de la République*. Paris, 1580. There is a revised Latin edition, *De Republica*, Paris, 1586. There is a good though partial translation in Coker, *Readings in Political Philosophy*, New York, 1934. See also the older translation by R. Knolles, London, 1606.
J. Baudrillart, *Bodin et son temps*. Paris, 1853.
E. Fournol, *Bodin prédécesseur de Montesquieu*. Paris, 1896.
R. Chauvire, *Jean Bodin*. Paris, 1914.
G. Fickel, *Der Staat bei Bodin*. Leipzig, 1934.
T. Hobbes, *English Works*, edited by W. Molesworth. London, 1839–1845. 11 vols. *Concerning Government and Society* in vol. II. *Leviathan* in vol. III. Citations in the text are from the Everyman edition of the *Leviathan*, London, 1911.
G. C. Robertson, *Hobbes*. London, 1886.
L. Stephens, *Hobbes*. London, 1904.
C. E. G. Catlin, *Thomas Hobbes*. Oxford, 1922.
J. Laird, *Hobbes*. London, 1934.
L. Strauss, *The Political Philosophy of Hobbes*. Oxford, 1936.

CHAPTER IV

THE DECAY OF ABSOLUTISM

THOMAS HOBBES represents the high-water mark in seventeenth century absolutism. By absolutism is meant the belief in the absolute right of the state to control the individual, and also the belief that the state itself should be controlled by a single person. On both points Hobbes must be regarded as an early but important precursor of Fascism.

At the time of Hobbes' death (1679) it must have appeared to most observers that his philosophy or some variation of his philosophy was likely to prevail in Europe for a long period. Everywhere there appeared to be a tendency to accept absolute monarchy as the ideal form of government. In Spain, in France, in Germany, even in Holland and the Scandinavian countries, the semi-democratic institutions of earlier days had lost their vitality. In many cases they had entirely disappeared. In Switzerland, to be sure, democratic institutions still prevailed, but the Swiss cantons were regarded as geographic curiosities. In Italy, Genoa and Venice were still republics, but these two city-states had lost their old virility. Their importance was over; they were museum pieces and their political institutions were but interesting relics of earlier times. In Poland the nobility preserved and even augmented their power over the king, with the result that Poland was always in a condition bordering on anarchy. Poland, in fact, constituted to most observers a classic example of how *not* to run a government.

It was only in England, Hobbes' own country, that there appeared any marked opposition to political absolutism; and even here, to the superficial spectator at least, it seemed that liberalism was on the wane. During the period 1640–1660, to be sure, the English Parliament and the English people had risen against their king; they had defeated, imprisoned, and finally decapitated him. For a brief period the monarchy itself had been abolished and supreme power entrusted to Oliver Cromwell, who as Lord Protector was supposed to be the delegate and the agent of the English populace. But the very violence of the revolution and of the revolutionary principles had brought an equally violent reaction. The people soon tired of republican government, and shortly after Oliver Cromwell's death the monarchy was restored and Charles II, the legitimate heir, placed upon the English throne.

The restoration of 1660 seemed to mark the passing of all the political ideals which had motivated the revolution. England was again ruled by an hereditary monarch, and royal rule was accepted with mad enthusiasm by all sections of the population. The new House of Commons appeared to be more zealous for monarchy than the monarch himself. Addressing Charles II, its members declared, "We submit and oblige ourselves and our posterities to your Majesty for ever." An act of Parliament provided that all officeholders must swear that it was unlawful, on any pretext whatever, to take arms against the king or his officers. The works of the republicans, such as Milton and Harrington, were publicly burned, and the booksellers declared themselves disgraced by the fact that some of their profession had been willing to sell such seditious books. The works of Filmer, of Hobbes, and of other advocates of divine or absolute right, enjoyed immense popularity. Freedom of conscience was a thing of the past. All political rights were made dependent upon conformity with the established church, the supreme head of which was the king. Freedom of speech on all matters, either ecclesiastical or secular, was outlawed by stringent licensing laws.

THE RISE OF LIBERALISM

Appearances are often deceptive. At the very time when absolutism seemed everywhere triumphant, the way was being prepared for the resurgence of liberal institutions and liberal doctrines. By an historic accident it was, once more, England which led the way. The idyllic honeymoon of Charles II and the English people, which started in 1660, did not and could not last. Before many years Charles' arbitrary actions aroused widespread discontent. Parliament, which at first had been so obsequious, began to throw obstacles in the king's path. Charles, in fact, had so much difficulty in securing money from the House of Commons that he was forced to rely upon a secret subsidy paid him by Louis XIV of France. Nevertheless Charles enjoyed the privileges of his position too much to be willing to endanger his throne by embarking upon headstrong measures, and on several occasions rescinded acts which proved to be universally unpopular. Fear of another period of civil disturbance kept the populace loyal to the monarchy as long as there was no extreme provocation, and Charles was able to rule for over a quarter of a century in comparative tranquillity.

In 1685 the merry monarch died, and James II, his brother, ascended the throne. From the beginning of his reign there was widespread restlessness, and after three years (1688) King James was forced to flee the country. The vacant throne was given to Mary, James' daughter, and her husband, William, Prince of Orange. This second, bloodless revolution was accomplished almost overnight, and this time the changes brought about by the revolt were to prove permanent. The legitimate line of the Stuarts was forever excluded from the throne, and with the passing of the Stuarts there also disappeared all belief in the divine right of kings. This doctrine, which had commanded general acceptance in the seventeenth century, soon came to be regarded as childishly ridiculous in the eighteenth century. Even the Hobbesian doctrine of the practical value of and need for an absolute monarch and an absolute state fell into disfavor, not to be revived again until the middle of the nineteenth century.

The leaders of the second, successful revolution soon felt the need of a system of political philosophy which would support and explain the actions which they had taken. By reason of the great dissimilarity of their ideals from those of the previous revolutionaries, it was impossible for them to use the writings which had been in vogue a few years earlier. Many spokesmen of the old revolutionary party had been Presbyterians, with a Calvinistic attitude towards all governmental problems, and to the leaders of the new revolution Presbyterianism was anathema. Many of the writers of the Cromwellian era, men such as Milton and Harrington, had been out-and-out republicans, and hence were immediately ruled out of court, for the new revolutionaries were sound believers in a constitutional monarchy even though they were opponents of absolutism. In a word, all the older writings had to be swept aside and provision made for a new political gospel which would embody the ideals of the men who had placed William and Mary upon the throne.

England did not have long to wait. A year after the expulsion of King James, John Locke (1632–1704) published his *Treatises on Civil Government* and these essays were at once accepted as the authoritative expression of the theoretical basis of the new system of government. Though they were composed as party pamphlets to defend the new order, Locke's essays were destined to become and remain classics in the literature of political philosophy. Quoted and requoted by later writers, they served as models for succeeding thinkers of the liberal tradition, and inspired the leaders of both the American and French Revolutions. These essays are of importance even to those persons whose primary interest is the study of the development of the absolutist or Fascist tradition, if only because most of the later defenders of absolutism went out of their way to attack Locke and all the basic principles of his political philosophy. If only by way of contrast, the doctrines of Locke bring the fundamental assumptions of the Fascists into sharp relief.

Locke's political philosophy starts with two fundamental doctrines. One is that men are rational; the other that men are "naturally" more or less equal. Hobbes, the absolutist, believed that man is normally irrational, in the sense that human action is motivated by impulse and passion rather than by reason. Locke, on the other hand, believed that reason was the dominant factor in human, certainly in social life. By the use of reason men learn to control their passions. At any given moment the passions may gain the upper hand, but after each such explosion reason sets in and strives to regulate human intercourse. To Locke it appeared obvious that all laws and all governments should be in accordance with rational principles. Locke was also convinced that naturally and innately men are more or less equal. He was willing to admit that some men are a little wiser, or a little stronger, or a little more industrious than others, but to him the differences between men are far less striking and far less important than their similarities. He was certain that many of the differences which seem to exist between men are arbitrary and artificial rather than natural. Locke was a strong environmentalist in the sense that he believed that a man's mental and moral ability are largely the result of the experiences, the sensations, or the education to which he is exposed. When, therefore, one man appears wise and another stupid, it may well mean nothing more than that one man has had a better upbringing than the other.

Locke agreed with Hobbes that all men once lived in a pre-political condition or a "state of nature" and that this state of nature continues to exist among primitive peoples even today. But there was a vast difference between Hobbes' state of nature and the one postulated by Locke. Hobbes' state of nature, it will be remembered, was really a state of war, with every man's hand raised against his fellows. Locke regarded the state of nature as normally peaceful because of man's social instinct. The state of nature was defined as "a state of peace, good-will, mutual assistance, and preservation." It goes without saying that in the state of nature as pictured by Locke all men were not only equal but also free.

Locke accepted Hobbes' doctrine of natural rights and natural law, but radically transformed both ideas, and in doing so went back to a position similar to that occupied by Grotius. According to Hobbes, a man has a "natural right" to everything he can lay his hands on. He has a perfect right to kill or enslave another and to seize the latter's property, if he can do so with impunity to himself. To Locke this doctrine was horrible. Locke assumed that moral order characterizes the whole universe and hence the state of nature. It follows from this assumption that in a natural state each man has a right to life, liberty, and property, and as each man possesses these rights, it is obvious that no man may rightfully interfere with the life, liberty, or property of another. Locke's doctrine of natural right necessarily led to a reinter-pretation of natural law. To Hobbes, natural laws were merely the maxims which each man should follow, the better to preserve his own life. To Locke, as to Grotius, natural law is the moral law, established by God, and discoverable by reason. In other words, natural law is the direct counterpart of natural right. Natural right insures each man his own life, liberty, and property; natural law forces us to respect the life, liberty, and property of other persons.

Locke was sufficiently optimistic to believe that in ordinary circumstances mankind will obey natural laws, even in the absence of force or sanctions. But he admitted that from time to time offenders will arise who will break the law by injuring their fellow men or by seizing their possessions. In a state of nature there are not and cannot be special officials charged with the punishment of breaches of natural law. Hence it is necessary for each man to take justice into his own hands. This situation necessarily brings about some injustice and confusion. It is this fact which makes the state of nature inconvenient and vexatious, and which eventually leads men voluntarily to frame a social contract and thereby institute a political state. The purpose of the state, in Locke's philosophy, is merely to see that natural rights are safeguarded and natural law executed more judiciously. To secure these ends, every state has for its fundamental aims, first, the transformation of the general unwritten precepts of natural law into established, settled, and known law, regarding the interpretation of which there can be no dispute; second, the establishment of known and impartial judges to settle disputes which may arise under this law, finally, the establishment of a police power to see that the decisions of the judges are carried into effect. According to Locke, in instituting the state, man gives up none of his natural rights save the right to decide and execute for himself the commands of natural law.

From these general assumptions Locke proceeded to draw a number of practical conclusions. These conclusions may be said to constitute the bulwarks of the defense of democracy and of individualism.

By democracy Locke meant merely the absence of despotism. He was not a republican and seems sincerely to have believed that a constitutional monarchy was the best form of government. He evinced no dislike for the House of Lords, and tacitly admitted its right to share in the machinery of government. He rather distrusted direct democratic control over the state. Nonetheless Locke was a democrat, as can be seen by his insistence upon the maxim that all government must rest upon the consent of the governed. This doctrine is, indeed, merely a necessary deduction from Locke's views regarding the social contract. In Locke's philosophy the state comes into existence only by the voluntary union of its individual citizens. Moreover, this consent to the contract must, according to Locke, be renewed each generation. Many other political philosophers, including Hobbes, had argued that the contract was made everlasting; that the promises made by the fathers were automatically binding upon the sons and upon all later generations; that by being born under any government, a man was naturally subject to it. Locke rejected this doctrine and held that every man is born "free," and that on reaching maturity he should have full liberty of choice as to whether or not he wishes to be a member of the community of which his parents formed a part.

Locke also accepted the well-known liberal maxim that all rulers and magistrates derive their authority from the people. He resolutely rejected the notion that kings rule by divine appointment. He also held that no just and legal government could be dependent upon force. The people, by the social contract, have formed the state, and the state, by majority decision, can institute any governmental organs it chooses. The state may well hand over the functions of government to a king or to an hereditary aristocracy, but even in an absolute monarchy, the king must be considered to derive his authority from a majority of the people. As an additional bulwark against despotism Locke invoked the doctrine of the separation of powers. To Locke the functions of government are threefold, one federative, one executive, one legislative. The legislative function is to frame and pass laws; the executive function is merely to see that the laws are put into operation; the federative function is the conduct of foreign affairs.

Though Locke insisted that the executive and federative functions are essentially separate and distinct, he was willing to permit a single person to perform both functions, and such a person might well be an hereditary monarch. But though the federative and executive functions could and should be thus united, he held that there is a vast gulf between these functions on the one hand and the legislative function on the other. To be sure, the state, if a majority of its citizens so wished it, could delegate both executive and legislative functions to a single individual. Hence absolute monarchy was perfectly legal and legitimate as long as it originated in the will of the community, but Locke obviously felt that such a union of governmental organs was extremely unwise and might well lead to disaster. Locke looked without disfavor upon the English Parliament with its two Houses, one of which represented not the people but the hereditary aristocracy. Nor did he object to the king sharing in the legislative function by his right to veto all bills. But he insisted that as the English state had granted the legislative function jointly to king and Parliament, it was illegal for the king to seek to deprive Parliament of any of its legislative rights.

As a final bulwark against despotic government Locke insisted upon the right of armed revolution against tyrannous government. If the king betrayed the trust which had been placed in him; if he tried to assume more power than that which had been delegated to him, the people, according to Locke, have a perfect right to revolt. Locke, moreover, was willing to admit that even Parliament, consisting of the elected delegates of the people, might at times become tyrannical, and so the right of rebellion was extended to cover this situation as well. "Though in a constituted commonwealth ... there can be but one supreme power which is the legislative, ... yet the legislative being only a fiduciary power to act for certain ends, there remains still in the people a supreme power to remove or alter the legislative, when they find the legislative act contrary to the trust reposed in them." [1]

Quite as important as the democratic or anti-despotic phase of Locke's thinking was the emphasis he laid upon individual rights inside the political state. It is essential to bear in mind, in this connection, the profound difference between Hobbes and Locke with respect to the rights given up by each person when he enters into the social contract. With Hobbes, the social contract implies that each person gives up *all* his rights and privileges to the "sovereign" — that whatever rights the private individual possesses thereafter are merely those granted him by the sovereign. The sovereign is thus free to dispose of a man's person, actions, and possessions as he sees fit. With Locke, the social contract entails none of these consequences. With him the institution of the political state does not interfere with the operation of natural law nor with the retention of nearly all of a man's natural rights. According to Locke, when a man joins or forms a state he preserves intact all his natural rights except the right to interpret and execute the commands of natural law. Each man retains full control over his own life, liberty, and possessions, and the community has no right to interfere with these things, except to punish a man who seeks to interfere with the life, liberty, or possessions of other persons.

From this general proposition Locke drew several important conclusions. To Locke it seemed obvious that it was not the function of the state to attempt to make its citizens better, wiser, or wealthier than they were originally. Hence he was opposed to all governmental paternalism. The function of the state he considered to be entirely negative: to punish crime and thereby preserve the natural rights of each of its citizens. It goes without saying that Locke believed that each man had a natural right to freedom of speech and of writing, and to freedom of religious belief, as long as a man's speech, writing, or religious belief did not seriously interfere with the rights of other men. Even more important was Locke's assertion that neither the legislative body nor the community as a whole could take from any man any part of his property save with his own consent. According to Hobbes, in a political state a man possesses no inherent right to private property. What property a man does "possess" is granted to him by the state and may be taken back by the state. According to Locke, property, being but the fruit of a man's own labor, belongs to him absolutely, and the state has no control over it, except, of course, to levy taxes upon it for the support of state functions.

The doctrine of the "natural right to property" was to have a profound effect upon later generations, and is worthy of special consideration. Though not exactly original with Locke, it was scarcely heard of in Europe prior to the seventeenth century, and it was Locke who gave it its clearest exposition. In the Middle Ages the ownership of property was universally held to imply duties as well as rights, and if the duties were not fulfilled, the rights were forfeited. It was everywhere agreed that the property-owner must provide for the support of the poor; in fact he must be ready to share his goods with the needy even if they were not in actual destitution. Most mediaeval thinkers held that the possession of property was a trusteeship or stewardship rather than outright ownership, and that the trusteeship would be forfeited if the owner neglected his social obligations. In the Middle Ages, as Tawney remarks:

> Just as the peasant may not cultivate his land in the way he thinks most profitable to himself, but is bound by the law of the village to grow the crops which the village needs and to throw his strips over to his neighbors' beats, so the lord is required both by custom and by statute to forego the anti-social profits to be won by methods of agriculture which injure his neighbor and weaken the state. He may not raise the rent nor demand increased fines, for the function of the peasant, though different, is not less essential than his own.[2]

The seventeenth century theorizers, with Locke at their head, changed all this. Property-ownership became ownership by inalienable right. It was claimed that a property-owner had the right to do as he pleased with his own. If a man found it advantageous to graze sheep rather than grow grain, he had a perfect right to oust his tenants from their farms, and the state was to be excluded from all interference with the exercise of this right. Religion or humanitarianism should, indeed, induce a man to be charitable, but it was no part of the state's functions to regulate what a man should do with his private possessions.

The first English revolution, the revolt against Charles I, aroused little sympathy on the continent of Europe. The execution of the king awakened a general feeling of horror, together with a belief that the English had gone out of their heads. Had the Commonwealth persisted, it is probable that it would eventually have had a profound effect upon continental Europe, but the sudden collapse of republican government and the restoration of the Stuarts made the Europeans believe that the revolution had been but a temporary local disturbance, of little value to serious students of political philosophy. The second revolution, followed by the expulsion of James II, was destined to have a far different effect upon the development of continental thought. At first, to be sure, the new revolt was received with silent and rather skeptical amazement. The Europeans were certain that before long King James or his son would be back on the throne, but as decade followed decade and the strictly limited monarchy of 1689 proved to be a strong and stable form of government, the peoples of Europe gradually came to realize that the English political system was worthy of serious consideration.

During the eighteenth century the prestige of England was constantly on the increase. The success of the armies led by King William and later by the Duke of Marlborough showed that a limited monarchy was able to fight on at least equal terms with absolute monarchies. The steady growth of English wealth, commerce, and industry at a time when most of the continental countries were commercially on the downgrade impressed the European public deeply with the idea that there might be something radically wrong with their own system and something fundamentally right with the British social, economic, and political organization. There was an immense curiosity about England and all things English, including the political principles which motivated the English system of government. Naturally enough, there arose, before long, a number of men who sought to interpret British institutions and British political philosophy to the European public. In most cases these interpreters were highly flattering to the British. In several cases these interpretations gave rise to new systems of political theory, systems based in large measure upon the ideas of Locke, but differing from him in several important features.

At this time France was the heart and soul of continental Europe. It is hardly surprising, therefore, to find that it was the French who were most curious about English institutions and that it was among the French writers that the foremost interpreters of these institutions and ideas arose. Chief amongst these interpreters was Charles Louis de Secondat, Baron de la Brède and de Montesquieu (1689–1755), best known to posterity by the simple name of Montesquieu. Montesquieu's best known book, *The Spirit of Laws* (published in 1748), enjoyed an immense popularity in European literary and political circles, and this popularity aided enormously in the spread of liberal ideas on the Continent.

Montesquieu was influenced by the English in general and by Locke in particular. But though Montesquieu agreed with Locke in most of the latter's conclusions, the two men differed radically in method, in attitude, and in fundamental assumptions. Locke based his political philosophy upon primordial individual rights and upon the supposed terms of the social contract. Montesquieu thought that the whole idea of natural rights was meaningless and that the doctrine of the social contract was absurd. Locke was theoretical and analytical; Montesquieu was practical and historical. Locke dealt with governments as they ought to be; Montesquieu with governments as they were, even though willing to indicate certain advisable reforms. Locke argued whether or not revolution was justifiable; Montesquieu took revolutions for granted and studied their causes.

Even in the field of practical politics there were important differences between Locke and Montesquieu. Locke was the prophet both of democracy and of individualism. Montesquieu was primarily concerned only with individualism and individual rights. He advocated a certain amount of democratic control only in order that individual rights might better be preserved. Where individual rights were seen to be endangered by pure democracy, pure democracy was immediately placed in the discard. But though Montesquieu's fundamental political postulate is the supremacy of individual rights, his views on individual rights differed radically from those which Locke has expressed on the subject. Locke believed in the eternal, absolute rights of the individual, which he was supposed to possess irrespective of whether he was or was not a member of a state. Montesquieu thought that the doctrine of natural rights was ridiculous. Even concrete *political* rights (the right to vote, etc.) were to him little more than matters of convenience or historical accident; but his whole political philosophy was based on a plea for actual human and personal rights, the right of each individual to lead a normal, decent life without being subjected to the whim of any person or any group of persons or even of the community as a whole. Montesquieu was, in fact, the founder of what is known as *guarantism*, the system designed to protect the real freedom of the individual against encroachment by the state or any group within the state.

To secure this freedom for the individual, Montesquieu advocated the doctrine of *check and balance* and the logical development of this doctrine, namely, the *separation of powers*. The idea of check and balance was based upon the idea that "constant experience shows us that every man invested with power is apt to abuse it, and to carry his authority as far as it will go. . . . To prevent this abuse, it is necessary from the very nature of things that power should be a check to power." [2a] Montesquieu thought that he had found a perfect example of check and balance in England, where the government of the country was shared between the king, the House of Lords, and the House of Commons, no one of these three factors being possessed of ultimate or sovereign power. It was right, according to Montesquieu, that the king should be the supreme magistrate, that the person of the king should be sacred and inviolable, and that the king should have an absolute veto upon all laws. It was right that the monarch should have the power to summon prorogue, and dissolve Parliament when he pleased, but lest he let too

great a time pass without summoning the legislative body it was desirable that money and supplies should be granted by Parliament for
only a limited period. It was, of course, necessary that all laws be
passed and all taxes voted by Parliament before being submitted to the
king for approval.

According to Montesquieu, in all states there are bound to be persons
distinguished by their birth, their riches, and their honors. There are
also bound to be a large number of people who possess none of these
advantages. Montesquieu felt that both these elements should have a
share in government. But if every man should have but one vote in
elections to a single assembly, the aristocratic element, being in the
minority, would certainly be oppressed. To protect the interests of
this group in the community it was advisable that the aristocrats
should form a separate branch of the legislature with a right "to check
the license of the people." It was well, moreover, that the nobles
should have certain judicial privileges.

> The great are always obnoxious to popular envy; and were they to be
> judged by the people, they might be in danger from their judges.... The
> nobility, for this reason, ought not to be cited before the ordinary courts
> of judicature, but before that part of the legislature which is composed of
> their own body.[3]

But while Montesquieu thus believed in granting power and special
privilege to the hereditary nobility, he also believed that the *plebs*, the
common people, should have the right to oppose any undue encroachment on the part of the nobility. In fact Montesquieu went even further
than his English contemporaries, for whereas in the eighteenth century
suffrage for the House of Commons was limited to a small group of
persons, Montesquieu urged that "all the inhabitants... ought to have
a right of voting at the election of a representative, except such as are
in so mean a situation as to be deemed to have no will of their own." [4]
Montesquieu, to be sure, had no great belief in the political sagacity
of the mob. "The people ... are incapable of conducting administration
themselves." [5] In fact they were considered unfit even to discuss public
affairs. Hence Montesquieu was a stern opponent of direct democracy.
Nevertheless he was convinced that the people are extremely well
qualified to choose persons to whom legislative authority may be
entrusted. The people know nothing of tactics, but "they can tell when
a person has fought many battles and has been crowned with success'
they are therefore capable of electing a general." The people know
little or nothing of law, yet "they can tell when a judge is assiduous in

his office, gives general satisfaction, and has never been charged with bribery." [6]   Hence it is all right for the people to have the power to elect their judicial officials.

From the belief that the people, though ignorant, are capable of choosing suitable representatives, Montesquieu deduced two important corollaries.   In the first place,

> the members of the legislature should not be chosen from the general body of the nation, but it is proper that in every considerable place a representative should be elected by the inhabitants.... The inhabitants of a particular town are much better acquainted with its wants and interests than with those of other places; and are better judges of the capacity of their neighbors than of that of the rest of their countrymen. [7]

From this statement it is clear that Montesquieu would have been strongly opposed to the electoral system in vogue in Germany under the Weimar Constitution, whereby the German people as a whole voted for general party lists.   Montesquieu would also have been opposed to class or group representation in the House of Commons, a scheme advocated by many modern functionalists.   Representation, according to him, should be on a strictly geographic basis.   In England then as now, though representation is nominally geographic in character, a man may stand for Parliament in any constituency in the realm and may be elected by a locality which he has never even seen.   It is probable that Montesquieu would greatly have preferred the American system, whereby, according to custom, a man must be an actual resident of the district he represents in Congress.

The other important deduction from Montesquieu's theory of representation is that all representatives should be entrusted with discretionary powers, or, in other words, be permitted to vote and debate as they themselves see fit.   "It is not at all necessary that the representatives who have received general instruction from their constituents should wait to be directed on each particular affair." [8]   In fact, representatives should be chosen because of their personal character and abilities, and once chosen they should be left free to decide political issues without further reference to the whims of the masses.

To Montesquieu the system of check and balance should be applied not only with reference to the different classes in a state, but also with respect to the different functions of the state.   It is, indeed, owing to Montesquieu's influence that the doctrine of check and balance has become intimately associated with the idea of separation of powers. Though the separation of powers was hinted at by earlier writers and formally developed by Locke, it was really Montesquieu who placed this doctrine on a secure and permanent basis. Locke had spoken of the three functions or powers as being legislative, executive, and federative, and though he claimed that they were separate functions, he believed that the executive and the federative functions should normally be united in the hands of a single person. It was Montesquieu who first enunciated the idea that the three functions should be the legislative, the executive, and the judicial, and he was also the first to argue that these three functions should forever be kept separate and distinct.

Locke had brought forth the ideas of the separation of powers largely as a means of bolstering his anti-despotic or democratic principles. For this reason his three powers were not co-equal; the executive and federative powers, which rested in the hands of the king, were definitely subordinated to the legislative branch of the government, which was elected by the people. Montesquieu advocated the separation of powers, not because of his belief in democracy, but because of his desire to maintain personal liberty, if necessary, at the expense of democratic institutions. For this reason he insisted that the three functions should be completely co-equal and that no one branch of the government should ever be subordinated to any other branch. For the liberty of the subject to be maintained, Montesquieu thought that it was advisable that the making of laws, the execution of laws, and the judicial decision of individual cases should be in the hands of three separate bodies, no one of which should be appointed or be held responsible to the others. It would be iniquitous, he argued, to have all three of these functions carried out by the king or by the personal agents of the king; it would be equally iniquitous to have these three functions carried out by the popular assembly. One of Montesquieu's principal objections to republics was that in all republics the three powers tend to be united in a single body.

Historically speaking, Montesquieu's doctrine of the three co-equal functions of government was based upon a misunderstanding and misinterpretation of the English system of government. Though the doctrine of cabinet responsibility was not as fully developed in the eighteenth century as it is today, it was not entirely absent. When Montesquieu was in England, the ministers of state, though nominally subordinate to the king alone, knew that the tenure of their office depended in large measure upon retaining the confidence of Parliament. As a result Montesquieu's version of the separation of powers was an anachronism when he wrote and was soon to appear ridiculous even to

the casual observer.   Locke's concept of the supremacy of the legislative over the other organs of government was far more in keeping with
the spirit of the British Constitution after 1689.   But though Montesquieu failed as an interpreter, he succeeded as a prophet.   His
doctrine of the separation of powers, though erroneous as a statement
of fact, was hailed by students of theoretical government.   It was due
in large measure to Montesquieu's influence that this doctrine was
accepted and applied by the inhabitants of the New World when the
Constitution of the United States was drawn up.

The writings of Montesquieu created a sensation in the literary and
intellectual circles of the civilized countries of Europe.   But great as
was Montesquieu's success, he was soon to be outshone in popularity
by his junior contemporary, Jean Jacques Rousseau (1712–1778).
Rousseau, like Montesquieu, was the idol of the literary salons, but
unlike Montesquieu, he became the inspiration of large sections of the
populace excluded from the higher circle, sections who felt that they
found in his writings a magic formula which would ease their troubles
and right their wrongs.   Rousseau was greatly indebted to Locke; in
fact the greater part of his political ideas are directly traceable to the
English theorist, Rousseau being content to popularize and develop
Locke's fundamental postulates.   But Locke's *Essay on Civil Government*
was a rather dull defense of a revolution which had already taken place,
and all that Locke wished to do was to cause the populace to accept the
status quo.   Where Locke was read by the hundred, Rousseau, whose
principal work, the *Social Contract*, appeared in 1762, was read by the
thousand, and wherever Rousseau was read, there was engendered a
vast discontent with existing conditions, and a feeling that something
radical should be done to correct existing evils.   Locke was a mild
defender of a bloodless revolution in the past; Rousseau was the ardent
apostle of a cause which was to lead to a violent revolution shortly after
his death.
Rousseau owed much to Locke.   He also owed much — more than
he would acknowledge — to Hobbes.   He attacked Hobbes' absolutist
conclusions, but he took over from Hobbes one of the most important
features of the latter's political philosophy, the doctrine of sovereignty.
Both Locke and Montesquieu had carefully avoided even the use of the
word sovereignty, feeling that the term was inextricably mixed up with
monarchist and absolutist ideas.   Rousseau, on the other hand, believed
that once sovereignty was postulated for the people rather than for the

monarch, the theory would prove to be the most potent weapon with which to bludgeon despots and despotism. Rousseau's belief on this point proved to be correct. After him, the theory of sovereignty became the rallying point of the advocates of democracy. There could be — nay, there was — an omnipotent ruler of the state, but this ruler was not the king, but rather the people taken as a whole.

But though Rousseau's doctrine of sovereignty was eminently successful in the war against despotism, it was to lead to many of the consequences which had so frightened Locke. It was soon seen that though sovereignty was compatible with democracy, it was not easy to fit this theory with the doctrine of individualism. Rousseau, to be sure, preached not only equality or democracy, but also liberty or freedom for the individual, but in actual fact this freedom in Rousseau's system became extremely tenuous. Man was to be free from the caprices of a tyrannous monarch, but he was to be subject to the absolute control of the democratic state. Locke, the founder of the modern liberal tradition, stressed both democracy and individualism. Montesquieu, in order to secure individual freedom, sacrificed the extremer forms of democracy. It was now the turn of Rousseau to emphasize the virtue and necessity of radical democracy at the expense of extreme individualism.

Much of Rousseau's belief in democracy was derived from his conception of the state of nature, the condition of man before the formation of political units. Hobbes had argued that the state of nature was a state of war; that the life of man at this stage was "solitary, poor, nasty, brutish, and short." In opposition to this view Locke had insisted that the state of nature was normally peaceful and pleasant. But even Locke had agreed that life in a state of nature was vexatious and inconvenient and that men had profited materially, morally, and intellectually by the formation of the political state. Rousseau accepted with a few modifications Locke's view of the state of nature, but emphasized even more strongly the peaceful, pleasant, idyllic condition of this natural state. Again and again, especially in his earlier works, Rousseau stressed the happiness which man enjoyed when everyone was free and equal, when nature provided abundant nourishment for all. He then proceeded to contrast with this early blissful state the inequality, the oppression, the poverty which is the common lot of the bulk of the inhabitants of most modern political states.

To be sure, Rousseau convinced himself in the end that it was advisable and even necessary to depart from the state of nature and form civil government. But though he admitted that the state was necessary, he continued to regret that it was impossible to return to the idyllic life enjoyed by the primitive savages. In fact Rousseau went even further and claimed that the closer man can approximate to the natural state, the better off he is. "Return to nature" is an axiom which cannot be carried out literally, but it can serve as a general guide in the conduct of human affairs. The conventionalities of so-called civilized life produce, according to Rousseau, only misery. Better a country of small farmers and simple shepherds living in close communion with nature than a land with vast cities teeming with hovels on one side and with palaces on the other.

Rousseau's plea for the natural life exerted a great influence upon his own generation. In Europe, especially in France, "naturalism" became the vogue, though this vogue was little more than a pose. The great lords and ladies of the court at Versailles felt that they were carrying out Rousseau's doctrines by staging elaborate pantomimes in which they dressed up and pirouetted as simple shepherds and shepherdesses. In the New World, especially among the English colonists, Rousseau's ideas won popular favor with the small farmers and the country folk. They became convinced that their life, close to nature, far removed from the luxuries and the sophistications of the Old World, made them members of an ideal community. They came to regard themselves no longer as pupils, but as the potential teachers of the effete Europeans.

Even more important were the conclusions which Rousseau and his disciples drew from naturalism with respect to the political potentialities of the common man. Most of the early liberals spoke eloquently in defense of the right of "the people," but they were convinced believers in the right and duty of the upper classes to lead the common herd. Though Locke and Montesquieu had advocated a wide suffrage, they had not hesitated to assert that the well-born, the rich, the cultured classes must take the leading part in political life. With Rousseau this belief in the superiority of the "well-born" was shattered. The upper classes, according to him, were probably corrupted by their contact with luxuries and the artificial conventionalities of social life. The simple peasant and ignorant worker in the field might be, and probably was, more imbued with civic pride and political sagacity than the much-vaunted members of the aristocracy.

The mere ignorance or illiteracy of the worker should not, according to Rousseau, be a barrier to his participation in political life. Rousseau did advocate universal education, but he set little store upon book learning or even upon the use of abstract reasoning. "Reflection and its practical results are the pernicious results of artificial society.... The man who reflects is a corrupt creature." On this point Rousseau differed radically from Locke, for Locke had argued that even in a state of nature man was rational and obeyed the commands of reason. To Rousseau man was naturally not a rational but an emotional animal, swayed in his actions by his feeling. But to Rousseau this was an advantage rather than a disadvantage, for man's fundamental emotions are not mere self-interest, but also pity for others. Hence reliance upon our natural feelings should give us peace and true liberty. In a word, Rousseau's naturalism was to exalt not merely the state of nature, but also the common man and his political capacity. With him "the people" meant no longer the common herd led by the magnates and the magistrates, but the mass of men acting in accordance with their natural emotions.

Rousseau took over the doctrine of the social contract from Locke, but in many ways the social contract he pictured was closer to the social contract of Hobbes than to the social contract of Locke. Whereas Locke had argued that in forming the contract men had given up only *some* of their natural rights, Rousseau following Hobbes believed that man's agreement to the covenant implied that he gave up *all* rights and prerogatives to the state. The social contract ordains "the total alienation to the whole community of each associate with all his rights ... This alienation being without reserve, the union is as perfect as it can be, and an individual associate can no longer claim anything...." [9] As nature gives every man an absolute power over his limbs, the social pact gives the body politic an absolute power over all of its members." [10]

In claiming that the social contract implies that a man gives up all his rights, Rousseau was in agreement with Hobbes. But he was in profound disagreement with Hobbes on one all-important point. According to Hobbes, the community, being unable to act for itself, is forced to transfer its supreme absolute power to a small group of individuals or preferably to a single individual. To Rousseau, the community or the state itself (meaning thereby the people as a whole) must always remain sovereign and cannot, even if it wished to, delegate or transfer to anyone else its sovereign prerogatives. Rousseau was at some pains to prove that the very concept of sovereignty implied that sovereignty was necessarily inalienable and indivisible. Though certain administrative functions might be granted to specific individuals, these individuals necessarily remained subordinate agents. Should the community seek to transfer all or even part of its sovereign powers to one of these agents, the body politic would thereby be destroyed.

In insisting that the community as a whole should always remain sovereign, Rousseau maintained that the state is not merely a collection of separate individuals, but that it is a new body with an identity, a life, and a personality of its own. Most important of all, in Rousseau's opinion, the state has a will of its own, the *volonté général* or general will, to which all separate and particular wills must be subordinated.

The theory that sovereignty was indivisible was aimed especially at Montesquieu's idea of the separation of powers, at least in the sense that the various branches of the government should be co-equal. In the first place, Rousseau insisted that Montesquieu's threefold division of governmental powers was inexact, for to him the executive and the judicial functions were merely different phases of the same thing, and he included both under the general heading of executive. Rousseau was perfectly willing to separate the executive and the legislative functions, but to him the executive function must always be subordinated to the legislative. Moreover, while the executive function had necessarily to be carried out by a few specially appointed agents, the legislative function, implying as it did full legislative powers, could not be carried out by a delegated body, but had to remain with the community as a whole.

The fact that Rousseau thought that legislative powers implied sovereign powers and that sovereign powers could not be delegated or transferred from the community acting as a whole, meant that he was forced to attack the theory of representative government, the idea that full legislative powers should be granted to an assembly, even though this assembly consisted of persons elected by the people. "Sovereignty cannot be alienated. ... The deputies of the people then are not and cannot be its representatives; they are only its commissioners and cannot conclude anything definitely. Every law which the people have not ratified is invalid; it is not a law." [11] From this passage it is clear that Rousseau stood for direct democracy as opposed to representative government. Though this phase of Rousseau's philosophy had little effect upon his contemporaries or his immediate successors, it was never forgotten and towards the close of the nineteenth century served as a stimulus to the political reformers who advocated the initiative and referendum.

Though Rousseau was convinced that supreme legislative power must always be kept in the hands of the community as a whole, he willingly admitted that it was necessary for the state to appoint agents or deputies to insure the carrying out of legislative acts, for the punishment of crime, and for the framing of minor ordinances and decrees. These agents, taken together, constituted, in Rousseau's system, the "government," as opposed to the "state." But though the governors, or the members of the government, should normally be entrusted with administrative control, they were merely "the depositories of executive power. They are not the masters of the people, but its officers. ... The people can appoint and dismiss them at pleasure." [12] The powers and the duties granted by the state (that is, the people) to the government (that is, the magistrates) might at any time be limited, modified, or resumed by the sovereign body.

Rousseau was convinced that even the best of governments tend to abuse the power granted them by the state. "Between the government and the sovereign [that is, the people] there is an unavoidable and incessant war, which sooner or later ends in the government suppressing the sovereign." Because all governments inevitably tend to usurp power, it is necessary for the sovereign people to be constantly on their guard.

> It is not sufficient that the assembled people should have once fixed the constitution of the state by giving their sanction to a body of laws. ... Besides the extraordinary assemblies which unforeseen events may require, it is necessary that there be fixed and periodical ones which nothing can abolish or prorogue, so that on an appointed day the people are rightly convoked by the law without needing for that purpose any formal summons. ... So soon as the people are lawfully assembled as a sovereign body, the whole jurisdiction of the Government ceases, the executive power is suspended.[12a]

According to Rousseau these periodic special assemblies of the whole body of citizens

> ought always to be opened with two propositions, which no one should be able to suppress, and which should be passed separately by vote. The first is "whether it pleases the sovereign to maintain the present form of government?" The second, "whether it pleases the people to leave the administration to those [at present] entrusted with it?" [13]

These proposals were destined to have an important effect in later years, especially in the New World. It was in accordance with the spirit, if not with the letter, of Rousseau that the Americans, in framing their system of government, provided for the election of officials for short rather than for long periods. It was in accord both with the spirit and with the letter of Rousseau that many nineteenth century liberals

demanded that the people be empowered to recall any unpopular magistrate even before his term of office had expired. It was the influence
of Rousseau which led to the system in vogue in some American states,
whereby special conventions (constitutional conventions) are called
at stated intervals to decide if the existing constitution is in need of
revision.

THE CONSERVATIVE REACTION IN EUROPE:

JOSEPH DE MAISTRE

The liberal tradition, founded by Locke, by Montesquieu, and by
Rousseau, had an immense effect upon popular opinion during the
middle and latter part of the eighteenth century. As this century drew
to a close, the liberal tradition gathered momentum and eventually led
to the outbreak of two great revolutions, the American Revolution,
which brought about the establishment of the United States, and the
French Revolution, which overthrew the Bourbon monarchy.

The excesses committed by many of the revolutionaries resulted in
a popular reaction against these revolutions and against the principles
upon which they had been based. In Europe, in England, even in
America, there arose systems of political philosophy which criticized
and attacked all the major items in the liberal ideology, and which
emphasized the need for law and order in contrast to demands for
freedom and equality.

But though the leaders of the conservative reaction attacked many
of the liberal principles, they were careful, for the most part, not to
revert to the Tory ideas of an earlier age. Very seldom did they refer
to the divine right of kings. Most of the conservative writers were
willing to admit the right of the people to a share in the process of
government. Conservatism was not incompatible with republicanism,
as is seen in the writings of the American Federalists. In a word, the
whole tenor of the anti-liberal reaction at the end of the eighteenth
century showed that certain phases of the old liberal tradition had
come to receive almost universal acceptance. The very nature of the
conservative reaction proved that liberalism, in some form, was destined to play an important role in nineteenth century history.

It is not surprising to find that the most violent criticism of the old
liberal tradition was in continental Europe, and especially in France,
the country which had suffered most severely from the ravages of the
revolutionary zealots. Among the most outstanding of the bitter

critics of the principles which had brought about the revolution were the Marquis de Bonald and, above all, Count Joseph de Maistre. De Maistre was a native of Savoy in northern Italy, but he wrcte in French and was in many ways the greatest exponent of French conservative thought during the period immediately following the revolution.

The basic principles of De Maistre (1753–1821) were *piety* and *tradition*. In the name of piety he assailed the secularism, the rationalizing, and the deism which characterized the writings of many of the liberal thinkers. The origin of all states, according to De Maistre, was centered in the religious instinct. "Examine history, which is experimental politics, and we shall invariably find the cradle of nations surrounded by priests and the Divinity constantly invoked in favor of human weaknesses." Religion, moreover, has always been the most important factor in giving permanence and stability to political institutions. "The duration of Empires has always been proportioned to the degree of influence which the religious principle had acquired in the political constitution. The cities and nations most addicted to Divine worship have always been the most durable and the most wise." Finally, it is the decay of religion which destroys the state. "As it is the religious principle which has created everything, so it is the absence of this same principle which has destroyed everything. The sect of Epicurus ... corrupted at first, and soon after destroyed every government which was unfortunate to give it admission." [14]

Arguing from the principle of religion, De Maistre goes on to claim that it was the rationalism of the eighteenth century which led to the era of chaos and anarchy ushered in by the French Revolution.

> It was only in the first part of the eighteenth century that impiety really became a power.... From the palace to the cabin, it insinuates itself everywhere and infects everything.... Entire Europe having been civilized by Christianity, the civil and religious institutions were blended.... It was then inevitable that the philosophy of the age should unhesitatingly hate the social institutions from which it was impossible to separate the religious principle.... Every government, and all the establishments were offensive to it because they were Christian. [15]

"Man in relation to his Creator is sublime and his action creative..., so soon as he separates himself from God and acts alone, he does not cease to be powerful, but his action is negative and tends only to destroy." [16] It is small wonder then that the impiety of the eighteenth

century led to the calamities, the wild excesses, the universal destruc-
tiveness of the French Revolution.

To De Maistre it was obvious that for civilization to be restored, for
law and order to be re-established on a permanent basis, it was first
of all necessary for the peoples of Europe to return to religion. It was
useless to try to reconstruct the outward forms of the old governments
unless the inhabitants of each country were inspired by religious convictions. De Maistre was, of course, a Catholic and he felt that political
as well as religious salvation was only to be found in the Catholic
Church.

De Maistre was convinced that a return to religion, to the Catholic
Church, would inevitably lead to a restoration of the monarchic form
of government. It is not mere chance that the history of the world
since the beginning of the Christian era has shown the dominance of
the monarchic principle in both church and state — in the church the
pope, in the state the king. Acceptance of the rulership of a single individual necessarily follows from a desire to follow the will of God.
Moreover, just as the church has the spiritual hierarchy of canons,
bishops, and archbishops, so does a well-ordered state have its temporal
hierarchy of the lesser and the greater nobility. The clamor for equality
will disappear when men are again imbued with the religious spirit.

In De Maistre's political philosophy the role played by tradition was
almost as important as that assigned to piety. A state could never be
artificially created; it could only grow slowly and unconsciously. The
true constitution of any country was its customary law plus the organs
of government which have gradually developed through the centuries.
This true constitution by its very nature could never be written. The
attempt to reconstruct governments on purely rational principles, the
transformation of the unwritten constitution based on custom and
tradition to a written constitution based on abstract ideas, was bound
to end in disaster.

A governmental system is like a language. As a living language cannot be artificially created nor even radically reformed by deliberate
planning, so must government be left to develop unconsciously and
spontaneously.

Quite naturally De Maistre was rather scornful of the much-vaunted
written Constitution of America. To his mind some of the provisions
of this Constitution might be of some value to the American people, but
only in so far as they were the expression of ideas and practices which
had long been familiar in the history and traditions of the people. The

really novel portions of the Constitution, those items which were the outcome of rational deliberation and planning, were foredoomed to failure.

It is interesting in the light of later history to examine into the truth of De Maistre's remarks.   It is certain that the most successful features in the American Constitution have been those which were modeled upon earlier institutions, and that the most unsuccessful feature of the Constitution, the college of electors, was the result of rational abstract planning, for which there was no prototype, at least in colonial or British history.   Nevertheless it must be added that some of De Maistre's prophetic strictures upon "planned politics" and "planned economics" have proved false.   When De Maistre wrote, the Americans were projecting the creation of a new city, which would serve as their political capital.   To De Maistre's mind "there was too much delibera-tion, too much of the human about the business, and it would be safe to wager a thousand to one, that the city will not be built, or that it will not be called Washington, or that Congress will not have its seat there." [17]

De Maistre's traditionalism made him a conservative, disliking all radical change, and skeptical even of moderate reforms.   Nevertheless this very traditionalism prevented De Maistre from joining hands with the Tory writers of the seventeenth century.   Bodin and Hobbes, for example, had argued for the placing of absolute power in the hands of a king at all times and places.   To such a conclusion De Maistre could not come.   To him, where tradition, the "unwritten constitution," provided for an absolute monarchy, it was heresy for the nobles or the people to demand political rights, but on the other hand where tradition, as in England, provided for the participation of the nobles and the people in the government, it would be dangerous and unwise for the monarch to try to secure unlimited powers.[18]

THE CONSERVATIVE REACTION IN ENGLAND: EDMUND BURKE

In England the outbreak of the French Revolution awakened vigorous opposition among many members of the British governing oligarchy, but nowhere was the dislike of the revolutionary ideals so forcibly and so plausibly expressed as in the speeches and writings of the great Anglo-Irish statesman Edmund Burke (1729–1797).

In many ways Burke occupies a unique place in English history. By some he has been described as the greatest thinker who ever devoted himself to English politics. Born and educated in Ireland, he is a superb example of what Anglo-Irish culture can produce, for he was of mixed English and Irish ancestry. His father was a Protestant, his mother a Catholic, and though Burke himself was brought up as a Protestant, he always maintained a keen sympathy for Catholics and the Catholic faith, a fact of some importance in considering his later political speculations. Burke's father was an attorney, a substantial and respectable citizen, but one lacking in influence or great wealth. On reaching maturity Edmund Burke quarreled with his father and was forced to shift for himself. This brought about great hardship, and for some years Burke lived from hand to mouth, eking out a precarious livelihood as a journalist and hack writer.

In 1765, at the age of thirty-six, he was fortunate enough to secure the post of secretary to the Marquis of Rockingham, and thereafter his path was much easier. Through his employer he secured a seat in the House of Commons and soon became one of the most eloquent and most distinguished members of that assembly. Lord Rockingham was the leader of a small but important party known as the "Old Whigs," and though Burke continued to act in a subordinate capacity, he was generally recognized as the real brain of this group.

Nevertheless Burke's later life was far from a bed of roses. During most of his parliamentary career his party was in opposition, and Burke was forced to serve as the impotent critic of other men's policies. Even when Rockingham became Prime Minister, Burke for some strange -eason was excluded from the cabinet, being given only the comparatively unimportant post of Paymaster General of the Army. In private life Burke was also unfortunate, though many of his troubles were the result of his own improvidence. Wishing to vie with the English landed aristocrats, he bought a large estate and was thereafter constantly harassed by debts. On his deathbed Lord Rockingham ordered the cancellation of Burke's notes for about £30,000, but Burke was so deeply involved that even this munificent action did not free him from financial worries.

In his old age Burke, at long last, became popular with the king and court. As a result he was offered a peerage. He was just about to be created the Earl of Beaconsfield when his only son died. The old man's grief was inconsolable. "The storm has gone over me and I lie like one of the old oaks which the late hurricane has scattered about me. I am stripped of all my honors. I am torn up by the roots and lie prostrate on the earth.... I am alone." Feeling that a peerage for a childless old man was ridiculous, Burke refused the proffered honor, and a life pension was all that he could be persuaded to accept.

Burke's importance in the history of thought is that he was the real founder of the political philosophy of the English Tory or Conservative Party during the nineteenth century. It was impossible for these later Tories to hark back to the old Tory tradition. During the seventeenth century the Tories had advocated monarchic absolutism and the divine right of kings. The true Tories were forced to remain loyal to the exiled Stuart family long after the House of Hanover was placed on the English throne. It was obviously impossible for the nineteenth century Tories to go back to these principles.

During the early portion of George III's reign there was a brief recrudescence of the Tory Party. The Tories at this time, though abjuring the doctrine of the divine right of kings, persisted in favoring a system in which the personal power and influence of the king was considered the paramount force in the national government. "The ministers were no longer to be members of a great party acting together ... they were to become nominees of the court answerable to the King." Even this position the nineteenth century Tories found it impossible to accept, for during this period the collective responsibility of the cabinet members to Parliament was taken for granted by all party groups, even the most reactionary.

If, therefore, the Tory Party was not to sink into insignificance, it was necessary for it to adopt a new political philosophy. This system it found in the writings of Burke, and it was its frank acceptance of Burke's fundamental principles which permitted the Tory Party — transformed into the Conservative Party — to remain an important and powerful factor in nineteenth century politics.

By a curious irony of history, Burke, the founder of philosophic nineteenth century Toryism, was not only a Whig but also one who gloried in the greatness of the Whig tradition and one who pointed the finger of scorn at the Tories of earlier days. When the violence of his remarks against the French Revolution caused some of his colleagues to proclaim that Burke had deserted the Whig cause, Burke wrote one of his masterpieces, the *Appeal from the New to the Old Whigs*, in which he endeavored to prove that it was he, and not the French sympathizers, who had held true to the glorious Whig tradition, in spite of the fact that it was the Whig Party which had engineered the English Revolution of 1689.

The arguments Burke used in this connection are not without interest to the student of political philosophy. He deplored the French Revolution because it was purely destructive. He applauded the English Revolution of the previous century because it had been constructive. He declared that the French people in rebelling against their king were wrong because this rebellion was also against the real, though unwritten, French Constitution, the immemorial institution in that country. He declared that the English had been justified in rebelling against King James, because King James had first been guilty of subverting the fundamental postulates of the British "Constitution." From the very nature of the case Burke could not deny the right of rebellion against a king, but such a rebellion to be justified must be shown to be necessary to preserve the country from illegal usurpation by a tyrant running roughshod over all the existing forms of government.

Burke's party, the Whig Party, had long accepted Locke as the Apostle of their political creed. Burke in his whole attitude to the fundamental problems of society and the state stood in direct antithesis to Locke, but being a Whig he could never attack Locke nor formally renounce any of Locke's political dogmas. But if he could not renounce them he could at least transform them to such an extent as to make them meaningless. As Hearnshaw remarks,

> One of the most interesting tasks that a student of political theory is called upon to perform in his perusal of the writings of Burke is to observe the way in which his author, when he comes face to face with a distinctive Lockian idea, bows down to it and worships, circumvents it, knocks it over from behind and then goes on his way rejoicing.[19]

Locke had based his political philosophy upon the social contract. Burke therefore could never specifically deny the social contract, but in his system the social contract becomes so ethereal, so vague as to be void of all meaning.

> Society is indeed a Contract. It is a partnership in all science, a partnership in all art, a partnership in every virtue and in all perfection. As the ends of such a partnership cannot be obtained in many generations, it becomes a partnership not only between those now living but between those who are living and those who are dead and those who are to be born.[20]

In so far as the social contract is accepted at all, it is used not, as with Locke, to justify revolution, but as an argument against revolution.

> The Constitution of a country being once settled upon some compact, tacit or expressed, there is no power existing or force to alter it without the breach of covenant or the consent of all the parties.[21]

The ultimate aim of Locke's philosophy was to stress individual rights — the "rights of man." Burke did not deny these rights, but the rights for which he pleaded were civil rights, not political rights.

> Far am I from denying the *real* rights of man. . . . If civil society be made for the advantage of man, all the advantages for which it is made become his right. . . . Men have a right to justice between their fellows. . . . They have a right to the fruits of their industry, and to the means of making their industry fruitful. They have a right to the acquisitions of their parents and to the nourishment and improvement of their offspring. . . . As to the share of power, authority, and direction which each individual ought to have in the management of the state, that I must deny to be amongst the direct original rights of man in Civil Society. It is a thing to be settled by convention.[22]

In contrast with his lip service to the old Whig doctrines, Burke's real devotion was to three quite different principles. Two of these were the same as those advocated by De Maistre, namely, *piety* and *tradition*. In addition he laid great emphasis upon *practical expediency*.

Like De Maistre, Burke was profoundly disgusted by the antireligious tone which was so intimately associated with the revolutionary movement in France. To him atheism or even skepticism was incompatible with peace and order. Though not a fanatic, he held that the very foundations of society consisted in the acceptance of the doctrines of God, free will, and immortality. "We know and it is our pride to know that man is by his constitution a religious animal. . . . We know, and what is better we feel inwardly, that religion is the basis of Civil Society." [23] Not only society in general, but political society or the state is of divine institution, and any state which ignores God and God's law is bound to meet with disaster.

Unlike De Maistre, Burke would permit religious toleration. He admitted that all forms of religion within the state might play a part in bearing witness to the validity of the religious impulse. He would even admit nonconformists and Catholics to political privileges — but he was firm in his belief that it was necessary for the state to avow its religious basis by formally establishing and supporting a national church. "The consecration of the state by a state religious establishment is necessary." [24]

Burke did not accept the idea that devout acceptance of the religious principle necessarily involved acceptance of absolute monarchy, or for that matter, any other form of government, but he did believe that religious devotion was incompatible with all revolutionary ideals and

that the truly devout, instead of aiming at the overthrow of society
and social distinctions in a wild desire for equality, would regard their
own status in life as assigned to them by God and hence would remain
satisfied.   "I may assume that the awful author of our being is the
author of our place in the order of existence and ... has subjected us
to act the part which belongs to the place assigned us." [25]

The traditionalism of Burke was very similar to the traditionalism
of De Maistre.   For all his nominal acceptance of the social contract,
Burke felt that the state was not a mechanism devised by the will of
man but a living organism.   The state is not an artificial creation of
man's rational will but the product of innate social instincts.   "The
state of civil society ... is a state of nature and much more truly so
than a savage and incoherent mode of life." [26]   After being created,
the civil state slowly grows and develops as the result of accumulated
experience.   "Our country is not a mere thing of physical locality.   It
consists in great measure of the ancient order into which we are born." [27]
In facing the problem of government, men should not forget that the
state is not the product of a single generation; they should remember
that "men come into a community with the social state of their parents,
endowed with all the benefits and loaded with all the duties of their
situation." [28]

To Burke as to De Maistre, the true constitution of a country is not
a written document drawn up by a body of men at a particular time and
place, but the organs of government which have arisen through the
centuries as the result of trial and error, through the survivals of those
institutions which have proved themselves most useful and most suitable for the nation as a whole.   It is not even necessary for a constitution to be embodied in ordinary statute law.   To his mind some of the
most important and valuable portions of the British Constitution are
to be found not in the formal acts of Parliament but in the unwritten
traditions based upon custom and precedent.

Burke did not, at least in theory, disapprove of all change.   "A disposition to preserve and an ability to improve, taken together, would be
my standard of a statesman." [29]   Occasional reforms or "improvements" were therefore necessary; in fact the very idea that the constitution was a growth implied the need of change, as growth without
change is impossible.   But improvements, to his mind, should be made
slowly and carefully, lest the growth, the whole social order be endangered.   In reforming, men should always bear in mind past experience
and the traditional spirit of the people.   "All the reformations we have

hitherto made have proceeded from the principles of reference to antiquity."

In judging governments and in instituting reforms it was above all necessary, in Burke's opinion, to be guided not by abstract principles but by expediency, and by expediency he meant consideration of the good of the whole community. Burke disliked all abstract theorizing. "One pure symptom of an ill-conditioned state is the propensity of the people to resort to theories." [30] He attacked the revolutionary thinkers because they were motivated by metaphysical theories of the state rather than by a desire to bring about concrete reforms. He disliked all theories of abstract rights, and all claims based upon these abstract rights. He assailed the French when they overthrew the government because of the "rights of man," but he was equally energetic in his indictment of the British government when it attempted to exercise its "legal rights" to tax the American colonies. When the matter came up for discussion in Parliament, Burke, who was opposed to taxing the colonials, was quite prepared to admit that England had a perfect "right" to impose taxation, but to him the question of right was quite beside the point. "The question with me is not whether you have the right to render your people miserable, but whether it is not to your interest to make them happy. It is not what a lawyer tells me you may do, but what humanity, reason and justice tells me you ought to do." [31]

In taking this attitude Burke placed himself alongside Montesquieu. Both were convinced that abstract rights were nothing and that concrete, personal, human rights were everything. But in emphasizing the supremacy of expediency as the basis of government, Burke went beyond Montesquieu and paved the way for the utilitarian doctrine which was to play such an important role in the nineteenth century.

Upon the basis of piety, tradition, and expediency Burke proceeded to evaluate the prevailing governmental institutions of his day. In his general attitude towards these institutions Burke remained in general accord with Montesquieu. Because of his emphasis upon tradition Burke agreed with Montesquieu that it is absurd to try to impose the governmental organs of one country upon an alien people, for it very seldom happens that the traditions of two countries are the same. "The circumstances and habits of every country, which it is always perilous ... to force, are to decide upon the form of its government." [32]

Like Montesquieu, moreover, Burke was convinced that though it was impossible to devise an ideal constitution suitable for all countries, yet the "mixed" government of England with its checks and balances in power was in many ways the highest embodiment of political wisdom. "These opposed and conflicting interests ... interpose a salutary check to all precipitate revolutions. They render deliberation a matter not of choice but of necessity. They make all change a subject of compromise, which necessarily begets moderation.... Through that diversity of members and interests, general liberty has as many securities as there are separate views in the several orders." [33]

By check and balance Burke did not mean the "separation of powers" — with that problem he did not greatly concern himself — but the system whereby the supreme political power in the state was to be divided between the king, the aristocrats, and the people.

Burke insisted that "there was nothing in his nature, his temper, or his faculties which should make him an enemy to any republic modern or ancient." But though he was not opposed to republicanism in the abstract, he was convinced that, in practice

> neither England nor France, without infinite detriment to them, could be brought into a republican form, but everything republican which can be introduced with safety into either of them must be built upon a monarchy — built upon a real, not a nominal, monarchy as its essential basis. [34]

Burke was no less convinced that the stability and greatness of a nation depended upon the existence of a strong and powerful aristocracy.

> To enable men to act with the weight and character of a people ... we must suppose them to be in that state of habitual social discipline in which the wiser, the more expert and the more fortunate conduct and by conducting enlighten and protect the weaker, the less knowing, and the less provided with the goods of fortune. ... To be bred in a place of estimation; to see nothing low and sordid from one's infancy; to be taught to respect oneself; to have leisure to read, to reflect, to converse; to be enabled to draw the court and attention of the wise and learned wherever they are to be found; to be habituated in armies to command and obey ... these are the circumstances of men that form a natural aristocracy without which there is no nation. [35]

Burke was not unmindful of the rights of the people taken as a whole. A member of the House of Commons for almost thirty years, he had an enormous interest in and respect for this august institution. Several of his most eloquent speeches were delivered with a view towards maintaining the power and the independence of the "popular" assembly. Unlike Montesquieu, who had advocated the complete separation of

the various organs of government, Burke wished to see the ministers
of the state responsible to Parliament in general and to the House ot
Commons in particular.

Nevertheless Burke was a democrat, not in the sense that Rousseau
was a democrat, but as the early Huguenots were democrats.   The
people were to be supreme in the sense that the true end of all legislation
was "to give a direction, a form, a technical dress ... to the general
sense of the community," [36] but he felt that all direct political power
should be in the hands not of the common herd but of the responsible
propertied classes.   The House of Commons "represented" the people,
but it should be elected only by the "better" elements in the community, persons who had a stake in the nation.   Burke was violently
opposed to majority rule in that he denied the right of the broad mass
of the ignorant populace to make and unmake constitutions at will.

For this reason he was opposed to universal suffrage.   So conservative was he, so much in love with the existing institutions in England,
that he was opposed to all efforts to secure parliamentary reform, to
the demand for shorter Parliaments, to the project for redistributing
seats in accord with the shifts of population, to the idea of abolishing
the "rotten boroughs."   As things were, great modern cities like
Manchester and Liverpool were completely unrepresented in Parliament, and obscure villages, the remnants of ancient towns — now
completely in the hands of a few great landed families — continued to
send members to the House of Commons.   With this system Burke
was perfectly content.   "Our representation is as nearly perfect as the
necessary imperfections of human creatures will suffer it to be."

Burke's dislike of radical and sudden change, his violent attack upon
the principles of the French Revolution, the reverence he felt for the
monarchy and the House of Lords, his opposition to a wide suffrage and
to parliamentary reform, tend to make us forget that after all Burke
belonged to the liberal tradition.   Burke made many heated attacks
upon the political ideas of Rousseau and Paine, the more extreme
liberals, but compared with the doctrines of King James I, of Filmer,
or of Hobbes, the political philosophy of Burke was truly liberal.

Though opposed to revolution, he was no less opposed to oppression.
A good portion of his public life was spent in attacking royal and governmental tyranny in Ireland, in America, and in India.   He was
constantly on guard lest tyranny and oppression be reintroduced intc
England.   Though a devoted believer in monarchy, "in a real, not a

nominal monarchy" as he tells us, he was violently opposed to monarchic absolutism.   To Burke more than to any other one man is due the defeat of George III's attempt to re-establish direct personal rule over the peoples of the British Empire.

Burke "looked with awe" to kings,[37] but he was determined that kings should never go beyond constitutional rights and willingly admitted that nations had a right to depose a king who sought to become a tyrant.   His whole life was bound up with "rendering all headlong exertions of arbitrary power, in the few or in the many, forever impracticable."   In his scheme of things the unlimited or absolute powers of kings had no place.   He assailed the system whereby the ministers of state were to be the personal friends and favorites of the monarch, "a faction ruling by the private instructions of a court, against the general sense of the people." [38]   He demanded a cabinet system of government in which the ministers were jointly responsible for their actions and their policy — and they were to be responsible not only to the king but also to Parliament.

Burke was anti-despotic, and to this extent a believer in democracy — one of the fundamental principles of liberalism.   Though an enemy of "the rights of man" in the abstract, he was keenly interested in the rights of man in the concrete, and thereby was a believer in individualism, the other great feature of liberalism.   It is interesting to find Burke attacking the French Revolution because it glorified the abstract rights of man, but also because it refused to recognize the real rights of the individual.   To him the revolutionary government was "wicked, immoral, oppressive," because to it "the will, the wish, the want, the liberty, the toil of individuals is as nothing.   Individuality is left out in their scheme of government.   The State is all in all."   In contrast with this system he insists that the state should be "made to the people, not the people conformed to the state." [39]   It is the duty of the state to cultivate the welfare of every individual.   His wants, his wishes, even his desires should be consulted.

Paradoxically enough, the English Conservative Party of the nineteenth century, by adopting Burke's political philosophy, unconsciously made themselves part of the old liberal tradition.

THE CONSERVATIVE REACTION IN AMERICA: THE FEDERALISTS

The conservative reaction was not confined to the countries of the Old World.   It had a powerful influence upon American public opinion.

Under the sway of this reaction American political institutions underwent a complete transformation. In Europe the conservative reaction was largely negative in character. Its leaders were opposed to the revolutionary ideals and to the governmental organs these ideals had created. Their war-cry was hold fast to the old, accept no change. In America this phase of the reactionary sentiment could not win support. The conservative movement was forced to be positive in character. It had to emphasize the need for creating a new system of government to overcome the political and economic anarchy which seemed to threaten the newly liberated colonies. In Europe the conservative reaction produced merely the thundering declamations of De Maistre and Burke against the Revolution and all its works. In America this reaction produced the Constitution.

The leaders of the conservative reaction were in many ways very remarkable men. They were almost unique in that they were both notable political theorists and also outstanding practical statesmen. Europe has produced many profound political philosophers. It has also produced many great statesmen. But very seldom have the European political philosophers been statesmen or the statesmen, political philosophers. In ancient times the outstanding political theorists, such as Plato and Aristotle, were closet philosophers. If legend be credited, the one time Plato attempted to interfere in practical politics by serving as the adviser of the ruler of Syracuse he was a complete fiasco. In modern times such notable theorists as Bodin, Hobbes, and Rousseau remained private citizens; Locke and Montesquieu held only minor political posts. Even the eloquent and practical Burke never attained cabinet rank. In America, on the other hand, political theory and the practice of politics were closely related, at least in the earlier period of the republic's history. Amongst the outstanding theorists of the post-revolutionary period were John Adams, and the authors of *The Federalist*, Alexander Hamilton, James Madison, and John Jay. Adams and Madison later became Presidents of the United States. Hamilton was one of the most notable Secretaries of the Treasury in American history, and Jay in addition to serving as a diplomat was at one time the Chief Justice of the Supreme Court.

Before and during the struggle between the colonies and the British motherland, the vast majority of the Americans accepted in some form or other the rather radical doctrines propounded by Rousseau and Paine and repeated the democratic dogmas laid down at an earlier time by Locke. The theory of the social contract and of natural rights was taken for granted, and great emphasis was laid upon the supremacy of the people in all governmental affairs. Most writers of the period insisted that, theoretically at least, direct democracy was the ideal form of government and that where it was necessary to legislate through elected representatives, these representatives were bound to keep in close accord with the wishes of their constituents.

The period subsequent to the Revolution was characterized by profound disillusionment with democracy as the basis of government. The more respectable elements in the community, the bankers, the merchants, the prosperous lawyers of the North, the slave-holding landed proprietors of the South, were frightened by the political and economic demands of the lower classes, the mechanics and petty merchants of the cities, the agricultural laborers and small farmers of the countryside. To them democratic control now seemed the rule of the rabble. The cry for cheap credit, easy bankruptcy laws, paper money, seemed to presage an attack upon the sacred rights of private property. The weakness and vacillation of the all-powerful legislative assemblies in the various states, assemblies which were directly dependent upon the people, made it difficult for trade to revive and for industry to prosper.

In the wave of reaction against naïve liberalism which set in at this time, many of the leaders of American thought expressed opinions which were surprisingly at variance with the doctrines these same persons had previously accepted. Hamilton "acknowledged himself not to think favorably of Republican government," [40] and definitely favored the establishment of some sort of monarchy. Even more numerous were those persons who believed that America should seek to institute a legislative body modeled upon the English House of Lords. John Dickinson wished the American Senate to consist only of men of rank and property and bearing "as strong a likeness to the British House of Lords as was possible." This view was shared by Gouverneur Morris. John Adams, who had once proclaimed that "where annual elections end, there tyranny begins," now stated that no well-ordered commonwealth had ever existed without aristocracy and hereditary nobility. Other writers were not prepared to go as far as accepting either a monarchy or an hereditary aristocracy. but they were equally frightened by the excesses of unrestrained democracy. John Randolph remarked, "our chief danger arises from the democratic parts of our constitutions." [41] The somewhat liberal Elbridge Gerry admitted that "the evils we experience flow from an excess of democracy." [42]   A large number of persons insisted that there was as much reason to entrust the suffrage to children as to the ignorant and dependent.

The majority of the fifty-five persons who composed the Constitutional Convention, entrusted with the task of drawing up a new system of government to take the place of the Articles of Confederation, were strongly influenced by these conservative doctrines.   Most of the members of this Convention were themselves men of substantial wealth. They represented the propertied classes rather than the people as a whole.   There was not a single person who could or would represent the mechanic or small farming groups.   As Beard remarks, "The overwhelming majority of members, at least five-sixths, were immediately, directly, and personally interested in the outcome of their labors at Philadelphia, and were to a greater or less extent economic beneficiaries from the adoption of the Constitution." [43]

The meetings of the Constitutional Convention were held *in camera*, and no reports of the speeches of its members were published until many years later.   The members were therefore free to express their views freely without regard to popular opinion.   We now know that many persons took advantage of this freedom to denounce popular movements and popular forms of government.   But the members were not fools.   They were aware that there was a limit to the curb which they would be permitted to place upon democracy.   Even the most reactionary knew that the people would not stomach a monarchy or an hereditary aristocracy, however excellent these institutions might be.   But they felt that it would be possible to do away with some of the extremer forms of democratic government, to limit and make more indirect popular control over the administration.   To the accomplishment of these ends they devoted their activities.

The result was the draft of the Constitution which was submitted to the states for ratification in 1787.   There was immediate and widespread opposition to the proposed new system of government.   Many men who had played a prominent part in the Revolution and who were still looked upon as national leaders, such as Samuel Adams and Patrick Henry, were among the opposition on the grounds that the Constitution was too anti-democratic in tone.   The new system was extraordinarily unpopular among the lower and lower middle classes.   Had universal suffrage prevailed, it is highly probable that the Constitution would never have been ratified.   But the franchise was still limited and large elements in the population could not vote.   The propertied classes had their way, and the new governmental institutions came into being.[44]

The long campaign for ratification brought forth many books and pamphlets of a propaganda nature, some for, some against, the proposed Constitution. Most of these writings have long since been forgotten, but one, *The Federalist*, has remained a classic in American literature. In fact it has been recognized as one of the major contributions to the field of general political theory. Many writers on politics have echoed the saying of Jefferson and declared it to be "the best commentary on the principles of government which has ever been written."

Though *The Federalist* was frankly a *pièce d'occasion*, written for a specific purpose, namely, to aid in the campaign to secure the support of New York State for the new Constitution, the book was soon recognized to be the best commentary on the spirit of the Constitution which has ever been penned. Being a polemical work, composed to secure popular support for an unpopular cause, *The Federalist* glosses over certain points, notably the anti-democratic bias of its authors, but in many ways it far transcended its immediate aim and became a document full of interest to all serious students of the science of government, irrespective of time and place.

The Federalist dealt, somewhat in detail, with a vast number of governmental problems, but the major portion of the work was devoted to the exposition of four major theses. The first of these was that human nature demanded a strong and not a weak government. The second was that indirect or representative government was far superior to direct democracy. The third was that good government necessitated an elaborate system of checks and balances. The fourth was that good government likewise necessitated a separation of powers. The first of these four theses was enunciated to meet an immediate and local need. The last three were obviously, and frankly, developments of ideas which had previously been laid down by Montesquieu.

The emphasis upon strong government was to counteract the idea then prevalent in most liberal circles that government should be kept as weak as possible. Rousseau had insisted that all governments, unless closely watched, tended to usurp power and oppress the people. This doctrine in itself was enough to make most radicals suspicious of all governmental activities. To the Federalists this doctrine was anathema. To their minds, the troubles which beset America in the post-revolutionary period were due, in large measure, to the extreme weakness of the central government and to the comparative weakness of the state governments. "Nothing is more certain than the indispensable necessity of government, and it is equally undeniable that, whenever and however it is instituted, the people must cede to it some of their natural rights, in order to vest it with requisite power." [45] The Federalists further insisted that the powers granted to the government

> ought to exist without limitation.... The circumstances which endanger the safety of nations are infinite, and for this reason no constitutional shackles can wisely be imposed on the power to which the care of it is committed.... Government ought to be clothed with all the powers requisite to complete execution of its trust.[46]

Many liberal thinkers asserted that the functions of the state should be negative, that a government should punish crime and arbitrate disputes between its citizens, but that otherwise its policy should be *laissez faire* or "let alone." Neither the Constitution itself nor *The Federalist* interpretation of the Constitution dealt at length with this problem, but it is obvious that underlying both documents was the belief that the state had positive as well as negative functions. Thus both documents speak of the duty of Congress "to provide ... for the general welfare of the United States ...; to promote the progress of science and the useful arts." Congress should also have the right to "regulate" national and interstate commerce.[47] When the Federalists came into power, it soon became evident that "regulation" also meant the duty of promoting and fostering many phases of commercial enterprises. At a later date, the propertied classes of America were to become the enthusiastic advocates of *laissez faire*, but during the early years of the republic this was far from being true, and the Federalists, as the foremost spokesmen of this class, were insistent that it was the duty of the government to be active and not merely passive.

The second point in the Federalist program was that the government should be only indirectly subject to popular control. The Federalists were perfectly willing to admit that ultimately all governmental authority is derived from the people. With Burke they paid nominal allegiance to the doctrine that all governments were created by a social contract through which individuals, previously free, voluntarily gave up some of their natural rights to form a political state. In fact they went further than Burke and declared that all power should emanate from and be delegated by the people and that the dependence of all officials upon the people should be secured by a short tenure of office.[48]

In view of the general tenor of public opinion at the time, it would have been exceedingly unwise for the Federalists to have argued other-wise.

But after this lip service to the cause of democracy, the Federalists proceeded to lay great stress upon the idea that popular control over the organs of government should be indirect rather than direct. With Montesquieu and with Burke, they claimed that even those office-holders directly elected by the people should decide on political issues in accord with their own reason and should not wait for specific in-structions from the electors. The views of the public were to be refined "by passing them through the medium of a chosen body of citizens whose wisdom may best discern the interests of their country." [49] They were convinced that to submit questions directly to the people would arouse the masses and disturb public tranquillity. The Federal-ists, therefore, thought that the function of the people ended with the selection of their betters to public office and were opposed to Rousseau's scheme for legislative activity by the people as a whole.

Applying this principle still further, the Federalists believed that it would be well to have only a small proportion of the governmental officials elected directly by the people — the others should be elected by other bodies at least once removed from popular control. In the new scheme of government the making and executing of laws was com-mitted to four different agencies: the House of Representatives, the Senate, the President, and the Supreme Court. Of these four bodies, only one, the House of Representatives, was to be directly elected by the people. The Senate was to be chosen by the state legislatures; the President was to be chosen by a special electoral college; and the mem-bers of the Supreme Court were to be appointed by the President "by and with the advice of the Senate."

Mention of these four governmental organs brings up the third feature of the Federalist program, the idea of check and balance. Though the principle of check and balance was taken over from Mon-tesquieu, the Federalists were forced to develop this principle and give it a very different application. Montesquieu's check and balance was the balance between the forces of monarchy, aristocracy, and democracy. As America possessed neither a monarchy nor an hereditary aristocracy, it was impossible for the balance of power to be adjusted on this basis. But were there not other forces which could be so nicely balanced as to hold one another in check?

The Federalists held that to a certain extent the various social and economic groups within the state would serve as contending powers which could be balanced one against the other.

> A landed interest, a manufacturing interest, a mercantile interest, a moneyed interest, with many lesser interests grow up of necessity in civilized nations and divide them into different classes, actuated by different senti ments and views.[50]

Good government should be based upon the proper balancing of these various classes in society.

In any one place, however, it is possible that one of these groups may outweigh all the others put together. In such a situation the principle of majority rule may well prove extremely oppressive to the minority, and the Federalists were extremely anxious to preserve the rights and privileges of these minorities. They thought that they had found a solution to this problem in a *geographic* check and balance. In a large country such as the United States, with a wide variety of economic areas, there should normally be a wide variety of interests and hence, to use the Federalist term, a large number of "factions." In any one area it is likely that a single faction may predominate — in one area an agricultural group, in another a commercial group, in still another an industrial group. Each of these groups seeks its own interests and tends to be tyrannical to the others, but in a large country these factions tend to cancel one another, so that no one group can secure complete supremacy over all the others.

> A religious sect may degenerate into a political faction in a part of the Confederacy; but the variety of sects dispersed over the entire face of it must secure the national councils against any danger from that source. A rage for paper money, for an abolition of debts, for an equal distribution of property, or for any other improper and wicked project will be less apt to pervade the whole body of the Union than a particular member of it; in the same proportion as such a malady is more likely to taint a particular county or district, than an entire state.[51]

The principle of geographic check and balance made the Federalists disagree on one essential point with Montesquieu, their great master in political philosophy. Montesquieu had argued that a republican form of government might be suitable for small countries but was illy adapted to large countries. The Federalists, by distinguishing between direct democracies (which they despised) and representative government (which they lauded), asserted that though direct democracies could only flourish in a small area, a representative republic could only thrive in a state of at least moderate size.

The principle of federalism, or the division of power between the central government and the local governments, an idea hinted at by Montesquieu, was fully developed by the fathers of the American Constitution, as is obvious from the very name Federalist, adopted by the potent defenders of the new system of government. To their minds federalism was but another and further application of the principle of geographic check and balance. A single powerful faction, by adroit propaganda might well be able to secure control over any one of the various states into which America was divided, but the check and balance system would prevent this state from embarking upon a wild orgy of demagogic legislation. No state could make any *ex post facto* law or a law impairing the sanctity of contracts, however much it might wish to do so. On the other hand, the existence of a large number of states subject only to a limited extent to the control of the central administration would serve as a check upon a tyrannous central government in case the national government should temporarily fall into the hands of a self-seeking majority.

The principle of special majorities for special measures, which played such an important part in the Constitution and in the Federalist philosophy, may be considered a further and more or less novel development of the check and balance idea. Locke had laid down the doctrine of majority rule, and this doctrine was accepted by most subsequent followers of the liberal school and was accepted even by the Federalists for the normal course of legislation. They saw, however, that this system was liable to lead to abuses and that there was need to check the unbridled power of a bare majority (say 51 per cent) over a minority only slightly less numerous than itself. The example of Poland showed that it was unwise to seek for unanimous consent on any governmental policy, but there might well be a provision requiring an unusually large majority in case any fundamental or any really radical change in the political or economic structure was intended. Thus the Federalists thought that it was wise that treaties with foreign powers should require the consent of two-thirds of the Senate and that changes in the Constitution itself should require the consent of two-thirds of both houses of Congress and in addition need the ratification of three-fourths of the individual states.

In this way no ordinary majority could interfere with the basic rights and privileges accorded all citizens by the fundamental law of the land.

The doctrine of the separation of powers, like that of check and balance, was taken over from Montesquieu and likewise was subjected to considerable modification. The doctrine itself was presented in no uncertain terms. "The accumulation of all powers, legislative, executive, and judiciary, in the same hands, whether of one, a few, or many, and whether hereditary, self-appointed, or elective, may justly be pronounced the very definition of tyranny." [52] But whereas Montesquieu presupposed that the three functions should be kept entirely separate and distinct, the Federalists argued that the smooth functioning of government required a certain amount of overlapping.

Locke and Rousseau had argued that the legislative branch ought to be superior to the other organs of government. This idea had found widespread acceptance, and most of the state governments in the period immediately following the Revolutionary War were characterized by strong legislative assemblies and by weak executives. The Federalists agreed with Montesquieu that such a system tended towards tyranny — the worst kind of tyranny, that of a mob — and insisted that steps be taken to prevent the legislative from dominating the executive and judicial branches. "The legislative department is everywhere extending the sphere of its activity, and drawing all power into its impetuous vortex. . . . Some more adequate defence is indispensably necessary for the more feeble [i.e., the executive], against the more powerful [i.e., the legislative], members of the government." [53]

To prevent the legislative from dominating the executive, the Constitution provided two solutions. One was to give the President, the chief executive officer, a suspensive veto over all acts of legislation; the other was to divide the legislative branch into two separate bodies. In England, as in most other monarchies, the king possessed an absolute veto over all legislation. In the first burst of republican enthusiasm most of the states had deprived their executive officers of all veto powers. The Federalists did not dare argue for an absolute veto, but they maintained the justice and propriety of granting the executive a conditional veto which could only be overridden by a two-thirds majority of the legislative organs.

The Federalists believed that a legislative assembly of a single house would be more powerful and more tyrannous than one consisting of two equal chambers, especially if the two chambers were rendered, "by different modes of election and different principles of action, as little connected with one another as the nature of their common functions and their common dependence on the society will admit." [54] The second chamber, the Senate, elected indirectly, was frankly conceived as a checking body or a brake upon the precipitancy and ambition of the lower house. "The necessity of a senate is not less indicated by the propensity of all single and numerous assemblies to yield to the impulse of sudden and violent passions, and to be seduced by factious leaders into intemperate and pernicious resolutions." [55]

While the legislative branch, which is normally strong, needs to be weakened by dividing its functions between two chambers, the executive branch which, according to the Federalists, is normally weak, needs to be strengthened by centering it around a single individual. Many of the early liberals had argued for a multiple executive as well as for a multiple legislative. In a system of government proposed by Harrington in the seventeenth century, the executive functions were to be carried out by a number of independently elected officials, and in several of the states the most important members of the governor's council or cabinet were elected and not appointed. Under the old Confederacy, the executive functions had been vested in a number of committees. The Federalists were rigorously opposed to all such systems. To their minds the government should have a single supreme executive officer, and to this officer all subordinate officials should be subordinated.

In addition to his ordinary duties the President was to be the commander in chief of the army; he was to have the right to negotiate treaties with foreign powers (though these treaties had to be approved by the Senate); and he had the power to appoint, with the advice and consent of the Senate, many of the lesser members of the executive branch of the government. The Federalists disapproved of the council or cabinet system which was already in existence in England, whereby the ministers of state were jointly responsible for executive policy. They insisted that all the executive officials should be separately and individually responsible to the President and should be bound to carry out his orders as long as they were not contrary to the law of the land. The Federalists likewise disapproved of the parliamentary system whereby the ministers of state were themselves members of Parliament and were forced to resign their offices when faced with an adverse vote in the legislative assembly. In the American system of government, approved by the Federalists, all executive officials were prevented from being members of either house of Congress, and the like or dislike of Congress had no effect upon their tenure of office, except in cases of formal impeachment.

The Federalists laid great stress upon the need for strengthening the power of the judiciary. Montesquieu was quite prepared to have the judges elected by the people. The Federalists on the other hand believed that the judiciary would be rendered stronger and more independent by having them appointed by the President. To render them free from executive control, all judges were to hold office for life. "From the natural feebleness of the judiciary, it is in continual jeopardy of being overpowered, awed, or influenced by its coordinate branches; and . . . as nothing can contribute as much to its firmness and independence as permanence in office, this quality may therefore be justly regarded as an indispensable ingredient in its constitution. . . . " [56]

The American system of government is famous for its doctrine of judicial review, or the right of the Supreme Court to invalidate acts of Congress on the ground that they are incompatible with the written Constitution. The Constitution itself makes no mention of this doctrine or of these powers. But it is obvious that the Federalists foresaw and approved of judicial review. "The complete independence of the courts of justice is particularly essential in a limited Constitution. By a limited Constitution I understand one which contains certain specified exceptions to the legislative authority: such, for instance, as that it shall pass no bills of attainder, no *ex post facto* laws, and the like. Limitations of this kind can be preserved in practice in no other way than through the medium of the courts of justice, whose duty it must be to declare all acts contrary to the manifest tenor of the Constitution void." [57]

There can be no doubt that the American Constitution, the text to which *The Federalist* papers were but a commentary, was composed by conservatives disgusted with the excesses of direct democracy. Nevertheless a system which provided for republican government, which provided for the ultimate control of all organs of government by the people, and which also provided numerous safeguards for individual rights must clearly be considered to be in accord with the liberal tradition — and the triumph of this Constitution meant a new triumph for the liberal cause.

NOTES TO CHAPTER FOUR

1. John Locke, *Of Civil Government*, sec. 149.
2. R. H. Tawney, *Religion and the Rise of Capitalism* (New York: Harcourt, Brace and Company, 1926), p. 149.
2a. Montesquieu, *The Spirit of Laws*, bk. II, chap. IV.
3. *Ibid.*, chap. VI.
4. *Ibid.*

5. Montesquieu, *The Spirit of Laws*, bk. II, chap. II.   6. *Ibid.*
7. *Ibid.*, chap. VI.
8. *Ibid.*
9. J. J. Rousseau, *The Social Contract*, translated by Tozer, bk. I, chap. VI. By permission of George Allen and Unwin, Limited.
10. *Ibid.*, bk. II, chap. IV.
11. *Ibid.*, bk. III, chap. XV.
12. *Ibid.*, chap. XVIII.
12a. *Ibid.*, bk. III, chap. XIII.
13. *Ibid.*, chap. XVIII.
14. Joseph de Maistre, *Essay on the Generative Principle of Political Constitutions*, secs. 30, 31, 60.
15. *Ibid.*, secs. 63, 65.
16. *Ibid.*, sec. 45.
17. De Maistre, *Considérations sur la France, Oeuvres*, I, 88.
18. It is interesting to compare De Maistre with Hotman, the author of *Franco-Gallia*. The methodology of the two men was very similar, even though their conclusions were different. Hotman in the sixteenth century argued against absolute monarchy in France because such an institution was contrary to French traditions. De Maistre, on the other hand, in the nineteenth century argued in favor of absolute monarchy in France because popular participation in government was contrary to the traditions which had grown up since Hotman's time.
19. F. J. C. Hearnshaw, *Social and Political Ideas of the Revolutionary Era*, p. 192.
20. Edmund Burke, *Reflections on the Revolution in France, Works*, III, 359.
21. Burke, *Appeal from the New to the Old Whigs, Works*, IV, 162.
22. Burke, *Reflections on the Revolution in France, Works*, III, 309.
23. *Ibid.*, p. 350.
24. *Ibid.*, p. 354.
25. Burke, *Appeal from the New to the Old Whigs, Works*, IV, 165.
26. *Ibid.*, p. 176.
27. *Ibid.*, p. 167.
28. *Ibid.*, p. 166.
29. Burke, *Reflections on the Revolution in France, Works*, III, 440.
30. *Ibid.*
31. Burke, *Conciliation with America, Works*, II, 140.
32. Burke, *Appeal from the New to the Old Whigs, Works*, IV, 109.
33. Burke, *Reflections on the Revolution in France, Works*, III, 277.
34. Burke, *Appeal from the New to the Old Whigs, Works*, IV, 109.
35. *Ibid.*, p. 175.
36. From *Letter to the Sheriffs of Bristol*.
37. Burke, *Reflections on the Revolution in France, Works*, III, 345.
38. Burke, *Thoughts on the Causes of the Present Discontents, Works*, I, 535.
39. Burke, *Regicide Peace, Works*, V, 375.
40. M. Farrand, *Records of the Federal Convention*, I, 424.
41. *Ibid.*, I, 26.
42. *Ibid.*, p. 48.
43. Charles A. Beard, *Economic Interpretation of the Constitution*, p. 149. By permission of The Macmillan Company, publishers.
44. It is estimated that only about 5 per cent of the inhabitants of the United States voted on the issue at all, but a majority of those who could and would vote was found to be in favor of the system proposed by the Constitutional Convention.
45. Alexander Hamilton, *et al.*, *The Federalist*, no. 2, p. 5.
46. *Ibid.*, no. 23, p. 11.
47. See Constitution, art. I, sec. 8.

48. *The Federalist*, no. **39**, pp. 190 **ff.**
49. *Ibid.*, no. 10, p. **45.**
50. *Ibid.*, p. 43.
51. *Ibid.*, p. 47.
52. *Ibid.*, no. 47, p. **245.**
53. *Ibid.*, no. 48, p. 252.
54. *Ibid.*, no. 51, p. 265.
55. *Ibid.*, no. 62, p. 317.
56. *Ibid.*, no. 78, p. 396.
57. *Ibid.*

BIBLIOGRAPHY

J. Locke, *Of Civil Government*. London, 1690. There are several modern editions. Citations in the text are from the Everyman edition, London, 1924.

Montesquieu, *The Spirit of Laws*, translated by T. Nugent, 2 vols., London, 1878.

J. J. Rousseau, *The Social Contract*, translated by H. J. Tozer. Third edition. London, 1902.

C. E. Vaughan, *The Political Writings of J. J. Rousseau*. 2 vols., Cambridge, 1915. (French text, with valuable introductions in English to each work.)

J. de Maistre, *Oeuvres*, 14 vols., Lyon, 1884–1886. Vol. I contains his most important work, *Essai sur le principe générateur des constitutions politiques*. An English translation, *Essay on the Generative Principle of Political Constitutions*, was published in Boston, 1847.

A. de Margerie, *Le Comte Joseph de Maistre, sa vie, ses écrits, ses doctrines*. Paris, 1882.

A. Albalat, *Joseph de Maistre*. Lyon, 1914.

G. Cogordan, *Joseph de Maistre*. Paris, 1894.

P. R. Rohden, *Joseph de Maistre als Politischer Denker*. Munich, 1929.

E. Burke, *Writings and Speeches*, 12 vols., Boston, 1901. See especially *Appeal from the New to the Old Whigs* in vol. IV, and *Reflections on the Revolution in France* in vol. III.

A. Cobban, *Edmund Burke and the Revolt against the Eighteenth Century*. London, 1929.

J. MacCunn, *The Political Philosophy of Burke*. New York, 1913.

R. H. Murray, *Edmund Burke, a Biography*. Oxford, 1931.

F. J. C. Hearnshaw, *Social and Political Ideas of the Revolutionary Era*. London, 1926.

A. Hamilton, *et al.*, *The Federalist*. There are several editions. Citations in the text are from the Everyman edition, London, 1911.

J. M. Jacobson, *The Development of American Political Thought*. New York, 1932, especially pp. 164 ff.

R. J. Mulford, *The Political Theories of Alexander Hamilton*. Baltimore, 1903.

C. A. Beard, *Economic Interpretation of the Constitution*. New York, 1913.

M. Farrand, *Records of the Federal Convention*. 3 vols. New Haven, 1911.

Part Two

THE IDEALIST SCHOOL AND
THE REVIVAL OF ABSOLUTISM

CHAPTER V

IMMANUEL KANT AND HIS ENGLISH DISCIPLES

AT THE beginning of the nineteenth century it appeared as if the old authoritarian-etatist tradition was slowly but steadily declining. Even in the most reactionary circles there was scarcely a soul who was willing to defend the doctrine of the divine right of kings, and the defense of absolutism itself was more or less half-hearted and apologetic. Following the French Revolution there was, indeed, a conservative reaction, but the leaders of this reaction, though attacking the more extreme forms of liberalism, were profoundly influenced by several of the liberal ideas.

Most of the conservatives were devout believers in monarchy, "a real not a nominal monarchy," but the vast majority of them now advocated a limited or constitutional monarchy rather than the unlimited and unchecked monarchy of former days. Such persons insisted that the hereditary nobility be allowed to preserve many of their ancient privileges, but they were willing to give a popularly elected House of Commons or House of Representatives a fair share in the framing and passing of laws. In a word, the authoritarianism of these conservatives was a rather milk-and-water affair. In like manner their attack upon individualism and their defense of etatism tended to be of a rather mild character. They denounced the theory that the individual possesses abstract natural rights with which the state may not interfere, but they were willing to grant the individual many concrete rights, if only for the sake of expediency. The vast majority of the conservatives believed in religious toleration, or the right of the individual to choose his own religion. They believed in the censorship of speech and of writing, but they insisted that this censorship should not be too rigorous or too harsh. Most of the conservatives were very skeptical about the governmental control of industry; some of them, like Edmund Burke, were avowed believers in *laissez faire*.

There were many persons, like the Frenchman, De Tocqueville, who rather disliked democracy and individualism, but who believed that there was an inevitable and irresistible tendency towards the realization of these two ideals — and hence argued that it was a useless waste of time to struggle against them.   For many decades political development in America, in England, and on the continent of Europe seemed to prove that De Tocqueville was right.   In America, the conservative Federalists fell from power in 1800 and were succeeded by the rather radical followers of Jefferson.   A few years later the ultra-democratic Jacksonians again put the conservatives to flight.   In England, Parliament was reformed and democratized in 1832, and every decade thereafter saw power gradually slipping from the hands of the monarch and the lords to rest in the hands of the bulk of the populace.   With increasing democracy came increasing belief in *laissez faire* and other forms of individualism.   Even on the continent of Europe there was a strong resurgence of the liberal tradition.   The French Revolutions of 1830 and 1848 enormously weakened the conservative position not only in France but in all other European countries.   In many of these countries absolutism, or what was left of absolutism, was swept away — some form of parliamentary government being put in its place.   With parliamentary government came increasing emphasis upon the sanctity of individual rights.

Towards the middle of the nineteenth century most observers of political conditions felt certain that belief in wholehearted authoritarianism and wholehearted etatism had gone forever.   And yet at the very time when liberalism seemed to be sweeping everything before it, there was arising a new school of political philosophy, the so-called idealist school, which aimed, very adroitly, at undermining the whole framework of the liberal creed.   At first the doctrines enunciated by the idealist school were little noticed by the world at large.   The leading members of this school had very little contact with the world of practical politics.   Most of its members were university professors and led quiet, more or less secluded lives.   For this reason they themselves and their doctrines were more or less ignored by the busy politicians of their own generation.   The active "men of affairs" of their own time either ignored, or misunderstood, or laughed at the idealist attacks on the basic assumptions of liberalism.   But the political theory of one day not infrequently becomes the political practice of a succeeding generation.   At first the teachings set forth by the idealists attracted only those persons especially interested in metaphysics or at least in a metaphysical approach to the problems of life and of politics.   But before long idealist doctrines began to infect many outstanding writers in the fields of history and law and thus came to appeal to a much

broader public. Finally, many of the theories advocated by the idealists were taken over and popularized by poets and essayists, men such
as De Quincey, Coleridge, and Carlyle, to mention only a few. As
decade followed decade, the idealist dogmas, in some form or another,
began to permeate many different levels of European culture until at
last they reached the man in the street.

In each and every case the spread of idealist doctrines in the spheres
of philosophy, or history, or law, or general literature coincided with the
spread of belief in *either* etatism or authoritarianism — very frequently
with the spread of belief in *both* etatism and authoritarianism. A great
many persons who had formerly been staunch advocates of individualism
and democracy were so won over by the charm of idealist theories
regarding life as a whole that they began to champion the idealist doctrines in the field of politics. It was thus in large measure due to the
work of the idealist philosophers and their immediate disciples that the
absolutist (we may as well say Fascist) tradition was revived in nineteenth century Europe. The idealists owed much of their success in
the political field to the subtlety of their methods. They were able to
revive faith in etatism and authoritarianism largely because they were
able to give both these doctrines such a new and attractive dress that
they were scarcely recognizable at first sight. They were careful to
avoid all the old arguments and all the old slogans of their predecessors
in the seventeenth century. Not once did the idealists quote Scripture
in defense of passive obedience; not once did they preach the divine
right of kings in the old sense of the word. To have done so would have
been impolitic. The words "liberty" and "freedom" had an immense
popular appeal at the time the idealists were preaching and writing.
Hence the members of the idealist school were careful never to attack
these terms — they were merely so reinterpreted as to become meaningless. Or rather the idealists distinguished between "false freedom,"
the freedom advocated by the liberals, and "true freedom," which
meant obedience to the dictates of the absolute state, a state run in
accordance with authoritarian principles.

Of very great importance is the fact that the type of etatism and
authoritarianism advocated by the members of the idealist school has
had a profound effect upon all subsequent political thought and has
led directly to the Fascist and Nazi ideology of the present day. Between the twentieth century Fascists and the seventeenth century
absolutists there is only a remote and indirect connection. But between
the twentieth century Fascists and the nineteenth century idealists the

connection is close and intimate. Had it not been for the idealists, the old absolute tradition might well have died a natural death. It was the idealists who played such an important part in the revival of absolutism at the beginning of the nineteenth century, and hence it is only natural that it was the idealists who exerted the greatest influence in shaping and moulding the absolutist tradition as it gradually expanded and developed in the middle and latter part of the nineteenth century. And after all, as we shall see, the Fascism and National Socialism of the present day are merely the concrete embodiments of the doctrines preached by the nineteenth century absolutists.

As we trace the "genealogy" of the Fascist and Nazi ideologies, we shall observe that Fascism and National Socialism have had many spiritual ancestors, but among these ancestors the idealists are not the least interesting or the least important. As we read the party programs and the propaganda statements of the present-day Fascist and National Socialist leaders, it is astonishing to find how often use is made of the arguments, the slogans, and the ideas of the nineteenth century idealists. It is not merely that the idealists and the Fascists agree in attacking individualism and defending etatism; more important is the fact that the type of etatism advocated by the Fascists is the type of etatism preached by the leading members of the idealist school. It is not merely that the Fascists and the idealists agree in attacking democracy and in defending authoritarianism; more important is the fact that the type of authoritarian government advocated by the Fascists today is almost identical with the type of authoritarian government advocated by the idealists nearly a century earlier. The main purpose of our present undertaking is not to study the dim and distant past; it is rather to understand the *real* meaning of contemporary Fascist and National Socialist ideology. It is for this very reason that we must, for the moment, ignore the present and embark upon a lengthy discussion of the political ideals of a group of philosophers long since in their graves.

IMMANUEL KANT

The idealist school started in Germany, and its first four major prophets, Kant, Fichte, Schelling, and Hegel, were all German professors of philosophy. In later years Germany still remained the home land of the idealist school, but as time went on the idealist movement gradually spread to many other countries and the idealist doctrines, in some form or another, were adopted by many prominent thinkers in France, in Italy, in England, and even in America.

It goes without saying that there were many important points of difference between the various idealist philosophers. Many of these points of difference were radical and far-reaching. Some of these differences were concerned with metaphysical problems; others had reference to social and political problems. Most of the later German idealists, men such as Fichte and Hegel and their disciples, were thoroughgoing etatists and thoroughgoing authoritarians. Other members of the school, however, men such as Kant, the founder of the idealist school, and the English followers of Kant, remained much closer to the liberal position. From the political point of view we may describe such persons as semi-etatists and semi-authoritarians. They emphasized the value and importance of the state, but they still retained a liking for certain phases of individualism. They emphasized the need for leadership and authority within the state, but they were willing to retain many features of democratic control. Such persons, in a word, constituted the connecting link between the liberal and the absolutist traditions.

There is a world of difference between such semi-etatists and semi-authoritarians as Kant and Green and Carlyle and such radical thoroughgoing etatists and authoritarians as Fichte and Hegel, and yet it is of great importance to note that Kant and Green and Carlyle played a very significant role in shaping the development of the later, more radical etatist-authoritarian tradition. In their political conclusions they remained under the influence of liberalism, but the metaphysical premises from which they started led directly to the conclusions of the radical anti-liberals, and it is impossible to understand the radical anti-liberal conclusions without an examination of the earlier, innocuous-looking premises. Kant, Green, and Carlyle are also of importance from another point of view. By the very mildness of their conclusions, they were able to win many converts from the ranks of true liberalism, converts who would have been shocked by the frank and brutal etatism and authoritarianism of the more radical idealists. Later on, after a suitable breathing spell, such persons, having been converted to semi-etatism and semi-authoritarianism, found it easier to accept the conclusions of the prophets of the radical etatist-authoritarian tradition. All unwillingly and unconsciously, Kant and his English disciples were thus forced to serve as the advance guard of the Fascist forces.

To many persons it must seem startling and even shocking to describe Kant as the forerunner of the neo-absolutist tradition.   In his
own time Kant regarded himself, and was generally regarded by others,
as a thoroughgoing liberal.   His fundamental postulate that each man
must be regarded as an end in himself and not as a means to an end
showed him to be a believer in individualism, one of the two cardinal
tenets of liberalism.   His dislike of hereditary nobility, his belief in
representative government, his dislike of despotism showed that he
was a believer in democracy, the other great tenet of liberalism, yet
Kant produced a system of political philosophy which was distinctly
out of keeping with the main current of liberalism.   This system had
a definite leaning towards etatism and authoritarianism and in the
hands of his most distinguished disciples, especially those of German
birth, many of Kant's most characteristic and fundamental dogmas
were twisted in such a way as to make them the foundation stones of
etatism and authoritarianism.

To the political scientists, Kant is far more important as the founder
of the all-powerful idealist school than as the creator of an independent
political system.   Kant's chief work lay in the domain of theoretical
or general philosophy.   In the field of politics he did little more than
analyze and resynthesize the doctrines previously enunciated by such
writers as Grotius, Montesquieu, and especially Rousseau.   If there
had been no Kantians, Kant himself could easily be ignored in a general
work on political theory.   But it so happens that there were a very
large number of thinkers in the nineteenth century who exerted an
enormous influence upon the political thought of their time and who
were consciously and confessedly influenced by Kant.   Many of these
disciples were to become the foremost advocates of etatism and authoritarianism, and as they adopted much of Kant's phraseology and claimed
that their own doctrines were merely logical developments of Kant's
ideas, no account of the etatist-authoritarian tradition would be adequate or even intelligible without a brief survey of Kant's basic assumptions in the field of politics.

Immanuel Kant (1724–1804) had a private life which was singularly
uneventful.   He was a closet philosopher, teaching at the then small
and relatively insignificant University of Königsberg in East Prussia,
a region which was then considered the eastern frontier of European
culture.   He had no contacts with the active world of politics, and was
generally regarded as a classic example of the impractical, unworldly,
and absent-minded college professor.   Heinrich Heine has very wittily
summarized the life of Kant in the following words.

The history of the life of Immanuel Kant is hard to write, inasmuch as he had neither life nor history, for he lived a mechanically ordered, and abstract old bachelor life in a quiet retired street in Königsberg, an old town on the northeast border of Germany.   I do not believe that the great clock of the cathedral there did its daily work more dispassionately and regularly than its compatriot Immanuel Kant.   Rising, coffee drinking, writing, reading college lectures, eating, walking, all had their fixed time, and the neighbors knew that it was exactly half past three when Immanuel Kant in his grey coat, with his Manila cane in his hand, left his house door and went to the Lime tree avenue, which is still called, in memory of him, the Philosopher's Walk. . . .

Strange contrast between the external life of the man and his destroying, world-crushing thoughts!   In very truth, if the citizens of Königsberg had dreamed of the real meaning of his thought, they would have experienced at his sight a greater horror than they would on beholding an executioner who only kills men.   But the good people saw nothing in him but a professor of philosophy, and when he at the regular hour passed by, they greeted him as a friend, and regulated their watches by him.   But if Immanuel Kant, the great destroyer in the world of thought, went far beyond Maximilian Robespierre in terrorism, he had many points of resemblance to him which challenge comparison between the twain.   Firstly we find in both the same inexorable, cutting, prosaic, sober sense of honor and integrity.   Then we find in them the same talent for mistrust, which the one showed as regarded thoughts and called it criticism, while the other applied it to men and entitled it republican virtue.   But there was manifested in both, to the very highest degree, the type of *bourgeoisie*, of the common citizen.   Nature meant them to weigh out coffee and sugar but destiny determined that they should weigh other things; so one placed a king, and the other a god in the scales — and they both gave exact weight.[1]

As has been said, Kant is chiefly known as a theoretical philosopher. His major work in this field, the *Critique of Pure Reason* (published in 1781), was destined to have an epoch-making, even a revolutionary effect upon later generations.   In Germany the vast majority of the professional philosophers became Kantians, to some extent at least, almost overnight.   The classic German philosophers of the following generation, such as Fichte, and Schelling, and Hegel, much as they might disagree with Kant as regards detail, and however much their ultimate conclusions might differ from those postulated by Kant himself, all started as disciples of Kant, and all used his ideas as foundation stones upon which they proceeded to erect their own systems.   Even the later iconoclasts amongst the German metaphysicians, men such as Schopenhauer, who dearly loved to criticize their contemporaries and predecessors, bowed down before the Kantian shrine and incorporated many phases of the Kantian philosophy in their own systems.   Even today, the cry "Back to Kant" is the phrase most heard in German philosophic circles. It was the revolutionary effect which Kant had upon the German method of thinking which caused some writers, such as Heine, to compare Kant with Robespierre, the foremost leader of the political revolution in France.

It is beyond the scope of the present undertaking to inquire into the details of the Kantian system of metaphysics. But some of Kant's basic ideas on the subject must be considered, as they throw a great deal of light on his views regarding ethics, jurisprudence, and politics. The first basic idea in Kant's philosophy was the supremacy of "the spiritual" over "the material" in all phases of human activity. The second basic idea was the supremacy of pure reason (mixed with a little intuition) over sensation or experience. The third basic idea was the supremacy of the universal moral law over the wishes, caprices, desires of the individual citizen. Each of these basic ideas had a purely metaphysical background, yet each of them was to exert an amazing amount of influence over subsequent social and political speculation.

The first basic idea, *the supremacy of the spiritual over the material*, is closely associated with the idea that "the soul" is superior to "the body" and that the mental is superior to the physical, notions which play an important part in the philosophizing of the various members of the idealist school. These notions have important implications in the field of social and political theory, but they are derived from the purely metaphysical doctrine, common to all members of the idealist school, that the physical or external world is either largely or wholly the product of the mind. Kant was far from being the first person to enunciate this doctrine, but he was the first philosopher in modern times to gain for this doctrine widespread popularity among the edu cated classes of his native country.

Kant insisted that the fundamental task of all philosophy was to answer the problems "How do we know?" and "What do we know?" In trying to answer these problems himself, Kant was willing to admit that a great deal of our knowledge regarding the objective world is derived ultimately from the impact of external objects upon our senses, but he insisted that the world *as we see it* is quite different from the world *as it really is* and that the world as we see it is caused quite as much by the working of our minds as by the impact of external objects. If we wear green glasses, everything in the world looks green whatever its true color. If we were always to wear such glasses and could never take them off, we could never have any knowledge of the true colors of

Nature   In Kant's philosophy the mind of man was likened to such a pair of glasses, because we can never sense things as they really are, but only as the mind presents them to our senses.   Or, to use an analogy drawn from modern science, we see before us what appears to be a brown table with a solid surface.   Yet the senses are deceptive, for the true table is not solid, as it consists of a large number of atoms, between each of which there is a considerable distance.   Likewise the table is not brown, as external objects, we are told, really possess no color — what we sense as color being so many corpuscles or so many light waves, moving at a particular rate.

Kant carried his analysis of sensations much further than does the orthodox science of today.   With orthodox science, Kant claimed that all colors, sounds, smells, and tastes are subjective, but in addition he insisted that practically everything else we know, or think that we know, about external objects is subjective in origin, or, in other words, is due to the working of the human mind.   Thus, for example, to Kant even space and time are really subjective ways of looking at things rather than objective realities.   In like manner, most of the relationships which appear to exist between external objects, such as the relation of cause and effect, are due to our mode of perception and conception, rather than to anything in the objective universe.   Kant believed that his analysis of the sensations constituted a "Copernican revolution" in philosophy.   Prior to Copernicus men believed that the sun moved around the earth; but Copernicus showed that in reality it was the earth which moved around the sun.   Men used to believe that the world of appearance was due merely to the action of external objects upon our passive minds.   Kant thought he had proved that the world of appearance was due quite as much to the workings of our own mind as to the action of external objects.

Kant's analysis of the cause of sensation, his "Copernican revolution," was to lead to important developments.   In spite of his "idealist" tendencies, Kant himself tenaciously clung to belief in the ultimate reality of external objects.   Among the later German philosophers, however, a study of Kant's system led to complete idealism.   These later philosophers ignored or rejected the notion that it is external objects which cause our minds to build up the world of appearance, and claimed that the mind was not merely the partial but was the sole cause of the world of appearance.   This doctrine in turn led to several important developments in the field of social and political theory.   In due course of time it will be necessary for us to examine these later developments, but for the moment we must confine ourselves to the ideas expounded by Kant himself.

The second basic doctrine in Kant's philosophy was *the supremacy of pure reason (mixed with a little intuition) over sensation or experience.* Kant was driven to defend this doctrine by the very nature of his whole philosophy. If the English philosophers were right in assuming that our senses give us a true picture of the external world, it would be perfectly correct to trust to sensation and to experience in trying to solve philosophical problems, including the problems affecting society and the state. But Kant, we know, rejected the English assumptions on this point. To him, the world of appearance was due far more to the functioning of the subjective mind than to the action of the external objects upon our senses. Hence he tended to ignore the senses, sensation, and sensual experience and looked to the mind and the action of the mind, that is, reason, to solve all the problems of reality. Above all, he insisted that some facts, and some of the most important facts, are known *a priori*, or prior to and independent of all contacts with the external world. Such, for example, are the truths given us by mathematics or pure logic. Having proved to his own satisfaction that it was possible to arrive at many general truths irrespective of sense impressions, Kant went on and tried to establish the supremacy of reason in all fields of human endeavor.

Kant was, indeed, willing to admit that there was a limit to the successful functioning of pure reason. According to Kant's philosophy, pure reason can never tell us the real nature of the external world. As space, time, and causality are subjective and not objective, it is useless for us to try, by abstract reasoning, to answer such questions as whether the real external world is finite or infinite, whether it is temporary or eternal, whether or not it is the work of an ultimate first cause. As a result of this belief, Kant's philosophy appeared to end in a sort of skepticism. But Kant refused to be a skeptic, and in order to avoid skepticism, he was forced to adopt a curious sort of *intuitionism*, somewhat out of keeping with his fundamentally rational nature. Certain basic ideas, he asserted, we can and do know, not by abstract reason, but by direct instinct or intuition, by immediate feeling or direct awareness. By means of this direct awareness, for example, we can be certain of the existence of the free moral will, and because of the existence of this free moral will we can also be certain of the existence of God and of the immortality of the soul, things which could not be proved by pure reason acting alone.

Kant's belief in, and use of, intuition played a relatively small part in his general philosophy, but this intuitionism was destined to exert a great deal of influence upon later speculation.   More important still, fate was to play a very significant role in the development of later theories regarding government and the state.   Most of the later idealists developed Kant's doctrines in such a way as to distinguish between *understanding*, the use of pure abstract reason alone, and *true reason*, which was said to consist of abstract reasoning plus intuition or "direct spiritual insight."   As time went on this definition led to the growth of philosophical and political systems which were openly and avowedly irrationalist in character, emphasizing the doctrine that intuition or instinct, far from being merely the subordinate ally of reason, is really the supreme guide in discovering what is true and false and what is good and bad.   It is this later irrationalism, derived indirectly, at least, from Kant, which has exerted such a profound influence upon Fascist and Nazi ideology.

With Kant, himself, however, intuitionism constituted only a relatively insignificant part of his philosophical system.   To Kant, intuition or "direct awareness" was of importance only in establishing the truth of certain fundamental assumptions.   Once these foundation stones had been laid, he believed that reason, and reason alone, was capable of erecting a complete body of doctrines capable of solving all the problems of human existence, including the problems affecting law, government, and the state.   In point of fact, much of Kant's energy was devoted to the exposition of a rational system of law or jurisprudence, a system which he confidently held must serve as the basis of all true or valid political action.   Politics to him was little more than the effective carrying out of the eternal rational principles embodied in the science of jurisprudence.   Kant insisted that pure reason could and did tell us what laws *should* govern human relations and that the chief function of the state, the chief political unit, was merely to see that these laws were applied and made compulsory.

Kant resolutely rejected the notion that law is merely "the command of a sovereign enforced by sanctions."   He believed that the idea law is merely the command of a sovereign, whether the sovereign be a single person or a popular assembly, was fundamentally immoral.   In issuing a command a sovereign, whether consisting of one or many persons, might well be swayed by selfish whims or momentary desires and caprices.   Hence the command itself might well be contrary to the dictates of pure reason.   Such a command, or any law based upon such a command, was fundamentally wrong and hence essentially invalid, however rigidly or brutally it might be enforced by the police and the law courts.   In like manner Kant refused to believe that true law could be based upon custom, or tradition, or precedent.   In many countries and at many times custom has permitted and condoned acts which are contrary to the dictates of pure reason; hence custom and tradition must be rejected in trying to frame the laws of any state which aims at being run on right or rational principles.

True law, according to Kant, must be based upon the dictates laid down by man's rational mind in accordance with *a priori* principles. Neither history nor personal experience can give us any sure guidance. "Reason commands us to act, even though no example of such action can be found."   Law, moreover, must be universal in character.   True law must be applicable to all persons and at all times.   It should serve primitive tribal communities and also modern civilized states.   True law exists prior to all governments and hence prior to all statutory legislation.   There are many points in common between Kant's theory of abstract rational law and the theory of Grotius regarding "natural" law.   Kant, in fact, not infrequently gives the name natural law to the scheme of abstract jurisprudence which he established.   There is, however, one important point of difference between Kant and Grotius. To Grotius, natural law was just law, primarily because it was "natural," that is, in accord with Nature.   To Kant, "Nature," that is, the external universe, meant little or nothing.   To him the value of a law system was not whether it was or was not in accord with Nature, but whether it was or was not in accord with abstract reason.   It was not through observance of Nature and her processes, but through a purely logical process that we arrive at the ideal system of jurisprudence.

According to Kant, all true jurisprudence must be based upon what he calls the principle of *Recht* or "right."   Now *Recht* is a curious German word, which sometimes means right (as opposed to wrong); sometimes it means a right or rights (such as the Right of man to do or possess something); sometimes it means law.   To Kant and to most other German philosophers the term *Recht* means all three things at the same time.   As a result Kant was convinced that he could establish a system of jurisprudence embracing all valid laws and all valid rights from a rational consideration of the problem, "What is and what is not Eternally Right?" or, in other words, from a rational consideration of the abstract principles of right and wrong.   It is unnecessary for us to go into the details of Kant's rather elaborate legal system

Suffice it to say that he attempted to deduce by "pure reason" all the 'aws which should govern such things as property, all contractual relationships, and even the laws regulating marriage.   Being by birth and tradition a West European, it is not surprising that Kant was certain that the only form of marriage which was in accord with "true juris prudence" was monogamy, ignoring the many Oriental countries which permitted polygamy.   When one analyzes Kant's system of jurisprudence, one soon discovers that most of its principles were derived more from the old private law of the Romans than from any *a priori* reasoning.

Kant insisted that all laws should be based on reason, but he also insisted that any system of laws implies compulsion, and likewise punishment in case any law within this system is broken.   Kant's views ɔn punishment seem rather peculiar to the modern mind, but are in full ιccord with his puristic and imperativistic philosophy.   To Kant an action was either good or bad, and if it were bad, eternal and absolute justice required that it be punished just because it was bad.   Punishment, to him, should be given, not primarily to reform the criminal, nor to deter others from criminal acts, but rather to see that the eternal principle of justice was not upset.   Kant's idea of justice smacks not a little of the old "eye for an eye, a tooth for a tooth" philosophy, and in view of his notions on the subject it is not surprising that he was distinctly suspicious of the pardoning power usually granted public officials and that he was violently opposed to those persons who wished to abolish capital punishment.

It is of importance to note the connection between Kant's doctrine of the supremacy of reason and the later authoritarian tradition.   In Kant's own time the doctrine that all laws to be valid must be in accord with rational principles might be and frequently was directed against despotic monarchs who made and unmade laws according to the caprice of the moment.   In later times, however, we find a number of authoritarians pointing out that this same principle can and should be used in combating many forms of democracy.   The late Lord Asquith, one-time Prime Minister of England, and one of the most prominent Liberal leaders of the last century, once declared that the chief function of the government was "to carry out the wishes, interests, and desires of every class and section of the community."   As Hastie, one of the leading exponents of the Kantian philosophy, points out,[2] this statement was in violent opposition to Kant's ideas regarding the functions of government.   Kant believed the wishes and desires of every class and every section of the community could well be ignored.   In preparing a new law, the government could well dispense with bother· ing about such details; it must consider rather "whether the law does or does not agree with a principle of right," [3] and this can be known by abstract reasoning, without referring to the wishes of the populace. "If a public law be thus conformable to right, it is irreprehensible, and hence it will give the right to coerce." [4]   In other words, the government has a perfect right to make and enforce any law it pleases, as long as it is in accordance with eternal abstract right, even though it be vigor- ously opposed by ninety per cent of the population.   With this proposi- tion of Kant's the later authoritarians are heartily in approval.   They merely add that surely the wise *one* or the wise *few* are in a better posi- tion to judge of what is and what is not in accord with the rational principles of abstract right than is a turbulent and stupid democracy.

The third basic idea in Kant's philosophy was *the supremacy of the universal moral law over the wishes, caprices, and desires of the individual citizen.*   Closely associated with this idea was the notion that mankind should be more concerned with its *duties* than with its *rights*.   To Kant the all-important thing was not what a man *wanted* to do, but what he *ought* to do, what the moral code says he *must* do.   All these notions are summed up in Kant's phrase, that all human conduct must be regu- lated by the "Categorical Imperative."   Kant's moralism made him violently opposed to the doctrine preached by the Epicureans in ancient times and by the Utilitarians in modern times, namely, that "goodness" is to be identified with happiness.   According to Kant man's animal wishes and desires tend to make him seek happiness or pleasure, to be sure, but true morality commands him to perform many acts which result in unhappiness; and in such cases man is obligated to abandon the search for pleasure and follow the commands of morality.

It is interesting to observe that Kant made full use of his rationalism (his second basic idea) even in the field of morals.   Many ethical phi- losophers taught that on all matters pertaining to morality man should be guided by his individual conscience, and by conscience they meant a moral *feeling*, or a moral *sentiment*, or a moral *sense* which is essentially non-rational in character.   To Kant, on the other hand, all moral codes, like all legal codes, must be based not on feeling but upon reason. To him the laws or ethics or morality must be eternal, abstract, and *a priori*, in no way derived from, or dependent upon, any experience or any sentiment.   In the Kantian philosophy, the moral law, being the product of abstract reason, is unconditionally binding upon all persons. It admits of no exceptions, and in applying it no attention should be paid to the tastes or inclinations of the individual. The moral law is universal in that it is obligatory on all rational beings, irrespective of the personal peculiarities, the class, the sex, or even the race of the person concerned.

The whole of the Kantian morality is based upon Kant's theory of the "free moral will." According to Kant, every man possesses a rational will at the very center of his being. This rational will is quite different from his impulses, his sensual appetites, his selfish desires. The rational will is a man's real self, the very essence of his being. Kant was thoroughly convinced that this rational will in each man is fundamentally moral. Led on by his appetites, his desires, or his passion a man may and frequently does commit immoral acts, but inevitably he feels remorse because his rational will tells him that he has acted contrary to the way he ought to have acted. Kant was also convinced that this moral will of each man is free. The very fact that we realize that we *ought* to do such and such means that we *can* do it, which in itself proves that we possess free will. The average man is frequently controlled by his appetites and passions, in fact is a slave to these appetites and passions, and hence is very far from being free. A man governed by the moral law, however, is free, because this moral law comes to us, not from outside (Kant will not admit that this moral law is dictated by an external deity), but from himself, from his own rational will, which is his own real self.

Kant's definition of freedom is of the very greatest significance because of its influence upon later philosophical and political speculation. Most of the classical liberal philosophers had argued that freedom or liberty meant the ability of each man to do what he wanted or wished to do. These philosophers argued that a man should be "free" to follow his wants or his wishes, even though these wants and wishes were low and unworthy, as long as he did not interfere with the life, or liberty, or property of other persons. To Kant, on the other hand, a man doing merely what he wanted or wished was a slave, a slave to his lower nature; *he was free only when he was doing what universal abstract reason told him that he ought to do.*

Kant himself, as we know, was far from being a thoroughgoing authoritarian, but the later authoritarians were destined to make full use of the Kantian philosophy and especially of Kant's moralism to bolster up their own cause. These later authoritarians insisted that the liberals were low and immoral because they talked about men's rights.

while they themselves (the authoritarians) were worthy disciples of Kant inasmuch as they insisted upon men's duties. The liberals, they argued, talked about what men wanted to do, while they, following Kant, talked about what men ought and must do. The liberals, they argued, were concerned with the wishes, caprices, and desires of the individual citizens, while they, with Kant, emphasized the supremacy of the moral law. These later authoritarians differed from Kant on only one important point. Kant himself believed that the moral law was regulated and inspired by the individual rational will; the later authoritarians, on the other hand, insisted the moral law was regulated and inspired by universal reason as embodied in the all-powerful state.

These later authoritarians were also able to make full use of Kant's numerous attacks upon the utilitarian doctrine that good government consists in seeking the greatest happiness of the greatest number of its citizens. Kant was as violently opposed to the happiness principle in the political as in the ethical field. According to Kant, a group of men, perhaps the majority of the citizens of the state, animated by selfish wishes and desires may well seek their own happiness, but the well-regulated state should certainly ignore these wishes and desires. Kant admitted the validity of the old adage that the welfare of the people should be the supreme guiding principle in running the state, "but by this is not to be understood the individual well-being and happiness of the citizens of the state. . . . The welfare of the state as its own highest good signifies that condition in which the greatest harmony is attained between the constitution and the principle of right." [5] If a law made by the state is in conformity with what the free moral wills of its citizens *should* wish, the law, according to the Kantian philosophy, is justifiable. "If . . . a people *should* agree to such a law, however unpleasant be its results in fact, it would be as such conformable to right." [6]

Kant's peculiar doctrine regarding the nature of freedom was also fated to prove an immense aid to the later authoritarians. Kant himself argued that as morality is based upon the dictates of the individual rational will, it cannot be enforced by any external authority, such as the state. Some of the later authoritarians, however, argued that though the state could not directly enforce morality, it could and should aid its citizens to be "free," that is, aid them to do the things which they ought to do. Kant had argued that if a man drinks or smokes or gambles to excess, he is not "free," as in such a case he is a slave to his lower nature. The later authoritarians, especially the English authoritarians, developed this line of thought still further and argued that the state might "remove the obstacles to man's freedom" by prohibiting the liquor traffic and suppressing all forms of betting. Under the guise of "aiding man to be free" there was no limit to the action which the state could take in interfering with the actions of the private individual. Some of the German authoritarians went even further in developing the implications of Kant's theory of freedom. Kant had argued that a man is free only when he obeys the dictates of the rational will. The later German authoritarians argued, as we shall see hereafter, that the dictates of the rational will are to be identified with the dictates of the state. Hence when the state forces the private citizen to follow its dictates (and suppress his own desires and wishes), it is only aiding these citizens to acquire true freedom.

To the student of the etatist-authoritarian tradition, Kant is of major importance largely because of the influence which his general philosophical system had upon the later thoroughgoing etatists and authoritarians. It is certain that Kant himself was neither a thoroughgoing etatist nor a thoroughgoing authoritarian. Yet there are many aspects of the political theory developed by Kant himself which show that Kant had broken with the genuine individualism and democracy of the old liberal tradition and was slowly drifting towards the etatist-authoritarian position.

Because of their emphasis upon individualism, many of the older liberal thinkers had regarded the state as a necessary evil. Kant was not at all of this mind. He argued that the state is, or at least should be, a positive good. The free moral will, he claimed, could only function effectively where men are protected by compulsory laws from the evil acts of their comrades, and such a condition is found only in the state; hence the state, instead of being a necessary evil, should be regarded as a necessary good) In fact Kant held that the state is so necessary to the functioning of the free moral will that every man has a moral obligation, dictated by the categorical imperative, to join the state, or to create a state if one is not already in existence. Surprisingly enough, in view of his love of "freedom," Kant added the statement that a man or a group of men is morally justified in forcing other men to abandon their wild lawless freedom and enter the body politic, even if they do not wish to do so.

Again and again Kant came back to the notion that all rights and all laws exist only abstractly and latently in the state of nature, that they can only become real and concrete when individual wills are fused into the common will, which is the state. Locke and the older liberals believed that private property and the right to own private property existed prior to the creation of the state. Kant modified this idea completely by claiming that the ownership of property in a state of nature is merely "provisory," based upon physical control or occupation, with a presumption of right. Real, lawful ownership of property, he held, is "possible only in a juridical or civil state of society, under the regulation of public legislative power."

Having argued that the state is necessary to the carrying out of the ideals of ethics and jurisprudence, Kant next proceeded to argue that the state should be all-powerful. Locke had claimed that when man formed the body politic he gave up to the state only a part of his innate rights. Kant, however, agreed with Hobbes and with Rousseau that when men create a state they give to it *all* their rights.[7] As a result of this grant of power Kant held that the state has and must have supreme absolute authority. "The will of the people is naturally ununified, and consequently it is lawless. Its *unconditional submission* under a sovereign will, uniting all particular wills by one law, is a fact which can originate in the institution of a supreme power, and thus is Public Right founded. Hence to allow a right of resistance to this sovereignty and to limit its power is a contradiction."[8]

Kant, following Montesquieu, divided the functions of the state into legislative, executive, and judicial. But whereas Montesquieu was anxious to protect the individual from absolute control by any one of these powers, Kant, in a burst of enthusiasm, declared "The will of the Legislator . . . is to be regarded as irreprehensible; the executive function of the Supreme Ruler is to be regarded as irresistible; the judicial sentence of the Supreme Judge is to be regarded as irreversible."[9]

As a necessary deduction from this principle of the absolute supremacy of the state over the individual, Kant argued that the state had certain absolute and not merely relative rights over private property. To Locke, private property was an inalienable personal right, existing prior to and independent of the state. According to Locke, therefore, the state had no right to confiscate private property for any reason whatsoever. To Kant, as we have seen, real, as opposed to provisory, property rights came into being only with the state. Arguing from these premises Kant then jumped to the conclusion that "all such rights must be derived from the Sovereign [State] and overlord and paramount superior of the soil, or, as it may be better put, the Supreme Proprietor of the Land."[10]

Kant was far from advocating socialization of the land. He believed that to deprive men of the actual ownership of land would reduce them to the status of serfs and hence would be reprehensible. But man should remember that his right to private property is derived from the state by assignment and that the state retains the right to assess private proprietors, to demand taxes, special services and even forced loans. In like manner, the state has a right to interfere, if it so wishes, with private property by abolishing primogeniture and entail.[11] In some cases, indeed, Kant would permit the outright confiscation of private property. In Kant's time some of the ancient knightly orders, which had long ceased to fulfill any practical purpose, still possessed large hereditary estates. This was, and still is, true of several great ecclesiastical corporations. Kant argued that the estates were originally granted the knightly orders in return for military protection. In modern times, when national armies have taken the place of the knightly orders as bulwarks of defense, these orders have lost their usefulness. Hence, Kant argued, the state has the right to abolish these orders and confiscate their property. "In like manner, the Church Lands... may be reclaimed by the state without scruple if Public Opinion has ceased to impel the members to maintain Mass for the souls of the dead, prayers for the living, and a multitude of clergy to protect themselves from eternal fire." Kant further argued that the state has the right to confiscate the property of such endowed institutions as charities, hospitals, schools, and universities, if and when they cease to perform functions compatible with the public will.

Kant's attitude towards all private corporations, whether temporal or ecclesiastical, shows very clearly his dislike of feudal ideas on the subject and his agreement with the defenders of "benevolent despotism" with respect to the *unitary state*. During the Middle Ages the trade guilds, the city corporations, the ecclesiastical orders, the hierarchy of nobles were considered to have certain innate powers and privileges with which no state could rightfully interfere. It was the function of such thinkers as Bodin and Hobbes, with their doctrine of sovereignty, to stress the dependence of all such organizations upon the state as the source of all power. The great thinkers of the liberal tradition, men such as Locke and Montesquieu, were so imbued with their dislike of absolutism in government that they ignored the demand for state sovereignty over lesser corporations, and Montesquieu, at any rate, welcomed the retention by the nobles and the burghers of their ancient rights as a bulwark against despotism. Kant, however, though more or less of a liberal, agreed with the great defenders of despotism in claiming that the state should have absolute supremacy over all subordinate groups within its territory. In fact the whole tenor of his political philosophy was to stress the immediate control of the state over every individual in the state and to look with suspicion upon every institution or group which served as an intermediary between the state and the individual.

It was largely for this reason that he deplored the granting of any special privileges to an hereditary nobility, arguing that the members of such a nobility tend to form a special group with an inclination to free themselves from many of the obligations imposed by the state upon its subjects. Kant's attitude towards the church was likewise based upon a desire to preserve the unity and supremacy of the state at all costs. Kant, to be sure, believed in religious toleration. He believed that the English of his time were unwise in excluding Catholics from political life. He thought it wrong for the state to try to force any religious dogma upon its citizens or upon any ecclesiastical organization, even upon an established church. Nevertheless, to him the field of the religious bodies was "the other world" and in all matters relating to this world the state should be supreme. "The state may throw off any burden ... imposed upon it by the church at will." [12] Moreover, he claimed, the state has the right "of regulating the influence of these public teachers [i.e., priests and ministers] upon the visible political commonwealth, that it may not be prejudicial to the public peace and tranquillity." [13] Kant's attitude towards all private corporations, whether temporal or ecclesiastical, is to be seen from his frank statement that they all should be subject to state inspection and control.[14]

In teaching the necessity, the supremacy, and the unity of the state Kant acted as the prophet of one very important phase of the absolutist philosophy. Most of the later absolutists went further than this and defended not only etatism but also authoritarianism. By this is meant that they were essentially undemocratic and believed that control over the state should rest, not with the broad mass of the citizens, but rather with a ruling group, sometimes a monarch, sometimes an aristocracy, sometimes a party. At first sight it would appear absurd to accuse Kant of being the spiritual father of the later dictatorships. He definitely favored a constitutional monarchy over a despotism. From his views on hereditary aristocracy, it is obvious that he was opposed to a House of Lords. Theoretically at least he favored placing legislative power in a representative assembly, elected on a fairly broad suffrage basis.[15] All these ideas were "democratic" and as such were contrary to the principles of authoritarianism in government. Nevertheless Kant enunciated several other political doctrines which contained, in a germinal form, many of the authoritarian theories which were later enlarged and developed by the outspoken opponents of democracy.

The first of these doctrines was Kant's denial that the state is, or necessarily should be, based upon the consent of the governed. During the seventeenth and eighteenth centuries, as we know, the theory that government should rest upon the consent of the governed was intimately associated with the theory of the social contract, the notion that a state comes into being by the voluntary compact of all its future citizens. Kant was a great admirer of Rousseau and he accepted many of Rousseau's ideas. With Rousseau, he admitted that the true state should best be regarded as representing the general will of the whole people. But Kant's historical sense forbade him to accept the notion that any historical state had actually originated as the result of a social contract. This led to several important consequences. The advocates of the social contract theory claimed that any government which did not derive its power from the people was *ipso facto* illegal. Kant vigorously attacked this doctrine. He insisted that "it is vain to inquire into the historical origin of the political mechanism," [16] but he was inclined to think with Bodin that the state probably originated with conquest or force. "It may be inferred from the nature of uncivilized men that they must have started from a state of violence." [17]

The state, to Kant, did not originate with the free consent of the governed. Nor could it be claimed, he argued, that in modern times the consent of the governed is necessary to make a state just or legal. "It is a duty to obey the law of the existing legislative power, be its origin what it may." [18] And again, "The people in order to be able to adjudicate with a title of right regarding the supreme power of the state ... cannot judge otherwise than as the present head of the state wills." [19] As a final slap at those who hold to the consent theory, Kant added, "The Supreme Power in the state has only rights and no [compulsory] duties towards the subject." [20]

Some political philosophers had claimed that even though the powers of the government were not derived historically or legally from the consent of the governed, nevertheless the people had a right to rebel against any government which proved itself hopelessly unjust or tyrannical. To Kant this doctrine was anathema. Unlike nearly all the great thinkers of the true liberal tradition, who made the "right of rebellion" an integral part of their system, Kant argued that active resistance to the *de facto* government was always wrong.

> Resistance on the part of the people to the supreme legislative power of the state is in no case legitimate.... There is no right of sedition and still less of rebellion belonging to the people. Least of all, when the supreme power is embodied in an individual monarch is there any justification, under the pretext of his abuse of power, for seizing his person or taking away his life.... It is the duty of the people to bear any abuse of the supreme power, even though it should be considered unbearable.[21]

Kant's attack upon the "consent" theory of government and his refusal to allow rebellion or even resistance for any reason whatsoever were important steps in the direction of authoritarianism. Equally important, in fact in view of later developments, even more important, was his theory that the general will, the supreme legislative organ of the state, might be embodied in and represented by a single individual. "The united will of the people ... is the sovereign, but the idea still requires physical embodiment in a person, who may exhibit the supreme power of the state and bring the idea actively to bear upon the popular will." [22]

Theoretically and ideally, the general will of the citizens is the supreme power in the state, but this, to Kant, did not necessarily mean democratic rulership. A single man or a group of men may be able to represent the general will quite as well as a popularly elected assembly. To put the matter more concretely, the supreme ruler of the country. according to Kant, should always legislate for the benefit of the community as a whole and never for the benefit of any special group within the community, for this is the only way in which his legislation may be said to be in conformity with the general will. But if aimed at the general welfare, any piece of legislation issued by an absolute monarch is morally and juridically right, even though it be contrary to the prevailing wishes of the majority of the population. Or as Kant himself put it,

> [The idea of the general will] is merely an idea of reason, but it had undoubtedly a practical reality. For it ought to bind every legislator by the condition that he shall enact such laws as *might have arisen* from the united will of the whole people.... This is the test of the rightfulness of every public law. If the law be of such a nature that it is impossible that the whole people could give their assent to it, it is not a just law.... But if it be merely *possible* that a people could consent to a law, it is a duty to regard it as just.

even supposing that the people were at the moment in such a position or mood that if it were referred to them, their consent would probably be refused.[23]

Here we find a clear exposition of the doctrine, so dear to the later authoritarians, that an absolute monarch or a dictator acting contrary to the known wishes of the majority of his subjects could still claim to be representing and carrying out the general will.

Before bidding Kant farewell, it is necessary to examine one further phase of his philosophy, a phase which was destined to play an important role in later political philosophy, namely, Kant's belief in the law of progress, sometimes known as the law of development or the law of rational evolution.

As we have seen, Bodin, in the sixteenth century, was the first thinker in modern times to enunciate the view that human history is the history of progress rather than the history of degeneration. Though this doctrine had little apparent effect upon Bodin's contemporaries, it was revived and re-emphasized in the eighteenth century by the French writers, Turgot and Condorcet. But it was Kant (in his *Natural Principles of Political Order*) who gave the principle definite and rational expression, and it was Kant who first attempted to make of the theory of progress an important cornerstone in the edifice of political science.

This law of progress or development, with suitable transformations, played a major role in the political speculations of the great German thinkers, Fichte and Schelling. More important still, it became the basic principle of Hegel's political system, and through Hegel's influence this doctrine dominated all the later etatist-authoritarian thinkers. Last but not least, this doctrine, with still further transformations (whereby the law of progress became dialectic materialism), became the cornerstone of the political theory of Karl Marx and of the later Marxian socialists and communists.

Kant's theory of progress has frequently been compared with Darwin's theory of evolution. Both presuppose a gradual development from a lower, simpler order to a higher, more complex order. There is, of course, the important difference that Darwin concerned himself primarily with organic evolution, the transformation of one species into another, while Kant was primarily concerned with developments inside the human species. But this difference is relatively unimportant, since Darwinism can be and frequently is applied to man's development since he became man and the Kantian law of progress could be and later was used to include the whole problem of organic evolution. Kant himself seems to foreshadow this development of his theory, for though he generally assumed that species are stable, once or twice he hinted rather vaguely that mankind developed or evolved from anthropoid apes.

Nevertheless, between Kant and Darwin there was a fundamental difference. Darwinian evolution was based upon the idea of the survival of the *fittest;* Kant's law of progress presupposed the survival of the *best.* In Darwin's system we see an overcrowded world in which those individuals which happen, *by chance*, to be the best adapted to their environment survive while the others perish. From the idealistic and moral point of view, those who survive may well be worse than those who perish. In the Kantian system, Nature (in this case another name for Providence) superintends the law of evolution and sees to it that there is a slow, steady development from inferior to superior groups. In this development there is no blind chance, no permanent survival of inferior types. At an early stage of development many horrible unethical traits may be revealed, but under Nature's powerful hands these traits are gradually eradicated; nobler and higher traits appear, at first in embryo and then fully developed.

Kant's main purpose was to show the workings of the law of progress within the human race. He tried to show how the law of progress makes possible a philosophy of history.

> When the play of the freedom of the human will is examined on the great scale of human history, a regular march will be discovered in its movements ... and in this way what appears to be tangled and unregulated in the case of individuals will be recognized in the history of the whole species as a continually advancing though slow development of its original capacities and endowments. ... Individual men, and even whole nations, little think while they are pursuing their own purposes, each in his own way and often in direct opposition to one another, that they are advancing unconsciously under the guidance of a purpose of Nature which is unknown to them, and that they are toiling for the realization of an end, which if it were even known to them might be regarded as of little importance.[24]

Kant firmly believed that all the higher capacities, such as reason "implanted in a creature by Nature, are destined to unfold themselves completely and conformably to their end, in the course of time." But he went even further than this in his optimism. He believed that even the evil traits serve unconsciously to drive men to certain actions which ultimately prove beneficial. Thus, for example, selfish motives are bad, but ultimately they lead to good results. These selfish motives impel a man to strive after honor or power or wealth. This seems bad, but in this way "the first steps are taken from the rudeness of barbarism to the culture of civilization." [25] Without these selfish motives "men might have led an Arcadian shepherd life in complete harmony and mutual love, but in that case all their talents would have remained forever hidden in the germ. . . . Thanks be to Nature for this . . . envious jealousy and vanity, for this insatiable desire of possession." [26]

Armed with this law of progress, Kant proceeded to sketch the historical development of social and political institutions in the past and then to prophesy regarding their probable further development in the future.

In his view of primitive man, of man in the pre-political state, Kant came far closer to Hobbes than to his beloved Rousseau. Kant insisted that even the savage had latent within him the faculty of reason and, along with reason, a certain moral sense. But as long as he remained in a savage state man was dominated, not by his reason or his moral sense, but by his desires and passions, his animal instincts. The dominant instincts were those for self-preservation and sexual desire, but he was also motivated by a desire for material possessions, a desire for glory, and a desire to dominate other persons. Yet mixed in with these purely selfish desires there was also a desire for company, for purely social intercourse with his fellow man.

Primitive society, according to Kant, was dominated by the "unsocial sociability" of mankind. Primitive man could not get on with his fellow man, and yet he could not get on without him. One instinct drove him to associate with others of his ilk, another forced him to try to dominate all other men with whom he came into contact. The result was antagonism, conflict, or at least keen competition between man and man. With Kant, as with Hobbes, the state of nature was a state of war. But this war, though horrible in itself, had good results. It forced man to develop the reasoning powers latent within him. As a result of competition and emulation, the arts, the crafts, the sciences gradually came into being. Last but not least, man eventually saw that even from his own selfish point of view, the state of nature was so horrible that he willingly sacrificed his own lawless liberty and voluntarily submitted to the political state in which all men are subject to uniform laws. "Universal violence and the evils arising from it at last force a people of necessity to resolve to subject themselves to the constraints of public law, which is the very means which reason itself prescribes, and thus enter a civil or political constitution." [27]

The creation of a strong state, one capable of repressing lawless and immoral acts, was thus seen to mark an important and necessary phase in man's progress upward from a condition of savagery to a life dominated by reason and moral law.   But Kant, unlike some of the later absolutists, did not stop there.   To him, the formation of a large number of separate states, the present situation in the political world, was only a halfway stage.   Eventually, for the rational and moral capacities of man to be fully developed, all these separate states must be amalgamated into a really powerful league of nations, capable of securing and maintaining eternal peace.

According to the Kantian philosophy, on forming a political state, man leaves the natural condition of war with his fellow man and submits himself to the reign of law.   But the individual states themselves are still in a "state of nature."   States are frequently involved in foolish and unnecessary wars with one another.   Most states are perpetually trying to secure influence or control over all other states, with the result that the lives and property of the citizens of all states suffer.   But Kant believed that just as the mutual antagonism of man eventually brought about the creation of the state, so must the mutual antagonism of states at last bring about the federation of the world.   It is not man's good qualities which will bring about this desirable result, but rather his bad qualities.

> Nature ... works through wars, through the strain of never relaxed preparation for them, and through the necessity which every state feels within itself, even in the midst of peace, to begin some imperfect efforts to carry out her purpose.   At last after many devastations, overthrows, and even complete internal exhaustion of their powers, the nations are driven forward to the goal which reason might well have impressed upon them, even without so much sad experience.   This is none other than the advance out of the lawless state of savages and the entering into a federation of nations.   It is thus brought about that every state, even the smallest, may rely for its safety and its rights, not on its own power or its judgment of right, but only on the great international federation, on its combined power and on the decision of the common will according to law.[28]

T. H. GREEN

Kant and his followers, men such as Fichte and Hegel, the founders of the German idealist school, had an enormous influence over political and social thought during the early part of the nineteenth century, not only in Germany but also in most other countries in continental

Europe. In England, however, this influence was very little felt during the first three quarters of the nineteenth century. A few writers, such as De Quincey and Coleridge, did their best to popularize Kant and Kantian ideas with the English public, but they met with little success. The English public was willing to read De Quincey's lighter essays or his *Confessions of an Opium Eater*; it was willing to read Coleridge's *Kubla Khan* or the *Ancient Mariner*, but it evinced slight interest when either writer commenced to lecture upon the glories of German philosophy.

Even in the English universities German philosophy was almost ignored. Philosophy at both Oxford and Cambridge consisted largely in reading Plato and Aristotle. One bold spirit admitted that there had been some speculation since Aristotle; another daring soul made reference to Locke, to Hume, or even to J. S. Mill; but German philosophical works were seldom read and almost never cited.

Shortly after 1870 a great change took place. Oxford, the lover of tradition, decided that Kant and Hegel had been dead long enough for them to be respectable. Oxford "dons" turned idly to peruse the pages of Kant and the German idealists and suddenly became converted. They came to scoff and remained to pray. The chief figure in the conversion of Oxford to German philosophy was Thomas Hill Green (1836–1882). At first he was a voice calling in the wilderness, but before long the influence of Green and Green's ideas became so strong that almost every Oxford fellow or professor who lectured on metaphysical or political philosophy was found to have absorbed many of the ideas current in Germany half a century previously. An Oxford school of philosophy, essentially an Oxford adaptation of German idealism, arose, and as Oxford men imbued with this system were given posts elsewhere, the Oxford school spread all over England and greatly influenced political thought in every corner of the land.

The list of men who formed part of the Oxford school is a long and important one. During the latter part of the nineteenth century the outstanding exponents, in addition to Green himself, were D. G. Ritchie, F. H. Bradley, B. Bosanquet.[29] The twentieth century saw the school increase rather than decrease in importance. The two leading writers on political philosophy at the present time, A. D. Lindsay and Ernest Barker, are both adherents of this school. Because of the stream of Rhodes scholars who constantly pass through Oxford, the idealist school of political thought has also had a marked effect upon modern American speculation in this field.

While many of the later members of the Oxford school departed radically from Green in regard to details, almost all of them used Green's system as a starting point for their own speculations; hence it is through Green that we can best approach the whole school.

The life of Green, like that of most university professors, was distinctly dull. His immediate ancestry was undistinguished, but he claimed to be descended in a collateral line from Cromwell. This fact seems to have been of some importance in Green's life, for though his father was an Anglican clergyman, and Green himself always remained a member of the established church, he was always deeply sympathetic with the Puritans and Independents of former times (Cromwell, it will be remembered was an "Independent") and this caused him to feel many close bonds with the nonconformists of his own generation.

Green was educated at Rugby and at Balliol College, Oxford. As a youth he showed himself to be a sound but not an especially brilliant student, and he might have found it difficult to get an academic post had it not been for his friend and patron Jowett, the translator of Plato and a notable figure at Oxford during his generation. Through Jowett's influence, Green secured a lectureship at Balliol and later became a tutor and fellow at this college. Even so, he remained little recognized by the world at large for many years. Feeling dissatisfied with his progress at Oxford he stood unsuccessfully for a professorship at St. Andrews University, and only the fear of another failure prevented his standing for a similar post at Manchester University. As time went on, however, his influence in Oxford became ever greater, and eventually he was elected to the Oxford Professorship in Moral Philosophy.

In addition to his academic work, Green dabbled in a number of other things. He toyed with politics and spoke at a large number of political meetings. He was never elected to Parliament but did manage to become a member of the Oxford City Council. He interested himself in problems affecting national education, became a member of the Oxford School Board, and was appointed an assistant commissioner to a Royal Commission on Secondary Education. He worked himself into a frenzy over the liquor problem (largely because his brother was a dipsomaniac), joined the United Kingdom Temperance Alliance, and constantly preached in favor of legislation cutting down or abolishing the traffic in "the demon rum." Not content with preaching, he opened up a model "coffee shop" in Oxford in the hope of luring the inhabitants away from places where liquor was served.

In order to understand Green's doctrines we must remember that he was violently opposed to the traditional English school of philosophy

the inductive, empirical school represented by such outstanding thinkers
as Locke, Hume, and John Stuart Mill. He looked with a jaundiced
eye at the biological philosophy of his great English contemporaries,
Darwin, Huxley, and Spencer. Though he was careful never specifically to deny physical evolution, he was determined that Darwinism
should never influence ethics, jurisprudence, or politics. At the close
of the nineteenth century most serious thinkers outside Oxford agreed
"to regard human life as essentially part of the larger whole of animal
life, and as something of which the goodness and badness is to be estimated on principles applicable — at least in some degree — to this
larger whole." [30] Green strenuously opposed this view. To him animals
were "merely sentient"; human morality was a thing apart, being determined by God-given self-consciousness and abstract reason, which
no animal did or could possess.

Considering Green's later philosophy, it is significant that as a student
reading poetry, with the whole world of literature open to him, he considered Wordsworth's rather prosaic *Ode to Duty* as the "high water
mark of modern poetry" and that as an undergraduate he wrote that
"a tendency to form societies and the reverence for supernatural
beings" afford the twofold evidence of the higher nature of man.

In its developed form, Green's philosophy is seen to be inspired by
three quite different sources. One was the German idealist school
represented by Kant, Fichte, and Hegel. On several points, especially
in the purely metaphysical field, Green adopted the Fichtean and
Hegelian developments of Kant rather than pure Kantianism itself.
Nevertheless in the ethical and political field it was Kant rather than
Fichte or Hegel who remained Green's chief inspiration, and hence we
must group Green with Kant and the other semi-etatists rather than
with the thoroughgoing etatists such as Hegel.

The second source of Green's political philosophy was the Greek
tradition, especially as represented in the writings of Plato and Aristotle.
Being brought up in Oxford at a time when "education" meant in large
measure reading Plato's *Republic* and Aristotle's *Ethics*, Green's use of
these sources is not surprising. Green, being what he was, ignored or
rejected Plato's defense of communism in women and in property and
Aristotle's defense of slavery. He took from these thinkers only what
he wanted to take. He took the doctrine that ethics and politics are
one and the same thing but approached from different points of view,
that the true state is a "partnership in a life of virtue." This phase
of Greek thought had also been adopted by Kant, but Green, unlike

Kant, accepted the other fundamental Greek postulate that man by his very nature is a social and political animal, that the state is not an artificial creation but a natural growth, that the state is as natural and as important as the individual.

The third, and in some ways the most important, source of Green's political thought was the nonconformists' attitude towards the problems of life. We have seen that Green was very proud of his descent from Cromwell, the great leader of the ecclesiastical independents. He was always fascinated by the ideas underlying the English Civil War and delivered a special series of lectures on the subject. He openly avowed his admiration for such men as Vane, Milton, and Lilburne. Even more to the point, he felt deep sympathy with the feelings and aspirations of the dissenting nonconformist bodies of his own day.

From the nonconformists, Green took his love for the two words "freedom" and "morality." The nonconformists called their churches "The Free Churches" as a partial indication that freedom was the most important thing in spiritual and also in political life. The state, since the restoration of 1660, had never been kind to the nonconformists. Sometimes the state actively persecuted them; sometimes it merely subjected them to petty but annoying handicaps. As a result the nonconformists looked with unfriendly eyes at the power of the state and at every attempt of the state to interfere with the private life of the individual.

At the same time, the nonconformists laid fierce emphasis upon morality. They were the descendants of the Puritans and had inherited the Puritan attitude towards the fripperies of life. The Anglican Church permitted card-playing, dancing, horse-racing, the theater. The nonconformists felt that none of these things were compatible with a moral life. Bishops and archbishops of the established church may and frequently do serve wine with their meals, but the modern nonconformists (in this respect unlike their Puritan ancestors) tend to regard the consumption of liquor in any form as immoral.

Many nonconformists, in keeping with their reverence for freedom, believe that morality and immorality, though of vital concern, should not come within the jurisdiction of the state. Many of the Free Churchmen, however, became convinced that it was the duty of the state to put down public vice. They demanded the legal prohibition of horse-racing, gambling, the liquor traffic.

Green's political philosophy marked an important epoch in the development of this line of thought. As deeply concerned with morality as the most fanatical nonconformist, he was convinced that the state *should* abolish institutions and conditions which lead to immorality. At the same time he was enamoured of the word freedom, and his whole system is really a study of how to combine theoretical freedom with state repression of immoral acts. As might be imagined, he reaches the conclusion that the word freedom must be reinterpreted. Freedom for Green does not mean "doing what one likes," it is rather "a positive power of doing and enjoying something worth doing or enjoying." Liberty shall be liberty not for the animal wishes and desires, but for the "*good* will." The state may not force a man to be moral, but it may do away with the conditions which tempt men to be immoral.

The latent political philosophy which the nonconformists had been vainly struggling to put into words for two centuries at length found expression in the writings of a member of the established church. Even many of the specific reforms which the nonconformists favored received the aid of Green's eloquent preaching and writing. Green joined with the nonconformists in urging some form of prohibition. Many, though not all, of the Anglicans were prepared to regard Negro slavery as a matter of little moral consequence. The nonconformists on the other hand (few of whom had ever owned slaves) found that slavery was iniquitous in the eyes of God. Green agreed with the nonconformists in this regard and told his contemporaries in England how wicked they were to side with the South instead of the North at the time of the Civil War.

Even in regard to his views on property, Green sympathized with the nonconformists. The great landowning aristocracy in England were members of the established church almost to a man. The leading spokesmen of this established church thought of the private ownership of land as something sacred and they defended the system whereby some persons owned thousands of acres, while thousands of other persons owned no land at all. They deprecated attacks upon primogeniture and entail, as such attacks tended to disturb the existing social system.

The nonconformist bodies, on the other hand, were chiefly recruited from the lower middle classes. Whereas the lord of the manor and his tenant farmers were members of the state church, the butcher, the baker, the candlestick maker — and the corner grocery man were nonconformists. More to the point, the vast majority of the new industrialists, the men who had taken advantage of the industrial revolution and made their fortunes in commerce and manufacturing, were also nonconformists. In fact these new industrialists were, for the most part, merely a group of the old butchers and bakers grown prosperous.

The members of these groups were for the most part landless. Their shops, their factories, even their homes were generally on land leased, not bought, from one or other of the great landowners. Even when he grew wealthy, the nonconformist merchant found it difficult to buy landed property and set himself up as a "gentleman." As a result he tended to think of the uncontrolled ownership of land as something iniquitous, as at least based upon an unjust principle. On the other hand property in the sense of capital, as money which was made by buying and selling, was good.

Green's ideas on property coincided completely with the nonconformist notions as here set forth. Green defended the principle of private property, as far as capital was concerned. Vast differences in wealth and poverty were also defended as being perfectly compatible with, in fact conducive to, morality. Ownership of land, however, was said to be a very different matter. Though not iniquitous in itself it might well lead to iniquity. The state, therefore, should exercise a very strict control over the rights associated with the ownership of land. The state, moreover, might do well to break up the great estates and create a class of small proprietors tilling their own land.

Green received an enormous stimulus from the nonconformist thinkers. At the same time, he and his disciples exerted an immense transforming influence upon the nonconformist thought. Largely for historic reasons the nonconformists regarded the state with suspicion and were thoroughgoing advocates of *laissez faire*. It was Green who showed them that the logical deduction from their own principles was etatism.

After this exposition of the various influences which led to the development of Green's philosophy we may now turn to a brief examination of the philosophical system in its finished form. As to the purely metaphysical phases of Green's philosophy, we need say only a word. With Kant, Green deprecated the purely empirical, inductive approach to the problem of reality and argued that the ultimate truth could only be known by the use of pure reason with occasional flashes of intuition. Green, moreover, largely as the result of the arguments used by Fichte and Hegel, was prepared to go far beyond Kant in accepting the findings of intuition and reason regarding the fundamental realities. Kant believed that there were certain limits which pure reason could not transcend. Though pure reason could teach us many things, it could not tell us the true nature of the immortal soul, of the objective universe, of God.

Green, following, though modifying, Fichte and Hegel, taught that Kant had been too skeptical in these matters. Starting from the immediate data of consciousness he argued that these data are intelligible only if we presuppose a permanent self — a philosophic counterpart of the theological "soul." From the content of the individual consciousness Green argued that the object of the consciousness must be of the same spiritual nature as the mind itself. Hence the cosmos, the real universe around us, must be spiritual, a world of ideas, not of material things. This intelligible world in turn implies "a Creator who is a self-conscious intelligence, in the same sense that I am a self-conscious intelligence. In Him the idea of the human spirit is completely realized." [31]

Though Green discarded many of the elaborate details of the Hegelian philosophical system he claimed that he took the "vital truth that Hegel had to teach . . . that there is one spiritual self-conscious being of which all that is real is the activity or expression; that we are related to that being . . . as partakers in some inchoate measure of the self-consciousness through which it at once constitutes and distinguishes itself from the world."

The effect of such views upon ethical and political issues is obvious. As the true permanent self of each man is a reproduction of the Divine Spirit, the true self of each man is fundamentally good and needs only favorable conditions to develop and express this goodness spontaneously. As we shall later see, Green insisted that the chief function of the state is to create, by force if necessary, the requisite favorable conditions.

Equally important is the notion that *all* persons are the reproductions of the same divine spirit. Hence each man is able to conceive the good of others as being also a personal good. In Green's view, a man is not an eternally separate atom, he is a part of a spiritual whole which includes all other human beings. Hence we are not surprised that he rejected all personal, individual rights in favor of group rights, and among group rights, the rights of society and the state become paramount.

Green agreed with Kant in basing the whole of his practical philosophy on the "free moral will." To Green the true personality of each man is his will. The will is not a separate faculty, coordinate with the other faculties; it is the man himself and is to be carefully distinguished from the animal desires and passions. The will is fundamentally moral, for it wishes its own well-being, and reason tells us, if we pause to reflect, that the true well-being of each will is only to be found in the "good life." Green, departing from Kant, taught that each will seeks above all things "self-satisfaction," but each will is truly satisfied only when it leads to and accomplishes moral actions. Self-satisfaction is not the same as pleasure. Many times a man can only feel truly satisfied when he performs actions which have seemingly unpleasant consequences. Moreover, the will which pursues the ideal of its own betterment necessarily aims at the betterment of the society of which each individual is a member.

The will, in Green's philosophy, is free because the moral code imposed upon the will is, and must be, self-imposed. True freedom, says Green, is not freedom to do as one likes, but is freedom from obstacles, so that a man can pursue those objects which the good will presents to itself. In other words freedom is the liberation of all the powers of men for the social good. The freedom of each man to follow a self-imposed moral code is only possible, according to Green, because the moral will of each person is but a reflection of the Divine Will and hence tends to develop the same type of ethical ideal. By a curious use of words, Green calls his "freedom to do the right thing" positive freedom, to distinguish it from the old liberal "freedom to do as one pleases," which he calls negative freedom.

Following Kant, Green proceeds to deduce from the free moral will the necessary content of ethics, natural jurisprudence, and politics.

Green agrees with Kant that ethics is essentially a study of *motives*, the motives which underlie human action. An action is good or bad morally because of the motives which stimulate such action. As external laws can deal only with acts and not with motives; as a good act is morally good only when it is done from a sense of duty, it is impossible for external organizations, such as the state, to bring about morality by force. But it is the function of the state "to maintain conditions of life in which morality is possible..." by the removal of obstacles to moral life.

Green disagrees with Kant on one major point with regard to ethics. Kant argued that ethics should ignore the *effects* of actions. An action to him could be morally good even though its effects were disastrous. To his way of thinking men should always tell the truth (truth being good in itself) even though telling the truth might, in certain instances, result in murder being performed. Green, on the other hand, believes that in making up our minds whether our actions are good or bad the effect of our actions should always be considered. An action is good if it results in the improvement of the individual and especially if it results in the improvement of the group of which the individual forms a part. "It is a falsely abstract view of virtue to take no account of the end in pursuit of which the self is devoted." [32]   Ethics to Green should not be abstract or individual — it must be concrete and social. The good will in other words is "the will of the good workingman, the good father, the good citizen." [33]   Moral life is only possible in a society in which man seeks the betterment not only of himself but also of society as a whole.

There is a great cleavage between Kant and Green regarding another fundamental ethical problem. Though Kant defended the theory of progress or evolution his ethics were essentially static. His categorical imperative was supposedly valid for all times and places. His moral code was equally applicable to the primitive savage and the citizen of the civilized state. Green, on the other hand, believes that ethics itself is evolutionary. "Goodness," to be sure, is in one sense always the same in that it means working for the betterment of oneself and of the group to which one belongs, but in another sense "goodness" must mean different things at different times, inasmuch as man slowly develops a deeper and richer sense of what the betterment of himself and the community implies.

In a primitive stage "goodness" consists only in a man working for the physical well-being of his family or his tribe. As time goes on and man's intelligence develops, the content of "goodness" develops, and man realizes that he must strive for certain spiritual qualities in himself and in his fellow tribesmen. "An interest has arisen over and above that in keeping the members of a family alive, in rendering them persons of a certain kind, in forming in them certain qualities." [34]

As civilization progresses and society becomes more complex, the content of the moral code must also be transformed. The development of new institutions, of new types of human relations necessarily means that a man to be "good" must be motivated by certain ideals and must strive for certain effects which would be completely unintelligible to persons still living in a state of savagery.

Of great importance is the fact that Green insists that the "moral sense" of the community in which a man lives has a great deal to do with the development or evolution of individual morality. Kant had argued that the true moral code is universal and abstract; that it could be known and should be observed by every human being irrespective of his time, his place, or his racial and national background. Green, on the other hand, stresses the idea that each community, at a certain stage in its evolution, develops its own standard of morality and that this particularized standard necessarily affects the moral outlook of all its citizens.

According to this view, the individual citizen is and should be more influenced by the moral code which has gained acceptance in his own community than by a purely abstract code which is timeless and space-less. With Green we witness a departure from belief in absolute ethics and the beginning of belief in relative ethics. According to Green, a Chinese in obedience to the Chinese code of morality would rightly regard a certain action as perfectly moral; while an Englishman, be-cause of his English background, would rightfully regard this same action as essentially immoral. In other words, according to Green's philosophy, it is for the community and not for the isolated individual conscience or the isolated individual reason to declare what acts should and what acts should not be committed. This doctrine, in a somewhat more developed form, was destined to play a very important role in later etatist speculation.

From ethics Green passes to "natural jurisprudence." It is inter-esting to find Green placing great emphasis upon natural jurisprudence. His views on this subject form far and away the most important element in his political philosophy. Under the savage attacks of Bentham and his fellow utilitarians upon the old doctrines of natural law and natural rights, belief in these ideas had slowly but surely dwindled in nineteenth century England. Natural law and natural rights were considered un-historical and unscientific, and to the average educated Englishman it seemed absurd to believe that these doctrines could ever again form part of a serious political philosophy.

Yet lo and behold, Green and his disciples, the leaders of the Oxford school of philosophy, resurrected these ancient shibboleths and based their whole political philosophy upon them. To be sure, the natural law and the natural rights of Green were very different from the natural law and natural rights of Locke and the older liberals. In Locke's system man lived prior to the social contract in a non-political state and as an isolated individual. As an isolated individual he possessed certain inherent rights, and in his contacts with other isolated individuals he was guided by certain rational principles which we can call natural law.

Green denied the historicity of the social contract. He went even further and denied that man had ever lived in a pre-political state. According to Green, man has never lived as an isolated individual. Agreeing wholeheartedly with Plato and Aristotle that man is a social and political creature, Green argued that prior to the rise of modern states man was already bound by certain social and political ties, that even savages are members of a clan or tribal organization which is essentially political in nature. At no time did man as an isolated individual possess inherent rights. In primitive times what rights he possessed were derived from his position in a family, a clan, or a tribe. In his contact with other men, he was guided not by rational or natural law but by the customary law which in some form or other is in vogue amongst all primitive communities.

But though Green denied the social contract, pre-political natural rights, and pre-political natural laws, he proclaimed that in another sense there really is natural law and that there really are natural rights. Natural law is the law which man as a moral personality *should* obey whether or not the particular state in which he lives enforces it or not. Better still, natural law is that law which reason tells us should be promulgated and enforced by the state whatever its actual statutory law may be. Natural rights are the rights the state *should* grant to each of its citizens in order that these citizens may best work for their own moral betterment, irrespective of whether the state in fact does or does not grant its citizens these rights. "There is a system of rights and obligations which should be maintained by law whether or not it is so, and which may properly be called 'natural'; not in the sense in which the term 'natural' would imply that such a system ever did or could exist independently of force exercised by society over individuals, but natural because necessary to the end which it is the vocation of human society to realize." [85]

In working out his theory of natural law and natural rights Green follows in large measure the fundamental postulates laid down by Kant. Green agrees with Kant that there is a necessary distinction between pure ethics and natural jurisprudence, and yet that there is and must be a close affiliation between the two sciences. Ethics and natural jurisprudence differ because ethics deals with moral duty — to act from certain dispositions and motives — which cannot be enforced by law; natural jurisprudence, on the other hand, lays down a system of law governing external acts which can and should be enforced by the state. Nevertheless there is a close connection between the two sciences

Ethics teaches us that it is our moral duty to obey the laws laid down by natural jurisprudence; natural jurisprudence, on the other hand, has for its chief aim the laying down of laws which bring about the conditions necessary for each man to carry out his moral obligations. "The question of how far rights and obligations as actually established by law correspond to the true *jus naturae* must be considered with reference to the moral end, as serving which alone law and the obligations of law have their value." [36]

Green further agrees with Kant that reason can and does tell us what the content of the natural law should be. It is not experience but reason as to what men ought to do and ought not to do which tells us what laws should be considered natural, that is, inherently obligatory. At the same time Green differs radically from Kant on the question of the changing content of natural law. Kant's jurisprudence, like Kant's ethics, is static. To Kant abstract reason gives us a body of law valid for all times and all places, a body of laws which should be applied by all states irrespective of the social or economic stages to which they have developed. Green, on the other hand, believes that jurisprudence like ethics is evolutionary, that the system of laws and rights which the state should enforce (another way of stating natural laws and rights) necessarily depends upon the intellectual and moral horizon of the citizens at any given time. Natural law in a small, primitive community must necessarily be simpler, less developed than in a large, complex, cultured state.

For Green, and this is a very important point, a law or a right is only part of the natural law and natural right if it meets with general acceptance or approval on the part of the community — if it is part of the "moral consciousness" of the community at the time in question. It is not necessary for the law to be on the statute books of the state for the law to be a natural law, but for it to be incorporated within the body of natural law, the community must be prepared to recognize that such a law "would be a good thing." An individual idealist or political reformer therefore has a twofold duty in regard to political life. He must strive to see that actual laws be made to conform with natural laws if in fact they do not coincide. He must also, by propaganda, seek to deepen and enrich the content of natural law — by convincing his fellow citizens that certain projects ought to be generally recognized as part of the "good life."

Natural law and natural rights vary from generation to generation in accordance with variations in the "moral consciousness" of the community — in accordance with what the community feels that a man ought to do or ought to have done to him. In times past a man had a natural right "to drive at any pace through the streets, to build houses without any reference to sanitary conditions, to keep his children at home, or send them to work analphabetic" [37] because society or the community believed that a man ought to have these rights. With the growth of moral consciousness in the community, however, a man ceases to have these natural rights, because a community comes to feel that he ought not to have them, irrespective of whether actual laws do or do not permit him to retain them.

Turning now from natural jurisprudence to the science of politics, the study of the actual state and the laws promulgated and enforced by this state, we find that Green is in accord with Kant in claiming that the state is a necessary good, and not a necessary evil. The existence of the state is necessary and good from the ethical point of view because human beings can only realize their ideal of moral perfection through civic institutions. The existence of the state is also necessary and good from the point of view of natural jurisprudence, for natural jurisprudence tells us what laws should be enforced and what rights should be granted, but it is only in an organized state that these laws can be enforced and actual rights granted and protected. The moral consciousness of the community tells us what we should and what we should not do, but there are always persons blind to this moral consciousness, and such persons must be restrained by force, force operated by an organized state.

Green further agreed with Kant that the state must be all-powerful, the only source of all actual laws and the only source of all actual rights. "The state is the source and the giver of our rights. Rights may have existed in the family before they existed in the state; when the state has come and guaranteed those rights they exist in the state and proceed from the state. Ideal rights may be conceived which are not in the state; only when they are in it do they become real rights." [38] Morally, that is, from the point of view of natural jurisprudence, an individual possesses those rights, and only those rights, which public opinion thinks he should have. As public opinion changes, the "natural rights" which a man previously enjoyed may be taken away. In like manner legally, that is, for the point of view of politics, a man enjoys those rights and only those rights which the state, the concrete embodiment of natural law, chooses to grant him. The state may and sometimes should take away some of the legal rights which an individual has previously enjoyed.

Kant, filled with a desire to glorify the state, demanded a unitary state, that is, a state which had immediate, direct control over all the individuals in it. He would allow no group, no corporation to mediate between the individual and the state. Corporations might serve a useful purpose, but the individual must not be allowed to divide his loyalty between the corporation and the state. Corporations must remain subservient to the state and must derive all their powers, even their right to exist, from the state.

Green, with his strong love for family, group, and community life, could not be quite as thoroughgoing in his statements about a unitary state, but though phrased differently his conclusions were in essential accord with those of Kant. In very un-Kantian language he argued "a state is not an aggregation of individuals under a sovereign, but a society in which the rights of men already associated in families are defined and harmonized." [39]   But shortly thereafter he added, "But though there may be rights outside the state, the members of the state derive the rights which they have as members of other associations from the state and have no rights against it . . . The other forms of community which precede and are independent of the formation of the state do not continue to exist outside it nor are they superseded by it.   They are carried on into it." [40]   Once the state is formed it becomes the supreme society, the society of societies which adjusts and harmonizes the claims of all lesser societies. As the adjuster and harmonizer of lesser societies the state must ultimately have supreme power over them. "Thus the citizen's rights, that is, as a husband or head of a family, or a holder of property, though such rights . . . existed when there was no state, are yet to the citizen derived from the state, from that more highly developed form of society in which the associations of the family and that of possessors who respect each other's possessions are included in a fuller whole." [41]

Green was thus in fundamental agreement with Kant in asserting that the state was a necessary good and that it should possess absolute power over its citizens both individually and collectively. On two further fundamental political problems, the question of "consent" and the question of sovereignty, he differed somewhat from his master.

The question of consent centered around the old problem, "Does and should the government rest upon the consent of the governed?" The classical liberals, such as Locke, answered unhesitatingly in the affirmative. With them all states originated with the social contract, whereby each man voluntarily agreed to enter into civil life. All gov-

ernments thus derive their power, their *raison d'être*, from the consent
of the people.   Moreover if they abuse this power the people have the
right to revolt.   Both in the past and in the present, therefore, government rests upon consent.

Green was unable to agree with this easy and simple solution of the
problem because he rejected in its entirety the doctrine of the social
contract, as being both false historically and absurd logically.   For all
his idealism he was realistic enough to recognize that as far as it is known
most governments have originated by conquest or force rather than by
the voluntary compact of their members.   Nevertheless he was unwilling to discard the old doctrine of consent in its entirety and set about
transforming and reinterpreting it.   At the base of this phase of his
philosophy was the doctrine of the general will, and he insisted that
will, that is, the general will and not force, was the basis of all true and
lasting states.

Green, it should be noted, gives a less metaphysical interpretation to
the term general will than that given by Rousseau or Kant.   To him
it is "that impalpable congeries of the hopes and fears of a people bound
together by common interests and sympathy," [42] or in other words the
common consciousness of a common good, or "a sense of possessing
common interests, a desire for common interests on the part of the
people." [43]   Rousseau had claimed that the general will, a transcendental entity, suddenly came into existence at the time of the social contract.   Green, on the other hand, believed that even before the formation
of the state, family and tribal groups had a feeling for the common good,
and thus possessed a general will, at least in embryo, though the general
will became fully developed or realized only with the creation of the state.

Green believed that man owed allegiance to a state and to the laws of
a state only when the state and the laws were in accord with the general
will, that is, only when the state was an institution devoted to the common good.   More to the point, he claimed that over any long period
of time men *do* pay allegiance to the state and obey the laws of states
only because they realize, perhaps unconsciously, that the state and
the laws of the state are for the common good.   Brute force and the
fear inspired by brute force may cause men to bow down before a conqueror and obey the commands of a conqueror for a limited period of
time, but in the long run institutions based merely upon force and fear
crumble to pieces.   Men habitually render obedience only to those
institutions which are felt to be in accord with the general good or the
general will.

For laws to be in accord with the general will or for the common good it is not necessary that everyone subject to the laws should take part in voting them, still less that each person should consent to their application to himself. The laws should, however, "represent an idea of common good, which each member of society can make his own, so far as he is rational." [44] Locke thought that "consent" implied the idea that in each state the citizens had voluntarily consented to join the state, and in the Lockian system, for laws to be valid they should be passed by the people either directly or through their representatives. Green denied both these doctrines — but he insisted that even in an absolute monarchy, established originally by conquest, government if it is to last must rest upon consent in the sense that no government can last which does not inspire loyalty in its subjects and voluntary submission to the established laws on the part of the majority. Force must be present in any state to repress the occasional rebel or to punish the occasional criminal; but for the machinery of government to run smoothly and permanently it must satisfy public opinion, another way of stating that it must be based upon the general will.

William the Conqueror may have been able to seize the royal power in England by force, but he and his successors were only able to consolidate their position because most of their later acts and laws were compatible with the public good. Even in modern states particular laws may be imposed and enforced by the government in conflict with the general will "in the sense that they tend to thwart those powers of action, acquisition, and self-development on the part of members of society, which there is always a desire to extend, and which it is the business of the law to extend." [45] But such laws are few and far between, and so far as they go they tend to lessen the habitual obedience of the people, and hence weaken the power of the government.

Having reinterpreted the old doctrine of consent, Green proceeds to discuss the problem of sovereignty. Many of the older liberals deliberately ignored the doctrine of sovereignty. Others, such as Rousseau, admitted the existence of sovereignty, but insisted that the only true sovereignty which political philosophers could admit was the general will of the people, a sovereignty which could neither be divided nor delegated. John Austin and the other utilitarians had a far more realistic approach to the problem. To Austin's mind "if a determinate human superior, not in the habit of obedience to a like superior, receive habitual obedience from the bulk of a given society, that determinate person or persons is sovereign in that society."

To Rousseau the only true sovereign in any state is the general will of the people. To Austin the sovereign is the person or group of persons who actually make and enforce the laws in any state. In a pure democracy the sovereign would be the people; in an absolute monarchy the sovereign is the king; in a mixed government such as England, the sovereign consists (according to Austin) of the king, the members of the House of Lords, and the electors who send their representatives to the House of Commons.

Green was forced to choose between the theory of sovereignty advocated by Rousseau and that advocated by Austin. After much discussion he attempts to effect a compromise between the two theories. The *legal* sovereign, he argues, must be the sovereign spoken of by Austin. The Austinians were "doubtless right" in supposing that in "a developed state there must be some determinate person or persons with whom in the last resort lies the recognized power of imposing laws and enforcing their observance." [45a] For a law to be a law, it must be formulated and enforced by a duly constituted and generally recognized organ of government.

But the ultimate *political* sovereign, as opposed to the mere legal sovereign, must, Green argues, be found in the general will of the people. By this he means that the people do render habitual obedience to the legal sovereign because they feel that this legal sovereign (however constituted) is working for their own good. "The institutions of political society ... are an expression of and are maintained by a general will." [45b] In this sense Rousseau is right in claiming that the general will is the ultimate sovereign.

Green agrees that, to avoid confusion, the word sovereign should normally be confined to the legal sovereign, the actual person or persons who make and enforce laws, but he insists that the legal sovereign must be regarded merely as the agent of the general will. It should be noted, however, that the legal sovereign may act as the agent of the general will irrespective of how this sovereign is appointed. The sovereign may be an hereditary monarch ruling with absolute powers and yet be considered the perfectly valid agent of the general will, as long as his actions and his laws are directed towards the common good.

After this brief examination of the general and more or less abstract principles underlying Green's political philosophy, it would be well to draw attention to some of the practical consequences which Green himself draws from these general principles.

The three most important consequences may be phrased as follows

(1) The good of the community or society must be regarded as more binding than the arbitrary dictates of the state.

(2) On the other hand, the good of the community as a whole is of far greater importance than the wishes and desires of the individual citizen.

(3) Society and its agent, the state, have the right to interfere with private actions in order to promote the moral and material betterment of their citizens.

The first of these consequences, namely, the idea that society is more important than the state, represents the non-etatist phase of Green's philosophy. On this point Green differs from Hegel and from his own disciple Bosanquet. Both Hegel and Bosanquet thought that society is included in and subordinate to the state, while Green insists that in certain cases the interests of society, based upon the general will, and the interests of the state, based upon the arbitrary dictates of a legal sovereign, might conflict. In such cases the interests of society must be considered paramount. It is this aspect of Green's thought that makes it necessary to class Green with the semi-etatists rather than with the thoroughgoing etatists.

Green is insistent that even in regard to national matters the interest of the community as a whole must outweigh the claims of the state. To him the state is merely the agent of society, the legal sovereign, the agent of the general will. If the agent should seriously and consistently betray its trust, its actions must be stopped. The chief function of the state is to enforce "natural laws" and secure "natural rights," that is, the laws which the moral consciousness of the community thinks ought to be in vogue and the rights which the general feeling of the community considers ought to be granted to its citizens. Should the actual laws of the state sharply conflict with "natural laws," should the state radically infringe upon "natural rights," it is the moral duty of the citizen to resist the state and, if necessary, overthrow the existing government. Normally disobedience to laws and active rebellion against the government should be based upon popular and widespread discontent with existing conditions — that is, upon the feelings of the vast majority of the population; but in some cases, where popular sentiment is amorphous and inert, it may be the duty of a hopeless minority to act in the interest of the common good.

In international matters Green also feels that society ranks higher than the state. The thoroughgoing etatists such as Hegel thought that the national state was the highest possible expression of the human mind. They denied the rights of mankind as a whole and looked upon all forms of internationalism with distrust. They argued that there was no natural or moral law regulating the intercourse of separate states. Most of them claimed that war, because of its quickening and vivifying effect upon national consciousness (enabling the state to realize itself), was a good thing.

Green, following Kant, violently disagrees with this position. Green admits that all men are members of national communities or societies which find their realization or actualization in national states. But man is also a member of an international community. There is a universal brotherhood of man and each man realizes that all other men, even men of different nationalities and different races, should enjoy certain rights and be subject to certain obligations. As yet this world society is not actualized in the form of a world state — the general will of mankind has not yet found expression or an agent in the form of a world sovereign. But Green insists that the "common moral consciousness of mankind" formulates certain moral or "natural" laws which should regulate the intercourse of different peoples, even though there is no legal machinery to enforce them. Under these laws the breach of treaties, wars, and other conflicts between states are bad and must eventually cease.

Green is not as explicit on these matters as Kant. In private life he was a cautious Oxford professor and had no desire to shock public opinion in England, but from several of his remarks it is clear that he sympathized with Kant's hopes for a world federation. On one occasion he remarked: "The dream of an international court with authority resting on the consent of independent states may yet come to be realized." [46] In another passage he was even bolder: "It is easy to conceive a better system than that of the great states of modern Europe with their national jealousies, rival armies, and hostile tariffs, but the condition of a better state of things would seem to be the recognition of a single constraining power." [47]

But if Green pleads that the interests of society are more important than the interests of the state, he is equally insistent that the interests of society as a whole are more important than the interests of any single individual. It is this phase of Green's thought which causes him to be classed definitely with the etatists. Locke and the older liberals had argued that individuals have certain innate rights with which no state may interfere. This, Green denied *in toto*. To him natural rights are merely the rights which a man ought to have, or rather the rights which society thinks he ought to have, and if society changes its mind and thinks that a man ought to have fewer rights than he previously enjoyed, the scope of natural rights is thereby narrowed. In like manner just as natural rights are derived from society, legal rights are derived from the state, and the state may increase or decrease these rights as it sees fit if such an increase or decrease is "for the common good."

Green reiterates this point of view from several different angles. "The members of a state derive their rights from the state and have no rights against it." [48] Though Green grants the right of the community to overthrow the state, he preaches that there can be no right to disobey the law of the state except in the interest of the state, "i.e. the true state, the agent of the general will." [49]

> There can be no right to disobey or evade any particular law on the ground that it interferes with any freedom of action, any right of managing his children or "doing what he will with his own." ... If upon new conditions arising or upon elements of social good being taken account of which had been overlooked before ... if in any one of these ways or otherwise the reference to social well-being suggests the necessity of further regulation of the individual's liberty to do as he pleases, he can plead no right against this regulation, for every right he has possessed has been dependent upon that social judgment of its compatibility with general well-being. [50]

Locke's version of the natural rights theory greatly weakened the power of the state over the individual. In his philosophy the state exercises only a limited sovereignty over its citizens. To him the state possesses only derived powers, the powers granted by its citizens at the time of the social contract, and these powers can never be increased or strengthened. The logical development of this line of thought was the system of *laissez faire* which dominated public thought during the early part of the nineteenth century. Green's version of the natural rights theory had just the opposite effect. To Green it is the individual who possesses derived powers, for all his powers and rights are granted by society and the state. These powers may at any time be curbed if they prove incompatible with the public interest. The logical development of this doctrine leads, with Green's wholehearted approval, to state regulation and control of all phases of the citizen's activity.

As a specific development of this line of thought we find the third of Green's three main dogmas of political philosophy, namely, that society and the state have the right to interfere with private actions in order to promote the moral and material betterment of their citizens.

Green agrees with Kant that it is impossible for the state directly to

enforce morality and that it is inadvisable for the state even to attempt
to do so.   Along with Kant he speaks of the evils of "paternal government," meaning by paternal government one which does seek by compulsion to make its subjects moral.   "The question sometimes put,
whether moral duties should be enforced by law, is really an unmeaning
one, for they simply cannot be enforced.   They are duties to act, it is
true, and an act can be enforced, but they are duties to act from certain
dispositions and with certain motives, and these cannot be enforced.
Nay the enforcement of an outward act, the moral character of which
depends on a certain motive and disposition, may often contribute to
render the motive and disposition impossible." [51]

From this premise it would seem as though Green would agree with
the older liberals that private morals lie outside the scope of state
action.   But this is far from being the case.   Green takes advantage
of Kant's definition of law as a hindrance to a hindrance of freedom to
promote a system in which the state is obligated to interfere with the
actions of its citizens in the cause of morality.

Briefly his argument may be summarized as follows: To Green, as we
have seen, true freedom consists in acting in accordance with the dictate
of the free moral will.   But under certain conditions it is impossible for
the free moral will to function.   Such conditions form a hindrance to
the activity of the free moral will, and it is the duty of the state to frame
laws to remove these hindrances or obstacles to freedom.   The forcible
removal of obstacles permits the moral free will spontaneously to develop along ethical lines.   "The function of the government is to maintain conditions of life in which morality shall be possible." [52]

"The effectual action of the state . . . seems necessarily to be confined
to the removal of obstacles.   Under this head, however, there may be
and should be included much that at first sight may have the appearance
of an enforcement of moral duties." [53]   Among the acts which the state
may well carry out, according to Green, in thus "removing obstacles" are
the establishment of compulsory education and the stringent regulation
or even abolishment of the liquor trade on the ground that ignorance
and drunkenness are obstacles to the functioning of the free moral will.

It should be remembered that Green grew up at a time when there
was no compulsory education in England and that many liberals
objected to state-enforced education because they said such a system
interfered with the freedom of the individual.   Green was scornful of
all such arguments.   "Without a command of certain elementary arts
and knowledge the individual is as effectively crippled as by the loss of

a limb. *He is not free to develop his faculties.*" [54]   Or as Barker, a disciple of Green, puts it "[a boy] has a capacity for doing things worth doing, worth doing for him, and worth doing for the community, which the community for his sake and for its sake has the right to liberate by removing the ignorance which hinders the action of his capacity." [55]

A similar line of thought dominated Green's remarks upon the liquor question.   To Green a man under the influence of his animal passions is not free, but a slave; domination by a passion for drink is the worst form of slavery; hence the state in curbing the liquor traffic is merely removing another obstacle to freedom.   "To argue that an effectual law in restraint of the liquor traffic would be a wrongful interference with individual liberty is to ignore the essential condition under which alone every particular liberty can rightly be allowed the individual, the condition namely that the allowance of that liberty is not . . . an impediment to social good." [56]

After discussing the moral obstacles to "freedom," Green goes on to discuss the material or economic obstacles.   To him, these are almost as important as the others.   The old liberals with their passionate belief in individual liberty argued that *laissez faire* is the only system which gives full expression to individual freedom.   Green, by changing the connotation of the word freedom, is able to argue that true freedom requires governmental regulation and control in the economic sphere. By freedom "we do not mean merely freedom to do as we like irrespective of what it is that we like. . . . We mean a positive power or capacity of doing or enjoying something worth doing or enjoying, and that something which we do or enjoy with others. . . . When we measure the progress of society by its growth in freedom we measure it by the increasing development and exercise of the whole of those powers of contributing to social good with which we believe the members of the society to be endowed. . . . The mere removal of compulsion, the mere enabling of a man to do as he likes, is in itself no contribution to true freedom." [57]

Once these premises are admitted, it is easy to follow Green when he claims that compulsory housing laws, factory laws, health laws are contributions to true freedom.   Man cannot be "free," in Green's sense of the word, if he lives in a crowded tenement, works in a factory where there is danger to life and limb, or dwells amidst completely unsanitary conditions.   It is the duty of the state, therefore, to promote "freedom" by compelling its citizens to build and live in houses which do not fall below a certain standard, to operate factories which are not deleterious to physical well-being, and to obey certain sanitary codes laid down by medical authorities.

Green was also in favor of regulating by law the hours, the compensation, and the conditions of the workers in factories. He believed that the employment of women and children should be radically curbed or even abolished. Even with adult men the state should step in and decide how many hours a day or week a laborer might work and what his minimum pay should be. Green frankly admitted that all these provisions were incompatible with the old liberal doctrine of the freedom of contract — and his answer was, so much the worse for freedom of contract.

Locke, Bentham, all the economists had argued that the state must enforce the carrying out of all contracts legally entered into, but insisted that the state had no right to prevent two persons entering into any contract they pleased. If a man voluntarily agreed to work for sixteen hours a day for ten shillings a week, it was no business of the state to prevent his doing so. If a woman wished to work in a crowded sweatshop, it would be an interference with individual liberty for the state to prohibit it.

Green protested violently against this philosophy. "Freedom of contract, freedom in the form of doing what one wills with one's own is valuable only as a means to an end. That end is what I call freedom in a positive sense, in other words the liberation of the powers of all men equally for contributions to the common good. No one has the right to do what he will with his own in such a way as to contravene this end." [58] So long as freedom of contract results in the common good, it should be permitted, but where its results are deleterious, it may and should be checked. "To uphold the sanctity of contracts is doubtless a prime business of government, but it is no less its business to provide against contracts being made which, from the helplessness of one of the parties to them, instead of being a security for freedom, become an instrument of disguised oppression." [59]

Green's attack upon freedom of contract was directed chiefly against the employment of labor by commerce and industry, but he applied the same principle in dealing with the contracts entered into by landlords and tenant farmers. "The peasant farmer is scarcely more free to contract with his landlord than is a starving laborer to bargain for good wages with a master who offers him work.... We must in some way give the farmers... by law that protection which as a rule they have been too weak to obtain for themselves singly by contract." [60]

As we have already had occasion to observe, Green was extremely unfriendly to the English system of large landed estates. Not only did he insist that the tenant farmers be protected against eviction and arbitrary enhancement of rents; in addition he urged that the state should prevent the wealthy landowner from keeping land out of cultivation or turning it into forest for the sake of his own enjoyment. Last but not least, he pleaded that the state should abolish entail and primogeniture and thus encourage the great landlords to break up their estates into small, tenant-owned farms.

From this brief survey of Green's political philosophy it is clear that Green departed radically from the old liberal tradition in regard to the sphere and function of the state. On such matters he was in agreement with the etatist thinkers of Germany. In Germany, however, the etatists were for the most part authoritarians, that is, opponents of democracy and believers in rule by a strong governing aristocracy. On this point, Green broke with his German confreres. Throughout his life he was a convinced, though mild, advocate of democratic control and the parliamentary system of government.

Nevertheless, there are in Green's philosophy the germs of authoritarianism, germs which could easily be made to develop in the hands of later thinkers. Locke, Bentham, and the other liberals were adamant in claiming that a government not directly subject to popular control was necessarily a bad government. Green was much more hesitant in pronouncing judgment on this point.

> Whether the legislative and administrative agencies of society can be kept in the main free from bias by private interests and true to the idea of the common good without popular control, whether again, if they can, that "civil sense," that appreciation of the common good on the part of the subjects which is as necessary to a free or political society as the direction of law to the maintenance of a common good, can be kept alive without active participation of the people in legislative functions — these are questions of circumstances which do not permit of an unqualified answer.[61]

Green thought that in most circumstances popular control of and participation in government was advisable, but he was far from claiming that it was necessary to good government. He insisted that the legal sovereign must be the agent of the general will, in the sense that this sovereign must work for the common good, but he admitted that this agency might exist in a dictatorship. For laws to be good laws it was not necessary that everyone subject to them take part in voting them, but only that they should represent an idea of the common good, and such laws might as easily be passed by an authoritarian as by a democratic state.

In fact, for all his democracy, Green was somewhat skeptical of majority rule. Even in cases where "the majority of the citizens have no share by law or custom in the supreme lawmaking and law-enforcing powers, they never can have a right, simply as a majority to resist that power...; resistance may be a duty before a majority of the citizens approve it, and does not necessarily become a duty when a majority of them do approve it.... It should be made, if at all, not because the majority approve it, but because it is for the public good." [62]

But who is to decide if rebellion or the forcible seizure of power is or is not for the public good? On Green's principles, might not a militant minority claim to be the true agents of the general will? It is hard to see on what theoretical grounds Green could have objected to the Fascist and Nazi denouements in Italy and Germany.

THOMAS CARLYLE

Before leaving the semi-etatists a word should be said regarding the political theories of some literary men who form logically, though not chronologically, a connecting link between the semi-etatists, such as Kant and Green, and the radical, thoroughgoing etatists, such as Fichte and Hegel. In England, at any rate, the purely literary men, the poets and the novelists, were never converted to the utilitarian doctrines of Bentham and his disciples who dominated the political, the philosophical, and even the scientific circles during the early part of the nineteenth century.

The natural and social philosophers might argue in favor of *laissez faire*, of manhood suffrage, of pleasure as the ultimate standard of value, all of which formed part of the utilitarian creed, but to the souls of the poets and novelists such ideas were revolting. The reaction from *laissez faire* and from the ideas which were associated with *laissez faire* did not seriously affect political and philosophical thought until the last quarter of the nineteenth century, but for decades the literary geniuses had been writing and preaching against the dominant Benthamite creed. Wordsworth, Southey, Coleridge during the latter portion of their lives were loud in their denunciations both of individualism and of democracy. Charles Kingsley and Mrs. Gaskell were equally opposed to the utilitarian position. Even Dickens, for all his Cockney sympathies, thoroughly disliked the industrial system which had grown up in an England so largely moulded by Benthamist doctrines and felt that something should be done about it — though he was not quite sure just what should be done.

By far the greatest and the most important of the literary prophets who preached against the old liberal tradition in general and against the utilitarian creed in particular were Thomas Carlyle and John Ruskin. Both these men had the faculty of writing in such a way that they were read by the broad masses of the population. Neither Carlyle nor Ruskin was a political philosopher in the strict sense of the word. Neither of them was willing, as were Green and the Oxford idealists, to study the detailed development of political theory, or to analyze and evaluate all the concepts which had been enunciated by previous political thinkers. But both Carlyle and Ruskin possessed definite political creeds which cut across many of the concepts held by professional political thinkers. Both, by their wit and their eloquence, were able to weaken and even to annihilate the blind acceptance by the masses of earlier doctrines. Green and the other members of his school were political philosophers in every sense of the word, but their works were read by a few hundred or at the most by a few thousand. Carlyle and Ruskin were political preachers or political prophets rather than political philosophers, but their works were read by the million and profoundly affected the political ideas of their own and succeeding generations.

Carlyle and Ruskin were men of quite different types; for the most part their writings appealed to quite different types of readers. On several points of detail their doctrines varied widely from one another. Ruskin, however, was quite frankly a disciple of Carlyle, and on all essential matters the two men were in agreement. For this reason it is possible for us to omit any detailed consideration of the political theories of Ruskin and confine ourselves exclusively to an examination of the life and doctrines of his master. The life of Thomas Carlyle was relatively uneventful. Born in Scotland in 1795, the son of a poor but terribly earnest and hard-working peasant, his early years were full of hardships. As a boy he displayed such talent and brains that it seemed unjust that he should be condemned to a life of manual labor; he was sent off to Edinburgh University, where he secured a sound but rather scrappy education. His parents hoped that he would become either a minister or a barrister, but young Thomas felt no call to either profession, and was determined to make a living by writing. At first he thought of staying in Scotland. He married and lived in a farm house inherited by his wife. Even so he remained desperately poor, and at times had less than five pounds between him and starvation. Even Edinburgh did not have scope for a would-be literary man (as Carlyle found by experiment), and in 1834 he moved to London where he continued to reside until his death in 1881.

Year after year Carlyle, the great apostle of silence, talked and lectured, and wrote. At first his works met with little success, but as the years went on his literary fame increased and in his old age he became mildly opulent. He was granted the Order of Merit by the Prussian government, an honor which he accepted, though he refused a knighthood offered him by Queen Victoria. His vogue continued long after his death. His own works continued to sell in large numbers, and his fame was enhanced by the appearance of many other books dealing with him or his relations with some of his contemporaries.

Carlyle wrote on all manner of things, his *Sartor Resartus*, his *French Revolution*, his *Heroes and Hero-Worship*, his *Frederick the Great* being perhaps the best known of his works. Even in these books there are numerous passages dealing with Carlyle's political ideas, but in addition he composed a number of volumes which aimed especially at expounding his political gospel, such as *Past and Present, Chartism*, and *Latter-Day Pamphlets*. Last but not least, mention should be made of some of his occasional essays such as *The Nigger Question* and *Shooting Niagara*, as some of his most important political opinions are embodied in these papers.

When we come to examine the background of Carlyle's political philosophy, the men who and the ideas which stimulated his own thoughts on political issues, we find that this background was very similar to that of T. H. Green, consisting as it did of Kant and Fichte, of Plato, and of Puritanism. But there was a great difference between Green and Carlyle with reference to this background. Green was a scholar who really had read and who knew the doctrines of Kant, of Fichte, of Plato, of Aristotle, and of Calvin. Carlyle, on the other hand, was too busy with his own genius to bother much with trying to understand all the obscure ideas of the men whom he admired.

Carlyle had a profound respect for German literature. As a young man he was best known as an interpreter of German thought to the English public. He translated one of Goethe's works, wrote a life of Schiller and essays on several other German writers. In connection with this type of work he naturally became acquainted with the writings of the German philosophers, and he frequently alludes to them in his own books. He was deeply impressed by Kant's ideas on ethics and by Kant's views on the subjectivity of space and time. But as Carlyle himself confessed, he found Kant terribly difficult reading. In fact it is doubtful if Carlyle ever succeeded in really reading through any of Kant's major works. It is certain that if he did read them through he never understood them, as his interpretations of Kantian ideas are singularly inaccurate. A similar story could be told of the relations between Carlyle and Fichte. Fichte, Kant's great successor in the German philosophical world, wrote both popular and scholarly works. We know that Carlyle read some of Fichte's popular works and was greatly stimulated by them. But from Carlyle's misunderstanding of Fichte, it is obvious that he never took the trouble to wade through Fichte's more serious contributions to metaphysical and political thought.

The case is similar with reference to Carlyle's indebtedness to Plato. If Carlyle had gone either to Oxford or to Cambridge he would undoubtedly have been forced to tackle Plato and Aristotle in the original. Going as he did to Edinburgh, where classical studies were far less highly developed, he had for many years only a second-hand knowledge of Plato.   Nevertheless we find in Carlyle many of Plato's most characteristic thoughts — the belief that the visible material world is a world of shadow, that the spiritual, ideal world is the real world, knowledge of which is attainable only to men of insight.   With Plato Carlyle ridiculed the idea that government should rest upon the consent of the governed; with Plato he insisted that man should be compelled to seek the true, the beautiful, and the good; with Plato he believed that moral education should be the basis of all political activity.   With Plato he preached that government should rest with a small group of spiritual aristocrats; with Plato he strenuously denied that individuals have any rights against the state.

There can be no doubt that the greatest motivating force in Carlyle's thought was Puritanism or Calvinism, even more so than in the case of Green and the Oxford idealists.   Carlyle has been well described as a Puritan who lost his creed. His doubts on certain crucial doctrinal matters, literal inspiration, the incarnation, miracles, prevented his seeking ordination.   But in one sense he was a Puritan preacher all of his life.   His thirty volumes are one long series of sermons.   That Carlyle was a preacher rather than a philosopher can be seen from the very style of his writings.   The philosopher argues, tries to convince by

reason. Carlyle never argues, seldom reasons. Almost invariably he
asserts, demands, denounces. Though Carlyle doubted many incidental
points in the Calvinist creed, he strenuously, even violently accepted
and preached to others the essential points — the omnipotence of God
and the necessity of obeying the moral code laid down by God. Carlyle
sometimes used strange terms for the deity. He spoke of the "World
Order" (a phrase borrowed from Fichte), or the "Eternities," the
"Immensities," the "Veracities" — but all of these terms were mere
pseudonyms for the God postulated by Calvin. Carlyle claimed to be
a disciple of Kant's moral philosophy, but Kant's moral philosophy was
based upon a *self-imposed* moral code. Carlyle's moral code, like that
of Calvin, was based upon the will of God, to which all men must render
blind, unwavering agreement.

On one point and one point only did Carlyle depart radically from the
Calvinist point of view. Calvin and the Calvinists, as we have seen,
leaned towards democratic as opposed to despotic government. Carlyle, while sweeping out the fine points of Calvinist theology, also swept
out these democratic leanings.

Carlyle was far from being a systematic or even a consistent thinker,
but as one reads through his books one finds that there were a few fundamental principles (principles more or less philosophical in character)
which motivated many of his concrete conclusions.

Take for example his attitude towards the problem of knowledge —
of *what* we can know and *how* we can know it. Carlyle's notions on
this subject were largely derived from the German philosophers, or
rather from his misconceptions regarding what the German philosophers,
such as Kant, had said. Carlyle, like Green, rejected the empirical
tradition which had long dominated English thought. To his mind
the mere accumulation of sense data (the basis of scientific investigation) was of little or no value. He took over from Kant the notion that
the world as we see it has little to do with the world as it really is. With
Kant he believed that both space and time were subjective — hence
the detailed study of spatial and temporal relations (and this is the
fundamental scientific technique) is of little or no objective value.

With this doctrinal situation in mind it is not surprising that Carlyle
was scornful of the physical sciences and of the theories of life based
upon scientific investigation. Carlyle was disgusted when he heard a
eulogy of the great scientific discoveries of Faraday, the English physi·
cist. "In sad fact I cared but little for these discoveries...; they are

not by any means the kind of discoveries I wanted to be made at the present. 'Can you really turn a ray of light upon its axis by magnet- ism?' — and if you could what would I care? This is my feeling towards most of the scientific triumphs ... so trumpeted abroad in these days." Carlyle was equally bitter towards the biologists. Re- garding Darwin's *Origin of Species* he remarked that he could never read a page of it or waste the least thought upon it. With his attitude towards sense data it was easy for him to dismiss the Darwinian theory of evolution with the words, "I have no patience with these gorilla damnifications of humanity."

Somewhat higher than sense data, in Carlyle's opinion, was the in- formation given us by the "understanding." Carlyle's "understand- ing" corresponds more or less to Kant's pure or theoretical reason. Just as Kant thought theoretical reason was valid within its own field but was incapable of answering all the problems of life, so Carlyle thought that understanding was good — at least it was better than grubbing around with sense data — yet understanding had its distinct limitations. Understanding was "logic chopping" — giving us dry, hard systems, while reality was greater than any such system. "Car- lyle identifies understanding with logic, implying a mere mechanical and uncreative deduction and inference from given premises, and as these premises are but appearances, the logical development of them cannot be of primary importance.... Understanding can attain only approximations." [63]

Carlyle applied his criticism of understanding to all systems, whether metaphysical or economic, which attempted to explain man's nature or man's actions on the basis of pure deductive rationalizing. He made fun of Hegel's attempt to solve the whole problem of the universe by logical dialectic. He made even greater fun of the economists who tried to explain all phases of human conduct by such laws as that of supply and demand. To him the relation between supply and demand was not a "law" or a "fact," but a theory, a none too accurate approximation of what sometimes happens. Carlyle indeed had a very low opinion of the value of theoretical economics. To his mind J. S. Mill's great work on *Political Economy* was "well done but not worth doing."

Carlyle believed that the real source of true knowledge was not "understanding" but "reason." Carlyle's "reason" corresponds to a certain extent to Kant's practical reason, but is definitely more in- tuitive in character. In fact what Carlyle called reason has very little to do with what we normally call reason — it is closer to "direct spiritual perception" — the ability to penetrate behind the shadows of logic and "see" the fundamental realities which lie beneath. His reason "senses" the fundamental unity behind all the apparent diversity of the phenomenal world. Carlyle's "reason" is really "insight" — sometimes it is little more than the dictates of conscience.

Armed with insight or "reason," Carlyle proceeded to give his views regarding the true nature of the universe. Carlyle was convinced that the world of reality was spiritual and not material. Our finite minds, with their spectacles of space and of time, give us but a very imperfect picture of the spiritual universe. Too often our vision is blurred, and we perceive only the shadows, the distorted shadows of reality. Occasionally, however, a man of vision arises who penetrates behind the veil of the senses and perceives the spiritual character of reality.

Carlyle was not an idealist in the sense that he denied the existence of the external universe. He never accepted the notion that the world is but a creation of an individual mind. (On this point he differed from some of his German teachers, such as Fichte.) But he *was* convinced that the real world was not the confused, disjointed, mechanical, ephemeral world such as appears to the senses, but a world of order, of purpose, "ideal" in character, unchanging in its essence. "The faithfullest, the most glowing word of a man is but an imperfect image of the thought, such as it is, which dwells within him . . . and then between his poor thought and nature's fact, which is the thought of the eternal, there may be supposed to be some discrepancies and shortcomings." [64]

Carlyle believed that if we could only peer behind the veils of space and of time (both subjective), we should be able to realize the essential ideality of the external world. "Sweep away the illusion of time. . . . Then sawest thou that this fair universe, were it the meanest province thereof, is in very deed the star-domed City of God; that through every star, through every grass blade, and most through every living soul, the glory of a present God still beams. But Nature, which is the time vesture of God, reveals Him to the wise and hides Him from the foolish." [65] Again and again Carlyle came back to the notion that Nature — Nature as it really is and not merely as we see it — is the Garment of God. "What is Nature? Ha! Why do I not name thee God? Art thou not the living Garment of GOD? Oh Heavens, is it, in very deed, HE, then, that ever speaks through thee, that lives and loves in thee, that lives and loves in me?" [66] At other times he declared that the universe was but the "symbol of God."

From these passages it is clear that Carlyle broke somewhat from the strict Calvinism of his childhood.   For the central concept of strict Calvinism was a God creating and ruling over the world, while to Carlyle, God manifests Himself through the world, the world of nature. Carlyle has been called a pantheist, but to the pantheist the world and God are one and the same thing, while to Carlyle the world was only one phase, one aspect of God.   Carlyle's God is not quite the personal God of his Puritan ancestors, but this God is not merely the general world-all of the Stoics, for He is above all the source of truth, of beauty, of holiness.

Carlyle was equally convinced that not only Nature but also the innermost soul of man is divine.   To him, the true soul of man is a spark of divinity.

> What is Man himself, and his whole terrestrial Life but an emblem — a Clothing or visible Garment for that divine ME of his, cast hither like a light-particle, down from Heaven?   Thus is he said also to be clothed with a Body....[67] To the eye of vulgar Logic what is man?   An omnivorous Biped that wears Breeches.   To the eye of Pure Reason what is he?   A Soul, a Spirit, a divine Apparition....[68]   There *is* no Space and no Time: We are — we know not what; light-sparkles floating in the ether of Deity....[69]   Man thereby, though based, to all seeming, on the small Visible, does nevertheless exten ! down into the infinite deeps of the Invisible, of which Invisible, indeed, his Life is properly the bodying forth....[70]

God, therefore, to Carlyle was not merely, as to the Puritan, the awful ruler and judge of man but the still small voice within man.   God was revealed not merely through nature but also through humanity.

Considering the idealistic and transcendental character of Carlyle's general philosophy, it is not surprising that Carlyle was also idealistic and transcendental in his views on ethical problems.   He rejected with scorn, a true Calvinist scorn, the view held by the utilitarians, that the standard of good and bad is happiness or pleasure and insisted that goodness consists in acting in accordance with the eternal laws of God. "Does not the whole wretchedness, the whole Atheism, as I call it, of man's ways, in these generations, shadow itself for us in that unspeakable, Life-philosophy of his — the pretension to be what he calls 'happy'?   We construct our theory of Human Duties, not on any Greatest Nobleness Principle, never so mistaken, no, but on a Greatest Happiness Principle." [71]

> Foolish soul!   What Pact of [divine] Legislature was there that *thou* shouldst be Happy?   A little while ago thou hadst no right to *be* at all.

> What if thou wert born and predestined not to be Happy, but to be Unhappy! ....
> There is in man a HIGHER than Love of Happiness: he can do without
> Happiness, and instead thereof find Blessedness. Was it not to preachforth
> this same HIGHER that sages and martyrs, the Poet and the Priest, in all
> times, have spoken and suffered; bearing testimony ... of the Godlike that
> is in Man, and how in the Godlike only has he Strength and Freedom. .... Love
> not Pleasure, love God.[72]

Carlyle admired Kant enormously because of the latter's insistence
upon the supremacy of moral obligations. Carlyle seemingly felt that
he was merely a disciple of Kant in these matters, but as we have already seen, there is a great gulf between Kant and Carlyle on the question of the basis of morality.[73] Kant's moral law is self-imposed; Carlyle's moral law is ordained by God and known to man through his
moral sense or his conscience. T. H. Green thought that moral goodness
was self-realization. Carlyle, with his belief that man is a spark of
the divinity, ought to have sympathized with this view — but his Calvinist upbringing was too strong for him. Morality, to him, was the
subjection of self to the divine will.

Carlyle's views on "jurisprudence" were in close accord with his ideas
on ethics. To be sure he had no interest in the technical side of the law,
and rather despised "attorney-logic" as he called legal reasoning. But
on many occasions he voiced the belief, shared with Kant, that human
law must be based upon "natural law," and to him natural law was the
same as divine law.

> A divine message or eternal regulation of the universe, there verily is, in
> regard to every conceivable procedure and affair of man.[74] ... The Maker's
> Laws, whether they are promulgated in Sinai Thunder, to the ear or imagina-
> tion, or quite otherwise promulgated, are the Laws of God; Transcendent,
> everlasting, imperatively demanding obedience from all men.[75]

Austin and the utilitarians denied the existence of natural laws and
asserted that positive laws, the laws passed by Parliament, were the only
valid laws. To Carlyle such views were blasphemous. He insisted that
there was a

> Law of Nature which the Law of England would vainly contend against
> in the long run.[76] ... Practically men have come to imagine that the Laws of
> this Universe, like the laws of constitutional countries, are decided by voting.
> ... It is an idle fancy. The laws of the Universe, of which the laws of England
> are not an exact transcript, though they should passionately study to become
> such, are fixed by the everlasting congruity of things, and are not fixable or
> changeable by voting. .... I tell you ... it is a miserable blunder, this self-
> styled "law" of theirs; and I for one will study either to have no concern with it,
> or else by all judicious methods to *diso*bey such blundering impious pretended
> "law." [77]

Carlyle constantly contended not only that positive laws should be in accordance with divine law, but also that in the treatment of particular criminals the divine need for punishment and retribution should never be lost sight of. The pardoning, the "molly-coddling" of criminals, the erection for them of luxurious model prisons, was contrary to the divine command that crime be duly punished and expiated. "God Himself, we have always understood, 'hates sin' with a most authentic, celestial, and eternal hatred. . . . Revenge, my friends! revenge, and the natural hatred of scoundrels, and the ineradicable tendency to *revancher* oneself upon them, and pay them what they have merited: this is forevermore intrinsically a correct, and even a divine feeling in the mind of every man." [78]

Carlyle was convinced that divine and natural laws are not inscrutable, but can be discerned by the minds and souls of man. "Intellectual insight is the discernment of order in disorder; it is the discovery of the will of Nature, of God's will." [79] Green thought that the content of natural law itself changed from time to time. Carlyle denied this. To him natural law, being divine law, was unchanging, but he readily admitted that our knowledge and understanding of divine law (and hence its application in statute law) increased as mankind gained in wisdom and insight. "An ideal of right does dwell in all men, in all arrangements, actions, and procedures of men. It is to this ideal of right that human Society forever tends and struggles." [80]

On most points Carlyle agreed with earlier thinkers in the matter of natural law. His doctrine that man should strive to make statute law coincide with natural law was a notion as old as Cicero. But on one point Carlyle introduced a relatively new idea — namely, that whether we wish it or not, whether we strive for it or not, statute law must inevitably become closer and closer to natural law, because by the mysterious workings of Providence "false" laws and nations which make "false" laws inevitably collapse. Only those nations which do seek to pattern their laws upon natural laws wax stronger and stronger. Faithfully following the divine law "said procedure or affair will prosper and have the whole universe to second it and carry it across the fluctuating contradictions to a victorious goal: not following this, mistaking this, disregarding this, destruction and wreck are certain for every affair." [81]

Turning now from jurisprudence to politics proper — the study of the functions of the state and how it should be governed — we find Carlyle to be equally eloquent — or shall we say, equally grandiloquent. Carlyle, of course, was not a systematic thinker and he completely ignored many of the problems discussed by previous philosophers, but during the course of his numerous books he touched incidentally upon most of the problems which interest political scientists.

Carlyle nowhere directly deals with the problem of the origin of the state, but it is easy to see that he completely rejected the doctrine of the social contract. On several occasions he hinted that the origin of the state was in force or conquest. "Politics are formed; the weak submitting to the strong; with a willing loyalty, giving obedience that he may receive guidance." [82] But this by no means implies that to Carlyle the state was an evil thing, because he was certain that in most instances the conquerors, the users of force, were the agents of Providence.

> Tancred of Hauteville's sons, some eight centuries ago, conquered all Italy; bound it up in organic masses, of vital order after a sort; founded thrones and principalities upon the same.... The Tancred Normans were some Four Thousand strong; the Italy they conquered in open fight... might count Eight Millions; all as large of bone, as eupeptic and black-whiskered as they. How came this small minority of Normans to prevail in so hopeless-looking debate? Intrinsically, doubt it not, ... because, in a dim, instinctive, but most genuine manner, they were doing the commandment of Heaven, and so Heaven had decided they were to prevail. [83]

In a vague and rather confused way Carlyle preached the doctrine so dear to T. H. Green, namely, that though the state starts with conquest, no state can endure unless the conquerors look after the welfare of the conquered. Sooner or later the conquerors lose their power as the result of revolution unless their actions make for the increase of the common welfare. To this extent, and to this extent only, did Carlyle accept the doctrine that government rests upon the consent of the governed.

> Conquest, indeed, is a fact often witnessed; conquest, which seems mere wrong and force, everywhere asserts itself as a right among men. Yet if we examine, we shall find that, in this world, no conquest could ever become permanent, which did not withal show itself beneficial to the conquered as well as to the conquerors.... The Romans, having conquered the world, held it conquered, *because* they could best govern the world; the mass of men found it nowise pressing to revolt; their fancy might be afflicted more or less, but in their solid interests they were better off than before. [84]

"Nothing which is unjust can hope to continue in this world." [85] As long as the conquerors rule justly and wisely, the conquered are content to be ruled by them, even though the rulers are not of the conquered's own choosing. But once the conquerors cease to be just, the conquered sooner or later rise up in revolt and the conquerors lose their power.

"Nakedness, hunger, distress of all kinds, death itself have been cheerfully suffered when the heart was right. It is the feeling of injustice that is insupportable to all men. No man can bear it or ought to bear it." [86] For this reason Carlyle felt that the French Revolution, being "a revolt of the oppressed lower classes against the oppressing and neglecting upper classes," [87] was both inevitable and justifiable. Apart from differences in phraseology, Carlyle and T. H. Green are very much alike on this point.

On the question of individualism versus etatism Carlyle occupied a very peculiar position. The older liberals, Locke and Bentham, thought that the individual was superior to the state, and that, apart from criminal actions, the state should exercise no control over the individual. The etatists, such as Hegel and his followers (presently to be considered) believed that the state was superior to the individual — that the individual's chief purpose in life was to serve as a subordinate unit in a greater whole; that the state was an end in itself, and that for the end of the state to be carried out, the state must control all individual actions. Carlyle accepted none of these ideas. His position can best be summarized as *state-regulated individualism.*

In many ways Carlyle was a thoroughgoing individualist. He was convinced that each man was an end in himself and not the means to an end. Not once did he glorify the state as an end in itself, to which the individual must be subordinated. To him the state was merely the means whereby the latent potentiality of each person could best be developed. Unlike even the semi-etatists, such as Kant and Green, Carlyle dismissed with scorn the notion of the general will. He denied even the very existence of the general will as a separate entity. To him the only true meaning that could be attached to the term general will was public opinion — the thoughts and desires of the people — and Carlyle was exceedingly disdainful of public opinion. One of his essays, *Signs of the Times,* was devoted in large measure to the notion that man should rely neither on nature nor on public opinion but on himself.

Carlyle was a reformer. But the reform in which he was primarily interested was not the reorganization of the state or of the machinery of government (though he had definite notions on these matters), but moral reform, a reform of the ideas and aspirations of each man — essentially an individualist concept. In his own time Carlyle was best known as an historian, but his view of history was essentially individualistic. He was not interested in the rise, growth, and decay of nations. History to him was "the biography of great men." To him Luther and Goethe were more interesting and more important than Germany; Cromwell more important than England. Carlyle's individualistic tendency was also evident in his views on immortality. Fichte, Carlyle's master on many points, was content with an impersonal immortality — the "little self" being merged with the "universal self." Not so Carlyle. To him immortality was valueless unless it meant the continued existence of the separate, discrete individual.

Carlyle was thus an ultra-individualist. But he differed radically from the old liberal individualists. The old liberals meant by individualism that a man had a right to do as he pleased as long as he did not interfere with the rights of other persons. To Carlyle, on the other hand (as to T. H. Green), "the primary fundamental right of man is the right to become what he is intended to be, the right to develop his inborn potentialities of goodness and beauty." [88] The individual, being a spark of divinity, should lead a divine life. If for any reason, such as ignorance or indolence, the individual refuses to live up to his potentialities, to his true self, he should be *compelled* to do so — either by his close associates or by the state.

Green stated that true freedom was the freedom to do the thing worth doing. Very close to this was Carlyle's own definition of freedom. "Surely of all rights of man this right of the ignorant man to be guided by the wiser, to be, gently or forcibly, held in the true course by him, is the indisputablest." [89]

> Liberty? The true liberty of a man ... consisted in his finding out, or being forced to find out, the right path, and to walk thereon. To learn, or to be taught, what work he actually was able for; and then by permission, persuasion, and even compulsion, to set about doing the same.... You do not allow a palpable madman to leap over precipices; you violate his liberty, you that are wise; and keep him, were it in strait-waistcoats, away from the precipices! Every stupid, every cowardly and foolish man is but a less palpable madman: his true liberty were that a wiser man, that any and every wiser man, could, by brass collars, or in whatever milder or sharper way, lay hold of him when he was going wrong, and order and compel him to go a little righter. [90]

The end of society is not the erection of an abstract entity called the state, but is the development, if necessary the forcible development, of the divine potentialities within each man. This was Carlyle's variation of the individualist doctrine. Carlyle proceeded to give many illustrations of his doctrine. The "true" development of the individual requires that he work; so Carlyle argued that every individual should be compelled to work. No man "who will not work according to what ability the gods have given him for working has the smallest right to eat pumpkin, or to any fraction of land that will grow pumpkin, however plentiful such land may be; but has ... a *right* to be compelled ... to do competent work for his living. .... If it be his own indolence that prevents and prohibits him [from working], then his own indolence is the enemy he must be delivered from: [that is] the first 'right' he has." [91]

With this concept of liberty, it is not surprising that Carlyle glorified the educational value of drilling and the moral role of the drill sergeant.

> Beyond all other schooling ... one often wishes the entire Population could be thoroughly drilled; into co-operative movement; into individual behavior, correct, precise, and at once habitual and orderly. .... The one Official Person, royal, sacerdotal, scholastic, governmental, of our times, who is still thoroughly a truth and a reality, and *not* in great part a hypothesis and worn-out humbug ... is the Drill-Sergeant who is master of his work, and who will perform it. [92]

Carlyle's belief in "regulated individualism" made him an enemy of *laissez faire* and all doctrines associated with *laissez faire*. To Carlyle *laissez faire* was "organized anarchy." "Is not *Laissez-faire* ... as good as an *abdication* on the part of governors; an admission that they are hencefore incompetent to govern?" [93] "To button your pockets and stand still is no complex recipe. *Laissez faire, laissez passer!* Whatever goes on, ought it not to go on; 'the widow picking nettles for her children's dinner; and the perfumed seigneur delicately lounging in the Oeil-du-Boeuf, who has an alchemy whereby he will extract from her the third nettle, and name it rent and law'?" [94] "Reader, did you ever hear of 'Constituted Anarchy'? Anarchy, the choking, sweltering, deadly, and killing rule of No-rule; the consecration of cupidity, and braying folly, and dim stupidity and baseness, in most of the affairs of men? Slop-shirts attainable three halfpence cheaper by the ruin of living bodies and immortal souls?" [95]

With the arguments, well known to present-day Americans from the pamphlets of the Liberty League, that *laissez faire* is identical with liberty and that to destroy *laissez faire* is to destroy liberty, Carlyle had no patience.

> What shall we do with all this of British Liberty, Voluntary Principle, Dangers of Centralization, and the like? ... For British Liberty it seems, the people cannot be taught to read. British liberty, shuddering to interfere with the rights of capital, takes six or eight millions [of pounds] annually to feed the idle laborer whom it dare not employ. For British Liberty we live over poisonous cesspools, gully-drains, and detestable abominations and

omnipotent London can not sweep the dirt out of itself.... If these are the results of British Liberty, I, for one, move we should lay it on the shelf a little, and look out for something other and farther.[96]

Carlyle vehemently rejected the notion, so dear to many of the older liberals, that the chief function of government is the protection of property. Government exists rather for the protection of the whole man, his body, his health, his capacity for work, his soul.[97] Carlyle was equally violent in his denunciation of the "freedom of contract" based upon the economic laws of supply and demand. Adam Smith and Bentham had argued that freedom of contract worked for the betterment of all classes, laborers as well as capitalists. Carlyle pointed out that in actuality freedom of contract worked out in the form of hopeless poverty and crushing misery for the underprivileged classes.

The master of horses, when the summer labor is done, has to feed the horses through the winter. If he said to his horses:

> "Quadrupeds, I have no longer work for you; but work exists abundantly over the world: are you ignorant (or must I read you Political-Economy Lectures) that the Steam-engine always in the long-run creates additional work? Railways are forming in one quarter of this earth, canals in another, much cartage is wanted; somewhere in Europe, Asia, Africa, or America, doubt it not, ye will find cartage, go and seek cartage, and good go with you." They, with protrusive upper lip, snort dubious; signifying that Europe, Asia, Africa, and America lie somewhat out of their beat; that what cartage may be wanted there is not too well known to them. *They* can find no cartage. They gallop distracted along highways, all fenced in to the right and to the left: finally, under pains of hunger, they take to leaping fences, eating foreign property, and — we know the rest. Ah, it is not a joyful mirth, it is sadder than tears, the laugh Humanity is forced to, at *Laissez faire* applied to poor peasants, in a world like our Europe.... [98]

Carlyle was convinced that where free competition, buying in the cheapest and selling in the dearest market, results in the mental, moral, or physical detriment of the population as a whole, it should be prohibited by law — that when freedom of contract results in the actual enslavement of the laboring classes it should be stopped. In place of the right of the laborer to hire himself out at will, the right of the capitalist to hire and fire laborers at will, Carlyle argued in favor of a permanent or at least a semi-permanent contract between laborers on one side and landlords and industrialists on the other.

In such an arrangement the laborer would be compelled to work, and to work hard, under pain of punishment or starvation. At the same time the capitalist would be forced to pay his laborers a living wage —

not merely a subsistence wage — provide for their health, for adequate living quarters, irrespective of what the world market might be at the moment.   In such an arrangement the capitalist would be able to discharge his workers only for deliberate shirking or gross moral turpitude. Last but not least Carlyle advocated some form of profit-sharing.   "May not your Master-Worker find it possible, and needful, to grant his Workers permanent *interest* in his enterprise and theirs?" [99]

Carlyle believed that much reform could come from private enterprise, quite apart from state intervention.   "Managing the Working Classes will, it is very clear, have to be solved by those who stand practically in the middle of it; by those who themselves work and preside over work." [100]   Not infrequently he alluded to the possibility of idealistic landlords and idealistic "captains of industry" doing an enormous amount of good, working voluntarily within their own domain.[101]   Nevertheless, Carlyle was convinced that the main responsibility for improvement of conditions rests with the national government — that it is the duty of the government forcibly to bring about reforms where private initiative fails.   "Not misgovernment, nor yet no-government, only government will now serve." [102]   After all "what is the end of Government?   To guide men in the way wherein they should go — towards their true good in this life, the portal of infinite good in a life to come?" [103]

Carlyle made no attempt to propose in detail all the things which an ideal government should engage in.   But from one or two suggestions he made, it is clear that he thought the government should assume a thoroughly paternalistic attitude towards its subjects.   He believed there was no sphere in which the state should not be permitted to function.   "The State as it gets into the track of its real work will find that same expand into whole continents of new unexpected, most blessed activity." [104]

Carlyle advocated compulsory education in state-run schools at a time when this was considered rather revolutionary.   "Legislative ... interferences not a few between the workers and the Master Workers ... are indispensable."   Factory inspectors, mine inspectors, sanitary inspectors are also necessary.   "The legislature, even as it now is, could order all dingy Manufacturing Towns to cease from their soot and darkness, to let in the blessed sunlight, the blue of Heaven ..., to burn their coal-smoke.... Baths, free air, a wholesome temperature, ceilings twenty feet high." [105]

It was the task of the government to go into the whole problem of

distribution.   "Let inventive men cease to spend their existence incessantly contriving how cotton can be made cheaper; and try to invent, a
little, how cotton at its present cheapness could be somehow justlier
divided among us." [106]   It was the task of the government to supervise
and regulate the operation of all private commerce and industry in the
interests of the common welfare.   In addition the government had a
further, more direct duty to perform.   The state should conscript all
paupers and idlers, make of them "soldiers of industry," and put them
to work in government-operated industries, keeping them at work there
until such time as they could find employment in private industry.
These government-operated industries would serve a twofold purpose:
— they would do away with unemployment and undeserving abject
poverty; at the same time they would serve as a model, a yardstick to
private industry.

> Mill-operatives, all manner of free operatives, ... they, seeing such example
> of its blessedness, will say, "Masters, you must regiment us a little; make our
> interests with you permanent a little instead of temporary and nomadic;
> we will enlist with the State otherwise."   This will go on, on the one hand,
> while the State-operation goes on, on the other: thus will all Masters of Work-
> men, private Captains of Industry, be forced to incessantly co-operate with
> the State and its public Captains; they regimenting in their way, the State in
> its way, with ever-widening field; till their fields *meet* (so to speak) and coal-
> esce, and there be no unregimented worker, or such only as are fit to re-
> main unregimented.... [107]

Turning now from the problem of the scope and functions of the state
to the other great problem of political philosophy — Shall the control
of the state rest with the many, the few, or the one? — we find that
Carlyle occupied a rather peculiar position.   He could agree neither
with the old Tories nor the old liberals in the answers they gave to this
question.

The old Tories defended absolute monarchy, kings ruling by divine
right, the iniquity of rebellion, the indefeasible rights of an hereditary
nobility, the duty of the lower classes to stay in the station where God
had placed them.   Many Tories, especially the Continental Tories,
were violent in their opposition to representative government, and
denounced Parliament and all its works.   The old liberals, on the other
hand, looked with deep distrust both on kings and on the aristocracy.
Many of them demanded that both monarchy and the order of nobility
be abolished.   They demanded that all power be placed in the House
of Commons, a house elected by universal suffrage.

Carlyle was vociferous in his denunciation of both these political philosophies. He agreed that certain kings, such as William the Conqueror or Tancred's sons, had secured their thrones through the mysterious workings of Providence (as shown by these monarchs securing military victories); hence, in one sense at least, it could be said that they ruled by "divine right." But Carlyle was not enamored of hereditary monarchy. He pointed out that many of the descendants of the rulers "by divine right" were cruel, unjust, or idle and dissipated men. Such men, in his opinion, certainly could not be said to rule by divine right, in fact, had no right to rule at all. Contrary to the Tories, contrary even to Kant, Carlyle preached that the people have a perfect right to rise up in rebellion against such rulers and depose them.

Similarly, Carlyle had no great love for the hereditary aristocracy. He felt a great respect for the earls and barons of earlier times and believed that they richly deserved the powers and the wealth granted them; but for the idle and dissipated descendants of these ancient lords, he had only words of scorn. In later life, when Carlyle, the peasant's son, became the dinner companion and friend of the nobility, he found that some of its members were not so bad, and even wrote: "Indeed, in spite of lamentable exceptions too visible all round, my vote would still be that . . . there was still no class among us intrinsically so valuable and recommendable [as our Aristocracy]." [108] For the most part, however, Carlyle looked with dislike and disdain upon the idle and effete aristocracy who drew vast revenues from their broad acres and served society in no effective way whatever. "What do these highly beneficed individuals *do* to society for their wages? Kill partridges. Can this last? No, by the soul that is in man, it cannot and will not and shall not. . . . Eleven thousand souls a day in Paisley alone living on three halfpence a day and the governors of England all busy shooting partridges." [109] Some of the older writers, such as Burke, claimed that the idle aristocracy was at least the backbone of literature and culture. Carlyle insisted that this so-called culture was worthless, that it was based upon and derived from novel reading.[110]

Carlyle was even more vehement in his attacks upon the new industrial aristocracy, the men who had made their money and acquired their positions as the result of success in commerce and industry. They constituted, to be sure, a working aristocracy as opposed to the landowning, unworking aristocracy, but most of the work they did was evil. "'My starving workers?' answers the rich millowner. 'Did I not pay them, to the last sixpence, the sum covenanted for? What have I to do with them more?' Verily Mammon-worship is a melancholy creed. When Cain, for his own behoof, had killed Abel, and was questioned, 'Where is thy brother?' he too made answer 'Am I my brother's keeper?'" [111] Surely the government of England could not be entrusted to such men as these. "Are these your pattern men? They are your lucky (or unlucky) Gamblers swollen big... Paltry Adventurers, for the most part, worthy of no worship."

Carlyle had many hard things to say about Parliament, but unlike many Tories, especially the Continental Tories, who wished to abolish all representative assemblies, he insisted that a popularly elected Parliament performed a useful and even necessary function.

> Surely not in England only, where the Institution is like second nature to us, but in all countries where men have attained any civilization, it is good that there be a Parliament. Morning Newspapers and other temporary or permanent changes of circumstances, may change and almost infinitely abridge its function but they can never abolish it.... Votes of men are worth collecting, if convenient. True, their opinions are generally of little wisdom...; but their instincts, where these can be deciphered, are wise and human; these, hidden under the noisy utterance of what they call opinions, are the unspoken sense of man's heart, and well worth attending to. [112]

In defending the right of revolution, in attacking the idle, landowning aristocracy and the selfish, money-grubbing "millocracy," in supporting parliamentary institutions, Carlyle departed from the old Tory beliefs and allied himself with the radical liberals. But Carlyle was far from being a liberal, for the liberals, especially the nineteenth century liberals, were thoroughgoing democrats and believed that the government of the people should rest in the hands of the people — and this belief Carlyle violently attacked.

To Carlyle democracy had only a negative, never a positive value. Democracy could and should destroy the evils of unjust despotism and arrogant and selfish oligarchy, but it could never create anything of value to take their place. Democracy is useful in that it aids to tear down the old evil, but it is only a halfway step, for it cannot create the new good.

> In democracy can lie no finality.... With the completest winning of democracy there is nothing yet won.... Democracy is, by the nature of it, a self-cancelling business; and gives in the long-run a net result of zero. [113]
>
> Historically speaking, I believe there was no nation could subsist upon Democracy. [114] Where no government is wanted, save that of the parish-constable, as in America with its boundless soil, every man being able to find

work and recompense for himself, democracy may subsist, not elsewhere, except briefly, as a swift transition towards something other and farther...
In Rome and Athens, as elsewhere, if we look practically, we shall find that it was not by loud voting and debating of many, but by wise insight and ordering of a few that the work was done. So is it ever, so will it ever be.[115]

Carlyle thought that good government meant wise government and wisdom was not to be found in the ignorant mob. To find out truth and wisdom by counting noses was ridiculous. To him the twenty-seven millions who then inhabited England were "mostly fools." To seek from them or their elected representatives the answers to the complicated problems of government was senseless. As for women, "the Lord made them fools to match the men." Democracy, being based upon the idea of equality, was absurd, blasphemously absurd. For could anyone argue that a Quashee Nigger was equal to Socrates or Shakespeare; Judas Iscariot to Jesus Christ?[116]

Carlyle, as we have seen, denied the Tory doctrine of rulership by hereditary monarchy and aristocracy, and the liberal doctrine of government by manhood suffrage. What then was his solution of the problem of government? We may answer in a word — government of the people, for the people, by a true aristocracy of talent. Carlyle agreed with the liberals, rather than with the Tories, in claiming that government should be for the benefit of the whole population rather than for a privileged few. He was democratic in believing that talent was to be sought — nay *must* be sought — from among all classes and sections and not merely from among the children of the rich and well-born. The old regime in France was wrong because the leaders in the army and in the affairs of state were chosen from a limited group. Many of the world's greatest men came from the lower classes — men such as Luther or Napoleon (Carlyle modestly refrained from adding his own name to the list). Granting ' The tools to him who can use them," irrespective of his social or financial background, was, in Carlyle's opinion, Napoleon's one great contribution to modern life.

But once this true aristocracy, this aristocracy of talent, has been selected, the management of affairs must be left completely in their hands, without interference on the part of the general populace or mob. "One thing I do know, and can assert with great confidence, supported by the whole Universe... that the few wise will have by one method or another to take command of the innumerable foolish; that they must be got to take it."[117] "Obedience, little as many may consider that side of the matter, is the primary duty of man.... Parents, teachers superiors, leaders, these all creatures recognize as deserving obedience. Recognized or unrecognized, a man *has* his superiors, a regular hierarchy above him, extending up degree above degree to Heaven itself, and God the Maker, who made His world, not for anarchy, but for rule and order." [118]

Some of the old liberals, such as Montesquieu and Jefferson, were perfectly willing to admit the natural inequality of man or even to admit that the wise and the talented are in the minority.   But they were optimistic enough to think that the many foolish, in a free election, would choose as their governors or representatives the few wise ones. Carlyle did not share this belief.   He thought the many foolish will invariably choose a fool or else an unscrupulous knave to represent them. "If of ten men nine are recognizable as fools, which is a common calculation, how, in the name of wonder, will you ever get a ballot box to grind you out a wisdom from the votes of these ten men?" [119]

As the nation could not secure its true governors, its real aristocrats by balloting, it was obvious that some other method of selection had to be adopted.   Carlyle was rather vague on this point, but he did offer one or two concrete proposals.   He wished to have an administrative hierarchy, a permanent civil service, with a great deal of independent power, appointed by the state on the basis of merit.   Moreover, the members of the cabinet, the secretaries or ministers of all departments, should be appointed because of their real ability and not from among the politicians.

Parliament, as we have seen, was not to be abolished.   Carlyle would, however, radically limit the franchise, and in addition to the elected members, the higher members of the civil service should automatically have a seat in the House of Commons.   These men, the intellectual aristocracy of the nation, should seek to guide the destiny of the ship of state.   Parliament, with its majority of elected members, might well be consulted on matters of general policy, but government, the drafting and administering of the laws, should be in the hands of the non-political administration.

Carlyle hoped to use this new aristocracy of talent as a nucleus in bringing about a reorganization of society.   In this reorganization he wished, above all, to revivify and revitalize the older aristocracies, the landowning and industrial aristocracies.   The landowning aristocracy was to be no longer idle, partridge-shooting, novel-reading parasites, but real leaders of the agricultural community.   The industrial aristocracy was to be lured away from the worship of Mammon, and its members were to become the captains of an industry devoted to the service of man.[120]

Carlyle preferred the few wise to the many foolish, but his passion for hierarchy drove him to look for an all-wise *one* at the top of his social and political pyramid. Carlyle rejected the blind worship of hereditary kings, but he insisted that real leadership must rest in the hands of a single person — a king, in fact, whether his title be that of monarch, dictator, president, or lord protector. "Yes, friends, Hero-kings, and a whole world not unheroic — there lies the port and happy haven, towards which, through all these stormtossed seas, ... the Supreme Powers are driving us." [121] Through all this period of messy democracy Carlyle looked forward to the time when "there will again *be* a King in Israel; a system of Order and Government; and every man shall, in some measure, see himself constrained to do that which is right in the King's eyes." [122] Once we are fortunate enough to secure for ourselves this leader, the whole government must be reorganized. Parliament will not, indeed, be abolished, but it will become an advisory not a governing body — the problem of governing being handed over to the Hero-king.[123]

Unfortunately Carlyle proposed no system for securing this hero-king. Hero-kingship was not and could not be hereditary. Democracy, being what it is, the people cannot be trusted to elect heroes to be their monarchs, though when the hero-king does arise the people will probably recognize and obey him. But though Carlyle refused to tell us how we *should* secure our king, we note that most of the men whom Carlyle recognized as hero-kings in the past secured their position through the force of their armies. Cromwell and Napoleon, two of Carlyle's hero-kings, rose from nothing to supreme power through military success. William the Norman and Frederick the Great, two other men recognized as hero-kings by Carlyle, both started as rulers by hereditary right, but both achieved their greatness, their right to be considered heroes, by conquest. Running all through Carlyle's books is the hint that at some period of national crisis, when the state seems near collapse, a hero will arise who will *seize* supreme power and install himself as dictator, ruling thereafter for the benefit of the whole people.

When we read Carlyle and then look to the later developments in European politics, no one can fail to be struck by the fact that Carlyle's works appear to be little more than a prelude to Naziism and Hitler.

Carlyle preached to the English, but his sermons were taken seriously not by the English, but by the Germans.

Hitler, like Carlyle, despises *laissez faire* and believes in an all-powerful state controlling and regulating the activities of both rich and poor. Hitler, like Carlyle, believes that agriculture, industry, and commerce should not be completely nationalized, but should be forced to submit to the dictates of the state. Hitler, like Carlyle, believes in the regimentation of labor and in the organization of labor on a national basis Hitler, like Carlyle, despises the machinery of democratic government, but Hitler, like Carlyle, has little use for the old hereditary monarchy or for the old hereditary aristocracy. Like Carlyle, moreover, Hitler believes that the hereditary aristocracy and the captains of industry, duly purged and revivified, can be made to fit into the new order of things, an order based upon an aristocracy of talent (the members and leaders of the Nazi Party), headed by an all-wise, all-powerful hero-dictator. Hitler, no doubt, feels that he has shown that Carlyle was right in supposing that in a time of crisis a hero-king can and will spontaneously arise.

The resemblance between Carlyle's political philosophy and Naziism is rendered even more striking by the fact that even in less important details there is a strong parallelism — in some cases complete identity.

Carlyle, like the modern Nazis, claimed that a sound state, a sound political organization, must be based upon *feeling*, not intellect; upon an unconscious urge to action, not upon a metaphysical analysis of ideologies. "In the body politic, as in the animal body, the sign of right performance is unconsciousness.... In all vital things men distinguish an artificial and a natural.... The artificial is the conscious mechanical; the natural is the unconscious dynamical.... The artificial society is precisely one which knows its own structure. Not in watching, not in knowing which, but in working outwardly to the fulfilment of its aim does the well-being of a society consist.... If the mystic significance of the state ... dwells vitally in every heart ... how should it stand by self-questioning. It must rush outward and express itself by work." [124]

Carlyle, like the modern Nazis, was a believer in force and strength. Running all through his writings was the notion that might and right tended to be identical. Carlyle did, indeed, reject the idea that might is necessarily right, but he did claim that right is mighty, that right in the long run is stronger and more forceful than wrong. As a result of this attitude, he came to believe that the victor, the conqueror was in·

evitably better than the defeated. "Might and right, so frightfully discrepant at first, are ever in the long-run one and the same." [125] "The strong thing is the just thing... It has the might and the right. By the same great law do Roman Empires establish themselves... and all extant Powers bear rule." [126]

Brute conquest of one nation by another was not, in Carlyle's opinion, necessarily wrong; in fact it was usually right. Taking English history as an example, he argued:

> Whose land was this of Britain? God's, who made it, his and no others. Who of God's creatures had the right to live in it? The wolves and the bison? Yes, they; till one with a better right showed himself. The Celt... arrived pretending to have a better right, and did accordingly, not without pain to the bisons, make good the same. He had a better right to that piece of God's land, namely a better might to turn it to use.... The bisons disappeared, the Celts took possession and tilled. Forever was it to be?... No property is eternal but God the Maker's; whom Heaven permits to take possession, his is the right; Heaven's sanction *is* such permission while it lasts.[127] Heaven permitted the Saxons to drive out the Celts; heaven permitted the Normans to conquer and rule over the Saxons, hence the Saxons and the Normans had a perfect *right* to do what they did. We may drop a tear of sympathy for the expelled Celts, for the conquered Saxons, and yet, on the whole, what can we say but that the cause which pleased the Gods has in the end to please Cato also.[128] [And by Cato, Carlyle meant any philosophical historian or statesman.]

Carlyle spoke in terms of English history; the Nazi talks in terms of German expansion in Central Europe — but the basic philosophy is the same.

With this attitude towards war and conquest, it is not surprising to find that Carlyle was an ardent imperialist. Most of the traditional liberals were opposed to the extension of the British Empire by force of arms. The utilitarians were "little Englanders" almost to a man and believed that England should liberate even those colonies which she already possessed. Carlyle was scornful of this attitude. He was convinced that England has been appointed by God to "civilize," that is, to conquer and administer a large portion of the world. "Sugar islands, spice islands, Indias, Canadas — these by the real decree of Heaven were ours." [129] He was horrified at the thought of letting the colonies slip away even though economically they were unprofitable. They must be retained at all costs. "Shame on us for unworthy sons of brave fathers if we do not. Brave fathers by valiant blood and sweat purchased for us from the bounty of Heaven rich possessions in all zones; and we wretched imbeciles cannot do the function of administering them." [130]

Carlyle argued that though the colonies might be costly for the moment, eventually they would form a bulwark economically for England. "Hostile tariffs will arise, to shut us out, and then again will fall, to let us in, but the Sons of England, speakers of the English language, will in all times have the ineradicable predisposition to trade with England." [131] Carlyle not only wished to keep the colonies in name; he also wished to keep effective control over them. The idea of granting them complete self-government (what is now called dominion status) was obnoxious to him. Carlyle was horrified to hear of an independence movement in Canada; more horrified still to hear that the British Governor General, England's agent in that region, did nothing about it. "Majesty's Chief Governor seeming to take it as a perfectly open question; Majesty's Chief Governor in fact seldom appearing on the scene at all except to receive the impact of a few rotten eggs on occasion and then duck in again to his private contemplation." [132]

Carlyle was perfectly willing to permit the establishment of colonial Parliaments to give advice to the various governors, but he felt that real control of affairs should remain with these governors sent out from England. "Wherever there are born kings of men, you had better seek them out and breed them to this work." [133] Were this done we should soon find that "the Imperial Mother and her constitutionally obedient daughters was not a red tape fiction provoking bitter mockery as at present, but a blessed God's fact destined to fill half the world with its fruits one day." [134]

Another marked point of resemblance between Carlyle and the modern Nazis is the belief in the innate superiority of certain races over others resulting in the notion that certain races are predestined to rule over others. The old liberals thought all mankind to be more or less alike, and one race as good as another. Not so Carlyle. He was convinced that the Negro was and always would be mentally inferior to the white man. Because of this fact Carlyle defended Negro slavery, on the ground that it was in accord with the eternal laws of God. [135] But even amongst the whites Carlyle felt that some peoples (we should now say races) were far superior to others. To his mind the Romans were intrinsically superior to the Greeks and hence were heaven-destined to conquer the latter.[136]

He was sure that the Germanic peoples (including the Anglo-Saxons) were far superior to the Celts.[137] For all his interest in and admiration of the French, he felt that they were definitely inferior to the modern Germanic peoples, the Germans and English. "That noble, patient, deep, pious, and solid Germany should at length be welded together into a nation and become Queen of the Continent instead of vaporing, vainglorious, gesticulating, quarrelsome, restless and ever sensitive France seems to me the hopefullest public fact that has occurred in my time." [138]   Last but not least, great as the Germans were, the English, in Carlyle's opinion, were even greater.   Let the Germans rule over Europe, but let the English rule over the world.

One final point of resemblance between Carlyle and the Nazis deserves to be mentioned.   Carlyle was a theoretical and not a practical man, so he never attempted to organize a political party which aimed at seizing control over the state and reorganizing it to suit his ideals. Nevertheless, from several of his remarks on minority parties and the sacred role such parties had played in history, one feels sure that Carlyle would have applauded the formation — and the tactics — of the Nazi group in Germany.

> I have known minorities, and even small ones by the account of heads, do grand national feats long memorable to all the world.... Witness Cromwell and his Puritans; a minority at all times...; yet the authors and saviors, as it ultimately proved, of whatsoever is divinest in the things we can still reckon ours in England.   Minority by tale of heads; but weighed in Heaven's balances, a most clear majority.... Indeed it is on such terms that grand national and other feats, by the sons of Adam, are generally done.   Not without risk and labor to the doers of them; no surely, for it never was an easy matter to do the real will of a Nation, much more the real will of this Universe in respect to a Nation.   No, that is difficult and heroic; easy as it is to count the voting heads of a Nation at any time, and do the behests of their beer and balderdash; empty behests, very different from their "will," poor blockheads, to say nothing of the Nation's will, and the Universe's will! [139]

One has only to substitute the words "Hitler" for "Cromwell," "the Nazis" for "the Puritans," and "Germany" for "England" to get an almost perfect exposition of the Nazi creed.

NOTES TO CHAPTER FIVE

1. H. Heine, *Germany, Works*, V, 136, 137.   By permission of Wm. Heinemann, Ltd. and W. Smith.
2. Immanuel Kant, *Principles of Politics*, in the translator's introduction, p. xxxix
3. *Ibid.*, p. 49.
4. *Ibid.*, p. 50.
5. Kant, *Philosophy of Law*, p. 173.   By permission of T. & T. Clark.
6. Kant, *Principles of Politics*, p. 50.   By permission of T. & T. Clark.

7. Kant, *Philosophy of Law*, p. 169.   8. *Ibid.*, p. 258
9. *Ibid.*, p. 170.
10. *Ibid.*, p. 182.
11. *Ibid.*, p. 185.
12. *Ibid.*, p. 252.
13. *Ibid.*, p. 188.
14. *Ibid.*, p. 185.
15. Kant argued that all *self-dependent* citizens should have the privilege of voting. He thought all children, all women, all servants, all agricultural workers, etc. are dependent for their livelihood upon the will of others and as such should not be considered worthy of political rights. (*Ibid.*, p. 167.)
16. *Ibid.*, p. 208.
17. *Ibid.*
18. *Ibid.*, p. 175.
19. *Ibid.*, p. 174.
20. *Ibid.*, p. 175.
21. *Ibid.*, pp. 176, 177.
22. *Ibid.*, p. 207.
23. Kant, *Principles of Politics*, p. 47.
24. *Ibid.*, p. 4.
25. *Ibid.*, p. 10.
26. *Ibid.*, p. 11.
27. *Ibid.*, p. 71.
28. *Ibid.*, pp. 16, 17.
29. Other persons of some note were: E. Caird, who carried the Oxford School to Glasgow; W. Wallace, Green's successor as Professor of Moral Philosophy at Oxford; J. MacCunn; J. H. Muirhead; Sir Henry Jones; R. L. Nettleship. All these men have written books dealing with political thought from the idealist point of view.
30. H. Sidgwick, *History of Ethics*, p. 259. By permission of The Macmillan Company, publishers.
31. W. H. Fairbrother, *The Philosophy of T. H. Green*, p. 24.
32. T. H. Green, *Prolegomena to Ethics*, sec. 246.
33. *Ibid.*, sec. 247.
34. *Ibid.*, sec. 243.
35. T. H. Green, *Principles of Political Obligation*.
36. *Ibid.*, sec. 11.
37. *Ibid.*, sec. 141.
38. E. Barker, *Political Thought in England*, p. 60. By permission of Oxford University Press, Oxford, England.
39. Green, *Principles of Political Obligation*, sec. 134.
40. *Ibid.*, sec. 141.
41. *Ibid.*
42. *Ibid.*, sec. 86.
43. *Ibid.*, sec. 85.
44. *Ibid.*, sec. 118.
45. *Ibid.*, sec. 93.
45a. *Ibid.*, sec. 85.
45b. *Ibid.*, sec. 93.
46. *Ibid.*, sec. 175.
47. *Ibid.*, sec. 119.
48. *Ibid.*, sec. 141.
49. *Ibid.*, sec. 142.
50 *Ibid.*
51 *Ibid.*, sec. 10.

52. Green, *Principles of Political Obligation*, sec. 18.
53. *Ibid.*, sec. 209.
54. Green, *Works*, III, 373.
55. Barker, *Political Thought in England*, p. 52.
56. Green, *Works*, III, 384.
57. *Ibid.*, p. 371.
58. *Ibid.*, p. 372.
59. *Ibid.*, p. 382.
60. *Ibid.*
61. Green, *Principles of Political Obligation*, sec. 119
62. *Ibid.*, sec. 108.
63. M. Storrs, *The Relation of Carlyle to Kant and Fichte*, p. 37.
64. Thomas Carlyle, *Latter-Day Pamphlets*, p. 203.
65. Carlyle, *Sartor Resartus*, p. 194.
66. *Ibid.*, p. 150.
67. *Ibid.*, p. 57.
68. *Ibid.*, p. 51.
69. *Ibid.*, p. 43.
70. *Ibid.*, p. 173.
71. Carlyle, *Past and Present*, p. 153.
72. Carlyle, *Sartor Resartus*, p. 153.
73. Carlyle, *Shooting Niagara*, p. 29.
74. Carlyle, *Latter-Day Pamphlets*, p. 17.
75. Carlyle, *Past and Present*, p. 229.
76. Carlyle, *Chartism*, p. 132.
77. Carlyle, *Latter-Day Pamphlets*, p. 235.
78. *Ibid.*, p. 78.
79. Carlyle, *Chartism*, p. 194.
80. *Ibid.*, p. 153.
81. Carlyle, *Latter-Day Pamphlets*, p. 17.
82. Carlyle, *Characteristics*, p. 11.
83. Carlyle, *Latter-Day Pamphlets*, p. 247.
84. Carlyle, *Chartism*, p. 146.
85. *Ibid.*, p. 154.
86. *Ibid.*, p. 144.
87. *Ibid.*, p. 149.
88. Storrs, *op. cit.*, p. 91.
89. Carlyle, *Chartism*, p. 157
90. Carlyle, *Past and Present*, p. 212.
91. Carlyle, *The Nigger Question*, p. 355.
92. Carlyle, *Shooting Niagara*, p. 41.
93. Carlyle, *Chartism*, p. 156.
94. *Ibid.*, p. 131.
95. Carlyle, *Latter-Day Pamphlets*, p. 29.
96. *Ibid.*, p. 30.
97. Carlyle, *Chartism*, p. 163.
98. *Ibid.*, p. 142.
99. Carlyle, *Past and Present*, p. 282.
100. *Ibid.*, p. 270.
101. Carlyle, *Shooting Niagara*, pp. 31 ff.
102. Carlyle, *Chartism*, p. 157.
103. Carlyle, *Past and Present*, p. 166.
104. Carlyle, *Latter-Day Pamphlets*, p. 16.

105. Carlyle, *Past and Present*, p. 265.
106. *Ibid.*, p. 183.
107. Carlyle, *Latter-Day Pamphlets*, p. 166. This doctrine of Carlyle's was taken over and greatly developed by Ruskin (see his *Unto This Last*, pp. xi ff.). Ruskin added that though the able-bodied paupers and idlers should be forced to work in government factories, the state should provide home and comfort, without forced labor, for the aged.
108. Carlyle, *Shooting Niagara*, p. 16.
109. J. S. Froude, *Life of Carlyle*, II, 67; III, 243.
110. Carlyle, *Sartor Resartus*, p. 22.
111. Carlyle, *Past and Present*, p. 147.
112. Carlyle, *Latter-Day Pamphlets*, p. 240.
113. Carlyle, *Chartism*, p. 159.
114. Carlyle, *Latter-Day Pamphlets*, p. 18.
115. Carlyle, *Chartism*, p. 158.
116. Carlyle, *Shooting Niagara*, p. 4.
117. Carlyle, *Latter-Day Pamphlets*, p. 34.
118. Carlyle, *Chartism*, p. 189.
119. Carlyle, *Latter-Day Pamphlets*, p. 238.
120. Carlyle, *Shooting Niagara*, p. 22 ff.
121. Carlyle, *Past and Present*, p. 36.
122. *Ibid.*, p. 250.
123. Carlyle, *Latter-Day Pamphlets*, p. 221.
124. Carlyle, *Characteristics*, pp. 12, 13.
125. Carlyle, *Chartism*, p. 147.
126. *Ibid.*, p. 174.
127. *Ibid.*
128. *Ibid.*, p. 173.
129. Carlyle, *Latter-Day Pamphlets*, p. 145; see also *Chartism*, p. 90.
130. Carlyle, *Latter-Day Pamphlets*, p. 150.
131. Carlyle, *Past and Present*, p. 269.
132. Carlyle, *Latter-Day Pamphlets*, p. 149.
133. *Ibid.*, p. 156.
134. *Ibid.*
135. See Carlyle, *The Nigger Question.*
136. Carlyle, *Past and Present*, p. 161.
137. Carlyle, *Chartism*, p. 173.
138. Carlyle, *Letter to the Times.*
139. Carlyle, *Latter-Day Pamphlets*, p. 246.

BIBLIOGRAPHY

FOR KANT

PRIMARY SOURCES. There are several editions of Kant's works in the original German. The latest and best edited is *Kant's Gessamelte Schriften*, Berlin, 1902–1938. Most of Kant's works have appeared in an English translation. For Kant's theory of knowledge and his metaphysics, see especially *Critique of Pure Reason*, translated by F. Max Müller, second edition, London, 1907. For Kant's ethics see *Critique of Practical Reason*, translated by T. K. Abbott, sixth edition, London, 1908. For Kant's views on jurisprudence and politics see *Kant's Philosophy of Law*, translated by W. Hastie, Edinburgh, 1887, and *Principles of Politics*, translated by W. Hastie, Edinburgh, 1891.

SECONDARY SOURCES. There are an enormous number of books dealing with various phases of Kant's philosophy. Among the most noteworthy are: W Wallace, *Kant*, Edinburgh, 1882; J. H. W. Stuckenburgh, *Life of Immanuel Kant* London, 1882; F. Paulsen, *Immanuel Kant, His Life and Doctrines*, New York, 1902; E. Caird, *Critical Philosophy of Immanuel Kant*, 2 vols., Glasgow, 1889. For Kant's political theories see J. Dewey, *German Philosophy and Politics*, New York, 1915 (especially chap. II); C. E. Vaughan, *Studies in the History of Political Philosophy*, Manchester, 1925 (vol. II, chap. II); E. L. Hinman, "Kant's Philosophy of Law," in *Immanuel Kant, Papers read at Northwestern University*, Chicago, 1925; R. Pound, "Law," in *Immanuel Kant, 1724–1924*, New Haven, 1925; C. E. Merriam, *History of the Theory of Sovereignty*, New York, 1900 (chap. II); L. Duguit, "Kant's Political and Juridical Doctrine," in *Harvard Law Review*, vol. XXI, 1917, pp. 40–56.

FOR T. H. GREEN

PRIMARY SOURCES. *Prolegomena to Ethics*, London, 1883. *Works*, 3 vols., London, 1885–1888. See especially *Principles of Political Obligation* in vol. II, pp. 335 ff. and *Liberal Legislation and Freedom of Contract* in vol. III, pp. 365 ff.

SECONDARY SOURCES. R. L. Nettleship, *Memoir of T. H. Green*, in Green, *Works*, vol. III, pp. xi ff. W. H. Fairbrother, *The Philosophy of T. H. Green*, London, 1896. H. Sidgwick, *Lectures on the Ethics of T. H. Green*, London, 1902. O. Gunther, *Das Verhaltnis der Ethik T. H. Greens zu derjenigen Kants*, Dresden, 1915. Y. L. Chin, *The Political Theory of T. H. Green*, New York, 1920. J. H. Muirhead, *The Service of the State, Lectures on the Political Teaching of T. H. Green*, London, 1908. There are also important sections or chapters on Green in the following works: J. MacCunn, *Six Radical Thinkers*, London, 1910 (chap. VI). D. G. Ritchie, *Principles of State Interference*, London, 1896 (chap. IV). E. Barker, *Political Thought in England, from Spencer to the Present Day*, London, 1915 (chap. II). R. H. Murray, *English Social and Political Thinkers of the Nineteenth Century*, Cambridge, 1929 (vol. II, chap. VII). A. D. Lindsay, "T. H. Green and the Idealists" in Hearnshaw, *Representative Thinkers of the Victorian Age*, London, 1933. E. F. Carritt, *Morals and Politics*, Oxford, 1935 (chap. X). C. Brinton, *English Political Thought in the Nineteenth Century*, London, 1933 (chap. IV, sec. 3). H. Sidgwick, *History of Ethics*, New York, 1931.

FOR CARLYLE

PRIMARY SOURCES. Carlyle, *Works*. Citations are from the Centenary edition, 30 vols. London, 1896–1901.

SECONDARY SOURCES. R. Garnett, *Life of Carlyle*, London, 1887. J. S. Froude, *Life of Carlyle*, 4 vols., London, 1882–1884. D. A. Wilson, *Life of Carlyle*, 5 vols., London, 1923–1929. N. Young, *Carlyle, His Rise and Fall*, London, 1927. M. Storrs, *The Relation of Carlyle to Kant and Fichte*, Bryn Mawr, 1929. T. Deimel, *Carlyle und der National Sozialismus*, Würzburg, 1936. W. A. Meseke, *Mensch, Geschichte und Staat bei Carlyle*, Munich, 1935. F. W. Roe, *Social Philosophy of Carlyle and Ruskin*, New York, 1921. B. E. Lippincott, *Victorian Critics of Democracy* (Carlyle, Ruskin, etc.), Oxford, 1938. The works of Murray, Brinton, and Barker, cited above, also deal with Carlyle.

CHAPTER VI

The Political Philosophy of Johann Gottlieb Fichte

KANT and the two English thinkers who took over many of Kant's ideas, Carlyle and Green, mark an important break in the old liberal tradition. With all these thinkers the old complete individualism was rejected and greater emphasis laid upon the importance and power of the state. All three, moreover, refused to give complete adherence to the old liberal doctrine of democracy and espoused to a greater or to a lesser extent the cause of authoritarianism. These three therefore, Kant, Carlyle, and Green, must be regarded as the forerunners of etatism, but none of these three were etatists in the modern sense of the word. Kant's objection to paternalism in government, his insistence that man be treated as an end in himself and not as the means to an end (the state), his dislike of a social or political hierarchy, were inconsistent with complete etatism. Green came far closer to etatism in stressing the supremacy of society over the individual, but even he rejected complete etatism by making society more important than the state, and by preferring democratic to authoritarian control. Carlyle came the closest to complete etatism with his drill-sergeant authoritarianism and his belief in regulation and control of all things by the state. But even Carlyle was a thoroughgoing individualist at heart and regarded the state as a means to an end and not as the supreme end in itself.

It was left for two German thinkers, strongly influenced by Kant, Fichte and Hegel, to take over the political philosophy of their master and develop it into complete radical etatism in a form so consistent and so persuasive that their systems served as models for all the later etatist thinkers both in the nineteenth and in the twentieth centuries. Nor was their influence confined merely to the world of speculation. Bismarck in the eighteen-sixties and seventies was merely applying in the realm of practical politics the principles of Fichte and Hegel. More important still, the present-day totalitarian and authoritarian governments in Europe, the Fascist regime in Italy, the Nazi regime in Germany, are little more than further developments and applications of the ideas enunciated in the Fichtean and Hegelian philosophies.

Fichte is one of the most interesting figures in political philosophy. Born in 1762 and dying in 1814, he was a son both of the eighteenth and of the nineteenth centuries. Not only in his life but in his philosophy and in his political ideas he represents an important link between the two eras. As a young man (in the eighteenth century) he was not merely an adherent but an eloquent preacher of the old liberal doctrines. He taught a rational "enlightened" approach to the problems of life as opposed to a traditional or a sentimental approach. He was a thorough-going individualist, limiting the power and the functions of the state in every possible way. He was a cosmopolitan, an internationalist as opposed to a nationalist, claiming to be a citizen of Europe rather than of any particular, petty state. He was an ardent democrat, assailing absolute monarchy and privileged aristocracy and demanding popular control over all the organs of government.

Beginning with 1800, the first year of the new century, Fichte's philosophical system underwent a decided transformation. At a time when most of his colleagues in the academic world were still content with the older outlook, Fichte became a fervent apostle of a new interpretation of the world and of the state. In place of the old cold rational approach to the problems of life he stressed the need for intuition, for sentiment, for emotion. In place of the old individualism Fichte began to lay greater and greater emphasis upon the state, and in the final exposition of his system the individual became little more than a pawn in the hands of an all-powerful government. In place of the old cosmopolitanism Fichte preached, with all the fervor of his being, in favor of nationalism in general and of German nationalism in particular. In place of the old democracy Fichte substituted a belief in authoritarianism. The people were to be ruled justly, to be sure, but not by themselves or their elected representatives, but by an all-powerful hierarchy of officials in whose selection they had no part.

When Fichte first began to preach his new gospel he was almost like a prophet preaching in the wilderness with no one heeding his voice. But as time went on the strange new gospel became the accepted creed throughout most of Germany and then spread from Germany to many other parts of Europe. It would, of course, be ridiculous to claim that Fichte was the sole or even the chief cause of the transformation in the intellectual and political thought of Germany in the generations following his death. But it is not without significance that most of the founders of the romantic movement in German literature were either disciples of Fichte's or else personal friends.   Though many of these disciples and friends later became personal enemies, they readily admitted the great part which Fichte had played in forming their opinions. It is also of significance to remember that many of the later prophets of etatism and authoritarianism, such as Hegel, were directly or indirectly followers of Fichte at some stage in their lives, and that most of the more extreme German nationalists in later times looked back upon Fichte as one of the founders and leaders of their cause.

FICHTE'S LIFE AND TIMES

Fichte according to tradition was descended from a Swedish dril! sergeant in the army of Gustavus Adolphus who settled in Germany during the Thirty Years' War.   His immediate forbears were poor hard-working peasants, or petty merchants, for the most part men of little or no education.   At the time of his birth he was definitely a membeɪ of the lower middle class, and all through his life he was given the nickname of "the peasant."   This circumstance, combined with the fact that he was a boy of great talent and boundless ambition, had a great influence upon his life and indirectly upon his social and political opinions.   It was not easy for a promising boy of his social position to rise in the Germany of his day.   Young Fichte bitterly resented this fact, and also the arrogance and superciliousness of his social superiors.

Through the patronage of a noble family Fichte was able to go to a school and later to a university where he met many scions of wealthy and aristocratic houses and his sensitive nature was deeply hurt by the occasional snubs he received at their hands.   These snubs produced in him what we would now call an "inferiority complex" which remained with him all through his life.   Metaphorically he went around with a chip on his shoulder, daring every man to knock it off.   He took violent offense at the slightest provocation and sometimes with no provocation at all.   Much of his life was spent in bitter quarrels not only with his enemies but also with his friends, even with such persons as Goethe, who had defended and aided him in times of dire need.

This inferiority complex profoundly influenced not only Fichte's life but also his ideas.   Fichte, for all his talk about the duty of unselfishness and self-abnegation, was completely self-centered — was in fact an egomaniac, and it is not surprising that the cornerstone of his philosophy, at least of his early philosophy, was the doctrine of the self or ego.

It was this inferiority complex which dominated his early political thought. Resenting as he did the prevailing absolute monarchy and privileged aristocracy, he was a violent advocate of democracy and the rights of man. To Fichte's hurt pride, justice demanded the curbing of kings and the abolition of the order of the nobility. To his mind at this time the state was little more than the organized agency whereby the monarch and the aristocracy maintained control over the bulk of the citizenry. Hence the state was to be regarded with suspicion. It could not, unfortunately, be abolished, but it was to be shorn of as many powers as possible.

Even Fichte's later political philosophy was greatly influenced by his psychological reaction to his surroundings. During his early life Fichte had been distinctly pro-French, but after 1800 this feeling rapidly changed. French armies had triumphed time and again over the various German forces. The French Emperor made and unmade German principalities and confederations to suit himself. Fichte, for all his cosmopolitanism, was a German, and he felt himself personally humiliated by this turn of events. He felt that he and his fellow Germans must show the world that they were just as good as if not a little better than these cocky French. In 1807 the French army occupied Berlin and took over control of the local administration. Fichte's blood rose to the boiling point and he chose this occasion to deliver the most impassioned of his appeals to German national feelings. In his *Addresses to the German Nation* delivered at this time Fichte set out to show how far superior the Germans were to all other peoples, and how the future of the world lay with them. To achieve actual supremacy the Germans had to give up their local and individual rights and unite to form a new strong state armed with autocratic powers.

By this time Fichte was a man of some name and fame. Moreover, the pride of the German ruling class had been somewhat humbled by their defeats at the hands of the French revolutionary armies. For this reason Fichte could now come into contact with the aristocracy without feeling his gorge rise. Fichte was no longer merely one of "the people," and so was content to abolish democratic control over the machinery of government. He was everywhere recognized as a scholar. It is not surprising, therefore, that it now became clear to him that autocratic control over the state should rest neither with the aristocracy nor with the people, but with the "scholars." These scholars in turn should choose a supreme ruler or dictator or master scholar, and from Fichte's description of what the qualifications of the master scholar should be

It is obvious that Fichte fancied that he himself was better fitted than any of his contemporaries to fill this role.

Fichte's life falls into four main periods. With the first period (1762–1784), his boyhood and the years spent as a student in Jena and Leipzig Universities we are not much concerned. His parents were anxious that Fichte should become a Lutheran pastor and as a result much time was spent in studying theology, but in the end Fichte found that he could not accept the dogmas of orthodox Lutheranism and so he was never ordained. In this connection it is interesting to note that three of the foremost apostles of etatism and authoritarianism, Fichte, Carlyle, and Hegel, started out as theological students, in marked contrast with the early life and training of most of the great liberal thinkers such as Locke who started out as a doctor, or Montesquieu who started out as a lawyer.

During the second period of his life (1784–1794) Fichte spent much of his time moving around from place to place, earning a precarious livelihood by tutoring the children of various well-to-do families. He was never a great success as a tutor. On one famous occasion he was dismissed after a few days' service because his noble patroness found his French accent atrocious and his independent nature unbearable. By threatening a lawsuit Fichte was able to secure as compensation a sum sufficient to last him several months. Fichte used this period of idleness to pursue his philosophical studies. It was at this time that Fichte became personally acquainted with Kant, an event which revolutionized Fichte's whole life. He was now determined to devote his activities to the exposition and interpretation and development of the Kantian principles. He composed a work, *The Critique of All Possible Revelation*, an application of Kant's critical method to the problem of religion. His chief conclusion was that if man *did* feel the need for revealed religion because of his weakness, the doctrines of such a religion to be acceptable must not be contrary to the postulates either of theoretical or of practical reason.

This book of Fichte's would probably have had little popular success had it not been for a trick played by the publisher upon the public. At the last moment he removed Fichte's name from the title page and had the book published anonymously. The literary critics of the time were stupid enough to think that the work was written by Kant himself and so gave it widespread publicity. When it was revealed that the author was not Kant but Fichte, the latter's reputation was immediately established. Encouraged by the success of this book Fichte married a lady some years his senior and brought out two further works, one defending the freedom of speech against political censorship, the other a defense of the principles underlying the French Revolution which had just broken out.

The third period of Fichte's life commenced in 1794 with his appointment to the chair of philosophy at Jena University, then the center of German culture. Fichte owed this appointment to his fame as the interpreter of Kant, but it showed a remarkable spirit of tolerance and broad-mindedness on the part of the Duke of Weimar, who controlled appointments to Jena, and of Goethe, the Duke's chief councillor. The lectures given and the books written during the next few years were instrumental in causing a revolution in German philosophical thought. In Fichte's hands the critical, skeptical, and agnostic philosophy of Kant was transformed into dogmatic idealism and this transformation was accepted by nearly all the later German metaphysicians. The later thinkers did not always agree with Fichte's detailed conclusions, but, due in large measure to Fichte's influence, German philosophy remained both dogmatic and idealistic. During this same period Fichte continued to be interested in political speculation and wrote his *Foundations of Natural Law*. Though less extreme than some of his earlier writings, this work was still liberal and even radical in tone and was largely a reinterpretation of Rousseau's doctrines, using Kantian phraseology.

But though Fichte's name and fame constantly increased during his stay at Jena, this period was characterized by many stormy scenes owing to Fichte's personal eccentricities. He was frequently engaged in violent quarrels with some of his colleagues. Among the persons with whom he disputed most violently was the great poet Schiller. Fichte's lectures were popular and well attended, but he became involved in a conflict with some of the students over their societies (or "fraternities" as we would call them) to which he was violently opposed. As a result some undergraduates attacked Fichte's house and broke several windows. For a little time thereafter his public lectures were interrupted by cat-calls, and fearing further trouble he resided some distance away from the town of Jena for several months. Scarcely had this excitement died down when a new and even more serious trouble arose. In a magazine article Fichte spoke of God as equivalent to the "moral order of the Universe." This article caused Fichte to be accused of atheism and there was much hubbub amongst the University authorities. The all-powerful Duke of Weimar was anxious to hush things up and all would have been well, except that Fichte was again guilty both of recklessness and of stubbornness, and in the end he was dismissed from the University.

The fourth period of Fichte's life extends from his dismissal in 1800 until his death in 1814. Fichte thought for a while that he would secure a post at a new university to be opened at Mainz under French patronage and designed to be the center of pro-French propaganda amongst the German youth. Had this university really been established Fichte would undoubtedly have joined the faculty. It is amusing to think that Fichte came within an ace of being a paid French propagandist instead of the inspired prophet of German nationalism. But the French abandoned their idea of establishing the Mainz University and Fichte was forced to look for refuge — and a source of livelihood — elsewhere. He found both in Berlin, the capital of the Prussian state, which was then the chief bulwark against the French plan to dominate all the German principalities. Through the aid of friends Fichte secured a post at the University of Erlangen, though he continued to reside in Berlin even while occupying the new chair. Some years afterwards (in 1809), when the University of Berlin was founded, he was given a professorship at this institution and in 1811 he was elected its rector (or president). As might be expected it was not long before he got into hot water. Violent disputes broke out between himself and his colleagues and also with the student body. Fichte felt forced to resign his rectorship after only four months of office, but he retained his professorship and continued to teach his classes until his sudden death in 1814.

During the years in which Fichte resided and lectured in Berlin he proceeded to modify and enlarge many of the metaphysical concepts which he had enunciated in Jena. But the style of his later lectures and writings on metaphysical problems was labored and obscure and they had little or no influence upon subsequent developments in German philosophy. Far different was it with Fichte's activities in the field of politics and jurisprudence. Influenced by his Prussian surroundings Fichte slowly but steadily transformed his early individualism into etatism, his early cosmopolitanism into nationalism, his early democracy into authoritarianism. Some of Fichte's new political ideas were delivered in the form of popular lectures to the general public, such as *Characteristics of the Present Age* and *Addresses to the German Nation*. At other times he chose a more learned setting for his doctrines and wrote such books as *The Closed Commercial State*, the *Theory of Law*, and the *Theory of State*. All these works exerted a considerable influence upon his contemporaries. More important still they were read and re-

read by later generations of Germans and played an important part in the moulding of subsequent political thought. In fact it may be said that in present-day Nazi Germany, Fichte exerts a greater influence than ever before.

FICHTE'S GENERAL PHILOSOPHY

Fichte was a thoroughgoing idealist in metaphysics, in ethics, and in politics. He violently objected to the classical English school of philosophy which sought to solve the problems of metaphysics by experience and observation, and the problems of ethics on the basis of self-interest and the pursuit of happiness. To his mind all such philosophizing was characteristic of a corrupt and degenerate age and needed to be remedied by a truer and purer system of philosophy.

Truth, according to Fichte, could only be ascertained by the use of reason and of "intellectual intuition." Theoretically, to be sure, Fichte laid great emphasis upon sensation or experience, but to him sensation is caused not by the working of the external world upon our organs of sense but by the spontaneous operation of our minds. All that sense experience can teach us therefore is to give an insight into the working of our minds, and once we have secured this insight the collection and observation of sense data have no further value. Reason, on the other hand, is to be regarded as the true source of all of our knowledge. The world of sense is but the creation of our minds, but as our minds are essentially rational, subject to the laws of reason, it follows that by the use of reason we can penetrate behind the illusions of sense impressions and grasp ultimate reality. To Fichte, the only knowledge which can be called true knowledge is that based upon pure *a priori* reasoning, completely independent of all sense experience. This statement holds true not only for the realm of metaphysics but also for the realms of ethics and politics.

Even Fichte admitted, however, that abstract reason has its limitations. Abstract reason can work out a complete logical system of the universe provided it starts with a few fundamental postulates or axioms. But these fundamental postulates or axioms can never be proved rationally — they must be perceived directly, by means of spiritual insight, or intellectual intuition.

> We cannot grasp the living reality by the discursive understanding and its spatial temporal causal ways; only when we (through an act of intellectual intuition) have seen through the nature of ordinary knowing, its superficiality

and relativity, can we grasp the living reality behind the surface, freedom, the moral world order, and God.[1]

This intuitional, more or less mystical background is a very important phase in Fichte's philosophy. It is this feature which distinguished Fichte from most of the rationalists of the eighteenth century and which endeared him to the new romantic movement in literature and politics. This intuitionalism was also all-important in Fichte's practical philosophy. His ideas on ethics, on jurisprudence, on politics, were all based upon the theory of the free moral will, and as Fichte himself admitted, the very existence of the free moral will is proved not by reason but by intuition. Once deny the validity of intuition, and Fichte's whole theory of the state falls to the ground.

In the realm of metaphysics Fichte, as we have seen, spent most of the time transforming the critical agnosticism of Kant into dogmatic idealism. According to Kant the world as we see it is partly the result of the real external world — the thing-in-itself — acting upon our senses, and partly the result of the creative activity of our own minds. As he developed his system Kant came to lay ever greater emphasis upon the part played by the mind in creating our sense impressions. Not only are colors, smells, tastes, subjective rather than objective, but even such things as space, time, and causal relationships are only ways in which our minds look at things rather than attributes of the real external world. When we come to analyze the world of appearance, the world as it *seems* to us is, if we follow Kant, ninety-nine per cent subjective, the creation of our own minds, and only one per cent objective, the result of the operation of external forces. Because of this fact Kant claimed that we can never know the true nature of the external world, and hence was agnostic.

To Fichte it seemed that the logical conclusion of Kant's analysis of the sensations would be to take away the one per cent objective element and make the subjective element one hundred per cent. If the creative activity of the mind by itself produces our notions of space, time, and causality; if the mind is the real cause of most of our sensations, such as color, sound, taste, and smell, what grounds have we for supposing that there really is an external objective world conditioning some of our other sensations? Surely the creative activity of the mind is sufficient to account for *all* our sensations. To prove his point Fichte argued that Kant's interpretation of sensation was itself contradictory. Kant claimed that objective reality was to some measure the *cause* of our sensations; yet in a later passage Kant also admitted that all causality

was only subjective, a product or category of the mind; hence the objective world causing our sensations must be false. The only true and
consistent explanation of our world of experience is that it is entirely
created by the mind.

The basis of Fichte's philosophy is the mind, or, as he prefers to call it,
the *I* or ego or self. If the cause of our sensations were some mysterious
thing-in-itself, we could never know anything about the true nature of
the universe, but as the cause of our sensations is mind, which is the only
reality, and this mind, being rational, follows a rational pattern, or
spontaneously obeys the laws of reason, it follows that we can by reason
solve all the problems of the universe. Through reason (and intuition)
we can know the nature of the creative self and hence can know the
nature of the creative world of sense impressions — which Fichte calls
the not-self.

Once we accept the idea that the external world, the not-self, is the
product of the spontaneous creative activity of the self, we at once ask,
Why does the self thus create the external world? To this Fichte
answered that the self can only become fully aware of itself by a process
of self-limitation — the limitation being the external world. In like
manner for the self, which is an active moral agent to realize its end, it
must set up an outer non-moral world. For the moral life means striving, activity, and this would be impossible if the self were infinite and
unlimited. By creating the outer world the self creates for itself a foil
by which it may become conscious of itself and a field for moral endeavor
in which the self by struggle may realize its own inherent freedom and
goodness.

By speaking of the mind as the self, Fichte would appear to be a complete individualist, but this is far from being the case. All men possess
selves, but in reality all these selves are but part of one Great Self, the
Universal Self, or Universal Mind or Reason.

> There is but one Life... one animating power, one living reason. That
> reason is the only possible independent and self-sustaining Existence and
> Life, of which all that seems to us to exist and live is but a modification,
> definition, variety, form.... It is the greatest error... that each individual
> imagines that he can exist, live, think, act for himself... whereas in truth he
> is but a single ray of the one universal and necessary thought.... It is only
> ... by earthly and finite perception that this one homogeneous life of
> reason is broken up and divided into separate individual persons.[2]

To Fichte the Universal Absolute Self is identical with God. God is
thus the one absolute life, the absolute unity, who can, however, only

become fully conscious of himself by self-limitation in the form of individual selves. Life, or God, becomes conscious of itself in individual forms and as an individual. In like manner man's individual will is only a manifestation of the one divine will. Fichte is thus an idealist in supposing that the external world is the creation of the mind, but he is also a realist in supposing that ultimate reality lies outside our individual selves.

It is not surprising, considering this theoretical background, to find that morality and the problems of morality played an all-important role in Fichte's philosophy. Just as Fichte's metaphysics was only a development of the ideas latent in Kant's *Critique of Pure Reason*, so was his ethics only a development of the ideas expressed in Kant's *Critique of Practical Reason*. To Fichte, as to Kant, ethics must be thoroughly idealistic and transcendental in character. He rejected with scorn the notion that a true system of morality can be based upon the principle of self-interest (in the narrower sense of that word) or of happiness, even the greatest happiness of the greatest number. In fact Fichte felt that no feeling, no emotion could be made the basis of a real ethical system. Ethics, to be true, must be founded upon the postulates of reason. In like manner it must be absolute, not relative in character. It cannot be based upon individual experience or collective custom and tradition. The moral code could not be based in any way upon the conventions or the accidents of time and place. It must be universal, eternal, known by *a priori* rationalization.

As with Kant, Fichte felt that the basis of all morality must be man's *free moral will*. With Fichte, as with Kant, the true essence of each man is his will, but whereas with Kant the will of each man is separate and distinct, with Fichte the individual is only one ray, one facet of the universal will, the will of God; for which reason it is obvious that the will is and always must be good, however corrupt the individual passions and desires may be. Freedom of the will, therefore, means the freeing of the will from the thralldom of the senses and from all sensual entanglements. To use other words, freedom means (1) the liberation of the individual from his own baser self, his purely natural instincts and promptings — internal freedom; and (2) the liberation of the individual from the arbitrary interference of others, the removal of all those obstacles which beset the realization of internal or moral freedom from without — external freedom.

It is very important to bear in mind this definition of freedom, for it has very significant consequences not only upon Fichte's moral theories

but also upon his political theories.   Fichte was always talking about
freedom and how it was the chief function of the state to secure the freedom of the individual, and we Americans, with our Anglo-Saxon traditions, are apt to think that by liberty he meant what we mean — freedom from external governmental control and the ability of each man to
choose whatever line of action he pleases as long as he does not interfere
with the actions of other persons (corresponding to Fichte's notion of
external freedom).   Fichte would have revolted against limiting freedom
merely to external freedom.   To do as one pleases, to his way of thinking, might well mean being a slave to the senses.   He became convinced
that in many cases it is the duty of our neighbors and the state to *compel
us to be free*, to compel us, against our wishes, to follow a certain course of
action on the ground that our wishes and our conduct are contrary to
the universal divine will and hence to our own true will.

In Fichte's philosophy the chief function of the state is "to set forth
the outward conditions under which moral freedom is to be achieved." [3]
In order to carry out this function the state may forcibly remove all the
external objects and institutions which tend to make men slaves to their
senses.   In addition the state can and should, through compulsory education, seek to transform the character and dispositions of its citizens.
Fichte contrasted his theory of education with the older systems of
education.   The older educators asked: "What more should one expect
from any education than that it should point out what is right to the
pupil and exhort him earnestly to it?   Whether he wishes to follow such
exhortation is his own affair, and if he does not, his own fault; he has
free will which no education can take away from him."

To Fichte, on the other hand,

> if you wish to influence him [the pupil] at all you must do more than merely
> talk to him, you must fashion him and fashion him in such a way that he
> simply cannot will otherwise than you wish him to will. . . . The recognition
> of and reliance upon "free" will in the pupil is the first mistake of the old
> system, and the clear confession of its impotence and futility.   By confessing
> that . . . the will still remains "free," i.e. hesitating, undecided between good
> and evil, it confesses that it neither is able nor wishes to . . . fashion the
> will. . . . On the other hand, the new system of education must consist es-
> sentially in this that essentially destroys the freedom of the will . . . and pro-
> duces on the contrary strict necessity in the decisions of the will. . . . Such a
> will can henceforth be relied upon with confidence and certainty. [4]

The strange part about all this is that to Fichte the will only becomes
really free when its freedom in the ordinary sense has been destroyed.
Distinct from but closely associated with the realm of ethics is the

realm of jurisprudence, centering around *Recht*, that curious German word which means both right, and rights, and law — meaning in this case what the old liberal thinkers called natural rights and natural laws. In his earlier writings, for example, the *Foundations of Natural Law*, Fichte stressed the difference between ethics with its code of moral obligation and jurisprudence with its codes of legal rights and legal obligations. Ethics, to Fichte, deals with what you *must* do; jurisprudence with what you *may* and *may not* do. Ethics holds good for a man whether living as an isolated individual or in a state of society; jurisprudence is only for men in a state of society. Ethics deals with motives, jurisprudence with acts. In his later writings, for example, the *Theory of the State*, Fichte emphasized the close association between the two sciences. Internal moral freedom can only arise in an external world regulated by law. Law, on the other hand, has for its chief end the setting up of conditions wherein man may achieve moral freedom. Hence law itself is an essentially moral principle.[5]

In his earlier writings Fichte sometimes spoke of absolute ideal law (the true study of philosophical jurisprudence) as *natural* law. At other times (under the influence of Rousseau) law was considered to be the product of the social contract, and therefore man-made. In the *Theory of the State*, the latest and most consistent of his political writings, both these ideas were rejected. Nature, to Fichte, was a product of the mind, and at the same time a limitation of the free activity of the mind and of the will. Man must seek to escape as far as possible from purely natural laws, the laws of external nature; hence to call the laws regulating how man should live "natural" laws was almost blasphemous.[6] In like manner, Fichte in his early days was a devout advocate of the principle of the social contract and felt, during this period, that the true basis of actual law should be the expression of the general will, the wishes of the united people. In later life Fichte radically changed his opinions in this regard. Man's true nature, his real will, might be divine, but the actual man with all his selfish passions and desires was a rather nasty animal and to derive true law from the united wishes and desires of such animals was a degrading thought.[7]

True law, like the moral code, must be derived from the dictates of pure reason — true law must be something which a man discovers, not something which he makes; it must be universal, eternal, *a priori* in character, not something upon which men agree merely as a matter of caprice. The thinker, the philosopher, will be able to understand the nature of true law immediately if he but use his reason, yet it may well be that at any given time and place true law may be contrary to the wishes and understanding of the vast majority of the population.   In like manner, the true rights of man, the rights which each man ought to have, are not necessarily those which he had in a state of nature, nor those which he received from any human compact, but the rights which pure reason postulates that he should have.

True law (the basis of all rights) is thus one and eternal, true for all times and places; but Fichte soon admitted that the embodiment of this true law in the world of sense in actual states is a matter of slow, gradual development.   In times past, when men were still in a state of barbarism, it was possible for them to gain only a faint and distant glimpse of the true nature of law; hence the legal institutions of those days had only a faint correspondence with true law.   In modern times, along with the other benefits of civilization, our legal concepts have improved, and come closer to reflecting the spirit of true law; but these concepts, at least as seen in the laws of actual states, are still far from perfect. In fact in the present state of mankind it would be impossible to apply true law in all its purity.   The philosophical reformer must merely seek to bring about a slow but ever increasing realization of the ideal.[8]

Actual law to Fichte, therefore (and this is a very important point), is and must be not static but dynamic and evolutionary, not something fixed once and for all, but a matter of slow growth towards a distant ideal.   Previous thinkers either regarded law as the command of a sovereign at some one place and time, or else had regarded law as the dictates of reason (*jus naturale*), but a reason which dictated its commands once and for all, and whose dictates could be applied at any period in the life of any community.   Fichte, on the other hand, though stressing the eternity, the universality, and the rationality of the ultimate ideal of law, felt that actual law must be an organic growth embodying to an ever greater degree the abstract principles of right.   Actual law, being thus an organic growth, should also, in Fichte's opinion, be *national* in character.   All spiritual activity must be expressed in a national form.   Each nation has its own language, its own traditions, its own past and its own future.   For this reason each nation must have its own national legal traditions.[9]   In expressing these views Fichte was unconsciously laying the foundations for Hegel's concept of law and for the historical school of jurisprudence which was to play such an important part in later legal and political thought.

But though law was to be derived from the dictates of reason and was to be regarded as the spontaneous and "free" expression of the soul or spirit of each community, Fichte was adamant in insisting that law must also contain a large element of compulsion or force.

> The establishment of compulsory law does not interfere with the freedom of men, for what is thereby taken away from men is not their freedom as moral beings or as members of a community, in which senses alone men may be said to be free or have a right to freedom.[10]

In fact, in the Fichtean philosophy, not only *may* a man be "free" when subject to compulsory law, but it is only when a man *is* subject to such law that he can really be "free."

Just as Fichte distinguishes between rational jurisprudence, a study of the law as it should be, and actual jurisprudence, the study of the law as it is actually applied, so does he likewise distinguish between rational politics, a study of the rational state, the state as it should be, and practical politics, a study of such states as exist in actuality. Actual jurisprudence should always bear in mind what abstract reason tells us the law should be; in like manner practical politicians should always bear in mind in governing states, or in preparing constitutions for states, what abstract reason or philosophy tells us that the true or rational state should be.

Actual states naturally differ in their power and functions and in the machinery of government which has been established to carry out their necessary functions, but Fichte believed that all these actual states might be judged and found good or bad by a rational standard, by the picture of the ideal or rational state to be deduced by abstract reasoning. In this workaday world no actual states are perfect, nor would it be possible or advisable to establish the rational state among mankind all at once. Nevertheless it is possible, at least for the philosophers, to construct the outlines of a perfect constitution, both as regards the functions of the state and the machinery of government. Once this construction has been made we should strive as rapidly as possible to transform the actual constitution to fit the ideal model.

Theoretically the realization of the rational or ideal state should come about through the spontaneous action and desire of the population, but Fichte was not above using force to achieve his ends, because of the ignorance and waywardness of actual mankind.

> Everyone who has both insight and power has not only the right but the sacred duty to compel mankind to adopt the rightful form of government. It may so happen that a single man may thus compel all mankind, for against him and what is right they have no rights and no freedom. ... Such a man might be considered a divinely appointed dictator.[11]

After this general survey of Fichte's philosophy we may turn to a more detailed consideration of one or two features of his social and political theory.   Of especial importance and significance was his *Philosophy of History*.   This philosophy of history was a development and an expansion of the old theory of Divine Providence combined with Kant's theory of the eternal progress of mankind from lower to higher forms of social and political organization.   What, however, is especially noteworthy about Fichte's philosophy of history is that it led directly to Hegel's historic determinism and indirectly to Karl Marx's theory of economic determinism.

Most of the old theologians argued that all human activities are controlled by Divine Providence — nothing happens by chance, all historic events are foreknown and foreordained by God.   Kant added the doctrine of progress, the idea that by the mysterious actions of Providence bad gradually gives way to good, lower forms to higher forms; that even those things which appear to be evil are but necessary stages in the slow, sure development of that which is good.   Fichte took this idea and tried to translate it into abstract and metaphysical language.

According to Fichte the whole universe is in a state of evolution.   The Universal Self or God, in order to become fully conscious of Himself, limits Himself by creating a large number of individual selves.   The individual selves, in order to be fully aware of themselves and their own moral perfectibility, limit themselves by creating the not-self, the illusory world of sense.   The individual self will eventually triumph over the illusory outer world and be completely moral and free.   The Universal Self will eventually be completely and perfectly reflected in all individual selves.   But Fichte felt sure not only that this ultimate goal will be achieved but also that the Universal Self and the individual selves must go through certain necessary logical stages before this achievement can be carried out.   Each person, without exception, must pass through the stages of babyhood, childhood, adolescence before he can become an adult.   Looking at any person we can tell how many stages he has behind and how many stages he has ahead of him.   In like manner the soul of man has to pass through certain necessary stages, and not merely the soul of man, but the outward expression of men's souls, the social and political life of humanity.   A man perfectly acquainted with the soul of man and the necessary stages of its unfolding could tell by examining men's souls today through what stages they have passed in former times and through what stages they still have to pass in the future.

Fichte set himself to accomplish this task and thought that he had thereby founded a new science — the philosophy of history. History was to be no longer the purposeless accumulation of isolated facts re garding human events at various times and places. Ordinary history is merely the study of what did happen in times past; philosophical history regards the events of the past merely as an expression of the dominant ideas which characterize the souls of mankind at different periods. Now these ideas of mankind develop logically and consistently out of man's inner consciousness. The philosopher who knows the nature of man also knows at what stage in human development each of these ideas will dominate the soul of mankind. As a result the philosophical historian, unlike the ordinary historian who relies merely upon experience, not only can give a rational interpretation of man's past but also can paint a clear picture of what ideas will dominate mankind in the future and thus foretell, at least in broad outlines, future history.

In Fichte's system no event, certainly no major historic event, ever happens by chance. For all his talk about freedom Fichte believed that man is bound by an inner necessity. All major historic events are merely the outward expression of the inner idea which necessarily develops at a certain stage in the evolution of the human soul. When we think that we are accomplishing some important historical act of our own will and accord, we are unconsciously being driven by inner necessity to carry out the spirit or the idea which dominates the age in which we live. Fichte was a great hero worshiper and also a great worshiper of the scholars and philosophers who have moulded and transformed the actions and the thoughts of man. But Fichte thought that even these heroes and scholars were, consciously or unconsciously, only the agents through which the world order or Providence, to use more theological language, worked out its scheme for human development.

Fichte's idea of the philosophy of history, his notion of historic determinism, his doctrine that true history is not the accumulation of ascertained facts but the logical and rational study of certain abstract principles, had an enormous influence upon later European thought. His particular view of the world plan and the five stages into which he divided the carrying out of this world plan — the five principal epochs in human history — had far less influence upon later speculation and hence need not detain us long. Nevertheless because of the light these details throw upon Fichte's political views, they are worthy of brief mention.

The world plan, to use Fichtean language, was the development of mankind from unconscious unity with the Absolute, through the break-up of this unity to the final conscious unity with the Absolute. This development falls into the following five great epochs: 1. The epoch in which man is governed by unconscious reason or instinct — the era of man's innocence. 2. The epoch in which external compulsive authority is substituted for instinct — the era of progressive sinfulness. 3. The epoch in which men revolt from external authority and become thoroughgoing individualists — the era of complete sinfulness. 4. The epoch of the increasing understanding of the rules of reason and voluntary submission to these rules — the era of progressive righteousness. 5. The epoch of conscious reason in which man has complete moral freedom and shapes all his actions in accordance with rational principles — the era of complete righteousness.

The first and the last of these epochs call for no special comment. They are both mythological. The first is the relic of a belief in the golden age in the dim and distant past, a belief incorporated in the story of the Garden of Eden. At this time man, being guided by blind instinct, needed no formal laws or political organization. The fifth and last epoch is a pious hope, corresponding to the Christian idea of the millennium. Man will be governed so completely not by instinct but by reason and the moral law that formal laws and political organization will again become unnecessary. In this connection it is interesting to note that Fichte and Karl Marx, two of the strongest advocates of state supremacy in actual politics, should both express the hope that state organization should eventually become unnecessary.

Far more interesting are Fichte's notions regarding the second, the third, and the fourth epochs. The second and third periods lay in man's historic past. Fichte felt that he himself lived at the end of the third period and at the beginning of the fourth period. Fichte being Fichte, his description of what life would be like in this epoch is really a picture of what he wished life to be like. The second epoch is the period usually known as ancient history. Man loses his unconscious reason or instinct and has not yet acquired conscious reason. Hence he is dominated by his passions and soon quarrels with his neighbors. Man is both culturally and socially a barbarian. To keep him in order it is necessary to establish strong compulsive authority, fixed rules of what to do and what not to do, and force him to follow these rules. In the sphere of religion it is the period of rigid dogmas which a man believes whether he understands them or not. In the realm of politics it is the period of the all-powerful state dominating and crushing individual activities and of despots ruling without check or hindrance over the mass of people.

In his younger days Fichte accepted the idea that the state originated as the result of a social contract.   In his more mature political philosophy Fichte completely rejected this notion.   In his later works all states are thought to have originated in force in the conquest of one people by another.   Fichte believed that from a very early period there was a marked inequality between the various races and peoples who inhabited the face of the earth.   He believed that at the beginning of time there was a superior race who dwelt somewhere in Central Asia. This people, being more rational than its neighbors, soon discovered the use of metals while the others were still living in the Stone Age.   As a result of its intellectual and technical advancement this superior race soon conquered the surrounding regions, enslaved the inhabitants, and formed great despotic empires such as Assyria, Media, and Persia.

In Europe the formation of states took place in a slightly different manner.   The superior race of Central Asia did not invade and conquer the European region — they were too busy in Asia to do that.   But small groups of this race, led by outstanding heroes, did come from Asia and colonize various parts of Europe.   As the result of their superiority over the savages among whom they settled, these colonists gradually "attracted the savages around them and gathered them into tribes; by their means erected towns and in these held them together; introduced more humane manners and established customs which gradually assumed the character of laws, and thus imperceptibly became their rulers." [12]   In Europe the members of the superior race were the leaders of the people rather than the conquerors of the people.   As a result the early states in Europe were not as dictatorial or despotic as those in Asia.   Nevertheless even these European states emphasized the supremacy of the state over the individual, the supremacy of the king and the aristocracy (descendants of the superior race) over the common herd.   To retain their supremacy the kings claimed to be descended from the Gods or claimed to rule by divine right.   The aristocrats, too, claimed that their station in life was due to Divine Providence.

The third great era in human history is characterized by the revolt of the individual against the external authorities placed over him in the second era.   The early workings of the rational impulse within him make man inquire into and finally reject the religious dogmas in which he had been taught to believe blindly. This same rational impulse make him rebel against the yoke of the omnipotent state in an attempt to express his own personality. It makes him reject the doctrine that he should render abject obedience to the commands of the absolute monarch. It makes him reject the idea that an hereditary aristocracy should always possess special rights and privileges. The first stirrings of this rational impulse is to be seen in ancient Greece with the revolt of the Athenians against despotic and oligarchic rule. Its further progress is evidenced in Rome with the overthrow of the monarchy by the patricians and then the constant struggle of the plebeians against the patricians. But the full working of this rational impulse is best to be found in modern times (eighteenth and nineteenth centuries), in the apostles of enlightenment preaching against dogmatic religion, with the advocates of liberalism preaching the sacred rights of the individual against the state, with the French revolutionaries, who not only preached but also acted against the king and the hereditary aristocracy.

Fichte thought that this third era was a great improvement over the second era, that the deliberate rejection of external authority was better than blind submission to it. Nevertheless he insisted that the ideas characteristic of this third age had been fraught with appalling consequences — in fact had brought about the "complete sinfulness" of mankind in his own generation. The rational impulse which led to the overthrow of authority was more impulsive than rational; it was the first stirrings of conscious reason rather than conscious reason itself. As a result man builds up for himself a completely false picture of the world and of himself. In his revolt against dogma he accepts only the facts of experience and hence becomes an empiricist, a materialist. Rejecting all the traditional moral codes, he thinks that goodness and happiness are identical and pursues pleasure as the only end in life. Rejecting all external control, his individualism becomes selfish individualism — each man for himself and the devil take the hindmost. Any system of government based upon such notions is bound to be disastrous. A blind mob composed of atheistic, pleasure-seeking, utterly selfish individuals can never build a rational state based upon the principles of eternal right.

The fourth great era in human history, the era in which mankind becomes clearly conscious of reason and has scientific understanding of its laws, is characterized by the reconstruction of all social and political institutions upon a purely rational basis. Fichte believed that this new era dawned in his own lifetime, somewhere between the years 1806 and

1809, and that he, Fichte himself, was the great prophet of the new dispensation. This new era would combine the individual freedom aimed at in the third era with the law and order aimed at in the second era. Man would no longer have blind faith in traditional unintelligent dogmas nor yet relapse into skeptical empiricism, but would have an intelligent faith in the doctrines of rational philosophy (Fichte's own philosophy). Morality would be based not upon a code supposedly handed down by Moses on Mount Sinai, nor yet upon selfish desire for pleasure, but upon the dictates of the free moral will. Man would no longer be the slave of the despotic state nor yet be content with anarchic individualism, but would find satisfaction and freedom in a rational or "absolute" state. Government in this state would not be in the hands of hereditary kings and noblemen nor yet rest with a blind, turbulent democracy, but be confided to heroes and scholars.

All this sounds very well, but when we analyze the details of Fichte's new scheme of things we find that in practice the rationalism of the fourth era does not differ greatly from the despotism of the second. The doctrines of Fichte's system of philosophy and of his system of ethics are just as rigid and unbending as those of the old theological systems. Any who disagreed with these doctrines, such as the great English thinkers, were immediately dismissed as being irrational. The state of the new era, Fichte's ideal state, was to be founded upon "freedom" and "equality," but the freedom he postulated was the freedom, not to do as one liked, but the freedom to do as one ought to do. The equality he postulated was largely a theoretical equality. All men, to be sure, are to be possessed of equal civil rights — but this equality is not to interfere with separate classes in society, nor does it mean political equality for all. In fact, in Fichte's ideal system of government the vast majority of the population possess absolutely no political privileges, government resting in the hands of a small specially appointed (not elected) minority. One is almost tempted to say that Fichte ostentatiously kicked despotism out the front door only to allow it to creep back in through the side entrance, but it would be truer and fairer to say that Fichte rejected not only Jeffersonian democracy but also the old dynastic state of the Habsburgs and the Hohenzollerns in favor of a new national authoritarian state — a foreshadowing of the states created by Mussolini and Hitler.[13]

THE ETATISM OF FICHTE

When one comes to analyze in detail Fichte's ideas regarding the power and function of the state one is more than ever impressed with the vast difference between the young Fichte, the Fichte of the eighteenth century, and the older Fichte, the Fichte of the nineteenth century.   The young Fichte was such an ardent individualist that his doctrine came close to philosophic anarchism.   In his two earlier works *Demand to the Princes for the Return of the Freedom of Thought* and *Correction of Some Views on the French Revolution*, this individualist phase of Fichte found vehement expression.   At this time Fichte believed in the origin of the state by social contract, and he followed Locke rather than Rousseau in teaching that man possessed certain natural and inalienable rights which were not and could not be given up to the state even after the social contract came into operation.   The only right which he gave up to the state, and thence by delegation of power to the government, was the right to punish crime.   Hence the only true function which the state could be said to have was the police function.   Property rights were prior to and independent of the state, but it was the duty of the state to protect these already existing rights — and almost its only duty.   It was *not* the function of the state to make men happy, virtuous, wealthy, or wise; such things must be left to the free and voluntary activities of the individual.   Every man must have complete freedom of thought and of speech.   It was no part of the function of the state to foster any religion or compel attendance at any church.   Church and state must be completely separated and religious belief and church membership kept entirely voluntary.   Even education lay outside the realm of the state and should be left in the hands of the private family.   There were to be no government-operated or government-controlled schools.

All these ideas were merely inherited by Fichte from some of the older liberal thinkers, but on one point Fichte went even further than his liberal predecessors.   The older liberals agreed that the people had the right, by revolution if necessary, to overthrow any existing government which acted in a way contrary to their wishes.   With this idea Fichte was in full accord.   But most of the old liberals were hesitant in claiming that a man had the right to withdraw from the state.   The social contract was made irrevocable.   Locke, to be sure, taught that before a man had assumed any civic duties or responsibilities he ~culd withdraw from the state, but only if he left the state's territory

when he did so. Fichte was more logical and more consistent in carrying
out the implications of the social contract in this regard — even though
his conclusions led to what appeared to be appalling results.   To him
the social contract, a voluntary compact between free individuals, could
be renounced at any time, irrespective of whether a man had or had not
assumed any civic obligations.   If a man does not approve of the state
and its laws, he may renounce his citizenship and revert to complete
liberty of action without being forced to change his residence.   Or if he
chooses he may make a new contract with others for the creation of a
new state.   If this new group remains within the physical borders of the
old state, there is created a state within a state or two states occupying
the same territory. Fichte was in no way shocked by this possibility
and pointed out that during the Middle Ages there were a number of
independent or semi-independent states within states such as the community of the Jews, the church, the military orders, and the orders of
nobility.[14]

This extreme individualism of Fichte's youth was gradually modified
with the passing of the years.   The first step in Fichte's progress towards etatism was to emphasize the importance, not of the state but of
society, and the necessity of subordinating the individual to the social
group.   In other words, Fichte gradually transformed his love for
humanity from humanity considered as a group of individuals to humanity considered as an organic whole.   As early as 1794 in his lectures,
The Vocation of the Scholar, Fichte revolted against the idea, so dear to
Rousseau, that man in a state of nature is better mentally, morally,
and physically than when he is a member of a large well-organized and
civilized community.[15]   Fichte had little use for a state of nature.   He
regarded primitive social organization as barbaric and savage, a condition which must be overcome as soon as possible.   He gloried in the fact
that he was a European, a member of the most cultured and most highly
integrated society in the world, and he looked forward to the time when
European social organization (purged of its many shortcomings) would
spread over the face of the earth.

Belief in the value of society and social institutions became ever
firmer with Fichte in the years which followed.   In his *Foundations of
Natural Law* he asserted that a man was fully a man only when he lived
with and among other men, that only in this condition can man develop
the latent potentialities for good within him.   The very concept of man
is wrapped up in the idea of the human species — man as an isolated
animal is completely unthinkable.[16]   Even morality (and Fichte was

always worked up over moral problems) was impossible or at least an empty and formal concept unless man freely associates with his fellow man, and mankind be regarded as a single whole, not merely as a group of scattered individuals.   As the years went by, Fichte's views on this subject became more extreme.   In his *Characteristics of the Present Age* he completely subordinated the individual to the welfare of the human species.

> It is the greatest error, and the real basis of all other errors ... when an individual imagines that he can exist, live, think, and act for himself. ... When one regards things truly and as they really are, the individual does not exist — he is worth nothing and must and should sink to nothing.   The species [or human race], on the other hand, really exists, and it alone should be regarded as the truly existent. ... Rational life consists in each person forgetting himself in the species, tying his own life up with the life of the whole, and sacrificing himself for the sake of the whole.   Irrational life, on the other hand, consists in each person thinking only of himself, loving only himself and in relation to himself, and spending his entire existence seeking his own personal welfare.[17]

With this increasing emphasis upon society rather than upon the individual it is only natural that Fichte's attitude toward the state underwent a slow but far-reaching transformation.   No longer was the state regarded with suspicion and dislike, as a necessary evil which could not be avoided.   Social life without some kind of political organization was unthinkable — the state, therefore, was a necessary and useful adjunct, enabling society to function smoothly and with a minimum of conflict. The state, therefore, came to be regarded as something inherently good. Nevertheless all through this, the middle part of Fichte's life, the state was regarded as a means to an end and not as an end in itself.   The end to be considered was mankind as a whole — the human species rather than any one political or national organization.   All states and all governments were good in so far as they fostered human welfare; they were bad if they looked only after their own selfish interests without regard to humanity as a whole.

Being thus converted from individualism to cosmopolitanism and internationalism, it is not surprising to find that Fichte took up and expanded some of the ideas enunciated in Kant's little pamphlet *On Perpetual Peace*.   Considering the large number of national and geographic units in the world, it is only natural that there should be a large number of political units.   It is quite right that this should be so, for the idea of a single empire embracing all mankind is no longer feasible.   At the same time it is a great misfortune that all these various states should frequently be at war with one another. Though war is sometimes useful and occasionally necessary, it is a great handicap to the progress of mankind as a whole and should be abolished. War can be abolished through the establishment of a world court and a league of nations.

Fichte's plan for these two institutions as outlined in his *Foundations of Natural Law* [18] shows remarkable similarity to the world court and the league of nations established more than a century after his work was written. In Fichte's scheme secret diplomacy was abolished. All treaties between states must be registered with the league of nations. Any disputes between nations must be referred to the world court, and its decisions must be binding on both parties. Should any nation fail to carry out its treaty obligations or decisions of the world court, or should it commit aggression against another nation, military sanctions must be applied. It will not be necessary for the league of nations to have a standing army of its own, for whenever sanctions become necessary the various member states must raise and equip armies to be used by the league for punishing the treaty-breaking or aggressor nations.

As time went by, Fichte gradually substituted nationalism for internationalism as his highest ideal. He never completely or formally abandoned his idea that mankind must be considered as a whole or that the highest purpose in life is the advancement of the human race, but in his later years Fichte felt that human beings can best serve mankind, not by a vague cosmopolitanism, but by complete and absolute devotion to the nation-state of which they happen to be members. Abstract cosmopolitanism — love of mankind in general — was considered "lazy" and "cold," therefore "vain," "useless," "absurd." Love of mankind must be particularized, made concrete by devotion to the country in which one is born. Mankind can best be served by serving one's own nation.

Associated with this idea was the notion, which became more and more dominant in Fichte's later thought, that the peoples of different nations differ radically from one another in their natural capacities. Not only were certain races superior, other races inferior, but even among the superior races, such as the peoples of Europe, there were many far-reaching, fundamental differences. Each nation possessed its own national character. The Germans, for example, showed a greater interest in and aptitude for philosophy than any other European people. Mankind could best be served, not by abolishing or ignoring these differences, but by letting each nation develop, to an even greater extent than at present, its own special capacity, its own special national

culture.   To reduce all mankind to a single uniform level, to force a
single culture pattern upon all the peoples of Europe, would be both
ridiculous and wicked.   Each nation has its own destiny, its own
"vocation," and each man can best serve mankind by aiding his own
nation to fulfill the "vocation" which Providence allotted to it.[19]

As a result of this line of reasoning Fichte came to the conclusion that
the nation as embodied in the national state must in practice be the
supreme object of man's devotion.   The state, at least the true state,
is not merely a legal or juristic organization, a group of individuals
bound together by the bonds of external law.   The state is and must be
a living whole, the concrete expression of the dynamic spirit of the
nation.   To illustrate this point Fichte compared the state to a living
organism, a metaphor very popular with later etatist philosophers.
The state is not like a heap of sand, to any single grain of which it would
be perfectly indifferent if the other grains were torn from it or trodden
under foot.   The state is like a tree, all parts of which are intimately
related.   The tree can exist without some of its leaves and branches,
but no leaf or branch can continue to live once it has been cut away from
the tree.   Serious injury to the tree as a whole automatically brings
injury to the leaves and branches.[20]

> In the same way, it is only as a member of the state that man attains a
> definite place in the series of living things, a resting point in nature.... In
> all organic bodies each part constantly contributes something to the main-
> tenance of the whole and thereby contributes to its own maintenance.   The
> relation between the citizen and the state is very similar.[21]

This concept, first formulated when Fichte still leaned towards cosmopolitanism, assumed even deeper meaning when he turned from
cosmopolitanism to nationalism.

With Fichte's gradual acceptance of nationalism as the supreme
motivating force in human behavior, his notions regarding the power
and the function of the state were radically transformed.   In his younger
days Fichte held that the chief function of the state was to protect the
rights which the individual possessed even prior to the formation of the
state.   In his later days he argued that all the rights which an individual possesses are derived from the state, it being the duty of the state
to grant to the individual those rights which he ought to possess for his
own best interests and for the community as a whole.   Among the
rights which the individual receives from the state are property rights.
"It is the function of the state to *give* to each man for the first time his

own, to *install* him for the first time in his property, and then to protect his possession of it." [22]

But the state must have even greater and more positive functions than these. It must also look after the physical and economic welfare of its citizens, "it must strive to quicken industry, to improve agriculture, to encourage inventions in the mechanical arts and in the natural sciences." [23] But the state is not merely an economic organization interested in the material well-being of its citizens. It is also the promoter of the higher things of life, the promoter of culture or civilization as opposed to barbarism. The state must, therefore, actively promote progress in the fine arts, and by the fine arts Fichte meant not merely painting and sculpture but also the drama, literature, and music.[24]

In the middle part of Fichte's life, when he willingly admitted that it was the function of the state to look after the material and the cultural interests of its citizens, he still felt that certain matters, such as morality, religion, pure science, and philosophy, lay outside the realm of state control, as they were essentially voluntary and international in character. In the last few years of his life even these were subjected to state domination — the state, in this instance, acting in the role of the national educator, moulding national morality and national intelligence through a rigorous state-controlled system of education. In his early days, it will be remembered, Fichte believed that education should be voluntary and entirely in the hands of the family, but after 1806 he was an ardent apostle of the opposite view that education should be compulsory and entirely in the hands of state-appointed officials. As far as possible children should not even be permitted to reside at home. In order that their character and intellects might be better and more completely moulded, they should reside in government-operated boarding schools.

Abstract morality might be based upon pure reason, but concrete morality was considered to be largely a matter of habits and customs, and habits and customs could be made to conform to rational principles by intensive training, that is, by education, and it is the function of the state to see that this is done. Pure science or pure philosophy could only be approached by the individual reason, but the state, by compulsory education, could compel men to use their reason and could force the minds of all youthful citizens to occupy themselves with certain necessary studies. If, therefore, the Germans had a certain proclivity to philosophy, the German state could and should force its citizens to develop their potential capacities along these lines. Incidentally it should be noted that Fichte, in the interests of truth and morality, was quite willing for the state to teach its pupils a number of things which can only be called lies. Education "should represent to each individual all the others as animated by a love of order exalted to the Ideal, which perhaps no one person really has, but which all ought to have." [25] "The tender age of man shall be maintained in simplicity and in quiet faith in his race. Let the knowledge of its knavery remain reserved for personal experience in mature and stronger years." [26]

On the question of religion Fichte was forced to proceed more cautiously. Though a deeply pious man, Fichte to the end of his days remained somewhat heretical in his theological opinions and the church authorities of his time regarded him with deep suspicion. But though he thus felt it necessary to speak cautiously about religious problems, he insisted that education to "true" religion was the final task of his proposed national system of education.[27] In one of the pamphlets of his later years Fichte also outlined his hopes for the eventual establishment of a truly national church. This national church, in Germany, was to take the place of the old Lutheran, Calvinist, and Catholic churches. This church was to teach belief in God and immortality, but most of its activities were essentially nationalistic in character. The church was to give special honor to those who died for the fatherland or who gave wise counsel to the state. At special services the local magistrate was to appear before the congregation and solemnly unfurl the national flag. By the side of the great altar were to be placed cannons and muskets, symbols of the determination of the people to maintain their national integrity by force of arms, if necessary. The sermons of the minister were to be directed chiefly towards making the church members good citizens. Nationalism in religion could scarcely go further.[28]

By his ardent and eloquent preaching of nationalism and the all-powerful state Fichte won a permanent place in the history of political thought. Scarcely less important was the fact that he postulated three conditions for smooth functioning of the national state and these three conditions have been favorite subjects of political discussion ever since. The first was that a national state must be based upon unity of language among its citizens. The second was that nationalism in the political sphere cannot function smoothly without nationalism in the economic sphere — the basic principle of economic nationalism. The third condition was that inside its own borders the state must assume far-reaching control over all the economic activities of its citizens.

The first condition — that language must be made the basis of political geography — was destined to be one of the most influential doctrines ever enunciated in political theory. The earlier political philosophers, both of the etatist and the liberal tradition, had thought of the state as a purely political and juristic entity. The national state in the modern sense of the word arose at the time and largely in consequence of the Reformation. But at this time and for nearly two centuries thereafter the meaning of the word "nation" as a community of persons speaking the same language was never thought of. Some theorists argued that the king should have absolute control over the people, others that the people should have absolute control over the king, but both groups thought of "the people" as the broad mass of the populace irrespective of whether it belonged to one or to several races or spoke one or several languages. Not once during the sixteenth, seventeenth, and eighteenth centuries did any political thinker of the first rank claim that political boundaries should coincide with linguistic boundaries.

Prior to the French Revolution and to Fichte it seemed normal and natural that the French king should rule over persons, some of whom spoke French, others a Celtic language as in Brittany, others German as in Lorraine. The Habsburgs might or might not be considered tyrants, but no one thought them tyrants merely because they, German-speaking rulers, controlled the destinies of persons of Slavic, Italian, and Hungarian speech. Even in the early days of the French Revolution the principle that states should be erected on the basis of linguistic unity was never thought of. When the French armies invaded Germany or Italy, they awakened little or no *national* hatred. Some of the conquered populace welcomed the French soldiers as the heralds of liberty; others disliked them as the heralds of mob rule or anarchy — but the fact that they spoke another language did not make them *ipso facto* enemies. Many of the German princes were perfectly willing to ally themselves with Napoleon against the Habsburgs and the Hohenzollerns and did not in the least feel that they were thereby betraying their "nation."

During the latter part of the Napoleonic era there was a revulsion of feeling in this regard. The inhabitants of all the petty states into which Germany was then divided experienced a common sense of shame and humiliation at being conquered by an alien monarch and by alien soldiers. It was felt that all the petty governments should unite in a close alliance and drive out the common enemy. One of the outstanding leaders of the new Pan-German movement was Fichte. He wished to sweep away the petty dynastic states and to unite the German-speaking peoples into a single great empire. Only thus could the German people be free, only thus could the all-important German culture survive. With this end in view he composed his *Addresses to the German Nation*, which from that day to this has been one of the chief stimulants to German nationalism.

Having argued that all German-speaking persons should unite to form one state, Fichte by logical necessity was forced to argue that other persons speaking a common language be united in one state. All persons speaking the same language formed part, whether consciously or unconsciously, of a single *Volk*, people or nation. The chief end of the state was to be the concrete embodiment of the nation. Hence the state was not a mere legal or political organization, ruling over persons of various linguistic backgrounds, but the living, forceful expression of the will and aspirations of a single homogeneous people. A nation not incorporated into a state was weak and impotent; a state not based on a nation is cold, abstract, lifeless. It was only in the creation and preservation of nation-states that man could carry out his spiritual destiny.

Some of the later etatists, especially the German etatists, claimed that the all-important factor in human affairs is not language but race — by race meaning, of course, the body structure of the various peoples of the earth. It is whether a man is a blond or a brunette, whether he has a long or a round head, whether a man has an aquiline or a flat nose, which counts, not whether he speaks French, or German, or Turkish. This idea was not unknown to Fichte, but he vigorously denied its validity. Fichte pointed out that, certainly as regards Europe, there was no such thing as racial purity; that the European peoples were formed by the blending of all sorts of racial strains, and that it was impossible to identify race and nationality or make race the basis of political boundaries. In France, in Italy, even in Spain there was a strong Germanic racial element (we should now say a strong Nordic element), but this was not sufficient to make them feel themselves German or make them wish to unite with the Germans. In Germany, on the other hand, there were many persons whose distant ancestors were Slavs (we should now say many persons of Alpine and other non-Nordic racial stock), yet, if they spoke German and considered German to be their mother language, they must be considered members of the German "nation." [29]

One exception, and one exception only, did Fichte make in identifying language and nationality.   In view of present-day developments, this exception is of great interest.   Fichte thoroughly disliked Jews, even those Jews who had been domiciled in Germany for centuries and whose mother language was German.   Jews, he declared, were not and never could be Germans in the full sense of the word.   He demanded that all civil and political rights in the German state be refused them.   If possible all Jews were to be deported from Germany and settled in Palestine, their original and proper home.   Fichte's hatred of the Jews was almost equal to that of the Nazis, Fichte's spiritual descendants. He would have great admiration, he claimed, for any Jew who had any sense of justice, humanity, or truth — but he doubted if there was or ever had been such a person.   The only way to make them worthy of citizenship was to cut off their heads and supply them with new heads which did not contain a single Jewish idea.[30]

But apart from the Jews, Fichte insisted that language was the all-important factor in determining human destinies.   Not only was race relatively unimportant, but even climate (contrary to Montesquieu) had very little influence in moulding human character.   Language, on the other hand, was neither accidental nor unimportant.   Language is the most fundamental expression of the soul of a people, revealing its true character.   Language not only reveals, it *creates* the national character.   Fichte's ideas on language and its political importance were destined to have far-reaching influence in the century following his death. The Greek, the Polish, the German, and the Italian national movements of the nineteenth century were all merely attempts to carry out in the realm of actual politics the linguistic-political philosophy first given clear expression in Fichte's writings.   His idea that political boundaries should coincide with linguistic boundaries continues to be a powerful weapon even in the twentieth century.   It is in accordance with this doctrine that Hitler justified his forcible annexation of Austria and the Sudeten areas in Czechoslovakia.   It is in accord with this doctrine that the Italian patriots of today demand the annexation of Corsica, Nice, and the other Italian-speaking areas of France.

Fichte's notions on the importance of language were so successful that the majority of semi-educated Europeans (and Americans) today go even further than Fichte himself went.   Fichte was careful to distinguish between race and language, even though he thought that language was more important than race.   The modern Europeans, on the other hand, unless specially educated in such matters, are apt to confuse race and language, and using language as the all-important factor, classify races upon a purely linguistic basis. There are frequent references to the "Latin race," the "Celtic race," the "Anglo-Saxon race," the "Slavic race." The scientist knows, of course, that there is no such thing as a Latin race or a Celtic race — but only peoples (of different racial stocks) who speak Latin or Celtic languages. But in politics it is not science but public opinion which causes votes to be cast and wars to be made. Fichteanism has triumphed to an even greater extent than Fichte himself would have imagined possible.

The second of Fichte's three conditions for the successful working of the national state was, as we have seen, economic nationalism. The fact that Fichte should have preached economic nationalism at the very beginning of the nineteenth century (his principal work on the subject, the *Closed Commercial State*, being published in 1800) is especially interesting because during the nineteenth century his views on the subject were very unpopular and it was not until the twentieth century that economic nationalism became the dominant factor in international relations. During the nineteenth century most political and economic philosophers (especially those of the liberal school) preached nationalism in the political sphere but internationalism in the economic. To their minds it was right and just that England, Greece, Portugal, Italy should be separate political units, each with its own separate and completely independent government, but it was wrong and unjust for these countries to form hard-and-fast economic units cut off from free and easy commercial and industrial intercourse with the rest of the civilized world. The vast majority of political philosophers during this period believed that there should be a general policy of low tariffs, "tariff for revenue only," or, better still, free trade for all the countries of the world. For any nation to prohibit the free import and export of goods, or to place artificial barriers in the way of international trade, such as special quotas or special taxation upon imported goods, was considered contrary to sound political and economic ideas.

Fichte was violently opposed to this whole philosophy. To him the whole idea of economic internationalism was a relic of the Middle Ages. In the Middle Ages there was a good deal of internationalism in politics. All persons felt themselves part of a single Christian community at the head of which stood the pope. Even in the purely political field the doctrine of national sovereignty was never developed. There was a graduated hierarchy of temporal officials with the emperor at the top.

It was only natural, therefore, that with this political internationalism, economic internationalism should have developed at least as an ideal after which men strived, however imperfectly carried out in real life. In modern times, however, where the old international Christendom has given way to national churches and national states, economic internationalism is completely out of place.

Fichte gave many arguments in favor of his plan for economic nationalism. One favorite argument was that the national state could not possibly hope to survive permanently even as a political unit unless it is more or less self-sufficient economically and not dependent upon foreign trade for its existence. If one nation depends for its manufactured goods upon another nation, it will tend to become politically dependent upon this other nation. In the long run economic domination results in political domination. Moreover, if one nation is dependent upon foreign nations for its raw materials or for its foodstuffs, it becomes very vulnerable in times of war, as the cutting off of these supplies by blockade or otherwise will bring such a nation to its knees. An economically self-sufficient nation, on the other hand, does not fear a blockade and hence is always better prepared to defend its independence.

Fichte, in fact, thought that international trade under modern conditions made for international discord and sowed the seeds of war. Foreseeing the rise of economic imperialism, he asserted that the constant and ever increasing struggle between nations for sources of raw materials and for markets for their surplus goods was the real though hidden cause of much of the political hatred between nations. Eliminate economic imperialism, abolish the struggle for outside sources of raw materials and for markets for surplus goods, and the whole international situation is cleared up. There is no longer any occasion for war. International trade instead of bringing peoples together makes them potential and frequently active enemies. Last but not least, freedom of international trade makes it impossible for the national state to improve the economic status of its own citizens. The flooding of the market by foreign goods may cause the collapse of local industries and the sudden but permanent impoverishment of thousands of citizens. In cases where one nation has a much higher standard of living than another, the "dumping" (as we should now say) of cheaply made goods from one nation upon another may destroy the high standard of living in the former country and reduce the workers to the economic level prevailing in the country with the low standard of living.

Under the weight of these arguments Fichte proceeds to argue for the most complete system of economic nationalism that the world has yet seen. Except for rare and special exceptions all trade between the various nations of the world was to be prohibited, and what little foreign trade was needed should not be left in the hands of private merchants but be handled as a government monopoly — an arrangement similar to that now in force in Russia. In line with this economic nationalism Fichte was violently opposed to the maintenance of an international standard of exchange such as gold. Each nation should possess its own type of currency, intrinsically worthless, and possessing purchasing power only within the limits of the issuing state. This idea is also interesting in view of the gradual abandonment by most nations of the gold standard in favor of an artificial paper currency and the limitation in several European countries of the free import and export of such currency. In such cases Fichte's dream of a national — and intrinsically worthless — currency has been realized. In Fichte's scheme not only was international trade to be prohibited but even international travel was strongly discouraged. Ordinary persons were not to be permitted to journey from country to country, traveling privileges being granted only to specially qualified persons, scholars and the like, duly authorized by the government.

Fichte was perfectly aware that his scheme for economic nationalism was possible only if each state was or could be made economically self-sufficient. Each nation should have enough agricultural land, land suitable for pasturage, forested land, and if possible enough coal and iron mines, etc., to enable it to live on its own resources without having to import either raw or manufactured products. Fichte was convinced that certain parts of the earth's surface were obviously destined by nature to form economically self-sufficient units and hence should be destined by man to form fixed political units. He argued that each state should possess what he called *natural* boundaries enclosing an area large enough and varied enough to support the economic activities of its citizens without recourse to the outside world.[31] Fichte was aware that in his own time political boundaries did not always coincide with natural boundaries. Especially was this true of the petty German states, many of which were too small to serve as self-sufficient units. To Fichte this fact presented no serious obstacle to his theory. Such small states were to be abolished, or rather incorporated in a great German Empire which was to be large enough and varied enough to be self-contained. Going from the particular to the universal, Fichte de-

clared that every state was justified in enlarging itself, by force and war
if necessary, until its political boundaries *did* coincide with natural
boundaries.[*]

For all his philosophical insight Fichte did not perceive that his views
on this subject were full of logical inconsistencies. To his way of thinking natural frontiers were eternal and once the political frontiers had
been altered to conform with these natural frontiers, they should never
be changed. He did not see that the growth of population in one
natural region or the decrease of population in another such region
might bring about conditions where the "natural" frontiers of one
generation might be the unnatural frontiers of another. In like manner
the growth of industry within each country might well produce an insatiable demand for certain new raw materials hitherto little used and
considered of small importance. The development of such a demand
might well make nations revise their ideas as to what constituted their
natural frontiers. Fichte's scheme whereby each state should seize its
natural boundaries by force, instead of resulting in eternal peace, would
probably result in new wars in each generation.

Far more serious was the inconsistency between Fichte's demand
that "national," that is, linguistic frontiers, be identical with political
frontiers and his demand that natural or economic frontiers be identical
with political frontiers. Theoretically at least it is perfectly possible
to fulfill either demand, but it is impossible to fulfill both demands at
the same time. One of the tragedies of history is that linguistic and
economic boundaries seldom have coincided. The middle Danubian
basin (the old kingdom of Hungary) formed a well-marked economic
area and seemed "destined by nature" to be included within a single
political unit. But there were and are several language groups within
this area, and on the basis of language we saw (in 1919) the northern
part cut off and given to Czechoslovakia, the eastern part given to
Rumania, the southern part given to Yugoslavia. The new reduced
state of Hungary had no natural frontiers, and with nothing except
purely agricultural land was no longer economically self-sufficient. The
conflict between linguistic and economic boundaries became even more
apparent in 1938 in the dispute over the Sudetenland. Prior to 1938
the Czech part of Czechoslovakia formed a perfect economic unit with a
well-marked natural frontier, though within this frontier was a fringe
of non-Czechish German-speaking persons. By ceding this German-
speaking area to Germany the linguistic frontier has been rectified, but
only by violating the natural geographic frontier and reducing Czecho-

slovakia to a position where it is no longer a self-sufficient economic area

But though Fichte's views on this matter were logically inconsistent, they were nevertheless vastly important, for they were shared by most of the national states which grew up during the nineteenth and twentieth centuries. During this period most states demanded that all their nationals — all persons speaking the same language — be included within their own borders. At the same time each endeavored to increase its territory so as to include within the area subject to its control all regions which would give it a natural frontier in the Fichtean sense of the word. Whenever it suited its purpose in gaining territory from a neighboring state, each state stressed the question of language and the linguistic frontier; but at other times and for equally serviceable purposes, the same state could and would ignore the alien minorities within its own area and insist that the area inhabited by these minorities be retained within the fatherland because of economic and geographic reasons. Logical inconsistency was not confined to the writings of the German professor of philosophy.

The third condition laid down by Fichte for the successful functioning of the national state was quite as important as the other two. This condition, it will be remembered, was that each state must assume far-reaching control over all the economic activities of its citizens. It was on this point that Fichte broke most radically with the *laissez-faire* doctrines of the old liberal thinkers and of his own youthful days. The old liberals thought that the sole function of the state was to protect the property rights which the individual possessed prior to and independent of the state. In this scheme the state had no right to dictate how an individual used his property. A man's property was *his*, in absolute possession, and the individual could do with it as he saw fit. Fichte, at least in his later years, had a very different idea regarding property rights. Legal ownership to property was derived from and granted by the state. Moreover, the state in granting property rights to individuals granted only the right of exclusive use of the property in question, not the outright and absolute ownership of this property. Even in granting the exclusive use of certain property to an individual and his heirs, this grant was made conditional. A man was granted exclusive rights to a piece of property only if he used it in a certain way; if he failed to use it well or according to the conditions laid down by the state, the property he had been granted could be taken away from him. The ownership of property, therefore, implies certain obligations as well as

certain rights and it is the function of the state to say what these obligations are and also to see that they are properly carried out. Thus, for
example, if a man allows his farmland to run completely wild, or otherwise misuses it, the state has the right to confiscate it — by taxation or
otherwise. To use a more modern illustration, if a man allows his land
to become a breeding ground for malarial mosquitoes, if he allows his
house to become the hiding place for infected rats, if he permits his cows
to contract tuberculosis, he cannot claim immunity from state control
on the ground that he has a right to do as he pleases with his own, for
he has not carried out his obligations as a property-owner and the state
can force him to make amends under threat of confiscation. Following this argument to its logical conclusion, it immediately becomes obvious that all property becomes subject to state control.[33]

This theory, important as it was, received even further and even more
far-reaching developments. Fichte was convinced that in a properly
organized state every man has a right to *live*, not only in the old Lockian
sense that the state must forestall and punish all attempts against his
life, but also in the sense that every man has a right to make a living,
and it is the duty of each state to see to it that conditions are such that
every man can make a living. To the old liberals, such as Locke, it
would have been a great calamity if a large number of citizens should die
of starvation, but it was not the duty of the state to feed these citizens —
such matters should be left to private charity. The state should step
in only if one of these unfortunate persons should steal from a member of
the propertied class — and then only to punish the offender. To
Fichte, on the other hand, the state owed to each of its citizens a living,
or at least the opportunity of making a living, provided always, of course,
that the citizen was willing to work.[34] The state was under no obligation to support idlers, but every industrious person should be insured
not only existence, but also a comfortable existence.

Carrying out this line of thought, Fichte believed that in cases of
sudden emergencies the state must grant direct subsidies or "doles" to
its citizens threatened with dire want, but he was convinced that such
subsidies would not be necessary except as temporary expediencies in
really well-regulated states. But he was equally convinced that for
each man to secure a living it was necessary for the state to assume rigid
control over the economic activities of all its citizens. Fichte started
with the basic assumption that there were enough natural resources in
each state to provide a livelihood for each citizen provided that no one
was permitted to take more than his fair share, and provided also that

the state saw to it that its economic machinery functioned smoothly Fichte has often been called the father of socialism. This is certainly not true if by socialism we mean modern state socialism — the belief that the state should own and operate all the sources of production and distribution. Fichte was a great believer in private ownership and private operation, but he wanted *all* persons to be private owners and private operators to a certain extent, and he felt that this condition could only be secured if the state maintained rigid control over all owners and operators.

Some of the ideas set forth in the *Closed Commercial State* as to the best methods the state should employ to carry out its control over private industry remind us strikingly of the methods which are now being used in such states as Germany and Italy. In Fichte's scheme the state should limit the number of persons who may enter any given profession.[35] If there are too many doctors and lawyers, some doctors and lawyers may find it difficult to make a living. To prevent such a situation Fichte would limit the number of persons who are permitted to practice either profession. This limitation holds good not only for the higher professions but also for all walks of life. The broad mass of the population, according to Fichte, are divided into three main groups: first, the producers including farmers, miners, fishers, etc.; second, the artisans and industrialists who take the raw products provided by the producers and manufacture them into finished goods; third, the merchants of all sorts who distribute the goods furnished by the producers and artisans. Fichte declared that each of these three classes and each division of these three classes should be limited to a number fixed by the state in the interests of the whole community. Though Fichte was rather vague upon the subject he strongly implied that the government should also regulate the conditions under which each man did his work. Curiously enough, Fichte made no actual mention of such matters as minimum wages and maximum hours of labor, nor the need for government control of sanitary conditions in factories, but undoubtedly he would have sympathized very strongly with governmental regulation of such matters because of his basic principle that the state owed each man not only a living but also a comfortable living.

Furthermore, the state, in Fichte's scheme, is to control the total amount of production of each basic commodity.[36] If too much wheat is grown the price falls and the farmer suffers. If too little wheat is grown the price rises and the consumer suffers. The same condition holds for all agricultural products and manufactured goods. The state, therefore, has the duty of trying to regulate the supply of each product so as to meet the natural and normal demand. For every article there should be a fairly definite quota fixed by the government, a quota which may not be exceeded under penalty of the law. If too much wheat is grown farmers may be required to grow other crops or turn part of their land into pasturage or woodland. Fichte hoped in this way to abolish the cycle of booms and depressions and guarantee a more or less permanent prosperity. He realized that certain practical difficulties lay in the way of carrying out his scheme in its entirety. In all farming communities, for example, there are good and bad years, dependent upon the weather. Fichte tried to overcome this difficulty by formulating a standardized average year. Credits were to be granted by the state to regions suffering in any one year, but these credits had to be repaid in good years. Government granaries always had to keep a supply of foodstuffs to be used in cases of famine.

Finally it was the duty of the state, according to Fichte, to regulate and stabilize all prices.[37] Cut-throat competition in prices might ruin a whole industry. Price-cutting by sweatshop manufactures might well bring ruin to workers in more legitimate establishments. On the other hand, where a small group of industrialists has almost exclusive control over the manufacture of a certain article, this group may demand outrageously high prices for its goods and the consuming public would thereby suffer great hardship. To obviate such conditions Fichte declared that the state must set the maximum and the minimum prices which were to be paid for all articles whether raw products or manufactured goods. Incidentally these prices were not merely to be fixed; they were also to be stabilized by the government. Under *laissez faire* the prices paid for all goods — the general cost of living — varies enormously from year to year and even from month to month. Moreover, even within this general price scale the cost of certain things becomes relatively greater than that of others. Fichte disliked this fluctuation and thought that it worked hardship upon the community. As far as possible both the general and the relative prices of articles was to be made permanent. To Fichte this task did not seem insuperable. With the total amount of production rigidly under control, the supply and demand for each article would always remain more or less the same, thus doing away with the chief factor in price fluctuations. Moreover, the money in Fichte's national state was not to be gold and silver, the value of which, in terms of foodstuffs, varied from time to time. Fichte's national currency, though actually only so much paper or leather, was really based upon the value of a bushel of grain and all other prices were to be stated and measured by this standard. What Fichte really was after was what we should now call "the commodity dollar," whereby a fixed amount of money would always buy a fixed amount of foodstuffs and other commodities. To keep the value of this national currency constant, Fichte was forced to give the state control over the credit structure of the community, but needless to say, he found no difficulty in taking this added step.

THE AUTHORITARIANISM OF FICHTE

Turning now from the nature and function of the state to the nature and proper organization of the governmental machinery within the state, it is interesting to follow the various stages through which Fichte progressed from belief in radical democracy to insistence upon complete authoritarianism in governmental matters.

In Fichte's early writings, especially in such works as *Correction of Some Views on the French Revolution*, he supported most of the democratic views enunciated by the French revolutionary writers. Fichte made no attempt in these works to outline a model constitution, or to give a systematic account of how much or how little power should be granted to the various organs of government. But during this period he was always insistent that ultimate political power must be derived from and be exercised for the benefit of the people. Governments originated by a transfer of power from the people, and this transfer is not irrevocable. Governments must always rest upon the consent of the governed. Revolution may sometimes, perhaps generally, be unwise, but there can be no doubt that the people have the *right* to change the form of their government, by force if necessary.[38] He was certain that sooner or later despotism must be destroyed. Even at this period, Fichte never argued in favor of complete democracy — the direct rule of the people over themselves. Having torn down the existing despotism the people will probably have again to delegate their power to some new government. Nevertheless he hoped that in this new government greater rights might be reserved for the people. On the whole the people can be trusted, and through experience they will learn to govern well.[39]

Writing as he did in 1793, when the French revolutionaries were fighting against absolute monarchy rather than for a republic, Fichte did not discuss the relative merits of republican and monarchic forms of government. He seemed to take it for granted that states will naturally and normally be governed by kings, but absolute monarchy or despotism (the two were synonymous to Fichte) must be rejected at all costs Fichte had little use for king-worship. "It is indecent for thinking men to crawl at the foot of a throne to beg permission to become the foot-stools of kings." [40] Rebellion against tyrannous monarchs might indeed result, temporarily at least, in anarchy and confusion, but surely this condition was no worse than life under absolute irresponsible despots. [41]

Fichte was even more bitter in his attack upon the powers and privileges granted the hereditary nobility. The only nobility whose existence can be rationally justified is a nobility of mind, of merit, of talent. But surely no one could claim that the existing European nobility represented an aristocracy of talent. The low intellectual and moral caliber of this group is apparent to every observer. In point of fact the present-day nobility has many privileges with no corresponding duties or services. It is therefore advisable that the present-day nobility be completely abolished, or if that be impossible that their privileges be radically limited. [42]

A few years later (during his professorship at Jena) Fichte departed somewhat from the radical democracy of his youth, but he was still far from being a thoroughgoing authoritarian. His views on governmental machinery at this time were incorporated in his *Foundations of Natural Law*. His theory at this period can best be described as advocating limited and indirect democracy with a strong hint that an hereditary monarchy with certain democratic and constitutional checks was the best form of government. In this work the state is still thought to originate logically, even if not historically, in the social contract, with the result that the general will of the people is regarded as the supreme political sovereign. All governmental bodies derive their authority from the general will or the people as a whole. These governmental bodies must be ultimately responsible to the people for their actions. If their actions become too tyrannical or too unjust, the people have the right to abolish these bodies and establish others to take their place. The right of revolution is, therefore, a sacred and natural right. But Fichte hoped that it would be possible for the people to establish a permanent check upon their government which would obviate the need for armed rebellion. This check was the creation of an institution, known as the ephorate, or the college of ephors.

The functions of the ephors were to correspond in large measure to those of the ephors in ancient Sparta, and more closely still to those of the tribunes during the Roman Republic. In the early days of the

Roman Republic, it will be remembered, all the highest officers of state, such as the consuls, the praetors, the senators, were chosen by and from among the patricians, the common people, the plebeians, having no right to such posts. But lest these patrician officials rule over the people unjustly, the plebeians were allowed to elect a certain number of tribunes (usually ten). These tribunes had no positive functions, either executive, judicial, or legislative, but they had the important negative function that they could veto the act of any of the higher officers of state. Fichte's ephors were to have the same function. They were to be chosen from among the oldest and wisest members of the population. They were to be elected for a limited period of years by the population as a whole, presumably by manhood suffrage. The ephors in Fichte's scheme were to be completely separate from and independent of other governmental organs. They might not be related nor even have close social intercourse with the members of the government proper, lest they be corrupted. Their sole function was to keep a close scrutiny upon the acts of the government, and should the government become tyrannical the ephors could place an "interdict" upon it, thereby suspending the heads of the government from their offices and placing a temporary veto upon all their acts. After such an interdict the people were to be called together, each town and village convoking an assembly of its own populace. These assemblies were to decide whether the ephors or the government should be given a vote of confidence. In other words, the government was to be impeached before a tribunal of the people, and if the people should find the impeachment justified the members of the government would automatically lose their positions and in addition be forced to go into lifelong exile.[43]

This sounds very democratic and entirely in keeping with the radicalism of Fichte's earlier years. But there is another side to the picture. The people in Fichte's scheme were to have the negative right of deposing unjust governors — or, to use modern language, the right of referendum and recall — but they were to have no positive rights. Neither the people nor their elected representatives, the ephors, were to exercise any of the ordinary functions of government. In fact, while Fichte insisted that the populace had the right to tear down bad governments, he claimed that for a people to rule directly over themselves was the worst tyranny of all. If the people ruled directly over themselves there would be no higher power before whom the people could be held responsible — and irresponsible government is bad. An irresponsible democracy is just as bad as an irresponsible monarchy. In a pure democracy one would always have to fear "the blind fury of an excited mob."[44] To prevent the tyranny of the mob it is not only advisable but also necessary that ordinary governmental functions be transferred or delegated to a smaller body of men, with whom the people as a whole have no direct contact.

Unlike the ephors, who were to hold office only for a limited period, the members of the government should hold office for life (unless they be impeached for tyranny).[45] In order to avoid partiality the members of the government should avoid entangling friendships, obligations, or associations with private persons.[46] In other words, the members of the government should keep themselves aloof from ordinary social intercourse with the populace. Fichte was a great believer in the centralization of power. Local and subordinate officials were to be appointed, not by the local population, but by the members of the supreme governing body, for this body is responsible for the welfare of the whole nation and cannot carry out its functions effectively unless all subordinate agents be entirely subject to its control.[47] Montesquieu had argued in favor of the separation of powers, claiming that the functions of government should be divided among an executive body, a judicial body, and a legislative body, and that these three bodies should be absolutely equal so that each could serve as a check upon the other. Fichte violently disagreed with this notion. He followed Rousseau in declaring that no distinction could be made between the executive and the judicial functions. In the lower ranks of the administrative hierarchy some persons might be granted executive, others judicial duties, but the supreme government must be given complete jurisdiction over both functions. Rousseau, however, still distinguished between the executive-judicial functions on the one hand and legislative function on the other, and declared that all legislative power must be reserved to the people. With this Fichte disagreed. Fundamental constitutional laws, determining the form of government the state should have, might be made by the people, but ordinary legislation was placed entirely outside the popular control. Fichte disliked representative government, the placing of law-making powers in an elective parliament, and declared that normal legislative functions should be carried out in the form of decree-making by the executive-judicial body or "government."[48] Fichte's "government," therefore, was an all powerful, more or less dictatorial body having complete control over the machinery and functions of the state, and was held in check only by the threat of an interdict on the part of the ephors.

How was this government to be constituted?

Fichte admitted that it was possible to place the governing powers in the hands either of one person or of several persons, and that many arguments might be advanced for both methods of procedure. If sovereign power be placed in the hands of one person, the government was called a monarchy, irrespective of the title given the ruler and irrespective of the method by which he came to power. If, on the other hand, rulership be entrusted to several persons, the state was called a republic, irrespective of how this governing body came to be chosen. Fichte refused to say that at all times and places a monarchy was better than a republic, or vice versa. But it is obvious that Fichte himself preferred a monarchic form of government. A republic, group government, was said to be more dilatory, less efficient than the rulership of a single person. Moreover, in group rule each person would always try to thrust responsibility on the shoulders of his colleagues. It was, therefore, more difficult to hold a republican government responsible for its actions. Where rulership was placed in the hands of a single person, on the other hand, though more mistakes might be made, the government was more efficient, and as the responsibility rests on his shoulders alone, he is apt to act with more circumspection. "A monarchic government has more strength and life." [49]

It next becomes necessary to decide how the governing body (whether consisting of one or of several persons) should be chosen. Fichte pointed out that the government might be *elected*, either by the population as a whole or by a small privileged section of the population; or the government might be *appointed*, that is, in the case of a group, the existing members might select additional members when necessary (a self-perpetuating board). In the case of a monarchy the heir or successor could be selected by the person in power. Finally the governor or the governing body might be *hereditary*. According to Fichte there are powerful arguments for all three methods of selection, yet curiously enough, in spite of his democratic leanings, Fichte decided that government by hereditary rulers was best. In the case of election there are apt to be bitter feelings between majority and minority groups, leading to permanent civil dissension. In the case of appointment there is apt to be much undesirable wire-pulling and political juggling. Where the choice of the ruler is on an hereditary basis it is easier for all parties to feel loyalty to the government and there is less room for scheming and crafty manipulation.

Moreover, there are other advantages in hereditary rulership which make its establishment advisable, such as the fact that the ruler is entirely cut off from the people and from birth to death has no private association with them.[50]

Fichte, the radical democrat, thus comes to the conclusion that the rulership of one is better than the rulership of many, and that rulership by right of birth is better than that by right of appointment or election. The defender of the French Revolution becomes the advocate of hereditary monarchy, of a kingship unfettered by an independent judiciary or by an independent legislative body, a monarchy held in check only by fear of a popular uprising (led by the ephors) in case it becomes too tyrannical.

In the second period Fichte still believed in the right of the people to curb and control its government. Not only had they the right to revolt, but through the ephors they had the right to stop, by legal means, the normal functioning of the governing body. In his last period, Fichte decided that it was necessary to do away with democratic control. He decided that the establishment of the ephorate would be useless and meaningless and he even went so far as to throw doubts on the rightfulness of revolution. The reason for this change in political opinions was in large measure the transformation of Fichte's attitude with regard to the goodness and intelligence of the average man, the "man in the street." In his youth Fichte had looked upon the common man as essentially good, and as intelligent even if not intellectual. In his later years he became thoroughly disillusioned regarding human nature. Man's true nature is no doubt divine. Potentially he is capable of mental and moral perfection, but in actual life all government and political thinking must rest upon the assumption "that all men are vicious and that without exception they will give expression to their viciousness as soon as they find certain opportunity for it." [51]

If common people taken individually are vicious unless controlled by the strong arm of the law and of government, little confidence can be placed in the wisdom and honesty of the mob, the people as a whole. Government should be based upon the eternal abstract *a priori* principles of right and justice. To identify abstract right and justice with the capricious wishes of an ignorant mob is ridiculous. "One can trust a select group of wise men far more than a majority which was constituted God knows how." [52] "As long as there are more evil than good men, one can be certain that it is not the proposals of the wise and of the good which will be accepted by the majority, but rather the proposals of the unwise." [53] Though the theoretical right of the people to rebel against a tyrannical government cannot be denied, one must not forget that in practice a popular revolution instead of abolishing evils generally leads to still greater evils. [54]

The ephorate is also expressly abandoned. Fichte sadly came to the conclusion that the ephorate, though a good idea, was not workable for several different reasons. In the first place there was the purely practical consideration that a government in order to be efficient had to be all powerful, and an all-powerful government would never permit itself to be crippled by a group of ephors which had no organized or armed force at its command. Even more important was the fact that the silly emotional mob, instead of electing the best and the wisest men to be ephors, would probably choose self-seeking rabble-rousers as their representatives. Such men, being self-seeking, might well be bribed by the government to acquiesce in all manner of injustice. In case such ephors did fall out with the government and bring about the overthrow of the latter, how could one be certain that the ephors would only overthrow a bad government? Might they not, with their own interests in view, overthrow a good government, one really devoted to righteousness and justice? [55]

Fichte was led by these considerations to abandon all semblances of democracy in his political system, and to deny to the people any right, in practice, to curb or check their government. The government, which in the second period was to be all-powerful, now became for practical purposes irresponsible as well, the only check upon its actions being "enlightened public opinion." But in coming to this opinion Fichte also changed his views regarding hereditary monarchy. As long as the people had a check upon the actions of the government, government might well rest in the hands of an hereditary king, but with this check removed the danger of tyranny and despotism once more became very real. To think that genius, talent, or righteousness is hereditary is ridiculous.[56] A wise and just monarch might well be succeeded on the throne by an idiot or a criminal if kingship automatically goes from father to son. Fichte even in this stage of his life was far from being a fanatical "republican" — in actual makeshift states it might well be that acceptance of the hereditary principle is advisable, but in a rational state (and all states should seek to become rational as soon as possible) it is imperative that the best and the wisest should rule,[57] irrespective of their parentage.

Fichte felt that the real progress of mankind had been brought about, not by the blind workings of the mob nor by the actions of hereditary despots, but by the creative genius of heroes and scholars, and that in an ideal state these heroes and scholars should be entrusted with the functions of government. "The civilized must rule and the uncivilized obey, if right is to be the law of this world." [58]

Who has united rude races together and reduced opposing tribes under the dominion of the law to the habits of peaceful life? Who has maintained them in this condition and protected existing states from dissolution through internal disorder or destruction by outward power? Whatever name they may have borne, it was Heroes who left their age far behind them, giants among surrounding men in material and spiritual power. They subdued to their idea of what *ought to be* races by whom they were on that account hated and feared.[59]

In times past heroes worked blindly and unconsciously, prompted by the inner workings of the Divine Spirit. In modern times, according to Fichte, the true heroes are the scholars who have seen through the sham of things, have realized the true nature of reality and the true nature and vocation of man. These scholars, like the heroes of old, devote themselves to the service of ideas and ideals, and force other men to become civilized, to become "free" (in the Fichtean sense of the word) even against their wishes. These scholars should be not merely the teachers of mankind; they should also be the rulers of mankind.[60] The mass of scholars, however, cannot rule the state directly. They must appoint one of their number, the wisest and the greatest of them all, to be a sort of supreme dictator in all governmental matters. This supreme dictator can and should use force to compel men to live in accordance with eternal right, the nature of which right he understands better than anyone else. He can and should use force to compel men to be "free," to give up the shackles of their wishes and desires and follow the dictates of their true moral will. In case the broad mass of humanity is unaware of what the true dictates of their own moral wills may be, the dictator will be kind enough to tell them.

Now in this sorry world of ours, where the bad far outnumber the good, can the rulership of the wise and the supreme rulership of the wisest be brought about? Fichte, like Carlyle, was a little vague on this subject, but he felt that sooner or later the hand of God, the working of Providence, would bring this about. "Sooner or later a man will arise who is both the ruler of his country and the most just of his countrymen. Such a man will certainly find a way to establish the succession of the best."[61]

A hundred years and more have elapsed since Fichte died. Today due partly at least to his influence many of the dreams which he dreamed — many of his wildest and most fantastic dreams — have become true. Germany is no longer a vast mass of petty principalities, which he hated, but a huge centralized national state, including within its borders most

German-speaking persons.　Germany was the first country in Europe to go in for a policy of economic nationalism (for which Fichte pleaded) and today, more than ever, it is Germany which tries to be completely self-sustaining.　The strict control over the economic activity of its citizens, so strongly advocated by Fichte, and which seemed absurd to his contemporaries, has been carried out by the Nazi government. Finally, the Nazi government has rejected the democratic rulership which Fichte detested and hereditary monarchy which (in his later days) he despised in favor of rulership by a group who consider themselves the most heroic and the wisest of their countrymen (whatever the rest of the world may think of them).　This select group of self-appointed heroes has delegated its power to a supreme dictator who does not hesitate to follow Fichte's advice and compel men to seek righteousness and "freedom" in accordance with the pattern of righteousness and freedom which he himself has laid down.

NOTES TO CHAPTER SIX

1. Thilly, *History of Philosophy*, p. 438.　By permission of Henry Holt and Company.
2. J. G. Fichte, *Characteristics of the Present Age*, pp. 21, 22.
3. Fichte, *Die Staatslehre*, p. 390.
4. Fichte, *Addresses to the German Nation*, pp. 20, 21.　By permission of the Open Court Publishing Company.
5. Fichte, *Die Staatslehre*, p. 432.
6. *Ibid.*, p. 364.
7. *Ibid.*, p. 436.
8. *Ibid.*, p. 393.
9. *Ibid.*, pp. 412 ff.
10. *Ibid.*, p. 433.　　　　　　　　　　11. *Ibid.*, p. 436.
12. Fichte, *Characteristics of the Present Age*, p. 185.
13. Fichte's philosophy of history and its application to politics is to be found in his *Grundzüge des Gegenwartigen Zeitalters*, and in a later and slightly modified form in his *Staatslehre* (pp. 460 ff.).
14. Fichte, *Beiträge*, pp. 149–154.
15. Fichte, *Bestimmung des Gelehrten*, pp. 335 ff.
16. Fichte, *Grundlage des Naturrechtes*, p. 39.
17. Fichte, *Grundzüge des Gegenwartigen Zeitalters*, pp. 23, 35, 38.　See *Characteristics of the Present Age*, pp. 21, 36, 33.
18. Fichte, *Grundlage des Naturrechtes*, pp. 379 ff.
19. Fichte, *Reden an die deutsche Nation*, pp. 311 ff.
20. Fichte, *Grundlage des Naturrechtes*, p. 203.
21. *Ibid.*, pp. 208–209.
22. Fichte, *Der Geschlossene Handlesstaat*, p. 399.
23. Fichte, *Grundzüge des Gegenwartigen Zeitalters*, p. 164.
24. *Ibid.*, p. 165.
25. Fichte, *Addresses to the German People*, p. 33.
26. *Ibid.*, p. 40.
27. *Ibid.*, p. 38.

28. See Fichte, *Die Republik der Deutschen zu Anfang des 22nten Jahrhunderts, Werke,* VII, 530 ff.
29. Fichte, *Reden an die deutsche Nation,* p. 314.
30. Fichte, *Beiträge,* p. 150.
31. *Ibid.,* p. 480.
32. *Ibid.,* p. 482.
33. Fichte, *Grundlage des Naturrechtes,* p. 206.
34. *Ibid.,* p. 213; Fichte, *Der Geschlossene Handlesstaat,* p. 422.
35. Fichte, *Der Geschlossene Handlesstaat,* p. 424.
36. *Ibid.,* pp. 411, 429.
37. *Ibid.,* pp. 431 ff.
38. Fichte, *Beiträge,* pp. 80 ff.
39. *Ibid.,* pp. 72, 73.
40. Fichte, *Zurückforderung der Denkfreiheit,* p. 15.
41. Fichte, *Beiträge,* pp. 96 ff.
42. *Ibid.,* pp. 157–244.
43. Fichte, *Grundlage des Naturrechtes,* pp. 171 ff.
44. *Ibid.,* p. 158.
45. *Ibid.,* p. 180.
46. *Ibid.,* p. 167.
47. *Ibid.,* p. 287.
48. *Ibid.,* p. 161.
49. *Ibid.,* p. 287.
50. *Ibid.,* p. 288.
51. Fichte, *Machiavelli als Schriftsteller* in *Werke,* XI, 420.
52. Fichte, *Das System der Rechtslehre,* p. 633.
53. *Ibid.,* 634.
54. *Ibid.*
55. *Ibid.,* pp. 632, 633.
56. Fichte, *Die Staatslehre,* p. 547.
57. *Ibid.,* p. 444.
58. Fichte, *Characteristics of the Present Age,* p. 46.
59. *Ibid.,* p. 45.
60. Fichte, *Die Staatslehre,* pp. 451–452.
61. Fichte, *Das System der Rechtslehre,* p. 635.

BIBLIOGRAPHY

PRIMARY SOURCES. The principal primary sources are Fichte's *Werke,* 11 vols., edited by his son, I. H. Fichte, Bonn-Berlin, 1834–1845. All references are to this edition. There is also an abbreviated edition of Fichte's works: *Werke,* 6 vols., edited by F. Medicus, Leipzig, 1911–1912.

Several of Fichte's works have been translated into English. For his general philosophy see *The Vocation of Man* (a translation of *Die Bestimmung des Menschen* by W. Smith), Chicago, 1925; and *The Science of Knowledge* (a translation of various versions of the *Wissenschaftslehre* by A. C. Kroeger), London, 1889. For his views on ethics see *System of Ethics* (a translation of *System der Sittenlehre* by A. C. Kroeger), London, 1907. For his views on politics see *Science of Rights* (a translation of *Grundlage des Naturrechtes* or *Foundations of Natural Law* by A. C. Kroeger), London, 1889; *Characteristics of the Present Age* (a translation of *Grundzüge des Gegenwartigen Zeitalters* by W. Smith), London, 1847; *Addresses to the German Nation* (a translation of *Reden an die deutsche Nation* by R. F. Jones and G. H. Turnbull), Chicago, 1922. With the exception of the last work, all the translations of Fichte, though accurate, are very wooden and not very intelligible to the English-speaking public. On several occasions, therefore (duly noted in the text), I have preferred giving my own versions of the German originals rather than copying from the existing translations.

Several of Fichte's most important contributions to political thought have never been translated into English. The following works are especially significant: *Zurückforderung der Denkfreiheit* (*Demand for the Restitution of the Freedom of Thought*); *Beiträge zur Berichtigung der Urteile des Publikums über die französische Revolution*, cited as *Beiträge* (or *Correction of Some Views on the French Revolution*). The two above-mentioned works reflect Fichte's early, liberal ideas. *Der Geschlossene Handlelsstaat* (*The Closed Commercial State*); *Patriotische Dialoge* (*Patriotic Dialogues*); *Die Republik der Deutschen zu Anfang des 22nten Jahrhunderts* (*The Republic of the Germans at the Beginning of the Twenty-Second Century*); *Über Machiavelli als Schriftsteller* (*Machiavelli as a Writer*); *Das System der Rechtslehre* (*Theory of Law*); *Die Staatslehre* (*Theory of the State*). The five above-mentioned works represent Fichte's later political doctrines and are to be found in Fichte's *Werke*, cited above.

SECONDARY SOURCES. In spite of Fichte's importance, there is surprisingly little written about him in the English language, at least as regards his political philosophy. Of especial importance are the following:

R. Adamson, *Fichte*, Edinburgh, 1881.

H. C. Engelbrecht, *Johann Gottlieb Fichte*, New York, 1933.

J. Dewey, *German Philosophy and Politics*, New York, 1915 (especially pp. 70 ff.).

W. A. Dunning, *Political Theories from Rousseau to Spencer*, New York, 1922 (pp. 137 ff.).

C. E. Vaughan, *Studies in the History of Political Philosophy*, Manchester, 1925 (vol. II, chap. III).

There is a large and ever increasing number of books dealing with Fichte both in French and in German. Out of this vast literature the following are of especial importance:

X. Léon, *Fichte et son temps*. 3 vols., Paris, 1922–1927. (The best work on Fichte. though it overemphasizes Fichte's liberal side.)

I. H. Fichte, *Fichtes Leben*. 2 vols., second edition, Sulzbach, 1862.

G. A. Walz, *Die Staatslehre des Rationalismus und der Romantik und die Staats philosophie Fichtes*, Berlin, 1928.

N. Wallner, *Fichte als politischer Denker*, Halle, 1926.

M. Wundt, *Johann Gottlieb Fichte*, Stuttgart, 1927.

E. Schenkel, *Individualitat und Gemeinschaft*, Zurich, 1933.

K. Reidt, *Das Nationale und das Ubernationale bei Fichte*, Giessen, 1926.

CHAPTER VII

THE POLITICAL PHILOSOPHY OF G. F. W. HEGEL

To AN American or Englishman who has grown up in the liberal tradition, the writings of Fichte, on first acquaintance, might well appear to be the last word in etatism. Surely, one might say, no one could go further than Fichte in glorifying the state at the expense of the individual or glorifying authoritarianism at the expense of democracy. But in reality the etatism of Fichte is only an introduction to the more radical and thoroughgoing etatism of Hegel and of his numerous followers who are usually grouped as the Hegelian school.

With Fichte abstract or universal ethics and abstract, universal law were considered higher than the ethical or legal dictates of any individual state. The laws of any one state, to be worthy of obedience, must be in accord with this abstract law and ethics. With Hegel and the Hegelians, on the other hand, abstract ethics and abstract or natural law are included in, but transcended, by the moral and legal codes laid down by the individual state. The individual should look, not to eternal abstract rational principles for guidance in his actions, but to the traditional morality evolved by his own nation and to the legal dictates laid down by his own state.

Fichte stressed the supremacy of the state over the individual, but the state in which Fichte was interested, the state to which the individual was to be subordinated and sacrificed was the rational, ideal state — the state as it should be, rather than the makeshift state as it actually is. To him the rational individual might well refuse to devote himself to the grasping tyrannical state in which he actually finds himself. To Hegel and the Hegelians, however, the actual state is the ideal state; the state to which the individual is morally bound to devote and sacrifice himself is the state into which he has been born and of which he finds himself, willy-nilly, a subject. Fichte glorified the state as it should be; Hegel glorified the state as it is. To Hegel many of the existing states are "stages in the self-revelation of the Absolute," or, to use theological language, the creations of God, and as such worthy of blind, passionate devotion.

Fichte, for all his glorification of it, regarded the state as a means to an end — the end being the creation of "morally free individuals." He stressed the power and strength of the state in the sinful present, but he believed that in some golden age in the distant future, when man has become morally perfect, the state would become unnecessary and all governmental machinery would disappear. Hegel and the Hegelians, on the other hand, thought that the state was the supreme end in itself, that all individuals were merely the means to this end. They believed that the more perfect man becomes, the more fully will he, of his own free will, subordinate himself to the dictates and purposes of the state. From the Hegelian point of view the state was not a necessary stage in human evolution, a stage to be eventually transcended, but was itself the supreme goal of human evolution, the highest expression of human activity.

Fichte eventually came to stress nationalism at the expense of internationalism or cosmopolitanism, but to the end of his days he still disliked war between states and hoped to avoid war forever by the creation of a league of nations and a world court of justice. Hegel, however, and most of his German followers glorified war. They claimed that war would always serve a useful and even necessary purpose in promoting patriotism and devotion to the national state. Hegel thoroughly disliked the notion of a league of nations and of a world court, as such bodies would tend to interfere with the complete sovereignty and independence of the individual state. Believing that each state was an end in itself, he ridiculed the so-called dictates of international law and international morality. Law and morality, being the creations of the state, held good only for the subjects within each state. Sovereign, independent states were not and could not be bound by any legal or moral code in their relations with one another. To Hegel each state had a perfect right to break or modify a treaty any time it served its purpose to do so.

Fichte was an ardent nationalist, identifying the "nation" with the state, and claiming that all the members of one nation should be included within the limits of a single political unit. To his mind all the Germans should be citizens of a single German state, all Italians of a single Italian state. He would permit the nation-state to make war so as to incorporate within its limits all its fellow nationals. Thus, for example, on Fichtean principles Germany was perfectly justified in annexing the German-speaking Austrians and the German-speaking areas of Czechoslovakia. But as he was such a consistent nationalist Fichte was opposed to imperialism, the rule of one nation over another. In Fichte's political philosophy all Germans should form a free and independent nation-state, but so should the Slavs, the French, and the other peoples of the world. Hence to Fichte the German nation-state should never seek to incorporate Slavs or Hungarians or Italians within its political boundaries. Hegel's attitude towards this problem was very different. Hegel agreed that normally the nation and the state should be identical and that most nations had the right to free and independent political existence. But he held that some nations are more virile than others, and that some nations have lost their virility, and hence have lost their right to political independence. On this basis he defended, for example, French rule over the Bretons, and English rule over the Welsh. But once this principle be admitted, there appears to be no limit in the applications to which it may be (and has been) put. Have not the Italians, a virile nation, a right to rule over the Ethiopians; have not the Japanese, another virile nation, a right to rule over the Chinese, on the ground that the Ethiopians and the Chinese have lost their virility and thereby their right to independent existence?

Fichte was an authoritarian in that he confined political rights to only a small section of the population. But he always opposed the theory of the divine right of kings and in his last years he attacked any and every form of hereditary monarchy. Hegel, on the other hand, believed that hereditary monarchy was the only *rational* form of government and the only form of government in accordance with the Eternal Spirit or God, a reinterpretation of the old divine right theory. Hegel insisted, moreover, that the king, though not absolute, should have real and not merely nominal powers.

Fichte was violently opposed to the old social and political hierarchy. He wished to abolish the old hereditary aristocracy and regarded even the great landowners and the industrial and the commercial magnates with an unfriendly eye. He insisted that all citizens should enjoy at least civil and legal equality, with no special privileges for any favored class. Hegel, on the other hand, felt that the division of mankind into social, economic, and political classes was part of the eternal and rational order of things, and that some classes should be given more, others fewer political privileges. In Hegel's model constitution, the national assembly was to represent, not individuals (one member for so many thousand persons, irrespective of who these persons might be), but groups and classes.   The upper and upper middle classes, the land-owners, the captains of industry, the professional classes were to be specially represented and in the national assembly these favored groups were to outweigh the representatives of all other groups and classes. The vast bulk of the population were to be shorn of real political power, in fact were to be dismissed from serious consideration on the ground that they constituted that element in the community which did not and could not think and which scarcely knew what it really wanted.

Fichte felt that at least in the field of morals all men are equal, having the same duties and obligations.   To Hegel and the Hegelians even this idea was dangerously radical.   To them every person was allotted by Providence a certain station in life.   The duties, even the moral duties, of each station differ enormously, and for a man to be effectively moral he must spend his time reflecting, not upon abstract universal moral codes, but upon his own station in life and upon the duties directly attendant upon this station.

HEGEL'S LIFE AND TIMES

Hegel occupied a very important, almost a unique position in the intellectual life of the nineteenth century.   In Germany, at any rate, he was regarded during this period more or less as Plato and Aristotle were regarded during the classical period.   He was to most of his fellow Germans not *a* philosopher, one among many; he was *the* philosopher, the man who had grasped for the first time the true nature of reality and to whose system later thinkers could only add postscripts and addenda.

Many writers and thinkers have to wait until they are dead before they win widespread recognition.   Hegel leaped to fame during his own lifetime, and in the latter part of his career was the uncrowned king of the intellectual world in Germany.   Hegel was the spiritual heir of Kant and of Fichte, but Kant in his own lifetime remained a professor with but a handful of students in an obscure university in the north-eastern frontier lands of Prussia.   Fichte, to be sure, led a far more active and varied life and taught in the larger and better known universities.   But Fichte, because of his irascible personality was never popular.   He left Jena in disgrace and even in Berlin he was always in hot water.   During his closing years he was admired but disliked and even distrusted by the higher Prussian authorities to whom he owed his appointment.   Hegel, on the other hand, though slow in making a start in the academic world, eventually became not only the most influential but also the most popular university professor in Germany. Three universities vied for his services, and when he eventually accepted a call to Berlin University it was generally felt that he was conferring as much honor upon Berlin by going there as Berlin conferred upon him by asking for his services. Though Berlin University was already a large and important institution, it had only recently been established and still lacked tradition and the prestige that goes with tradition. During Hegel's professorship, and in large measure owing to his presence and influence, Berlin came to be considered for the first time the intellectual center of Germany. In Berlin Hegel always stood in high favor with the Prussian king and the Prussian ruling bureaucracy — becoming not only the king of philosophers but also the philosopher of kings. He was more, he was the official philosopher, the official spokesman in academic matters for Prussia and Prussianism.

Hegel was not cursed with false modesty. He was convinced that he had solved all the problems with which previous speculators had wrestled in vain. He was equally convinced that further progress in science and philosophy could add but little to the truths contained in his system.

> Although I could not possibly think that the method which I have pursued ... might not be capable of much perfecting, of much thorough revising in its details, I know that it is the only true method.... It is clear that no method can pass for scientific that does not go the gait of this method.

Several times Hegel expressed the opinion that he was not merely a person arguing and reasoning about the World Spirit, but that his thoughts and ideas were really the thoughts and ideas of the World Spirit itself; or, to use theological language, he felt that he was an inspired prophet, voicing the thoughts of God. It is not surprising, considering Hegel's temperament, that he convinced himself of his own importance, but it is rather surprising that he was able to convince so many of his contemporaries. On his death many of his disciples earnestly debated the question whether or not there was anything left to do — for had not philosophy been perfected and completely manifested in the writings of the master?

To be sure, this attitude did not last long. Every self-respecting professor of philosophy, be he ever so humble, feels it necessary to improve on his predecessors and bring forward one or two novel ideas of his own. Before many years had passed, even the most ardent disciples felt called upon to attack some details of the Hegelian system, to modify others, to add not a few notions of their own. After a few decades the Hegelian school had broken up into a number of different branches, each violently inimical to the others.   Nevertheless the Hegelian school in some form or other remained the dominant system in the German universities during the greater part of the nineteenth century.   Even those philosophers who attacked orthodox Hegelianism were, for the most part, strongly influenced by many of the Hegelian concepts.   Towards the close of the nineteenth century there was indeed a general reaction against the Hegelian tradition, and for a while it appeared that the long reign of Hegel was over, but in the twentieth century there arose a new group of thinkers and teachers with the cry, "Back to Hegel," and the last few years have seen a flood of new books re-expounding and reinterpreting the basic Hegelian assumptions.

Nor should it be forgotten that Hegel's influence in Germany was not confined to the realm of pure philosophy or professional philosophers. Directly or indirectly he influenced many writers in other fields, especially in history and jurisprudence.   Many of Germany's foremost historians during the nineteenth century, notably those with a strong nationalist bias, such as Ranke, Droysen, and Treitschke, were deeply affected by their reading of Hegel, even though they ignored or rejected many of Hegel's metaphysical notions and even differed from Hegel in their interpretation of the nature and function of history.   Not less important was the effect of Hegelian ideas upon many of Germany's leading writers on law and jurisprudence.   From the long list of such writers it is necessary to cite only such a name as that of Savigny, the real founder of the historical school of jurisprudence, who was long a colleague of Hegel's at the University of Berlin and who borrowed many of his ideas from the Hegelian theory of the state.   Even more important is the fact that there has grown up in Germany a special and very powerful school of jurisprudence which frankly called itself Neo-Hegelian, whose leading exponent was Joseph Kohler, generally considered the greatest of the German writers of juristic problems.

Considering the enormous influence exerted by Hegel and Hegelian concepts upon the intellectual life of Germany during the nineteenth and twentieth centuries, it is not surprising that many of the Hegelian ideas became realized in the world of practical politics.   It would, of course, be ridiculous to blame (or praise) Hegel for all the subsequent developments in German political life.   There were undoubtedly many causes and many contributing factors behind these developments.   But it is worthy of note that many of the subsequent German political leaders were admittedly influenced by Hegelian doctrines (especially Hegel's doctrines with reference to the state) and that many of the changes which these leaders brought about were little more than the practical application of these doctrines.

It has long been recognized that Hegel is the spiritual father of Bismarck and the Bismarckian notions regarding the duties and the functions of the national state. As Merbach[1] puts it: "At the portal of Bismarck's century stands the life, thought, and activity of Hegel like the thought before the deed. . . . It is not too much to say that Bismarck carried out in fact what Hegel and his disciples expressed and demanded." Bismarck's emphasis upon the nation-state based upon force or power as the supreme goal of human activity; his belief that the state is not a collection of individuals but a single organic whole; his advocacy of an all-powerful monarchy and bureaucracy in opposition to democracy; his notions of international relations — were all rooted in Hegelian principles.

By a curious paradox, Bismarck's most violent opponents, the socialists Karl Marx, Friedrich Engels, and Ferdinand Lassalle, were also disciples, though aberrant ones, of Hegel. Lassalle, for many years the head of the parliamentary Socialist Party in Germany, was an avowed follower of Hegel and wrote a book defending Hegel from some of his opponents. Lassalle, in fact, regarded himself largely as an interpreter or reinterpreter of Hegel, though Hegel must have turned in his grave at some of the constructions put upon his words. The case of Engels and Marx (the joint authors of the *Communist Manifesto* and *Capital*) is somewhat different. In their younger days both were definitely members of the Hegelian school, and one of Marx's first works was a *Critique of Hegel's Philosophy of Law*, in which he disagreed radically with many of Hegel's conservative conclusions, but insisted that the Hegelian system was "the most logical and the richest" philosophy of the state which had ever been devised. In later years Marx and Engels became more violent in their disagreement with Hegel and rejected the Hegelian idealistic philosophy entirely, but to the end of their days both remained strongly stamped by their Hegelian background. In many ways we may say that the Marx-Engels philosophy of the state and of history was the Hegelian doctrine turned topsy-turvy. The "dialectic materialism" or economic materialism of Marx and Engels was only the dialectic spiritualism or idealistic determinism of Hegel turned around. It is the Hegelian aspect of Marxian socialism and communism which so strongly distinguishes this school from the more "liberal," empirical socialism which developed in England and in America.

Last but not least, it is easy to find in the Nazi Party of present-day Germany many elements of Hegelian ideology. Most of the Nazi leaders have quietly discarded the clumsy framework of the Hegelian meta·physics. But after all, even with Hegel, this framework was merely the scaffolding used in building the philosophy of the state, and the finished edifice has been taken over by the Nazis almost in its entirety. It should not be forgotten that the word Nazi is an abbreviation of the term National Socialist Party. The Nazi Party is both nationalistic and (in the broader sense of the word) socialistic. Bismarck developed the nationalism which was *explicit* in Hegel; Lassalle, Marx, and Engels developed the socialism which was *implicit* in Hegel. Hitler and his cohorts have combined the nationalism of Bismarck with many features taken from the socialism of Lassalle, Marx, and Engels to form the Nazi philosophy of the state. Hitler, to be sure, regards Marx and the Marxians with loathing. He is disdainful even of Lassalle, but it is obvious that he has taken many of his ideas from these thinkers. That he out-Bismarcked Bismarck in his emphasis upon nationalism goes without saying.

So far we have spoken only of the effect of the Hegelian philosophy upon Germany, but it must be borne in mind that Hegel's influence spread over the continent of Europe. Translations of his works appeared in a number of languages, and a host of enthusiastic Hegelian disciples arose in France, in Holland, and in the Scandinavian countries. But by a curious freak of fortune the two countries most influenced by Hegelian doctrines were England and Italy. In England, Hegelianism did not find widespread acceptance until the last quarter of the nineteenth century. One of the first persons to attract general attention to the Hegelian system was T. H. Green, the founder of the Oxford idealist school, but Green, though deeply impressed by Hegel, could not stomach all the features of Hegel's radical etatism. Many of Green's successors, however, were willing to go much further than was Green himself. Gradually there arose a powerful school of thought which adopted most, though not all, of Hegel's philosophical principles, including his philosophy of the state. Among the numerous writers of this group it is necessary to mention only two persons, Bernard Bosanquet, famous for his *Philosophical Theory of the State*, and F. H. Bradley, well known for his *Ethical Studies*, with its emphasis upon "My Station and Its Duties."

To the followers of the old liberal tradition it seems a pity that Hegel and his theory of the state should find so many disciples and exponents in England — their rejection of the old English tradition appearing almost like treason.   But the fact that an Hegelian school arose in England has at least one advantage to the student of the history of political philosophy, namely, that many of the Hegelian concepts became presented in an interesting and intelligible form.   In France for any writer, even a great philosopher, to command an extensive following, it is necessary that he present his ideas in a clear and precise manner.   In England and in America we sometimes demand that a man prove his scholarship by loading his writings with numerous footnotes and cross-references, but we think none the less of him if his text is lucid or at least understandable.   In Germany, on the other hand, a tradition has grown up (a tradition seemingly started by Kant) that for a man to be profound he must be obscure; that depth and intelligibility are contradictory terms.   No one was more affected by this tradition than Hegel, with the result that he devised a vocabulary and a method of expression which render his writings completely baffling to the average reader.   The typical Englishman or American is as much mystified by Hegel in literal translation as he is by Hegel in the original German.   Many a devout student of Hegel has willingly admitted that he has spent twenty years in the study of Hegel and still fails to understand all that Hegel meant.

This obscurity of Hegel was one secret of his success in his native land. Many a good German feels that Hegel must be a great philosopher, largely because of the fact that when he reads Hegel he can understand only one page in ten.   The good German is deeply impressed when he reads Hegel's definition of the state as the "realized substantive will having its reality in the particular self-consciousness raised to the plane of the universal." [2]   He is not quite certain what it means, but it sounds so profound that he feels it must be true, and nods his head in quiet acquiescence when Hegel deduces from this definition the notion that the state, therefore, must have the "highest right," that is, complete control, over the individual, and that the "highest duty [of the individual] in turn is to be a member of the state." [3]

The average American or Englishman when presented with a page of Hegelian jargon feels either annoyance or amusement.   The English Hegelians, therefore, realizing this fact, felt it necessary to interpret and paraphrase the Hegelian writings in such a way as to make them reasonably intelligible.   As a result, students of Heglian etatism find it advisable to turn to the works of the English Hegelians when attempting to discover the real principles upon which the Hegelian philosophy of the state was based.

In Italy, Hegel and the Hegelian principles have had even greater vogue than in England. In England, Hegelianism gave rise to a school of political philosophers, but these philosophers had only an indirect influence upon practical politics. The English Hegelians, moreover, found it advisable to reject some of the more extreme features of Hegel's political theory, such as his emphasis upon monarchic and authoritarian principles. In Italy, on the other hand, Hegelianism has had a profound effect not only upon theoretical but also upon practical politics. In addition the Italians were willing to accept not merely some but all of Hegel's authoritarian conclusions, and in some cases have even out-Hegeled Hegel himself. Hegelianism was first popularized in Italy about the middle of the nineteenth century by Augusto Vera, a professor at Milan University, later at the University of Naples. Following Vera there sprang up a large number of Italian Hegelians and semi-Hegelians who applied their principles not only to philosophical but also to historical, to juristic, and to political problems. In the first two decades of the twentieth century, two Hegelians, Benedetto Croce and Giovanni Gentile, attained widespread fame and popularity. Both followed Hegel in emphasizing and glorifying the state, insisting upon the supreme part it plays in forming worthy individuals.

There are many features of Italian Fascism which are non-Hegelian in origin, but there can be no doubt that the spread of the Hegelian school paved the way for the acceptance and triumph of Fascism. Nor can it be doubted that Fascism has incorporated within its doctrines a number of the political ideas first clearly enunciated in modern times by Hegel. It was not an accident that Gentile, formerly a preacher of Hegelianism, found no difficulty in suddenly becoming one of the foremost exponents and interpreters of Fascism. Equally interesting is the fact that when we read the writings of Alfredo Rocco, perhaps the most important of the "official" Fascist philosophers, we almost feel that we are reading Hegel's *Philosophy of Right* denuded of its metaphysical background.

In Fascist Italy, as in Nazi Germany, there is the same emphasis upon nationalism, etatism, and authoritarianism which were such characteristic features of Hegel's philosophy of the state. In Fascist Italy, even more than in Nazi Germany, there is emphasis upon the role to be played in the state by "corporations" as opposed to individuals, another distinguishing feature of Hegelian political theory. In Fascist Italy as in Nazi Germany there is a violent denunciation of Marx and of Marxian socialism, but under Mussolini, a former socialist leader, there is the same quiet adoption of certain phases of the socialist system, which itself was a curious and aberrant outgrowth of the Hegelian philosophy of history and of the state.

The life of Hegel, like that of most university professors, was not especially dramatic or exciting, but certain phases of his career throw a good deal of light upon his social and political ideas and are worthy of mention.

Hegel was born in 1770, six years before the American Declaration of Independence; nineteen years before the outbreak of the French Revolution. His birthplace was the city of Stuttgart, the capital of the duchy, later the kingdom, of Württemberg. The place of his birth is mildly interesting. Württemberg was a South German state, and during the early part of his life Hegel felt himself far more at home with the South Germans, such as the Bavarians and the Austrians, than with the Germans of the north, such as the Prussians. Considering his later career it is amusing to find that for many years he regarded Prussia and the Prussians with active dislike. He witnessed the decay of the Habsburgs and the rise of the Hohenzollerns with dismay, and in one of his earlier writings (*Die Verfassung Deutschlands*) he pleaded that Austria rather than perfidious Prussia should take the lead in re-creating a strong German Empire. When the Napoleonic armies crushed Prussia at the battle of Jena, Hegel spoke and wrote of the Prussian humiliation with great glee. Fortunately for Hegel none of these writings saw the light of day during his own lifetime.

In later life his attitude towards North Germany in general and Prussia in particular was completely transformed. This was partly due to the religious situation, regarding which Hegel became more acutely conscious as the years went by. Most of the South German states were Roman Catholic. Württemberg, on the other hand, like most of the North German states, including Prussia, was Protestant, which meant that not only the religious outlook, but also the literary, historical, and social traditions of the Württembergers had more in common with North Germany than with South Germany. In his early years Hegel, who felt himself above such petty matters as the difference between Protestantism and Catholicism, ignored this difference, but in middle life he suddenly discovered that he had far more in common with Protestant Prussia than with Catholic Bavaria or Catholic Austria. To Hegel the very fact that he felt more at home in Prussia than in Austria meant that Prussia, not Austria, must become the leader of the German people in the formation of a strong national state. Personal matters were not un-

mixed with this change of attitude.   Catholic Austria consistently ig·
nored him.   Catholic Bavaria employed him, but only as the director
of a gymnasium (principal of a high school as we should say) in one of
the cities which happened to be Protestant.   Prussia, on the other hand,
made Hegel the leading professor in its highest institution of learning.
Small wonder that Hegel came to regard Prussia and the Prussian system of government as the concrete expression of the same eternal verities
which underlay his system of metaphysics.

Hegel's social position is also deserving of attention.   Fichte, by birth
a member of the lower middle classes, long regarded "the people" as the
bulwark of the state and the supreme arbiter of governmental affairs.
Hegel, on the other hand, was the son of upper middle class parents.
Brought up in such a family it is small wonder that he looked upon the
bulk of the population with disdain.   Not being an aristocrat he was
somewhat dubious as to the value of an hereditary nobility, but he was
certain that the upper and upper middle classes, taken as a whole,
formed far and away the most important element in the population and
that this group should lead the ignorant masses.   More to the point,
Hegel's father was a civil servant, a member of the petty bureaucracy of
the state of Württemberg, and this fact seems to have made a profound
impression upon Hegel's mind.   In different stages of his career Hegel
held widely different views regarding certain political problems, but he
never abandoned the notion that the welfare of the state demanded a
strong well-trained hierarchy of permanent officials, chosen on an appointive and not an elective basis.   His ideal state was a monarchy but a
constitutional monarchy, a monarchy held in check not so much by the
elected representatives of the people as by the members of the permanent bureaucracy.   He was insistent that the civil service should not
merely be entrusted with the task of executing and administering law,
but also that the members of the bureaucracy should have a large part
in the making of laws.   He thus advocated having a large number of the
higher officials made *ex officio* members of the legislative assembly.

Hegel's boyhood and youth are of no concern to us.   As a student at
the Stuttgart gymnasium or high school he was considered a slow,
plodding, conscientious, and hard-working boy with a retentive memory
and sound intelligence, but with no signs of genius or even of brilliance.
Of greater significance were the years spent as a student at the University of Tübingen.   Hegel was destined by his parents to be a Lutheran
minister and with this end in view his college studies were largely theo·
logical in character.   It is curious to note that three of the greatest

etatists of the nineteenth century, Fichte, Carlyle, and Hegel, were all theological students and that all three reacted to their theological studies in much the same way.   All three were profoundly religious by nature, but all three found it impossible to accept the orthodox dogmas.   All three refused to lapse into skepticism or agnosticism, but attempted to reinterpret traditional doctrines in terms of a general metaphysics acceptable to the rational mind.   Carlyle rejected the ancestral God, but believed fervently in the Eternal Verity.   To Fichte, God was but a popular and inadequate way of expressing the Universal Self.   To Hegel, what the populace called God should be called the Absolute or the Absolute Spirit or Mind.   All three rejected revelation in the ordinary sense of the word, but all three believed that the nature and the purposes of God could be known to philosophers gifted with insight.   All three rejected miracles, but all three accepted Providence, the guidance and control of human destinies, the rise and fall of nations by the hand of the Supreme Being.   All three regarded human history as the truest revelation of God.

Fichte, Carlyle, and Hegel, moreover, transferred to the field of political and social life the religious enthusiasm, sometimes the religious fanaticism, that is normally reserved for a discussion of theological problems.   All three were as dogmatic in political matters as orthodox theologians are supposed to be in religious matters.   All three failed to become "ministers of the gospel," but all three became and remained preachers directing their eloquence to converting mankind to an acceptance of their political creed.   Hegel was especially insistent that the so-called religious impulse should be applied to the solution of political problems.   In his younger days Hegel, the Lutheran theological student, thought that in many ways Christianity was far inferior to Greek religion.   Christianity had accepted too literally the saying, "my kingdom is not of this world"; had concentrated attention too exclusively upon God above the world, upon the immortal soul and the far-off kingdom of Heaven.   Greek religion was superior because it dealt to a greater extent with the affairs of this world, thought of religion as part of the state and not as above the state.   Greek religion was part and parcel of political and social life.

> To the Greek the idea of his fatherland, the state, was the invisible, the higher reality for which he labored and which formed his persistent motive. This was his end and aim of the world, or the end and aim of *his* world, which he found expressed in reality and which he helped to express and to maintain. In comparison with this idea, his own individuality was as nothing; it was

its endurance, *its* continued life that he sought, and this he was himself able to realize. To desire or pray for permanence of eternal life for himself as an individual could not occur to him, or at least it was only in moments of inaction and despondency that he could feel a stronger wish and relation to his individual self.[4]

In later life Hegel departed from this rather antagonistic attitude towards the spirit of Christianity, but his belief that the religious impulse should be directed towards the things of this world and find its fullest expression in political life was never changed. The state is declared to be the "actual God," or God made manifest. Religion, which is based upon intuition, feeling, and imaginative thought, has a very important part to play in human life, but the devotees of religion should never forget that the object of their worship is not or should not be a transcendant. God, a God beyond the world, but an immanent God, a God manifested or revealed in the world, and that the state is the most perfect manifestation of the deity in the world of men. "The state is the divine will as a present spirit which unfolds itself in the actual shape of an organized world." [5] The state, instead of being denied or despised by religious enthusiasts, should be revered as an "earthly God."

Indirectly at least, the theological training which Hegel received at Tübingen had a tremendous influence upon his opinions, but he regarded his rather pompous and rigidly orthodox professors with suspicion, and would never discuss with them the fundamental problems which perplexed his brain. As a result they, in turn, looked upon him as a rather dull fellow, a youngster with sound enough scholarship, but with no gift for expressing himself and with little or no imagination. But the stimulus which he failed to find in his professors he did receive from long talks with some of his fellow students, and above all from his wide and varied reading of books. Among the writings which most influenced his later opinions were the works of Kant and Fichte, the works of the Greek philosophers, especially Plato and Aristotle, and the writings of such French thinkers as Montesquieu and Rousseau. From all these authors he extracted those notions which fitted in best with his already strongly developed etatist tendencies.

It is not surprising that Hegel should be affected by the writings of Kant and Fichte, for these two men were then the two great lights in the German philosophical firmament. The young students of Hegel's generation regarded both men as Titans in the world of thought. In later life Hegel sharply criticized both these masters and regarded himself as their superior. Nevertheless he remained deeply indebted to

both the Kantian and Fichtean systems, and many of his own doctrines
are intelligible only in the light of the ideas thrown out by these two
men. In common with Kant and Fichte, Hegel rejected the English
type of philosophizing, with its reliance upon sensation, experience, and
experiment. Like his predecessors Hegel believed that ultimate reality
could and should be known by abstract reason — and a touch of intuition. Hegel also learned to dislike the somewhat tentative and
skeptical character of the English tradition. In common with Fichte
and Fichte's interpretation of Kant, Hegel believed that the problems
of the universe could be solved, in fact had been solved, through his own
philosophic system. Though Hegel differed radically from Fichte in
details, he agreed that the whole universe is spiritual or mental in character. Hegel, moreover, took over from Kant and from Fichte the all-
important doctrine that "freedom" meant action in accord with reason,
freedom to do the right thing rather than freedom to do as one chose.
Using this notion as a starting point, Hegel developed the implicit
etatism and authoritarianism of Kant and of Fichte's earlier writings
into the explicit etatism and authoritarianism of his own system.

Scarcely less important was the influence exerted upon Hegel by the
Greek philosophers, especially by Plato and Aristotle. From boyhood,
Hegel was strongly attracted by the ancient Greek civilization and mode
of life and thought. To him the Greek dramatists were the greatest
the world has ever seen and, as we have already observed, he felt for
many years that the spirit of Greek religion was in many ways better
than the spirit of Christianity. It is not surprising, therefore, that he
was very susceptible to the teachings of Greek philosophy. In the field
of metaphysics he strove to incorporate in his own system a reinterpretation of Plato's doctrine of ideas and of Aristotle's doctrine of forms.
In the field of politics the influence of Plato and Aristotle was equally
strong. In common with these great thinkers of antiquity he proclaimed
that "man is a political animal"; that the state is not an artificial
creation, but the natural and necessary outgrowth of human activity;
that man's "natural" state is political, not prepolitical. Both Plato
and Aristotle were etatists; both believed that the state should have
control over the individual; that the individual can have no rights
against the state. Hegel, for all his philhellenism, rather disliked the
democratic features of ancient Athens. He preferred to accept the ideas
of Plato and of Aristotle that the government should be in the hands of
the "better classes." In Rome, as opposed to Greece, we find, at least
in an elementary state, the doctrine of individual rights. In Roman

political and legal philosophy we find the doctrine that "government should rest upon the consent of the governed" and that all officials derive their authority from the people. It is small wonder that Hegel felt far more drawn to the Greek than to the Roman tradition.

Finally, during his university career and in the years immediately thereafter Hegel was greatly affected by the ideas and doctrines current in France. In Hegel's time French was for all Europe not only the language of diplomacy but also of society and polite literature. Even in Germany to be a polished gentleman meant being acquainted with the works of the leading French writers. Hegel, with his yearning for "culture," could not escape French influence. In the young, fresh, romantic years of college life even Hegel, the stodgy, matter-of-fact Hegel, known to his fellow students as "the old man," felt for some months a warm sympathy for the aims and ideals of the French revolutionaries. There is even a tradition that he was one of a group of students who planted a tree of liberty in the market place at Tübingen. Hegel's enthusiasm for the French Revolution soon died away, but he later became, and remained, deeply impressed by the meteoric career of Napoleon. To Hegel, Napoleon was the personification of the "Soul of the World." In his later years Hegel was thoroughly ashamed of his youthful sympathy with the Revolution. He thought it advisable even to hide his admiration for Napoleon, but to the end of his days he remained deeply influenced by certain features of French political thought, especially as expressed in the writings of Montesquieu and Rousseau. Hegel, to be sure, was little impressed by Montesquieu's individualistic tone and was only half converted by Montesquieu's advocacy of the system of check and balance and the separation of powers. To Hegel, Montesquieu's real contribution was the idea that each nation in the course of its historic development acquires a tradition, a spirit, a genius, all its own, and that the laws of that nation should be an expression of that spirit and should not be based upon abstract reasoning. This idea strongly influenced Hegel's doctrines on the philosophy of law and the philosophy of history. In like manner Hegel was horrified by Rousseau's idealization of the "state of nature," by his doctrine of the social contract, and by his emphasis upon democracy. For Hegel, Rousseau was important because the latter had stressed the significance of the rational will as the basis of human activity, and of the general will, as opposed to the will of all, as the basis of the state.

For six years after leaving his university Hegel served as a private tutor in aristocratic private homes, first at Berne in Switzerland and later at Frankfort, the old imperial city of Germany. Hegel was not especially successful or popular as a tutor and though he wrote numerous essays and articles during this period, none of these early writings were published. Hegel felt that he should stand under the aegis of some well-known university before trying through printed works to convince the general public of the genius he felt sure lay within him. In 1800 the long-sought-for opportunity arrived. Hegel's friend Schelling, formerly a fellow student at Tübingen, inherited Fichte's professorship of Philosophy at the University of Jena. Through Schelling's influence Hegel received an appointment as *dozent* or lecturer at the same institution. At that time it was the custom in German universities to pay full professors a regular salary. *Dozenten* or lecturers, on the other hand, had to depend on the fees from whatever students they were able to attract to their courses. Hegel's financial prospects at Jena were therefore very dubious. Just at this time, however, his father died and he inherited from the paternal estate the princely sum of about fifteen hundred dollars. Using this as capital, Hegel accepted the Jena appointment and thereby officially entered upon his academic career.

Hegel remained at Jena for seven years (1800–1807). During this period he evolved in his own mind all the essential features of his elaborate and complicated system of philosophy. In addition to his teaching he composed (and this time published) numerous essays and also his first great book, the *Phenomenology of Mind*. With this record of achievement Hegel had high hopes of being promoted to a regular salaried professorship, but at this time his hopes were in vain. There were few vacancies and the few which did exist were filled by other men. To make matters worse the Napoleonic wars came closer and closer to Jena. Eventually a great battle took place just outside the little university town. The wars affected Jena University disastrously. There was a great decrease in the number of students and Hegel's income fell to almost nothing. His little capital was long since exhausted. He, the Napoleon in the world of thought, was faced with starvation.

With bitterness in his heart Hegel left Jena (1807) and became the editor of a small daily newspaper in the town of Bamberg. A year later he again entered the academic world, but this time not as the member of a great university but as the director of a secondary school in the old world city of Nuremberg, the city of Hans Sachs and the Meistersingers. This time Hegel was quite successful.

> He was a strict disciplinarian and altogether opposed to the Pestalozzian ideas of education then in vogue, according to which the teaching must ac-

commodate itself to the individuality of the pupil.... The basis of **sound** education was for Hegel obedience and self-surrender — the submission of the mind to an external lesson which must be learned by everyone even by rote with utter disregard of individual tastes and desires.[6]

In other words, the authoritarianism which Hegel preached in the world of politics he himself applied in the world of education.

In Nuremberg, Hegel married the daughter of a local aristocrat. Now reasonably happy, Hegel nevertheless felt himself humiliated by his lack of recognition in the world of higher learning. He therefore determined to write a new book which would prove once and for all his greatness in the realm of philosophy. The book took the form of a three-volume treatise on the *Science of Logic*. Never before had such a work seen the light of day. All books on logic are more or less abstruse, but all previous books on logic were nursery rhymes compared to Hegel's monumental undertaking. The concept of being was found to lead logically to the concept of essence; the concept of essence to the concept of notion; and notion itself was found to consist of subjective notion, of objective notion, and of subjective-objective notion or idea, which in turn was the same as self-activity. The worthy pedants of the German academic world were delighted with this book. Here at last was something incomprehensible. It must therefore be deep.

Hegel, the obscure director of a provincial high school, now became one of the most celebrated philosophers of Germany. Universities vied with one another to secure his services. After much consideration Hegel accepted a professorship at the famed University of Heidelberg (1816). Here he composed the *Encyclopedia of the Philosophical Sciences*, the greatest and most comprehensive exposition of his whole philosophical system which he ever wrote. In addition he occupied himself with other more practical tasks, such as the political problems of the day. One of the most interesting essays was *On the Constitution of Württemberg*, dealing with the political situation of the little kingdom in which he had been born. The Napoleonic wars had wrought great changes in Württemberg. Its duke was given the title of king, and his domain considerably enlarged. The old system of government had been abrogated and the king tried to force a new constitution on his subjects in which the royal powers were considerably enlarged. The representatives of the people refused to accept this new constitution and there was much popular clamor about the whole matter. At the suggestion of one of the officials of the royal court, Hegel wrote a long article in which he exhorted the people of Württemberg to accept the new system of government. Hegel undoubtedly believed in the ideas he set forth, but he also had an ulterior motive in making his passionate plea. He knew that he was being considered for the post of chancellor of the University of Tübingen, a post in the hands of the King of Württemberg, and he wished by his essay to win favor in the royal eyes.

The Tübingen scheme came to nothing, but the high officials in another even more powerful kingdom, the Kingdom of Prussia, discovered that Hegel would make a superb "official philosopher," one whose lectures and writings on political philosophy would give strong moral support to an all-powerful monarchic and bureaucratic state. Hegel was invited to take the professorship of Philosophy at the University of Berlin (a post left vacant since Fichte's death). This offer Hegel accepted with alacrity. He took up his new work in 1818 and continued in active service at Berlin until his death (from cholera) in 1831. At Berlin, Hegel was considered the greatest teacher at the most important university in Germany. He was generally recognized as occupying the same position in the world of thought that Goethe occupied in the world of letters. But Hegel's influence was not confined to the academic world. He also played an important part in the Prussian administrative hierarchy. In 1830 he was chosen rector (or president) of the University of Berlin. For years he was employed by the Prussian government in testing candidates for the scholastic profession and was often consulted with reference to academic appointments of all sorts. In all such matters Hegel was careful to see that posts were given only to sound, worthy persons — persons who accepted the Hegelian system of philosophy and wholeheartedly supported the Prussian system of government.

Considering the high favor in which he was held by the Prussian government, it is not surprising that Hegel came to regard the Prussian state as the concrete embodiment of his ideal and rational philosophy. Abstract philosophizing could tell us what the function of the state and the machinery of government ought to be. But if we want a concrete as opposed to an abstract model we have only to look to the Prussia of his own day. To be sure, the concrete model was not perfect in all respects; there were certain improvements that might be made, but such improvements must be merely the further development of the essential features which were already latent or implicit in the Prussian system. It was the task of Hegel's successors in political philosophy to show that the logical development of these essential features led directly from the Prussia of 1820 through Bismarck's Germany of 1870 to Hitler's Germany of 1933.

During his professorship at Berlin, Hegel wrote very little in the field of general philosophy, being content to bring out new and somewhat revised versions of his *Science of Logic* and his *Encyclopedia of the Philosophic Sciences*. Most of Hegel's energy at this period was devoted to applied or practical philosophy, the realm of ordinary human activities. His chief work after coming to Prussia was the *Philosophy of Right*, an encyclopedic book giving the Hegelian solution to all legal, ethical, and political problems. Equally important were the lectures he gave on the philosophy of history. This lecture material, though not published during Hegel's lifetime, was brought out shortly after his death and is important for the light thrown on many aspects of Hegel's political views. Though his earlier works cannot be neglected, it is to these two books, the *Philosophy of Right* and the *Philosophy of History*, that we must turn as the basic sources for the study of Hegel's philosophy of the state.[7]

HEGEL'S GENERAL PHILOSOPHY

In order to understand Hegel's philosophy, including his philosophy of the state, it is necessary to know something of his methodology, or the methods he thought serviceable for ascertaining truth and for judging of the goodness and badness of human activities and of social and political institutions.

In common with the other major German philosophers, Hegel thoroughly despised the methodology used by the classical English philosophers. The English thinkers took it for granted that knowledge of external reality was to be derived from sensation and experience; by the careful observation and accumulation of sense data; by the analysis and grouping together of these sense data in such a way as to build up tentative theories and hypotheses; and finally by testing these tentative theories and hypotheses by experiment and by further observation. This method of procedure was supposed to hold good both for the study of nature (the field of physics and chemistry) and for the study of man and his social and political relations. Hegel had little or no use for this type of philosophizing. As a young man he wrote a book violently attacking Newton and the Newtonian physics because of its empirical and experimental character. As an old man he wrote another work dealing with the English system of government and again attacked the English method of treating political problems by a slow, seemingly irrational, trial-and-error method.

In place of the English empirical method Hegel relied partly upon abstract reason, partly upon instinct or intuition, and partly upon tradition. Theoretically, at least, he placed supreme emphasis upon abstract reasoning. All the classical German philosophies emphasized the rational as opposed to the empirical approach and the Hegelian system was even more radical and thoroughgoing in its rationalism than the others. To Hegel, "the rational is the real and the real is the rational." Anything in the universe which is irrational or contrary to the laws of reason is *ipso facto* false — a delusion of the senses. From this premise it follows that the rational is the good and the good is the rational — that any system of government (such as the English system) which has no rational basis is *ipso facto* bad, that any system which is (consciously or unconsciously) based upon reason is *ipso facto* good — and Hegel felt that he had proved that the Prussian system of government was more or less ideal when he had proved that it was essentially rational in character.

Hegel, as we shall presently see, had the curious notion that "thought and being are one," by which he meant that thought was the only ultimate reality in the universe. Once this position is accepted, it follows that a knowledge of thought and of the laws of thought will solve all the vexed problems of existence. Earlier philosophers had distinguished between logic or the study of the laws of thought and metaphysics or the study of the ultimate nature of the world around us. To Hegel this distinction was useless. As thought and being (or reality) are one and the same, logic must obviously be the same as or at least include metaphysics. For this reason it is not surprising that Hegel's most important philosophical work, in which he claimed to have solved the ultimate secrets of reality, was his *Science of Logic*. To Hegel all true science was merely the concrete application of logical principles. Hegel had a great deal to say regarding the philosophy of nature (corresponding to the physics, chemistry, and biology of empirical science), but in everything which he wrote on this subject he was dominated by the idea expressed by Schelling, his friend and one-time teacher:

> Those theories alone can be true which are established absolutely *a priori*, for if the principles are certain in themselves and nowhere need experience to confirm them, they must be completely universal, and as nature can never contradict reason, must suffice for all possible phenomena, known or unknown, present or future.[8]

If in the Hegelian system the principles of reasoning or logic are found applicable to the philosophy of inanimate nature, they are of even greater importance in the understanding and interpretation of mankind (man being a rational animal) and of all human activities. The fields of art, ethics, economics, jurisprudence, and politics are all subject to rational logical laws and can best be studied by the rational logical approach. Some persons might object that in all these fields we are faced with an irrational element in the form of values and the standard of values. Surely in saying that this picture is beautiful or ugly or that this form of state or government is good or bad, we are dealing with something outside the scope of purely logical or rational categories. Not so, to Hegel and the Hegelians. The Hegelian school resolutely "rejects the view that judgments of value are incapable of being logically supported. It is true that values are relative to feeling. But feeling can be subjected to criticism.... This means that there is a logical standard by which standards of value are determined." [9]   In other words, reason or logic can tell us not merely what is false or true in the field of society and the state but also what is good and bad in art.

By his reliance upon reason for solving all social and political problems, Hegel seems to be in close accord with his predecessor, Fichte. But in reality there is an enormous difference between the rationalism of Fichte and that of Hegel. The rationalism of Fichte was revolutionary, that of Hegel was conservative. By the use of reason Fichte created in his own mind a picture of an ideal state — of the state and government as it should be — and then contrasted this picture with the states and governments he saw around him. Again and again he emphasized that existing states and governments were far from rational and hence far from ideal, and he also insisted that we should strive to transform the irrational makeshift states of the present into conformity with the ideal picture of the state given by reason. To Hegel this was a very dangerous doctrine and smacked too much of the principles laid down by the French revolutionaries. States and governments, to him, should of course conform to rational principles, and in point of fact he frequently did accord praise and blame to existing political institutions on the ground that they did or did not agree with the dictates of reason. But to Hegel the primary purpose of reason and logic in the field of social and political studies is to show logically and rationally how existing economic, social, and political institutions have originated and to give a logical and rational analysis of these institutions as they exist at present. Above all, and this is the important point, Hegel strove to show that existing economic, social, and political institutions rest upon an essentially rational basis — and being rational they are *ipse facto* good, and must be joyfully accepted by all thinking human beings.

In the field of economics, to take an example, Hegel and the Hegelians thought that it is not the function of reason to build up some idealistic Utopian scheme for the equitable production and distribution of goods. Rather it is to analyze the existing economic order and to show how this order is not a blind chaos, but is based upon the working of a number of rational economic laws (the "laws" of supply and demand, etc.). Having satisfied himself that these laws are rational, the thinking man will come to the conclusion that they are also good. This leads Hegel to the startling conclusion that "the insight to which ... philosophy is to lead us is that the real world is as it ought to be." [10] Or as a critic of the Hegelian system has remarked,

> Just as in a simple religion the powers that be are ordained of God, so with the metaphysician who starts from the belief that things are what they should be, the fabric of social life, and in particular the state system, is a part of an order which is inherently rational and good, an order to which the lives of individuals are altogether subordinate.[11]

In his very curious use of the powers of reason Hegel appears to adopt a decidedly static and conservative attitude towards political affairs. Hegel was, indeed, a strong defender of the powers that be, and he and most of the later Hegelians were genuinely in favor of preserving the *status quo*. But this is not the complete story. In point of fact Hegel himself was strongly in favor of many changes in the social and political fabric of his own time. On several occasions he reminded his contemporaries that they were no longer living in the Middle Ages and that it was useless and even ridiculous for them to try to preserve institutions which had come down from mediaeval times and which were no longer suitable to existing conditions. In 1802 (shortly before its abolition) he violently attacked the existing organization of the Holy Roman or old German Empire, and demanded radical changes in its constitution.[12] In 1816 he warmly defended the proposed new constitution for Württemberg and vigorously attacked those persons who clung blindly to the political institutions of the "good old days." In 1830, shortly before his death, he discussed the English Reform Bill (eventually passed in 1832) and though he radically disagreed with many of its detailed items, he willingly admitted that some kind of reform was necessary.

How can one reconcile Hegel the conservative with Hegel the re former?   Hegel, like most persons in a similar position, claimed that he wished neither stagnation nor revolution, but evolution — that he welcomed change, but that the change, in most cases, must be slow and gradual, the gradual dropping of outmoded institutions, the gradual development of new institutions to fit the exigencies of the times.   In no case should reformers seek to destroy or violently dislocate the existing social structure.   More especially, and this is the really vital point, these changes should come spontaneously, more or less unconsciously, not in reliance upon abstract principles, but in accord with an intuitive or instinctive feeling demanding improvement.   In a word, Hegel, the super-rationalist, declared that all real progress in human affairs is not based upon conscious reason, but upon blind instinct.

In order to defend this position and make it more or less compatible with his essentially rationalist philosophy, Hegel was forced to declare that reason and intuition are ultimately and fundamentally identical. Hegel, like Carlyle, sharply distinguished between understanding and reason.   Understanding, it will be remembered, was to Carlyle "the mere mechanical and uncreative deduction and inference of given premises."   Reason, on the other hand, was "direct spiritual perception, the ability to penetrate behind the shadows of formal logic and *see* the fundamental realities which lie beneath."   Hegel's distinction between understanding and reason, though not identical, was very similar.   Understanding to Hegel was "the mode of mind which seeks precision above all things and insists upon clear distinctions.   As such it is a necessary factor of every philosophical method. . . . But its truth is not the whole truth.   Beneath these distinctions there is identity; and to see this is the work of reason." [13]   Reason, therefore, gives us a deeper insight into the real nature of things than understanding with its formal ratiocination.   But Hegel was convinced that most persons, especially most political philosophers, based their doctrines upon understanding rather than upon reason — with disastrous consequences.   Hence his dislike for pseudo-rationalism in political discussion.

Equally important was the distinction which Hegel made between creative and reflective reason.   Creative reason to Hegel was unconscious reason, reason unaware of itself.   Most of what we call experience, most of what we call the artistic or active instincts of the mind, were called by Hegel creative reason.   "As a creative power reason builds up the world of sensation, art, conduct, and religion in which man habitually lives and moves." [14]   It is unconscious reason which has built up the family, society, the state.   It is unconscious creative reason which permits and will permit further development of human institutions. Reflective or conscious reason, on the other hand,

> reconstructs in thought and by a conscious effort of thought the fabric which, blinded by the very force of its creative power, it has ceased to recognize as its own. It reviews with open eyes the ground it had originally traversed blindfold, retracing the whole circle of progress and marking how each step necessarily follows from those that had gone before.[15]

It is creative reason, in other words, which brought the state into being, which allowed it to grow, which sustains it at the present time, which will permit its further development in the future — and this creative reason is unconscious and instinctive. Reflective reason, because of the very fact that it is conscious and reflective, cannot be creative. It can only analyze and comprehend the work which the creative reason has already accomplished. It can show that the work of the creative reason was essentially rational even though unconscious. But to try to make reflective reason do the work of creative reason might well prove disastrous. Hence, says Hegel, away with all idealistic theories of government based upon abstract reflective reasoning! Philosophy is, of course, the work of reflective reason, hence

> philosophy does not appear until reality has completed its formative process and made itself ready.... When philosophy paints its grey in grey, one form of life has become old, and by means of its grey it cannot be rejuvenated but only known. The owl of Minerva takes its flight only when the shadows of evening are fallen.[16]

Hegel's doctrine that political progress must be made unconsciously and instinctively and not in dependence upon logical systems was, of course, directed against the rationalists of the French Revolution and their demands for a state based upon the laws of reason. In preaching his political intuitionism Hegel doubtless felt that he was attacking the roots of all revolutionary doctrines. Considering this fact it is amusing to note that this very intuitionism in a slightly modified form was to serve as the cornerstone of much of the revolutionary thought of modern times. More especially was it used by Sorel, the intellectual leader of the French syndicalists, in his demands for bloody revolution and class warfare. More interesting still, this intuitionism of Hegel has been incorporated into the Fascist creed. Fascism

> disparages the political philosophy that would have action wait until a formulation of some systematic program has been agreed upon among theorists and understood and approved by the populace. Thus Fascism is described and widely applauded as empirical and pragmatic; acting first, theorizing when it does theorize, afterwards![17]

Another phase of Hegel's methodology is vitally important in view of later developments. This is the fact that Hegel, in addition to relying upon reason and instinct, also emphasized the need of history and tradition in trying to solve political and all other problems. In stressing tradition Hegel broke sharply not only with such liberal thinkers as Locke, Bentham, and Rousseau, to whom history is the story of past abuses, but also with such thinkers as Kant and Fichte with whom Hegel had otherwise much in common. The reverence for tradition Hegel took over from Montesquieu and from Burke, but he developed their doctrines very considerably and in this modified form traditionalism became an integral part of the Hegelian system.

To Hegel the best way to study philosophy or religion or science is to study the history of philosophy and religion and science. To him the history of philosophy is itself philosophy, for the history of philosophy, the study of the appearance and development of philosophic concepts, gives us the only possible solution of most philosophic problems. The historic attitude is equally important in approaching the problems of ethics, of society, of government. "The wisest men of antiquity have laid it down that wisdom and virtue consist in living conformably to the customs of one's people." [18] Most of the liberal thinkers contrasted the dictates of reason with the dictates of tradition. To the Hegelians this contrast was false.

The tradition of today is the result of the rational activities of yesterday. It has been built up from the conscious and purposeful activities of countless men and is the embodiment of the collective reason of the past.[19]

Kant, rejecting tradition, thought that the only true basis of morality lay in the dictates of the individual conscience, or the "practical reason" of each person. To Hegel this idea was anathema. To him the individual conscience tells us that we should do right and avoid wrong, but as to *what* is right and *what* is wrong — on this point the individual conscience gives us no aid. The content of our conscience is derived from the conscience of the community as embodied in family, tribal, or national traditions. In like manner, in judging the goodness or badness of codes of law or systems of government, appeal must be made to the fundamental laws of human nature and these can best be known, not through the speculation of individual philosophers, but through the study of human nature as embodied in the human institutions which have gradually come into being through the course of ages.

Hegel's emphasis upon history or tradition did not make him a reactionary in the strict sense of the word, that is, a man opposed to all change or one who wished to resurrect the life and institutions of an earlier age. Hegel believed in growth, in development, in evolution.

He realized that all communities and all institutions must grow and hence must change. It was impossible for any people to stay still, much less to push back the clock and return to an earlier condition of society But he insisted that all growth to be healthy must be continuous. For a tree to grow it must be rooted in the ground and it must not be trans- planted carelessly or too often. New branches may grow, but they must grow out of the old trunk. In like manner communities, peoples, nations, if they are to prosper should and must change with the times, but they must have their roots in the past and in building new branches should and must utilize the trunk of tradition.

Hegel's emphasis upon history and tradition is very significant and had an enormous influence upon later political and legal speculation. With his general principle we are bound to sympathize. But this should not blind us to the fact that Hegel, though a great master of historical fact, always twisted his facts to suit his metaphysical theories and his national prejudices. History to him was not a mistress but a handmaiden, to whom he insisted upon giving orders. He was con- vinced that history must be rational, so he *made* it rational. It suited his purpose to teach that India was greater than China and Japan, and Persia greater than India. Poor history, by emphasizing some facts, by misrepresenting other facts, by ignoring still others, is made to sup- port this plea. It need not surprise us, therefore, that in Hegel's hands history is made to prove that Germany and especially Prussia is the heir of all the ages, the Germans chosen people of the World Spirit, and that the social and political aspirations of past ages have reached their fruition in the Prussian system of government.

It is unnecessary to go into the intricacies of the Hegelian system of metaphysics, but attention should be drawn to five of the principal features of his philosophy as a whole because of the light they throw upon his attitude toward social and political problems:

(1) Throughout the whole course of man's history action is dominated by thought, and in the long run it is only thought which counts.
(2) The whole universe is a creation of reason or thought or spirit.
(3) Thought or reason, the only ultimate reality, is not static but dynamic; reason is a principle of growth and development; hence no one of its manifestations is intelligible unless it be studied along the lines of its continuous development.
(4) Among social institutions that must dominate mankind, society is higher and more important than the family, but the state is higher and more important than society.

(5) The national state is greater than humanity as a whole; war between the various national states is useful and inevitable.

The first characteristic, the belief that man's actions are dominated by thought, is in marked contrast with the materialistic notion that men's thoughts are dominated by their environment, or by their racial or economic background. Karl Marx, though a disciple of Hegel on many points, violently opposed his master in this regard. Marx thought that man's ideas and ideals, their religious and philosophic opinions, are largely a product of economic forces and conditions. Many non-Marxists have reached a similar conclusion, though they may stress other than mere economic factors. Sait, for example, an outstanding Liberal, proclaims: "Ideas are not commonly the result of conscious thought. They are imposed on us by circumstances. They arise out of our environment as a consequence of our spontaneous reaction to it." [20]   To Hegel and the Hegelians such concepts are anathema. To Hegel,

> Reason is the sovereign of the world. The history of the world therefore presents us with a rational process. . . . This Idea or Reason is the True, the Eternal, the absolutely powerful Essence. It reveals itself in the world and in that world nothing else is revealed but this and its honor and glory. [21]

Though the later Hegelians differed from Hegel himself in many respects, this notion was accepted by practically all of them, with the exception of the Marxists. Again and again we come across such passages as "the distinctive feature of human life is that it is not swayed by blind impulses only, but is guided and controlled by ideas and it is ideas after all that rule the world." [22]   In fact this doctrine of the supremacy and creativeness of ideas was adopted by many sober historians who rejected the Hegelian metaphysic. Thus we find Lord Acton, the famous English historian, declaring that "it is our function to keep in view and to command the movement of ideas, which are not the effect, but the cause of public events."

In addition to stressing the importance of ideas in general, Hegel and the Hegelians introduced and popularized the notion of *Zeitgeist*, or "spirit of the times," and of *Volksgeist*, or "spirit of the people." By the spirit of the times the Hegelians meant the complex of ideas and thoughts which dominate, consciously or unconsciously, the minds of mankind at any given time. Each successive wave of history is but the carrying out in the world of fact the ideas which have arisen and captivated men's thoughts at this period. The dominating ideas of each age find expression first in the thoughts and then in the actions of the great men of the epoch in question, and through their activity the condition of the whole of humanity is thereby transformed. In contrast to Carlyle, who thought that great men created new ideas and thereby led and controlled the world, Hegel believed that great men were great merely because instinctively they identified themselves with and became the organs of expression for the complex of ideas which together constituted the spirit of the times.

In like manner, to the Hegelians each nation and each people is dominated, whether consciously or not, by a special group of ideas, and it is this fact which causes each people, each nation, to have a specific genius, a specific character and tradition of its own. The spirit of each people finds embodiment in its legal and political institutions. "The constitution of a people makes one substance, one spirit with its art and philosophy, or at least with its concepts and thoughts — its culture generally." [23] As each nation possesses its own spirit, its own complex of ideas, it is ridiculous to try to impose the legal and political institutions of one people upon another — all such institutions should be the spontaneous expression of the national mind.

The second characteristic of the Hegelian system, the doctrine that the whole universe is a creation of thought or reason or spirit, is obviously only a rather radical development of the preceding notion. Though this doctrine may seem purely metaphysical and hence its discussion beyond the scope of the present book, yet the acceptance of this doctrine had an overwhelming influence upon the political outlook of the Hegelian school and hence merits brief mention.

In contrast with the old common-sense notion that the universe consists of matter and mind, or possibly of matter and mind and of God, the creator of both matter and of mind, the Hegelians think that there is only one ultimate reality. We can call this ultimate reality God or the Absolute; we might conceivably call it matter; but because it is essentially spiritual in nature we can best call it mind, or spirit. In Hegel's view

> the distinction between spirit and nature, between reason and knowing and the world as known is not a final and absolute but a partial and relative distinction. They are the terms of a process each of which is inseparable from and is necessary to the existence of the other.... In one sense reason and matter, nature and spirit, are co-ordinate elements in our world of experience. In another and fuller sense, reason is all in all.... Matter itself, the world that we call external, is the creation of reason.[24]

The Absolute, which the vulgar call God, is Pure Thought, Pure Reason. This Absolute is therefore knowable by reason. "The content of Logic is the representation of God as he is in his eternal essence." [25] The world of matter or nature is a partial and one-sided manifestation or embodiment of reason or mind. It is mind in its spatial and temporal form. Hegel also calls it unconscious intelligence or petrified intelligence. But being essentially rational the world of nature obeys the laws of thought and can be known by rational thinking. In man, an essentially rational being, thought or reason becomes for the first time conscious of itself. When a man thinks rationally he follows the universal laws of reason — he is thinking the thoughts of God, who is Pure Reason. "Subjective reason is identical with objective world-reason. Our reason *is* the Absolute Reason." [26]

In many ways this Hegelian philosophy bears a striking resemblance to the idealist philosophy enunciated by Fichte. This is not surprising when one remembers that in his younger days Hegel was strongly influenced by Fichte. Nevertheless there are several very important differences between the Fichtean and the Hegelian systems. In the first place Fichte, at least in the earlier phases of his thinking, inclined towards "subjective idealism," while the Hegelian system emphasizes "objective idealism." Let us illustrate the difference between the two systems. I see a tree. Subjective idealism claims that the tree and the image of the tree are only modifications of my mind. Fichte with his belief that the self creates the not-self comes close to this doctrine, though it would perhaps be fairer to say that according to Fichte the tree is a product of the Universal Self working in the individual consciousness. Objective idealism, on the other hand, claims that both the tree and the mind which perceives the tree are equally real, but that both are only manifestations of the Universal Mind or the Absolute. Objective idealism does not deny the existence of the external objective world, but insists that this world is essentially spiritual or mental or ideal in character, and is only a phase of a greater reality.

Equally important is the fact that the Hegelian system is far more monistic, universalistic, and absolutistic than the system developed by Fichte. Fichte believed that the universe consists of an infinite number of finite egos or selves, though he admitted that all these selves are only reflections or manifestations of the one Universal Self. With Hegel such emphasis is laid upon the essential unity of the Absolute Mind that the finite selves, the human personalities, are almost even though not completely ignored. To most interpreters of Hegel the human personality or finite self is "only a transient modification of the Absolute, as evanescent and unsubstantial as the passing waves of the ocean." "All things in heaven and earth are parts of one thought or subject within which are included even the human selves whose separate existence ordinary pluralism affirms." [27] "In reality there is ultimately only one ultimate individual, the Universe, and the human soul can work out its destiny, not as a separate entity, but as a member of the Universe." [28]

The influence of this doctrine upon social and political speculation is enormous. The liberal thinkers, such as Locke and Bentham, thought of human beings as separate and distinct personalities and claimed that the state should be merely the voluntary association of these separate and distinct personalities, no one of which should be crushed in the wheels of governmental machinery. Even Kant, the founder of German idealism, declared that each person should be treated as an end in himself and not as a means to an end. To the Hegelians all such views are "atomistic" and therefore bad. To the Hegelians sin itself is but the assertion of the particular will of the individual, his isolation of himself from the world order. In the world of politics the particular will of the individual must conform to the general will for civilized life to be realized. A solitary individual is not a whole in himself; he is only a fragment of a greater whole, and is of interest and importance only because he *is* a fragment of this greater whole. From this metaphysical doctrine it is but a step to the political doctrine that the state, the concrete embodiment of the Universal Mind, is far more real and far more important than are the individual citizens of the state.

The third characteristic of the Hegelian system is, as we have seen, the doctrine that reason, the only ultimate reality, is not static but dynamic, that it is essentially a principle of growth and development. It was this doctrine which sharply distinguished Hegelianism from the older forms of idealism, such as the Platonic philosophy. In Plato's system the world of appearance or experience, to him the shadow world, is full of change, of growth, and decay, but the true world, the world of ideas, the world of pure reason, is eternal and changeless. In this ideal world there is no becoming, there is only being. In this world there is and can be no growth or development or evolution. In Hegel's philosophy, on the other hand, the world of pure thought, the world of ultimate reality, is not fixed or rigid or changeless. It is itself the principle of eternal becoming rather than of pure being. By its very nature pure reason has to develop or unfold itself — and the universe itself is but a part of the eternal self-unfolding of the Universal Mind. Change, growth, development, evolution are not an illusion, as taught by Plato, but a vital part of the everlasting world process undergone by mind or reason.

At the lowest stage Universal Mind, in its process of spontaneous self-development, embodies itself or reveals itself in the form of seemingly inert matter, the inorganic world of physics and chemistry. But this seemingly dead world of matter has pulsing within it a vast creative energy. As this creative energy, which is essentially spiritual in character, further unfolds itself, as from its nature it must, it reveals itself in the form of the organic world, first the world of plants, and then the world of animals. Still later this creative energy or creative reason (the two, to Hegel, are identical) unfolds itself in the form of man in which for the first time Universal Mind becomes conscious of itself. In one sense we may say that Hegel's philosophy is a universal and cosmological interpretation of the idea expressed in Lowell's lines —

> Whether we look, or whether we listen,
>   We hear life murmur, or see it glisten;
> Every clod feels a stir of might,
>   An instinct within it that reaches and towers,
> And, groping blindly above it for light,
>   Climbs to a soul in grass and flowers.

save that for Hegel "life" or mind in its "groping" and "climbing" neither begins nor ends with grass and flowers, but embraces the whole cosmic process from beginning to end.

Vitally important in the Hegelian system is the doctrine that Universal Mind, being itself rational, necessarily follows a logical or rational pattern in its process of self-unfolding or self-development. Hegel, moreover, thought that he had discovered the nature of this rational pattern. This pattern he called the *universal dialectic*. The Hegelian dialectic in its details is an exceedingly abstruse and metaphysical concept, but it is necessary to give a brief summary of its general character because of its influence on later political speculation. Not only did it play a part in etatist philosophy, but, in a somewhat modified form, it was also made the keystone of Marxian socialism and communism. In fact, without an understanding of the principle of the Hegelian dialectic, Marx's whole political philosophy remains unintelligible.

Briefly, the dialectic states that all development and evolution proceeds not in a straight line but in a zigzag or spiral, following the formula of *thesis*, *antithesis*, and *synthesis*. **In** other words, action is followed by reaction; from the opposition thus engendered a harmony or synthesis results. All this sounds rather technical, but it is easy to elucidate the general principle with a few concrete illustrations. From early Greek times some philosophers noted that historical processes tend to go by opposites. Every tendency when carried out too radically breeds an opposite tendency which destroys it. Absolute monarchy leads to despotism and this in turn leads to a reaction, frequently a revolution, producing a democratic form of government. But democracy ends in license and mob rule. This in turn leads to a reaction, the emergence of a single strong man, a dictator, who usually becomes a monarch. Hegel accepted the principle of "opposition," or action and reaction, but felt that this was not the whole story. By this principle there could be no real growth or evolution, but merely a pendulum-like swing from one tendency to another.

Other philosophers from ancient times on have thought that there is visible in human affairs not a twofold but a threefold rhythm. Monarchy, according to this view, generally leads to government by an aristocracy. Aristocratic government generally leads to democratic government. Democratic government in turn, when carried to an extreme, leads to the emergence of the dictator such as Caesar or Napoleon, and hence to the emergence of monarchy once more. Hegel was much taken with this idea. He, too, thought that there is a triple and not merely a double rhythm in human affairs. But he was convinced that the old triple rhythm is an inadequate explanation of the historical process. The old rhythm meant going in a circle like a squirrel in a revolving cage and led to no real progress or evolution.

To Hegel, human history shows that men go from despotism (the thesis), then by reaction from despotism to democracy (the antithesis). Finally reaction from unlicensed democracy leads, not back to despotism, but to constitutional monarchy (the synthesis), which combines certain features of both despotism and democracy, but which transcends both the older forms of government. This means that man proceeds not in a circle, but in a spiral, a spiral that leads ever upwards and onwards. The law of action, reaction, and counter-reaction in this form, unlike the older view, does permit real growth and development. Hegel's so-called law of thesis, antithesis, and synthesis was applied by him, not merely to the problem of political institutions, but also to all other phases of human activity Social institutions start with the family (the thesis) based upon mutual love and mutual self-sacrifice. The growth of the family leads to the emergence of general society (antithesis) dominated by universal competition, each man struggling to buy in the cheapest and sell in the dearest market.   The growth of society in turn leads to the emergence of the state (synthesis), the institution which includes but transcends the family and society and which has room both for the principle of mutual love and for universal competition.   Hegel's dialectic in fact was applied not merely to the sphere of mankind and human activity, but to the whole history of the universe.   Cosmically speaking, the first category is pure thought or Universal Abstract Mind (the thesis).   Pure thought negates itself and thereby reveals itself as the world of matter (antithesis).   Universal Mind then returns to itself and thereby reveals itself as the world of spirit, embodied in mankind (synthesis).

To many persons Hegel's doctrine of the Universal Mind and the dialectic unfolding of this mind seems absurdly abstract and unrelated to the world of reality.   But Hegel's beliefs on these matters led him to assume a very positive attitude towards the concrete problems of everyday human existence.   Curiously enough this same attitude was adopted by an enormous number of persons who ignored or rejected Hegel's metaphysical background.   This attitude, with especial reference to human history or the development of human affairs, may be summed up as follows:

Hegel was an enthusiastic supporter of the doctrine of human progress. He definitely rejected the doctrine of the fall of man as taught by ortho- dox Christianity and the idea that man has slowly degenerated from a golden age in the distant past as taught by many of the classical philos- ophers.   Not only did he take over the doctrine that man slowly but surely becomes better and wiser from such thinkers as Bodin and Kant and Fichte, but he greatly developed the idea and made it a central point in his system.   Hegel, in fact, transformed the theory of progress and made it part and parcel of a general theory of evolution.   Living as he did in pre-Darwinian days, Hegel himself denied or ignored the doctrine of organic evolution, the physical evolution of one species from another, but his followers soon discovered that he had been inconsistent on this point and most of them became as enthusiastic supporters of the doc- trine of the origin of species by organic evolution as the most zealous Darwinian biologists, however much they disagreed with the Dar- winians as to how and why this evolution took place.

Hegel, himself, accepted the notion that superior races evolve from inferior races within the human species and that the rich and elaborate language structure of modern times has developed from the primitive sounds used by savages. More especially did he emphasize the idea that there has been a slow but steady evolution of social, legal, and political institutions, and of ethical, artistic, religious, and philosophical ideals. The concept that human ideals have constantly evolved was made a cornerstone of the whole Hegelian system. Hegel did, indeed, think that the average Prussian of his own day was a better and nobler man than the average Athenian of 400 B.C. But more important, to Hegel, was the fact that the ideals upon which the good and noble Athenian moulded his character were less advanced than the ideals which motivate the modern Prussian. The Athenian, for example, had for his ideal the city-state; the Prussian the far higher ideal of the nation-state. The Athenian accepted slavery as a matter of course; the modern Prussian demands "civic freedom" for all human beings.

The Hegelian school, unlike many "scientific" exponents of evolution, insisted that progress and evolution are inevitable, constant and never-ending. Many non-Hegelians believe that though progress and evolution are the general rule, yet we ourselves and the community in which we live may hinder evolution; we may even refuse to progress and insist on going backwards. Hegel, on the other hand, taught that though some groups may progress more rapidly than others, this was all part of the cosmic scheme and that no individual and no group of individuals could check or curb the omnipotent upward surge of the world process, of mind unfolding itself. To the Hegelians, progress and evolution are no more voluntary than is the growth of the individual from childhood to adulthood. The doctrine of inevitable development along a certain direction has always been a powerful weapon in the Hegelian advocacy of certain political institutions. The Hegelian claim that the strong, national authoritarian state is the inevitable goal of human evolution was a telling argument with many persons for the immediate acceptance of such a state, on the principle of "eventually — why not now?" As Sabine remarks, "Nothing strengthens the sinews like believing that one stands at Armageddon and battles for the Lord; that the issue is not really in doubt, because one is ranged on the side of eternal right" — and one might add, of "eternal might." [29]

Many persons, not imbued with Hegelian ideas, believe that evolution and progress have been the dominant notes in world history, but claim that at certain periods man has degenerated rather than progressed. They point out the general collapse of civilization following the fall of the Roman Empire and declare that the passing of man from classical times to the Dark Ages can scarcely be called progress.   In other words, while admitting progress to be a general rule they refuse to admit that it is constant or unceasing.   This position is also attacked by the orthodox Hegelians.   To Hegel and his followers the constant stream of progress has never stopped — all seeming exceptions to this rule are purely illusory.   To their minds the passage of world history from one stage to another necessarily involves a break with old institutions, a period of seeming anarchy, but this break, this collapse of the old, is merely a necessary stage in the passage from a lesser to a greater good. Hence this period of anarchy is itself a sign of progress.

Most empirical scientists, geologists, biologists, and the like admit that there has been genuine progress and evolution in times past. They see no reason to doubt that evolution will continue for an indefinite period in the future.   But they refuse to admit that the "upward" movement will or must continue forever.   They point out that in all probability the sun and the earth will eventually cool to such an extent that all animal and all human life will be extinguished.   The Hegelians ignore all such considerations.   They are firm in their cosmic optimism.   They are firm in their belief that evolution is not only constant but also never-ending.

Darwin and most other evolutionary biologists think that chance or accident has had a great deal to do with the course which evolution has taken.   In a given litter of rabbits it so happens that some are lighter in color than others.   It so happens that at that particular time climatic or environmental conditions are such that the light-colored rabbits have a better chance of survival than dark rabbits.   The dark rabbits die out in that region; the light-colored rabbits survive and breed.   Before long a new species of rabbits, one exclusively light in color, has emerged. The emergence of this new species is not part of a rational cosmic process; it is the result of a series of accidents.   It is not the result of a survival of the *best;* it is the result of the survival of those which by chance were the fittest at that particular time and place.   To the orthodox Hegelians such notions were horrible; such notions were blasphemous against the Universal Spirit.   Evolution to the Hegelians must mean the survival, not of those which happened to prove fittest, but of the best — the survivors were fittest because they were the best. Evolution is not the result of chance or caprice, but of fixed, determined iaws of development, the unfolding through an inner necessity of unconscious mind in the direction of a definite goal.   Evolution, to the Hegelians, must mean an evolution towards something, and this something is the realization of the rational ideal. Evolution to the Hegelians "ceases to be a mechanical, it becomes a spiritual law." Progress is not mere change, but change according to fixed principles and for the better. "Development is no mere formal process — development of nothing in particular. It is the gradual working towards a determinate end. That end is the realization of Spirit." [30]

Other writers have given a deterministic interpretation of history. Some have advocated the belief that all history is the result of purely material factors, such as climate or the nature of the geographic environment. Some have stressed the idea that human development is entirely dependent upon the racial factor. Others have defended the thesis that human history and the development of human institutions have depended entirely upon the economic background. Many of these writers have been profoundly influenced by Hegel's advocacy of historic determinism. But to Hegel himself and to orthodox Hegelians all such ideas were completely heretical. To Hegel, human development is indeed determined, but it is determined only by Universal Mind and the spontaneous unfolding of Universal Mind. Philosophy, to Hegel, shows that the world has an ultimate rational design; it further shows that this design has been actually realized in cosmic and in human history. This in turn shows that the world was formed and grew through the activity of reason, even though this reason was creative and unconscious rather than reflective and conscious. Reason, therefore, is the "sovereign of the world." The world is not abandoned to chance and external contingent causes, for "reason directs the world. Reason is the infinite energy of the universe." [31]

Hegel admitted that there was a close association between his doctrine of rational determinism and the old theological doctrine that the world is governed by Divine Providence. The idea "that a Providence (that of God) presides over the events of the world, consorts with the proposition in question; for Divine Providence is wisdom endowed with an infinite power which realizes its aim, namely, the absolute rational design of the world." [32] There were, however, several differences between Hegel's rational determinism and the orthodox view of Providence. To Hegel, God was an impersonal principle rather than a concrete personality (in the ordinary sense of the word). Hegel rejected, moreover, though with great caution, the notion of miracles or direct supernatural intervention in the laws of the universe. Divine Wisdom to him worked through the laws of the universe rather than by interfering with their operation. God was immanent in the process of history

rather than ruling it from without. Finally Hegel objected to the idea
that the workings of Providence are mysterious and beyond the reach
of human understanding. Divine Wisdom, and the world plan designed
by Divine Wisdom, if still unknown, are not unknowable. God, to
Hegel, is Reason and the world plan is rational. Hence man, by using
his reason, "penetrates even into the deep things of Godhead." [33]

To the student of political thought one of the most important phases
of Hegel's philosophy of evolution and of history is his doctrine that one
of the chief goals, not only of human but also of cosmic development, is
the creation and gradual perfection of the national state. The state,
we are told, is the last and "most perfect embodiment of Spirit." [34]
The ultimate actualization or realization of the Universal Mind "is to be
found in the state, in its laws, its universal and rational arrangements." [35]
As a separate organism the pinnacle of evolution is to be found in man.
The cosmic process which evolved through inert matter, next through
plant life, and then through animal life finds its culminating point in
the emergence of human beings. To Hegel there will and can be no
further physical evolution. To the question, "Beyond man — what?"
Hegel answers decisively, "Nothing."

But though physical evolution reached its goal with the emergence
of mankind, the process of spiritual evolution was not yet completed.
The line which spiritual evolution has taken subsequent to this period
has been the creation and development of human institutions, first the
family, then civic society, then the state. The state is above all "the
Divine Idea as it exists on earth." Even as regards the form of the
state there has been a progressive evolution. The World Spirit working
through man has passed through the despotic empire of the Orientals,
the small city-state of the Greeks, the amorphous world-state of the
Romans, and now has reached the final and most perfect development
of political institutions in the form of the national state. Just as
Hegel refuses to believe that there can be any further physical evolution
beyond man, so does he likewise refuse to believe that there can be any
further social or political evolution beyond the national state. This
national state is, therefore, the supreme goal of cosmic development.

THE ETATISM OF HEGEL

The study of Hegel's philosophy of history has already given us a
general insight into his philosophy of the state. It only remains to
describe a few of the more detailed features of Hegel's political system
as outlined in the *Philosophy of Right.*

The first of these features is that in the Hegelian philosophy the state is regarded as essentially divine in origin. Hence the state must be looked upon with reverence and awe. In one sense this idea must be considered a revival and reinterpretation of the attitude so common in the sixteenth century when the dogma of the divine right of kings held almost universal sway. To the early Lutherans and Anglicans it seemed obvious that governments are not the work of men but are instituted and ordained by God and hence have absolute and divine right to rule over the destinies of individuals. During the seventeenth and eighteenth centuries most civilized Europeans completely broke with this doctrine. It was the task of Hegel to revivify a doctrine which seemed long since dead. The fact that Hegel's God was impersonal rather than personal, that Hegel was exceedingly dubious about revelation in the ordinary sense of the word, and that he denied miracles or the direct intervention of God in human affairs, did not in the least prevent his undertaking the task.

Hegel started with a violent attack upon the doctrine which had long stood in opposition to the theory of the divine origin of the state, namely, the idea that man originally lived in a pre-political condition, a condition characterized by liberty and equality, and that the state originated with the social contract to which each person gave voluntary allegiance. Hegel was equally vehement in his rejection of the doctrine of "consent," denying both that the state originated with the consent of individuals and that in modern times states must or should rest upon the consent of the governed. To Hegel the notion that in a primitive state of nature men were free and equal was ridiculous. Primitive life, or the state of nature, is "predominantly that of injustice and violence, of untamed natural impulses, of inhuman deeds and feelings." [36] In this state of savagery men live as groups rather than as individuals. Hence "however rude and simple their condition, they involve social arrangements which (to use the common term) restrain freedom." [37] Among savages the strong rule over the weak, the wily over the stupid; hence there is no equality among them. The state, therefore, did not and could not originate in the voluntary union of free and equal individuals. To claim that it commenced with a social contract between its members, or between subjects and their ruler, is historically absurd. The doctrine that the state ever has depended upon the conscious voluntary consent of its subjects is shown by the facts of history to be equally without foundation. [38]

Hegel agrees with Aristotle in claiming that states arise because man is naturally and instinctively a social and political animal.   But Hegel unlike Aristotle, insists that man is thus innately a political animal because of a divine spirit (Universal Mind) moving within him, a divine spirit which can find adequate expression only in the formation of political units.   The state was not the conscious creation of man at one time and place; it is the product of a long process of evolution.   Man being a social animal, even in a primitive state he lived in groups. Slowly but surely under the stimulus of divine wisdom man developed more or less unconsciously from lower, less adequate group life to higher and more perfect institutional life.   Out of the family developed the tribe, out of the tribe the state, at first in a lower, then in a higher form. At each stage of development Hegel sees the workings of Universal Mind, another way of saying divine guidance.   Hence this creation of the perfect modern state must be considered the work of God rather than of man.

Hegel was perfectly aware that the creation of some states was the result of force, of conquest, rather than of slow spontaneous development.   Some of the later Hegelians went even further and suggested that all higher political institutions have originated with the conquest of one people by another, or the seizing of power by some one outstanding individual.   But this fact, or this claim, in no way invalidated Hegel's central thesis that human history is the march of God in the realm of time.   "World history is world judgment" is Hegel's way of stating Carlyle's proposition that might and right are fundamentally identical.   The victory of one nation over another, the subjugation of a people by a world hero, is a sure sign that the victorious nation or the conquering hero was the unconscious agent of the World Spirit in its process of self-unfolding.   Alexander the Great, Caesar, Napoleon were consciously motivated by love of glory or love of gain, but behind their actions there was really

> an unconscious impulse that occasioned the accomplishment of that for which the time was ripe. . . . They may be called heroes in as much as they have derived their purposes and their vocation . . . from a concealed fount . . . , from that Inner Spirit which, impinging on the outer world as on a shell, bursts it in pieces.[39]

The end of such heroes may be tragic; "they die early, like Alexander, they are murdered, like Caesar, transported to St. Helena, like Napoleon."   But they meet this end only when their purpose has been attained — and this purpose is to act as "agents of the World Spirit."[40]

With a philosophy such as this, it is no wonder that Hegel claims that "the state is the march of God in the world." [41] "The state is the divine will as a present spirit, which unfolds itself in the actual shape of an organized world." [42] "The state is the Divine Idea as it exists on earth." [43]

The second outstanding feature of the Hegelian political philosophy is the idea that the individual must be completely subordinated to the state, and the wishes and desires of the individual must be rejected in favor of the will of the state. In one sense this doctrine is a revival of the old sixteenth century idea of the duty of passive obedience, of the old notion that "such subjects as are disobedient or rebellious against their princes disobey God and procure their own damnation." The worthy writers of the sixteenth century had no need to argue this point. They were content to give numerous scriptural quotations proving that complete subjection to the powers that be is ordained by God, and the vast majority of the population as a result accepted this doctrine as true. In the nineteenth century such tactics were no longer possible, so Hegel, brushing Scripture aside, prepared an elaborate network of metaphysical arguments.

Hegel begins his defense of the absolute state by recasting the wording of the old doctrine. In the nineteenth century, after the work of the English, the American, and the French Revolutions had been accomplished, it was impossible to use the old words "passive obedience." These words stank in the nostrils of the multitude. Even the restored Bourbons who "learned nothing and forgot nothing" found it impossible to use such terms. Hegel, therefore, silently passed over the words passive obedience, and then developed in their place the doctrine of the supremacy of the state over the individual. The old liberals had stressed the notion that the state is not an end in itself, but only the means to an end — the end being the happiness and the welfare of the individual. Hegel, on the other hand, declared that the state *was* an end, or rather the end in itself, and that individuals were merely means to an end, the end being the glorification of the state of which they happened to be members. [44]

> Were the characteristic features [of the state] to be regarded as the security and protection of property and personal freedom, the interest of the individual as such would be the ultimate purpose of the social union. It would then be at one's option to be a member of the state. But the state has a totally different relation to the individual. The state is the objective spirit [an Hegelian expression meaning that the state is the incarnation or embodiment of the Universal Mind or World Spirit] and the individual has his truth, his real existence and ethical status only in being a member of it. [45]

Hegel expressly warns us that in our political thinking "we must not take our departure from individuality or individual self-conscious-ness." [46]   The individual and individual self-consciousness has only an indirect and reflected existence. [47]   Ultimate reality is possessed only by the Universal Mind directly embodied in the state.   "All the worth which the human being possesses, all spiritual reality, he possesses only through the state." [48]   The state "has the highest right over the in-dividual, whose highest duty in turn is to be a member of the state." [49] In short, we may, with Hobhouse, sum up the Hegelian theory of the state by saying that the state is "a greater being, a spirit, a super-personal entity in which individuals with their private consciences or claims of right, their happiness or misery, are merely subordinate elements." [50]

All this, of course, was distinctly shocking to the adherents of the liberal tradition, with their belief in individualism.   Even more shock-ing to them was the fact that Hegel defended his extreme etatist posi-tion by adopting and then slightly misconstruing several of the old liberal terms and formulas.   One of the watchwords of the liberals was liberty or freedom.   In the name of liberty the liberals had fought against absolute monarchs; in the name of liberty they defended the rights and privileges of the individual against the absolute powers of the state — even a state democratically organized and democratically governed.   The old defenders of absolutism, the defenders of the divine rights of kings, made passionate attacks upon the principles of liberty or freedom, and claimed that it led straight to anarchism.   Not so Hegel and the Hegelians.   Hegel claimed to be as passionately at-tached to the principles of freedom as any liberal; he proclaimed that freedom was the keystone to his whole political philosophy.

> The essence of Spirit is Freedom.... The history of the world is none other than the progress of the consciousness of Freedom.... The Orientals have not attained the knowledge that Spirit — man as such — is free.... They only know that one [their despotic ruler] is free.... The Greeks... and the Romans... knew only that some are free — not man as such.... The Ger-man nations... were the first to attain the consciousness that man, as man, is free. [51]

From this it follows that "the state as a completed reality [i.e., the state in its perfected form] is the actualization of Freedom." [52]

These words were as sweet music to the liberals and many persons were foolish enough to think, because of these expressions, that Hegel was a liberal at heart.   But Hegel then proceeds to demonstrate to his own satisfaction, and to the satisfaction of his numerous followers, that true freedom means voluntary but complete subservience to the dictates of the state. In order to prove this point Hegel adopts and develops the definition of liberty laid down by Kant and accepted in one form or another by Fichte, by Carlyle, and by Green, namely, that liberty consists in the ability to do what one ought to do. This Kantian-Hegelian notion of freedom may be more fully summed up in the follow ing words:

> By freedom is meant not the mere absence of external restraints; not the liberty of the individual to do what he wills with his own faculties and his own possessions ... , but the untrammeled *development* of man's powers, moral, intellectual, and spiritual, according to the fundamental laws of his own nature.[53]

So far Kant and Hegel are in complete agreement. They further agree that as man is essentially rational, action in accord with "the fundamental laws of man's own nature" means action in accord with right reason. But here Kant and Hegel diverge. To Kant rational action (or free action) means action in accordance with man's individual reason. To Hegel rational action (or free action) is action in accordance with universal reason — universal reason both in the abstract sense and also as embodied in rational institutions, such as the state, with its system of universal rational laws. To obey the laws of the state, therefore, means merely to act in accord with reason, the inner essence of each man. Hence by obeying these laws man becomes for the first time free.

Man in a state of isolation is not free to Hegel, for in isolation man cannot develop his material or moral or intellectual faculties. Such development can take place only in community life where man associates with his fellow man. Man is not free in primitive communities ruled by irrational dictates of barbarism and savagery. Limitation of individual action is certainly produced by more advanced stages of society and the state, but "it is a limitation of mere brute emotion and rude instincts ... , of self-will, of caprice, and passions. ... Such limitation is the indispensable provision of emancipation. ... To the ideal of Freedom, law and morality are indispensably requisite." [54] Or, as Vaughan, the devout disciple of Hegel on political matters, puts it,

> It is impossible for the soul, as a principle of action, to unfold its powers to any degree without the submission of the individual to certain specific duties which he himself had no share in imposing, and which he only comes gradually to recognize as the adequate and the necessary expression of his own freedom and personality.[55]

To Hegel and the Hegelians, freedom is largely a feeling or consciousness of freedom, an awareness of the fact that in obeying the laws of
the state, the external embodiment of reason, one is really obeying the
laws of one's own true rational self.

This doctrine, the very kernel of Hegel's political philosophy, was
greatly expanded by some of the later Hegelians, especially by Bernard
Bosanquet, the most outstanding of the English Neo-Hegelians, whose
book, the *Philosophical Theory of the State*, is regarded almost as a bible
by the majority of modern etatists.   Bosanquet's political philosophy
may be summed up as follows: (1) The individual is free only when he
acts in conformity with his real will as opposed to his "actual" or apparent will.   (2) The real will of the individual is identical with the
general will of the community in which he lives, and by general will
Bosanquet means the real will of the community and not the apparent
or "actual" will of the majority of the population.   (3) Finally, the
general will is embodied in the state and in the laws laid down by the
state.   Or to put the idea in another way, when a man obeys the laws of
the state in which he is a citizen, he is obeying the general will of the
community.   In obeying the general will of the community he is really
obeying his own rational or true will.   In obeying his own rational will
a man is obviously free.   Hence a man is more free when he obeys the
dictates of the state than when he obeys the dictates of his own momentary desires and passions.

Bosanquet's political ideas are obviously a rehash of Rousseau's
theories (minus the social contract) reinterpreted in the light of
Hegelian philosophy.   Bosanquet, like Rousseau, thinks that all valid
political thought must start with the rational will of each individual.
This will (Bosanquet calls it the real will), being rational, always seeks
to defend and expand the true best interests of the individual.   But
man, because of his lower animal instincts, is sometimes led into error.
He wishes or desires a particular object (such as a bottle of gin), though
the possession of such an object may be hurtful to him or at least not be
in accord with his own best interests.   Hence these wishes and desires
are the expressions of his apparent or actual will and not of his rational
or real will.   The self is free, therefore, only when it is master of its
passions, or, in other words, when the real will is master of the actual will.

But how can the real will be induced to assert itself and become
master of the actual will?   To Bosanquet the only acceptable answer to
this question is by saying "through the agency of the general will."

To Bosanquet, as to Rousseau, each community does possess such ?

general will, which is the union of the individual wills of all its citizens, though Rousseau believed that the general will was created by the social contract, while Bosanquet asserted that the general will is the product of a long social development. To Rousseau and to Bosanquet the general will invariably seeks to safeguard the true interests of the community as a whole, and the true interests of all the persons whose wills unite to form the general will. To Bosanquet, as to Rousseau, "the general will is always right and always tends to the public advantage" — though, in order to maintain this position, both thinkers were forced to distinguish between the real general will and the actual general will, the wishes and desires of the majority of the population at any given time.

To Bosanquet as to Rousseau it was necessary that the general will be realized in a concrete form (Hegel's doctrine of objective as opposed to subjective spirit). To a certain extent this general will is concretely expressed in the moral and social traditions of society (i.e., non-political society) in which we live. But the most complete and perfect embodiment of the general will is in the all-powerful state, with its will expressed in laws, and its administrative machinery to see that these laws are enforced. As Bosanquet himself informs us, the real purpose of Rousseau's doctrine and of his own, was to show that

> the negative relation of the self to the other selves begins to dissolve away before the conception of the common self [i.e., the state]; and the negative regulation of the self to law and government begins to disappear in the idea of a law which expresses our real wills as opposed to our trivial and rebellious moods.[56]

Considering this curious definition of liberty, it is small wonder that Rousseau could say "whosoever shall refuse to obey the general will shall be constrained to do so by the whole body, which means nothing else than he will be forced to be free." Nor need we be surprised when we find that according to Bosanquet's principles when a thief runs down the street pursued by a policeman, the thief *really* wills that the policeman catch him, that the judge sentence him to prison so that he may expiate his crime against society — although his actual or apparent will is, of course, that he get away scot-free. The thief would be considerably astonished to learn that his real will ran so contrary to his actual will. But Bosanquet blandly assures us that we must not be led astray by the criminal's ignorance of his own real will. The criminal, he says, "doubtless ... would think it cruel nonsense. ... But after all we are dealing with social logic and not with empirical psychology."[57]

In the light of this philosophic background it is not surprising that

Hegel himself, that great apostle of freedom in the abstract, thought that true freedom had nothing to do with political freedom in the ordinary sense, the right of the people to elect their own officials or to make their own laws.   Nor did his abstract freedom have anything to do with everyday freedom of speech or freedom of the press.   "To define the liberty of the press as the liberty to speak and write what one pleases is parallel to the definition of liberty in general as liberty to do as one pleases." [58]   On Hegel's own principles, therefore, freedom of speech and of the press means the freedom to say and to print what one should say and write, or rather what the general will (embodied in the government) tells us that we should say and write.

The third feature of the Hegelian political philosophy is the idea that the dictates of the state are higher and more important than the dictates of natural law and of subjective morality.   This phase of Hegelianism stands in marked contrast with the teachings of practically all the earlier political philosophies.   From early classical times men drew a distinction between law as it is (whether customary law or statutory law) and law as it ought to be.   Among the Romans, law as it ought to be came to be called natural law.   It was also called rational law or the law of reason.   Throughout the Middle Ages it was a common axiom of faith that civil law, the statutory law imposed by the state, must be based upon the eternal principles of natural law or rational law, and that any civil law which violently conflicted with natural law was *ipso facto* invalid.   In the seventeenth and eighteenth centuries the doctrine of the supremacy of natural law was adopted by all the great liberal thinkers such as Locke and his followers.   In fact it became one of the foundation stones of liberalism.

In the hands of the liberals the idea of natural law became an excuse for rebellion against despotic governments.   If the laws laid down by such governments were contrary to natural law, the citizens had a right to ignore or break them and to overthrow the government which sought to impose them.   Of great importance is the fact that the liberal thinkers closely associated the concept of natural law with the concept of natural rights, such as life, liberty, and property, or life, liberty, and the pursuit of happiness, which each individual should enjoy under the dictates of natural law, whether the existing government recognized such rights or not.   According to the liberals, if a government did not grant such rights it was acting against the fundamental precepts of natural law and might legitimately be overthrown by armed rebellion. As the doctrine of natural law and natural rights was made the cornerstone of individualism against the arbitrary encroachments of the absolute state, it is only natural that Hegel should regard the whole idea with deep suspicion and hostility.

Equally dangerous to the Hegelian view of the power and function of the state was the old doctrine that the dictates of morality are higher and more binding than the dictates of positive law as formulated and enforced by the government. The early Christians were willing to render unto Caesar the things which were Caesar's, but they were equally insistent upon rendering unto God the things which are God's. In case of conflict, in case Caesar claimed that which rightly belonged to God, there could be no doubt as to where the Christian's duty lay. He must resist Caesar in the name of God, even though he suffer martyrdom for so doing. During the Middle Ages almost unanimous consent was given to the doctrine that the laws of the secular states must never be contrary to the religious and moral codes (the two were considered more or less identical) as laid down and safeguarded by the church. The Reformation shattered the control of the church in such matters, at least in Protestant countries, but in place of the infallible church there arose the doctrine of the supremacy of the individual conscience. The good Lutherans and Anglicans were told that they should render unquestioning obedience to the demands of the state, save where a question of conscience was concerned; but should the state demand that which was contrary to conscience, the good Christian should offer at least passive resistance. The later Protestant bodies, the French Calvinists, the Scotch Presbyterians, the English Puritans and Congregationalists went even further and declared that when a government sought to impose laws which are contrary to conscience the citizens might lawfully arise and overthrow the government. The classical liberals, even those not especially concerned with theological matters, eagerly adopted this doctrine. Their whole concept of liberty, liberty of speech, of the press, of religious opinion, was based upon the notion that the state must not seek to override the conscience of the individual citizen.

For the Hegelian doctrine of the absolute supremacy of the state over the individual to win acceptance it was necessary for Hegel to attack the supremacy of natural law and natural rights and also the supremacy of the individual conscience in matters of morality. Hegel entered into the fray with relish and enthusiasm, but it is typical of him and his methods in general that his attack on both doctrines was a flank and not a frontal attack. When Hegel entered into conflict with the liberals he almost never directly denied the arguments or even the conclusions

of his adversaries.   His policy was to accept the liberal position and
then show that it meant something completely different from what the
liberal philosophers thought it meant.   When the liberals pleaded for
freedom as opposed to tyranny, Hegel shouted, " I, too, believe in freedom
as much as you do if not more," and then proceeded to show that freedom meant blind obedience to the dictates of the state.   In like manner,
when the liberals proclaimed their belief in natural law, in natural
rights, and the sanctity of conscience, Hegel proclaimed, " I, too, believe
in these things," and then proceeded to prove to his own satisfaction
that the dictates of natural law and of the individual conscience are not
and never can be contrary to the dictates of the modern state.   In fact
he goes even further and claims that all that which is worthy or valid
in natural law or individual morality is included in but transcended by
the dictates of the absolute state.

In order to prove his point Hegel brings in the aid of his famed
dialectic, the development of logical thought from thesis, through antithesis, to synthesis.   The World Spirit in the process of self-unfolding
passes at first (thesis) through the stage in which it concerns itself with
abstract right and abstract rights.   This is the sphere of natural law
and natural rights — rights for rights' sake.   Eventually the World
Spirit, the mind of mankind, evolves beyond this state and reaches
the state of (antithesis), *subjective morality*.   This is the stage where
man concerns himself with moral right and wrong, and convinces himself
that there are some things which are right and some which are wrong.
This is the sphere of duty for duty's sake — the sphere of the individual
conscience, calling upon each man to perform what he feels he ought to
perform.   Finally the World Spirit passes to the third and last stage
(the stage of synthesis), or *social ethics*, where man no longer concerns
himself merely with abstract right and abstract wrong, but is zealous
for the concrete social and ethical codes laid down by such institutions
as the family, society, and above all, by the state.

In the lowest category, the sphere of abstract right, Hegel deals with
the concepts advocated by the old natural-law philosophers.   To Hegel,
as to most other German writers, right (the German *Recht*) means
right (as opposed to wrong), and also law, and also a right or rights.
In dealing with his doctrine of abstract right, Hegel constantly shifts
from one meaning of the term to another, but for the most part he emphasizes the notion of abstract right as meaning abstract rights, the
right or rights which an individual ought to possess on the basis or
reason (or natural law).   Hegel finds that a man, *qua* man, does and

should possess rights. He has the right to be considered and be treated as a person and not as a thing. In order to make his personality complete, reason dictates that he should be permitted to own property of some sort (real or personal). To make ownership complete, a man must be permitted to acquire, give away, and exchange his property. This in turn means that man must be permitted to enter into contractual relations with his fellow man.

All this is or seems to be in accord with the teachings of the old liberal defenders of natural law and natural rights. But Hegel then proceeds to state that abstract right, or rights for rights' sake, mark a low and imperfect phase of reason. When man thinks about his rights and nothing else, the result is endless discord leading to universal conflict and anarchy. For man to make real progress, he must not deny, but he must transcend, the idea of rights for rights' sake and enter the moral sphere in which he learns to value duty for duty's sake; he must learn what he *must* do, not merely what he has a right to do. For a man to exercise his rights, he must also perform his duties, and his duties, as we shall presently see, are those laid down, not by the individual conscience, but by the community of which he is a member. Even within the sphere of abstract rights we soon find that the rights which Hegel gives the individual are not the rights which any "actual" person claims. True rights are the rights which reason says that a man ought to have in order that he may best develop the divine capacities within him. But the person who lays down and defines these rights is not and should not be the private individual with his mass of petty wishes and desires, but the general will, the rational will behind all individuals, embodied in the dictates of the state. The rational will, as embodied in the state, recognizes that men, to develop the best that is in them, should be permitted to own property and enter into contractual relations with one another. Hence men have rational or "natural" rights in such matters. But the same rational will, as embodied in the state, also lays down the conditions under which man may enjoy these rights. It lays down the conditions under which men may enter into contractual relations or acquire, sell, and exchange property. And these conditions are just as rational, just as "natural," as the rights themselves. Above all, "private possession must be kept subject to the higher spheres of right, to a corporate body, or the state." [59]

Having thus dismissed the argument of those who pleaded that natural rights are different from and higher than the rights and duties laid down by the state, Hegel and the Hegelians next turn to combat the notion that the claims of morality and the individual conscience are higher than the dictates of organized society. Hegel's arguments are directed against the "intuitionists" or those who claim that each person is possessed of moral feeling or a conscience which invariably tells him (and tells him rightly) what is right and what is wrong. Hegel's arguments are also directed against the slightly different but basically similar doctrine of Kant, namely, that in the field of morals a man must be guided not by feeling but by reason — the practical reason of each man being to Kant the agent which tells a man what he should and what he should not do, and which, when consulted, invariably gives him the right answer. To the intuitionists and to Kant there is no need to consult external authority when faced with a moral problem, and should the state or any other external agent seek to impose any line of conduct against which our own moral sense or our own reason rebels, we are morally bound to resist the state.

To Hegel all such doctrines were horrible, but following his usual procedure he began by accepting his opponents' premises. The intuitionists are right, say Hegel and the Hegelians, in claiming that men have a moral sense or conscience which tells them that there is a difference between good and bad, and makes them obligated to follow the good. Kant, moreover, is right in claiming that the dictates of conscience are ultimately derived from and depend upon reason or the rational will. Goodness consists in willing and doing the rational. But, says Hegel, this is only the beginning, not the end of the ethical problem. Conscience is right in saying that there is a good and a bad. On this all men are agreed. But conscience alone cannot be considered the eternally valid basis of action because the consciences of different people tell them different things. More especially does the conscience of one time and one place differ from the conscience of another time and another place. Conscience at all times and at all places agrees that there is a good and a bad, and thus far is valid. But the content of the conscience, the feeling that *this* is good and *that* is bad, differs from age to age and from nation to nation, hence to claim that the content of my conscience or your conscience is eternally and absolutely true or valid is absurd. In like manner Kant was right when he claimed that reason, individual reason, tells us that there is a difference between good and bad and that we are obligated to seek the good, but he was wrong when he claimed that abstract reasoning on the part of the individual will enable him to deduce a complete moral code, binding upon him throughout life. The average man is so full of caprice and prejudice that when he claims to think rationally, he is frequently guilty of "wishful thinking," of defending by pseudo-reasoning his own capricious likes and dislikes.

From the Hegelian standpoint, abstract or subjective morality can give us only the blank concept of goodness, of duty, of moral obligation. In order to fill out this blank concept, in order to find out *what* is good, or where our duty lies, we must leave the realm of abstract or subjective morality and enter the realm of concrete social ethics. The German word for social ethics is *Sittlichkeit*, which is ultimately derived from the term *Sitte* or custom, a fact which throws a great deal of light upon what Hegel really meant by social ethics. Social ethics, as opposed to subjective morality, is the moral code based upon the customs, traditions, dictates of the group, whether family, social, or political, in which one happens to be born. Older thinkers claimed that true morality consisted in departing from that which is merely customary and seeking to judge all conduct by an eternally valid subjective standard. Hegel denied this claim. To him subjective standards led only to confusion or empty abstractions. True ethics consisted in being motivated by the inner conscience, but also in conforming to the ethical standard of the group of which one formed a part. "It is from the conscience of the community and from that alone that any specification of duties can come." [60] "Virtues and duties have no meaning apart from the institutions which give them concrete form. . . . Man is not a lonely being cut off from his fellows, and his moral ideas are not to be found ready-made within his mind. They grow along with the development of customs and institutions and are inseparably connected with them." [61]

The Hegelians insist that ethical intuitionism — "my conscience is my only guide" — is contrary to the principle of progress and evolution. At any given time a man does have a conscience and this conscience does have a specific content. It does tell him that it is right to do this and wrong to do that. But whether he is aware of it or not, the content of this conscience is derived from his environment, his childhood experiences, the teachings of his parents, the praise or blame of his comrades. The intuitionist takes this conscience with its specific content and assumes it to be forever valid. In doing so he forgets that the conscience of the savage is on a different and a far lower level from the conscience of a man living in a civilized community. Worse still he fails to realize that the conscience of a man in the distant future, with a more perfect social organization, will be on a level different from and far higher than the conscience of present-day man. Intuitionism tends to "fossilize the principles of conduct at the particular stage of social development which

commends itself to the particular intuitionist." [62]   The same argument
holds good against the doctrines of Kant.   Kant was right in claiming that
the ethical code must be an expression of the rational will, but he was
wrong in identifying the deductions of the subjective understanding with
the postulates of the rational will.   The true rational will is the universal will embodied in human institutions and expressing itself in the
form of custom, of tradition, and of state-made laws.

The fourth feature of the Hegelian political philosophy is the doctrine
that among the social institutions that must dominate mankind society
is higher and more important than the family, but the state is higher and
more important than society.

The first phase of this doctrine, the idea that the family is transcended
in importance by society, calls for little comment.   In China, certainly in
old China, such insistence was laid upon the family that the average
Chinese grew up with the idea that the welfare of the family was more
important than the welfare of society in general or the state in particular.
Among nearly all modern peoples, however, and especially among the
European peoples, the notion that the well-being of the family must be
subordinated to society as a whole is so widespread that it is unnecessary
to deal in detail with Hegel's defense of this proposition.   It is, however,
of some interest to see what Hegel thought the family and family life
should be.   Among most Oriental peoples, and even among the Greeks
and Romans of European antiquity, the word family meant the great or
patriarchal family.   All the descendants of a single male ancestor constituted the family in the true sense of the word.   In this type of family
organization the father has control over the lives and fortunes of his sons
not only when they are small but even after they have reached maturity
with wives and children of their own.   In China today one finds many a
household consisting of three or four generations living together, with the
lives of the whole group dominated by a single person, the ancestor of the
people by whom he is surrounded.   To Hegel's mind the true family is
very different from this.   To him the family means a man, his wife, and
their immature children.   When children come of age, certainly when
they marry, they cease to be members of the parental family and create
new family groups of their own.   A man's first loyalty, therefore, must be
to his wife and his own children, and not as in China or ancient Rome to
his parents, his brothers, or his uncles.   Parental control of and responsibility for their children should cease when they reach maturity.

St. Paul preached celibacy as the highest ideal for all persons.   The

Catholic Church believes that the bulk of the population should marry, but that many persons, specially called by God, should remain free from family ties. Hegel, on the other hand, thought that it was the duty of all men and of all women to marry. "That an individual may fulfill his ethical duty, he should marry." [63] Ignoring the polygamous customs of the Orient and even of the ancient Jewish people, he claims that monogamy is the only true and rational form of married life. Marriage is a contract, but it is more than a contract, it is a divine institution. Hence weddings should take the form of a public ceremony, preferably a religious ceremony. For the same reason divorce, though permitted, should be made as difficult as possible. More interesting is the fact that he held old-fashioned German views as to how marriages should be arranged. Marriage and the family should be based upon love, but not upon "subjective passion." "Marriage as an ethical institution is an embodiment of the universal and as such has a higher right than the particular inclinations, whims, caprices of the individual." [64] From this it follows that marriage should not be the result of "the falling in love" of two young people. The bride and the groom should consent to their wedding, but in general marriages should result from the arrangement of the parents. Provided the husband or wife is wisely selected, "love" will spring up in due course. Hegel strongly objects to having the young people know one another too well before marriage. "Familiarity, intimacy, habituation due to the same course of action ought not to occur previous to marriage, but should be found for the first time in the married state." [65] To be thoroughly consistent Hegel should have urged us to go back to the good old custom whereby the bride and groom meet for the first time on their wedding day. Divine wisdom, plus German tradition, revealed to Hegel that marriage should be associated with the *dot* or dowry and marriage-settlement system. He was also convinced that reason demanded that the family fortune should be treated as a unit, the administration of which should lie entirely with the husband. The modern system, whereby the wife maintains control over her own fortune, would have struck him as "irrational."

Hegel, like the modern Nazis, was an earnest apostle of the theory that a woman's place is in the home.

> Women can, of course, be educated, but their minds are not adapted to the higher sciences, philosophy, or certain of the arts. These demand a universal faculty. Women may have happy inspirations, taste, elegance, but they have not the ideal [i.e., the gift of universality]. The difference between man and woman is the same as that between animal and plant.

The animal corresponds more closely to the character of the man, the plant
to that of the woman.... If women were to control the government, the state
would be in danger, for they do not act according to the dictates of universality, but are influenced by accidental inclinations and opinions.[66]

But though the scope of women should be confined to family matters,
it is the inevitable destiny of men to emerge from the narrow limits of the
family circle and deal with the world of society.   It is part of Hegel's
philosophy that the very growth and development of the family ends in
its own destruction.   The chief object of the family is the procreation
and nurture of children, but the nurture of children brings them to
maturity, whereby they automatically leave the family circle and enter
the world of society, in which the individual units are no longer bound
together by ties of affection, but struggle, each person for himself, for
survival and for dominance over his fellow men.

This very statement shows Hegel's rather peculiar attitude towards
the nature of society, and foreshadows his arguments as to why society
must be curbed and controlled by the state.   To the old liberal writers,
society was the world of voluntary cooperation, to Hegel it was the world
of universal competition, needing a higher power to keep this competition from getting out of hand.   To Paine, one great representative of the
liberal tradition, man's social instincts, his tendency to settle near his
neighbors even when not forced to do so, was a sign that naturally and
normally men liked one another and that their relationship with one
another was based upon friendship and affection.   To Paine the state or
government with its reliance upon force was necessary only to provide for
those few persons devoid of social instincts who tried to defraud or do
violence to their neighbors.

> Society is produced by our wants, government by our wickedness.   The
> former promotes our happiness positively by uniting our affection, the latter
> negatively by restraining our vices.... The first is a patron, the last is a
> punisher.   Society in every state is a blessing, but government even in the
> best state is but a necessary evil, in the worse state an intolerable one....
> Government is no further necessary than to supply the few cases to which
> society and civilization are not conveniently competent.

Even such an avowed semi-etatist as T. H. Green, strongly influenced
though he was by Hegel, had still enough of the liberal feeling to subordinate the state, based upon force, to society, based upon voluntary
cooperation.   To Green society as a whole is of far greater importance
than the individual.   But this society is based upon man's natural instincts, his instinctive desire to live in harmony with his fellow beings,

not upon armed might or political subjection. Society has its "natural laws," or the standard of conduct which the community feels should hold sway between its members, its "natural rights," the rights which the general community feels the individual ought to have. To Green these natural laws and natural rights were all-important. To him, the state was merely an agent, frequently an imperfect agent, of society. The positive laws of the state and the legal rights granted by the state are merely attempts and frequently very imperfect attempts to embody the natural laws and the natural rights of society in a concrete form, in a form enforceable by physical sanctions. If the state as the agent of society should betray its trust, its actions must be stopped. Should the actual laws of the state sharply conflict with the natural laws of society, should the state radically infringe upon the natural rights granted by society, it is the moral duty of the private individual to resist the state and, if necessary, to overthrow the government.

All such notions were anathema to Hegel and to the orthodox Hegelians. To Hegel, society, if not a state of conflict (Hobbes' state of war), was at least a state of limitless and ruthless competition. Hegel's view of society was strongly influenced by the science of economics which, in Hegel's own lifetime, was beginning to attract widespread public attention. To Hegel, society, was characterized, not by affection and friendship, but by the "laws" recently enunciated by such men as Adam Smith and Ricardo. It was these economic laws which constituted the natural laws of society and not natural laws in the sense of ideal laws — laws as they should be. The "economic man" of the economists was the same as Hegel's normal man in a state of society. Such a man did not necessarily go about murdering and robbing his neighbors, but naturally and normally he did tend to buy in the cheapest and sell in the dearest market, irrespective of how such a course of action might affect the general welfare of the community as a whole. In his intercourse with his fellow human beings (apart from members of his own family) the average man was chiefly concerned with the profit motive. In buying or selling property, in making a contract to labor or for the hire of labor, a man's main interest was in how much he was to get out of the deal. Society then is dominated by the principle of self-seeking and "individuals in society are private persons who pursue their own interests." [67] Such an institution can surely not be considered the goal and aim of evolution.

Hegel thought that a great forward step is taken when men depart from the pure individualism of society as a whole and group themselves together in the form of voluntary associations, which he calls corporations.   By the word corporation Hegel means not a business firm but such institutions as the guilds of the Middle Ages, or the employers' associations and the trade unions of the present day.   To Hegel the tendency of mankind to form such groups was an excellent sign — the sign not of its social instinct (for to Hegel the social instinct meant competition) but of its "state instinct," a blind groping towards the perfect union of mankind in the form of the state.   In the corporation "the particular and self-seeking end" of society becomes transformed into "something actively universal." [68]   When a man joins a corporation "it is also recognized that he belongs to and has active interest in a whole, whose aim is to promote the welfare of society in general." [69]   Speaking of the decay of the mediaeval guilds, he says, "In modern times the corporation has been superseded, with the intention that the individual should care for himself. . . . It is, however, needful to provide the ethical man with a universal activity, one above his private ends.   This universal, with which the modern state does not always supply him, is given by the corporation." [70]   Hegel, of course, insists that the state is higher than the corporation, that the corporation must be subject to state control and regulation, but he is equally convinced that the corporation has an all-important part to play as the link between the individual and the state.

This stress upon the corporation is a very significant phase of the Hegelian political philosophy.   Most of the older etatists, such as Bodin, Hobbes, and even Kant, had looked upon guilds and corporations with a very suspicious eye as tending to conflict with the supreme loyalty which the individual owed to the state.   They insisted that the state should have immediate and direct control over and contact with the individual rather than indirect control through the agency of an intervening group.   In Hegel we find nothing of this attitude.   In the Hegelian system the state is so all-important that it has no need to be jealous of lesser groups; rather does it aid and sponsor such groups because through them the private person learns to forget his selfish individualistic point of view and merge himself in the activities of a greater whole — a necessary stage to the understanding and appreciation of the God-created state.   It is this phase of the Hegelian philosophy which was later developed into the theory of the corporative state in the Fascist and Nazi ideology.

But though the corporation marks a valuable step in the gradual evolution of mankind from the ruthless individualism of society, it is impossible for humanity to pause at this stage.   The corporation rests and must rest upon voluntary action, upon codes and principles freely accepted by its members, and this is not enough. For the many iniquities of society to be overcome it is necessary to use force. This all-important force finds itself embodied in the form of the courts of justice and the police. Owing to Hegel's rather peculiar terminology, he regards these two institutions as separate from and subordinated to the state proper, or rather as two social institutions created, preserved, and regulated by the state in the latter's attempt to curb and control the vicious tendencies inherent in society as a whole.

Hegel's attitude towards the courts of justice calls for only brief mention. He insists that courts derive their authority not from society but from the state and from the state only. In society, apart from the state, there is no way of securing justice save by the iniquitous system of private vengeance. The law that they administer, moreover, must be the law which has been formulated and commanded by the state. Some thinkers, including some of the later Hegelians, thought that law owes its origin and much of its validity to custom. Such persons show a marked partiality to the English type of common law, based upon tradition and precedent. To Hegel himself, however, this idea was obnoxious. It was too much like saying that law owes its validity more to its acceptance by society than to its expressing the commands of the state. Law, to Hegel, should be based upon the principles of abstract right, but abstract right, as interpreted by the rational will, to him is another way of expressing the term state.

Abstract right, moreover, has no vitality and hence no validity until it is embodied in the commands and the statutes of the state. Many laws may, in point of fact, have originated as customs. But customs, unlike laws, "are affected with accidentality and contingency. They are subjective and partial in their application." [71] For customs to pass into laws they must acquire universal application and be definitely "instituted," and this can be done only by the action of something higher than society, namely, the state. Incidentally, Hegel thought that laws should not only be embodied in state-made statutes; these statutes should also be included in a series of rational codes worked out and made definitive by the state.

Passing from the courts of justice to the police, we find that Hegel gives an even wider interpretation of the police power of the state than does modern American constitutional law. Its chief function is "to oversee and foster the ways and means calculated to promote the public welfare." [72] Hegel admits that in the exercise of their functions "the police may go to work in a pedantic spirit and disturb the moral life of individuals. But great as the nuisance may be, an objective limit to their action cannot be drawn." [73] To Hegel the prevention and punishment of crime is one function but only one of the less important functions of the police power. The police power as the agent of the state (we in America would say the state, using its police power) may and should: (1) Make public improvements, "lighting the streets, building bridges," etc. (2) Control education. Hegel, along with Fichte, was one of the earliest advocates of universal compulsory education. (3) Control public health. Hegel specifically mentions only its right to compel all persons to be vaccinated, but he leaves the field open to all other forms of medical legislation by the phrase "police control ... take charge of health." [74] (4) Look after poor relief. Hegel ridicules the idea that care for the needy should be left to private charity.

> Haphazard almsgiving, and such foundations as the burning of lamps beside holy images, are replaced by public poor houses, hospitals, etc. ... To charity enough still remains. It is a false view for charity to restrict its help to private methods and casual sentiment and knowledge, and to feel itself injured and weakened by regulations binding upon the whole community. On the contrary the public system is to be regarded as all the more complete, the less remains to be done by special effort.[75]

Last but not least, the police, acting for the state, must regulate and control commerce and industry. In defending this position Hegel argues that if it is the duty of the state to look after the poor, it is also its duty to check the cause of poverty — the free, unbridled individualism witnessed in unregulated society. Sometimes this control is to be exercised merely over irresponsible individuals.

> The community has the duty and right to take under its guardianship those who wantonly squander their subsistence and that of their family. In place of this extravagance it substitutes their real end, which it seeks to promote along with the purpose of the community.[76]

At other times the state, acting through the police power, must regulate trade and industry as a whole.

> The individual, it is true, must have the right to earn his bread in this or the other way, but on the other hand, the public has the right to ask that what is necessary should be done. ... Freedom of trade should not be of such a kind as to endanger the general weal. [77]
> The different interests of producers and consumers may come into conflict, and although the right regulation between the two may arise of its own accord, yet the adjustment of the two calls for a regulation standing above both sides and put into operation consciously. The right to make such a regulation in any particular case ... consists in this that the public offer of

goods in wide and general use is not to the individual as such but to him as a universal, i.e., to the public. The peoples' right to honest dealing and inspection of goods to prevent fraud may be enforced by a public functionary. But more especially does the dependence of great branches of industry upon foreign conditions and distant combinations, which the individuals engaged in these industries cannot themselves oversee, make necessary a general supervision and control. . . . Private interest summons the principle of freedom against interference from above, but the more blindly it is sunk in self-seeking ends the more it stands in need of regulation in order that it may be led back to the universal.[78]

To sum up, we may say that Hegel believed that the family must be transcended by society; and society in turn must be curbed and regulated by the courts of justice and the police force, two agents of the state. But these two institutions are merely the external organs of the state. Behind these agents or organs stands the ultimate reality which they represent, the state itself, which Hegel conceives as a mystic transcendental entity, the mysterious union of all with all, the great whole which embraces, but is greater than, any or all of the individual selves. Compared with this supreme reality, the state, all other things, whether the individual, the family, the corporation, society as a whole, sink into insignificance.

This belief in the supremacy of the state over lesser groups and over society itself is reflected in the teachings of nearly all the later Hegelians. It dominates the writings of Bosanquet. Bosanquet, like Hegel, distinguishes between society "on a lower level," society considered as the sphere of anarchic individualism, and society "on a higher level" which is identical with the state. "By the state we mean society as a unit recognized as rightly exercising control over its members through absolute physical power." [79] In the course of evolution "the characteristics of society pass gradually into those of the state." [80] "Society after all is within the state and it has its meaning in the state." [81] The state "includes the entire hierarchy of institutions by which life is determined, from the family to the trade, and from the trade to the church and the university. It includes all of them, not as a mere collection of the growths of the country but as the structure which gives life and meaning to the political whole." [82] These lesser institutions and organizations play and should play an important part in everyday life, but only as subordinate parts of a greater whole. "As exclusive objects they are a prey to stagnation and disease — think of the temper which lives solely for the family or solely for the church; it is only as taken up into the movement and circulation of the state that they are living spiritual beings." [83]

The fifth and last characteristic of the Hegelian theory of the state is the belief that the national state is greater than humanity as a whole; and war between the various national states is useful and inevitable. This conclusion seems somewhat surprising to those who have followed the general trend of the Hegelian philosophy. Hegel always seems to be more preoccupied with the "universal" than with the "particular"; he always emphasizes the "all-embracing whole" as opposed to the individual parts which make up the whole; reality is and must be to him "a totality"; he is perpetually talking about the "World Spirit" as reflected and embodied in man *qua* man. We are not surprised that Hegel took over from Fichte the notion that a state should naturally and normally coincide with a nation (a group of persons speaking the same language). But we are surprised when Hegel refuses to subordinate the national state to a greater and more comprehensive unit, such as a world state or even a league or confederation of nations. But Hegel, for all his universalism, is just as violent and as vehement in his insistence that the national state is the ultimate goal of evolution, that it must not be subordinated to any higher unit, as he is in his insistence that the individual and the smaller groups must be subordinated to the national state. What is even more extraordinary, the vast majority of the later Hegelians, including the English, followed him in stressing nationalism at the expense of internationalism.

To Hegel the World Spirit is embodied not in the form of a world-state, but in the form of world history, which is the story of the rise and fall of various states, each of which has its individual mission and each of which furnishes its specific contribution to the life of humanity as a whole. "Each state stands for and embodies an idea, or to be more exact, each state embodies a particular phase of the Universal Idea " [84] — but for a single world-state to try to embody the world idea in its entirety would be ridiculous — it would be false as opposed to true universality. The ever more perfect revelation and realization of the universal idea can only come about through conflict, the conflict of one national state with another. "In history the Idea unfolds its various phases in time and the dominant phase at any epoch is embodied in a dominant people " [85] — a people who dominate but never can conquer the whole of the civilized world. The same idea is expressed in less metaphysical language by Bosanquet, "the Nation-State is the widest organization which has common organization necessary to found a common life." [86] "It has no determinate function in a larger community, but is itself the supreme community; the guardian of a whole moral world, not a factor within an organized moral world." [87] To suppose that humanity as a whole is or ever can become an organized moral world is regarded as ridiculous.

Hegel brushes aside with contempt the plea for a world-state or a league of nations put forward by Kant and Fichte and supported by such men as Green. He treats with equal irreverence the Kantian-Fichtean plea for a world court before whose bar individual nations can be brought for judgment, for the non-observance of treaties or for other breaches of international law. To Hegel the idea of such a world court passing judgment upon separate independent nations is and ever must remain visionary. Hegel does indeed insist that there is an ultimate and final tribunal or world court, but this world court is no man-made institution, it is the World Spirit itself in the form of world history. In the eternal competition and conflict between states, the state which survives and triumphs over the others is obviously more in accord with the World Spirit than the others. Its very triumph shows that the world court of history has granted judgment in favor of this nation. *Die Welt Geschichte ist das Weltgericht.*

Putting aside all this charming metaphysical verbiage, Hegel's doctrine of the world court of history boils down to this: nation-states must eternally be in conflict with one another; the only way to settle these conflicts is by war; the nation which triumphs in war proves itself to be *ipso facto* right. Hegel and the Hegelians had no use whatever for Kant's dream of perpetual peace. The British Hegelians, to be sure, have been somewhat milder in their praise of war. But even they are indignant with those who denounced war as a national crime.

> A public act which inflicts loss, such as war..., is wholly different from murder or theft.... It is not a violation of law.... It is not a breach of an established moral order by a being within it.... It is the act of a supreme power which has ultimate responsibility for protecting the form of life of which it is the guardian. [88]

Hegel and the German Hegelians were far less milk-and-watery in their defense of war. War, to Hegel, was not only necessary, it was also good. It was an invaluable instrument in aiding the moral advancement of mankind.

> Just as the movement of the ocean prevents the corruption which would be the result of perpetual calm, so by war people escape the corruption which would be occasioned by perpetual peace. [89]

War, to Hegel, is essentially and intrinsically good because it inspires men to patriotism. It awakens men from their individualistic selfishness, their lethargy regarding public affairs, and makes them acutely aware of the nature and functions of the great whole, the state, in which they live and move and have their being, but do so, in times of peace, unconsciously. War by inspiring love of country indirectly inspires morality or ethics: for ethics, as we have seen, is not something individual, but is based upon "my station and its duties" within the state. Without devotion to the state true ethics is impossible. Moreover, "peoples who have been unwilling or afraid to endure internal sovereignty have been subjugated by others." [90]   In other words, in warfare peoples with a strong central government triumph over peoples unwilling to submit themselves to the dictation of the all-powerful state. To Hegel the all-powerful state is the end all and be all of evolution, so that war by promoting the triumph of such an institution directly aids evolution.   Again, wars are good because external wars "have prevented civil broils and strengthened the internal powers of the state." [91]   Finally Hegel declares that war is a great aid to morality in bringing vividly to our minds the vanity and transiency of all earthly things and all temporal possessions. "It is necessary that what is finite, such as life and property, should have its contingent nature exposed." [92]   Surely there is no quicker and more vivid way of pointing out this great moral lesson than the horrors of war.

Considering their defense and even advocacy of war, it is not surprising that Hegel and the Hegelians are very cold-blooded and ruthless in their treatment of international obligations. The liberals thought that there really is such a thing as international morality; that individual states are bound to obey the principles laid down by international morality. To the liberals, a state is morally bound to observe the treaties it signs with other nations and to respect the rights of other nations. To the Hegelians this whole notion of international morality is nonsense. True morality to them is "social ethics," and social ethics can only develop inside an organized community such as the family, the corporation, or the state. Humanity as a whole does not constitute an organized community; it is not a "moral organism." Hence there can be no true morality based upon humanity as a whole. As a consequence moral law holds good only within each state. It does not apply to the relations between states. This attitude is summed up by Bosanquet as follows: "Moral relations presuppose an organized life, but such a life is only within the state, not in relations between the state and other communities." [93]   As morality can only exist within the state, "the state as such certainly cannot be guilty of personal immorality, and it is hard to see how it can commit theft or murder in the sense in which these are moral offenses." [94] "We deny ... that someone is guilty of murder when a country carries on war, or of theft when it adopts a policy of repudiation, confiscation, or annexation." [95]

Stace, another prominent exponent of the Hegelian philosophy, expresses the same idea in slightly different words. "Between states there is no objectively existent sphere of universal right as in the case between persons. Hence the acts of states are governed by their arbitrary will." States may, of course, sign treaties between themselves,

> but because there is no authority above the states and because the relations between them are governed not by universality but by contingency, these relations are continually shifting, and treaties, even if they purport to be binding in perpetuity, become in fact obsolete when the conditions which produced them change. [96]

A state may, therefore, violate any treaty it pleases on the plea that conditions have changed. This, incidentally, was exactly the defense Germany made in 1914 when invading Belgium. The idea that a treaty is "only a scrap of paper" is thus seen to rest on sound Hegelian philosophy.

THE AUTHORITARIANISM OF HEGEL

After this rather lengthy discussion of the Hegelian doctrine regarding the nature and function of the state, we may now turn to an examination of the Hegelian views respecting the nature and functions of government, or the problem of who shall guide and control the state. Many of the British and American Hegelians, because of their liberal environment, broke with their master and indicated their belief in a democratic or at least a semi-democratic form of government. Hegel himself, however, and the vast majority of the German and other Continental Hegelians, were thoroughgoing authoritarians. To them government was not and should not be based upon the consent of the governed. Governmental officials do not acquire their power by delegation of authority from the people. The broad mass of the people should be excluded from participation in political activities. Sovereignty resides not in the people but in the person of the ruler. In short, Hegel's ideal form of government is a political pyramid with power centered at the top and gradually sinking downwards, rather than rising from the bottom to the top. Or, to put the matter in other words, Hegel, like Carlyle, craved a social and political hierarchy, the many being guided and controlled by the few; and the few in turn being subordinated to the one — the supreme head of the state.

Hegel's own method of approaching the problem of government was by reinterpreting and modifying some of the basic doctrines of Montesquieu. Montesquieu, it will be remembered, proclaimed that good government should be based upon the principles of check and balance and the separation of powers. Instead of granting absolute power either to a monarchy, or to an aristocracy, or to a democracy, Montesquieu advocated that control over the machinery of government be divided among the monarch, the aristocracy, and the bulk of the people. Each element in striving to protect its own interests would prevent the others from securing despotic control over the state. In like manner, by dividing the functions of government among an executive, a judicial, and a legislative body, each separate from the others, and supreme in its own field, the dangers of absolutism might be avoided. To Hegel the doctrines of Montesquieu are valuable but imperfect. The principles of check and balance and of the separation of powers are valuable, just as the division of labor in the economic field is useful, but it must not be carried too far. Absolute separation of powers leads to anarchy. If the various organs of government were independent entities constantly opposing and checking one another, the whole fabric of the state would dissolve. There must be a unity behind this diversity. There must be an organ within the state which transcends and harmonizes the other organs.

In place, therefore, of the old division of government into legislative, executive, and judicial organs, each with equal powers, Hegel insists that the true and rational separation is into legislative, executive, and monarchic organs, in which the legislative and executive check and balance one another, but both are transcended and find their final harmony in the person of the monarch, who symbolizes the essential unity of the state. The legislative branch represents the element of universality in the state, its chief function being to lay down general laws. The executive represents the element of particularity in the state, its chief function being to apply general laws to individual concrete cases. For this very reason Hegel includes the judiciary under the head of the executive, as the element of particularity applies to judicial as well as to ordinary executive functions. The monarchic branch, sharing in and supervising both the legislative and the executive functions, brings the element of particularity into harmony with the element of universality and makes of the state a living organic whole. Hegel's division of powers thus follows the general pattern of his dialectic, for we have the legislative as the thesis, the executive for the antithesis, and the monarchic as the synthesis

These three governmental bodies also embody the essential elements of democracy, of aristocracy, and of monarchy. Monarchy represents the supreme rule of one. The executive, to Hegel, consists of the administrative hierarchy within the state and represents the guidance and leadership of the few, the true aristocracy. The legislative represents the collective wisdom of the many, even though Hegel's "many" constituted only a small portion of the total population.

In his detailed treatment of the problems of government, Hegel devotes, as we should expect, a great deal of attention to the nature and functions of the monarchic element. Anyone who reads through Hegel's various political writings must come to the conclusion that in his heart of hearts Hegel really favored absolutism or a dictatorship, even though the exigencies of the time prevented him from giving free rein to his opinions. The real, though half-hidden, absolutism of Hegel is revealed in such passages as

> He who tells the time what it wills and means and then brings it to completion is the great man of the time. In his act the inner significance and essence of the time is actualized. Who does not learn to despise public opinion, which is one thing in one place, and another in another, will never produce anything great.[97]

This sympathy with absolutism made Hegel a great admirer of such great dictators in the past as Alexander, Julius Caesar, and Napoleon, whose names he always mentions with reverence. Most of Hegel's German contemporaries regarded Napoleon, the French conqueror, as a horrible tyrant, trampling down the liberties of mankind. Not so Hegel. To him Napoleon was *die Weltseele*, the incarnation of the soul of the world. The World Spirit is indeed "the inmost soul of all individuals. but in a state of unconsciousness which the great men in question aroused. Their fellows, therefore, follow these soul-leaders, for they feel the irresistible power of their own inner Spirit thus embodied."[98] Hegel admits that his heroes frequently "treat other great and sacred objects inconsiderately; conduct which is indeed obnoxious to moral reprehension. But so mighty a form must trample down many an innocent flower — crush to pieces many an object in its path."[99] After reading Hegel's descriptions of the functions and character of heroes, one feels sure that Mussolini and Hitler would certainly be included with Alexander, Caesar, and Napoleon in his galaxy of great men, concrete embodiments of the Divine Idea, God made manifest in the flesh.

Hegel was convinced that monarchy in some form was absolutely essential to good government, though his definition of monarchy would include present-day Germany, with its *Führer*, as it included ancient Rome with its *Imperator*. All forms of government other than monarchic are necessarily imperfect. "In the government regarded as organic totality the sovereign power is . . . the all-sustaining, all-decreeing will of the state." Now this will of the state, the sovereign power, must be embodied in a "person." This "person" may be a theoretical or fictitious person, such as a House of Lords, or a popular assembly, but in a perfect form of the state this all-sustaining, all-decreeing will must be embodied in an actual or real person — the monarch. "The monarchic constitution is therefore the constitution of developed reason; all other constitutions belong to the lower grades of the development and realization of reason." [100] In a modern state "the element which implies absolute decision is not individuality in general, but one individual — the monarch." [101]

Hegel insists that sovereignty must be embodied in the person of the sovereign, and thus definitely denies the idea, so dear to the liberals, that sovereignty resides with the people.

> It may be said that internal sovereignty resides in the people, if we speak in general terms and mean that sovereignty accrues to the whole state. But . . . the people, apart from their monarch and the common membership necessarily and directly associated with him is a formless mass. It is no longer a state. . . . When a people having passed from the primitive condition which made the forms of aristocracy and democracy possible and is represented not as in a willful and unorganized condition, but as a self-developed organic totality, in such a people sovereignty is the personality of the whole, and exists too in a reality, in the person of the monarch. Even in the imperfect forms of the state the summit must be occupied by an individual. . . . Under aristocratic or more especially under democratic government he appears in the form of statesmen and generals, according to accident and the particular needs of the time. Here all actions and all reality have their origin and completion in the unity of the leader's decision.[102]

Monarchy, therefore, is only the carrying out in the sphere of politics of the principle that in all social organizations one person, whether called general, or statesman, or chairman, must stand at the apex and direct the activities of the whole.

Considering Hegel's passion for the great dictators of the past, and for Napoleon, the great dictator of his own age; considering his belief that the all-sustaining, all-decreeing will of the state must be embodied in a single individual; that all worth-while action is based upon the decision of a single outstanding person, it is rather surprising that he did not come out and openly espouse the cause of absolute monarchy or absolute dictatorship. But it must be remembered that Hegel lived and wrote at a time when the open advocacy of such a principle was extremely unpopular. Even the restored Bourbons were unable to preach a return to the absolute monarchy of Louis XIV's time. When Hegel was formulating his systematic political philosophy, Napoleon was a prisoner at St. Helena. The year of the publication of the *Philosophy of Right* was also the year of Napoleon's death and at such a time it was ridiculous to lecture in favor of popular dictatorship, the absolute rule of one man who rises, by force of arms and by popular acclaim to supreme power in the state. Hegel was, therefore, forced to accommodate his principles to the demand of the times, and advocated the cause, not of absolute monarchy, but of limited or constitutional monarchy.

Hegel could at least be true to innate convictions in proclaiming that a constitutional monarchy was at least better than a republic or any other democratic form of government. Some of the more advanced liberals of Hegel's own times argued that constitutional monarchy was only a passing phase, a halfway stage between despotism and a republic. Hegel calls in his dialectic to prove that such a view is false. The movement of history is not, he says, from despotism to limited monarchy, to a republic, but from despotism (the thesis) to a republic (the antithesis) to a constitutional monarchy (the synthesis).[103] Constitutional monarchy, therefore, instead of being a provisional and temporary stage, is the final and perfected form of government, a form of government to which all states must come when they attain a certain degree of development.

In defending constitutional monarchy Hegel was also forced to defend the hereditary principle in such monarchies. Forgetting for the moment his heroes, Caesar and Napoleon, who won rather than inherited their thrones, Hegel called upon divine, universal reason to prove that the true monarch was monarch by right of birth and not by election or the choice of his subjects; "the election of a monarch is the worst of proceedings." A desire to elect one's own ruler "proceeds from the will of the multitude in the form of inclination, opinion, and caprice." [104] "The ultimate self of the state's will is in this, its abstraction, an individuality which is simple and direct. Hence its very conception implies that it is natural. Thus the monarch ... is appointed to the dignity of monarch in a directly natural way, by natural birth." [105] To the lowly unphilosophical person this line of argument seems perilously close to sheer nonsense, but to the good German Hegelians this doctrine seemed a direct revelation of divine wisdom.

Hegel freely admits that an hereditary monarch may in private life be

a selfish, pleasure-seeking, ill-educated boor.   But, he argues, in a con·
stitutional as opposed to an absolute monarchy, the private character of
the monarch is of no importance.   In a constitutional monarchy the
king "is bound to the concrete content of the advice of his councellors,
and when the constitution is established he often has nothing to do but
sign his name." [106]   Moreover, for the modern office of king "is needed
only a man who says yes, and so puts the dot upon the i." [107]   All this
would be very well if by constitutional monarchy Hegel meant a monarchy such as exists at the present time in England, where all the actions
of the king are determined by the advice of his ministers who are in turn
responsible to the House of Commons.   But Hegel's idea of a constitutional monarchy was not at all that of the English model. He disliked the
thought of parliamentary government where the ministers of state are
dependent for their office upon having the confidence of the popular assembly.   Hegel's constitutional monarchy was patterned after old
Prussia and not after modern England.   The ministers of state and all
the members of the administrative hierarchy are to owe their appointment and dismissal to "the unlimited, free, arbitrary will" of the monarch.[108] The king is to act upon the advice of his ministers, but these
ministers are to be men of his own choosing, in no way dependent upon
the wishes and desires of parliament or of the people.   This, plus the
fact that the king in his own person is to have an absolute veto upon all
legislation, shows that Hegel is distinctly optimistic in claiming that the
private character of his monarch is a matter of no significance.

Having disposed of the power and functions of the monarch, Hegel
proceeds to discuss the essential character of the so-called executive
branch of the government.   As we have already seen, what Hegel calls
the executive is really the administrative hierarchy or organized bureaucracy which for so long had actual and practical control over most of the
functions of government in Germany and especially in Prussia.   This
administrative hierarchy included, of course, the ministers of state, the
various departmental heads, down to the rank and file of the civil service.
It included all the judicial officers of the state, both judges and such persons as district attorneys and public prosecutors.   It also included the
heads of the national gendarmery or national police force.   From the
purely governmental point of view, Hegel's executive consists of the
whole body of bureaucrats, who thus constituted the political aristocracy
of the country.   As Hegel himself admits, his executive was to take the
place of the aristocracy of ancient times.

It is difficult for us in America to understand the prestige and impoɪ·

tance of the bureaucracy in Germany, and the significant role it played and still plays in everyday governmental life. Many of the persons who in Germany would be members of the national administrative hierarchy are, in America, elected by the local communities, such for example as the various state officials, the governor, frequently the secretary of state, and the treasurer of each state. Our state judges, our district judges, our boards of education are locally elected and hence are persons who are more or less professional politicians. Many, if not most of the higher posts in what administrative hierarchy we do possess, are considered to be political plums which must be given to deserving friends of the party in power. Most of the lower posts in this hierarchy are awarded to the friends and relatives of senators and representatives and other political patrons whose political service needs to be rewarded. In the last few decades we have organized and developed our permanent non-political civil service, but as yet this civil service plays a minor role in the affairs of state and its members have little or no social prestige and little or no influence in the shaping of national policies.

With the growth of the national bureaucracy under the New Deal, and the establishment of such institutions as the School of Public Administration at Harvard University and elsewhere, conditions have changed considerably from the way they were a few years ago, but in America we still regard the members of the civil service as the servants of the state and of the public rather than as the leaders and guides of public affairs. With us the young men from what are called "the better families," that is, families socially and financially prominent, usually aim at going into business or following a profession. Occasionally, very occasionally, such young men aim at going into politics, but almost never do they have for their life's ambition going into "public service." A few may be tempted by thoughts of joining the diplomatic corps, but to be a member of the domestic civil service seems a very drab life indeed.

In Germany conditions were, and still are, very different. There, a large number of socially prominent young men, after specializing in public law and the problems of public administration during their university days, enter the service of the state and proceed to work their way up the administrative hierarchy. Throughout their lives they enjoy a great deal of social and political esteem. During the nineteenth century most of the highest ministers of state, foreign ministers and imperial chancellors were recruited from this group. Bismarck was only one of the many persons who reached the peak of political power after a long career in the public service. General laws had of course to be passed by the Reichstag, but the bureaucracy had a great deal to say about the formulation and shaping of these laws.   Moreover, many things which with us would be covered by laws were in Germany regulated by administrative decrees or "police orders," the framing of which lay entirely in the hands of the administrative hierarchy.

The Prussian bureaucracy as it slowly developed during the nineteenth and twentieth centuries was little more than a practical application of the ideas on the nature of the executive as sketched by Hegel in his *Philosophy of Right*.   The function of the executive (always spoken of in the plural) is "the execution and application . . . of the existing laws, regulations, establishments for common ends and the like. . . . It is their duty to care for each particular thing in the community and in these private ends make to prevail the universal interest." [109]   The members of the executive, unlike the head of the state, are not to owe their positions to "natural personality or to birth."   They are to be appointed by the king (without reference to the Diet or Parliament) but on the basis of their "knowledge and proof of fitness." [110]   In their guidance of the population as a whole the administrative hierarchy should work, as far as possible, through the corporations (trade and professional groups) into which the people are to be organized, rather than with separate individuals.   The leaders of these corporations may well be nominated by the members of the corporations themselves, but subject to confirmation (and possible veto) by the national authorities. [111]

Hegel sometimes speaks of his executive or body of state officials as being members of the middle class, but they are middle class only in the sense that they mediate between the members of the royal family and the highest members of the landowning aristocracy on the one side and the bulk of the population on the other.   They represent what would be called by us the upper middle and upper classes, according to their position in the hierarchy.   Even in Hegel's system of classification they constitute the most important element of the highest of the three classes into which Hegel divides the population as a whole.   According to him society is divided into, first, the agricultural class, second, the industrial and commercial class, and third, the universal class.

The agricultural class includes both the landless agricultural laborer and the small peasant farmers who own their own land.   This class is characterized by simplicity, living as it does in direct contact with Nature and receiving what she gives in a spirit of trust and dependence.   In this class, reflection plays only a small part in daily life.   The industrial and commercial class includes both the artisans or handworkers, the clerks and other employees of commercial undertakings, and also the employers and the heads of industrial and commercial firms, especially those working on a small scale. This class depends less on Nature and more on its own efforts. It is the class dominated by reflection or understanding which it uses to analyze wants and to mould the materials of Nature to its own satisfaction. According to Hegel the essential element in this class is "particularity" or the emphasis placed upon individualism and individual enterprise, each man seeking his own interest, the profit motive being the all-important factor. It is the class, therefore, which most demands "subjective" or "negative" freedom — the kind of freedom which Hegel thinks is the false kind of freedom, the freedom to do as one wishes rather than the freedom to do as one ought.

The universal class has for its work and purpose the universal interests of society and the state. It concerns itself with the state as a whole rather than with the interests of the individual. It is the class dominated, not by abstract understanding, but by reason, that is, understanding plus spiritual insight. It includes, of course, the administrative hierarchy (or executive), as the members of this hierarchy serve the public as a whole; the officers of the army and navy, as they too work for the state rather than for the particular interest; the clergy who minister to the spiritual needs of the whole nation. Apparently the professional classes (doctors and lawyers) are also included in this class. It is certain that it included the large landowners and the great commercial and industrial magnates whose wealth is such that they can live on their incomes and hence devote themselves to society as a whole rather than struggle to secure their own livelihood.

> The business of the universal class is with the universal interests of society Hence it must be relieved of the direct task of providing for itself. It must possess private means or receive an allowance from the state. His private interest may thus find satisfaction in his labor for the universal.[112]

Hegel does indeed differ from the old eighteenth century conservatives in insisting that neither birth nor pedigree is an essential consideration in deciding to what class a man is to belong. Normally the son of a peasant will be a peasant; the son of a petty tradesman a petty tradesman; but Hegel accepted the principle so dear to Napoleon, "the tools to those who can use them" — a principle accepted also by Mussolini and Hitler. If a boy of genius should arise among the agricultural class, he should be permitted to qualify himself for entrance into the universal class. But though Hegel thus adopted the doctrine of equality of opportunity, he was insistent that the universal class must be the dominant or governing class in the whole community. This class must direct and control the activity of the other classes, at least in so far as this activity has reference to the general welfare. The direction of military and naval affairs should not lie in the hands of the common soldiers and sailors, but with their officers. The direction of financial, social, and political movements should lie, not with the broad mass of the population, but with the members of the universal class as a whole. Among this class the normal conduct of governmental affairs should lie with the administrative hierarchy, those members of the universal or governing class who devote all their time and energies to the service of the state.

To Hegel the vast majority of all governmental matters should be regulated, not by laws requiring the consent of the legislative assembly, but by administrative decrees framed and executed by the administrative hierarchy on its own initiative. Laws should be few, simple, and universal in character. They should merely lay down general principles. The application of these principles to the complicated world of everyday activity must rest entirely with the bureaucracy, which must, therefore, be given a free hand in working out all matters of detail. A law should merely say, for example, "the police are to control health." On the basis of this "law" the administration, on its own responsibility, should work out a series of detailed regulations as to what the individual citizen must and must not do to preserve public health.

Equally interesting is the fact that Hegel urged that the administration be given almost a free hand in financial matters. General financial policy, such as the type of taxes to be raised, might be considered legislative in character and thus need the consent of the legislative assembly, but the normal year-to-year raising and spending of money should be controlled by the executive.

> To give the name of law to the annual fixing of financial requirements only serves to conceal the fact that the legislative power when it makes a decree about finance is really engaged in strict executive business. The importance attached to the power of from time to time granting "supply" on the ground that the assembly of the estates [i.e., parliament] possesses in it a check on the government and thus a guarantee against injustice and violence — this importance is rather plausible than real.[113]

But though the normal conduct of governmental affairs can thus be safely entrusted to the official bureaucracy, even Hegel admits that general laws should be made only after consultation with a larger body. This brings us to a consideration of his ideas regarding the legislative body, the third and last governmental organ.

Montesquieu with his belief in the absolute separation of powers urged that the monarch (to him the head of the executive hierarchy) and all other executive or administrative officials should be rigidly excluded from the process of legislation. To Hegel this proposal was ridiculous. To his mind there should be a legislative body in addition to the monarch and the bureaucracy, but both the monarch and the bureaucracy should play an important role in the shaping of all laws. In legislative matters the monarch "gives the final decision." [114] In actual practice this means that the monarch has the right to propose laws and also the right to veto laws passed by the legislature. Incidentally the all-important matters of making war and peace are taken from the legislature and placed entirely in the hands of the monarch.[115] The cooperation of the administrative hierarchy in the function of legislation is considered especially important, because "the executive element has concrete knowledge and oversight of the whole in its many sides and in the actual principles firmly rooted in them." [116] "The highest state officials have necessarily deeper and more comprehensive insight [than the ordinary legislator] into the working and needs of the state and also greater skill and wider experience." [117]

The administrative hierarchy, therefore, should aid the legislature by proposing legislation and shaping the bills when they come to be considered. But in addition it is advisable that the higher ministers of state should have the right to speak and to vote in the legislative assembly. Hegel commends the English system wherein the members of the cabinet are always members of Parliament, but he fails to point out the important difference between the English system and the type of government he advocates. In England the cabinet members are not trained administrators who have worked their way up the bureaucratic hierarchy, but professional politicians who owe their posts to the fact that they are the leaders of the majority party in the House of Commons. The executive is thus guided and controlled by the legislative assembly. In Hegel's scheme the ministers of state are professional administrators in no way responsible to or controlled by the popular assembly. They are to have *ex officio* seats in the legislative assembly in order that they may enlighten the assembly as to the real needs of the government, and by their advice and votes help steer the course of legislation in the right direction. The position of Hegel's ministers in the legislative assembly is analogous, not to conditions in England, but to conditions in British India under the old (Minto-Morley) constitution, where the legislative councils of the various provinces consisted half of "official members" appointed by the crown from among the members of the Indian Civil Service, and half of "unofficial" members selected in various ways by the community as a whole.

Hegel hoped that the bureaucratic or "official" members of the legislative assembly, though possessing less than a numerical majority, would dominate the process of legislation. Nevertheless he, like the Indian constitution makers, had to make provision for unofficial members and lay down rules as to how they should be chosen. In this portion of his work Hegel again shows his strong dislike of democracy. In the first place he insists that though the legislative assembly should represent "the many," it is not at all necessary that it represent "the all" — or all sections of the population. If, says Hegel, it were necessary that "the all" be represented in parliament it would be necessary for women and children to be represented, which, in his opinion, is manifestly absurd. If women and children are to be excluded, there is no reason why all men should be represented; the ignorant, stupid, self-seeking bulk of the male population should also be kept from interfering with the proper functioning of the state. To his mind, "the people" — the broad mass of the population — "does not know what it wills. To know what we will, and further what the absolute will, namely, reason, wills is the fruit of deep knowledge and insight and is therefore not the property of the people." [118]   When, therefore, Hegel tells us that the legislative assembly should represent "the many," we find that his "many" constitutes only a small portion of the population.

To be quite sure that the people as a whole do not seize control over the legislative body Hegel provides that his diet or parliament shall be divided into two chambers. By this means "an accidental decision secured on the spur of the moment by a simple majority of the votes is rendered far less probable." [119]   Moreover, one of these chambers, the upper house, bears a strong resemblance to the English House of Lords. It is to consist exclusively of the great landowners, who acquire their right to sit in this house by reason of birth or at least by the inheritance of the paternal estates. The great landowners constitute a group "whose ethical character is natural. As its basis it has family life and as regards subsistence it has possession of the soil." [120]   This group has a more "independent volition" than any other group within the state. Its very wealth gives it this "independent volition." It is more independent than the public officials, for the latter secure their livelihood from the state and constantly fear dismissal from office. It is more independent than the members of the industrial and commercial class. for the desires of the latter depend upon "the uncertainty of trade, the desire for gain, and the fluctuation of property [i.e., commercial capital]." This group of landowners and this group alone is "secure from the favor at once of the executive and of the multitude." For this reason it should be given a special share in the process of legislation and made to constitute one of the two houses which shall pass upon all proposed bills. This group shall be "further secured even from its own caprice" by having its members automatically become members of the upper house rather than undergo the whims and accidents of any elective process. To keep this group intact Hegel provides for entail or the law whereby the great landlords may not sell or otherwise dispose of their estates, and each such person must leave all his real property to his eldest son.[121]

Whereas the upper house is to consist of a single group within the community, the lower house is to be somewhat more general and more inclusive in its make-up. It is to consist of representatives of all the "estates" or classes and of all the principal "corporations." This phrase must not be misunderstood. Hegel violently disapproved of manhood suffrage. He even disapproved of granting the vote to all persons who possessed a certain property qualification. To his mind a man merely as an individual or private citizen had no right whatever to vote. He had a right to vote only as a member of some group or corporation, and the members of the lower house should represent not merely a mass of individuals who happen to live together in a certain locality, but the various functional groups into which the organic unity of the state is divided. To Hegel the very thought that a single person should or could represent all persons living within a certain geographic district was ridiculous. Persons living within this district have nothing in common save territorial propinquity, surely a very inadequate basis for parliamentary representation. No, the lower house should consist of one or more representatives of what we should now call trade unions, and such organizations as farmers' cooperatives. The great majority of the members of the lower house, however, should consist of representatives of the higher and more important corporations, such as the chambers of commerce, manufacturers' associations, trade associations, bar associations, medical associations, and the like.

Hegel was willing to permit a few representatives of the lower orders, such as peasants and artisans, organized into groups, to have a wee small voice in the councils of the nation, but the number of such representatives must always be small, since he would impose a property qualification upon members of parliament and would, moreover, force them to serve without pay and thus make them have an independent income or else be supported by the group they represent. The vast majority of the corporations to be represented in the lower house are to consist of persons who belong to what we should call the middle and upper middle classes. Every class in the community is to be represented, but represented separately and in such a way that the representatives of upper and middle groups — the numerical minority in the community — will be able to outweigh and outvote the representatives of the great unwashed, the bulk of the population. In almost any given territorial district the poor enormously outnumber the rich; the rank and file, the socially and intellectually prominent. To give the bulk of the population the right to vote and to have them vote in territorial units means that the rich, the prominent, the intellectually able have no way in which they can be directly represented in the councils of the nation. Such a system of government, says Hegel, leads inevitably to national calamity. If the nation is to survive and grow strong, it must see that each group within it be given adequate representation, and by adequate Hegel means the system whereby the higher and more important can control the lower and less important.

Hegel's theory of corporate representation is an important landmark in the history of political theory. In Hegel's own time his arguments on this matter were largely ignored, and territorial representation remained the order of the day. Towards the close of the nineteenth century, however, there arose in Germany and even in England and America a number of thinkers who felt that territorial representation had proved inadequate for the needs of the community and who demanded "functional representation," which is really Hegel's corporate representation under another name. And, be it noted, this demand for functional representation was frequently made, not by the reactionaries, but by men with extremely liberal views. It is, moreover, likely that this demand will secure even greater attention in the not distant future. To a certain extent, but to a certain extent only, Hegel's views on class representation were incorporated in the old Prussian Constitution of 1850. According to this system all voters were arranged in three classes, according to the amount of direct taxes they paid. Each group elected an equal number of "electors," who in turn elected the members of the lower house. In this manner the members of the upper or wealthier classes, though numerically in the minority, acquired equal representation with the middle and lower classes. The Prussian system, however, made no arrangement for corporate representation, which is the kernel of the Hegelian system. The first attempt in modern times to embody this idea in concrete legislation was made by the Italian Fascists with the abolition of the old territorially elected parliament and the substitution of a special "Chamber of Corporations." In this, as in so many other respects, Hegel has proved to be the great forerunner or "morning star" of the Fascist theory of the state.

NOTES TO CHAPTER SEVEN

1. In his Introduction to Hegel's *Der Staat*, pp. 71, 82.
2. G. F. W. Hegel, *Philosophy of Right*, p. 256. 3. *Ibid.*
4. Quoted in E. Caird, *Hegel*, pp. 31, 32.
5. Hegel, *Philosophy of Right*, p. 260. By permission of G. Bell & Sons, Ltd.
6. Caird, *Hegel*, p. 72. By permission of Wm. Blackwood & Sons Ltd., original publishers.
7. The foregoing account of Hegel's life is based upon Caird, *Hegel*; Rosenkranz, *Hegels Leben*; and Haym, *Hegel und seine Zeit*. A great deal of light on Hegel's intellectual development is thrown by such books as Dilthey, *Die Jugendgeschichte Hegels* and Haering, *Hegel, sein Wollen und sein Werk*.
8. F. W. J. Schelling, *Werke*, XIV, 530.
9. H. Haldar, *Neo-Hegelianism*, p. 265. By permission of Heath Cranton, Limited.
10. Hegel, *Philosophy of History*, p. 38.
11. L. T. Hobhouse, *Metaphysical Theory of the State*, p. 17. By permission of The Macmillan Company, publishers.
12. See Hegel's *Verfassung Deutschlands*.
13. W. T. Stace, *The Philosophy of Hegel*, p. 101. By permission of The Macmillan Company, publishers.
14. C. E. Vaughan, *Studies in the History of Political Philosophy*, II, 147. By permission of the Manchester University Press, Manchester, England.
15. *Ibid.*
16. Hegel, *Philosophy of Right*, p. xxx.
17. Coker, *Recent Political Thought*, p. 473. By permission of D. Appleton-Century Company.
18. Hegel, *Phänomenologie des Geistes*, p. 258.
19. Haldar, *Neo-Hegelianism*, p. 334.
20. Sait, *Political Institutions*, p. 10.
21. Hegel, *Philosophy of History*, pp. 9, 10.
22. Haldar, *Neo-Hegelianism*, p. 333.
23. Hegel, *Philosophy of History*, p. 48.
24. Vaughan, *Studies in the History of Political Philosophy*, II, 145.
25. Hegel, *Logik*, p. 33.
26. Stace, *The Philosophy of Hegel*, p. 103. By permission of The Macmillan Company, publishers.
27. H. Sturt, *Idola Theatri*, p. 17.
28. Haldar, *Neo-Hegelianism*, p. 270.
29. G. H. Sabine, *History of Political Theory*, p. 636. By permission of Henry Holt and Company.
30. Hegel, *Philosophie der Geschichte*, p. 69; see Sibree's translation, p. 58.
31. Hegel, *Philosophy of History*, pp. 9, 10.
32. *Ibid.*, p. 13.
33. *Ibid.*, p. 15.

34. Hegel, *Philosophy of History*, p. 40.
35. *Ibid.*, p. 41.
36. *Ibid.*, p. 42.
37. *Ibid.*
38. *Ibid.*, p. 45.
39. *Ibid.*, p. 31.
40. *Ibid.*, p. 32.
41. Hegel, *Philosophy of Right*, p. 247.
42. *Ibid.*, p. 260.
43. Hegel, *Philosophy of History*, p. 41.
44. Hegel, *Philosophy of Right*, p. 240.
45. Hegel, *Philosophie des Rechtes*, p. 306; see *Philosophy of Right*, p. 240.
46. Hegel, *Philosophy of Right*, p. 246.
47. *Ibid.*, p. 240.
48. Hegel, *Philosophy of History*, p. 41.
49. Hegel, *Philosophy of Right*, p. 240.
50. Hobhouse, *Metaphysical Theory of the State*, p. 27. By permission of The Mac millan Company, publishers, and George Allen and Unwin, Limited.
51. Hegel, *Philosophy of History*, pp. 18, 19.
52. Hegel, *Philosophy of Right*, p. 244.
53. Vaughan, *Studies in the History of Political Philosophy*, II, 153.
54. Hegel, *Philosophy of History*, pp. 42–45.
55. Vaughan, *Studies in the History of Political Philosophy*, II, 172.
56. Bernard Bosanquet, *Philosophical Theory of the State*, p. 101. By permission of The Macmillan Company, publishers.
57. *Ibid.*, p. 226.
58. Hegel, *Philosophy of Right*, p. 325.
59. *Ibid.*, p. 53. For a full discussion of this whole subject from the Neo-Hegelian point of view, see D. G. Ritchie, *Natural Rights*.
60. Vaughan, *Studies in the History of Political Philosophy*, II, 171.
61. Haldar, *Neo-Hegelianism*, p. 194.
62. Ritchie, *Natural Rights*.
63. Hegel, *Philosophy of Right*, p. 167.
64. Stace, *The Philosophy of Hegel*, p. 409. By permission of The Macmillan Com pany, publishers.
65. Hegel, *Philosophy of Right*, p. 174.
66. *Ibid.*, p. 172.
67. *Ibid.*, p. 190.
68. *Ibid.*, p. 235.
69. *Ibid.*, p. 236.
70. *Ibid.*, p. 238.
71. Stace, *The Philosophy of Hegel*, p. 419. By permission of The Macmillan Com pany, publishers.
72. Hegel, *Philosophy of Right*, p. 227.
73. *Ibid.*, p. 226.
74. *Ibid.*, p. 228.
75. *Ibid.*, p. 231.
76. *Ibid.*, p. 229.
77. *Ibid.*, p. 228.
78. *Ibid.*, p. 227.
79. Bosanquet, *Philosophical Theory of the State*, p. 184.
80. *Ibid.*, p. 185.
81. E. Barker, *Political Thought in England from Spencer to the Present Day*, p. 71.

82. Bosanquet, *Philosophical Theory of the State*, p. 150.
83. *Ibid.*, p. 151.
84. Stace, *The Philosophy of Hegel*, p. 438. By permission of The Macmillan Company, publishers.
85. *Ibid.*
86. Bosanquet, *Philosophical Theory of the State*, p. 320.
87. *Ibid.*, p. 325.
88. *Ibid.*, p. 326.
89. Hegel, *Philosophy of Right*, p. 331.
90. *Ibid.*
91. *Ibid.*
92. *Ibid.*
93. Bosanquet, *Philosophical Theory of the State*, p. 325.
94. *Ibid.*, p. 323.
95. *Ibid.*, p. 328.
96. Stace, *The Philosophy of Hegel*, p. 437. By permission of The Macmillan Company, publishers.
97. Hegel, *Philosophy of Right*, p. 325.
98. Hegel, *Philosophy of History*, p. 32.
99. *Ibid.*, p. 34.
100. Hegel, *Philosophy of Mind*, p. 269. By permission of the Oxford University Press.
101. Hegel, *Philosophy of Right*, p. 286.
102. Hegel, *Philosophies des Rechtes*, p. 361; see *Philosophy of Right*, pp. 288, 289.
103. Hegel, *Philosophy of History*, p. 48.
104. Hegel, *Philosophy of Right*, p. 294.
105. *Ibid.*, p. 290.
106. *Ibid.*
107. *Ibid.*, p. 292.
108. *Ibid.*, p. 296.
109. *Ibid.*, p. 298.
110. *Ibid.*, p. 302.
111. *Ibid.*, p. 299.
112. *Ibid.*, p. 202.
113. Hegel, *Philosophy of Mind*, p. 273.
114. Hegel, *Philosophy of Right*, p. 309.
115. Hegel, *Philosophy of Mind*, p. 270.
116. Hegel, *Philosophy of Right*, p. 309.
117. *Ibid.*, p. 310.
118. *Ibid.*
119. *Ibid.*, p. 320.
120. *Ibid.*, p. 315.
121. *Ibid.*, pp. 315, 316.

BIBLIOGRAPHY

PRIMARY SOURCES

Hegel, *Der Staat*. Leipzig, 1934. (Consists of excerpts from all of Hegel's writings which deal with political matters. Also contains a valuable introduction by P. A. Merbach.)

Hegel, *Theologische Jugendschriften*. Edited by H. Nohl, Tübingen, 1907. (Hegel's early unpublished writings on theological matters, containing many important remarks on political problems.)

Hegel, *Schriften zur Politik und Rechtsphilosophie.* Edited by G. Lasson, Leipzig, 1913. (Contains many of Hegel's early essays on politics, not otherwise available. Includes his articles on the constitution of Germany, on the constitution of Württemberg, and on the English Reform Bill. None of the foregoing works are as yet available in English.)

Hegel, *Werke.* 19 vols., Berlin, 1832–1887. This edition of Hegel's works contains all his major writings. Of especial importance are (a) *Phänomenologie des Geistes* (English translation by L. B. Baillie, *The Phenomenology of Mind*, London, 1910). (b) *Encyclopädie der philosophischen Wissenschaften* (part one translation by W. Wallace, *The Logic of Hegel*, Oxford, 1892; part three translation by W. Wallace, *Philosophy of Mind*, Oxford, 1894). (c) *Philosophie der Geschichte* (translated by J. Sibree, *Philosophy of History*, London, 1878). (d) *Philosophie des Rechtes* (translated by S. W. Dyde, *Philosophy of Right*, London, 1896). The last two works, *Philosophy of History* and *Philosophy of Right*, are of especial importance for the study of Hegel's later and more mature system of political philosophy. The above-mentioned translations are all sound, but are rather wooden and not always intelligible to the English reader. This is especially true of Dyde's version of the *Philosophy of Right*. For this reason, in my citations from Dyde I have occasionally slightly altered the wording in order to bring out more fully the meaning of the original. Such instances are indicated by references both to the translations and to the German original. The general student will find Hegel, *Selections*, edited by J. Loewenberg, New York, 1929 (excerpts from several of the above-mentioned translations) a very useful work.

SECONDARY SOURCES. An enormous number of works have been written about various aspects of Hegel. Those especially useful for the student of politics include:

E. Caird, *Hegel.* Edinburgh, 1883. (For Hegel's life and a brief account of his philosophy.)

J. H. Stirling, *The Secret of Hegel.* London, 1865. (This was the first work to popularize Hegel in the English-speaking world. Valuable, but as some wit remarked, Stirling guarded his secret very well.)

W. T. Stace, *The Philosophy of Hegel.* London, 1924. (The best and clearest exposition of the Hegelian philosophy as a whole. By an ardent disciple.)

B. Croce, *What is Living and What is Dead in the Philosophy of Hegel.* London, 1915. (A reinterpretation of Hegel, by a prominent Italian Neo-Hegelian.)

H. A. Reyburn, *The Ethical Theory of Hegel.* Oxford, 1921. (Almost as obscure as Hegel himself, but valuable in spots, especially on political phases.)

G. S. Morris, *Hegel's Philosophy of the State and of History.* Chicago, 1887. (Very useful, but glosses over those points in Hegel's philosophy likely to antagonize Anglo-American readers.)

A. D. Lindsay, "Hegel, the German Idealist," in F. J. C. Hearnshaw, *Social and Political Ideas of the Age of Reconstruction.* London, 1932 (pp. 52 ff.).

C. E. Vaughan, *Studies in the History of Political Philosophy.* London, 1925 (vol. II, chap. IV). (Very valuable, though written by an ardent Neo-Hegelian.)

W. A. Dunning, *History of Political Theories from Rousseau to Spencer.* New York, 1922 (pp. 154 ff.).

G. H. Sabine, *History of Political Theory.* New York, 1937 (chap. XXX). (Valuable, critical.)

J. Dewey, *German Philosophy and Politics.* New York, 1915 (especially pp. 107 ff.).

Those familiar with French and German will find the following works very valuable:

P. Roques, *Hegel, sa vie, ses oeuvres.* Paris, 1912.

V. Basch, *Les Doctrines politiques des philosophes classiques de l'Allemagne.* Paris, 1927. (Most of this work is devoted to a candid but sympathetic interpretation of Hegel, see especially pp. 111–323.) (Valuable.)

K. Rosenkranz, *Hegels Leben.* Berlin, 1844. (The standard biography. By an ardent disciple.)

R. Haym, *Hegel und seine Zeit.* Second edition, Leipzig, 1927. (Critical, valuable, very readable.)

T. Haering, *Hegel, sein Wollen und sein Werk.* Leipzig, 1929.

W. Moog, *Hegel und die Hegelsche Schule.* Munich, 1930. (An excellent outline of the whole Hegelian philosophy.)

F. Fosenzweig, *Hegel und der Staat.* 2 vols., Munich, 1920. (The standard work on Hegel's political philosophy.)

H. Heller, *Hegel und der nationale Machtstaatsgedanke in Deutschland.* Leipzig, 1921.

F. Dittman, *Der Begriff des Volksgeistes bei Hegel.* Leipzig, 1909.

W. Dilthey, *Die Jugendgeschichte Hegels.* Leipzig, 1905.

THE NEO-HEGELIAN MOVEMENT IN ENGLAND. The best general works on the subject are as follows:

H. Sturt, *Idola Theatri.* London, 1906. (Critical, very readable.)

H. Haldar, *Neo-Hegelianism.* London, 1927. (By a devout Hegelian, but very lucid and valuable.)

L. T. Hobhouse, *Metaphysical Theory of the State.* London, 1918. (A critical, lucid, valuable interpretation of the Hegelian theory of the state in general and of Bosanquet's theory in particular.)

E. Barker, *Political Thought in England from Spencer to the Present Day.* London, 1915. (See especially chap. III for Bradley and Bosanquet. Sympathetic but critical.)

B. Pfannenstill, *Bosanquet's Philosophy of the State.* Lund, 1936. (By an ardent disciple. Deals with the Neo-Hegelian movement as a whole, but with especial reference to Bosanquet.)

The following works by individual Neo-Hegelians are especially noteworthy:

F. H. Bradley, *Ethical Studies.* London, 1876. (See especially Chap. V, "My Station and Its Duties.")

B. Bosanquet, *Philosophical Theory of the State.* London, 1899. (There are several more recent editions.) (The most important work of the Neo-Hegelian school dealing primarily with politics.)

B. Bosanquet, *Social and International Ideals.* London, 1917.

B. Bosanquet, *The Principle of Individuality and Value.* London, 1912.

D. G. Ritchie, *Principles of State Interference.* London, 1891.

D. G. Ritchie, *Darwin and Hegel.* London, 1893.

D. G. Ritchie, *Darwinism and Politics.* London, 1889.

D. G. Ritchie, *Natural Rights.* London, 1895.

Sir H. Jones, *Working Faith of the Social Reformer.* London, 1910.

Part Three

THE DEVELOPMENT OF ABSOLUTISM
IN THE NINETEENTH AND
TWENTIETH CENTURIES

CHAPTER VIII

TRADITIONALISM AND THE TRADITIONALISTS

HEGEL died in 1831; Mussolini seized control of Italy in 1922; Hitler became the master of Germany in 1933. In many ways Mussolini's Fascism and Hitler's Naziism may be regarded as little more than rather radical developments of the theory of the state and of government advanced by Hegel. But in the century or so which elapsed between the death of Hegel and the triumphal emergence of Mussolini and Hitler upon the political stages, much water flowed under the bridge. The orthodox Hegelian tradition was considerably modified by the later Neo-Hegelians. In addition many powerful and able writers completely broke with Hegel's metaphysical background even though they remained profoundly influenced by many of Hegel's political and legal ideas. As a result of this break with the Hegelian metaphysics even the ideas taken over from Hegel underwent a radical transformation. These later modified and developed ideas had an even greater and more direct effect upon the formation of the Fascist and Nazi ideologies than the doctrines derived from the orthodox Hegelian tradition, and hence deserve our especial attention.

In the realm of general political speculation we may say that there are three characteristic Hegelian doctrines which were especially important in later philosophizing about the state. These three doctrines, moreover, enormously influenced many persons who disliked Hegel, and who resolutely rejected the orthodox Hegelian system. All three, in one form or another, have been incorporated in both the Fascist and Nazi ideologies. The first of these doctrines is *traditionalism*, the belief that legal and political institutions must have an historical background and must be in accord with the specific genius or culture of the people concerned, as shown in their national tradition. The second doctrine is *irrationalism*, the belief that political action must be based, not on reason, but upon feeling, instinct, intuition. The third is *evolutionism*, the belief that all social and political institutions, to be useful, must be the result of a long line of evolution or development. In later times the rather idealistic interpretation of evolution given by Hegel was transformed into what is usually called *Social Darwinism*, the idea that the keynote to social and political progress is eternal conflict between groups and the ultimate survival of the fittest.

It is our duty to examine each of these three main lines of thought. Of these the simplest and in many ways the most intelligible is that of traditionalism, which may be defined as respect for the past and the political and social traditions handed down by the past. In this connection a sharp line of contrast must be drawn between the old traditionalism and the new type. Old traditionalism was violently opposed to all theories of progress, or improvement, or evolution. Political life was pictured as in a continual state of decline and the only hope of civilization was to cling resolutely to the old ways and to avoid dangerous modernistic tendencies. Not infrequently the old traditionalists went even further and demanded that we discard the iniquitous changes which have been made in recent generations and go back to the glorious days of the distant past.

In contrast with this old traditionalism was the new traditionalism of Hegel, the type which was to become dominant during the nineteenth and twentieth centuries, especially among those thinkers who leaned towards etatism. Hegel, as we know, believed in evolution, in perpetual, inevitable progress. To him, in theory at least, the present is better than the past, the future must be better than the present. To cling blindly to old outworn institutions, to wish to revive institutions of an earlier age when mankind was in its childhood was ridiculous — it was blasphemous against the Universal Spirit which is ever leading mankind to higher goals. Yet with all this progressivism and evolutionism Hegel was profoundly conservative. He was convinced that progress in the present and future can only be made in dependence upon traditions handed down from the past. A healthy tree shows perpetual growth; each year it should tower higher and higher towards the sky. Yet this growth is only possible if the tree is well rooted in the ground, if the sap can rise from its roots to the new-growing twigs and branches. In like manner a nation can progress only if it is acutely conscious of the glorious traditions of its past, only if it follows these traditions in all essential respects, however much individual institutions may be changed to suit a new and different age.

It was Hegel, moreover, who pointed out that there is and must be a close connection between traditionalism and etatism. Earlier thinkers had failed to see the inevitability of such a connection. Many of the earlier traditionalists, such as Hotman and Montesquieu. had been ardent liberals. Some of the greatest etatists, on the other hand, men such as Bodin and Hobbes, had despised tradition and traditionalism. They ignored all problems of historical background and defended the omnipotent state and authoritarian government on the basis of pure abstract reason. There were some thinkers, to be sure, men such as De Maistre and Burke, who were both traditionalists and etatists, but with such men there seemed to be no logical or necessary link between the two. It was Hegel who supplied this link. It was Hegel who took the methods of Hotman and Montesquieu and combined them with the conclusions of Bodin and Hobbes. This startling synthesis has had an immense effect upon subsequent political thought.

The basis both of Hegel's traditionalism and of his etatism (and the connecting link between the two) is the idea that the individual as an eternal separate entity, as an indestructible spiritual atom, does not exist. Man is what he is because of his membership in a community. His mode of life, his food, his drink, his clothing are not individual discoveries or inventions, but the gifts of his spiritual mother, the community. His religious and philosophical ideas, even the dictates of what he calls his conscience, are only to a slight extent the results of his own speculations or activities; they come to him from the great whole of which he is only an insignificant and evanescent part. Moreover, and this is the important point, the community consists not only of the living but also of the dead. The living and the dead are inseparably linked in every phase of human life. We are what we are, not only because of our neighbors, but also because of our ancestors and our neighbors' ancestors. Instead of blindly fighting for our individual rights we must accept the suzerainty of the community, both present and past.

> The individual, bare, naked, and unqualified by social pressure and social tradition, is a thing unknown to history or experience; that which we loosely call the individual is always and everywhere a being moulded by those around him and those who have gone before him, a being who may please to think himself independent and isolated from his fellows, but who in reality is little more than a puppet in their hands, a being whose conception of the world he sees around him, whose moral and social standards, whose belief about nature and the unseen powers behind nature, whose very reason, will, and conscience are determined almost entirely by the beliefs, customs, and traditions into which, with no choice of his own, he happens to be born. It is to society and not to the phantom which he calls his individuality that he owes all which is definable in his being; if all he thus owes were taken away, nothing tangible, certainly nothing distinctly human, would be left.[1]

Concepts such as these led Hegel to worship at the shrines both of tradition and of the state. In marked contrast with earlier periods, during the nineteenth and twentieth centuries nearly all the advocates of traditionalism believed in a strong and active state, and nearly all the apostles of etatism preached that man should listen to the voice of tradition.

Somewhat more startling and far less logical was the alliance established by Hegel between traditionalism and authoritarianism. At first sight it might seem as if belief in tradition should go hand in hand with belief in democracy, for tradition is usually associated with custom, and custom is what the populace as a whole does rather than the habitual action of a minority group within the community. It was Hegel who insisted that sound tradition could only grow up in a well-ordered community, and a well-ordered community meant one which was controlled by its upper classes. It was Hegel who insisted that though tradition should be reverenced by all, the really fine things in the tradition of each country were the creation of a few superior minds, which were the special embodiments of the World Spirit. Some of these arguments may seem a little far-fetched, but it is a remarkable fact that during the nineteenth century traditionalism and authoritarianism, in the vast majority of cases, went hand in hand.

JOSEPH MAZZINI

The influence of Hegel and especially of his form of traditionalism was very widespread and affected many persons who were directly opposed to orthodox Hegelianism and even to orthodox etatism. It is especially interesting to observe this influence upon the great Italian leader Joseph Mazzini (1805–1872). Hegel was the great conservative of his generation, Mazzini the great reformer and revolutionary of his. Hegel was the pillar of the Prussian bureaucracy and of the Prussian throne; Mazzini was the great iconoclast assailing both the bureaucracies and the monarchies of his time. Yet this "symbol of revolution," this "terror of principalities and powers," was profoundly affected by the Hegelian political philosophy and more especially by the traditionalism inherent in this philosophy. Mazzini did, indeed, reject Hegel's authoritarianism, but he accepted most of Hegel's etatism. It was the task of Mazzini to show that traditionalism meant nationalism, that traditionalism was perfectly consistent with armed revolt against the powers that be when these powers were, or seemed to be, in conflict with the historic national ideal.

In his own lifetime Mazzini was known as a liberal; by many he was regarded as the foremost apostle of liberalism on the continent of Europe. It is undoubtedly true that there are many liberal elements in Mazzini's philosophy. Liberalism, as we know, is a combination of individualism and democracy. In so far as he believed in freedom of speech, of thought, of religious belief, Mazzini was an individualist. It is beyond question that Mazzini was a fervent advocate of democracy, assailing both aristocratic and monarchic rule. Yet there are many elements in Mazzini's thought which stand in marked contrast to historic liberalism, elements which he took over from the German philosophers, especially from Hegel. It is these elements which sharply distinguish Mazzinian liberalism from English liberalism. It is these elements which permit Mussolini and the Fascists to proclaim that Mazzini was the great precursor of Fascism and that Fascism is only the logical and consistent application of the great fundamental principles which underlie the Mazzinian philosophy, however much Fascist doctrines may disagree with the superficial aspects of Mazzini's thought.

In Mazzini's own lifetime most English liberals were utilitarians, followers of Bentham and James Mill. Mazzini abhorred Bentham's notion that "goodness" and "happiness" were synonymous, that men should be guided by enlightened self-interest, that the aim of government should be merely the greatest happiness of the greatest number. To Mazzini goodness was something far different from happiness — in fact was frequently inconsistent with happiness — and it was the duty of man to pursue goodness at all costs. This meant that man should forget all thought of happiness, all thought of enlightened self-interest, if self-interest meant only the pursuit of pleasure or material advantages. In like manner the thought that government should merely aim at the greatest happiness of the greatest number was considered profoundly immoral. It was the duty of the government to aim at the moral as well as the material betterment of its subjects, and this moral betterment might well make the people unhappy, at least temporarily. Each nation has its own special vocation, its own special mission to perform, and it is the duty of the government to see that this mission is duly carried out however much such an action interfered with the material pleasure of the populace.

Mazzini was equally opposed to the old classical liberalism, the liberalism of Locke, of Paine, of Jefferson, the liberalism based upon natural rights. The liberals of this school thought that every man *qua* man had certain innate inherent rights with which no government whether autocratic or democratic, should interfere. It was upon the basis of natural rights that these classical liberals advocated a system of rigid individualism, and in accordance with this individualism were ardent apostles of *laissez faire*. Mazzini had no use whatever for the doctrine of natural rights. In fact the very word rights irritated him. As opposed to natural right he preached the doctrine of natural duty. Each and every man is bound by duty, by duty to himself, to his neighbors, to the community in which he lives. It is true that a man's neighbors also have duties towards him, that the community has duties towards its citizens, and these duties give birth to what we call rights, but the whole world of politics is clouded when we think of rights instead of mutual duties. Any rights which a man may have are not "natural," but are derived from the community, and are due him only in so far as he worthily fulfills his duties as a member of the community. In rejecting the doctrine of natural rights, Mazzini also rejected the rigid individualism of the classical liberals. To him the group, the community, the nation, are of far greater importance than the individual and it is the duty of the individual to subordinate himself to and even to sacrifice himself for the great whole of which he is a part. In rejecting individualism Mazzini also rejected *laissez faire*. To his mind the state not only might but should regulate and control the activity of the individual in the interests of the community as a whole.

Mazzini also broke with the liberals, both the utilitarian and the classical liberals, in his attitude towards internationalism or cosmopolitanism. The liberals as a group were not only individualists; they were also cosmopolitans. They proclaimed that they were more interested in the rights of each and every man, whatever his nation or his race, and of humanity as a whole, than in the specific rights of any one community. The liberals were more interested in the rights of "Man" than they were in the rights of Englishmen, or Frenchmen, or Americans. A man was a man and should have all the rights of a man irrespective of whether he had a yellow or a white or a black skin, or whether he spoke English or Greek or Italian. A state for them was merely a convenient political unit; its boundaries were flexible and should be based largely upon geographic considerations. Within these boundaries all citizens should be equally free whatever their racial or linguistic backgrounds might happen to be.

Mazzini's views formed a sharp contrast to those of the liberals on this point. Mazzini was not so extreme an opponent of internationalism as was Hegel. He was willing to admit that humanity constituted a single "collective being" for whose welfare every person should work, but with Fichte, Mazzini felt that each person could best serve mankind by complete and absolute devotion to the nation-state of which he formed a part. He was opposed to the "cold, abstract, vain cosmopolitanism and internationalism" of the other liberals. Each nation, he claimed, has its own special vocation, its own special mission, its own special duties to perform, and each citizen should first and foremost concern himself with the vocation, the mission, the duty of his own nation rather than bother about mankind as a whole. Mazzini felt that he could best serve humanity by working for the greater glory and power of Italy, by aiding Italy to triumph over Austria, by enabling Italy once more to assume the political and spiritual leadership of the world.

One of the most important phases of Mazzini's political philosophy was his combination of pseudo-liberalism with Hegelian traditionalism and his ability to convert thousands of liberals to his own point of view in this regard. As we have already seen, there is no necessary opposition between liberalism and traditionalism. Both Hotman and Montesquieu were devout traditionalists, yet both were supporters of liberal doctrines. During the eighteenth century, however, most of the classical apostles of liberalism were violent in their opposition to traditionalism, and in Mazzini's time it was generally felt that liberalism and traditionalism were mutually contradictory. Both Locke and Bentham ignored history and historical precedents. To them it was of no consequence how long political institutions had been in existence. We must, they argued, get down to rational first principles, and upon these principles, ignoring the past, erect the ideal constitution for the state. Rousseau and Jefferson were equally violent in their opposition to the voice of tradition. To Rousseau political history is largely a history of human abuses. "From what has been done, the jurist infers a right to do. The result is a theory of the state conformable with the most ardent wishes of tyrants." Jefferson protested against "government by the dead instead of the living," and insisted that each generation should frame its own form of government, rather than be guided by past precedents.

It is not surprising that conservatives such as De Maistre, Burke, and Hegel, defenders of the *status quo*, protested against this irreverent anti-traditionalism. What is surprising is that Mazzini, the arch-revolutionary, the enemy of the *status quo*, should have insisted upon tradition and the need of following tradition in all social and political

matters.   When Mazzini began his career, most of Italy was divided
into a number of petty states.   To him this was contrary to the Italian
tradition, a tradition which declared that all Italians must be unified
in one state (when and where came this tradition, Mazzini does not tell
us).   When Mazzini began his career, most of the Italian states were ruled
over by hereditary monarchs.   But Mazzini fought for a republic on the
ground that republican government alone was in accord with the true
Italian traditions.   "Monarchy has no tradition.   It has never been a
source of national life." [2]   Ancient Rome in the period of its glory was a
republic.   The transformation of the republic into the empire was a sign
of degeneration, a sign that Italy was false to her national tradition.
Hence this transformation "hastened the work of dissolution" and
"opened the way to the invaders of the north."   The true Italian tradition of the Middle Ages was represented by its republics, such as Genoa,
Venice, Florence.   The modern Italian monarchies were created by
self-seeking blackguards supported by foreigners.   As the creation of
these monarchies went contrary to Italian tradition, they never prospered.
In the holy name of tradition the Italians must arise, overthrow the
existing order of things, and create a strong unified republic.

It was because of traditionalism that Mazzini insisted that Rome be
made the capital of the Italian state.   Rome must be the capital of
Italy, not because of its geographic advantages, but because of the great
traditions which centered in this city.

> We look on Rome as the sanctuary of the nation, the sacred city of Italy,
> the historic center whence, by providential mission, came Italy's message
> to men. . . .[3]
> Rome of the Caesars gave the unity of civilization that force imposed upon
> Europe.   Rome of the Popes gave a unity of civilization that authority
> imposed on a great part of the human race.   Rome of the People will give . . .
> a unity of civilization accepted by the free consent of the nations for Hu-
> manity.[4]

The Rome of the future must be different from the Rome of the past,
but its greatness will depend upon its using the traditions handed down
from the past.   "From Rome must come, must permeate humanity
that message that two earlier worlds have baptized and consecrated." [5]

With the German philosophers, Mazzini was convinced that the task
of the future is not to destroy the past but to fulfill it.   For the proper
fulfillment of the past it is necessary that each people be keenly aware of
its own national tradition.   It is necessary that scholars devote much
time to the study of national origins, to the language and history of the

nation of which they are members, for only thus can a nation become aware of its true vocation in life, only thus can a nation unfold its true genius. It is this thought which gives us a clue to the nature of Mazzini's traditionalism. To De Maistre and Burke traditionalism meant only conservatism, the abhorrence of change and especially of revolution. To Mazzini traditionalism was only another word for nationalism, a nationalism which demanded change and even bloody revolution. For us it is of especial importance that the Fascists and Nazis are traditionalists, and that their traditionalism is the traditionalism of Mazzini and not that of De Maistre and Burke.

To Mazzini we are what we are because of the group, especially because of the nation in which we live. Our acts, our thoughts, our aspirations are merely a reflection of the group or nation. Destroy the nation as a nation and the individual talents and capacities which constituted it dwindle and eventually die away. It is equally true that a nation is what it is because of what it has been, because of the experiences it has undergone, because of the store of traditions it has stored up. As a consequence of this belief Mazzini, for all his humanitarianism, refused to be an internationalist. Though he loved England and the English, he insisted that an Englishman because of his national background and national tradition was essentially a different sort of animal from a Frenchman or an Italian. In like manner each nation because of its separate history and traditions has a distinct and everlasting personality of its own, and any attempt to ignore or to merge or to subdue these separate national personalities would end in disaster.

But if Mazzini was thus an ardent traditionalist, he was a traditionalist of the Hegelian school, for combined with a profound reverence for the past was a fixed belief in eternal, unceasing, inevitable progress. To Mazzini, as to Hegel, there is this constant progress not only in material, but also in spiritual things, in morals, in politics, in religion — but to Mazzini, as to Hegel, this progress is possible only by building upon the past. Mazzini did not claim to be a metaphysician. Hence his phraseology differed radically from that of Hegel, the professional logician, but underneath the apparent differences in words there is a remarkable resemblance between the ideas of the two writers. Mazzini, in spite of his Catholic upbringing, followed Hegel in rejecting the infallibility of the church and of the Bible. He denied, though very guardedly, the divinity of Christ, miracles, and special revelation in the old sense of the word. But Mazzini, like Hegel, was a firm believer in the existence and omnipotence of a great World Spirit, though, unlike

Hegel, he preferred to give to this impersonal World Spirit the old-fashioned, orthodox name of God. To Mazzini, as to Hegel, God reveals Himself to mankind, not through special scriptures (or at least only partially so), but through history. His action is seen, not through miracles, but through the slow, constant development of the human race. All history is dominated by Divine Providence. It is because of this Divine Providence that man inevitably evolves or progresses — whether or not he wishes to do so.

Mazzini, like Hegel, tried to evolve a new philosophy of history, based upon the belief that human history is not a blind series of haphazard and inconsequential events, but the continuous development of mankind under divine guidance from lower to successively higher stages according to a fixed pattern, a pattern invisible to the ignorant masses, invisible even to the average historian, but clearly to be recognized by the man with spiritual insight. To be sure, the divine pattern sketched by Mazzini differed radically from that revealed by Hegel, but in spite of many differences the two have certain underlying features in common. Both patterns were secured by twisting and turning historical details so as to make them fit into a beautiful general scheme. To Hegel the whole of human history was the gradual development of such a perfect political institution as the Prussian monarchy. To Mazzini it was the gradual development of such a perfect political institution as the Mazzini-inspired Italian Republic of the future. There is a strong family resemblance between the two political ideas.

Mazzini, as we have seen, disliked the idea of rights and liked the idea of duty; he disliked individualism and liked what he called the principle of association. Such being the case, it was easy for him to devise a historical scheme whereby the whole of human history was shown to be a slow development of mankind from devotion to rights to devotion to duty, from adherence to individualism to adherence to associationism. To put it more bluntly, Mazzini saw in history only the development of the perfect all-powerful state, to which the individual with his plea for individual rights is completely subordinated — surely a point of view not very different from that postulated by Hegel.

In Mazzini's historical scheme, the whole of history is divided into two great periods. The first starts with the rise of the Greek republics (everything before that is merely prehistory) and goes down to and through the French Revolution. The second starts with the close of the French Revolution and will lead (under Mazzini's tutelage) to the new reformed world of tomorrow. All through the first period man was dominated in some form or other by the idea of rights, individual rights. By a curious perversion of history Mazzini insisted that not only Rome but also Greece emphasized liberty, meaning by liberty individual rights. "Ignorant of the unity of life ... they focused the work of the intellect on the individual and saw in him only the subjective existence of the ego — that is, liberty." [6] As human progress continued, it was the task of Christianity to add the doctrine of equality to the old pagan doctrine of liberty.

> The Mosaic religion had already established the vital doctrine of divine unity. Christianity appropriated this dogma, and advancing a step further withdrew it from the privilege of the *chosen* people in order to diffuse it among all nations. The God of Moses was the God of Israel. The God of Christianity was the God of men, who were necessarily brothers in Him. The slow abolition of slavery was a consequence of the triumph of Christianity. [7]

Even the Reformation was only a further development of the doctrines of liberty and equality laid down by the classical world.

> Sixteen centuries had exhausted the vigor of the Christian philosophy. The human spirit was bound to move again towards a newer and vaster philosophy, hence the necessity for a strong assertion of the individual and for that right of private judgment without which every attempt to pass the limits of the old beliefs would have failed. Protestantism unconsciously asserted it, and that was its sole mission in the world. The sovereignty of the individual, arbitrarily confined within the limits of the Bible, was its last word, re-echoed in the arts, the economics, the politics it inaugurated. [8]

Looking at history from this point of view, Mazzini came to the conclusion that the French Revolution was only the logical carrying out of the old doctrines of individual liberty and equality. The French Revolution, therefore, was not the beginning of a new epoch, but the summing up, the conclusion, of an old one. It did not give to mankind a new ideal or a new formula, but transplanted to the practical political sphere the formulas inherited from the pagan, the Christian, and the Protestant worlds.

With the end of the French Revolution, however, there was ushered into the world a new epoch, destined to give new formulas, new ideals to the world. Mazzini himself was to be regarded as the chief prophet of this new epoch. Eventually these new ideals would lead to a new and greater revolution which would bring man to the promised land, a goal looked for but in vain by the promoters of the French Revolution. The leaders of the new epoch would not entirely discard the ideals of the old era, liberty and equality, but these were to be transformed in the light of the new superior ideals of duty and association.

Mazzini argued that the course of events during the French Revolution showed conclusively the need for these new ideals. Demand for individual rights led to confusion, to anarchy, and then from anarchy to despotism. As long as men struggle merely for rights (as opposed to duties) we shall witness, as in the past, the struggle of man with man, of class with class. It is only when man turns from belief in rights to belief in duty that cooperation can take the place of conflict, and justice the place of domination of one group by another. Moreover, the very doctrine of progress or evolution (the all-important dogma in Mazzini's creed) demands that we abandon the pursuit of rights for the pursuit of duty. The doctrine of rights is static; the doctrine of duty is dynamic, progressive. The old defender of natural rights taught that these natural rights were always the same, at all times and at all places. An understanding of the doctrine of duty, on the other hand, shows that though man is always bound by duty, the duties of one time and place may be very different from those imposed in a different country and at a subsequent era. It may well be that in the future we may owe to the state certain duties of which we are at present unaware. It may well be that the state will owe to its citizens duties (such as the duty to see that each man gets an adequate wage) of which existing states are equally unaware.

To Mazzini the doctrine of duty in no way interferes with the principle of freedom or liberty, for following the German school of philosophers he insisted that true freedom consists in doing or in being able to do what one ought to do. In fulfilling all our obligations to our fellow countrymen and to the state, therefore, we are gaining, not losing, our freedom.[9] From this doctrine there follows the important conclusion that we ought to help other persons to be "free," that is, to induce them to do the things which they ought to do, whether or not their momentary caprice makes them wish to do so.

> The time has come to convince ourselves that we can only rise to God through the souls of our fellow men, and that we ought to improve and purify them, even though they do not ask it of us themselves.[10]

Another important phase of Mazzini's philosophy is the belief that duty is not merely obedience to the individual conscience, but is also and more especially obedience to the collective conscience, as voiced in the ideas and aspirations of the community as a whole. To most Protestants, and to the followers of Kant, duty meant obedience to the voice of the individual conscience or to the dictates of the individual reason. Mazzini had associated too much with the liberals for him to

deny completely the usefulness of individual conscience or reason.
But after paying lip service to the old liberal individualism,[11] he
hastened to add that the individual conscience and individual reason
by themselves form very inadequate guides for conduct.   With Hegel,
Mazzini insisted that though the blank form, the abstract idea, of duty
may come from the individual conscience, the filling up of that form,
the concrete application of the idea of duty, must come from the conscience of the whole community.

> Conscience can only teach us that the law exists, not the nature of the
> duty which it imposes. . . . The conscience of the individual speaks in accord-
> ance with his education, his tendencies, his habits, his passions. . . . Evidently
> the voice of the individual conscience is not enough in all conditions of things
> and without any other guide to reveal the law to us.[12]

What is true of the individual conscience is also true of the individual
reason.

> Your individual intellect will not be enough to teach you the law of God. . . .
> Your life is short, your individual faculties are weak, uncertain, and need
> support.[13]

Mazzini was convinced that our individual consciences and intellects
must be supported by the group conscience and intellect.

> God has placed beside you a being whose life is continuous, whose faculties
> are the sum of the individual faculties which have been exercised for perhaps
> four hundred centuries, a being which amid the errors and faults of individuals
> ever advances in wisdom and morality, a being in whose development God has
> written and writes in every epoch a line of his law.   This being is Humanity.[14]

From this passage it would appear that our consciences and intellects
should seek to conform with the beliefs of humanity as a whole.   As
Mazzini developed his arguments, however, we find that our real guide
in moral and intellectual matters is not humanity in the abstract, but
the particular group or nation of which we happen to be members.

> Humanity is a great army moving to the conquest of unknown lands. . . .
> The Peoples (or Nations) are the different corps and divisions of that army.
> Each has a post entrusted to it, each a special mission to perform, and the
> common victory depends on the exactness with which the different operations
> are carried out.   Do not disturb the order of battle.[15]

In other words, as private soldiers fighting in the ranks we need not and
should not concern ourselves with the general tactics for the whole army.
Enough for us to take our commands from our divisional and regimental
commanders.   As long as we do this, our duties and obligations are fulfilled.

Considering what Mazzini has to say regarding duties versus rights, it is not surprising to find him preaching that in the new era, which dawned at the end of the French Revolution, individualism must give way to the principle of association. As long as we thought only in terms of rights, we thought only of our individual selves. Once we begin to think of duties, we must think of others, and of the need of co-operating with others. We must think of ourselves not as eternally separate units, but as parts of a greater whole, to the welfare of which each one must devote and if necessary sacrifice himself.

> We part forever from the exclusively individualist Age, and with greater reason from that individualism which is the materialism of that Age.[16] We believe in association ... as the only means possessed by us to realize truth as the method of progress, as the only existing road to perfection.[17]

In accordance with this principle of association, Mazzini rejects the idea that government is a necessary evil and insists that it is a necessary good; he rejects the idea that he governs best who governs least and insists that we should have a strong, active government, one which seeks to mould and guide its citizens, not one which merely seeks to prevent and punish crime and disorder. He attacked what he called the American political theory (really the Jeffersonian theory) which

> centers itself in the sense of liberty alone, smothers the principle of association under the omnipotence of the ego ..., plants mistrust in the civil organization ..., introduces materialism, individualism, egotism, and contradiction through the doctrine of the atheism of the law and the sovereignty of rights and interests.[18]

In place of the old Jeffersonian *laissez faire*, Mazzini demanded "legislation tending to advance the intellectual and economical progress of those classes that need it most." [19]

As a result of his belief in a strong government Mazzini had little use for the old doctrines of check and balance and the separation of powers. Montesquieu in insisting upon these doctrines was "vitiated by a fundamental error." By advocating the separation of the executive, legislative, and judicial powers, he

> destroys the conception of national Unity. The theory of rights and hence of acquired rights compelled Montesquieu to discover powers where they did not exist, and found a political tri-theism which has survived even to this day and impairs every conception of national organization.[20]

In the name of the great God, Association, Mazzini demanded a highly centralized and unified political organization.

The doctrine of association led Mazzini, in the economic sphere, to denounce not only the old liberal *laissez faire*, but also socialism and communism, and to demand an economic organization very similiar to that which the Fascists now call the corporative state. The old liberal doctrine was each one for himself and liberty for all.

> If they were right the disease of poverty would be incurable and God forbid, my brothers, that I should ever agree with them. . . . Under the exclusive régime of liberty which they preach . . . the poverty of the working classes remains unchanged. Freedom of competition for those who possess nothing, for those who are unable to save anything from their daily wages . . . is a lie.[21]

But Mazzini was equally opposed to the Marxist and other forms of socialist doctrines which were becoming popular in his time. *Laissez faire* is bad, but communism "touches the opposite extreme, denies the individual, denies liberty, closes the way to progress, and, so to speak, petrifies society." [22] Even were Communism possible (which is doubtful) existence in a communist state

> would be a life of beavers, not of men. The liberty, the dignity, the conscience of the individual would all disappear in an organization of productive machines. Physical life might be satisfied by it, but moral and intellectual life would perish and with it emulation, the choice of free association, stimulus to production, joys of progress and all incentives to progress.[23]

To Mazzini economic progress is possible only by rejecting both extreme individualism and extreme collectivism. With the Socialists he agreed that private property is badly constituted at the present time and that there is need for economic reform. With the individualists he insisted that the desire to own private property of some sort is one of "the true elements inseparable from human nature. . . . The principle of property is rooted in human nature itself and you find it existing and protected throughout the whole existence of humanity." [24] Nevertheless, and this is the important point,

> the methods by which property is governed are subject to change and destined like every other manifestation of human life to obey the law of progress. Those who, finding property already established in a particular form, declare that form to be inviolable and oppose all attempts to transform it, deny progress itself . . . and those who, because they find it badly constituted at a certain epoch, declare that it must be abolished and wiped out of the social system deny an element of human nature, and, could they ever have their way, they would only succeed in retarding progress by mutilating life.[25]

In other words, Mazzini insisted that the principle of private property and the private ownership and operation of commerce and industry must be kept inviolate, but he was equally insistent that the community or the state might regulate and control the conditions under which private property might be retained. Moreover, the state might and should radically change the present conditions of property-holding in accordance with the laws of economic progress with the aim of securing more equitable distribution of wealth. In place of the old "free" capitalism, he demanded state-controlled capitalism and state supervision over all commercial and industrial undertakings.

Equally important was the emphasis laid upon group as opposed to individual and state enterprises, though, of course, according to Mazzini, the state must reserve the right to control these group enterprises. Like Hegel, Mazzini was a great advocate of group or corporate action. The state represents, of course, the supreme group, but inside and subordinate to the state there should exist a large number of smaller groups in which the citizens might practice the principles of association.

> The state, the nation, represents the association of the citizens in those things and in those aims which are common to all the men who compose it. But there exist aims and ends which do not embrace all the citizens, but only a certain number of them. And as the aims and ends common to all constitute the nation, so the aims and ends common to some of the citizens ought to constitute the special association.[26]

Mazzini was hopeful that the development of a group or corporate life would solve the economic problem of the age. Private property and private enterprise were not to be abolished, but in place of the old cut-throat individualism he hoped to substitute group action, the voluntary grouping of workers and producers into guilds, corporations, associations. Cooperation was to take the place of relentless competition. With this end in view, Mazzini urged the formation of various forms of cooperative enterprises, farmers' cooperatives, producers' cooperatives consumers' cooperatives.

> Association of labor, division of the profits of labor amongst the laborers in proportion to the amount and the value of the work accomplished; this is the social future. In this is contained the secret of your emancipation. You were slaves once, then serfs, then wage earners. Before long you shall be, if you will it, free producers and brothers in association.[27]

The corporate state in modern Italy has departed radically from certain aspects of Mazzini's doctrine of association — notably in the distinction between workers' associations and employers' associations — but in its emphasis upon the idea that all economic enterprises should be carried out by state-regulated corporations, it has been profoundly influenced by the Mazzinian ideology.

HEINRICH VON TREITSCHKE

The influence of Hegelian traditionalism was enormously strengthened by the writings of the powerful Prussian school of historians which arose about the middle of the nineteenth century. In other countries historians, at least the leading historians, have been respected and popular members of the literary world. Their works have been read with interest and admiration, but very seldom have their books brought about a transformation in the political views of the bulk of the population in their respective countries. In Germany, however, many of the historians looked upon themselves as political prophets. They sought to make history, not merely to record it. They wrote of the past in order to influence the present and the future.

Among these writers, Droysen, Sybel, Treitschke, members of the so-called Prussian school, were especially successful. Their works on history were looked upon as political gospels. In large measure as the result of their writings German public opinion came to welcome Prussian domination over the other German states, to welcome the creation of a new strong paternalistic and militaristic German Empire under Prussian hegemony. Last but not least, they succeeded in quenching the republican and ultra-democratic feeling which had been rampant in Germany during the 1830's and 1840's, and they popularized authoritarian government, control of the state by an hereditary monarch, and a strongly entrenched civil and military bureaucracy.

The creation of the new German Empire was largely the work of civil bureaucrats, such as Bismarck, and of military leaders, such as Moltke. The widespread enthusiasm for the new order of things was due in no small degree to the books and lectures poured forth by the Prussian school of historians. Of especial importance is the fact that the doctrines they preached have survived the empire they glorified and the monarchy they flattered. The German Empire as they knew it fell in 1918 and with it hereditary monarchy and the House of Hohenzollern, but their views on the nature and the function of the state and the need for autocratic rule remained popular with a large section of the German population and aided in the subsequent development of the Nazi ideology. The Prussianism of Droysen, of Sybel, and of Treitschke has given way to the Germanism of Hitler, but there is a strong logical and historical link between the two systems.

Of these three writers, Heinrich von Treitschke was by far the most interesting, the most eloquent, and the most influential. His life (1834-

1896) corresponded with some of the most stirring events in German history and in many of these events he was called upon to play a personal part.   He was a personal friend of the Prussian monarch and of Bismarck, the empire builder, and during every major political crisis he was called upon or felt himself called upon to write an essay or a monograph outlining and defending the Prussian point of view.   Almost total deafness prevented his taking an active part in military or administrative life, but this deafness did not interfere with his university lecturing nor with the production of a flood of polemical writings.   Nor, strangely enough, did it interfere with his serving actively for many years as a member of the German Reichstag or Diet.   The fact that he could not hear the speeches of his opponents made it all the easier for him to expound his own views and those of Bismarck, his master.

It is rather amusing to find that Treitschke, the great apostle of German nationalism, was himself of Slavic (Czechish) ancestry.   It is equally amusing to find that Treitschke, the great apostle of the doctrine that Prussia must conquer and control the smaller German states, was himself a native of Saxony, one of these smaller states, and that he was the son of a general in the Saxon army who was opposed to Prussian domination.   It is not without interest to note that for years Treitschke preached his gospel of Prussianism outside Prussia, while teaching in such non-Prussian institutions as the Universities of Leipzig, Freiburg, and Jena.   At these universities his glorifications of Prussia, his demands that Prussia demolish the smaller states, including the states in which he taught, caused conflict with his colleagues and some of his students, but these lectures helped pave the way for the subsequent acceptance of Prussian overlordship.   It was only in 1874, after the establishment of the German Empire (under Prussian control), that Treitschke went to Berlin University, where he continued until his death to serve as a guiding star and political oracle to German youth.

In studying the political philosophy of Treitschke, it is necessary to distinguish between the ideas of Treitschke as a young man and the ideas of Treitschke as an old man.   Throughout his life Treitschke was consistent in being an ardent nationalist and a devoted advocate of a strong unified state.   But in his younger days he tried to combine his nationalism and etatism with certain beliefs taken from the creed of the liberals.   In his younger days Treitschke was a nationalist without being an imperialist.   In defending German nationalism he thought it necessary to make allowances for nationalist movements elsewhere.   Each nation should have complete control over its own political destinies.

Later, nationalism was combined with wholehearted support of imperialism. The German people should, of course, control their own destinies, but in addition the Germans had a mandate to guide and control the destinies of other peoples, the many lesser breeds unworthy of self-government.

In his younger days Treitschke demanded a strong paternalistic state, but he wished to retain a certain amount of liberty for the individual, at least in the religious and economic sphere. In his later days the state was to be all-powerful even in these fields. He became an ardent supporter of Bismarck's anti-Catholic laws and of Bismarck's attempts to control commerce and industry and to establish economic nationalism. In his younger days Treitschke tried to combine nationalism and etatism with democracy. His strong national state was to be democratically controlled. Though a fiery apostle of Prussianism, he refused to enter the service of the Prussian state because Prussia was too much in the hands of the Junkers or hereditary aristocrats and because the Prussian monarch was not sufficiently "constitutional" in his actions. In later days, Treitschke glorified the Junkers and Junktertum — the guidance of the state by the aristocrats. He declared that the elected diet was the weakest part of the German Empire and insisted that the ministers of state must be responsible to the king-emperor and not to the popular assembly.

The philosophy of the younger Treitschke was very similar to that of Mazzini. The philosophy of the older Treitschke was very similar to that of fully developed Fascism and Naziism. This fact is of great importance. There would seem to be no necessary or logical connection between individualism and democracy, the combination of which constitutes liberalism. In like manner there seems to be no necessary connection between etatism (belief in the supremacy of the state over the individual) and authoritarianism (belief in control of government machinery by a non-democratic administrative hierarchy), the combination of which constitutes the core of Fascism and Naziism. T. H. Green and Mazzini advocated etatism, yet defended democracy. Pareto defended authoritarianism, yet disliked etatism. But such instances are rare. In most cases belief in etatism has led sooner or later to belief in authoritarianism and belief in authoritarianism has led to a belief in etatism. The liberal nationalism of Mazzini has led to the imperialism and authoritarianism of modern Italy. The liberal nationalism of the younger Treitschke has led, through the teachings of the later Treitschke, to the radical Nazi doctrines of modern Germany. It is because he serves as the missing link between two seemingly antithetical worlds of thought that Treitschke deserves a special place in the history of political philosophy.

We have called Treitschke a traditionalist and in point of fact he was the most eloquent exponent of traditionalism in modern times. At the same time it must be remembered that he was a traditionalist in the Hegelian and Mazzinian sense of the word. Treitschke, like Hegel and Mazzini, was a great believer in progress. Under God's guiding hand the history of mankind is on the whole a history of the ascent from lower to higher stages of culture. Far from being a standpat conservative, Treitschke was frequently in favor of change, even of violent or revolutionary change. Respect for tradition did not prevent his wishing to wipe out the small states of Germany, most of which had had an independent or semi-independent existence for many centuries. No reform was too radical for Treitschke if this reform could find a suitable place in his system of political thought.

Nevertheless Treitschke insisted that political speculation and action must be based upon respect for history and tradition (to his mind the two terms were more or less synonymous). Changes and reforms are not only possible, they are necessary; but these changes and reforms must be in accord with the lessons and traditions of the past. Treitschke was at times a professor of history, at other times a professor of political science, but to his mind the two posts were more or less identical. The professor of history should always apply the lessons of history to the present. The professor of political science must always seek a solution of his problems in the lessons taught by the past. For Treitschke, his two greatest works, *German History* and *Politics*, were only separate parts of one connected work.

Hegel, the founder of modern etatism, based his science of politics partly upon intuition or unconscious reasoning, partly upon reflection or conscious reasoning, and partly upon tradition or the lessons of history. Treitschke was very skeptical of the value of both intuition and conscious reasoning, and would rely almost entirely upon history as the source of valid political thought. To Hegel, when men acted "spontaneously" and nations developed "organically," they were really being guided by intuition or "creative unconscious reason." Treitschke had little use for either spontaneous or organic developments.

  We have come to realize that whenever this unhappy word "organic" finds its way into politics, all thought disappears. But the cradle song of indolence which has rocked the German world in comfortable slumber only too long can no longer delude us. Look back a hundred years at the Confederations of the Netherlands and Switzerland and then look at our own Holy Roman Empire. These indeed were states that developed organically until at last a foreign power trampled disdainfully on the decaying fragments that remained of them. We may be absolutely certain that a reforming and, if necessary, an energetically revolutionary will is essential to every state.[28]

Spontaneous organic development guided by unconscious reason is not enough. But neither is abstract conscious reasoning, doctrinaire philosophizing about the ideal form of government. The attempt to base political science upon reasoning apart from historical experience is bound to end in disaster.

> The historic sense was innate in the Greeks and what we call doctrinairism was unknown to them. It was for this reason that the theory of politics was brought by them so early to such a height.[29]

The Middle Ages were barren politically because political thinking was based upon barren metaphysical and theological dogmas instead of being guided by a sense of history. The Reformation under Luther broke the old dogmatism, but even so, most political philosophers turned away from the study of historical facts and pursued rationalistic or philosophical phantoms, such as natural law, natural rights, the social contract, and tried by theorizing to evolve a perfect system of government. Small wonder that this theorizing led to the horrors of the French Revolution. Instead of philosophizing upon abstract principles. we must devote ourselves to the study of the underlying political principles revealed by history, especially the history of our own nation.

> Politics becomes applied history.... The task of Politics is threefold. It must first seek to discover, through contemplation of the actual body politic, what is the fundamental idea of the state. It must then consider historically what the nations have desired in their political life, what they have created, what they have accomplished, and how they have accomplished it. This will lead on to the third object, the discovery of certain historic laws and the setting forth of some moral imperatives.[30]

Treitschke was a traditionalist in that he thought the truths of political science must be learned by a study of the past. He was also a traditionalist in the sense that he believed that the state must be an organic being with its roots in the past, an organic being in which yesterday, today, and tomorrow are firmly linked. The state

> aims at establishing a permanent tradition throughout the Ages. A people does not only comprise the individuals living side by side, but also the successive generations of the same stock. This is one of the truths which

Materialists dismiss as a mystical doctrine, and yet it is an obvious truth. Only the continuity of human history makes man a ζωον πολιτικόν [a political animal]. He alone stands upon the achievements of his forebears, and deliberately continues their work in order to transmit it more perfect to his children and children's children. . . . It is just a play upon words to talk of a bee State. Beasts merely reproduce unconsciously what has been from all time, and none but human beings can possess a form of government which is calculated to endure. There never was a form of Constitution without a law of inheritance. The rational basis for this is obvious, for by far the largest part of a nation's wealth was not created by the contemporary generation. The continuous legalized intention of the past must remain a factor in the distribution of property amongst posterity. In a nation's continuity with byegone generations lies the specific dignity of the state. It is consequently a contradiction to say that a distribution of property should be regulated by the deserts of the existing generation. Who would respect the banners of the State if the power of memory had fled. . . . Genuine patriotism is the consciousness of cooperating with the body-politic, of being rooted in ancestral achievements and of transmitting them to descendants.[31]

Treitschke's wholehearted acceptance of traditionalism as a political philosophy is obvious when we find him stating:

There is no truth more important for the political development of a people, than the old one that a State is maintained by the same forces which have helped to build it up. This is the reason why all healthy States have always had a conservative tendency. . . . We hear much of the inconstancy of the Athenian Democracy, but in actual fact, when a crisis arose, they reiterated the decree that the ancient custom and law of the State should still hold good. The same conservative inclination swayed the Romans, who held by their existing institutions in doubtful cases. All great nations have this true political instinct, the very opposite of the shallow Radicalism which loves novelty for its own sake.[32]

To some persons England and America seem characterized by a love of change, but in England the old laws

stand unrepealed, merely with new clauses added to them, so that we may find the English Parliament appealing to precedents dating from the fifteenth century. The Americans display this turn of mind very strongly, their Constitution has only once been changed by a couple of paragraphs in a hundred years. They pay a worship to their forefathers which may be overdone, but which is right in the main. A people which fails in respect to an existing dynasty or to great inherited institutions is politically unfit.[33]

A casual reading of these remarks might lead one to suspect that Treitschke was a traditionalist like De Maistre and Burke. But whereas Burke and De Maistre deplored change and reform of any sort, Treitschke urged changes and reforms as long as they were in accord with the national traditions. Moreover, while Burke and De Maistre were horrified by the thought of bloody revolution, Treitschke insisted that such revolutions are frequently necessary and useful if they are carried out with due reverence for the past.

> There is no principle in Revolution, either for good or evil.... The constitution of some States is so at variance with reason that their peaceful development is impossible.... History affords no instance of a State which has accomplished its development without revolution.[34]

The older traditionalists made a great point of defending "legitimate" governments against "illegitimate" usurpers. The new traditionalists, Treitschke among them, thought that such distinctions are absurd.

> It is a doctrinaire interpretation to force a distinction between a legitimate and a revolutionary State.... If we define a legitimate government to be one which has acquired its actual possessions ... through an acknowledged title, or by inheritance, or by wars admittedly righteous, we ask ourselves what State in Europe to-day deserves the name. It would be mockery to bestow it upon France; the English succession rests upon a violent revolution.... Belgium's whole existence is due to the same cause;... and in Germany the glorious Prussian State must thank the [violent] secularization of the lands held by the Orders for its very being.... A lawful development is the normal, but to every state without exception moments arrive when it can go no further upon peaceful lines, and war without or revolution within becomes inevitable.[35]

The relation between Treitschke's views on the subject and those of the Fascists and Nazis are very close. Both the Fascist and the Nazi states are revolutionary or semi-revolutionary in origin. Both constantly use revolutionary methods — yet both insist upon a blind reverence for tradition.

Traditionalism led Treitschke, as it led Mazzini, to become an ardent exponent of nationalism as the supreme governing principle in politics, for it is the unity of tradition which makes a nation out of a miscellaneous collection of individuals. A nation without a national tradition is not a true nation, and tradition which is not embodied in a national spirit is powerless and ineffective. Treitschke was convinced that traditionalism transformed into nationalism is the basis of all great and noble action.

> It is of the essence of political genius to be national.... The truly great maker of history always stands on a national basis. This applies equally to men of letters. He only is a great writer who so writes that all his countrymen respond, "Thus it must be. Thus we all feel," — who is in fact a microcosm of his nation.[36]

As an historian Treitschke was aware that the terms nation and state do not always correspond. There are some nations which have never achieved independent statehood. There are, on the other hand, many states consisting not of one but of several nationalities. In Treitschke's own lifetime the Turkish and Austro-Hungarian Empires were classic examples of multi-national states. But Treitschke pointed out the inherent weaknesses of such states. Because of the absence of unitary national tradition behind such states, they were unable to pursue a strong effective policy in either domestic or foreign concerns. Moreover, in such countries economic, literary, and artistic culture tends to stagnate. For political, social, and economic progress to take place it is essential that the state have as its core a single strong nation proud of itself and proud of its glorious past.

> We may say with certainty that the evolution of the [true] State is broadly speaking nothing but the necessary outward form which the inner life of a people bestows upon itself, and that peoples attain to that form of government which their moral capacity enables them to reach.[37]

Looked at in this light, national traditions as unfolded in the life of the state must be regarded as "the objectively revealed will of God."[38]

Treitschke was scornful of the view that nationalism is only a passing phase and will sooner or later be replaced by cosmopolitanism.

> The notion that a universally extended culture will finally replace national customs for all mankind and turn the world into a cosmopolitan primitive hash has become a common place. Yet the same law holds good with nations as with individuals — that their differences appear less in childhood than in riper years. If a nation has the power to preserve itself and its nationality through the merciless race struggle of history then every progress in civilization will only develop more strikingly its deeper national peculiarities. We Germans acquiesce in Paris fashions, we are bound to neighborly nations by a thousand interests. Yet our feelings and ideas are undoubtedly at the present day more independent of the intellectual world of the French and the British than they were seven hundred years ago when the peasant all over Europe lived in bondage to primitive customs, when the priesthood in all countries drew its knowledge from the same source.[39]

Treitschke, like Mazzini, was always able to twist the doctrines of nationalism in such a way that they served the cause for which he was arguing at the moment. As a practical politician Treitschke thought that it was unwise to advocate the forcible annexation of Holland and German Switzerland, although the Dutch and the German Swiss spoke Germanic languages and hence theoretically belonged to the German nation. Because of practical considerations he argued that these peoples had best be left outside the German Empire. At the same time he spoke passionately in favor of the annexation of the provinces of Alsace and

Lorraine on the ground that the inhabitants of these regions rightfully belonged to the German nation even though they were bitterly anti-German in their personal sentiments.

> These provinces are ours by the right of the sword and we will rule them in virtue of the right of the German nation to prevent the permanent estrangement from the German Empire of her lost children. We Germans who know both Germany and France know better what is good for the Alsatians than they do themselves, who in the perverse conditions of a French life have been denied any true knowledge of modern Germany. We desire, even against their will to restore them to themselves.... The spirit of a nation embraces successive as well as contemporary generations. Against the misguided wills of those who are living now we invoke the wills of those who lived before them... Before the nineteenth century is ended the world will recognize... that in disregarding the wills of the Alsatians today we are only fulfilling an injunction imposed by our national honor.[40]

Treitschke's treatment of the Alsatian problem is not out of keeping with the spirit of Mazzini, but in one or two essential elements Treitschke did depart radically from Mazzinian ideology. According to Mazzini each nation has its own separate and special mission, but each nation is equal in the sight of God, and each nation has the right to work out its own destiny, unhampered by other nations. To Treitschke such thoughts were anathema. In the Mazzinian philosophy if, say, the German Empire possesses a region inhabited chiefly by non-Germans, such as the Poles, it is the duty of the Germans to permit such persons to secede from the empire and form a state of their own. Treitschke was vigorously opposed to this notion. He admitted that the existence of a strong Polish minority was a weakness to the German state, but his solution of this problem was forcibly to Germanize the Poles, annihilating all traces of the Polish language and all traces of the old Polish tradition. After all, nationality is not the same thing as race. In Eastern Germany a large section of the population is really of Slavic origin and has only slowly been Germanized through the centuries. Such persons are now good sound Germans, worthy members of the German nation. What has been done slowly and unconsciously may be done quickly and by force. Let us rigidly, ruthlessly, relentlessly Germanize the Polish and other minorities in order that the German nation and thereby the German state may increase in splendor and in strength.

To Treitschke the doctrine that all nations are equal was sheer moonshine. Inequality is the law of the universe. Just as individuals are unequal, so are nations unequal. Some are strong, others weak; some superior, others inferior; some worthy to survive and to dominate other nations, others rightly destined to subjection or to extinction. Needless to say, Treitschke is thoroughly convinced that the Germans as a nation are far superior to all the other peoples of Europe. His books are full of examples of phrases in which he pours scorn upon the English, the French, the Italians, and the other "lesser nationalities" and lauds the Germans.

The Germans are declared to be a profound, the English a shallow people. We hear of "the want of chivalry in the English character which strikes the simple fidelity of the German nature so forcibly." [41] The Germans are declared to be "more reasonable and more free" in character than the French.[42] Speaking of the Latin peoples as a whole (in contrast to the Germanic peoples), he says, "the Latin has no feeling for the beauty of a forest; while he takes his repose in it, he lies on his stomach, while we rest on our backs." [43] The Americans are characterized by "an energetic materialism on economic lines combined with an indifference to the intangible possessions of intellectual life." [44] The Russians are little more than barbarians masquerading as civilized persons as opposed to the Germans who are naturally cultured. In justice to Treitschke it should be added that in glorifying the Germans and the German national character at the expense of other peoples, he was only following the example set by a large number of other German historians. Among the works of most of the German historical writers one finds almost universal use of such terms as "German love of freedom," "German loyalty," "German profundity," and "German thoroughness," and disparaging remarks about surrounding peoples.

In view of this attitude it is not surprising that in Treitschke's hands the liberal nationalism of Mazzini is gradually transformed into national imperialism. If the Germans are such a manifestly superior people, surely it is only right and fair that such a people be permitted to extend their domination over other persons. We are assured that "no people was ever more justly annihilated than the Poles." [45]

> The civilizing of a barbarian people is the best achievement. The alternatives before it are extirpation or absorption into the conquering race. The Germans let the primitive Prussian tribes decide whether they should be put to the sword or thoroughly Germanized. Cruel as these processes of transformation may be, they are a blessing for humanity. It makes for health that the nobler race should absorb the inferior stock.[46]

In the Middle Ages the Germans performed a great cultural benefit by conquering the Baltic provinces (the sometime republics of Latvia and

Estonia) and bringing German culture to this area. Unfortunately

> in these two countries the Teutonic immigrants only formed as it were a
> thin crust over the mass of the population, who remained un-Germanized.
> The nobility and the upper classes were German, and assumed dominion over
> a people who were not. But since every nation is rejuvenated from below,
> it is the peasant population which decides nationality.... There was no
> other course open to us but to keep the subject race in as uncivilized a condi-
> tion as possible and thus prevent them from becoming a danger to the handful
> of their conquerors.[47]

Treitschke insisted that the German nation was the greatest of the European nations. He also insisted that all of the European nations taken together were immeasurably superior to the nations which have arisen among the black and yellow races. The yellow races possess neither aristocratic nor political aptitude. It is obviously the function of the Negroes to serve as the servants of the more privileged groups.[48] As a result of these facts, it is not only the right, it is the duty of the white nations to invade and dominate the areas inhabited by these inferior stocks.

> A nation shows the courage of its faith in God when it seeks to capture
> new areas of production wherewith to nourish its increasing numbers.[49]
> Upon the whole the white races have a great faculty for overcoming climatic
> conditions; this is the physical foundation for the call of the European
> nations to dominate the whole world as one great aristocracy.[50] All great
> nations in the fullness of their strength have desired to set their mark upon
> barbarian lands.... Those who take no share in this great rivalry will play a
> pitiable part in time to come.[51]

Though Treitschke was the ardent advocate of nationalism, or at least of imperialistic nationalism, he differed radically from some of his fellow nationalists in refusing to admit the complete identity of the terms nation and state. As we have seen, many states arose and persisted for centuries which had no national basis. On the other hand, many nations have existed and still exist without political or state organization. The Welsh, for example, constitute a well-defined nation, with a national language, a national tradition and culture, and yet for centuries Wales has formed part of the completely alien English state, nor is there among the Welsh people any widespread desire for the establishment of Wales as an independent political unit. It is doubtless true that natu- rally and normally a nation wishes to evolve for itself a state in which it can find adequate self-expression. It is equally true that a state needs to be connected with a nation and a national tradition for it to be completely successful — but history shows us that nation and state are separate terms and must be studied separately.

The state, Treitschke tells us, is "the people legally united as an independent entity," [52] while a nation may exist without independence or legal union. The state is not merely the totality of the people or a concrete embodiment of the national mind as the orthodox Hegelians would have us believe, it is "the public *force* for offense and defense. It is above all *Power* which makes its will to prevail." [53] The doctrine that the essence of the state is force or power is the key to the Treitschkean theory of the state. The liberals taught that the state must be based upon the consent of the governed. Even the state-worshiping Hegelians declared the state to be based, not upon force, but upon reason (conscious and unconscious). To Treitschke, however, such notions were ridiculous. To him the state

> does not ask primarily for opinion, but demands obedience, and its laws must be obeyed, whether willingly or no. A step forward has been taken when the mute obedience of the citizens is transformed into a rational inward assent, but it can not be said that this is absolutely necessary. Powerful, highly developed Empires have stood for centuries without its aid. Submission is what the State primarily requires; it insists upon acquiescence, its very essence is the accomplishment of its will. [54]

Treitschke completely rejected the old liberal notion of a prepolitical state of nature and the doctrine that the state originated with a voluntary contract among its members.

> The State is primordial and necessary, ... it is as enduring as history and no less essential to mankind than speech.... Creative political genius is inherent in [man] and ... the State, like him, subsists from the beginning. The attempt to present it as something artificial, following upon a natural condition, has fallen completely into discredit.... We can imagine humanity without a number of important attributes; but humanity without government is simply unthinkable.... Man is driven by his political instinct to construct a constitution as inevitably as he constructs a language. [55]
>
> This natural necessity of a constituted order is further displayed by the fact that the political institutions of a people, broadly speaking, appear to be external forms which are the inevitable outcome of its inner life. Just as its language is not the product of caprice but the immediate expression of its most deep-rooted attitude towards the world, so also the political institutions regarded as a whole, and the whole spirit of its jurisprudence, are the symbols of its political genius.... [56]

So far this doctrine smacks very strongly of Hegelianism, but Treitschke distinguished his theory from the Hegelian position by adding that the evolution of a state, unlike the evolution of a language, cannot be entirely spontaneous, unconscious, organic. The evolution of the state must be the result of the conscious creative compelling will of the rulers, imposing many conditions not desired nor even liked by the bulk of the population.

> We must guard against the abuse of this parallel between speech-construction and State-construction. The great historical jurists have often erred in this respect. They have too often failed to see that the conscious will cooperates in the building up of a State in far greater measure than in the formation of a language.[57]

This creative will which moulds the state is best expressed in men of action. The real creators of the German Empire were not thinkers and dreamers, such as Fichte and Hegel, but men of deeds like the Emperor William and Bismarck.[58] This leads us to Treitschke's final conclusion. The state is born in a community whenever a group or an individual has achieved sovereignty by imposing its will upon the whole body.[59]

But whereas the state is thus seen to rest upon force, it does not mean that it is a necessary evil. Far from it. The state must be regarded as a necessary good. "We have to deal with it as a lofty necessity of nature." [60] Treitschke agrees with Aristotle, "The State arose to make life possible. It endured to make *good* life possible." [61] Some persons, such as T. H. Green and Paine, glorified society at the expense of the state, and claimed that it is society and not the state which is the supreme good. To Treitschke this idea was absurd. Anyone can see for himself that society, unlike the state, is intangible. We know that the state is a unit and not a mere mythical personality. Society has no single will and we have no duties to fulfill towards it. "Society is composed of all manner of warring interests, which, if left to themselves, would soon lead to a *bellum omnium contra omnes*, for its natural tendency is towards conflict, and no suggestion of any aspiration after unity is to be found in it." [62] The state, on the other hand,

> is the legal unity which counterbalances this multiplicity of interests, and it is only playing with words to speak of political and social science as two separate things. Law and peace and order can not spring from the manifold and eternally clashing interests of society, but from the power which stands above it, armed with the strength to restrain its wild passions. . . . The State it is which brings justice and mercy into this struggling world.[63]

If, as Treitschke insists, the essence of the state is force or power, it follows that the stronger and more powerful the actual state, the more closely it approximates the ideal state. "The State would no longer be what it has been and is, did it not stand visibly girt about with armed might." [64] "The State cannot legitimately tolerate any power above its own." [65] From this it follows that a state cannot subject itself to a higher power, such as a universal church, or a league of nations, and remain a true state. Moreover, the state cannot be bound by the dictates of ordinary abstract, pseudo-universal morality. The Hegelians, it will be remembered, claimed that the whole moral code was created by the state, and hence applied within the state, but not to the state itself, especially in its dealings with other states, which had and must have different moral codes. The Lutheran conscience of Treitschke would not allow him to go quite this far. He continued to pay lip service to the universal ethic laid down by Christianity. But in practice his ideas on national morals were very nearly the same as Hegel's. The state, to Treitschke, is not entirely devoid of moral obligation, but it must not be judged by the same standards as private individuals. As

> its very personality is power, we see its highest moral duty is to uphold that power. The individual must sacrifice himself for the community of which he is a member, but the State is the highest community existing in exterior human life, and therefore the duty of self-effacement can not apply to it.... The injunction to assert itself remains always absolute. Weakness must always be condemned as the most disastrous and despicable of crimes, the unforgivable sin of politics. [66]

Treitschke was adamant in insisting that the private citizen has no right to resist the will of the state on the ground that such resistance is based upon the voice of conscience or obedience to a higher law with greater claims than the dictates of the state.

> The pure individualism of the Natural Law teaching came to the preposterous conclusion that the citizen has the right to desert the State if it declares a war which he holds to be unjust. But since his first duty is obedience such unfettered power cannot be granted to his individual conscience. For me the upholding of the mother country is a moral duty. The machinery of the political world would cease to revolve if every man made bold to say "the State should not; therefore I will not."... The individual should feel himself a member of his State, and as such have the courage to take its errors upon him. [67]

Even in religious matters personal beliefs should bow before the will of the state. There was a "tragic guilt" about the French Huguenots who left their fatherland rather than change their theology.

Considering the cavalier way in which Treitschke treats the dictates of abstract super-national morality, we need not be surprised at his views regarding international law. The idea that intercourse between nations should be regulated by an abstract, unchanging universal law, a law discoverable by reason, is rejected with scorn.

> Here we find the State regarded as if it were a good little boy, who should be washed, and brushed, and sent to school, who should have his ears pulled to keep him obedient.... Our doctrinaire professors of international law think that they have only to formulate a few axioms, and the nations, as reasonable beings, will be bound to agree to them; it is again and again forgotten that stupidity and passion have been among the great powers in history. ... There can never be an international law which will impose itself on the Great Powers as a practical restraint, by the mere fact of its theoretic scientific existence.[68]

Nevertheless Treitschke does not completely reject international law. He holds it to be a useful body of ideas and practices which the great powers have developed in order to aid themselves in their contacts with one another. It must be based upon

> a mutual recognition of personal advantage. Every State will realize that it is an integral part of the community of other States in which it finds itself placed, and that it must live with them on some kind of terms, bad or good, as the case may be. These reflections will arise from very real considerations of reciprocity, and not from love to mankind.[69] A State which went upon the principle of despising faith and morality would be constantly threatened by enemies and would consequently be unable to fulfill its purpose of being physical power.[70]

As nations frequently engage in war with one another, they find it to their mutual advantage to lay down certain general conditions under which warfare shall be waged. To this extent and to this extent only, the dictates of international law should be considered sacred.

Treitschke was sharply critical of the older forms of international law on the ground that these forms were evolved by small rather than by great nations.

> Countries like Belgium and Holland, which, to the great detriment of that science, have unfortunately so long been the home of international jurisprudence, adopted a sentimental view of it, because they lived in constant fear of aggression. In the name of humanity, demands were made upon the victor which were unnatural, and unreasonable, and irreconcilable with the power of the State.[71]

The theory of international law must be rooted in practice, the actual conduct of nations in their relations with one another. Now the actual conduct of European affairs is really regulated by the great and not by the small powers. Consequently the development of international affairs should rest with these powers. In point of fact, true international law is the line of conduct which the great powers have come to regard as to their mutual advantage.

Because of this attitude towards international law, it is not surprising to find that Treitschke was lenient in such matters as the violations of treaties. States find it convenient to sign treaties with one another. Each state in making a treaty limits its powers in certain directions for its own sake, but such limitations are not absolute. They are but voluntary self-restrictions. Moreover, all such treaties must be regarded as temporary self-limitations.

> All treaties are concluded on the tacit understanding *rebus sic stantibus* [conditions being as they are]. No State ever has, or ever will, exist which is willing to hold to all eternity to the agreements it signs. No State will ever be in a position to pledge its whole hereafter to a treaty, which cannot fail to be a limitation of its sovereignty; it always intends that the contract shall eventually be annulled, and shall only apply so long as the present circumstances are not totally altered.[72]

Should circumstances change, each nation has a right to change treaties made in earlier times. Moreover, each nation reserves to itself the right to judge whether these circumstances have or have not changed.

> Every State reserves to itself the right to judge of its own treaties.[73] Hence, it follows that the establishment of a permanent international Arbitration Court is incompatible with the nature of the State....[74]

Treitschke also held very lax views on the conduct of war. International law should try to ameliorate war conditions, but after all war is war.

> It is, therefore, perfectly equitable to wage war in the most effective manner possible, so that the goal of peace may be reached as quickly as may be. For this reason the blow must be aimed at the enemy's heart, and the use of the most formidable weapons is absolutely justifiable.... Philanthropists may declaim as much as they like against explosive shells fired into powder magazines of wooden battle ships, but still facts remain unchanged.... It is permissible to take advantage of all the enemy's weak points, and a State may turn treason and mutiny within its enemy's borders to serve its own ends.... It is equally impossible to deny to a belligerent State the right of employing all its troops in the field, whether they be savages or civilized men.... It is mere mockery to apply these [ordinary] principles of warfare in wars against savages. A negro tribe must be punished by the burning of their villages, for it is the only kind of example which will avail. If the German Empire has abandoned this principle today it has done so out of disgraceful weakness....[75]

As the essence of the state is power, Treitschke had little use for the small state. Small states are powerless, hence unworthy imitations of the true state. Moreover, only in large states "can that truly national pride arise which is a sign of the moral stamina of a people." [76] It is the duty of small states to seek to become greater and bigger. Not only the size but also the shape of the state must be taken into consideration.

If it does not make a compact whole the State must try to round it off more conveniently. This, however, applies only to great States who are keenly conscious of themselves, and take pride in the belief in their great future. They can not allow raggedness in their territory.

But though Treitschke advocated great as opposed to small states, he rejected any notion of a world-state, or even such an idea as an inclusive league of nations.

The idea of one universal empire is odious — the ideal of a State coextensive with humanity is no ideal at all. . . . All nations, like all individuals, have their limitations, but it is exactly in the abundance of these limited qualities that the genius of humanity is exhibited. The rays of the Divine light are manifested, broken by countless facets among the separate peoples, each one exhibiting another picture and another side of the whole. . . . The grandeur of history lies in the perpetual conflict of nations, and it is simply foolish to desire the suppression of their rivalry. . . . [Many] examples show clearly that there is no prospect of a settlement of international contradictions. [77]

Not only did Treitschke reject the ideas of a league of nations, of a world court, and the arbitration of international disputes, he also argued that frequent wars between nations were good and salutary.

Without war no State could be. All those we know of arose through war, and the protection of their members by armed force remains their primary and essential task. War, therefore, will endure to the end of history. . . . The laws of human thought and of human nature forbid any alternative, neither is one to be wished for. The blind worshipper of an eternal peace falls into the error of isolating the State, or dreams of one which is universal, which we have seen to be at variance with reason. . . . The great strides which civilization makes against barbarism and unreason are only made actual by the sword. . . . Most undoubtedly war is the one remedy for an ailing nation. Social selfishness and party hatreds must be dumb before the call of the State when its existence is at stake. . . . The grandeur of war lies in the utter annihilation of puny man in the great conception of the State, and it brings out the full magnificence of the sacrifice of fellow-countrymen for one another. In war the chaff is winnowed from the wheat. . . . The historian who moves in the world of the real Will sees at once that the demand for eternal peace is purely reactionary. He sees that all movement and all growth would disappear with war and that only the exhausted, spiritless, degenerate periods have toyed with the idea. . . . God above us will see to it that war shall return again and again, a terrible medicine for mankind diseased. [78]

The theory that the state is power led Treitschke to radical na
tionalism and chauvinism in the realm of international affairs.   The
same doctrine led him to thoroughgoing etatism in domestic affairs.
Within its own borders the state was to have absolute and unquestioned
supremacy over its individual citizens.   The state was not to be the
means to an end, but an end in itself, or, as Treitschke put it, the state
"must seek its own goal within itself," [79] and again:

> No individual has the right to regard the State as a servant of his own aims.
> but is bound by moral duty and physical necessity to subordinate himself to
> it.[80]   Forgetting himself, the individual must only remember that he is a part
> of the whole and realize the unimportance of his own life compared with the
> common weal.[81]

To the old liberals the state was merely a convenient organ established by its citizens to protect their own life and property.   To
Treitschke such a view was ridiculous.   "If we simply look upon the
State as intended to secure life and property, how comes it that the
individual will also sacrifice life and property to the State?" [82]   If
nations went to war only to protect the life and property of their members, it would be possible to defend the old liberal concept, but such
is not the case.

> It is a false conclusion that wars are waged for the sake of material ad-
> vantage.   Modern wars are not fought for the sake of booty.   Here the high
> moral ideal of national honour is a factor handed down from one generation
> to another enshrining something positively sacred, and compelling the indi-
> vidual to sacrifice himself to it.[83]

The true purpose of the state is far different from that talked about by
the liberals.

> The State is a moral community called to positive labours for the improve-
> ment of the human race, and its ultimate aim is to build up real national
> character through and within itself.... We may, then, shortly call the State
> the instrument of civilization, and demand of it positive labour for the eco-
> nomic and intellectual welfare of its members.[84]

The functions of the state, the amount of control it exercises over its
citizens, vary from place to place and from time to time.   We can
indeed "fix the theoretic minimum for its activity and decide what
functions it must at the least fulfill before it can be given the name of
State." [85]   This absolute minimum "includes maintaining power without and law within, [hence] its primary obligations must be the care
of its army and its jurisprudence."   This further implies the existence

of some fiscal system in order to provide for the upkeep of its military and juridical staff.

But though we can thus outline the minimum functions of the state, we cannot hope to give a definition of the maximum number of functions it can be called upon to fulfill.

> Theoretically no limit can be set to the functions of the State.... History shows us how the sphere of the State's activity increases with the growth of culture.... In Homeric times the prince was content with pronouncing judgment and when necessary, conducting war. Even in the Middle Ages an administration was still non-existent and the State concerned itself with the most elementary necessities. Not until the splendour of the Holy Roman Empire was in German hands did German kingship begin its fuller, richer expansion. Then the growth of the cities forced the State to adopt new aims and wider activities. Experience teaches that the State is better fitted than any other corporate body to take charge of the well-being and civilizing of the people. Briefly put, what was the great result of the Reformation? The secularization of great portions of the common life of men. When the State secularized the larger portion of the Church's lands it also took over its accompanying public duties, and when we reckon how much the State has accomplished for the people's culture since the Reformation, we recognize that these duties fall within its natural sphere.[86]

When Treitschke demanded of the modern civilized state "positive labor for the economic and intellectual welfare of its members," he necessarily implied that the state must regulate most of the economic and intellectual activity which goes on within its borders. Treitschke was far from being a socialist, but he did believe that there are many phases of economic enterprise which can best be directly owned and operated by the state. He defended the system of crown lands, under which the king or the government directly owns a considerable portion of the agricultural land within the country.[87] He thought it advisable that the state should own and operate the greater part of the forested area within its boundaries. "Forest land is intended by nature for extensive cultivation, therefore the management on a large scale by the State in forestry is necessary and usual." [88] There are in addition many trades "which belie the doctrine formerly laid down by the Manchester school of the State's incapacity to conduct business of any kind." [89] Not only should the postal service be run by the government, but the telegraph and railroad system might well be taken over by the state.

In opposition to the socialists, Treitschke insisted that the bulk of agriculture, commerce, and industry had best be left in private hands. But even here the state was to have its full measure of regulation and control. Actual creative work in these fields can well be relegated to private enterprise, but "the State can do great things in protecting, guiding, and opening new fields for economics." [90] With Mazzini, Treitschke held that private property in some form or another is an indispensable phase of human society, but with Mazzini he also held that the conditions under which property is owned, the obligations which property-owners owed the community, varied from generation to generation, and should be regulated by the state to suit existing conditions. Property

> has no absolutely invariable form; in the last resort the State must be the judge of the conditions under which it will best express the legal instinct and satisfy the economic requirements of the nation.[91]

In like manner "every constituted State must have some voice in the organization of industry and will impose certain conditions." [92] Normally business enterprise can best be controlled by economic or non-political laws, such as the law of supply and demand, but this no longer holds true "when whole classes of the population are suffering from the effect" of such laws. Treitschke was violently opposed to equalitarianism in the economic sphere, the belief that the distribution of wealth or of goods should be the same for all persons. He believed that there always would be and always should be the rich, the moderately wealthy, and the poor in every community. Nevertheless the state "must take care that the gulf between the heights and the depths of society does not become dangerously great, and that the lower classes are not exploited for the benefit of those above them." [93] In case the strong gain undue advantage over the weak, the state is

> compelled to readjust unfair divisions of property. This interference on the part of the State is perfectly justifiable, for all private rights of ownership are subject to it. . . . Moreover, the historian cannot conceal from himself that certain gigantic upheavals of property have been wholly beneficial to mankind. Who is there to-day who would condemn the secularization [i.e. confiscation] of the Church's goods in the sixteenth century. . . . The public good may require that the procedure which was possible and necessary in the case of the Church should be equally applied to the private ownership of land and capital.[94] It is very possible that the State may some day be obliged to step in to prevent such unnatural accumulations of capital.[95]

In view of this attitude towards economic problems, we are not surprised that Treitschke thought that certain enterprises, such as stock markets, should be subject to rigid government control. "We may lay down as a principle for reform that the Stock Exchanges must be organized into corporations under the control of an official of the state and

must conform to stern fixed rules." [96]   Nor is it surprising that Treitschke
was a warm defender of Bismarck's attempts at social legislation.

> Bismarck, with his usual astuteness, saw that the weak spot in the existence
> of the modern working man was the insecurity of his means of livelihood.
> He took the first step towards remedying it and providing a possibility of
> sound social development for the working classes when he instituted the
> system of health-insurance. [97]
> The State must see that work is forthcoming for those who are honestly
> seeking it, and must also care for the physically unfit in some way or an-
> other. [98]

Treitschke refused to follow Fichte in advocating complete economic
nationalism, but he did claim that a state "can do an immense amount
for its own internal economy by means of a commercial policy which
protects the nation as a whole against the foreigner." [99]   In other words,
he advocated a system of high tariffs, not for revenue only but designed
to create and preserve national industries against foreign competition.

> To-day we have cast aside as a prejudice that axiom which declares the
> protective Tariff only necessary for the defense of young nations. As a matter
> of fact it is far more needful for the long-established industries.   The history
> of Italy under the republic and empire of Rome affords us a terrible warning
> of its necessity. If protection against the import of corn from Asia and
> Africa had been introduced at the right time the old Italian agricultural
> class would not have perished, and social conditions would have remained
> healthy.   Instead of this Roman merchants were suffered to buy the cheap
> African grain, thus bringing distress upon the peasants of Italy and causing
> the incredible state of affairs which made a desert of the Campagna, the very
> heart of the country, and encircling the capital city of the world. [100]

Treitschke's demand that the state "labor for the intellectual welfare
of its members" led to some rather far-reaching results.   It was the duty
of the state consciously and actively to foster and guide the arts, such as
painting, music, and literature.

> It savors of barbarism to regard the State's fostering of art as a luxury.
> The State is there to set before art its great work for the nation's monuments. [101]
> We must maintain that a State which fails to regard the encouragement
> of art as one of its essential duties has no claim to be called civilized. [102]

State guidance in such matters was to be carried out by state art institutes and museums, state theaters and operas, state academies of
letters and fine arts.   It must be admitted that Treitschke wished to
preserve a certain amount of liberty in the artistic world.   "The State
may not meddle with the inner life of art, which has an existence of its

own." [103]   Treitschke, after all, did not advance to the position of the Nazis in this respect.

The state's control over the intellectual activity of its citizens was to be insured by the system of universal compulsory education and state-owned and operated schools and universities.   Treitschke objected to the system of private or denominational schools.   To his mind state schools were to be the only educational institutions permitted and all teachers and professors were to be appointed and dismissed by the government.   Treitschke retained too much of the Liberal traditions of his youth to wish to suppress freedom of speech and freedom of the press in its entirety, but as he grew older he had less and less use for these hallowed doctrines.

> It is not to be denied that freedom of the press has not brought the blessings in its train which enthusiasts once looked for.[104]   Every man may speak the truth, and the State must not prevent him, but Truth is a subjective conception, and the right to declare it openly is accompanied by the no less binding duty to refrain from doing public harm by the spoken word.   The right to strengthen the spoken word a thousandfold through print by no means follows from the right to speak the truth; nor is the right of absolute freedom for the press a necessary consequence. . . .[105]

Treitschke disliked both the old Catholic doctrine that the church was superior to and should control the state, and also the prevailing American doctrine that the church should be a purely voluntary organization within the state, having no special relation to the government. To Treitschke's mind there should be a fairly intimate connection between the church and the state, but he was equally convinced that the correct policy was that of maintaining the supremacy of the state.

> The Church received privileges as a corporation and is therefore to that extent brought into subjection to the State which supervises and decreases its legal status in civil society.[106]   The education of the clergy is a matter which properly concerns the Church, but the State must supervise it. . . . The State must keep a particularly watchful eye on the religious Orders.   Since it guarantees personal freedom for all its citizens, it may on no account permit any one of them to surrender his whole life to servitude by any sacred vow. . . . The State cannot afford to surrender its share in the patronage of the highest offices of the Church. . . . Schools must remain secular.[107]

In his earlier days Treitschke was an enthusiastic advocate of complete freedom of conscience for the individual.   As he grew older his belief in this doctrine visibly weakened.

> It is not permissible for any one to make his religious convictions a reason for disobeying the law or neglecting his duty as a subject.   A State decreeing

monogamy must punish Mormons as immoral polygamists. Similarly it cannot tolerate the resistance of the Mennonites against military service or the taking of the oath.... From the standpoint of the State, atheists, strictly speaking, are an anomaly.[108]

Treitschke insisted that religious instruction (supervised by the state) must be given in every school. This instruction must be Christian even though the parents of many of the children were Jews or skeptics.

> Heaven preserve us from the fashionable vapourings of the present day, which would fain prevent Protestant children from hearing of the glorious deeds of Luther, and would suppress all open and honest mention of Jesus Christ out of consideration for a few Jews.... Every father has the right to have his children instructed in the religious creed of his own choice, but he is not entitled to allow them to grow up without any religion at all.[109]

From many passages in his writings it is obvious that at the close of his life Treitschke came to the conclusion that the state could not afford to be really tolerant in religious matters. He was firmly of the opinion that while the state may tolerate such religious differences as those which separate one Christian confession from another, the unity of the state is impossible when its subjects are divided between radically different religions.

> The consciousness of national unity is dependent upon a common bond of religion.... Ritual differences may indeed be endured by a great nation, although with difficulty... but the coexistence of several religions within one nationality, involving an irreconcilable and ultimately intolerable difference of outlook upon life can only be a transitional phenomena. Spain was not a nation until Christianity had conquered and driven the adherents of another faith into a corner. Our State is the state of a Christian people, therefore in the regulation of civil life it presupposes the Christian Church to be the Church of all.[110]

From the foregoing citations it is obvious that Treitschke was a thoroughgoing etatist, even though not as thoroughgoing or as ruthless an etatist as the later Fascists and Nazis. A perusal of his writings shows that he was also a convinced authoritarian. The doctrine of the inequality of man, socially, politically, economically, lay at the basis of Treitschke's whole philosophy.

> When we examine more closely the whole fabric of these conditions of mutual interdependence which we call society we find that under all its forms it tends naturally towards aristocracy.... Just as the State pre-supposes an irremoveable distinction between those in whom authority is vested and those who must submit to it, so also does the nature of society imply differences of social standing and economic condition amongst its members. In short, all social life is built upon class organization.... To put it simply: the masses

must for ever remain the masses. There would be no culture without kitchen-maids. . . . Millions must plough and forge and dig in order that a few thou-sands may write and paint and study. . . . It is precisely in the differentiation of classes that the moral wealth of mankind is exhibited.[111]

In conformity with this position Treitschke strongly disapproved of higher education for the bulk of the people. In Germany university education was open to only a small fraction of the population, but to Treitschke it was already too easy for the masses to enter them and hence to forget their proper station in life. "We have already over-stepped the limits of prudence in this direction, and it would be a disaster if still more Germans wished to matriculate." [112]

Treitschke ridiculed all democratic theories in the political sphere.

All civil society is, as we have seen, aristocratic by nature. A monarchy as well as an aristocracy becomes part of this naturally ordained aristocratic division, while all democracy is rooted in a contradiction of nature, because it premises a universal equality which is nowhere actually existent. . . .[113]

The very notion of democracy contains a *contradictio in adjecto*. All governing implies the existence of the governed, but if all are to rule, who is to be ruled? . . . All inequalities between individuals are to be violently levelled, so much so that a point is reached at which even sex distinctions are to be abrogated by enactment. For the sake of conforming to a principle every possible difference between human beings is to be bludgeoned out of exist-ence.[114]

Treitschke did not completely reject parliamentary government. He thought it well that the state should have a national representative assembly with some voice (though not an all-powerful one) in legislation. He was, however, horrified at the thought that this national assembly should be elected by universal suffrage.

It remains a sound principle to exclude the wholly irresponsible section of society from the exercise of a right which implies a capacity for independent judgment. . . . It remains true that in Universal Suffrage a disproportionate share of influence is given to stupidity, superstition, malice and mendacity, crude egoism and nebulous waves of sentiment. . . . The strongest lungs always prevail with the mob, and there is now no hope of eliminating that peculiar touch of brutality and that coarsening and vulgarizing element which has entered into public life. . . . Beyond this comes the further danger that the really educated classes withdraw more and more from a political struggle which adopts such methods.[115]

For similar reasons the secret ballot was also deplored.

Treitschke thought that an aristocracy (or an aristocratic republic as he called it) was far superior to a democracy. In fact he was willing to admit that at certain times and places an aristocracy was the best

form of government. He cited the Roman Republic, Genoa, and Venice
as examples of illustrious and successful aristocracies. He pointed out
that England rose to world greatness when it was really ruled by its
Whig aristocracy. But he was certain that monarchy supported by
and depending upon an aristocracy was the ideal form of government,
at least under modern conditions.

> Since the State is primarily power, that State which gathers authority
> most completely into the hands of one and there leaves it most independent,
> approaches most nearly to the ideal.[116] It is an ancient experience that
> monarchy presents more perfectly than any other form of government a tangi-
> ble expression of political power and national unity.... Monarchy implies the
> idea of equal justice for all, which is realized in the person of the King....
> Even to-day it may be said with truth that in spite of all hostile agitators the
> mass of the people have more confidence in the Crown than in parliament.[117]
> A perfect military organization is undoubtedly an easier task for a monarchy
> than for a republic.... What is true of the army is equally true of the Civil
> Service. No republic is as well fitted to train competent public servants as a
> healthy monarchy.... Official incompetence is as frequent under democracy
> as are ability and integrity under genuine monarchical rule.[118]

In defending monarchy as the ideal system of government, Treitschke
made it clear that by monarchy he meant *real* monarchy, the system by
which the king had immediate personal control over the affairs of state.

> In a republic, authority is founded upon the will of the governed, while
> in a monarchy it is derived from the historical claim of a particular family, and
> concentrated in the hands of one man who wears the crown and who, though
> surrounded by more or less responsible advisers, ultimately decides every
> question himself. It is idle to toy with metaphors: the minimum test of
> monarchy is whether or not the will of the monarch can be overruled.[119]

For this reason the English system of government was declared to be
not a real but a sham monarchy, unworthy of serious consideration.

> In Belgium [the king is not quite so impotent as the British monarch.
> Nevertheless in that country] the Monarchy is a shadow raised into transient
> importance by the great political ability of Leopold of Coburg.... Under the
> Belgian Constitution all authority emanates from the people; a king hemmed
> in by such an axiom is no longer a Monarch in the true sense.[120]

Because of his views on the true nature of monarchy, Treitschke
rejected Montesquieu's doctrine of check and balance and the separation
of powers.

> To Montesquieu England... appeared as the paragon State combining
> the advantages of monarchy, aristocracy, and democracy. He believed that
> she had solved the problem of maintaining while co-ordinating these three
> elements in the State....[121]

To Treitschke this was, historically, a completely erroneous interpretation of the English Constitution.   In Montesquieu's own time democracy, in the true sense of this word, was completely non-existent in
England and the royal power illusory.   England, far from being a land
of check and balance, was a classic example of a country ruled by its
aristocracy.   To Treitschke a real system of checks and balances between the monarch, the aristocracy, and the democracy is impossible.

> All states, closely examined, reveal distinctly where their true center of
> gravity lies and whether they are genuine monarchies or genuine republics.
> A mixed State, belonging to neither kind, does not exist.[122]

During modern historic times England has possessed a king, a House of
Lords, and a House of Commons.   Yet there can be no doubt that
Tudor England was a genuine monarchy, eighteenth century England
an aristocracy, and nineteenth century England a democracy.   Real
check and balance is impossible over any lengthy span of time.

In like manner Montesquieu's doctrine of the separation of powers
was declared to be historically unsound and theoretically unwise.
Montesquieu based his doctrine of the separation of powers upon a
study of the English Constitution and asserted that in the British Isles
the legislative, executive, and judicial functions lay in separate hands.
Treitschke thought that "rarely has a more stupendous error been
enunciated; beyond all question it is precisely in England that this
division was not to be found." [123]   In reality the cabinet, the executive
branch, was little more than a committee of the House of Commons, the
legislative branch.   It is, moreover, ridiculous to insist that the three
branches of government should be differentiated.

> This whole doctrine of the three authorities in the State and their division
> is the toy of theory and playful fancy.   The essence of the State is in its unity,
> and that State is the best organized in which the three powers are united in
> one supreme and independent head.[124]

In Prussia, the ideal state, "all authority is centered in the King.   Without his assent no law is valid, in his name justice is administered; his
instructions direct foreign policy and internal government." [125]

From his whole attitude towards the true nature of monarchy it is
not surprising to find that Treitschke was opposed to the theory of
responsible government, the theory that ministers of state should hold
office only as long as they enjoy the confidence of the parliamentary
assembly.

> Under a monarchy in which the whole authority of the State is centered
> in the person of the King, it follows that the choice of ministers must lie

with him and that they must become the instruments of his will. Only on these terms can the monarchy perform its duty of standing above party.[126]

Treitschke was of the opinion that all the essential functions of government should be carried out by "a monarchical civil service," a permanent administrative hierarchy or bureaucracy, independent of legislative control. The offices of state, both great and small, should not be filled with political appointees (as in America in the old days). Nor should the lesser officials, on permanent tenure, be controlled by a few parliamentary officials who change with each ministry. Rather should the civil service, like the army and the navy, be governed by an ascending hierarchy of officers, whose apex is formed by the prime minister, who in turn is responsible only to the monarch, the supreme ruler of the land.

To Treitschke it was clear that the officers of the civil service, like the officers of the army and navy, should be recruited from the upper classes within the state. In fact the chief function of the aristocracy is to provide capable men devoted to the service of the state.

> From out of the aristocracy there is evolved in process of time what are vaguely called the ruling classes. "Optimates" arise to eminence who generally have a share in the civil or military government of the State.... [The German nobility] set store by having a position, real or apparent, in the framework of the State.... In England we find the purely aristocratic ambition, with us [Germans] it takes monarchic-bureaucratic form. Whatever it be, some kind of tradition is necessary in the guidance of the State. Our ruling class comes of good families, who bring up their children with definite notions of what is honourable and what is not. A stock of inherited conceptions of integrity and morality is a necessity for government, which does not depend primarily upon knowledge but upon capacity to rule....[127]

Treitschke was certain that all the ordinary functions of government could best be left in the hands of the monarch and his civil and military bureaucracy. The conduct of foreign affairs was to be exclusively in their hands as well as all executive and judicial functions. In addition many of the matters which in America are settled by legislative bills were to be carried out by administrative decrees, framed by the bureaucracy on its own responsibility. Finally the monarch and his bureaucrats were to have an important part in general legislation. Not only should all bills require their full consent, but in addition it was their duty to frame or draft all acts of legislation. Nevertheless Treitschke did not wish to do away with parliamentary institutions completely. The key to Treitschke's thoughts on this subject can be found in the following remark:

> The test of what our Provincial and Imperial Diets have accomplished is to be found not in what they have achieved but in what they have prevented. Political experience shows that every governing class, if left to itself, becomes either stereotyped or corrupt. The rough-and-tumble of a popular Assembly is well calculated to resist this tendency....[128]

In other words, diets, parliaments, congresses can accomplish little constructive, but by questions to ministers of state, by criticism of governmental acts, by debates on general policy, they can prevent the governmental hierarchy from becoming completely stagnant — but that is their only proper function.

Treitschke, in common with most of his contemporaries, favored a parliament or diet consisting of two chambers.

> The Lower House should principally stand for the mass of tax-payers and be the specifically popular Assembly ... while the Upper House should represent the ruling classes, upon whom fall the more complicated tasks of public life.[129]

In other words, the ideal parliament should consist of a House of Commons, elected by the well-to-do members of the community, and a House of Lords or Peers, limited to representatives of the nobility and the other really outstanding groups within the state.

As we have seen, Treitschke thought that the chief function of parliament was to interrogate and appraise the actions of the administration.

> We are indebted to the watchful care of our Parliament, cantankerous though it may sometimes be, for the virtual elimination of corrupt practices from our administration.... Army administration must exert itself to avoid everything which could lay it open to criticism, because there is always a group of privileged cavillers in Parliament ready to beat the big drum about every little failing.[130]

But, it should be noted, in Treitschke's scheme parliament could not bring about the fall of the ministers it criticized, nor could members of parliament themselves hope to be ministers of state. The criticism of parliament was to have mere publicity value.

Parliament, moreover, according to Treitschke, should have a share in legislation. All general legislation should require its consent, but it should not be forgotten that in Treitschke's ideal state a great deal of legislation was accomplished by administrative decrees, in the framing of which parliament had no share. In addition, the initiation of legislation had best be left to the bureaucracy. Parliament should content itself with accepting or rejecting the proposals put forward by the king's ministers. Finally the king should have an absolute veto on all legislation — if the king refused to sign a measure, it was automatically vetoed.

Treitschke admitted that parliament should cooperate with the government in exercising financial control over the country. In other words, it should have the right to grant (or refuse to grant) supplies. But it is important to bear in mind that Treitschke taught that parliament should have only a limited control over the national finances. Standing obligations of the state, money to pay interest on the public debt, money for the salaries for officers and officials should not be subject to the whim of a parliamentary majority in any one year. Expenditures for such items should be placed outside parliamentary control. In such cases the function of parliament "is merely supervisory, it audits accounts, and sees that all is in order, but its actual sanction is not required." [131] Moreover, when new legislation has been passed providing for such things as a new tribunal or a new cavalry regiment, the government has a right to appropriate money for their upkeep, nor can parliament veto such appropriations. It is only in such matters as expenses which are not fixed in amount or sanctioned beforehand by law that parliament can be said to have a free hand, and such items constitute only a small portion of the annual budget.

In like manner Treitschke argued that it was ridiculous to claim that parliament should have exclusive control over the revenue of the state. Revenue from the crown lands (an important item in Prussia) should be completely outside its control. Income from certain state properties, such as the post office and the state railroads, is regulated by previous laws and can be collected by the government without the consent of the existing parliament. Even over ordinary taxes the parliament of any one year is to have only a small measure of control. Taxes should be voted not annually but for an indefinite period. It is only when these taxes need to be changed that parliament should be called into consultation.

When we come to review Treitschke's political philosophy as a whole, we find it to be little more than the Hegelian system, denuded of its metaphysical background, except for the important distinction that while Hegel looked upon the state as an embodiment of reason, Treitschke, preaching in a more practical age, called it the embodiment of force or power. Treitschke was neither as completely etatist nor as completely authoritarian as the modern Nazis, but the widespread popularity of his *Politics* was an important factor in preparing the German public to accept the later Nazi ideology.

THE HISTORICAL SCHOOL OF JURISPRUDENCE

It is impossible to conclude our survey of traditionalism in the nine teenth century without a brief discussion of the doctrines laid down by the leaders of the historical school of jurisprudence. Although these thinkers were primarily concerned with the origin and nature and function of law rather than directly with political issues, their ideas were of the utmost importance in moulding the general development of political thought and of political action.

By way of summary it may be said that the historical school of jurisprudence was little more than an application of Neo-Hegelian traditionalism to legal problems, an exposition of the idea that laws, like political institutions, must be based upon the two principles of progress and tradition. The historical school of jurisprudence originated in Germany. Its two leading exponents, Savigny (1799–1861) and Puchta (1798–1846), were both junior contemporaries of Hegel, and though neither of them was an orthodox Hegelian, the influence of Hegel was very marked in the legal theories evolved by both these men. More to the point, the historical school, in one form or another, became the dominant school among the legal writers of the latter part of the nineteenth century, and among these later thinkers the Hegelian doctrine regarding the function of tradition in national life was just as marked as with their predecessors.

About the middle of the nineteenth century there arose in England and in America another form of the historical school of jurisprudence, which was able to exert a widespread influence among the lawyers and judges of their respective countries. The chief exponent of this school in England was Sir Henry Maine (1822–1888), whose most famous work, *Ancient Law*, became a classic in English literature. In America the most eloquent advocate of the historical interpretation of law was Carter, and though Carter never secured the general popularity of Maine, his influence upon juridical thought was almost as profound.

It should be noted, however, that though the English and American members of the historical school were in keen sympathy with many of the ideas enunciated by their German predecessors and contemporaries, they rejected several of their characteristic doctrines, with the result that the Anglo-American and the German branches of this school differed both in their premises and in their conclusions. To the English and American writers the historical approach meant little more than an emphasis upon custom and tradition in the formation and development

of laws.   The German school, with its Hegelian or semi-Hegelian background, thought that both laws and customs are the concrete embodiments of the *Volksgeist* or national mind.   Because of this basic difference the German writers tended to emphasize nationalism, etatism, and,
incidentally, authoritarianism.   The German members of the historical
school were, in fact, the leading advocates of the political philosophy
which was later to develop into Fascism and Naziism.

The historical school of jurisprudence stands in marked contrast to
the analytical and to the natural law or philosophical schools of law.
The analytical school goes back in some measure to the teachings of
Bodin and Hobbes, though in its developed form it is the product of
the great utilitarians, Bentham and Austin.   To the analytical school
each and every law is a law because it is the command of a sovereign
(whether a king or parliament) enforced by sanctions.   To this school
statute law is the only true law.   In England, for example, any law
passed by Parliament and signed by the king is a perfectly valid law
enforceable by the courts, even though this law be completely irrational
and even though it be completely contrary to all British customs and
traditions.

Bodin and Hobbes espoused this theory of law largely because it
fitted in with their ideas regarding the divine, or at least the absolute,
right of kings, who to their minds, should be the only lawmakers.   The
utilitarians, on the other hand, were thoroughgoing democrats and espoused this theory of law for very different reasons.   They were in
favor of rapid and widespread legal and political reforms.   They wished
to have a free hand, once Parliament was in their control, in the making
and unmaking of laws, irrespective of whether their ideas were or were
not in accord with the inherited notions of natural right or with the
customs and unwritten laws of the country.   The sovereign people
through their parliamentary representatives were to abolish all time-
honored abuses both in the political and in the legal machinery of the
country.

The members of the historical school were opposed to the reforming
zeal of the utilitarians and to the utilitarian desire to remedy the evils of
society by hasty legislation, hence they opposed the whole analytical
concept of law.   They pointed out that in early times law had little or
nothing to do with the definite commands of a definite sovereign, but
arose as an embodiment of the customs and traditions of the community.
They pointed out that even in such developed countries as England and

America, common law, based upon precedents, customs, traditions, is much more important than statute law.   It is, moreover, far better for a country to be governed by common law than by statute law, for statute law is really only enforceable if it is in accord with the customs and traditions of the community.   Should the will of the sovereign legislature conflict sharply with prevailing social conditions (i.e., with existent customs), the law after being promulgated remains a dead letter, and is not applied.   The historic school admitted that statute law had a place in political and social life, but only a very limited place.   The legislative body should merely decide what customary rules of conduct need formal definition in order to secure better observance.   In addition, it may well attempt to clarify the existing laws and indicate certain particular applications and sanctions to social rules already in force.

In a word, the historical school emphasized that law, to be healthy, must be a growth or an unconscious development, rather than be the product of the conscious will of a person or a group of persons at any one particular time.

The historical school was thus in violent conflict with the analytical school of jurisprudence.   It was no less violent in its opposition to the natural law and philosophic schools, which in fact were merely branches of the same general movement.   According to the school of natural law, true law is to be found — not made.   The positive or actual laws of existing states are only imperfect attempts to apply the universal, eternal laws of nature, and it is the only duty of legislators and judges to try to make positive laws coincide ever more perfectly with the everlasting dictates of natural law, which is the same for all times and all peoples.   Any positive law which is contrary to natural law is *ipso facto* invalid and can and should be ignored by the citizens of any existing state, whatever the statute books may say.

The belief in natural law, which was inherited from the Romans, was revived in modern times by Grotius and adopted by Locke and most of the other classical liberal thinkers.   It was accepted by the early American political philosophers and was frequently used by Daniel Webster in arguing cases before the federal courts.   Closely associated with the natural law school were the doctrines of the philosophical school represented by such writers as Kant and Fichte.   These thinkers agreed that there are certain eternal abstract legal principles with which concrete laws should be made to conform, but they insisted that these abstract principles are not so much the laws of nature as the laws formulated by pure abstract reason as divulged by a study of philosophy.

The historical school assailed the doctrine of natural laws and of abstract principles on the ground that all such laws and principles are purely imaginary, based upon a false concept of nature and upon a false interpretation of the powers of the reason — the holding of that which is peculiar to ourselves as common to humanity in general. The so-called laws of nature are not really universal natural laws, but the product of a legal philosophy which grew up in the Roman Empire and which was profoundly influenced by the social, economic, and metaphysical principles peculiar to that time. Natural laws also evolved in the Near East, in India, and in China. The natural law of Europe looks upon monogamy as the only natural or valid form of marriage. The natural law of Asia looks upon polygamy as equally natural and equally valid. In like manner, to claim that philosophy or abstract reason will give us an eternal standard of justice is equally absurd. There are as many philosophies as there are philosophers. Abstract reason gave to Kant one set of legal principles, to Fichte quite another; to an English or to a French philosopher reason would give even more divergent answers to legal problems.

The natural law and philosophic schools, in addition to being false, have also worked out disastrously in the actual world of politics. Ignoring positive laws and existing political institutions, the advocates of natural law or the law of reason have generally argued in favor of widespread, utopian, impossible reforms. Attempts to carry out such reforms have frequently resulted in revolutions which have swept away the bulwarks of society and led to semi-anarchic conditions.

> Looking back to the period at which the theory of the state of nature acquired the maximum of importance, there are few who will deny that it helped most powerfully to bring about the grosser disappointments of which the French Revolution was fertile.[132]

In opposition to the analytical and the natural law or rational schools, the members of the historical school claim that their own approach to the problems of law is the only sound and valid one, but, as we have already seen, there is a sharp difference between the Anglo-American and the German members of the historical school as to the true teachings of the school. To the English and American writers, true law is merely the customs and traditions which have spontaneously grown up in a community, clarified and enunciated, when necessary, by the legislative body and applied with police help by the judicial organs of the state. But though the judicial and legislative organs thus aid the application and enforcement of law, law itself is only custom.

The clearest exposition of this point of view is found in Carter's work on *Law, Its Origin, Growth and Function.*

> In associating custom with justice, we do not dethrone the latter but seat custom beside her. Justice is the felt necessity of doing that which secures order and peace. Custom furnishes the rule which answers to that necessity. ... Justice is not an absolute but a relative virtue, finding its play in that field of our conduct which relates to our dealings and intercourse with each other in society and enforcing in that field the things necessary to the existence of society. This existence is assured when and only when persons receive from all the treatment he may fairly expect. ... Justice may therefore be defined to be the principle which dictates that conduct between man and man which may be fairly expected by both and as none may fairly expect from another what is not in accordance with custom, justice consists in compliance with custom in all matters of difference between men. ... To each his due, but as we can know the due of each only from the common feeling of what is due, and this is dependent upon custom, the identity of justice with conformity to custom is implied.[133]

On one point and one point only the Anglo-American members of the historical school fell under the influence of the analytical school, thereby breaking away from their German confreres. Though they admitted and even insisted upon the customary origin of the content of law, they refused legal validity to national customs until these customs had been willed by the national legislature or judiciary. They thus, unlike the Germans, distinguished between custom and morality, with mere social sanctions and law proper, with external or police sanctions.

The German members of the historical school started with the fundamental assumption that the basic unit of all social, political, and legal action is the *Volk* or nation, a great super-organism which is something different from and higher than the sum total of the individual citizens of which it is composed. Each *Volk* has its own line of material, social, and cultural development. In the course of this development each *Volk* evolves its own manners and customs, its own standards of morality, and of justice. Each *Volk* has a soul of its own, and the manners and customs of each nation are merely the outward expression of the gradual evolution of this inner soul. Moreover, each *Volk* has a mind (*Geist*) of its own, and each such national mind evolves for itself its own standards of what is true and false, of what is good and bad. It evolves for itself its own standard of what is right, both in the moral and also in the legal sense of the word. This standard of right is the basis of true law. Law, therefore, has its origin neither in the commands of contemporary agencies of government (as taught by the analytical school) nor in the dictates of universal and unchanging human reason (as taught by the philosophical school), but in the national mind as revealed in the orderly practice of the nation. According to this view both custom and law are the embodiments or unconscious emanations of the national mind, and by a study of custom we can gain an insight into the national standard of right, in accord with which all law cases ought to be decided.

Savigny, the most famed member of the German historical school, tries to express this position by saying:

> In the earlier times to which authentic history extends the law will be found to have already attained a fixed character, peculiar to the people, like their language, manners, and constitutions. Nay, these phenomena have no separate existence; they are but the particular faculties and tendencies of an individual people inseparably united in nature and only wearing the semblance of distinct attributes to our view. That which binds them into one whole is the common conviction of the people, the kindred consciousness of an inward necessity.... Law grows with the growth and strengthens with the strength of the people (*Volk*) and finally dies away as the nation loses its nationality.... Law merits praise in so far as it falls in, or is adapted to fall in, with the feelings and consciousness of the people (*Volk*).[134]

This same position is outlined even more clearly by Puchta.

> Peoples (or Nations) are to be regarded as different individualities, dissimilar and unequal in nature and tendency. This individuality forms what we call the national or popular character. Hence the Rights (i.e. Law Systems) of peoples are different, and the peculiar characteristics of a nation are exhibited in its system of Right (of Law) just as in its language and customs. ... A principle of Right (or Law) becomes a fact by being recognized as such in the common conviction of those to whom it is applicable.... Through this common consciousness of right (or Law), as by a common language or a common religion the members of a people (or nation) are bound together in a definite union.... The consciousness which permeates members of a people in common is born with them and makes them spiritually members of one whole. It constitutes, in a word, the National Mind or spirit of the people and is the source of human or natural Right, and of the convictions which stir and operate in the minds of individuals.
> The share which usage has in connection with the origination of this form of Right is frequently represented so that Right (or Law) is said to arise out of custom.... The true view is just the reverse. Usage is only the last fact of the process by which the Right which has arisen and is living in the members of the people completely externalizes and embodies itself. The influence which custom has upon conviction only amounts to this, that the conviction may be brought by it into distinct consciousness and so confirmed.[135]

It goes without saying that all the members of the historical school were traditionalists. Law was regarded as the work of many generations and not the product of the arbitrary will of any person or group of persons at any one time.   They thought that they must reverently delve into the past to understand the "soul of the nation," the only true law-giver.   They had a horror of great or violent change.   Nevertheless they were traditionalists in the Hegelian sense of the word, for they did believe in progress and evolution.   They thought that we should be guided by the past, but not shackled by it.   The mind of the nation, like all other organisms, must grow and develop, and development necessarily implies change.   This attitude was summed up by Savigny in the words,

> To talk of going back to this past time were a vain and idle proposition, but it is a wholly different affair to keep its distinguishing excellences in view and thus fortify our minds against the narrowing influence of the present.[136]

Puchta is even more explicit:

> As a people changes throughout its whole sphere of life in the course of time, the same condition holds true of the system of Right [or Law] as a branch of that life.   Right is not fixed or stable at any time.   It develops with the people.   It attaches itself to the national character at its different stages of culture and it adapts itself to the changing wants and requirements of the people.[137]

It is largely because of this insistence upon perpetual growth that the members of the historical school broke with Hegel on one point and attacked the idea of codifying the laws.   A code of laws, however well it might embody the collective wisdom of the past, would stultify contin-uous growth in law, and without growth, law, like other manifestations of the national mind, would ossify and become lifeless and meaningless.

For our present purposes it is of the utmost importance to observe that the German branch of the historical school tended to emphasize nationalism as opposed to internationalism and cosmopolitanism.   In like manner it emphasized etatism or state control in opposition to in-dividualism.   Law was no longer to be based on universal abstract reason, common to all countries and all peoples; it was the product of the national mind of a single people.   To be consistent they had to argue that not only law but also morality were national rather than interna-tional in character.   Each nation evolves its system of moral as well as legal rights, but this standard is binding only upon its own citizens.   In the light of this doctrine not only international law but also interna-tional standards of ethics become meaningless words.   For one nation to borrow the legal or moral standards of another nation would be absurd.   Any attempt to do so would be a betrayal of its own national soul.

With such a philosophy it is small wonder that the members of the German historical school became ardent nationalists in politics as well as in the field of law.

In like manner the German historical school exalted the state, the embodiment of the nation, at the expense of the individual. The goodness or badness of a law was not to be judged by any individual reason or any individual conscience. To them true law should and could not be made by individuals or mere groups of individuals. It is a product of the collective or national mind taken as a whole, and to this collective mind all individual minds and individual wills are to be subordinated. In legal and political activity the conscious will of the individual was reckoned inferior to the unconscious, spontaneous creations of the community. To the members of this school the individual, as an individual, was of no importance. It was only as a member of a group, and more especially of a national group organized as a state, that he has real significance.

Considering the fact that the historical school regarded law as the emanation of the *Volk*, it is not surprising that its members supported nationalism and etatism. What is surprising is that they were all vigorous opponents of democracy and supporters of authoritarianism. If law is not the command of an individual or group of individuals but dictates of the mind of the nation taken as a whole, it would appear that political as well as legal control should rest with the people rather than with a select aristocratic group. No, exclaimed the members of this school. Political and legal sovereignty does indeed rest with the nation as a whole, but this does not in the least mean majority rule or even that the broad mass of the population should have any direct control over the machinery of government. Common or customary law is based upon the manners and customs of the general population, but the interpretation and administration of customary law should lie in the hands of a small select group of judges appointed by the king. These judges are better exponents of the legal conscience of the nation than are howling mobs in the market place who are more liable to lynch than to think judicially. In like manner the will of the nation must be regarded as the supreme political sovereign, but this will must be guided and controlled by a small select group of political aristocrats. The will of the nation does not mean the whim of the ignorant crowd. A nation is a nation with a corporate will of its own only when it ceases to be a formless aggregate of individuals and becomes organized into an organic whole with its classes and estates, its social and political pyramid, and with all administrative power concentrated at the top of this pyramid.

It is interesting to observe that though the English and American members of the historical school were unable to stomach the radical nationalism and etatism of their German brethren, they heartily agreed with the Germans in the latter's attack upon democracy. In fact one of the best defenses of monarchic and aristocratic as opposed to democratic control ever penned was Sir Henry Maine's *Popular Government*.

NOTES TO CHAPTER EIGHT

1. Vaughan, *Studies in the History of Political Philosophy*, II, 39, 40. By permission of the Manchester University Press, Manchester, England.
2. Joseph Mazzini, *The Duties of Man and Other Essays*, p. 228.
3. *Ibid.*, p. 223.
4. *Ibid.*, p. 222.
5. *Ibid.*, p. 223.
6. *Ibid.*, p. 263.
7. *Ibid.*, p. 264.
8. *Ibid.*, p. 265.
9. *Ibid.*, p. 269.
10. *Ibid.*, p. 47.
11. *Ibid.*, p. 34.
12. *Ibid.*, pp. 36, 37.
13. *Ibid.*, p. 37.
14. *Ibid.*
15. *Ibid.*, p. 55.
16. *Ibid.*, p. 173.
17. *Ibid.*, p. 176.
18. *Ibid.*, p. 193.
19. *Ibid.*, p. 246.
20. *Ibid.*, p. 271.
21. *Ibid.*, pp. 98, 99.
22. *Ibid.*, p. 105.
23. *Ibid.*, p. 106.
24. *Ibid.*, p. 103.
25. *Ibid.*, pp. 103, 104.
26. *Ibid.*, p. 92.   27. *Ibid.*, p. 109.
28. Quoted in H. W. C. Davis, *The Political Thought of H. v. Treitschke*, p. 51. By permission of Charles Scribner's Sons.
29. H. v. Treitschke, *Politics*, I, xxxiii. By permission of The Macmillan Company publishers, and Constable and Company, Limited.
30. *Ibid.*, I, xxxii–xxxiii.
31. *Ibid.*, I, 13–15.
32. *Ibid.*, I, 124.
33. *Ibid.*, I, 125.
34. *Ibid.*, I, 126, 127.
35. *Ibid.*, I, 128–130.
36. *Ibid.*, I, 13.
37. *Ibid.*, I, 12.
38. *Ibid.*, I, 13.

39. Quoted in Davis, *The Political Thought of H. v. Treitschke.* p 14
40. *Ibid.*, p. 111.
41. Treitschke, *Politics*, II, 395.
42. *Ibid.*, I, 66.
43. *Ibid.*, I, 206.
44. *Ibid.*, II, 317.
45. *Ibid.*, I, 12.
46. *Ibid.*, I, 121.
47. *Ibid.*, I, 122.
48. *Ibid.*, I, 275.
49. *Ibid.*, I, 231.
50. *Ibid.*, I, 205.
51. *Ibid.*, I, 116.
52. *Ibid.*, I, 3.
53. *Ibid.*, I, 22
54. *Ibid.*, I, 23.
55. *Ibid.*, I, 3–7.
56. *Ibid.*, I, 10.
57. *Ibid.*
58. *Ibid.*, I, 25.
59. *Ibid.*, I, 26.
60. *Ibid.*, I, 10.
61. *Ibid.*
62. *Ibid.*, I, 46.
63. *Ibid.*, I, 47.
64. *Ibid.*, I, 18.
65. *Ibid.*, I, 27.
66. *Ibid.*, I, 94–95.
67. *Ibid.*, I, 104–105.
68. *Ibid.*, II, 588–590.
69. *Ibid.*, II, 591.
70. *Ibid.*, II, 588.
71. *Ibid.*, II, 594.
72. *Ibid.*, II, 596.
73. *Ibid.*, I, 96
74. *Ibid.*, I, 29.
75. *Ibid.*, II, 609, 614.
76. *Ibid.*, I, 36.
77. *Ibid.*, I, 19, 21.
78. *Ibid.*, I, 65–69.
79. *Ibid.*, I, 61.
80. *Ibid.*
81. *Ibid.*, I, 66.
82. *Ibid.*, I, 15.
83. *Ibid.*
84. *Ibid.*, I, 74.
85. *Ibid.*, I, 63.
86. *Ibid.*, I, 74, 75
87. *Ibid.*, II, 291.
88. *Ibid.*, II, 492.
89. *Ibid.*, II, 494.
90. *Ibid.*, I, 390.
91. *Ibid.*, I, 391.

92. Treitschke, *Politics*, I, 165.
93. *Ibid.*, I, 397.
94. *Ibid.*, I, 392, 393.
95. *Ibid.*, I, 404.
96. *Ibid.*, I, 405.
97. *Ibid.*, I, 401.
98. *Ibid.*, I, 166.
99. *Ibid.*, I, 402.
100. *Ibid.*, I, 403.
101. *Ibid.*, I, 76.
102. *Ibid.*, I, 382.
103. *Ibid.*, I, 387.
104. *Ibid.*, I, 175.
105. *Ibid.*, I, 167.
106. *Ibid.*, I, 351.
107. *Ibid.*, I, 355–359.
108. *Ibid.*, I, 334.
109. *Ibid.*, I, 359.
110. *Ibid.*, I, 334.
111. *Ibid.*, I, 41–43.
112. *Ibid.*, I, 44.
113. *Ibid.*, I, 53.
114. *Ibid.*, II, 17.
115. *Ibid.*, II, 196–198.
116. *Ibid.*, II, 13.
117. *Ibid.*, II, 59–61.
118. *Ibid.*, II, 73.
119. *Ibid.*, I, 59.
120. *Ibid.*, II, 162.
121. *Ibid.*, II, 145.
122. *Ibid.*, I, 16.
123. *Ibid.*, II, 4.
124. *Ibid.*, II, 5.
125. *Ibid.*, II, 4.
126. *Ibid.*, II, 176.
127. *Ibid.*, I, 316–317.
128. *Ibid.*, II, 200.
129. *Ibid.*, II, 193.
130. *Ibid.*, II, 200, 201.	131. *Ibid.*, II, 204.
132. Sir H. S. Maine, *Ancient Law*, p. 75.
133. J. C. Carter, *Law, Its Origin, Growth and Function*, pp. 159–163. By permission of G. P. Putnam's Sons.
134. F. v. Savigny, *The Vocation of Our Age for Legislation and Jurisprudence.*
135. G. F. Puchta, *Outlines of Jurisprudence as a Science of Right*, pp. 26, 30, 38–39 By permission of T. & T. Clark.
136. Savigny, *loc. cit.*
137. Puchta, *loc. cit.*

BIBLIOGRAPHY

FOR MAZZINI

J. Mazzini, *The Duties of Man and Other Essays*, Everyman edition, London, 1907. See also *Life and Writings of Joseph Mazzini*, 6 vols., London, 1890–1891:

E. A. Venturi, *Joseph Mazzini, A Memoir*, London, 1875; B. King, *Mazzini*, London, 1902; G. V. Griffith, *Mazzini, Prophet of Modern Europe*, London, 1932; C. E. Vaughan, *Studies in the History of Political Thought*, Manchester, 1925 (vol. II, chap. VI); R. H. Murray, *History of Political Science*.

FOR TREITSCHKE

H. v. Treitschke: *Politics*, 2 vols., London, 1916; *Historische und Politische Aufsätze*, 2 vols., Leipzig, 1871; *Zehn Jahre Deutscher Kämpfe*, Berlin, 1897. E. Barker, *Nietzsche and Treitschke*, Oxford, 1914. H. W. C. Davis, *The Political Thought of H. v. Treitschke*, New York, 1915. A. Hausrat, *Treitschke, His Life and Works*, London, 1914. A. Guilland, *Modern Germany and Her Historians*, London, 1915 (chap. IV).

FOR THE HISTORICAL SCHOOL OF JURISPRUDENCE

F. v. Savigny, *The Vocation of Our Age for Legislation and Jurisprudence*, London, 1831. G. F. Puchta, *Outlines of Jurisprudence as a Science of Right*, Edinburgh, 1887. Sir H. S. Maine: *Ancient Law*, fourth edition, London, 1870; *Early History of Institutions*, London, 1875; *Popular Government*, London, 1884. J. C. Carter, *Law, Its Origin, Growth and Function*, New York, 1907. R. Pound, *Interpretations of Legal Theory*, New York, 1923. R. G. Gettell, *History of Political Thought*, New York, 1924 (chap. XXIV). E. Freund, "The German Historical School." in *Political Science Quarterly*, V, 468–486.

CHAPTER IX

IRRATIONALISM AND THE IRRATIONALISTS

It is obvious that traditionalism has played an important part in the shaping of the Fascist and Nazi ideologies. Equally important is the part which has been played by the school of thought which we may call irrationalism. To the serious student of political thought it is clear that modern irrationalism, like modern traditionalism, has its roots in the Hegelian philosophy. At first sight, to be sure, it does seem rather absurd to class Hegel among the founders of political irrationalism. In the realm of metaphysics Hegel was a thoroughgoing rationalist. To him thought and being were the same thing; reason was not only the sovereign of the universe, but the universe itself was nothing more than the concrete embodiment of universal reason. Nevertheless, Hegel's political philosophy was based upon a revolt against rationalism in the affairs of state. In the first place, Hegel insisted that his guiding principle was not mere understanding, but reason — that is, understanding plus "spiritual insight" — thus introducing the non-logical or intuitional element. In the second place, Hegel stressed the difference between reflective or conscious reason and creative or unconscious reason, and insisted that all true political developments, the creation and transformations of states, must be based upon unconscious and not upon conscious reason. From a belief in unconscious reason to a belief in pure intuitionism or pure irrationalism is only a short step and this step was soon taken by many of the later political philosophers, especially by those who had leanings towards etatism and authoritarianism.

IRRATIONALISM IN GENERAL PHILOSOPHY

As Hegel's rational premises seemed inconsistent with his irrationalist political conclusions with which the later etatists so warmly sympathized, these later thinkers quietly dropped the whole of the Hegelian metaphysics with its logical and rationalist background, and looked for moral support to the teachings of some of the non-Hegelian philosophers, especially of those philosophers who had stressed the importance of irrationalist elements in the operations of the universe. There was no lack of such persons during the last portion of the nineteenth century and during the first portion of the twentieth century. Most of these thinkers disagreed radically among themselves in regard to details, but the majority of them agreed on three points in violent opposition to orthodox Hegelianism. The first of these three points is the belief that reason alone cannot solve the problems of the universe or give us a true standard in judging the good and bad of social institutions. The second point is the belief that the universe itself is essentially irrational; that reality does not and never will obey rigid logical laws. The third point, the most important to the student of politics, is the belief that man is essentially an irrational animal, and that social and political activity must be based upon this fundamental assumption.

There were numerous philosophers who adopted these doctrinal points, but it was the American, William James, the Frenchman, Henri Bergson, and the German, Friedrich Nietzsche, who are worthy of especial attention because of their widespread popularity, their influence upon public thought and opinion, and more particularly because all three had an important part in the shaping of later etatist-authoritarian thought. In one sense it is distinctly amusing to find that it was these three writers who were most influential in establishing the philosophical background of later etatist speculation, for none of the three were themselves etatists. Bergson ignored political problems, but certainly had no etatist leanings; James, when dealing with political matters, was an ardent defender of individualism and of democracy, the two pillars of liberalism; Nietzsche, to be sure, violently attacked democracy and all of its ways, but even he was an enthusiastic individualist and was vociferous in his onslaughts on the authoritarian state. These facts did not prevent the later etatists from elevating these three men to the rank of philosophical deities. The philosophical ideas of these three men were developed and modified in such a way as to make them fit in perfectly with the etatist attitude. It is indeed one of the remarkable ironies of history that the later etatists were able to take the irrationalist premises of James, of Bergson, of Nietzsche and associate them with the political conclusions and deductions of Hegel, generally regarded as the greatest of all rationalists.

William James (1842–1910) was one of the few Americans to win an international reputation in the realm of philosophy. This is partly due to the fact that he possessed a very charming and lucid style which rendered his writings intelligible and interesting to vast multitudes normally incapable of enjoying metaphysical discourse. There are many phases in James' philosophy. He was a believer in "radical Empiricism" as opposed to the rationalism of the classical German school. To him it is *not* true (as it was true to Hegel) that whatever is rational is real, but rather that whatever is experienced is real. He was a pluralist, as opposed to a monist. The world to him was not a "block universe," the transformation of a single primordial substance in which all separateness and individuality are illusory, apparent rather than real. The universe was regarded as an aggregate, even though a harmonious and interconnected aggregate, of a limitless number of individual be- ings, each of which has its own real and independent existence. James called himself a tychist (from the Greek word *tyche*, meaning chance), as opposed to a determinist. To him the universe and mankind are not governed by fixed, rigid determined laws, which cannot be broken. He saw rather in the working of the universe and in human activities a large element both of chance and of free will. To James a man may be strongly influenced by his environment, his racial or his historical back- ground, or by economic factors, but he always remains a free agent, able to shake off these influences and control his own destiny. The Hegelian philosophy was essentially a philosophy of observation; the Jamesian philosophy is essentially a philosophy of action, and man cannot act unless he feels free to act as he chooses.

James was neither an optimist, as was Hegel, nor a pessimist, as was Schopenhauer, another great German philosopher, but a meliorist, a believer that things are bad but may be improved. Schopenhauer taught that life is essentially evil and that little or nothing can be done to make it better. Hegel taught that all reality is a manifestation of the Universal Mind and hence is essentially good. It was difficult for him and his followers to admit the positive existence of evil. In place of the old "God's in his heaven, all's right with the world," he taught that the world is God and hence must be perfect to the eye of reason. James re- fused to admit that the world is either essentially good or essentially bad. He claimed that some things in the world are good, others bad, and that it lies in our power to diminish the bad and increase the good. Good will eventually triumph, but only if we struggle on its behalf.

These doctrines had a great effect upon later political speculation But James' greatest influence on politics was due, not to these doctrines, but to his ideas regarding the nature of truth and how truth can be ascertained. James insisted that truth can never be known merely by logical reasoning; that truth is essentially irrational; that there are many basic facts which transcend logic, which are seemingly irrational and yet fundamentally true. We must, he said, "learn to give up the logic, fairly, squarely, and irrevocably," as a philosophic method; for "reality, life, experience, concreteness, immediacy, use what word you will, exceeds our logic, overflows and surrounds it." [1] In place of the old doctrine of truth as being based upon logical consistency, James postulated his famous doctrine of pragmatism, that an idea is true if it works and that the goodness and badness of an object must be judged, not by an abstract rational standard, but by its concrete effectiveness, a variation of the old saying, "by their fruits shall ye know them."

James insisted that all scientific hypotheses are purely pragmatic in character; that scientists believe in their hypotheses merely because they "work"; that is, merely because these hypotheses aid them in further experimentation or in controlling material objects. No one has ever seen an atom; presumably no one ever will. But we believe in the truth of atoms because the atomic theory aids us in forming many new chemical compounds. Reasoning from these premises, James proclaimed that we may believe, at least provisionally, in the validity of any hypothesis, whether scientific, religious, or political, if it seems to aid us in improving our everyday life. If the belief in God is useful, we should accept the existence of God at least as a working hypothesis. If belief in determinism leads to a blind acceptance of things as they are, while belief in free will aids us in our struggle against evil, the belief in free will turns out to be "true." Considering the flexible character of pragmatism, it is small wonder that it was taken over and applied by the later etatists in ways which must cause the liberally inclined James to turn over in his grave. On pragmatic grounds, say these etatists, the divinity of a given state or race must be true if belief in this divinity increases the power and prestige and effectiveness of this state or race. Dictatorship must be better, represent a "truer" form of government, if dictatorial Germany becomes progressively stronger and democratic France becomes progressively weaker.

A very important aspect of the pragmatic doctrine of truth as expounded by James was the emphasis laid upon the "will to believe," or, as James expressed it, "Our passional nature not only lawfully may, but must, decide an option between propositions whenever it is a genuine option that cannot by its nature be decided on intellectual grounds." James pointed out that our acceptance or rejection of certain hypotheses frequently depends, consciously or unconsciously, upon our emotional background — in other words, much of our thinking is wishful thinking.

James was not the first person to point out this fact, but whereas earlier thinkers deplored this condition and urged that we seek to eliminate our emotional likes and dislikes when we set out in search for truth, James welcomed the emotional or passional phase in man's attempt to investigate and evaluate reality.   Man's beliefs should not go contrary to reason, but there are so many things which reason cannot decide; in such matters it is the right and duty of man to adopt beliefs which best satisfy his inner emotional nature.

James himself applied his "will to believe" largely to religious and moral problems.   We have, he said, the right to believe in God and in certain moral standards which are logically unprovable if these beliefs satisfy our emotional needs and thereby make us better and more useful citizens.   Here again the later etatists took over James' methodology and applied it in their own fashion to very different problems and reached conclusions at which James would have stood aghast.   "We have a right to believe in any doctrine which satisfies our emotional needs" has proved a very popular and much-used argument in defense of many Fascist and Nazi doctrines which are patently and admittedly irrational and even absurd.

Closely related to the ideas of William James, though dissimilar in many important details, are the doctrines put forward by Henri Bergson (1859–1941).   The central point in Bergson's philosophy is the emphasis laid upon intuition as opposed to intellect or reason.   Bergson approached the problems of philosophy from the standpoint of biology, and his whole system is largely a reinterpretation of the theory of evolution.   Just as the body, through a long line of evolution, has developed such organs as the eye and the ear to establish contact with the external world, so the mind has developed the special organ of the intellect that it may satisfactorily cope with and control material forces.   We know that the eye is a very valuable organ, but we also know that it is imperfect.   We know that it is subject to many optical illusions; we also know that there are many things which remain invisible to the human eye (such as infra-red and ultra-violet lights), although the existence of such things has been scientifically proved.   Our eye is what it is because of the evolution it has undergone.   By a process of adaptation and by reason of the survival of the fittest, it has trained itself to see those sights and those colors which were useful to the human organism and to ignore those sights and those colors which were or which seemed to be more or less useless.

In like manner, reason or the intellect, the organ which the mind or consciousness has developed during the course of evolution, is extremely valuable, but it, too, is subject to many limitations and is far from perfect. There are many phases of reality which the intellect is unable to grasp, and even of those phases which it does grasp it is apt to give a distorted picture, a picture based upon the need for action rather than on the search for abstract truth. Bergson likened the action of the intellect to a cinematograph film giving us a series of mental pictures, which, when strung together and passed rapidly before our minds, gives us an illusion of reality. But reality itself, though similar to, is never the same as the moving-picture version of it created by the intellect. We must, according to Bergson, transcend the intellect if we wish to gain a direct glimpse of reality.

Bergson declared that a study of animal life shows that mind is capable of developing other mental organs in addition to and quite different in character from the intellect. Such, for example, is the instinct found in many animals, and especially developed in such insects as bees and ants. Certain instincts are still found in man, but on the whole man in developing his intellect has lost most of his powers of instinct. It is, says Bergson, inadvisable and impossible for us to turn our backs on intellect and re-create our instinctive faculties. We must continue to use our intellect or reason, but we must also make use of something akin to instinct—namely, direct insight or intuition—in order to correct the distorted picture of reality which the intellect gives us. Physical science, based as it is upon intellect, gives us a very valuable and useful picture of the world, but it is still only a picture and a very imperfect picture. Philosophy, true philosophy, must use the data of science, but it must correct these data by the use of intuition, for to use intuition is to seize reality itself. By the use of intuition, "and only by so doing, can we have a real metaphysic, a science which is both before and beyond the sciences." [2] Intuition, not intellect, is the basis not only of philosophy but also of all forms of artistic endeavor. "The clearest evidence of intuition is in the works of great artists. What is it we call genius in great painters and poets and musicians? It is the power they have of seeing more than we see and of enabling us by their expression to penetrate further into reality." [3] What is true of the artists is also true of the leaders of society and the state. The heroes of human history are those who have had a greater direct insight into reality than their fellows.

On the basis of his "new" method, Bergson proceeds to sketch for us the outlines of a new metaphysics, the type of philosophy which must dominate men's minds in the present and the future. A careful analysis of this system shows that in spite of its new terminology and its general air of novelty, it is largely a re-edition of Hegel's philosophy, minus the elements of rationalism and of determinism. The only ultimate reality, says Bergson, is *life* (which thus takes the place of Hegel's Absolute). This ultimate reality is essentially spiritual or "vital" in character, and can best be considered as a consciousness which unceasingly "becomes" or changes and yet which forever endures. Both matter and intellect are to be derived from this ultimate reality. But though this ultimate reality or life is one, there are apparent in it two different currents, one a descending, arresting, or retarding current, the basis of our concept of matter; the other an ascending, advancing, creative current, the basis of our concept of mind (and by mind, Bergson means, of course, something far more comprehensive than intellect or reason). The universe around us is the result of the interplay of these two currents or forces. In all forms of organic life, whether vegetable, animal, or human, we find traces of these two currents. In man, of course, we find intellect, instinct, memory, intuition — the mental faculties on the one side, and the physical organs on the other. But there is a similar distinction in all other forms of organic life. A rudimentary or dormant form of consciousness is to be found even in plants and in the lowest forms of animal life, in addition to their purely physical or material framework.

Bergson is especially interested in the "ascending, advancing, creative" current. In fact, though his term life in the broader sense includes both currents, that is, both matter and mind, yet when he speaks, as he so frequently does speak, of "the stream of life," "the life process," "the life impulse," he usually has reference to this advancing, creative current. To him, this upward truly vital stream is in no way caused or created by matter, the downward stream. Mind or consciousness, the upward stream, is essentially different from and independent of matter, but in the world around us we find that mind has become ensnared or enmeshed in matter. Mind struggles to arrange and organize matter; not infrequently it finds itself hopelessly caught in the instrument it seeks to dominate. The whole history of evolution is the history of mind groping upward, trying to achieve a sphere of free activity. In the vegetable world mind is least able to express itself, for among plants there is a tendency towards immobility and unconscious torpor. In the animal world there have been not one but several lines of evolution. On many lines progress has been arrested or even turned back, but along two main lines it has found free way.   One is the line of the bees and the ants, which has led to the development of instinct; the other is the line of the vertebrate animals, which has led to the development of the in- tellect and which finds its highest expression in man.   "Everywhere else the current of life has been turned back by the weight of the dead matter that confronted it; in man it has won free way." [4]   Moreover, man as he is at present, though the highest, is not the final stage of evolution. Man may, probably will, continue to evolve and become even more free in his creative activity.   Humanity as it evolves may be able to beat down every resistance offered it by matter, may even be able to over- come death.

Hegel, it will be remembered, thought of the whole universe as the self-unfoldment of Universal Mind.   Bergson's position is not far differ- ent.   But to Hegel, mind was essentially reason or intelligence, and it necessarily followed a determined, logical pattern as it unfolded.   Berg- son believes that mind is far deeper and broader than reason, and refuses to believe that mind, as it gropes upward for free expression, follows a logical or predetermined pattern.   He refuses to see in evolution noth- ing more than the unrolling in time of a plan previously conceived and once and for all determined.   Evolution for him is the free creative ac- tivity of mind which creates new and unpredictable forms as it surges upwards.   In evolution there is tendency towards something, but never a fixed goal, nor does evolution follow a fixed path; rather in its upward surge it creates a fresh path for itself.   Every moment in our lives is a fresh creation.   Man, like the universal stream of life of which he is a part, is also basically free, a center of creative activity, and the path of human evolution is towards an ever greater and more perfect expression of his free creative action.

Bergson is, like James, a philosopher of action and not, like Hegel, a philosopher of observation.   This in itself is a fact of prime importance when we come to examine Bergson's influence upon political philosophy. But we should not forget that Bergson himself has little to say about the sphere of ethics and almost nothing about the spheres of law and politics. At most, Bergson tries to stimulate a sort of romantic heroism in all fields of human endeavor.   With his emphasis upon "creative activity," it is easy to see how his teachings could be used in attacking the old principles of *laissez faire*, but from Bergson's own words it would be dif- ficult to know if greater emphasis should be placed upon the individual, the group, or the state.   "Society, which is the community of individual energy, benefits from the efforts of all its members and renders effort easier to all.   It can subsist by subordinating the individual: it can progress only by leaving the individual free; contradictory requirements which have to be reconciled." [5]   With a statement of political action so charmingly ambiguous as this, it is small wonder that Bergson has served as a stimulus to liberal reformers, to syndicalists and revolutionary socialists, and to the advocates of a totalitarian state governed by a dictator.   To us, at the moment, the fact that Bergson exercised a strong influence upon Mussolini and the other apostles of the totalitarian state is of especial importance.

The third outstanding member of the irrationalist school of philosophers, Friedrich Nietzsche, differs in several important respects from James and Bergson, especially in the deductions he draws from irrationalism with respect to ethics and politics.   There are many phases to Nietzsche's philosophy, but most of these phases are merely developments of his central position, the doctrine of the will to power, a doctrine he evolved by combining certain aspects of Schopenhauer's philosophy with the Darwinian theory of evolution.

Schopenhauer (1788–1860), Nietzsche's great predecessor, was a junior contemporary of Hegel, Schopenhauer's masterpiece, *The World as Will and Idea*, being written in 1818 when Hegel was still alive.   Nevertheless Schopenhauer remained almost unrecognized until after the middle of the nineteenth century, when he suddenly leaped to fame and inspired many of the later German thinkers.   Schopenhauer's fundamental doctrine, the doctrine which had the most effect upon Nietzsche, was the idea that the only ultimate reality in the universe is *will*, blind struggling will, which manifests itself in all of the multitudinous phenomena we see around us.   Schopenhauer, like most of the classical German philosophers, was a thoroughgoing monist.   He thought that there was and could be only one fundamental substance, from which all other things are derived.   He rejected with scorn the idea of the materialists that this ultimate reality was matter.   He accepted from Kant the idea that space, time, causality are not objective but subjective, the product of the mind, or rather the way in which the mind looks at reality.   This idea led him, as it led Fichte and Hegel, to the doctrine that the mind, in some form or another, is the only ultimate reality, but he differed from Fichte and Hegel in refusing to identify this universal mind with reason or intelligence.   The idea that the mind of man or of the universe is essentially rational was to him an enormous error, which must be rectified before we can understand reality.

Even the term consciousness is too broad a term to give to this fundamental universal mind. "Consciousness is the mere surface of our
mind, of which, as of the earth, we do not know the inside but only the
crust." [6] According to Schopenhauer, under the conscious intellect is
the unconscious will, a striving, persistent, vital force, a cause of spontaneous activity. Schopenhauer's universal will is very much like
Bergson's life impulse or the stream of life, and, like Bergson, Schopenhauer sees this will or vital force behind all the phenomena in the universe. Even in inert matter Schopenhauer sees the action of this will,
disguised as blind energy or force. In the vegetable kingdom we find
more obvious traces of this unconscious striving or impulse. Plants
desire light and push upward; they desire moisture and push their roots
into the soil. When we come to the animal world, the part played by
will or desire or impulse is obvious to all. All animals, high or low, are
dominated by a blind, remorseless will to live. With the higher animals
and with man this primitive, fundamental will becomes consciousness
and with consciousness there develops intelligence and reason. The
intellect, however, is merely the organ which the will of man has created
in order that it may the better grapple with the external world and sub-
jugate it to its control. To call man a rational animal is ridiculous.
Even in man the will to live, the desire for food and comfort, the desire
to reproduce himself, is superior to all intellectual proclivities. Even in
man the intellect always remains in the service of the will; the will is the
master, the intellect is the servant.

To Schopenhauer, as to Bergson, reason or the intellect is a very mar-
velous and a very useful organ, but it is necessarily incomplete and imperfect, giving us only a partial picture of truth. Even the knowledge
that the will is the ultimate reality comes to us by direct awareness or
insight and not through reasoning. In all true wisdom there is invariably an intuitive element in addition to the purely intellectual element.

> In real life, the scholar is far surpassed by the man of the world, for the
> strength of the latter consists in perfect intuitive knowledge.... Philosophy
> must be brought back to the recognition of the richness of an immediate and
> direct knowledge of reality. It must learn that the meaning of things is
> to be realized more by living than by thinking.[7]

Nietzsche (1844–1900), the most outstanding of the modern disciples
of Schopenhauer, takes the doctrine of the will and develops it even further. To Nietzsche, as to Schopenhauer, will, blind will, is the only ultimate reality, but to Nietzsche this will is not merely the will to exist or
survive, but also the will to dominate and control one's environment

and other wills. Or, as Nietzsche himself puts it, the universal will is not merely the will to live but the will to power. Every living thing strives to increase its power by vanquishing other things; life itself is essentially a striving for surplus power.

> Whereever I found a living thing, there found I the Will to Power, and even in the will of the servant, there found I the will to be master. Neither necessity, nor desire, but the love of power is the demon of mankind. You give men everything possible — health, food, shelter, enjoyment, but they are and remain unhappy and capricious, for the demon waits and waits, and must be satisfied.

In the second place there is a sharp contrast between Schopenhauer, the master, and Nietzsche, the disciple, in their attitude towards the external world and the universal will which underlies and creates this world. Both men saw the world as an entity without fixed goal or purpose. This caused Schopenhauer to lapse into pessimism, while in Nietzsche it caused the creation of an attitude which may be called "tragic optimism." Schopenhauer saw in the world the eternal conflict between wills and thought it horrible. Nietzsche saw in life the same conflict and thought it magnificent, even though this conflict were futile and led to no permanent goal. To Nietzsche, man does not instinctively seek happiness and avoid unhappiness. Rather does he seek to overcome obstacles; and he finds joy (not happiness) in thus overcoming obstacles, even though this struggle entails pain and even death. To Nietzsche life is indeed a tragedy, for it ends in sickness, sorrow, and death. But we should and can find an exuberant joy in living this tragedy. Like the warriors of old, we must find our chief joy in the battlefield, even though the battlefield leads, sooner or later, to death.

Finally, there is an important difference between Schopenhauer and Nietzsche with reference to the doctrine of evolution. Schopenhauer rejected the idea of the transmutation of species, while Nietzsche warmly welcomes the Darwinian theory of biological or organic evolution and makes it an integral part of his will to power. To him, the will to power is the real cause of evolution, the real cause of the emergence of new species. Darwin's idea of evolution through the struggle for existence and the survival of the fittest is only another way of stating Nietzsche's basic theory of will. Evolution, itself, is merely the dramatic story of the history of the will to power.

Of great importance is the fact that Nietzsche took the doctrines of evolution and the will to power and applied them to a solution of the problem of good and evil and also to the problem of what is true and how we know it to be true.   To both these problems he gave a distinctly irrationalist solution.   In the realm of morals, Nietzsche denied that there is an eternal absolute standard of right and wrong, to be known either by an inner moral sense or by reason.   According to Nietzsche, there is not one but there are many moral standards; each of them has merely a relative value and each of them is the product of evolution. Each moral code is but a weapon in the struggle for power.   Most living beings, both human and animal, have discovered that they have a better chance in the struggle for existence if they live and act in groups rather than as individuals.   Hence they develop a herd instinct.   Each group or herd develops a standard of action, based primarily on its desire to preserve and universalize its own type; this standard of action becomes a moral code.   At first each group or community compels its members to follow a certain line of conduct.   Later this line of conduct becomes custom; still later it becomes almost an instinct and takes the form of "moral sense" or conscience.   But it should never be forgotten that all moral valuations are in reality nothing but the expressions of the needs of the particular community or herd, of that which is to *its* advantage. As the conditions for the maintenance of one community have been very different from those for the maintenance of another community, there have been different codes of morality at different times and places.

A similar attitude characterizes Nietzsche's theory regarding the nature of the true and false.   Not only goodness but also truth is merely that which has, or is considered to have, survival value.   "All our senses and organs of knowledge are evolved with a view to the maintenance and development of the species." [8]   Nietzsche, like Bergson, thinks that the eye and the intellect have learned to perceive what is useful, not necessarily what is true.   Hence what the eye and the intellect tell us are invariably distortions of reality.   To say that an idea is true is merely to state that it has proved useful to the preservation of the race. The eternal truths postulated by the philosophers, the eternal laws of nature postulated by the scientists, are merely subjective creations of the intellect, an intellect consciously or unconsciously motivated by the will to power and not by a yearning for absolute reality.

> Humanity, finding itself in certain conditions of existence, required knowledge as a necessary means of persisting.   The ideas of causality, of space and time are ideas which under the actual conditions of existence prove most beneficial to humanity as a means of acquiring knowledge, consequently as a means of maintaining itself in the struggle for life.   These ideas have no reality whatever in themselves; they represent the truth for humanity under

certain conditions . . . and should perchance the actual conditions change, the truths of today would no longer be the truths of tomorrow. . . . These ideas have no reality in themselves; in the beginning it is possible that many different concepts of reality were in existence; and if the concepts which we regard today as immutable, those of causality, of space and time, have survived it is because these concepts are the best adapted to the conditions of existence.[9]

In other words, in the realm of concepts as well as in the realm of physical organisms it has been not a survival of the best, but merely the survival of the fittest.

To Nietzsche there is only one ultimate reality, only one ultimate truth — the will to power. All else is illusion, even though these illusions sometimes serve a very useful purpose. Moreover, on the same principle, if any illusions serve our purpose, if they aid us in the will to power, they must be accepted, even though they be palpably false. After all, the ultimate aim of life is not knowledge of reality through thought, but *action*, struggle, combat. Only in action can we lead a full life, and anything which aids us in leading this full life, whether conscious illusions, or instincts, or intuitions, or even ordinary emotions, must be welcomed.

Some of the social and political conclusions which Nietzsche drew from his irrationalist premises are of great interest to the student of political thought. Nietzsche was far too much of an individualist, far too interested in giving free scope to the individual will to power, for him to become an apostle of thoroughgoing etatism. But many features of his political philosophy were extremely popular with the etatists and were taken over and incorporated in the etatist creed.

One of the features which proved very acceptable to the etatists was Nietzsche's reverence for struggle, for conflict, for war.

> War and courage have done more great things than charity. . . . Every natural gift must develop itself by contest. . . . One will have to forgive my occasionally chanting a paean of war. Horribly clangs its silvery bow, and although it comes along like the night, war is nevertheless Apollo, the true divinity for consecrating and purifying the state. . . . Against the deviation of the State Ideal into a money ideal . . . the only remedy is war and once again war, in the emotions of which, this at least becomes obvious . . . that in love to fatherland and prince it produces an ethical impulse indicative of a much higher destiny. . . . We rejoice in everything which like ourselves loves danger, war, adventure, which does not make compromises, nor let itself be captured or conciliated.

Even more significant is Nietzsche's violent denunciation of democracy and his defense of aristocracy. To Nietzsche, democracy means the rule of the base, the sordid, the mean. It means the crushing of creative genius by the numbing weight of mediocrity. Democracy, to him, is the contrary of the whole principle of evolution, for evolution is the development and survival of the fittest, while democracy is the control of the fittest by the great mass of the unfit. Nietzsche is convinced that the most certain thing about human beings is that they are unequal, fundamentally and biologically unequal. Once this inequality be granted, it follows as a matter of course that the best and not merely the greatest number should rule. "Every elevation of the human type has until now been the work of aristocratic society — and thus will it always be — the work of a society which believes in the necessity of the hierarchy of rank and values, and which necessarily has slavery in some form or another."

Carlyle wished to have government *of* the people, *for* the people, *by* the aristocracy. Nietzsche frankly wished to have government *of* the people, *by* the aristocracy, and *for* the aristocracy.

Nietzsche desires the systematic cultivation of a race of masters, similar to that of the patricians in Rome and of the "aristoi" in Athens. He desires the re-establishment of the system of castes, rigidly separated from one another, with just sufficient connection between them to enable a renewal of the race to take place periodically. The sufferings and toils of humanity are necessary in order to permit of the existence of a few creators, supreme masters of the destinies of mankind, sublime Olympian artists who constitute the justification of humanity. The progress of civilization has not for its aim the emancipation of the masses. Nietzsche will not hear of such a thing as an "Arbeiterfrage" [the labor problem] and is even prepared to denounce Prince Bismarck himself as a democrat and as a socialist, because of his social legislation.... The real progress of civilization will be realized first when the aim of the state will be the cultivation of a superior race. The State which devotes itself to this object will be a real state — that is to say one wielding authority and able to command. The real interests of civilization demand the existence of a vast confused mass of humanity which shall serve as the instrument whereby the race of the elite, of the masters may be cultivated.[10]

The utilitarian liberals demanded that all government and all legislation should have as its aim the greatest happiness of the greatest number. To Nietzsche this is a horrible ideal, signifying the triumph of mediocrity. He believed all government and all legislation should aim at the happiness and improvement of the elite, and this elite will always constitute the minority in any community. "Humanity as a mass sacrificed for the benefit of a single race of strong men — that is what would constitute progress." Humanity exists for the benefit of the superior race, of the elite, and Nietzsche is convinced that the new strong government of the future will make this the guiding principle in its administration.

Closely associated in Nietzsche's mind with his plea for aristocracy is his demand for a new morality — a new moral code which shall guide the elite or aristocracy in the government of the world. Nietzsche divides all mankind into two main groups — the race of masters, the elite, on the one side, the race of slaves or the broad masses of mankind on the other. He insists that each of these two groups must have its own religion and philosophy and its own type of morality. Nietzsche agreed with Karl Marx, his arch-enemy, that orthodox religion is an opiate to the people, but unlike Marx, Nietzsche thought it well that the masses should have this opiate. The race of masters, however, must see through the fraud of religious dogma and realize that the only enduring reality is the will to power and must act accordingly. In like manner there is a sharp contrast between slave morality and master morality. The idea that the poor, the meek, the humble are especially holy; the idea that pity, sympathy, charity are high virtues are sure signs that customary morality is a product of slave mentality. It is well for the masses to retain this moral code, for the slaves, the herd, need such ideas and one must not take from them "the pillars of their existence, and the soporific appliances towards happiness." The masters, the elite, on the other hand, must reject this slave morality and invent or adopt a new master morality. A peasant may well be bound by Christian morality, but a gentleman should be bound by something different and higher, the code of a gentleman.

In Nietzsche's philosophy, as we have seen, all moral valuations are merely the expressions of the need of the community or group of that which is to its advantage. It is only natural, therefore, that the race of slaves should adopt a moral code with sympathy for the weak, the poor, the oppressed as its standard of action. The race of masters, however, has nothing whatever to do with the race of slaves. They belong or ought to belong to a different group. They should, therefore, adopt a moral code which is to their advantage, and should not be bound by a moral code which works only to the advantage of the masses. The aim of the master morality should be to preserve the power of the masters over the masses and to preserve and improve the racial strain of the masters, looking forward to the time when the masters will produce a race of supermen. Christian or slave morality protects and preserves the unfit and the weak. Master morality seeks to eliminate the weak and unfit. Master morality is concerned only with increasing the power and the happiness of the masters. "No greater or more fatal misfortune could happen than if the strong and powerful and healthy in mind and body should begin to doubt of *their* right to be happy." In master morality *good* is synonymous with brave, powerful, beautiful, but it is also synonymous with ferocious, hard, cruel when it comes to handling slaves. Master morality demands that masters know neither pity nor sympathy in their treatment of the multitude. "A man loses power when he pities. Pity thwarts the law of development which is the law of selection. It preserves that which is ripe for death; it fights in favor of the disinherited and the condemned of life. By multiplying misery, quite as much as by preserving all that is miserable, it is the principal agent in promoting decadence."

It is not without significance that Mussolini admits the strong influence which Nietzsche's writings exerted in the formation of his own political opinions.

IRRATIONALISM AND SOCIAL PSYCHOLOGY
IN ENGLAND AND AMERICA

The emphasis upon irrationalism was not confined to the realm of pure philosophers. Towards the close of the nineteenth century and in the first two decades of the twentieth century, there arose a group of writers whose primary interest was the psychological interpretation of the problems of social and political science. In their hands there gradually evolved a new science, the science of social psychology, a study of the psychological motivations which underlie all human activity, especially all social and political activity. Practically all these men stressed the fact that human behavior is determined far more by irrational and unconscious impulses or instincts than by conscious reflections or reason. It is of special interest to note that whereas none of the outstanding exponents of irrationalism in the realm of pure philosophy were etatists in the strict sense of the word, many though not all of the social psychologists, the exponents of irrationalism in the realm of the social sciences, tended to draw etatist conclusions from their studies. A few of the social psychologists remained staunch liberals, especially those who arose in England and America, but the majority of these men, especially those who flourished on the continent of Europe, tended to emphasize the importance of the group at the expense of the individual and also the need for autocratic leadership and control within the group.

Two of the most interesting exponents of the new science of social psychology are the Englishman, Graham Wallas, the author of *Human Nature and Politics*, and his American disciple, Walter Lippmann, the author of *Public Opinion* and numerous other works. Lippmann has devoted himself to a study of the American political scene, but on all essential points he has remained in accord with his English master. Graham Wallas' main thesis has been very ably summarized by Gettell in the following words:

> Wallas lays stress upon the fact that politics is only in a slight degree the product of conscious reason. He argues that it is largely a matter of subconscious processes, of habit and instinct, of suggestion and imitation. He points out the importance of names and symbols, of party shibboleths and of the emotional connotations of political devices. He believes that the art of politics consists largely in the creation of opinion by a deliberate appeal to non-rational inference and to emotional suggestion. Accordingly, great political decisions do not represent a general will, resulting from clear thought and reason. They are more likely to result from a confusion of impulses, inferences, habits, and prejudices.[11]

In spite of these conclusions Wallas remains at heart both a democrat and a rationalist. Democracy in practice may be pretty bad, but at least it is better than government by an irresponsible dictator or oligarchy, and the one or the few are apt to be as irrational as the many. Moreover, Wallas is optimistic enough to think that mankind, though normally irrational, may be trained or educated to act more or less rationally. In fact much of Wallas' work is concerned with discovering within the democratic framework effective methods of substituting rational control of social processes for the unreasoning group action of the herd. In like manner we find Lippmann lauding such American institutions as the League of Women Voters which attempts to lay before its members an impartial survey of political facts as an antidote to the irrational propaganda employed by all the major political parties.

Far closer to the etatist position are the conclusions of William McDougall (1871–1938), the Anglo-American author of *Social Psychology* and *The Group Mind*. McDougall, like Wallas, starts with an attack upon the theory that man's social and political actions are based to any large extent upon reason. He attacks both the abstract rationalism of the idealist school and the rational hedonism of the utilitarian school. It is not true, as the idealists claim, that society and the state are built upon reason, or that man's "practical reason" has given him the moral code to which he seeks, however imperfectly, to conform. It is not true

that man's rational interpretation of the good has created his social and
political machinery. It is not true that man normally does what his
reason tells him he ought to do. The idealists (Kant and his school)
were wrong and the utilitarians were right in claiming that man's activity is motivated much more by his passions and desires than by reason.

The utilitarians in turn were wrong in supposing that these passions
and desires were based upon logical or rational principles. The utilitarians supposed that man is motivated by rational self-interest. According to them man always seeks to secure for himself the maximum of
pleasure and the minimum of pain. Closely related to this view is the
doctrine of the classical economists that in his business transactions man
intelligently seeks his own advantage — buying in the cheapest and selling in the dearest market. According to McDougall, all these basic
assumptions are wrong. Man is indeed dominated by his passions and
desires, but these passions and desires are seldom rational. Man frequently does things which any reasoning shows are not to his best interests. Man frequently and voluntarily does things which cause him pain
rather than pleasure, as may be seen by observing persons dominated by
the paternal or maternal instinct. It is false to say that the average
man is always rational enough to buy or even to try to buy in the cheapest and sell in the dearest market.

> Mankind is only a little bit reasonable and is to a very great extent unin-
> telligently moved in quite unreasonable ways. The economists neglected
> to take account of the suggestibility of men which renders the art of the
> advertiser, of the pushing of goods generally so profitable and effective.
> Only on taking this character of men into account can we understand such
> facts as that sewing machines which might be sold at a fair profit for £5
> find a large sale at £12, while equally good ones are sold in the same market
> at less than half the price.[12]

No, says McDougall, man is motivated neither by abstract rationalism
nor by rational hedonism. A few of his acts may be dominated by
reason, but for the most part man is the slave of a few primary irrational
emotions and a certain number of basic irrational instincts. McDougall
is a firm believer in physical evolution and argues that all the human
emotions and instincts are but developments of similar emotions and
instincts to be found among the higher animals. Man, to him, is a
creature that has "been evolved from the animal world, whose nature
bears so many marks of this animal origin and whose principal springs
of activity are essentially similar to those of the higher animals." [13]

McDougall insists that the number of basic or primary emotions is very small, and claims that most of the human emotions of which we so frequently talk are really compounds or derivatives of these few basic emotions. After a careful psychological analysis he discovers that there are only seven basic emotions — fear, disgust, wonder, anger, subjection or humility, elation, and tenderness. All the other so-called emotions are really compound and derivative. Thus, for example, the feeling of awe is really a compound of subjection and fear. It is interesting to note that to McDougall such feelings as love, hate, happiness, sorrow, envy, resentment are compound and derivative rather than primary. Hence, if his analysis be true of social and political action, none of these feelings can be regarded as the true and ultimate bases.

To McDougall the seven primary emotions are extremely important, but even more important are the fundamental instincts of mankind. In his psychological system an instinct is an innate tendency to *act* in a certain way, while a primary emotion is an innate tendency to *feel* in a certain way. To McDougall these innate tendencies to act in a certain way are just as basic and fundamental as the innate tendencies to feel in a certain way. Some of the primary instincts are closely associated with the primary emotions. Thus the instinct to flee from danger is closely associated with the emotion of fear; the instinct of repulsion with the emotion of disgust. But it is not true that the emotion causes the instinct. Their relation is merely that of association; both are products of a long line of evolution. When a man suddenly confronts danger, he has the emotion of fear and the instinct to run away, and so on. Moreover, there are more instincts than there are primary emotions, and some of these extra instincts have aided in the development of the derived or secondary emotions.

McDougall has no doubt whatever that mankind does possess a certain number of fundamental instincts.

> The human mind has certain innate or inherited tendencies which are the essential springs or motive powers of all thought, whether individual or collective, and are the bases from which the character and will of individuals and of nations are gradually developed....[14]
>
> All agree that man has been evolved from prehuman ancestors whose lives were dominated by instincts, but some hold that as Man's intelligence and reasoning powers developed his instincts atrophied until now in civilized man instinct persists only as troublesome vestiges of his prehuman state.... Others assign them a more prominent place in the constitution of the human mind; for they see that intelligence as it increased with the evolution of the higher animals and of man did not supplant and so lead to the atrophy of the instincts but rather controlled and modified their operation.[15]

McDougall himself goes even further than this and insists that man, even modern man, "has at least as many instincts as any of the animals,' and that even with civilized man these instincts

> play a leading part in the determination of human conduct and mental proc-
> ess.[16] [With man as with animals,] some sense impression or combination of
> sense impressions excites some perfectly definite behavior, some movement or
> train of movements, which is the same in all individuals of the same species and
> on all similar occasions. And in general the behavior so occasioned is of a kind
> either to promote the welfare of the individual animal or of the community
> to which he belongs, or to secure the perpetuation of the species.[17]

McDougall goes on to tabulate an elaborate list of the fundamental instincts in man and attempts to show how they motivate most human actions, both individual and collective. To him, the primary instincts are: (1) the instinct of flight when confronted with danger; (2) the instinct of repulsion when confronted with some disagreeable object; (3) the instinct of curiosity when confronted with something new; (4) the instinct of pugnacity or the tendency to fight to overcome obstacles; (5) the instinct of self-abasement or subjection when the individual confronts another individual seemingly more powerful; (6) the instinct of self-assertion or self-display when the individual associates with persons supposedly his equals; (7) the parental instinct, i.e., the paternal and maternal instincts; (8) the sexual instinct, the instinct to reproduce oneself; (9) the gregarious instinct, the tendency of men to live in groups; (10) the instinct of acquisition or the tendency to collect and hoard various objects; (11) the constructive instinct, the tendency to make things, "from a mud pie to a metaphysical system or a code of laws."

In addition to these eleven specific instincts, McDougall believes there are also five general or non-specific "innate tendencies." One of these is sympathy, meaning the tendency to experience certain feelings and emotions "when and because we observe in other persons the expression of that feeling or emotion." The second is suggestibility, the tendency of mankind to act on suggestions from outside sources — the acceptance with conviction of communicated propositions even in the absence of logically adequate grounds for their acceptance. The third is the tendency to imitate or the copying by one individual of the actions and body movements of another. The fourth is the tendency to play. The fifth is the tendency to form habits, "the tendency for every process to be repeated more readily in virtue of its previous occurrence and in proportion to the frequency of its previous repetitions." [18]

McDougall insists that his primary emotions and his primary instincts and innate tendencies were the essential factors and the only essential factors in the development of social and political institutions.   In this development intellect and reason, whether conscious or unconscious, played a very insignificant role.   To him reason has usually had a pernicious and destructive effect upon social organization.   Large powerful and stable communities have evolved under the blind workings of the reproductive and parental instincts.   When man begins to act rationally, to question whether it is "wise" and to his advantage to encumber himself with a wife and children, social and political decay have set in.   "A weakening of the social sanctions of the parental and reproductive instincts by developing intelligence has played a great part in the destruction of some of the most brilliant and powerful societies of the past.   Notably those of ancient Greece and Rome." [19]

In like manner, McDougall admits that many manifestations of the fighting or pugnacious instinct are completely irrational.   Among most primitive peoples intertribal warfare serves little or no rational purpose. "No material benefits are sought, a few heads and sometimes a slave or two are the only trophies gained." [20]   The same is largely true of most civilized peoples.

> The history of Christendom is largely the history of devastating wars from which few individuals or societies have reaped any immediate benefit and in the causation of which the instinct of pugnacity of the rulers or of the masses of the people has played a leading part.[21]

But this fighting instinct, though irrational, has had beneficial results for mankind.   In Borneo there are some tribes which are peaceful, others more or less warlike, others extremely warlike.

> It might be supposed that the peaceful people would be found to be superior in moral qualities to their more warlike neighbors, but the contrary is the case. In almost all respects the advantage lies within the warlike tribes.   Their houses are better built, larger and cleaner; their domestic morality is superior; they are physically and mentally more active and in general are more trustworthy.   Above all their social organization is firmer and more efficient. Each man identifies himself with the whole community and loyally performs the social duties laid upon him.[22]

A similar situation is evident amongst the civilized peoples.   India and China which are more or less pacifistically inclined have shown less social progress than the European peoples who are notoriously pugnacious.[23]   In fact all through history the operation of the irrational fighting instinct, "far from being wholly injurious, has been one of the essential factors in the evolution of the higher forms of social organization and in fact of those specifically social qualities of man, the high development of which is an essential condition of the higher social life." [24] In 1908, McDougall was worried by the fact that the European peoples were losing their instinct for pugnacity, since pacifism "would bring to an end what has been an important, probably the most important factor of progressive evolution of human nature, namely the selection of the fit and the extermination of the unfit (amongst both individuals and societies) resulting from their conflicts with one another." [25]

The same defense of irrationalism is witnessed by McDougall's remarks upon the subject of religion. McDougall believes that most dogmas of orthodox religion are absurd. Most of the dogmas are the result of the blind operation of the emotions of reverence and awe combined with a ridiculously false interpretation of social phenomena. Nevertheless

> the strength of the social sanctions derived from the belief in the supernatural powers ... was a main condition of the strength and stability of society; and no society has been able to survive in any severe and prolonged conflict of societies without some effective system of such sanctions. . . . In the main these societies which have been most stable and capable of enduring have been least tolerant of the spirit of inquiry; on the other hand the flourishing of scepticism has been too often the forerunner of social decay, as in ancient Rome. . . . At the present time it may seem that in one small quarter of the world, namely Western Europe, society has achieved an organization so intrinsically stable that it may with impunity tolerate the flourishing of the spirit of inquiry and give free rein to the impulse of curiosity. But to assume this to be the case would be rather rash.[26]

McDougall himself is a firm believer in natural as opposed to supernatural causation, but he is equally convinced that the general rejection of the doctrine of supernatural causation might well lead to the collapse of all our social and political institutions.

It is interesting to note that upon the basis of his irrationalism McDougall proceeds to erect a system of political philosophy which bears strong family resemblance to that of the thoroughgoing etatists, in spite of his protest to the contrary. He is an eloquent advocate of the need for aristocratic leadership of and control over the group.

The study of psychology convinces McDougall that the mental processes of the adult man are partly the result of the working of his own irrational emotions and instincts, but that they are also in large measure the result of "the moulding influence exerted by the social environment." [27] "Each man is an individual only in an incomplete sense; he is but a unit in a vast system of vital and spiritual forces which are expressing themselves in the form of human societies and working towards ends which no man can foresee." [28]   When a man thinks that he is reasoning logically, using nothing save his own intellect, he is really using the thought patterns which have been laid down by the group to which he belongs.   These thought patterns are the product of an immensely long line of evolution, are patterns which have been produced by the mental activities of countless generations and are but very little modified by the members of society living at any one time.   "Society consists of the dead as well as the living and the part of the living in determining its life is but insignificant as compared with the part of the dead." [29]

Not only is the mental life of the individual conditioned consciously or unconsciously by the group of which he is a member, but so also are his conduct and the moral standard by which he judges his own conduct and that of his neighbors.   In fact, the group in socializing man has also moralized him.   Man is naturally "a creature in which the non-moral and purely egoistic tendencies are much stronger than altruistic tendencies." [30]   Under the pressure of the group, man has developed a behavior pattern which is both moral and more or less altruistic.   What we call our conscience is largely the result of the group working upon our minds. The group spirit is

> the principal if not the sole factor which raises a man's conduct above the plane of pure egotism, leads him to think and care and work for others as well as himself.[31]   It is only by participation in the life of society that any man can realize his higher potentialities.   Society has ideals and aims and traditions loftier than any principles of conduct the individual can form for himself unaided, and only by the further evolution of organized society can man be raised to higher levels....[32]
>
> The collective actions of the well organized group become truly volitional actions expressive of a degree of intelligence and morality much higher than that of the average member of the group, and even, by reason of exultation of emotion and organized co-operation in deliberation, above that of its highest members.[33]

McDougall rejects Hegel's doctrine of the World Spirit, but he does believe in the Hegelian doctrine of the group mind.

> The aggregate which is a society has in virtue of its past history positive qualities which it does not derive from the units which compose it at any one time, and in virtue of these qualities it acts upon its units in a manner very different from that in which the units interact with each other....[34]
>
> A society when it enjoys a long life and becomes highly organized acquires a structure and qualities which are largely independent of the qualities of the individuals who enter into its composition and take part for a brief time in its life.   It becomes an organized system of forces which has a life of its

own, a power of moulding all its component individuals and a power of perpetuating itself as a self-identical system, subject only to slow and gradual change.[35]

McDougall is such a believer in the excellence of group life that he urges that each person should be a member of several groups — one local, one occupational, and at least one recreational — a parallel to Hegel's advocacy of "corporations." But McDougall, like Hegel, declares that the supreme group, which coordinates and controls all the other groups, must be the national state. The national state is the group at the top of the hierarchy of other groups and also the great organization which embraces all other organizations.

Not only does McDougall's irrationalism lead him to a worship of the national state; it also leads him to advocate aristocratic leadership and control of the state, the other distinguishing feature of the etatist political philosophy. McDougall arrives at his aristocratic authoritarianism by distinguishing between the actions of the "well-organized group" and the actions of the mob or crowd. Whereas the actions of the "well-organized group" are more intelligent and more moral than those of the average member of the group, the actions of the simple crowd, being merely impulsive or instinctive, imply "a degree of intelligence and morality far inferior to that of the individual member of the crowd." [36] Now the chief difference between the crowd and the "well-organized group" is that in the latter "while the common end of collective action is willed by all, the choice of means is left to those best qualified and in the best position for deliberation and choice." [37] Pure democracy, to McDougall is equivalent to mob rule; for the state to be a "well-organized group" it must be controlled by the "better minds" of the community. It is indicative of McDougall's leaning towards authoritarianism that he cites the modern army as an always perfect example of a "well-organized group."

> Deliberation and choice of means are carried out by the commander in chief and his staff, the persons who have shown themselves the best able to execute this part of the army task. But ... the private soldier in the ranks remains a free agent performing truly volitional actions. ... He wills the common end, and believing that the choice of means to an end is best effected by the appropriate part of the whole organization, he accepts the means chosen, makes of them his proximate end, and wills them.[38]

Again and again McDougall returns to a defense of the aristocratic principle in government.

To follow and obey a leader is the simplest, most rudimentary fashion in which the crowd's actions may become more effective, consistent, controlled. Not any one can be a leader, exceptional qualities are necessary.... If a people is to become a nation it must be capable of producing personalities who will play the part of leaders.[39]

The measurement of a great number of skulls of different races

has shown that any large collection of skulls from one of the peoples who have formed a progressive nation invariably contains a certain small number of skulls of markedly superior capacity... while any similar number of skulls from one of the unprogressive peoples like the negro differs not so much in the smaller average size of the brain as in the greater uniformity of size, that is to say the absence of individuals of exceptionally large brains....[40]

Let us imagine the fifty leading minds in each great department of activity suddenly removed from among us. Clearly we should be reduced to intellectual, moral, aesthetic chaos and nullity in a very short time.[41]

Incidentally McDougall agrees with the Nazi ideologists not only in claiming that certain individuals are greater, finer, and more intelligent than other individuals, but also in asserting that certain races are inherently superior to others and always will be so. It is only right, therefore, that certain races, such as the white races, and especially the Nordic race, should be "the leaders" of the inferior races, and especially of the Negro race. Moreover, while cross-breeding between closely related races results in the advancement of civilization, cross-breeding between unrelated races, especially between superior and inferior races, has disastrous results.

IRRATIONALISM AND SOCIAL PSYCHOLOGY
IN FRANCE AND ITALY

The study of social psychology was not confined to England and America; it also attracted widespread attention on the continent of Europe. Numerous works on this subject appeared in Germany and elsewhere, but for some curious reason the most outstanding contributions in the field were made in France and Italy. Especially notable were the works of Tarde, Durkheim, and Le Bon. In the writings of these men there is a strong emphasis upon the irrational element in human thought and conduct, and while none of these authors are out and out etatists, their conclusions give strong moral support to the etatist cause.

Gabriel Tarde (1843–1904), like the other social psychologists, stressed the importance of the background of group life in interpreting individual thought and action. Such thought and action is nearly always determined, not by individual reason or individual valuation, but by the mental interaction of the various members of the group to which the individual belongs. To Tarde nearly all phases of human behavior are motivated by three innate tendencies or instincts, the tendencies of imitation, of opposition, and of adaptation. Especial importance is attached to the imitative instinct, and in imitation Tarde includes both imitation proper and what McDougall calls suggestibility. Tarde admits that occasionally man is capable of original or inventive thought and action, which may or may not be based upon reason; but he is certain that the vast majority of our thoughts and actions are mere repetitions or imitations of the thoughts and actions of others. In many cases, moreover, this imitation has no logical or rational basis. "In general extra logical influences . . . interfere in the choice of the examples to be followed and often . . . the poorest innovations — from the point of view of logic — are often selected because of their place or even the date of their birth." [42]   To Tarde imitation is the basis of all social and political institutions; in fact, as he frequently remarks, "Society is imitation." Tarde is far from being a radical etatist. He ridiculed the ideas of the group mind and the national mind, so dear to the etatist thinkers, but his emphasis upon the group as shaping the thoughts and acts of the individual was warmly welcomed by the etatist philosophers. They also welcomed Tarde's suggestion that new thoughts and new inventions are apt to start with the aristocracy and then spread by imitation to the common herd.

Émile Durkheim (1858–1917) differs radically from Tarde in many important respects, but he agrees with Tarde in claiming that most of man's thoughts and acts are of non-rational origin and are imposed on him by the group or society to which he belongs. When we reason, or think we reason, we use such concepts as time or space or force, but all such concepts are not the creation of the individual mind, but have, without our knowing it, been imposed upon us by the group. Unlike Tarde, Durkheim is a great believer in the real existence of "collective consciousness," or the group mind, which differs radically from the minds of the individuals which compose the group. This group mind has ideas of its own, called by Durkheim "collective representations" which exist outside the individual and come to his mind as something exterior in the form of certain moral, legal, and logical rules. These "collective representations" are endowed with a power of coercion which allows them to impose themselves upon the individual irrespective

of the individual's own desires.   To Durkheim "collective consciousness is the highest form of psychic life. . . . Being placed outside of and
above individual and local contingencies it sees things in their permanent and essential aspects. . . . Society sees better than individuals." [43]
Durkheim himself was more interested in the smaller regional and occupational groups (Hegel's corporations) than he was in the larger groups,
such as the state, and argued for the restoration of the ancient occupational associations as definitely recognized public institutions.   Economic life was considered too specialized to be handled directly by the
state with any chance of success.   The activities of any given profession
should be regulated by special guilds or corporations consisting of persons intimately acquainted with its functions and needs.   Nevertheless
Durkheim admitted that it was necessary for the state to serve as the
supreme arbiter of the corporations, regulating and controlling their
interactions.   He was an advocate of what is now known in Italy as the
corporative state.

Gustave Le Bon (1841–1931) the third member of this group shows
many interesting points of agreement and of disagreement with Durkheim.   With Durkheim and the other social psychologists, Le Bon emphasizes the fact that man is not a logical animal.   Man is apt to believe the most illogical and unreasonable things if they correspond to his
emotions and feelings.   Moreover, most men find it impossible to live
without many illogical and absurd beliefs.   Most religious doctrines are
ridiculous, but it is useless to try to sweep them away.   A certain God
or a certain form of religion may be overthrown, but before long a new
form of God and a new set of dogmas, equally irrational, will inevitably
arise.   However, man's beliefs, though irrational, have played an
enormous part in moulding human history, and any radical modification of these beliefs is bound to be followed by a great change in the
whole social and political life of the people concerned.

Le Bon, like Durkheim, believes in the existence of a group mind
distinct from the minds of the individuals composing the group.   In
contrast with Durkheim, however, who thought that the group mind was
better than the individual mind, Le Bon teaches that the group mind
tends to a lower moral and intellectual level than the individual mind.
Working by himself, a man may occasionally act and think rationally,
but a group or a crowd always acts and thinks irrationally.   The group
mind is dominated by instinctive and subconscious emotions rather than
by conscious thought.   The group mind, moreover, is easily influenced
by suggestion.   As a result, the group or crowd is characterized by

emotional instability, by impatience, by intolerance, and by a sense of irresponsibility. McDougall distinguishes between well-organized groups, which are good, and unorganized groups, which are bad. To Le Bon all groups tend to be bad, though some are worse than others. Because of his attitude towards the group and the group mind, Le Bon tends to stress the need of individualism as opposed to collectivism or socialism. Far more important from the point of etatist tradition is the fact that Le Bon constantly preaches the need for authoritarian control by the select few — the true aristocrats of the country. To Le Bon democracy is the rule of the turbulent crowd. For civilization to advance, the crowd must be curbed, controlled, regulated by a small rational minority.

The doctrines of Tarde, of Durkheim, of Le Bon played an important part in the shaping, or rather in the reshaping, of the etatist tradition. But the influence which these men exerted was largely indirect. Far more important and far more direct was the influence of the writings of two unique personalities, the French political writer, Georges Sorel, and the Italian sociologist, Vilfredo Pareto.

Georges Sorel (1847–1922) played a significant but very peculiar role in the development of political philosophy. Sorel was a socialist, but his greatest influence was exerted upon political groups which violently assailed the whole foundations of socialism. Sorel was not only a socialist, but also a revolutionary socialist, yet many of his doctrines were hailed with delight by the French monarchists who wished to restore the Bourbons and the divine right of kings. These opinions were equally important in shaping the opinions of the Fascists in Italy and of the Nazis in Germany.

As might be imagined, Sorel's socialism was of a very peculiar sort. Most socialists have been enthusiastic defenders of extreme democracy. Sorel violently attacked democracy and all its works. He believed in autocratic control or dictatorship, though his dictatorship was to lie in the hands, not of the old effete aristocracy, but with a small, select group from the proletariat. Most socialists have been believers in an omnipotent state, which not only controls but also operates the means of production. Sorel, at least during his earlier years, disliked the state. The state, to him, has usually been the instrument of capitalist operation and was to be regarded with distrust. The means of production was not to be owned by the state, but directly by the workers organized in syndicates or trade unions. In England and in America, at any rate,

most socialists, as opposed to communists, have advocated socialization by evolution, not revolution, by political, rather than by "direct,"
action.   Sorel, on the other hand, was the apostle of violence, of revolution, of socialization through the general strike rather than through
control of the voting booths.   Sorel, in short, was not a socialist in the
ordinary sense of the word, but a believer in syndicalism, a movement
which has been ably summarized by Coker as follows: "Syndicalism
holds that the workers alone must control the conditions under which
they work and live; the social changes they need can be achieved only
by their own efforts, by direct action in their own associations, and
through means suited to their peculiar needs." [44]

But though Sorel was a syndicalist, it would be a great mistake to
identify Sorel and syndicalism too closely.   Sorel was an acute observer
rather than an active participant in the syndicalist movement.   Moreover, strange though it may seem, his syndicalist conclusions are the
least important phase of his philosophy.   Sorel's main interest was
advocating irrationalism and romantic heroism in political life, and to
these two doctrines his other ideas are subordinated.   For a while
Sorel saw in syndicalism the finest embodiment of irrationalism and
romantic heroism, and hence preached syndicalism.   But he was prepared to admit that he might be mistaken on this point; that irrationalism and romantic heroism might be better expressed in some other
political creed, in which case he was perfectly willing to change from
syndicalism to the new ideology.   Late in life he switched from pure
syndicalism, with its anarchic dislike of a sovereign political unit, to
bolshevism, with its ideology of an omnipotent and despotic state.   At
other times he flirted with the French revolutionary monarchists.   It
is highly probable that, had he lived, Sorel would have been a passionate
defender of Fascism and Naziism.   It is certain that the Fascist and
Nazi leaders, discarding Sorel's non-essential syndicalism, have been
deeply influenced by his interpretation of irrationalism and romantic
heroism.

At the basis of Sorel's political philosophy were the theories of
knowledge expounded by James, Bergson, and Nietzsche.   He was
convinced that reason or logic would never give us an insight into reality.
With Bergson he argued that truth can only be ascertained by spiritual
insight or intuition.   In common with most of the social psychologists,
Sorel insisted that man's actions were only to a slight extent influenced
by his reasoning, most human actions being motivated by irrational
feelings, prejudices, sentiments.   But whereas many of the social psy-

chologists regarded man's irrational nature with sorrow, Sorel regarded man's irrationality as his chief redeeming feature. As long as man is motivated by reason, or rational self-interest, man is selfish and ego- istic. It is only when man is dominated by irrational impulses that he is capable of good or great or heroic actions. What we call heroic actions are heroic largely because they are foolish, certainly from the point of view of calculating logic. This is true both of men individually and also of man collectively. In opposition to those who think that every truth is useful and every superstition harmful, Sorel stresses the point that this belief is false. History shows us that the widespread acceptance of a truth may have disastrous social consequences, while the blind acceptance of an irrational dogma may be and frequently has been of the greatest benefit to mankind. These considerations led Sorel to formulate his most famous doctrine, the doctrine of the *social myth*.

A myth, to Sorel, is "a body of images capable of evoking sentiment instinctively." Every effective social movement known to history has been the result of the widespread acceptance of a myth. The fact that many of these myths were and are absurd is of no consequence whatever. Largely because they are irrational they supply an emotional drive that gives cohesion to a group and enables it to undertake positive action. The early Christians expected the immediate return of Christ and the inauguration of the kingdom of the saints at any moment. This doc- trine was ridiculous, but it gave the Christians a driving power which enabled them to Christianize Europe. The hopes which Luther and Calvin formed of the religious exaltation of Europe were vain dreams, but these vain dreams brought about important and permanent changes in both church and state. The eighteenth century ideals of equality and liberty were irrational, yet these doctrines radically transformed the whole course of history. As in the past, so in the present. If we wish to change or improve the world, we must invent a new myth capa- ble of inspiring mankind to heroic action.

To Sorel, the best myth for the workers to adopt was the myth of the general strike, the belief that the millennium would arrive when the proletariat should arise and by a swift universal strike overthrow all the established organs of government. In point of fact the myth of the general strike had very little effect upon subsequent political thought. Even among the proletariat it met with only a feeble response. What is of real importance is that Sorel's doctrine of the existence and value of myths was taken over by the Fascists and Nazis and made an integral part of their philosophy. Thus we find that one of the most important expositions of Nazi ideology is Rosenberg's *The Myth of the Twentieth Century*, which is a reinterpretation of Sorel's doctrine of myths in the light of Hitlerism. We find Mussolini making use of the following words: "We have created our myth. The myth is a faith, it is passion. It is not necessary that it shall be a reality. It is a reality by the fact that it is a goad, a hope, a faith, that it is courage. Our myth is the Nation, our myth is the greatness of the Nation!" [45]

Sorel's irrationalism made him accept and reinterpret Nietzsche's doctrine of the artificial basis of all moral standards. Morality is not an eternally valid code of right and wrong to be known by reason or revelation or conscience. Every moral code is merely a standard created by a group to protect its own interests, to aid it in the struggle for survival or in dominating other groups. No group can hope to be successful unless it imposes a stern discipline upon its members; this discipline takes the form of a code of morals. Sorel was keenly interested in moral problems, but he rejected the old traditional code of morality as being the product of a group of which he disapproved — bourgeois society dominated by capitalistic ideals. He demanded that the workers realize they formed a group apart and that they should construct for themselves a new morality and a new code of morals and no longer rely upon traditional morality.

This new morality, which the working classes must create to protect their interests as a group, must discard many of the moral maxims of the past. The new morality must reject the sentimental humanitarianism of the old morality. The new morality must be based upon the class war and it must be realized that anything which weakens the workers as a group is *ipso facto* immoral. Hence pity, kindliness, gratitude of workers towards employers, must be rejected. The new morality demands that the workers learn to bite the hand which feeds them. Only thus can the workers learn group solidarity, which is the basis of group discipline, the basis of true morality. The new morality demands that the workers learn the art of violence, of sabotage, of confiscation. The new morality teaches the workers how to expel the capitalist from the productive domain and how to seize and operate for their own advantage the workshops created by capitalism. The sentimental humanitarianism of the traditional morality is really based upon middle class cowardice and must be despised and not revered.

It is interesting to see how Sorel's doctrine of the new morality was taken over and transformed by the apostles of Fascism and Naziism.

Both historically and logically the ethics of proletarian violence advocated by Sorel led to the ethics of etatist violence advocated by Mussolini and Hitler. As Sorel himself said, "Proletarian violence ... seems to be the only means by which the European nations, at present stupified by humanitarianism, can recover their former energy. ... Everything can be saved if the proletariat by their use of violence manage to re-establish the division into classes and so restore to the middle class something of its former energy." [46] Sorel, to be sure, wished to quicken the middle classes into energetic action only that they might be the more quickly destroyed. The Fascists and Nazis transformed Sorel's doctrine into the notion that the middle classes, rejecting their old sentimental humanitarianism, might be quickened into energetic and violent action in order that they might not be destroyed. The revolutionary syndicalism of post-war Italy and the threat of communist revolution in depression-ridden Germany made the Italian and German middle and lower middle classes flock to the banners of the Fascist and Nazi leaders, who preached that proletariat violence must be met by middle class violence, and that the middle classes must strike first — and hard.

Of especial significance is the fact that most of the Fascist and Nazi leaders have adopted an attitude similar to that of Sorel towards the problems of morals. With Sorel, they agree that a code of morals is merely the discipline which a group in its struggle for power imposes upon its members. With Sorel, they agree that the only real standard of good and bad is whether or not the action in question tends to increase the power and prestige of the group. With Sorel, they agree that the traditional morality with its sentimental humanitarianism must be discarded in favor of a new, vigorous, and realistic morality. They disagree with Sorel only in proclaiming that the all-important group is not the proletariat but the nation-state. To the Fascists and the Nazis, violence, confiscation of alien property, the breach of solemnly made treaties, and aggressive warfare are perfectly moral if these actions can be shown to add to the power and prestige of nation-states which undertake them.

The third and last feature of the Sorelian political philosophy is the idea that what is most needed by mankind is heroism, and that heroism consists, not in thinking or talking, but in acting. As mere logic or reason gets us nowhere, the persons who devote themselves to thinking and theorizing are to be despised. Sorel admits that talking and talkers have a place in human affairs, but only in so far as eloquence leads men to action. The important social myths have been spread by talking, but it should never be forgotten that these myths, in so far as they have value, "are not descriptions of things, but expressions of a determination to act." [47]   Sorel assailed democracy and parliamentary or representative institutions because all such institutions are much more suited to talking than to acting.   To Sorel, as to Carlyle, parliamentary discussion is largely idle chatter and parliamentary assemblies time-wasting debating clubs.   But whereas Carlyle wished to preserve parliamentary institutions in an attenuated form, Sorel wished to destroy them altogether, thereby assuming an attitude which the Fascists and Nazis could adopt with little or no modification.

If civilization is to be saved, mankind must be inspired, not only to action, but to heroic action.   Men

> must be convinced that the work to which they are devoting themselves is a serious, formidable, and sublime work.   It is only on this condition that they will be able to bear the innumerable sacrifices imposed on them by a propaganda which can procure them neither honors, profits, nor even immediate intellectual satisfaction.[48]   There would never have been great acts of heroism in war if each soldier, while acting as a hero, yet at the same time claimed to receive a reward appropriate to his deserts.   When a column is sent to an assault the men at the head know that they are sent to their death and that the glory of victory will be for those passing over their dead bodies to enter the enemy's position.   However, they do not reflect on this injustice, but march forward.[49]

Heroic action necessarily implies the willingness to live dangerously, to take risks, to play for gigantic stakes, knowing, but not caring, that at any moment all may be lost.   True heroes seek out the hazardous in their enterprises.   Sorel despised the bourgeois, democratic, liberal movement because the members of this movement, the typical "Babbitts" (as we should say), always wish to play safe.   Such persons are afraid of the new, the unknown, of taking risks.   Economically they avoid farseeing schemes which involve the possibility of financial loss; politically they are terrified of any change which might disturb the fixed balance of political forces in the country.   Because of this cowardice on the part of the middle class liberals, they can be terrified into giving up most of their rights by a resolute minority which is willing to take risks.   In fact, social and political advances in the past have usually been accomplished by the granting of rights by the bourgeoisie in abject fear as an insurance against violence or revolution.

> Experience shows that the middle classes allow themselves to be plundered quite easily, provided that a little pressure is brought to bear, and that they

> are intimidated by the fear of revolution; that party will possess the future which can most skillfully manipulate the spectre of revolution. . . .[50]
>
> Syndicalist leaders teach the workers that it is not at all a question of demanding favors, but that they must profit by middle class cowardice to impose the will of the proletariat.[51]

Middle class cowardice very much resembles the cowardice of the English Liberal Party which constantly proclaims its absolute confidence in arbitration between nations. Arbitration nearly always gives disastrous results for England. Many Englishmen believe that by humiliating their country they will arouse more sympathy towards themselves. This supposition is not borne out by the facts. "But these worthy progressives prefer to pay or even to compromise the future of their country rather than face the horrors of war." [52] In other words, success is bound to come to the resolute, heroic minority who know what they want and have the will to act when the opportunity comes.

Sorel preached his doctrine of heroic action, of getting what you want by threats, to the members of the French proletariat. The members of the French proletariat paid him only scant heed, but his sermons found a warm response in the breasts of the Fascist and Nazi leaders. Mussolini and Hitler, at the head of a resolute minority willing to risk all, not only have made themselves the masters of their own countries, but also have been able to "profit by middle class cowardice" and to impose the will of the dictators upon a large portion of the civilized world. England is no longer governed by the Liberal Party, but in 1938 Hitler found "the worthy Conservatives prefer to pay or even to compromise the future of their country rather than face the horrors of war."

Sorel's doctrine of the need for heroic action made him reject the optimism adopted by so many of the earlier political philosophers. Optimism, the belief that men and conditions are fundamentally good in spite of certain imperfections, is incompatible with the instinctive feelings of the hero, for the hero wishes to transform everything around him. The hero feels and must feel (like the early Christian) that ordinarily mankind left to itself is wicked, but that with heroic action it can be saved. The hero feels and must feel that present-day social, political, and economic conditions are horrible, that to reform them needs gigantic effort and the overcoming of many obstacles; but the hero welcomes gigantic efforts; he is thrilled, not discouraged, by the prospect of obstacles to overcome.

Along with optimism, Sorel also rejected the theory of inevitable progress. Formulated by Kant and Fichte, developed by Hegel, the doctrine of inevitable progress had been taken over by many socialists and occupied a central position in the Marxist political creed. To Sorel, however, the belief in romantic heroism seemed inconsistent with the belief that progress is continuous and inevitable. If we believe that progress is inevitable, we are content to float along with the tide; we are sure that we improve whether we make a violent effort to do so or not. Belief in inevitable progress means paralysis of the will — the heroic will to act and to create. Sorel agreed with Bergson that man is free and not determined; that man may be influenced but not controlled by his racial, geographic, or economic background. Man being free, man's future cannot be determined nor even scientifically forecast. Man not only is but must be made to feel free to carve out his own future. The hero is a genuine creator, not merely a pawn moved by some mysterious power forcing him and his fellow beings ever upwards and onwards. Progress is possible, but it is not certain. It is not even probable unless man be reawakened to the need for irrational but heroic action.

Even more important than Sorel in the transformation of the etatist tradition was his great friend, Vilfredo Pareto (1848–1923), called by many the morning star of the Fascist movement, by others the Karl Marx of Fascism, as his writings have been accepted with almost as much reverence by the Fascists as the writings of Marx have been accepted by the socialists and communists. We know that Mussolini was strongly influenced by Pareto and claims to have studied under him. It was Pareto who converted Mussolini from socialism; it was Pareto's doctrine of the elite and the circulation of the elite which paved the way for the Fascist theory of the totalitarian state.

Pareto's mother was a French woman, and he himself was born in France, but his father was an Italian of a distinguished bourgeois family which had been ennobled by Napoleon, and most of Pareto's early life was spent in Italy. During the latter part of his career, Pareto held the post of Professor of Economics and Sociology at the University of Lausanne in Switzerland. When Mussolini came into power, Pareto was offered the post of Italian delegate to the Disarmament Conference held under the auspices of the League of Nations, a post which he declined, but he did accept appointment as a member of the Italian Senate, and wrote several contributions for Mussolini's personally owned newspaper. His death in 1923 makes it impossible for us to know how he would have greeted the later developments of Fascism.

Pareto occupies a very peculiar position in political philosophy — a position which can best be described as that of a disillusioned rationalist and a disillusioned liberal. Unlike many of the other philosophical irrationalists, Pareto believed that ultimate truth, as far as it can be known at all, can never be known through instinct or intuition, but only by reason, or at least by rational or logical experimentation (differing thus from Hegel, who believed in logic minus experimentation). In later life, however, Pareto became convinced that the vast majority of human actions have very little to do with logical experimental motivations and that all social and political studies must be based upon the fact that human behavior is, by and large, completely irrational. In like manner, Pareto in his younger days was an ardent liberal and resigned from the service of the government of Italy because of the Italian government's departure from the orthodox liberal policy of *laissez faire* and free trade. In later years he became more and more disgusted with the weakness and corruption of the so-called liberal-democratic governments of Italy and France, and felt that European civilization could only be saved from destruction by having a new aristocracy seize power and rule over the stupid mob with an iron and relentless hand.

Pareto was the author of many books and articles, the most important being his great treatise on sociology, known in the English translation as *The Mind and Society*. In this work he deals with many different phases of economic, social, and political life, but all the phases of his thought are dominated by two central doctrines, the first being that men are irrational, the second that men are, always have been, and always will be, unequal in their capacities and potentialities.

Pareto's belief in man's irrationality came from a profound, though rather unsystematic, study of the motivations underlying human conduct. Pareto admitted that occasionally, very occasionally, human conduct is regulated by reason, but he pointed out that in many cases the stimulus to activity is not logic, but such factors as geographic environment and racial, historic, and economic background. More important still are the roles played by the two factors to which he gives the rather peculiar names of *residues* and *derivations*. By residues Pareto means what others (such as McDougall) call the basic instincts and emotions, or rather the manifestation of these basic instincts and emotions and sentiments, as witnessed in human actions. By derivations Pareto means the patterns of thought, the pseudo-rational "myths," ideas, and ideologies which most men think are rational, but which are really derived from the residues and which have no sense apart from them.   The derivations, to Pareto's mind, are instances of wishful thinking.

It is interesting to note that though Pareto places as much emphasis upon the basic instincts and emotions as does McDougall, the list of the basic instincts and emotions as given by the two writers differs very considerably, a sure sign that the social psychologists are still far from the establishment of their theories upon a strictly scientific basis. Pareto gives us a long and complicated list of fundamental residues, into the details of which it is unnecessary to go.   It is, however, important to observe that these residues are classified into six main groups, a classification that becomes very significant when we come to a consideration of Pareto's views on politics.   The first of these groups is "the tendency to form combinations," the instinctive tendency to combine things and thoughts into a group.   This tendency towards combination (McDougall would call it the instinct of construction) sometimes produces absurd notions, such as the association of certain numbers with good luck and bad luck; it sometimes produces a great scientific system; it is the tendency which produces the creative, progressive, inventive element in human affairs.   The second group Pareto calls the residue or tendency towards "the persistence of aggregates," the tendency to worship, defend, and protect the combinations which have been made by an earlier generation.   This tendency leads to religious and political conservatism, a resistance to the disintegration of old combinations and opposition to the formation of new ones.   Sometimes this tendency is based upon the rational protection of combinations (political institutions, scientific theories) which have proved useful.   At other times this same tendency leads to a fanatical faith that makes man ready to kill and be killed for his opinions, however grotesque these opinions may be and however disadvantageous they may be to the believer himself.

The third group of residues consists of a tendency to express sentiments by external acts, though these acts frequently have little or no logical relation with the sentiments or emotions which inspire them. A dog wagging its tail at the sight of its master is an example of this type of residue.   Another example is the action of human beings at a revival meeting when they howl and weep and dance and laugh because they imagine that they are in the presence of their God.   The fourth group of residues is the residues of gregariousness or sociability, the tendency in mankind to form groups, the desire of mankind to be like everyone else, the desire of men to impose their manners, mode of life, and beliefs on other people.   Also included in this group by Pareto is the feeling for hierarchical social position in which a man has a fixed place with reference to his fellow beings. The whole etatist philosophy is an example of the working out of the residues of sociability. The fifth group of residues consists of those tendencies which aim at the protection of the integrity of the individual — the tendencies to promote individualism as opposed to etatism. Every individual who is a member of a group has certain notions regarding his proper relations with other members of the group and with the group as a whole. When these relations are disturbed, he feels acute distress, and he tries either really or symbolically to restore the former equilibrium. The sixth and last group of residues consists of the various manifestations of the sexual instinct.

It will be noticed that the first and second and again the fourth and fifth groups of residues are more or less mutually contradictory. The first group, the tendency to change, to find and accept new combinations, is opposed by the tendency to preserve old combinations. The residues of sociability form a contrast to the residues aiming at the integrity of the individual. Nevertheless, Pareto feels that all the residues are to be found to some extent in every normal person. At the same time he stresses the fact that the strength or distribution of these residues in various individuals and in various groups is not the same. Some persons and some groups are more dominated by the residues of combination (desire for change); others by the residues leading to the persistence of aggregates (conservatism); and so on with the other groups. Even within a single community, in the course of time, through various circumstances, the domination of one or the other of the residual groups may greatly change. When this change occurs, the social and political organization of the community invariably changes its form.

Pareto believes that the residues, whether or not we are conscious of their existence, are the most important factors in the motivation of human conduct. Nevertheless the average man feels a hunger and thirst after reason, even though his actions are in reality completely irrational. As a result he invents all manner of pseudo-logical reasons to explain his own conduct. The pseudo-logical, the would-be rational myths and ideas in which men believe, are what Pareto calls the derivations. The residues, the basic emotions and instincts, disguise themselves as derivations or would-be rational beliefs and explanations. Men think that they are rational when they accept this or the other type of derivation or ideology, but in the majority of cases an ideology is accepted or rejected not so much because it is true or false, but because of its agreement or disagreement with their residues. To Pareto all the old liberal notions of democracy, justice, equality, freedom, progress, are merely non-logical derivations, and are just as fallacious as the crudest superstitions.

The derivations of Pareto correspond to, or at least include, what Sorel called the social myths. Like Sorel, Pareto stresses the fact that belief in non-logical derivations (or myths) frequently serves a very useful purpose. The acceptance only of rational truths might well lead to the disintegration and breakdown of society, while the belief in a non-logical or even absurd derivation may well have a stabilizing effect upon social institutions. There is, however, one difference between Sorel and Pareto. Sorel thought that myths are just as important and just as powerful as the basic instincts and emotions. Pareto denies this and insists that the instincts and emotions (his residues) are more stable, more constant, and more potent than most derivations. Nevertheless, Pareto admits that human history has been profoundly influenced by the derivations and even admits that the derivations may influence the residues of a people, or at least bring about the domination of certain residues at the expense of others.

Pareto believes that the ruling class of each country should make a profound study of the residues and derivations. By knowing which derivations are and which are not in accord with the residues, they can choose and promote (by propaganda) derivations which will find widespread acceptance. Thus the derivation of "the nation" or "the honor of the nation" is much more powerful and much more easily accepted than others, such as the general strike, because of its intimate association with such residues as the persistence of aggregates and sociability. By the wise use of such derivations the ruling class can keep its control and induce the masses to follow their leadership with a minimum of difficulty and with a minimum use of armed force.

Turning now from Pareto's irrationalism to his other basic doctrine, the belief in the inequality of human beings, we find that this doctrine is associated with two concepts to which Pareto devotes a great deal of attention. One of these is the concept of the elite. The other is the concept of the circulation of the elite. In examining the question of the elite, Pareto points out that mankind, far from being equal or uniform, shows an enormous amount of divergence. Some are stronger, others are weaker; some are wiser, others more stupid; some tend to be law-abiding, others are more or less criminally inclined; some have more others less, artistic, musical, and literary ability. As a result there are in every community special groups of persons outstanding for their ability in some particular line. Such groups Pareto calls groups of elite. Thus there is in every civilized community an artistic, a sporting, a scientific elite, and also a relatively small group of persons who dominate the political and economic forces of the country. In his detailed study of the elites, Pareto pays especial attention to this governing elite, which includes not only persons occupying the higher posts in the machinery of government, but also the powerful financiers and industrialists, who directly or indirectly exert an enormous influence upon governmental activity. Pareto would include in this elite the high ranking officers of the military forces, though in modern times such persons take an active part in governmental affairs only in times of crises.

Pareto is thoroughly convinced that each and every country is really dominated by an elite, however democratic its political organization may be in theory. As Sorokin, paraphrasing Pareto, puts it, "There never has been any social or political system in which equality or real democracy has been realized. What is styled democracy is rather plutocracy, the control of the governed principally through deceit, machinations, and combinations, and by demagogues, capitalists, hypocrites, and cynical persons." [53] The followers of Pareto, like many so-called radicals, claim that America, far from being a true democracy, is in large measure controlled by the "60 families," the representatives of the great industrial and financial interests, such as the Rockefellers and the Morgans. But Pareto would also have included in the American governing elite such rabble-rousers as Huey Long, Father Coughlin, and Dr. Townsend; such clever political manipulators as James Farley; and of course such shrewd masters of political technique as Presidents Theodore and Franklin Roosevelt. Pareto believes that there is a real biological difference between the elite and the masses. Pareto was not and did not claim to be an anthropologist. He ignored the problem as to whether one race or body type was superior to others (though it is probable that he did believe in such racial differentiation). It is certain, however, that he did believe that within each race there are certain groups which are innately and inherently superior, more intelligent than others. Generally, though not invariably, this group tends to climb to the top of the social, economic, and political pyramid. Thus, the followers of Pareto point with glee to the fact that intelligence tests in a large number of schools have shown that the average intelligence of the upper and middle class students is higher than that of the children of the poor.

In short, Pareto claims that at all times and at all places a community, whatever its nominal constitution, is dominated by a small group of elite But he also contends that there is always a "circulation of the elite" — the fall of certain members from the group of the elite to the rank of the masses, and the rise of certain outstanding members of the masses into the ranks of the elite. Sometimes this class transformation or circulation takes place freely and rapidly ("three generations from shirt sleeves to shirt sleeves"); at other times, because of artificial barriers, this circulation takes place slowly and imperceptibly. But it can never cease entirely or the civilization of the community concerned decays and the existing organization is eventually swept away either as the result of external aggression or of internal revolution. A community must indeed be governed by an elite, but no one fixed group of elite has or can have a permanent existence. History, says Pareto, is the graveyard of aristocracies. Any one group of aristocrats sooner or later loses its power by being overthrown or else loses its identity through the constant adoption of prominent members of the masses into its own ranks.

Much of Pareto's political theory is closely associated with his theory of the circulation of the elite and as a result this phase of his system has for us especial significance. Pareto stresses the fact that though no elite is permanent, some elites are far more enduring, more stable, and more successful than others, depending upon the methods they use to maintain their integrity and to preserve their domination over the masses. There are, he says many types of elite, but there are three main types. Pareto himself gives no names to these types, but we may, for the sake of convenience, call them type A, the elite of the old regime; type B, the liberal-democratic elite; and type C, the Fascist-Nazi elite. Type A, the elite of the old regime, was the type of elite found in France in the eighteenth century. Here the governing class formed a more or less closed group; the free circulation of the classes was hindered and almost prevented. As a result stagnation and dry rot set in, a condition which soon led to the French Revolution. Type B we call the liberal-democratic elite as it is the type of elite most often found in countries with a Liberal (favoring individualism) or democratic constitution. With this type of governing class the circulation of the elite is made easy and rapid, but this type also breaks down before long because of its selfishness, inefficiency, and corruption. Type C we call the Fascist-Nazi type of elite, because the description which Pareto gives us of this type corresponds almost exactly to the group which, subsequent to the composition of Pareto's book, came into power in Italy and Germany. In some ways this type is halfway between type A and type B. Class circulation is permitted, but only slowly and under closely guarded conditions. Individual initiative is permitted (as in type B), but great stress is laid upon authoritarian and hierarchic principles (as in type A). An attempt is made to win the favor of the masses by the use of derivations and propaganda (as in type B), but no hesitation is felt in using brute force to command obedience (as in type A). Pareto feels that even this type of elite will sooner or later break down, but compared with the other types, it is stable, efficient, and successful. If, after all, we have to choose between these three types, there is no doubt in Pareto's mind that we should choose the Fascist-Nazi type of elite rather than either of the others.

Pareto spends very little time discussing the merits and defects of type A, the elite of the old regime, probably because this type of elite is now only of historic importance. But he is insistent that any elite which constitutes a completely closed group is bound to decay. "If human aristocracies were like thoroughbreds among animals, which reproduce themselves over long periods with approximately the same traits, the history of the human race would be something altogether different from the history we know." [54] If men, like thoroughbred animals, bred true to type, it would be possible for an elite of type A to continue indefinitely; but they do not, and as a result an elite of this sort is exceedingly unstable. An hereditary aristocracy invariably decays in numbers and eventually dies out. The ancient aristocracies of Athens and of Rome have vanished without leaving any descent.

> Where in France are the descendants of the Frankish conquerors? The genealogists of the English nobility have been very exactly kept; they show that very few families still remain to claim descent from the comrades of William the Conqueror. In Germany the aristocracy of the present day is very largely made up of descendants of vassals of lords of old. [55]

These hereditary aristocracies "decay not in numbers only. They decay also in quality, in the sense that they lose their vigor, that there is a decline in the proportion of the residues which enabled them to win their power and hold it." [56] It is certain that some of the sons of the elite will be less able than their fathers, and in the long run the ruling group will contain an increasing percentage of unfit members. If the elite remains closed, there is an accumulation of inferior elements in the governing class and of superior elements in the lower classes. Prestige, customary veneration, or the use of force may keep such an elite in power for a considerable length of time, but sooner or later there is a revolution, a crash. "Revolutions come about through the accumulation in the higher strata of society ... of decadent elements, no longer possessing the residues suitable for keeping them in power, and shrinking from the use of force, while meantime in the lower strata of society elements of superior quality are coming to the fore, possessing residues suitable for exercising the functions of government and willing enough to use force." [57] Hence the French Revolution, ending one classic example of an elite of the old regime, came about.

Quite different in character, but in Pareto's opinion, not much better, is the elite of type B, the liberal-democratic elite, or rather the type of elite which flourishes in countries which have nominally a liberal-democratic form of political organization. "Whether universal suffrage prevails or not, it is always an oligarchy that governs, finding ways to give to 'the will of the people' that expression which the few desire." [58] Nevertheless, in a country which has universal or even a wide suffrage, a peculiar type of oligarchy or elite tends to arise, quite different in aims and character from the governing group which exists in theocratic or authoritarian states. According to Pareto, democratic countries tend to produce a governing class of what he calls "speculators." To Pareto the word speculator has rather a peculiar significance. To him, most men may be divided into two main types — one the "speculator," the other the "rentier." [59] The speculator is one who would rather work on a commission; the rentier is one who would rather work on a fixed salary. The speculator is interested in new enterprises and likes to buy stocks; the rentier prefers the old established, the safe and sound, enterprises, and likes to buy bonds. The speculator is progressive; he likes to make new combinations, or, to use Pareto's phraseology, he is dominated by the residues of group one. The rentier is conservative; he wishes to preserve the existing combinations, or he is dominated by the residues of group two. The speculator tends to have a keen inquiring mind and is rather skeptical in matters of religion and philosophy. The rentier tends to keep a simple faith in existing dogmas and theories.

The speculator tends to be an individualist, dominated by the residues of group five (the integrity of the individual). The rentier tends to be a collectivist, as he feels greater security in group action, and is dominated by the residues of group four (sociability). The speculator tends to be more corrupt and dishonest than the more simple rentier, who blindly clings to the existing code of morals. Finally, and this is a

very important point, the speculator, being himself a cunning person, puts more faith in brains than in brawn. He is terrified of violence and hesitates to use violence himself. The rentier, on the other hand, is more terrified of cunning than he is of force. He has less hesitation in using force or violence when he sees his security endangered or his favorite ideologies attacked.

In Pareto's political philosophy a liberal-democratic state is pictured as one in which the masses or the bulk of the population tend to be of the rentier type, while the ruling oligarchy tends to be of the speculator type. What Pareto calls the speculator type is what we in America, using the language of the street, call the "hustler," the "man of pep," the "wide-awake individual," the "live wire." [60] In most democracies ample opportunities are given such persons to rise in the social, economic, and political hierarchy, while the rentier type, being more passive, less aggressive, tends to stay in the station in which he is born. Pareto points out that there are many advantages to a social system in which the bulk of the population are of the rentier type and the governing elite of the speculator type. The rentier element provides the community with its necessary cohesion and stability; the speculator element provides the community with the initiative necessary for growth, expansion, reconstruction. For a time, at least, the leadership of the speculator type, through the establishment of new industries and new forms of business combinations, promotes the economic welfare of the country. But sooner or later, and sooner rather than later, an elite of this sort is bound to fall — first, because this type of elite has an inevitable tendency to become corrupt and, also, because this type of elite is apt to be weak and vacillating, unable and unwilling to use force even when faced with loss of power.

Pareto admits that many persons of the speculator type may be personally honest. Among this group have been found some of the greatest idealists and reformers the world has ever seen, but he insists that in a normal democracy governmental control tends to pass more and more into the hands of the crafty, self-seeking manipulator. In fact, the public, the stupid masses, prefer to be led by a person who "bamboozles" them rather than by one who is rigidly honest, who tells them uncomfortable truths, and who tries to make them do what they ought to do (in their own self-interest) instead of what appeals to their illogical sentiments. From time to time "reform" administrations come in, but they are seldom popular, and before long are succeeded by another long period of "machine" administration. Pareto is convinced that a liberal-democratic form of government invariably leads to government by such institutions as Tammany Hall, to the rise of such men as Huey Long, to real control through lobbying and secret deals on the part of the "vested interests." Even the would-be honest leader finds it difficult to fight against such influences.

> In the United States Wilson and Bryan went into power as professed and probably sincere opponents of trusts and financiers, but actually they worked in their favor in maintaining anarchy in Mexico with a view to securing a President there who would be subservient to American finance.[61]

Pareto naturally makes a more detailed study of Italy, his native country, analyzing at great length the type of corruption in vogue in Italian politics in the pre-war liberal-democratic period. Pareto claims that Depretis, one of the most successful prime ministers, "was a past master at utilizing the sentiments and interests then prevailing in the country.... He made many speculators rich men by protective tariffs, railway deals, government contracts in which the state was robbed right and left, banking irregularities that were later exposed." [62] Giolitti, another prime minister,

> extended the franchise to strike terror into the hearts of the bourgeoisie and make himself its protector, meanwhile doing his utmost to look like a patron of the popular parties.... He did not want the war with Turkey [of 1911] and fought it only as a sop to certain sentiments, using it as an instrument of governing.... He refused to increase army and navy appropriations in the degree required because he did not care to exasperate the taxpayers. On the other hand, he made loud boast of the fact that in spite of his war [with Turkey] he had maintained or increased expenditures on public works and in subventions of various sorts to voters. He concealed the amounts the war had cost by disguising them in his budget reports, postponing payment of them to the future. He increased the public debt clandestinely by using long term treasury bonds, so filling the coffers of commercial and savings banks, but with grave risks of dangers to come.[63]

To Pareto's mind the actions of Depretis and Giolitti are typical of all popular leaders in all liberal-democratic states.

In addition to being corrupt, the government — or the elite — in a liberal-democratic country forms an essentially unstable group, one that soon disintegrates in times of crisis. This instability is partly due to the fact that in a liberal-democratic regime there is too rapid a circulation of the elite. In such a government it seldom happens that power rests with the same groups of persons for more than two or three generations. This rapid turn-over in the elite creates a very unstable equilibrium. Since this elite is of the speculator type, one interested in new combinations and new enterprises rather than dominated by the desire to maintain the old combinations, it makes for instability. This type of elite neglects tradition and hence is easily swept away. Finally its inherent corruption tends to bring about its own destruction. Craft and cunning can go a long way, but eventually there is a day of reckoning. The liberal-democratic type of elite tends to be pacifistic, but frequently its political machinations lead to war, and in the chaos of war and post-war conditions, it is usually thrust out of power and forced to give way to a more powerful and more vigorous type of elite. Even without a war the corruption of a liberal-democratic elite leads to rapid disintegration. To Pareto a democracy is only a plutocracy in disguise, and in a plutocracy the rich get richer and the poor get poorer. Eventually the poor become restive; workers form unions; these unions gradually resort to sabotage, to strikes, to violence. As time goes on, the violence becomes greater. Peaceful picketing becomes bloody picketing; the ordinary strike is succeeded by the sit-down strike or the forcible seizure and illegal operation of the factories by the workers.

Even at this stage the governing elite, being far more intelligent than the revolting rabble, could easily retain its power if it would only resort to force. But to Pareto the great weakness of the liberal-democratic type of elite is its spinelessness, its unwillingness to meet violence with brute force, its milk-and-watery humanitarianism in times of crisis. "In the majority of cases people who rely on their wits are or become less fitted to use violence." [64] As the liberal-democratic type of elite relies almost entirely on its wits (or its cunning) it is easily corroded by the "poison of humanitarianism." Again and again a governing group has been overthrown because of its supine unwillingness to employ force.

> If the class governing in France [in the eighteenth century] had the faith that counsels the use of force and the will to use force, it would never have been overthrown, and procuring its own advantage would have procured the advantage of France. ... If the victims of the September massacres, their kinsmen and friends had not, for the most part, been spineless humanitarians without a particle of courage or energy they would have annihilated their enemies instead of waiting to be annihilated themselves. [65]

The ruling elite of modern democracies are very different from the old French aristocracy, but they, too, are threatened with extinction because of their chicken-heartedness.

> If a government sets out to protect employers or strike-breakers from violence it is accused of "interfering" in economic matters that do not concern it. If the police do not allow their heads to be broken without using their weapons

they are said to have "shown poor judgement," to have "acted impulsively," "nervously." Like strike breakers they must be denied the right to use arms whenever they are attacked by strikers, for otherwise some striker might be killed. . . . Court decisions are impugned as "class decisions."[66]

In a democracy, in a word, we find "an appeal to sentiments of pity for the sufferings that are caused by the use of force, disregarding entirely the reasons for which the force is used and the utility or harm that results from using it." [67]   Small wonder, with such wishy-washiness on the part of the governing classes that we find chaotic conditions, such as existed in pre-Mussolini or liberal Italy, and (Pareto would have added) in pre-Hitler or liberal Germany.   Such chaos is followed either by a "red" revolution, mob or communist rule, or else by a "white" revolution in which the more vigorous and energetic members of the middle and lower middle classes, fearful lest they lose their stake in the community, seize the reins of power, put down the turbulent multitude and the striking workers with an iron hand, and, thrusting the old effete liberal-democratic elite aside, proceed to rule in their own right — a scene witnessed in the rise of Fascism and Naziism in Italy and Germany.

This new elite differs from the old liberal-democratic elite not only in its personnel, but also in its whole structure, and in the type of persons who are allowed to come to the top.   The new elite is what we have called type C, or the Fascist-Nazi type of elite.   Pareto, of course, wrote when Fascism was in its infancy and Hitler was an unknown figure, and so could not apply this terminology, but the description he gives of the "new elite" fits almost perfectly with the governing groups which have grown up in the last few years in Italy and Germany.   This new elite contains and must contain a small number of speculators, as otherwise the community would become completely stagnant.   But the bulk of the new elite belongs to the rentier type, with the result that their attitude towards all economic and social problems is completely different from that of the old liberal-democratic elite.   As the rentier wishes security above all else, he lashes out savagely at anyone who threatens his security.   Unlike the speculator, he has no hesitation in using force to protect his interests, real or imaginary.   The rentiers, to be sure, are generally more conservative than the speculators, but "there are evolutions, revolutions, innovations that the rentiers support, especially movements tending to restore to the ruling classes certain residues of group persistence." [68]   Being believers in force themselves, they treat with scant courtesy the theories of the humanitarians and not infrequently persecute the humanitarians themselves, "and in so doing, to tell the truth, they are performing a useful public service, something like ridding the country of a baneful animal pest.... The country is saved from ruin, and is reborn to a new life." [69]

The old liberal-democratic elite tended to be rather skeptical of traditional religious and social dogmas. The new Fascist-Nazi elite assumes a very different attitude towards these matters. A few of the more enlightened may despise these dogmas, but they are careful to use them as instruments in governing the populace. The bulk of the new elite, however, because of their rentier background and their love for "the persistence of aggregates," sincerely cling to traditional ecclesiastical and social conventions. Very frequently this type of elite is not only rigid and "narrow-minded" in such matters; it also tends to become fanatical to the extent of persecuting those who are skeptical of its beliefs. For this reason the new elite has little use for rationalists or "intellectuals." The intellectuals are either killed off or are forcibly silenced. Pareto rejoices to see such a development take place.

> The "intellectuals" of Europe, like the Mandarins of China, are the worst of rulers and the fact that our intellectuals have played a less extensive role than the mandarins in the conduct of public affairs is one of the many reasons why the lots of European peoples and the Chinese have been different, just as it explains why the Japanese led by their feudal chieftains are so much stronger than the Chinese. [70]

Religious and social dogmas may be and usually are sheer nonsense, but their blind acceptance constitutes a strong stabilizing influence.

Pareto believes that the Fascist-Nazi type of elite tends to be more stable and permanent than the liberal-democratic type, which may be accounted for in several ways. First of all is the willingness of the Fascist-Nazi type of elite to use force. In a lengthy historical survey, Pareto cites the story of Sparta, of the Roman Empire, and of Venice, to prove that an elite, which corresponds in some ways to that of the Fascist-Nazi type and which is prepared to govern by force, may give a community security and enable it to survive for long periods. Even when a regime has lost all popular approval, it can persist for an indefinite period if it is prepared to use force to the limit. From Pareto's point of view, it is perfectly clear that there are other reasons why the Fascist-Nazi type of elite should be more stable than its rivals. As opposed to the restless running after novelty characteristic of the liberal-democratic type, an elite of the Fascist-Nazi type is dominated by sentiments of group persistence and a desire to maintain established institutions. This in itself is a strong stabilizing influence. The

Fascist-Nazi type of elite, moreover, permits a certain amount of class circulation, thus preventing internal decay; but it insists that this circulation take place slowly and cautiously, thus escaping the unstable equilibrium of a too rapid circulation of the elite witnessed in most democratic countries.

The Fascist-Nazi type of elite emphasizes the hierarchic principle in government, the social, economic, and political pyramid with power centered at the top, and this, according to Pareto, makes for both a more stable and a more efficient type of government. Finally, Pareto thinks that a Fascist-Nazi type of elite is more honest than its liberal-democratic rival if only because of the fact that the Fascist-Nazi type is too stupid and too lacking in enterprise to go out and make money for itself. Pareto believes that corruption is bound to take place in all forms of government. But under the rule of the Fascist-Nazi type of elite there is greater emphasis upon and belief in rigorous moral codes (however stupid these codes may be), and there is less willingness and less possibility of departing from these codes than in democratic countries. The very fact that an elite is more honest makes it, in Pareto's opinion, more stable.

In his heart of hearts, Pareto is more of an authoritarian than he is an etatist. From his voluminous writings it is obvious that Pareto desires all political power to be centered in a small, vigorous elite, an elite governing by force rather than by consent. In other words, he advocates a political dictatorship by a small select class. But he is not so certain that his dictator state should seek to control and regulate the non-political, that is, the social and economic activities of its citizens. There are in fact many indications that Pareto would like to combine political dictatorship with economic liberalism. The aristocrats should control the state, but the state should not interfere with private enterprise in the economic sphere. As an old-line economist, Pareto would like, if possible, to have free trade and *laissez faire* ("let the government keep out of industry"). It is interesting to observe that the Fascists, the disciples of Pareto, in the first years of their rule tried to carry out his idea of authoritarianism without etatism. Fascism "simply wanted to change the existing political regime in order to preserve the existing social structure and its main institution, private property in the means of production. Fascism in the first years of its reign was more liberal in economic policy than the liberal governments previous to it, abandoning a good deal of state subventions, and so on." [71]

Before long, as we all know, the Fascists abandoned this policy and went in for thoroughgoing etatism. In one way this change was due to local economic conditions at the time, but in another sense it may be said to be only a further and more consistent application of Pareto's own principles. If Pareto's philosophy be correct, the main difference between the liberal-democratic type of elite and the Fascist-Nazi type of elite is that the former consists mostly of speculators and the latter mostly of rentiers. Pareto tells us that the speculators are the progressives who wish to make new combinations (residue one); the rentiers are the conservatives who wish to preserve group aggregates (residue two). But Pareto also admits that the speculator, *qua* speculator, places a great deal of emphasis upon individual or private enterprise. In order to gain wealth he may advocate a protective tariff or seek government aid or government subvention, but he can remain a speculator only as long as he is not too well controlled or regulated by the government. The speculator does and must emphasize the integrity of the individual (group five of the residues) as opposed to the residues of sociability.

The rentier, on the other hand, is above all things interested in security. He is satisfied with a small fixed income, but he is terrified lest he lose his job, his income, or his social position. Now security is possible only if the government steps in and artificially regulates prices, conditions of employment, methods of operation, and the total amount of production. As a result, the rentier is far more willing to accept control of his activities by the group than is the speculator, or, in other words, is far more dominated by the residues of sociability (group four) than he is by the problem of the integrity of the individual. If, therefore, Pareto is right and the Fascist-Nazi type of elite means the government of the country by rentiers, we need not be surprised that this type of elite tends to insist upon etatism or collectivism as well as upon authoritarianism as fundamental articles in their political philosophy. Pareto's system, therefore, is the key not only to the earlier, but also to the later, phases of the Fascist theory of the state.

NOTES TO CHAPTER NINE

1. William James, *Pluralistic Universe*, p. 212.
2. H. W. Carr, *Henri Bergson*, p. 46. By permission of Thomas Nelson & Sons. Ltd
3. *Ibid.*, p. 49.
4. *Ibid.*, p. 88.
5. Henri Bergson, *Mind Energy*, p. 33
6. Schopenhauer, *The World as Will and Idea*, II, 328.

7. M. Beer, *Schopenhauer*, p. 80. By permission of the Dodge Publishing Company.
8. Friedrich Nietzsche, *Werke*, XV, 273; see *Will to Power*, II, 26.
9. G. Chatterton-Hill, *The Philosophy of Nietzsche*, p. 158.
10. *Ibid.*, p. 207.
11. R. G. Gettell, *History of Political Thought*, p. 447. By permission of D. Appleton-Century Company.
12. William McDougall, *Introduction to Social Psychology*, p. 11. By permission of John W. Luce and Company.
13. *Ibid.*, p. 18.
14. *Ibid.*, p. 19.
15. *Ibid.*, p. 23.
16. *Ibid.*, p. 24.
17. *Ibid.*, p. 26.
18. *Ibid.*, p. 116.
19. *Ibid.*, p. 271.
20. *Ibid.*, p. 280.
21. *Ibid.*, p. 281.
22. *Ibid.*, p. 289.
23. *Ibid.*, p. 291.
24. *Ibid.*, p. 28.
25. *Ibid.*, p. 295.
26. *Ibid.*, p. 319.
27. *Ibid.*, p. 16.
28. McDougall, *The Group Mind*, p. 6. By permission of G. P. Putnam's Sons.
29. *Ibid.*
30. McDougall, *Introduction to Social Psychology*, p. 18.
31. McDougall, *The Group Mind*, p. 78.
32. *Ibid.*, p. 20.
33. *Ibid.*, p. 53.
34. *Ibid.*, p. 7.
35. *Ibid.*, p. 9.
36. *Ibid.*, p. 53.
37. *Ibid.*, p. 32.
38. *Ibid.*, p. 52.
39. *Ibid.*, p. 135.
40. *Ibid.*, p. 137.   41. *Ibid.*, p. 138.
42. Gabriel Tarde, *The Laws of Imitation*, p. 141. By permission of Henry Holt and Company.
43. Émile Durkheim, *Elementary Forms of Religious Life*, p. 444. By permission of The Macmillan Company, publishers.
44. F. W. Coker, *Recent Political Thought*, p. 229. By permission of D. Appleton-Century Company.
45. Quoted in Finer, *Mussolini's Italy*, p. 218.
46. Georges Sorel, *Reflections on Violence*, pp. 90, 98. By permission of George Allen and Unwin, Ltd.
47. *Ibid.*, p. 23.
48. *Ibid.*, p. 152.
49. *Ibid.*, p. 290.
50. *Ibid.*, p. 58.
51. *Ibid.*, p. 69.
52. *Ibid.*, p. 73.
53. R. Sorokin, *Contemporary Sociological Theories.* p. 56. By permission of Harper and Brothers.

54. Vilfredo Pareto, *Mind and Society*, section 2055. By permission of Harcourt Brace and Company.
55. *Ibid.*, sec. 2053.
56. *Ibid.*, sec. 2054.
57. *Ibid.*, sec. 2058.
58. *Ibid.*, sec. 2183.
59. "Rentier" is a French word, indicating one who lives off his *rentes*, or income from bonds or public securities, with a fixed rate of interest.
60. Pareto, *Mind and Society*, section 1563.
61. *Ibid.*, sec. 2256.
62. *Ibid.*, sec. 2255.
63. *Ibid.*
64. *Ibid.*, sec. 2190.
65. *Ibid.*, sec. 2191.
66. *Ibid.*, sec. 2189.
67. *Ibid.*
68. *Ibid.*, sec. 2235.
69. *Ibid.*, sec. 2191.
70. *Ibid.*, sec. 2299.
71. F. Borkenau, *Pareto*, p. 197.

BIBLIOGRAPHY

FOR IRRATIONALISM IN GENERAL PHILOSOPHY

From among the enormous number of books on this subject see especially W. James: *Pragmatism*, New York, 1907; *Pluralistic Universe*, New York, 1909; *Essays in Radical Empiricism*, New York, 1912; *The Will to Believe and Other Essays*, New York, 1927. E. Boutroux, *William James*, New York, 1912. T. Flournoy, *The Philosophy of William James*, New York, 1917. Henri Bergson: *Creative Evolution*, New York, 1911; *Mind Energy*, London, 1920. A. D. Lindsay, *The Philosophy of Bergson*, London, 1911. H. W. Carr, *Henri Bergson*, London, 1913. A. Schopenhauer, *The World as Will and Idea*, 3 vols., Boston, 1883–1886. M. Beer, *Schopenhauer*, London, 1914. T. Whittaker, *Schopenhauer*, London, 1909. H. Zimmern, *Arthur Schopenhauer, His Life and Philosophy*, second edition London, 1932. Friedrich Nietzsche: *Werke*, 20 vols., Leipzig, 1895–1926; *Complete Works*, 18 vols., London, 1909–1913, especially *Thus Spake Zarathustra* and *The Will to Power*. (The English translation is not always to be trusted.) G. N. Dolson, *The Philosophy of Friedrich Nietzsche*, New York, 1901. H. Lichtenberger, *The Gospel of Superman, The Philosophy of Friedrich Nietzsche*, New York, 1926. G. Chatterton-Hill, *The Philosophy of Nietzsche*, London, 1913. H. Hartle, *Nietzsche und der Nationalsozialismus*, Munich, 1937.

FOR ANGLO-AMERICAN SOCIAL PSYCHOLOGY

G. Wallas: *Human Nature and Politics*, New York, 1909; *The Great Society*, London, 1914. W. Trotter, *The Instincts of the Herd in Peace and War*, London. 1916. W. Lippmann, *Public Opinion*, New York, 1922. W. McDougall: *Introduction to Social Psychology*, London, 1908; *The Group Mind*, New York, 1920; *Is Democracy Safe for America?* New York, 1921.

FOR CONTINENTAL SOCIAL PSYCHOLOGY

M. M. Davis, *Psychological Interpretations of Society*, New York, 1909.　G. Tarde: *Social Laws*, New York, 1899; *The Laws of Imitation*, New York, 1903. M. M. Davis, *Gabriel Tarde*, New York, 1906.　É. Durkheim: *Elementary Forms of Religious Life*, New York, 1915; *On the Division of Labor in Society*, New York, 1933; *Rules of Sociological Method*, Chicago, 1938.　C. E. Gehlke, *Émile Durkheim's Contribution to Sociological Theory*, New York, 1915.　H. Alpert, *Émile Durkheim and His Sociology*, New York, 1939.　G. Le Bon: *The Crowd*, second edition, London, 1897; *Psychology of Peoples*, New York, 1898; *La Psychologie politique*, Paris, 1910.　G. Sorel: *Reflections on Violence*, New York, 1914; *Les Illusions du progrès*, Paris, 1908; *La Décomposition du Marxisme*, Paris, 1908; *Matériaux pour une théorie du prolétariat*, Paris, 1919.　F. D. Cheydleur, *L'Évolution des doctrines de Georges Sorel*, Grenoble, 1914.　G. Piron, *Georges Sorel*, Paris, 1927.　P. Lassère, *Georges Sorel*, Paris, 1928.　R. Soltau, *French Political Thought in the Nineteenth Century*, New Haven, 1931 (pp. 444 ff.).　V. Pareto, *Mind and Society*, 4 vols., New York, 1935.　G. H. Bousquet, *Vilfredo Pareto, sa vie, et son oeuvre*, Paris, 1928.　G. C. Homans and C. P. Curtis, *An Introduction to Pareto*, New York, 1934.　L. J. Henderson, *Pareto's General Sociology*, Cambridge, Mass., 1935.　F. Borkenau, *Pareto*, London, 1936.

CHAPTER X

THE SOCIAL DARWINISTS AND THEIR ALLIES

ONE of the most important events in the intellectual life of Europe during the nineteenth century was the publication of Charles Darwin's two major books, the *Origin of Species* (in 1859) and the *Descent of Man* (in 1871). In one sense, to be sure, the theory of evolution expounded in these books was far from being new. The theory of evolution in the broadest sense of the word underlay the whole of the Hegelian philosophy and had important effects upon Hegel's political ideas. Hegel, rather inconsistently, did deny physical or organic evolution, the rise of one species out of another, but even this idea in one form or another was preached by a large number of persons during the early part of the nineteenth century. Nevertheless Darwin caused a revolution in European intellectual circles. Evolution, which formerly seemed to be merely an idle philosophical theory, now appeared to be established as a scientific fact. Before Darwin one could deny the transmutation of species and be a perfectly sound and orthodox scientist. After Darwin the special creation of each species was maintained only by a few zealous and rather reactionary theologians.

Of even greater importance was the particular slant given to the doctrine of evolution by Darwin. To Hegel, evolution was merely the gradual self-unfoldment of the Universal Mind according to a divinely prearranged plan. Many of the other early evolutionists refused to accept Hegel's idealism, but most of them agreed in giving a rather pleasant and optimistic interpretation of evolution and of the causes of evolution. Some insisted that the development from lower to higher forms, from imperfect to perfect organisms, was due to the workings of Divine Providence. Some insisted that all living beings have within them a peculiar "life urge" which impels them constantly to strive after nobler and higher forms in the evolutionary scale. Somewhat more scientific were the claims that evolution took place because of the direct influence of the environment upon organisms (the doctrine of Buffon) or as the result of the transmission of acquired characteristics (the doctrine of Lamarck). Even these ideas would have had only a casual effect upon social and political speculation. Darwin, on the other hand, taught that evolution took place because of the blind struggle for existence and because of the fact that in this struggle it is only the biologically fittest which survive. It was this doctrine, transferred to the social and political sphere, which caused such a revolution in political philosophy, producing the school of thought which is usually called Social Darwinism.

So important are the terms struggle for existence and natural selection (or the survival of the fittest) that it is well to pause for a moment and see what Darwin meant by them. The struggle for existence meant, to Darwin, the universal competition which goes on between all organic beings for the means of livelihood. Everywhere and at all times we can observe that there is, in a state of nature, a fierce, relentless struggle both between the various species and also between the various members of each species.

> The rivals may in an unthinking way absorb the limited supply of nutriment, moisture or light, leaving the less successful competitors to perish of starvation; it may take the form of a conscious and deliberate extermination of rivals by the method of slaughter, or it may take the less deadly form of gracious social intercourse which accompanies courtship and leaves the less fortunate competitors to go unmated and eventually to perish without reproducing themselves.[1]

Among human beings this struggle takes the form of frequent conflicts and wars between different tribes and different countries. Inside any one country we find men in bitter economic competition with one another. Among the lower animals we find that one species preys upon another species and is in turn preyed upon by a different type of animal. This relentless struggle for existence is obvious even in the plant world.

> We behold the face of nature bright with gladness...; we do not see or we forget, that the birds which are idly singing around us mostly live on insects or seeds, and are thus constantly destroying life; or we forget how largely these songsters, or their eggs, or their nestlings, are destroyed by birds and beasts of prey.... A plant which annually produces a thousand seeds, of which only one of an average comes to maturity, may be more truly said to struggle with the plants of the same and other kinds which already clothe the ground.... Several seedling mistletoes, growing close together on the same branch, may... truly be said to struggle with each other. As the mistletoe is disseminated by birds, its existence depends on them; and it may metaphorically be said to struggle with other fruit-bearing plants in tempting birds to devour and thus disseminate its seeds [rather than those of other plants].[2]

Darwin further argued that things being what they are, this universal struggle for existence is not only natural, it is also inevitable.

A struggle for existence inevitably follows from the high rate at which all organic beings tend to increase. Every being, which during its natural life time produces several eggs or seeds, must suffer destruction during some period of its life..., otherwise, on the principle of geometrical increase, its numbers would quickly become so inordinately great that no country could support the product. Hence as more individuals are produced than can possibly survive, there must in every case be a struggle for existence, either one individual with another of the same species, or with the individuals of distinct species, or with the physical conditions of life.... There is no exception to the rule that every organic being naturally increases at so high a rate, that, if not destroyed, the earth would soon be covered by the progeny of a single pair. Even slow-breeding man has doubled in twenty-five years, and at this rate, in less than a few thousand years, there would literally not be standing-room for his progeny.[2]

What is true of man and of the other higher animals is even more true of the lower animals and of plants. There are some fish which in the course of their life lay from sixty to one hundred thousand eggs apiece. If all these eggs were to hatch and come to maturity the ocean would literally be overflowing with the descendants of a single pair of fish. It is obvious that only a small percentage of the individuals of any one species have a chance in the struggle for existence. It is equally obvious that the motto, conscious or unconscious. of every organic being must be, "I must outwit and defeat — if necessary kill — the other members of my species lest I lose out in the struggle for existence, and be outwitted, defeated, or killed by them."

The second point in Darwin's system is that the struggle for existence leads to the principle of natural selection or the survival of the fittest. Everyone knows that there are small individual differences or variations between the different members of the same species. Even among puppies in the same litter these differences or variations are apparent. As a result of these variations some members of the species are stronger, others weaker; some faster, others slower; some more cunning, others duller-witted than the others. In the course of the struggle for existence it is clear that normally the strongest, the swiftest, and the most cunning have the best chance to survive, while the weak, the slow, and the dull-witted tend to be killed off. It is important to note, however, that it is the fittest and not necessarily the best which survive. On some occasions the fittest may also be the best, but not always. In the relentless struggle for existence the individual who is more gentle, more kindly, more humane is apt to lose out to his cruel, self-centered rivals.

In many cases the question of survival depends not upon the possession of higher or lower qualities, of greater or less strength and intelligence, but merely upon the possession of certain qualities or variations which happen by chance to be best suited to a particular time and place. There is nothing higher or lower about the colorations of animals, but in times and places where snow is abundant those rabbits which are white have a better chance of survival than dark-colored rabbits, as they are less visible to their enemies. On a brown prairie, on the other hand, the possession of white coloration is a disadvantage and white rabbits tend to be killed more rapidly than those rabbits which happen to be brown. In some cases it is the possession of certain physical defects which give the individual a better chance of survival. In modern states, for example, perfect physical specimens of humanity are apt to be conscripted and sent off to be killed in battle, while those persons who are lame or who possess bad eyesight or other physical disabilities are left at home to survive — and reproduce their kind. The law of the survival of the fittest, therefore, does not necessarily imply material or moral progress; it merely means that those individuals which by accident are best adapted to life at a particular time and place will survive and that those individuals less adapted to such conditions will die.

But though the struggle for existence and the survival of the fittest does not necessarily imply material or moral progress, it does, in Darwin's opinion, serve as the principal though not the only cause of organic evolution. For unknown reasons all species tend to produce occasional "sports," that is, individuals with marked variations, which cause them to differ radically from other members of their species and even from their own parents. In many, though not in all, cases, these marked variations tend to be reproduced in the offspring of these "sports." Thus in a litter of wolves one wolf cub may be unusually long-legged and may well become in later life the sire of other unusually long-legged wolves. If this marked variation serves no useful purpose, the individual possessing it may well be killed in the struggle for existence and the marked variation will lead to no permanent result. If, on the other hand, the marked variation is of real advantage to its owner in life's struggle, enabling him to overcome his competitors, this individual will live to a ripe old age and will probably be the parent of many other individuals who will inherit this same marked variation; and as time goes on a new breed of animal will arise. Among wolves where longleggedness is of advantage, a new unusually long-legged breed will be formed. Bit by bit the breeds will become still further differentiated until eventually entirely new species will arise. From the primitive eohippus of early geologic time, there arises the horse as we know him today. From some primitive ape-like being of the dim and distant past, there arises man, the *genus homo*, as we know him today.

The important point about the Darwinian theory of evolution is the idea that the chief though not the only cause of organic evolution is the struggle for existence and the survival of the fittest. If there had been no struggle for existence and if the unfit as well as the fit had survived, there would have been no evolution in the past. If evolution is to go on in the present and in the future, the same factors — the struggle for existence, the wiping out of the unfit, the survival of the fit — must continue. If for any reason these factors were eliminated, evolution would cease. If a species reproduces itself so slowly that there is a tendency to underpopulation rather than to overpopulation, the struggle for existence becomes less acute. There is room for the unfit as well as for the fit — and the process of evolution is retarded. Remove in some other way, say by human agency, the principle of the survival of the fittest; let man see to it that the unfit as well as the fit survive, and evolution will practically cease. It was this phase of Darwinism which was destined to have such a widespread influence upon social and political speculation during the latter part of the nineteenth century.

THE GENERAL IMPLICATIONS OF SOCIAL DARWINISM

Though Darwin was a genius he was not a universal genius. He was and remained a biologist and made no attempt to apply his theories to social and political fields. With the widespread acceptance of his theory, however, it was only natural that other thinkers, themselves immersed in social and political problems, were strongly influenced by Darwinism and endeavored to reinterpret social and political philosophy in the light of the Darwinian hypothesis. It is also natural that among such thinkers there was a sharp clash of opinion as to the proper deductions to be drawn from Darwinism in their own particular field. Among the many apostles of Social Darwinism three in particular stand out as especially worthy of notice, namely, Herbert Spencer, Walter Bagehot, and Ludwig Gumplowicz. None of the three were thoroughgoing etatists in the modern sense — Spencer, in fact, was a rabid advocate of individualism; but all three produced theories which had an enormous influence upon the later development of the etatist philosophy.

Herbert Spencer (1820–1903), like so many other English men of science, was a self-made and even a self-educated man.   He never attended a university, never held a professorial or other academic post, and consistently refused to receive academic honors when in later life they were offered to him.   Nevertheless, he was one of the most popular and most important of the European thinkers during the latter part of the nineteenth century.   Spencer's philosophy has now lost something of its former vogue, but it must not be forgotten that many of Spencer's ideas have become part of the accepted background of educated opinion, a background so taken for granted that we frequently fail to remember that it originated in Spencer's writings.   Nor should it be forgotten that Spencer exerted an enormous influence upon subsequent thinkers, including those who opposed him most vigorously upon individual issues.   In the course of his numerous writings (his monumental *Synthetic Philosophy* alone occupies ten ponderous volumes), Spencer enunciated a large number of theories, most of which call for no mention here.   Many of these theories constituted a defense of democracy and more especially of individualism and hence were fiercely attacked by etatist writers.   But among his ideas which were to have the greatest influence upon subsequent social and political thought were two general theses which were accepted by practically all of the later adherents of the theory of evolution, including those who were rabid etatists.   In fact, after undergoing a suitable transformation, these two theses were made foundation stones in the edifice of etatist political philosophy.

The first of these general theses was that man is, after all, an animal, though the highest of the animals.   Consequently the laws of evolution apply as much to man as to all other members of the animal kingdom. This in turn means that not only man's body but also his mental, moral, and social traits must be regarded as the products of evolution.   Spencer used this general thesis in an attempt to solve several of the great problems which had perplexed philosophers during the preceding centuries.

One of the perennial disputes among philosophers was that between the empirical school led by Locke and the transcendental school led by Leibniz and Kant.   According to Locke all our knowledge is derived from experience.   According to the transcendentalists, we have also certain innate ideas or at least certain innate forms of thought which are prior to and independent of experience.   Spencer with his evolutionism aimed to mediate between these two schools.   He agreed with the transcendentalists that it is false to say that with any one individual the mind is an absolute blank prior to experience, for every newborn infant possesses *potentially* certain rational instincts or forms of thought which enable him later to organize his experiences into a rational pattern. But to Spencer, the transcendentalists were wrong in claiming that these instincts, ideas, and forms of thought are prior to *all* experience — the products of a mind created in the image of God. These rational instincts or innate ideas are the product of experience — the experience of the race, of the vast chain of ancestral experiences running back through ages of barbarism and animality to the lowest beginnings of life. What Kant and his fellow idealists regarded as *a priori* principles were to Spencer *a priori* indeed to the individual, but *a posteriori* to the race. In other words, these principles were regarded as the results of race experience which appeared in individuals in the form of intuitions.

What is of importance to the political scientist in this connection is that Spencer differed from the old empirical school regarding the innate mental capacity of different individuals and of different races. The empirical school taught that each person irrespective of class and of race comes into the world with a mind which is a *tabula rasa*, a blank page. Upon this environment, experience, and education are supposed to work, so that the difference between a stupid and a wise man, the criminal and the saint, is to be accounted for by the difference in their upbringing. The empiricists were mostly democratic in their sympathies, largely because they believed in the potential equality of all men. Spencer, on the other hand, not only believed in innate ideas and innate instincts, but also taught that these innate ideas and innate instincts differ from person to person and from group to group, according to their heredity. Good or bad training will help or retard the intellectual and emotional development of the individual — but Spencer was a great believer in the old adage, "you cannot make a silk purse out of a sow's ear."

Spencer made a similar attempt to mediate between the two traditional schools of ethics. One of these schools, the intuitional school claims that we possess a God-given conscience which tells us there is a difference between good and bad and also teaches us infallibly what is good and what is bad. The other school, the utilitarian school, claims that what we call our conscience is merely a reflection of the training and moral education we receive during the formative period of childhood. Spencer completely rejected the idea of a God-given conscience, but he sided with the intuitionists to the extent that he also rejected the idea that our moral sense is the product of an individual's experience

or training during a single lifetime.   Though the content of our conscience may be in large measure the result of our environment or our
education, man does possess a certain moral sense prior to and independent of his training or education.   "There have been and still are
developing in the race certain fundamental moral intuitions; and though
these moral intuitions are the results of accumulated experiences of utility, gradually organized and inherited, they have come to be independent
of conscious experience." [4]   Just as in the case of the rational instincts,
Spencer holds that the moral instincts differ from person to person
and from race to race because of the difference in hereditary background.   The moral instincts of a savage are quite different from
those of a highly developed Caucasian, and no amount of training or
education can obliterate this training in the course of a single generation.   In like manner, in our modern civilization a man is usually a
criminal, not because of bad environment or defective upbringing, but
because by some quirk of heredity he has inherited a moral sense out
of keeping with that of most other members in his community.

It is important to note that though Spencer claimed that we all
possess an inherited moral sense in some form or another, he is equally
emphatic in asserting that this moral sense has ultimately a purely
selfish and hedonistic basis.   In the early stages of evolution man, like
all other animals, aims merely at preserving his own existence, at reproducing himself, at securing the greatest amount of happiness, at avoid-
ing the greatest amount of pain.   Any action which results in carrying
out these aims he comes to regard as "good," any actions which result
in retarding these aims he regards as "bad."   This valuation, frequently
an unconscious one, is transmitted to posterity in the form of instincts.
Even today a man instinctively regards as "good" anything which
benefits himself or his dependents.   The parental instinct and the feeling that the parental instinct is good are easily accounted for by the
laws of evolution.   Those individuals which were so callous as not to
nurse and look after their offspring left no descendants, as the offspring
perished in the struggle for existence.   Those individuals who did nurse
and look after their offspring aided them to survive.   We who are
obviously the descendants of persons with parental instincts have inherited the feeling that to look after our own children is "good," not to
look after them is "bad."

Even the altruism, the willingness to serve our fellow man, which is
seemingly mixed up in our moral sense, has, to Spencer, a selfish foundation.   At an early stage of evolution man found that he could find

greater safety in group, as opposed to individual, action. The several weak by combining together could protect themselves from the single bully, however strong. But for the group to persist, a certain amount of altruism had to exist between its members. Each member had to sympathize with, and look out for, and fulfill his obligations to the other members of the group, lest he himself be left in the lurch in time of danger. Those persons who were entirely selfish remained isolated individuals and perished; those persons who were loyal to the group and who held to the code of conduct laid down by the group survived. We are the descendants of the latter class of persons; hence we find in ourselves certain social instincts which we call our moral sense. It was the struggle for existence which led man, willy-nilly, to develop a certain sense of altruism.

The second main thesis in Spencer's philosophical system is the idea that not only is man as an individual the product of evolution, but human groups and society as a whole are the products of evolution, and in the course of their evolution must and do obey certain fundamental natural laws. It is the function of biology and psychology to study the physical and mental evolution of man as an individual. It is the func- tion of the new science of sociology, the queen of the sciences, to study the evolution of human groups and the laws which govern this evolu- tion. In adopting this position, Spencer placed himself in opposition to the believers in the social contract and agreed with the traditionalists that society and the state cannot be "manufactured," but must be the result of long, slow, and unconscious growth. This means that society must be dealt with, not as a mechanism, but as a living thing.

In asserting that human groups, whether social or political, are the results of evolution and are controlled by the laws which govern evolu- tion, Spencer not only opposed the old doctrine of the social contract, but also Carlyle's doctrine that history is the biography of great men, the idea that history or the development of social groups is to any large extent dependent upon the conscious actions of individuals at any time or place.

> What are the causes that make communities change from generation to
> generation — that make the England of Queen Anne so different from the
> England of Elizabeth, the Harvard College of today so different from that of
> thirty years ago? ... The Spencerian school replies, The changes are irrespec-
> tive of persons, and independent of individual control. They are due to the
> environment, to the circumstances, the physical geography, the ancestral
> conditions, the increasing experience of outer relations; to everything in fact,
> except the Grants and the Bismarcks, the Jones and the Smiths.[3]

In developing this phase of his system Spencer asserted that society has many of the attributes of an organism and can best be considered as a special type of organism. According to Spencer there are four important analogies between physical organisms and the social organism:

> (1) Commencing as small aggregations, they insensibly augment in mass: some of them eventually reaching ten thousand times what they originally were.
>
> (2) While at first so simple in structure as to be considered structureless, they assume, in the course of their growth, a continually increasing complexity of structure.
>
> (3) Though in their early undeveloped states there exists in them scarcely any mutual dependence of parts, their parts gradually acquire a mutual dependence; which becomes at last so great, that the activity and life of each part is made possible only by the activity and life of the rest.
>
> (4) The life of a society is independent of, and far more prolonged than the lives of any of its component units; who are severally born, grow, work, reproduce, and die, while the body politic composed of them survives generation after generation, increasing in mass, in completeness of structure, and in functional activity.[6]

In enunciating the doctrine that society is a social organism analogous in many respects to the physical organism, Spencer put forth an idea which was hailed with joy by most of the etatists of his own and of subsequent generations. These etatists pointed out that Spencer was only saying in biological language what Fichte and Hegel had already said in metaphysical language. Spencer, however, was not an etatist, in fact was a violent enemy of etatism; and lest his doctrine of the social organism give too much support to the etatist cause, he immediately added that though society did constitute a kind of organism, there are several marked differences between the physical and the social organisms. Two of these contrasts are of especial importance. One is that "the parts of an animal form a concrete whole, but the parts of a society form a whole which is discrete." [7] Still more important is the fact that

> in the one (the physical organism) consciousness is concentrated in a small part of the aggregate. In the other (the social organism) it is diffused through the aggregate; all the units possess the capacity for happiness and misery, if not in equal degrees, still in degrees that approximate.[8]

Spencer thus rejected the notion, so dear to the etatists, that the social organism has feelings of its own, a mind of its own, a soul of its own, quite distinct from the feelings, the minds, the souls of its component parts.

For this very reason he also rejected the etatist doctrine that in the social organism the parts must be made subservient to the whole.

> While in individual bodies the welfare of all other parts is rightly subservient to the welfare of the nervous system ... in bodies politic the same thing does not hold, or holds but to a very slight extent. It is well that the lives of all parts of an animal should be merged in the life of the whole, because the whole has a corporate consciousness capable of happiness or misery. But it is not so with a society, since its living units do not and can not lose individual consciousness, and since the community as a whole has no corporate consciousness. And this is an everlasting reason why the welfare of the citizens can not rightly be sacrificed to some supposed benefit of the state: but why on the other hand the state is to be maintained solely for the benefit of citizens. The corporate life must here be subservient to the lives of the parts, instead of the lives of the parts being subservient to the corporate life.[9]

The later etatists took over from Spencer the doctrine that individual man and social groups are the products of evolution, of evolution governed by the struggle for existence and the survival of the fittest, even though they rejected with horror Spencer's doctrines of extreme individualism and of absolute *laissez faire* in politics. These later etatists found greater consolation in the teachings of Walter Bagehot (1826–1877), one of Spencer's contemporaries.

Bagehot was a university graduate (being a product of the University of London), but, like Spencer, he never filled an academic post, spending most of his time either as a successful small-town banker or as the editor of the well-known financial magazine, the London *Economist*. He was also the author of several books which had an enormous influence over the intellectual life of his contemporaries. Of these the most important was *Physics and Politics*. It should be noted that the title of this book is misleading, as its main theme is the relation, not between physics and politics, but between biology and politics, and thus marks another important milestone in adapting the Darwinian theory of evolution to the field of social and political activity.

Bagehot thought of himself as a Liberal, and even stood (unsuccessfully) as a Liberal candidate for Parliament, but there were many things in his political philosophy which gave support to several of the fundamental tenets of the etatist cause. The later etatists were, as we know, traditionalists, and we find that Bagehot, in contrast with Spencer, was a profound believer in traditionalism. Though Spencer thought of society and the state as an organism, the product of slow, steady growth, he had little or no respect for the past or the teachings and traditions of the past. Bagehot, on the other hand, was essentially conservative in most of his political attitudes. "The first duty of society is the preservation of society." You cannot, Bagehot maintained,

> improve the living by political change, unless you contrive to regulate change to a slow and sober pace, quiet, almost insensible, like that of the growth of grain. If you cannot do that, perhaps it is better to hold steadily to the old present ways of life under a strong, unshaken government, capable of guidance and command.

The later etatists we found to be greatly influenced by irrationalism, the idea that man's political actions are motivated much more by the instincts and emotions than by reason. It is of significance that Bagehot, unlike Spencer, was an early but enthusiastic supporter of political irrationalism. Spencer was well aware of the absurd actions and ridiculous beliefs prevalent among primitive peoples and even among the civilized peoples of his own day, but he could never get away from the notion that the basis of all human action was rational self-interest. He insisted that most of man's religious and social creeds were crass superstitions, but he also insisted that men arrived at these creeds by reasoning upon false premises or without adequate data. Bagehot, on the other hand, was convinced that man's actions only to a very slight extent were based upon rational self-interest.

> No orator ever made an impression by appealing to men as to their plainest physical wants, except when he could allege that those wants were caused by some one's tyranny. But thousands have made the greatest impression by appealing to some vague dream of glory or empire or nationality.[10]

Bagehot insisted that the vast majority of human beliefs and human actions are not founded upon reasoning at all, but upon unconscious imitation, thus anticipating the doctrine of Tarde.

> The truth is that the propensity of man to imitate what is before him is one of the strongest parts of his nature.... We must not think that this imitation is voluntary or even conscious. On the contrary, it has its seats mainly in very obscure parts of the mind, whose notions, so far from having been consciously produced, are hardly felt to exist; so far from being conceived beforehand, are not even felt at the time.[11]

Because of this imitation man tends to render blind obedience to the beliefs and institutions handed down to him from his ancestors.

> Society is not then formed upon a "voluntary system," but upon an involuntary. A man in early ages is born to a certain obedience, and cannot extricate himself from an inherited government. Society then is made up, not of individuals, but of families; creeds then descend by inheritance in those families.[12]

Of even greater importance for our present study is the fact that Bagehot was far more radical and far more consistent than Spencer in the application of Darwinism to social and political problems. Spencer, to be sure, frequently spoke of the struggle for existence and the survival of the fittest, but this doctrine played a rather subordinate role in his detailed study of the origin and development of social and political institutions. Spencer thought that the principle of evolution was innate and inevitable in human affairs, that all social organisms because of an inner urge were bound to grow from "indefinite, incoherent, homogeneous units into definite, coherent heterogeneous units" irrespective of whether or not the units were engaged in the struggle for existence. Bagehot, on the other hand, thought that all social and political progress has taken place at first because of the eternal conflict between individuals and later because of the conflict between social groups. It was not the inevitable tendency towards progress but the struggle for survival which has produced the culture, the morality, the advanced social and political institutions of modern times. Of great significance to the etatist cause is the fact that Bagehot taught that social progress took place only because the struggle for existence caused men to form strong, compact social groups having despotic control over the entire conduct of their members.

The first basic doctrine in Bagehot's theory of political evolution is that in the struggle for existence those individuals survive which are able to cooperate with other individuals to form a compact group. According to Bagehot in very early prehistoric times men lived either as isolated individuals or else in small loosely knit family groups. Bagehot's picture of man's condition at this stage of evolution is very similar to that drawn by Hobbes in speaking of "the state of nature." To Bagehot, as to Hobbes, life amongst the primitive savages was a *bellum omnium contra omnes*, the war of all against all. "Whatever may be said against the principle of natural selection in other departments, there is no doubt of its predominance in early human history. The strongest killed the weakest as they could." [13] Certainly as regards primitive times Carlyle's dictum is true: "The ultimate question between every two human beings is, 'Can I kill thee, or canst thou kill me.'" [14] Rousseau was wrong in his idyllic picture of primitive savage life. Dryden likewise was wrong in writing, "When wild in woods the noble savage ran."

"When lone in woods the cringing savage crept" would have been more like all we know of that early, bare, painful period. Not only had they no comfort, no convenience ... , but their mind within was as painful to them as the world without.   It was full of fear.   So far as the vestiges inform us, they were afraid of everything; they were afraid of animals, of certain attack by near tribes, of possible inroads from far tribes.[15]

Bagehot agreed with Hobbes that even in modern civilized man the old wild primeval passions lie sleeping and may be reawakened when well-organized social and political institutions break down.

> We now understand why order and civilization are so unstable even in progressive communities.   We see frequently in states what physiologists call "Atavism" — the return, in part, to the unstable nature of their barbarous ancestors.   Such scenes of cruelty and horror as happened in the great French Revolution, and as happen, more or less, in every great riot, have always been said to bring out a secret and suppressed side of human nature, and we now see that they were the outbreak of inherited passions long repressed by fixed custom, but starting into life as soon as that repression was catastrophically removed, and when sudden choice was given.[16]

Hobbes thought that the state of nature was so horrible that man voluntarily gave up his isolation and his independence and formed the social contract.   To Bagehot the whole idea of the social contract was an absurdity.   But his own doctrine was not fundamentally different in its essence.   To Bagehot the horrors of early primitive life eventually led to the formation of groups, or to the strengthening of whatever loose group life may have existed at the time.   It is not so much that the horrors of isolated life are so great that man voluntarily goes in for group life, but rather that in the early universal period of conflict those individuals who wish to remain isolated and independent succumb to those individuals who form themselves into groups, or to those in whom the primitive group spirit is strongest and most active.

> I need not pause to prove that any form of polity is more efficient than none; that an aggregate of families owing even a slippery allegiance to a single head would be sure to have the better of a set of families acknowledging no obedience to any one, but scattering loose about the world and fighting where they stood.   Homer's Cyclops would be powerless against the feeblest band. ...[17]

Because of the struggle for existence, "the first thing to acquire is, if I may so express it, the legal fibre; a polity first — what sort of polity is immaterial; a law first — what kind of law is secondary; a person or set of persons to pay deference to — though who he is or they are, by comparison, scarcely signifies."[18]

The second basic doctrine in Bagehot's political philosophy is that groups once having been formed, the struggle for existence between these groups has as a consequence that those groups survive and prosper which are most compact, are best disciplined, and are the most homo-geneous in character.

> Unless you can make a strong co-operative bond, your society will be con-quered and killed out by some other society which has such a bond.... The members of such a group should be similar enough to one another to co-operate easily and readily together. The co-operation in all such cases depends on a felt union of heart and spirit; and this is felt only where there is a great degree of real likeness in mind and feeling, however that likeness may have been at-tained.[19]

> The most obedient, the tamest tribes are, at the first stage in the real struggle of life, the strongest and the conquerors.... What makes one tribe to differ from another is their relative faculty of coherence.... The compact tribes win, and the compact tribes are the tamest.[20]

By "tamest" Bagehot obviously means not the weakest or the meek-est, but those most willing to submit to the discipline ordained by the group.

For a group to be compact and coherent it is necessary that all its members act, talk, and even think more or less alike.

> The needful co-operation and this requisite likeness I believe to have been produced by one of the strongest yokes... and the most terrible tyrannies ever known among men — the authority of "customary law." In its earlier stages this is no pleasant power — no rose-water authority... — but a stern, incessant, implacable rule.[21]

As is well known, all primitive communities are completely subject to customary law. What the member of such a community wears, what he eats, where and how he dwells, all the most minute details of his daily life are dictated by custom, and in Bagehot's opinion, rightly so.

> What you want is a comprehensive rule binding men together, making them do much the same things... — fashioning them alike, and keeping them so. What this rule is does not matter so much. A good rule is better than a bad one, but any rule is better than none.... How you get the obedience of men is the hard problem; what you do with that obedience is less critical.[22]

In order to have blind obedience to the customary law of the group, it was necessary to have not only political but also religious sanctions.

> To gain that obedience the primary condition is the identity — not the union, but the sameness — of what we now call Church and State.... What is there requisite is a single government — call it Church or State, as you like — regulating the whole of human life. No division of power is then endurable without danger — probably without destruction; the priest must not teach

one thing and the King another; King must be priest, and prophet King; the two must say the same, because they are the same. The idea of difference between spiritual penalties and legal penalties must never be awakened. Indeed, early Greek thought or early Roman thought would never have comprehended it.... We now talk of political penalties and ecclesiastical prohibition, and the social censure, but they were one then.[23]

Many of the early religions were a mass of crude superstitions and were accompanied by odious and horrible rites, "but one use they assuredly had; they fixed the yoke of custom thoroughly on mankind. ... They put upon a fixed law a sanction so fearful that no one would dream of not conforming to it." [24]

It is all very well for us moderns to talk about liberty and equality, but such notions

are fitted only to the new world in which society has gone through its early task: when the inherited organization is already confirmed and fixed; when the soft minds and the strong passions of youthful nations are fixed and guided by hard transmitted instincts. Till then not equality before the law is necessary, but inequality, for what is most wanted is an elevated *élite* who know the law; not a good government seeking the happiness of its subjects, but a dignified and overawing government getting its subjects to obey: not a good law, but a comprehensive law binding all life to one routine.[25]

Considering this fact it is small wonder that in most early communities we find a powerful oligarchy, a patriciate "which alone could know the fixed law; which alone could apply the fixed law ... had then sole command over the primary social want." [26]

It is small wonder that most early communities, at least those which were pre-eminently successful, had a strong, ruthless despot at the top of the social and political pyramid.

Travellers have noticed that amongst savage tribes those seemed to answer best in which the monarchical power was most predominant, and those worst in which the "rule of many" was in its vigor. So long as war is the main business of nations, temporary despotism ... is indispensable. Macaulay justly said that many an army has prospered under a bad commander, but no army has ever prospered under a "debating society"; that many headed monster is then fatal.[27]

As early groups live in an almost constant state of war, it is only natural that they tend towards a despotic form of government.

Once it is granted that the more compact, coherent groups triumph over the less compact, coherent groups, it follows that early groups must do everything possible to secure coherence and compactness. This in turn means that early states to be successful must seek after cultural isolation. It also means that groups must persecute those of its members who do not follow the established pattern.

The necessity of thus forming co-operative groups by fixed customs explains the necessity of isolation in early society. As a matter of fact all great nations have been prepared in privacy and in secret. They have been composed far away from all distraction. Greece, Rome, Judaea were framed each by itself; and the antipathy of each to men of different race and different speech is one of their most marked peculiarities, and quite their strongest common property. And the instinct of early ages is a right guide ... for the needs of early ages. Intercourse with foreigners then broke down in states the fixed rules which were forming their characters, so as to be a cause of weak fibre of mind, of desultory and unsettled action; the living spectacle of an admitted unbelief destroys the binding authority of religious custom and snaps the social cord. Thus we see the use of a sort of "preliminary" age in societies, when (foreign) trade is bad because it prevents the separation of nations, because it infuses distracting ideas among occupied communities, because it brings "alien minds to alien shores." [28]

For the same reason the need for persecution was equally obvious.

The persecuting tendency of all savages, and, indeed, of all ignorant people, is even more striking than their imitative tendency. No barbarian can bear to see one of his nation deviate from the old barbarous customs and usages of their tribe.... In early ages the act of one member of the tribe is conceived to make all the tribe impious, to offend its peculiar god, to expose all the tribe to penalties from heaven.... The early tribe or nation is a religious partnership, on which a rash member by a sudden impiety may bring utter ruin. If the state is conceived thus, toleration becomes wicked. A permitted deviation from the transmitted ordinances becomes simply folly. It is a sacrifice of the happiness of the greatest number. It is allowing one individual, for a moment's pleasure or a stupid whim, to bring terrible and irretrievable calamity upon all. [29]

This attitude and the persecution which follows from this attitude may strike us as odious, but it served a very useful purpose. A group could only survive if it were coherent, and coherency demanded uniformity in action and even uniformity in speech and thought. A group permitting individual variations perished at the hands of a group which acted as a single homogeneous unit.

The third basic doctrine in Bagehot's political philosophy is that in the conflict between groups which are equally compact it is the higher and nobler group which generally wins. The law of conflict or the struggle for existence thus leads not only to material but also to moral progress. As we have already seen, the struggle for existence means that the isolated man perishes and the group survives, that the incoherent group perishes and the coherent group survives.   But even among coherent groups conflict goes on.   In this conflict the fittest survives, and (this is the important point) Bagehot was convinced that broadly speaking the fittest is also the best.

> In every particular state of the world those nations which are strongest tend to prevail over the others and in certain marked peculiarities the strongest tend to be the best. . . .[30]
>
> Every nation is an "hereditary co-operative group," bound by a fixed custom; and out of those groups those conquer which have the most binding and most invigorating customs, and these are, as a rough rule, the best customs. The majority of the "groups" which win and conquer are better than the majority of those which fail and perish, and thus the first world grew better and was improved.[31]
>
> It is only by the competition of customs that bad customs can be eliminated and good customs multiplied.   Conquest is the premium given by nature to those national characters which their national customs have made most fit to win in war, and in many most material respects those winning characters are really the best characters.[32]

Not only does conflict make for progress, but without conflict progress would be impossible.   "This principle explains . . . why western Europe was early in advance of other countries because there the contest of races was unusually severe." [33]

Take, for example, the case of morals.   Early primitive man undoubtedly had a very low moral standard, but in the conflict of groups with different moral standards, the groups with the higher standard tend to prevail.

> There are cases in which some step in intellectual progress gives an early society some gain in war; more obvious cases are when some kind of moral quality gives some such gain.   War both needs and breeds certain virtues, not the highest but what might be called the preliminary virtues as valor, veracity, the spirit of obedience, the habit of discipline.   Any of these and others like them, when possessed by a nation, and no matter how generated, will give them a military advantage and make them more likely to stay in the race of nations . . . and the success of the nations which possess these martial virtues has been the great means by which their continuance has been secured in the world, and the destruction of the opposite vices also. . . . The hard impact of military virtues beats meanness out of the world.[34]

It was the conflict of groups which brought about the evolution of the present family system.   Bagehot was convinced that a very low form of sexual morality prevailed among early mankind.   He thought early man was more or less promiscuous, with the result that descent was and could only be traced on the female side.   In contrast with this, those nations which developed a strong family system tended to prevail, and hence the modern family system is now more or less universal.

> A coherent family is the best germ for a compaigning nation. In a Roman family the boys from the time of their birth were bred to a domestic despotism which well prepared them for a subjection in after life to a military discipline. ... They conquered the world in manhood because as children they were bred in homes where the tradition of passionate valor was steadied by the habit of implacable order.   And nothing of this is possible in loosely bound family groups (if they can be called families at all) where the father is more or less uncertain. .... An ill knit nation which would be conquered like a mob by another nation which had a vestige or a beginning of the *patria potestas.*[35]

As with morals and family life, so also with religion.   Bagehot, we know, laid great emphasis upon the role played by religion and religious fears in the formation of strong, compact groups.   He was equally convinced of the importance of religious sanctions and religious motivations in more developed social and political life.

> Whatever may be the fate of his fame, Mr. Carlyle has taught the present generation many lessons and one of these is that "God fearing" armies are the best armies.   Before this time people laughed at Cromwell's saying, "Trust in God and keep the powder dry."   But now we know that the trust was of as much use as the powder if not more.   That high concentration of steady feeling makes men dare everything and do anything.[36]

The conflict, the martial conflict, of nations has also brought it about that the lower, more primitive forms of religion have perished, and the higher, purer forms of religion have survived.

> The better religions have had a great physical advantage over the worse. ... The savage subjected to a mean superstition is afraid to walk simply about the world. ... But under the higher religions there is no similar slavery and no similar terror. ... The belief of the Roman that he was to trust in the Gods of Rome for these Gods were stronger than all others; the belief of Cromwell's soldiers that they were to "trust God and keep the powder dry" are great upward steps in progress. ... More directly what I call the fortifying religions ... have had plainly the most obvious effect in strengthening the races which believed them and in making those races the winning races.[37]

The fourth fundamental doctrine in Bagehot's political philosophy, the one which made him depart from the etatist tradition and join the liberals, was the notion that in the later stages of evolution the old form of government, government by despotism and government by customary law, does and should give way to "government by discussion," in which the individual is permitted a greater amount of personal freedom and in which some form of democratic control is introduced into governmental machinery. In claiming that all progress is the result of armed conflict, in claiming that the group is stronger and therefore better than the individual, that the compact, coherent group is stronger and therefore better than the loose group, Bagehot preached doctrines which were thoroughly acceptable to the radical etatists. But when he claimed that the strong, compact group was necessary and useful only at an early stage of evolution and that in later, more progressive ages a certain amount of individualism and democracy should be introduced into social and political life, the etatists raised a howl of disapproval. They pointed out that conflicts between nations are still just as important as the tribal conflicts in the past, that strong compact nations, nations organized on an etatist and authoritarian basis, still have a better chance of survival than nations which have been "corrupted" by liberal tendencies.

Even Bagehot himself was rather cautious and sometimes even skeptical in his advocacy of liberal principles. In the first place he admitted that a certain amount of liberalism in modern states was permissible in modern society only because we have inherited a strong sense of law and order from our etatist forefathers. "We reckon as the basis of our culture upon an amount of order, of tacit obedience, of prescriptive government." [38]   In other words, we in modern times can afford to be liberals after a fashion only because we have not lost our etatist instincts acquired when mankind was still very young. In the second place, Bagehot insisted that liberal institutions were not fitted for all countries or for all peoples, but only for a small number of specially capable nations. It seemed obvious to him that the French, for example, for all their quick-wittedness and vivaciousness, were ill-adapted to "government by discussion."

Bagehot happened to be in Paris in 1851 at the time when Napoleon III overthrew the French Republic and made himself dictator of France. Instead of being shocked by these proceedings, we find Bagehot writing a series of articles [39] defending Napoleon's actions, stoutly supporting the use of military violence, attacking the freedom of the press, and maintaining that France was wholly unfit for parliamentary government. At all costs the political fabric must be kept together and to do so Bagehot was willing to sacrifice both individualism and democracy. Bagehot did defend liberal institutions in England, but only because of the peculiar character of the English people. Individualism, *laissez faire*, worked very well in England only because the English were too stupid to take undue advantage of their freedom. Democracy worked very well in England, but only because the bulk of the people were instinctively deferential to their social and economic betters. Thanks to the Englishman's innate respect for rank, the apparently democratic changes of the nineteenth century have not altered the real position of the ruling classes. This is fortunate because the higher classes can still rule, and the higher classes have more political ability than the lower classes.[40]

Bagehot, moreover, disagreed with most of his liberal friends and claimed that a liberal government was less strong and less stable than a despotic etatist government. "Though government by discussion has been a principal organ for improving mankind, yet from its origin it is a plant of singular delicacy." [41] Unless well-integrated and well-coordinated, governments by discussion are apt to fall in their conflicts with compact authoritarian governments.

> Their internal frailty is even greater. As soon as discussion begins, the savage propensities of men break forth; even in modern communities, where these propensities have been weakened by ages of culture and repressed by ages of obedience, as soon as a vital topic for discussion is well started, the keenest and most violent passions break forth. Easily destroyed as are early free states by forces from without, they are even more liable to destruction by forces from within. On this account such states are rare in history.[42]

It is curious to find that one of the chief arguments which Bagehot used in defense of "government by discussion" is used by the etatist school as a weapon in the fight against liberal institutions. Bagehot (and the etatists) claim that liberal institutions, "government by discussion," lead to inaction, or at least to the slowing up of action.

> If you want to stop instant and immediate action, always make it a condition that the action should not begin till a considerable number of persons have talked it over and agreed on it.... Each kind of person will have its spokesman; each spokesman will have his characteristic objection and each his characteristic counterobjection, and so in the end nothing will be done, or at least only the minimum which is plainly urgent.[43]

It so happens that Bagehot was opposed to overmuch and to overhasty action. "An inability to stay quiet, an irritable desire to act directly is one of the most conspicuous failings of mankind." [44] To Bagehot therefore liberal institutions, by delaying action, are good. To the etatists, on the other hand, action, quick decisive action, is good, and to their minds authoritarian government is valuable if only because it permits and even aids such quick. decisive action.

Among the most influential apostles of Social Darwinism were the members of the so-called Austrian school of sociologists of whom the most important was Ludwig Gumplowicz (1838–1909). Though the school is called the Austrian school, it should be noted that Gumplowicz had numerous disciples in other countries, among them Franz Oppen heimer, professor at Frankfurt, and Lester Ward, professor at Brown University and the real founder of sociological studies in America.

Gumplowicz marks an important phase in the development of the radical etatist tradition. Considering that many of the later etatists were and are markedly anti-Semitic in tendency, it is rather amusing to note that Gumplowicz, one of their spiritual ancestors, was a Polish Jew. In spite of this Jewish background, Gumplowicz, as a young man, was an ardent supporter of the Polish national movement, and it was only after the collapse of this movement that Gumplowicz turned from active politics to academic life, becoming first an instructor and later a professor at the University of Graz. With this institution he remained connected for over thirty-three years. In his old age Gumplowicz contracted cancer of the tongue; his wife had been an invalid for several years. Unwilling to bear their miseries any longer, the devoted couple committed suicide together in 1909.

The basis of Gumplowicz's whole sociological theory is that the state and all other political institutions originate in the conflict between groups and more especially in the conquest of one group by another. As the result of this doctrine Gumplowicz felt that it was necessary to accept etatism, the authority of the state over the individual, and authoritarianism, the control of the state by a small number of its citizens.

Bagehot, for all his etatist leanings, retained a touch of old English individualism in his political philosophy. In Bagehot's view, originally, in some very early and primitive state of nature, man lived a more or less isolated and non-social existence. To Bagehot it was only as a result of the fierce struggle for existence that man learned the value of cooperation and thus came to form small, compact groups. Gumplowicz, on the other hand, claimed that man has always been a gregarious and social animal and that from the earliest times on down, he has lived in groups; that the individual as a separate unit has never had any real existence. With Gumplowicz, therefore, the whole history of mankind has been the history of groups, of the conflict between groups, and of the eventual domination of one group by another. In this group struggle it is, of course, the fittest which survive, and Gumplowicz along with Bagehot thinks that the eternal struggle between groups and the domination of the less fit groups by the more fit groups has resulted not only in material but also in social and intellectual progress.

After some hesitation Gumplowicz came to the conclusion that all the numerous races of men may at some very early period have had a common origin, that all the various human races may have sprung from a single branch of some ape-like stock; but he was firmly convinced that for untold ages the various branches of this common human stock lived in complete isolation from one another with the result that all these various branches became highly differentiated both as regards body type and also with respect to such important matters as manners, customs, language, and religion.[45] At the dawn of human history, when we first become acquainted with the condition of mankind, we find it split into a large number of separate groups, each with its own physical type, its own social and moral pattern, its own language, its own religion. Each one of these groups Gumplowicz calls a *race*, giving to the word race a rather peculiar significance. To Gumplowicz it is certain that all these races looked upon one another with marked hostility, that each race regarded the members of the other races as complete and absolute aliens, as beings who were scarcely human. For this reason to rob, to enslave, or to kill the members of an alien race was not considered as in any way a moral evil.

To Gumplowicz these early groups or races were necessarily small; almost invariably the members of each group were united by ties of blood. In other words, these early units were merely small, compact, kinship groups. But though small the influence of such groups upon their members was overwhelming. The actions, the speech, even the thoughts of the individual were dominated by the group of which he was a member.

> It is not man himself who thinks but his social community; the source of his thoughts is in the social medium in which he lives, the social atmosphere which he breathes, and he can not think aught else than what the influences of his social environment concentrating upon his brain necessitate.... What we think is the necessary result of the mental influences to which we have been subjected since childhood.[46]

To Gumplowicz this is more or less true even in modern times; it was absolutely true when the kinship group was the only social influence to which the individual was subjected.

In these early "races" or kinship groups there was no political organization in the modern sense of the word. A vague sort of leadership may have been exercised by the group elders or the group chief, but this leadership was not important, as all members of the group were considered more or less equal.   There were no castes or classes, no distinctions between rulers and subjects; all members of the group were considered members of the same family, with a right to equal privileges. In such groups there were no laws or legal rights in the modern sense of the words, for to Gumplowicz all true laws and all true legal rights are the product of the state, which came into existence only in comparatively modern times — many thousands of years after the evolution of mankind and of the various kinship groups.   Among these early groups the place of true law, the dictates of the state, was taken by customary law, enforced by social and religious sanctions.   To Gumplowicz the early customary law has served as the basis of all later "morality" and "moral sense."   Every community or group, in order to preserve its own existence, created for itself a rigid code of conduct which it imposed on all its members.   This code had, of course, a purely naturalistic origin, the desire of the group to insure discipline and thus succeed in conflicts with other groups; but man is a "myth-maker and poet by nature," and soon learned to ascribe a divine origin to the code which he himself invented as an aid to himself in the struggle for existence.

In this attitude towards the origin of morals, Gumplowicz is only echoing the ideas enunciated by Bagehot, but Gumplowicz soon departs from Bagehot on one very vital point.   To Bagehot the herd or the tribe developed into the state as the result of slow, internal evolution. To Gumplowicz, on the other hand, the state originated as the result of cataclysmic action, the conquest of one group by another, or rather by the conquest of several weaker groups by one powerful dominating group.

> Every political organization, and hence every developing organization, begins when one group permanently subjects another.   Subjection of some to others is the source of political organization, is the condition essential to social growth.   This proposition constitutes the corner stone of the author's theory.[47]

Gumplowicz is convinced that from very early times, from the period when the previously isolated human groups or "races" first came into contact with one another, they frequently came into armed conflict, and that from this conflict, especially from the triumph of the stronger over the weaker, there have arisen many important social, economic, and political consequences.   As the result of tribal raids the women of

the weaker groups were seized and brought home to serve as the con-
cubines of the triumphant warriors. This, to Gumplowicz, was the
origin of the modern family. In the early primitive horde, says Gumplowicz, there prevailed a system of sexual promiscuity, and descent
and kinship were necessarily traced exclusively on the female side.
The triumphant warrior, however, insisted upon having exclusive sexual
rights over the alien women he captured, and this fact eventually led
to the tracing of descent on the father's side. Just as tribal wars led
to "father-hood, father-family, father-right," [48] so did such wars also
lead to the institution of private property, a notable step in economic
progress. To Gumplowicz the primitive horde was essentially com-
munistic, all property being held in common; but in tribal conflicts
the victorious warrior was allowed to keep the goods he had looted from
the neighboring tribes. This dealt a deathblow to the earlier communism and indirectly led to the distinction between rich and poor.
Finally the conflict between groups led to slavery. The defeated
tribesmen, instead of being killed, were forced to labor for their victorious rivals, which led not only to rigorous class and caste distinctions,
but also to the appearance of a leisure class, a group of persons who
could live upon the exertions of others. Gumplowicz, like Aristotle, is
convinced that it was the existence of this leisure class which in time
permitted the growth of art, literature, science, and civilization.

In very early times tribal conflicts were in the nature of casual raiding
or looting parties and did not lead to permanent conquest or subjugation
of peoples on a large scale. According to Gumplowicz, during this
period we cannot, therefore, speak of the existence of fully fledged
states, for the true state only emerges when one group gains complete
and permanent control, both economic and political, over other groups.
In insisting that practically all the historic states have come into existence through conquest, Gumplowicz makes a very interesting contribution to political theory. Gumplowicz rejects as absurd the notion
that the state was a divine creation, ordained and instituted by God
for the control of sinful man. He rejects as equally absurd the idea
that the state came into existence as the result of a voluntary compact
or social contract between previously isolated individuals. He likewise
rejects the Aristotelian doctrine that the family gradually and peace-
fully expanded into the tribe and the tribe into the state.

In claiming that the state originated in force, Gumplowicz had many
predecessors, notably the French thinker, Jean Bodin. But most of
these predecessors thought that the force used was the force employed

by an individual to secure control over the other members of his group. To Gumplowicz this individual force might bring about a change of rulers or a change in dynasty, but it would not account for the origin of the state as such. States as states have originated only when one group has by forceful means secured control over other groups.

> The state, ... during the first stages of its existence, is a social institution, forced by a victorious group of men on a defeated group, with the sole purpose of regulating the dominion of the victorious group over the vanquished. ...[49]

Gumplowicz himself is content to lay down the general proposition that the state originates in conquest. His pupil, Oppenheimer, goes into greater detail and attempts to point out the various stages which take place in the formation of the state. To him most great states in the historic past have been formed as the result of the perpetual inroads of nomadic herdsmen into the territories occupied by peaceful agriculturalists. During the first stage the invaders are content to kill, to rape, to loot, and to enslave. In the second stage,

> it begins to dawn on the consciousness of the wild herdsman that a murdered peasant can no longer plow, and that a fruit tree hacked down will no longer bear. In his own interest ... he lets the peasant live and the tree stand [50]

in order that he, himself, may collect fresh tribute at some future time. It was really this stage which

> gave birth to nation and state, to right [i.e., law] and the higher economics. ...[51] The third stage arrives when the "surplus" obtained by the peasantry is brought by them regularly to the tents of the herdsmen as "tribute." ... By this means the peasantry is relieved entirely from the little irregularities connected with the former method of taxation, such as a few men knocked on the head, women violated, or farmhouses burned down.[52]

The fourth stage is reached when the conquering or invading group settles down and resides permanently in the territory inhabited by the subjugated group, instead of visiting it periodically to collect tribute. At the fifth stage the conquerors insist on arbitrating the various disputes which arise among the subjugated peoples, especially quarrels between neighboring villages, as such quarrels, if fought out, would impair the capacity of the peasants to render service and tribute. In the sixth stage the conquerors and the conquered gradually amalgamate to form one nation, and the full-fledged state is born, with the conquerors no longer regarded as aliens, but merely as the upper or governing class.

In modern historical times many states have arisen more directly, that is to say without going through all the six separate stages, but

Gumplowicz, and with him all of the members of the Austrian school, is convinced that all or practically all the great historical states have arisen through the conquest of one group by another, with the sole exception of those states which have arisen (like the states of the New World) by rebellion against previously existent states. In some cases the record is clear. Sparta we know arose from the Dorian conquest of an earlier autochthonous population; France from the Frankish conquest of the Latinized Celts; England in the first place from the Anglo-Saxon conquest of the early Britons, and then in a new form from the Norman conquest of the Anglo-Saxons; Russia from the Varangian conquest of the Slavs. In some cases, as for example Athens and Rome, the real origin of the state is unknown or is beclouded by myth and fable, but even here, Gumplowicz asserts, we have strong indirect evidence that conquest played an important part in the formation of political institutions.

Gumplowicz is convinced that law, in the modern sense of the word, and all legal rights and duties are the creations of the state and are the result of the attempt on the part of the conquerors to impose rigid living conditions upon the subjected populations. The old customary law of the kinship group, the root of modern morality, was quite different in character. It was imposed by the group upon itself. It was egalitarian in its nature, imposing the same duties upon all persons. It was imposed not by force, but by tradition and by social and religious sanctions. Modern or state law, on the other hand, is essentially the command of the political sovereign and is enforced by the police and the judges are appointed by the sovereign. The Austrian school thinks that this modern type of law originated in the following way:

> After the conquest of one group by another, the conquered or tributary group is at first controlled by arbitrary military rule, but sooner or later such personal government grows wearisome, and some change is demanded. It is found that authority may be generalized and that rules may be adopted for the repressions of certain general classes of acts such as are most frequently committed. When this is found to be economical, still larger groups of conduct are made the subject of general regulation.[53]

In this fashion certain elementary legal principles were established which gradually grew into elaborate systems of jurisprudence.

> [Legal] rights are not the product of the individual and his nature and constitution, nor are they the creation of the folk or of a common will or national spirit. . . . Rights are a social creation, a form of communal life produced by the conflict of unlike social groups of unequal power; such unlike

ness and inequality is the necessary precondition of all rights. ... Thus family right subjects the wife and children to the control of the father. ... Property rights regulate the inequality between owner and non-owner in respect to the thing owned; the rights of inheritance regulate the inequality between the heir and the non-heir in respect of the inheritance; the rights of debtor and creditor regulate the inequality between them in respect of the obligation. In short every right comes from an inequality and aims to maintain and establish it through the sovereignty of the stronger over the weaker. In this respect every right is a true reflection of the state, to which it owes its existence.[54]

Gumplowicz agrees with Thrasymachus in Plato's *Republic*, "my doctrine is that justice is the interest of the stronger." [55] He is equally convinced that all talk of natural rights, alleged to exist outside the state, beyond its borders and superior to its authority, is ridiculous. The doctrine of natural rights is "overthrown, dead, and buried." [56] The doctrine of natural rights being absurd, it follows that all talk of innate or inalienable rights, such as the right to live or the right to work, is equally absurd.

That man is a free being is pure imagination. ... The premises of "inalienable human rights" rest upon the most unreasonable self-deification of man and overestimate the value of human life, and upon complete misconception of the only possible basis of the existence of the state. This fancied freedom and equality is incompatible with the state and is a complete negation of it.[57]

To Gumplowicz it seems obvious that the state originated in conquest and is maintained by power or force. Without power or force the state would cease to exist; and that state is most successful and hence is the best which is the most powerful and most forceful in its operations. To talk of the private rights of the individual against the state is nonsense. As all rights are derived from the state, the state has the "right" to treat its subjects in any way it pleases. Freedom and equality are myths which should be dismissed from serious political discussion. Arguing as he does from these premises, it is not surprising that Gumplowicz dismisses all international or cosmopolitan ideals with a sneer. To him, as we know, the normal relation between two alien groups is that of conflict. In primitive times the conflicting groups were tribes or "races." In modern times states have taken the place of the earlier "races," but the principle of conflict still remains. When two states are in contact with one another they are bound to compete with one another either in the political or in the economic sphere or in both. So long as the state has aggressive power, it strives to augment and increase its territory, to conquer, and to colonize. "This continues until strength fails from internal or external causes or until the state is surpassed by other states or crippled. Only when strength fails does strife cease." [58]

When one remembers that Gumplowicz thinks the state begins with ruthless conquest and is maintained by the relentless use of force, one would think that to Gumplowicz and his followers the state would be regarded as something inherently evil. Such is far from the case. The state to them is not only necessary, the inevitable outcome of social evolution, but it is also something inherently good. Without the state, brutal though it is, there would be no industry, no commerce, no material progress. Without the state and its forceful inequalities, there would be no literature, no art, no science. In the primitive horde there was indeed equality, but equality in misery. In the state there is inequality, but at least some of its subjects, usually the strongest or the cleverest, have a chance to improve their living conditions and to develop their higher faculties.

> The only choice for men here below is between the state with its necessary servitude and inequality and — anarchy. There is much unavoidable evil in the former, but on the other hand it promotes and protects the greatest good that man can experience on earth. Anarchy raises infinitely the evil which is unavoidable in the state without affording even the least of its advantages, for the greatest human evil here below is human stupidity and baseness. Scarcely can the state hold it in check; in a condition of anarchy it rages without restraint, heaping horror upon horror. There is no third choice, for it is impossible to return to the primitive horde, and between these two modes of social existence, the state and anarchy, it is not hard to choose. [59]

Gumplowicz' theory of the state as force or power gives strong though indirect support to the etatist cause. Equally important is another phase of Gumplowicz' political philosophy, the theory of class conflict, which serves as a support of authoritarianism, the belief that a small minority of the citizens should and must control the organs of government. Briefly stated, Gumplowicz' theory is that the historical development of the state gradually brings about the superficial assimilation of all the heterogeneous groups within the state and eventually produces what appears to the casual observer a single homogeneous people or nation. In reality, however, each people, each nation, continues to consist of a number of separate groups — the so-called social and economic classes. These groups or classes are always in bitter, though hidden, conflict with one another, and the political history of each state is really the story of these group or class conflicts. In these conflicts it is, of course, the fittest which succeed in dominating the less fit groups, which means that it is the fittest which seize and maintain control over the governmental machinery.

The process of integration or superficial assimilation which goes on within the state is, to Gumplowicz' mind, obvious to all students of history. At first the conquerors (the ruling class within the state) differ in body type, in language, in religion from the conquered (the subject classes). But as time goes on these differences tend to disappear.

> The two dialects become one language; or one of the two, often of an entirely different stock from the other, becomes extinct. This, in some cases, is the language of the victors, but more frequently that of the vanquished. Both cults amalgamate to one religion, in which the tribal god of the conquerors is adored as the principal divinity, while the old gods of the vanquished become either his servants, or, as demons or devils, his adversaries. The bodily type tends to assimilate, through the influence of the same climate and similar mode of living. Where a strong difference between the types existed or is maintained, the bastards, to a certain extent, fill the gap — so that, in spite of the still existing ethnic contrast, everybody more and more, begins to feel that the type of the enemies beyond the border is more strange, more "foreign" than is the new co-national type. Lords and subjects view one another as "we," at least as concerns the enemy beyond the border; and at length the memory of the different origin completely disappears.[60]

This process of integration or assimilation is greatly aided by the fact that the state in the course of its development produces a number of new groups or classes, and the very existence of these new groups tends to blur the sharp line of demarcation between the highest (or conquering) and the lowest (or conquered) classes. At first the state has only the rulers or landowning lords on the one side and the land-tilling, rent-paying peasants on the other. But before long there appears a middle class of merchants and industrialists. To Gumplowicz and his school, this new merchant class originates by immigration or the settlement within the state of foreigners who are attracted to the towns and villages by the possibilities of trade. Gumplowicz tries to show that in primitive states the bulk of the traders are aliens. In Athens most of the trade lay with the metics or resident strangers; in mediaeval England most of the merchants were Flems, or Germans, or Italians. Even in more modern times the merchant classes of Turkey, of Hungary, of Poland have been foreigners, either Armenians or Jews or Germans.

As states develop, this middle class group also becomes assimilated, adopting the language and the religion of the country in which it resides. Usually it begins to recruit new members from the other groups of classes, from the poorer members of the lordly class and from the more ambitious members of the peasant class, until in the end the middle class is completely "nationalized." In most cases economic and social progress means that many new classes or groups develop, such as the priestly class and the various professional groups. For the most part the members of the new groups are likewise recruited from among the members of the older groups, and hence from the very beginning are not regarded as alien elements within the community.

In this way the fully developed state, though really formed from many different ethnic elements, eventually secures a simple homogeneous appearance. The teaching of and the belief in rabid nationalism tend to emphasize this illusion. In reality, however, each group within the state, whatever its origin, remains or becomes a separate element. "Each has its own interests which it represents, its own power which it strives to increase, and each bears down upon the others according to its strength and their resistance." [61] Above all, each group tries to secure a dominating influence over the state and the machinery of government. However uniform it may appear, "every state in history was or is a state of classes, a polity of superior and inferior social groups, based upon distinctions either of rank or of property." [62] However much each class or group pays lip service to the ideal of national solidarity, each group naturally and normally endeavors to keep the others in their place by seeking its own advantage through the exploitation of the others and keeping its own interests intact. "The struggle between social groups, the component parts of the state, is as inexorable as that between hordes or states. The only motive is self-interest." [63]

Gumplowicz and his school make an elaborate attempt to interpret all political history in terms of group or class struggle. The internal history of Athens or of Rome is largely the story of the struggle between the *eupatridae* and the commoners, or between the patricians and the plebeians — later on between the rich and the poor. Rome changed from a republic to an empire because the Caesars managed to get the organized support of the great unwashed. In mediaeval times class struggles involved such separate elements as the central authority (the emperor or king), the higher feudal nobility, the lower nobility, the burghers, the common freemen, and the serfs. The conflicts and the coalitions between these various groups account for the developments which took place during the Middle Ages. In the sixteenth century we find a coalition between the king and the rising middle classes to put down the power of the feudal nobility — thus producing centralization and "benevolent despotism." During the eighteenth century a change of coalitions took place. The king and the nobility banded together to keep the middle classes in their place. The middle classes in return secured for themselves the support of the lower classes, with crises such as the American and French Revolutions as the inevitable result.

Some of the adherents of the Austrian school, men such as Oppenheimer and Ward, hope that the class state of the past and present will eventually give way to a utopian, classless state. Gumplowicz, however, the patriarch of the school, insists that such views are completely visionary. To him, classes, groups, and group conflicts are eternal and necessary elements in human society. A classless society is sheer nonsense and wherever, as in revolutionary France, an attempt is made to establish such a society, the result is always anarchy, followed by reaction and the re-establishment of classes, of class conflict, and the domination of the less efficient by the more efficient classes. A state is and always will be

> the organized control of the minority over the majority. This is the only true and universal definition; it is apt in every case.[64] The rulership of a majority over a minority is as unthinkable as it is absurd. It lies in the nature of things that a pyramid must rest on a broad basis, becoming smaller and smaller as it rises to the top. It is impossible to place a pyramid upside down, with its broad base suspended in the air. In like manner it lies in the nature of rulership that it can only exist in the domination of the minority over the majority.[65]

The establishment of parliamentary machinery or of universal manhood suffrage does not, to Gumplowicz, affect the truth of this statement. "The outer form of the government is not the decisive factor; the fight of the classes is carried on and leads to the same result in a republic as in a monarchy." [66] In a democratic republic the great mass of the population must continue to live in poverty, earning their living by hard labor while a minority of "exploiters" gather in the tribute. In a democratic republic, real effective political control is not with the masses, but with the plutocratic wire-pullers or with rabble-rousing demagogues. The socialists aim at a classless democratic state, but in point of fact the triumph of socialism means either the rule of a small number of bureaucrats or the dictatorship of the proletariat — and the proletariat means, in practice, not the broad mass of the workers, but a small and highly organized group within the working class. Make what legislative reforms we will, the world is and will continue to be dominated by a minority.

If a state must necessarily be dominated by a minority, the question then arises which minority, which group or coalition of groups, should control the state? To this question Gumplowicz refuses to give a direct answer. A scientist, according to Gumplowicz, should lay aside all questions of value. He should dismiss from his mind all thought of what should or should not take place. But behind this mask of objectivity we soon see that Gumplowicz is in favor of dictatorial control by the upper and middle classes. To Gumplowicz the struggle for existence results in the survival or rather the domination of the fittest — and broadly speaking the fittest are also the "best." The struggle between the groups or classes has brought the fittest, the "best" elements to the top of the social, political, and economic ladder. In "the subjection of one social group by another and the establishment of sovereignty . . . the sovereign body is always less numerous. But numerical superiority is supplemented by mental superiority." [67] There may, of course, be many individual exceptions, but as a general rule each group in the social pyramid occupies the place which it has proved itself the fittest to occupy. Once we grant these premises; once we admit that the state must always be dominated by a small minority; once we further admit that the upper and middle strata of society are not only the fittest, but also inherently the best — it should follow that we must take the further step and accept the doctrine that the upper and middle classes should constitute the minority entrusted with the control of the machinery of government. Such at least were the conclusions drawn from Gumplowicz's political philosophy by later authoritarians.

EUGENICS AND THE DOCTRINE OF CLASS SUPERIORITY

Closely associated with the doctrines of Social Darwinism, though differing in one or two essential respects, are the teachings of the group of men whom we may call the eugenists, the originators of the science of eugenics. This school came into existence through the efforts of two Englishmen, Sir Francis Galton (1822–1911) and Karl Pearson (1857–1936), but the work of these two men has been supplemented by a large number of other persons, some biologists, some psychologists, some sociologists, in all the principal countries of the world. Last but not least, the eugenic doctrine has been taken over by a number of social and political philosophers who have tried to make eugenics the basis for a new start in political speculation. Of these one of the most popular and widely read is the American, Lothrop Stoddard, the author of *The Rising Tide of Color* and *The Revolt against Civilization*.

The eugenists agree with the older generation of Social Darwinism in accepting the doctrine of evolution and in teaching that evolution has taken place largely through the struggle for existence and the survival of the fittest. But whereas the older Social Darwinists, men such as Bagehot and Gumplowicz, took it for granted that the survival of the fittest meant, broadly speaking, the survival of the best, the eugenists are far more skeptical and far more pessimistic. They are convinced that a careful study of sociological data shows that under a system of purely natural selection, the survivors in the struggle for existence may be, and frequently are, the inferior rather than the superior breed. They are even more insistent in claiming that under the prevailing social, economic, and political systems the superior types of human beings are tending to die out, while the inferior types are tending to multiply. From these premises the eugenists draw the conclusion that the state should step in and counteract the workings of natural selection by aiding or forcing the better stocks to multiply and by forceful elimination of the worse stocks. This doctrine may be said to constitute a new variation of the old etatist theme. Equally important is the fact that most eugenists show a strong tendency to assert that social and political leadership should be placed in the hands of the biologically better stocks — and thus give voice to a variation of the old authoritarian theme.

The first basic doctrine in the eugenists' creed is that men are naturally and innately unequal. It is obvious to everyone that men differ in their bodily characteristics, such as stature, weight, pigmentation, and health. Careful psychological tests show that they also differ in their energy, their power of seeing and hearing, their sensitivity to sensations, their mental imagery, their sociability, their creative ability, and their native intelligence. These differences, these inequalities, physical, emotional, and mental, are declared to be inborn and not merely the result of differences in environment and education. It is readily admitted that environment and education do play a part in developing or suppressing natural abilities, but neither environment nor education is sufficient to account for the obvious differences in human types. A white man born and brought up in the Congo does not grow up to be a Negro. A Negro born and brought up in England does not become a Caucasian. In the English public (or boarding) schools the boys eat the same food. wear the same clothes, are usually given the same personal allowance, live in the same buildings, and attend the same classes, yet show an enormous variation in their mental abilities.

> The idea of natural equality is one of the most pernicious delusions that has ever afflicted mankind. It is a figment of the human imagination. Nature knows no equality. The most cursory examination of natural phenomena reveals the presence of a law of inequality as universal and inflexible as the law of gravitation.... Not only are the various life types profoundly unequal in qualities and capacities; the individual members of each type are similarly differentiated amongst themselves. No two individuals are ever precisely alike.... Individual inequalities steadily increase as we ascend the biological scale. The amoeba differs very little from his fellows; the dog much more so; man most of all. And inequalities between men likewise become ever more pronounced. The innate differences between members of a low grade savage tribe are as nothing compared with the abyss sundering the idiot and the genius who co-exist in high grade civilization. Thus we see that evolution means a process of ever growing inequality. There is in fact no such word as equality in nature's lexicon. With an increasingly even hand she distributes health, beauty, vigor, intelligence, genius — all the qualities which confer on their possessors superiority over their fellows.[68]

Even among persons with very similar body type or outward appearance and with very similar environmental background, there are enormous differences with respect to innate intellectual ability. Take for example the American people. With the exception of the Negroes, the American Indians, and a few persons of Oriental extraction, the Americans are racially more or less homogeneous, at least to the extent that they are all Caucasoids. Americans tend more and more to adopt a uniform culture pattern. In America class differences are far less binding and far less rigid than in Europe. In America we have universal compulsory education, so that practically all persons receive at least a grammar school education, and yet numerous psychological tests (the so-called intelligence tests) show that Americans differ widely with respect to innate mental capacity. The eugenists stress the point that these tests are tests of innate intelligence and not of knowledge. A person with an imperfect education may well have only a very scanty stock of knowledge, and yet this person may show himself to have a very high potential intelligence. A large number of intelligence tests, taken in various parts of America, seem to show that less than five per cent of the population possess very superior intelligence; that about nine per cent possess superior intelligence; that about twenty-five per cent of the population show either inferior or very inferior intelligence; and that the remainder of the population may be said to possess "average" in· telligence. According to Stoddard these tests

> have conclusively proved ... that individuals come into the world differing vastly in mental capacities; that such differences remain virtually constant throughout life and cannot be lessened by environment or education ...; that the number of really superior persons is small and that the great majority of even the most civilized populations are of mediocre or low intelligence.[69]

To the eugenists these facts are remarkable because they so flatly contradict so many of the older theories regarding the essential equality of all human beings. To the early Christians all souls were equal in the sight of God. To the Stoic philosophers all men were fundamentally and "naturally" equal, all seeming inequalities being the result of accident or artificial convention. This same egalitarianism dominated philosophical thought during the seventeenth and eighteenth centuries and continued to prevail during the early part of the nineteenth century. The great English philosophers, Hobbes and Locke and Hume, differed radically from one another on many points, but they all agreed that man in "a state of nature" is more or less equal; that the mind of all human beings at birth is a blank sheet which, through education, experience, association, habit, can be moulded and developed to an unlimited extent in any manner or direction. Some minds have been better, others worse moulded — and that is the only difference between the intelligence of various men and of various classes of men. In the middle of the nineteenth century J. S. Mill could still declare,

> Of all vulgar modes of escaping from the consideration of the effects of social and moral influences on the human mind, the most vulgar is that of attributing the diversities of conduct and character to inherent natural differences.

Of great importance is the fact that the classical expositions of liberalism with their emphasis upon democracy were all based upon the assumption that men are "naturally" more or less equal. If the eugenists be right, if men are naturally and innately unequal, it seems obvious that the old liberal creed must either be abandoned or else radically reinterpreted.

The second basic doctrine in the eugenists' creed is that the innate differences which exist between men are hereditary. Just as the children of blond parents are blond and the children of brunette parents are brunette, so, in like manner, the children of "superior" parents are superior and the children of "inferior" parents inferior.

> A man's natural abilities are derived by inheritance under exactly the same limitations as the form and physical features of the whole organic world. ...[70]
>
> If two children are taken, of whom one has a parent exceptionally gifted in a high degree ... and the other has not, the former child has an enormously greater chance of turning out to be gifted in a high degree than the other.[71]

In fact the whole eugenic creed may be summed up in the words of Karl Pearson, "Man varies, and these variations, favorable and unfavorable, are inherited." [72] Members of the same stock inherit not only the physical but also the psychological and pathological characteristics of their ancestors. Not only may we say that able fathers produce able children in a much larger proportion than the generality, but we may also say that specific ability, like that of a mathematician, a musician, an eminent lawyer, or a statesman, is commonly inherited.

In their efforts to emphasize the importance of heredity, the eugenists consistently ridicule the idea that environment is in any way as important as directly inherited capacity in the formation of superior or inferior individuals.

> I acknowledge freely the great power of education and social influences in developing the active powers of the mind, just as I acknowledge the effect of use in developing the muscles of a blacksmith, and no further. Let the blacksmith labor as he will, he will find that there are certain feats beyond his power that are well within the strength of a man of herculean make, even although the latter may have led a sedentary life.[73]

To the eugenists, of course, a man is of "herculean make" because of his hereditary background.

Some of the older biologists, such as Spencer, were earnest apostles of the importance of heredity, but claimed that environment or education had at least an indirect effect upon the future of a nation through the inheritance of acquired characteristics. According to Spencer, there are indeed innately superior and inferior human stocks, because of the difference in their respective ancestors. But to Spencer the inferior stocks are not doomed to remain forever inferior. If we take a child of inferior stock, and by careful education improve his qualities of body and mind, by the Spencerian theory, many of the good qualities and good instincts he acquires in this way will be transmitted to his offspring. Conversely, if we take a child of superior stock and allow him to debauch his talents through sloth or riotous living, the progeny of this child will tend to display a similar degeneration in virtue and health, and will be born with lower, coarser instincts than their father originally possessed.

Many of the social reformers, both liberals and socialists, during the nineteenth century, found great solace and great inspiration in the doctrine of the transmission of acquired characteristics. Departing from the complete egalitarianism of the eighteenth century, they admitted that at any one time and place some persons are superior, others inferior; but they insisted that this disparity need not be permanent. In the course of a few generations the inferior stock might improve, the superior degenerate, so that the relative position of the two strains might be completely reversed.

> The comfortable and optimistic doctrine was preached that we had only to improve one generation by more healthy surroundings, or by better education; and by the mere action of heredity the next generation would begin on a higher level of natural endowments than its predecessor. And so from generation to generation, on this theory, we could hope continually to raise the inborn character of a race in an unlimited progress of cumulative improvement.[74]

In marked contrast to all such notions, the eugenists are vehement in their insistence that acquired characteristics are not and cannot be transmitted by inheritance. To them the characteristics, the habits, the instincts which a person acquires during his lifetime have no effect whatever upon the character, the qualities, or instincts inherited by his children. According to the eugenists, some human stocks are superior, others inferior; and they retain their superiority or inferiority throughout the centuries. If, say the eugenists, we take a boy of inferior stock, a son of dull-witted parents and himself rather dull-witted, we may, by changing his environment, by careful, scientific education enormously improve his normal mental capacity. Such a person might even become a reasonably good scholar, but such improvements would be limited to a single generation. Because of his ancestral strain the children of all such persons would be born dull-witted and all the work of special education and improvement would have to be done over again. Conversely a person of good stock might, because of bad environment or bad education, appear stupid to the casual observer, but the children of such a man would be born with their innate mental qualities unimpaired and with favorable opportunity might prove themselves to be geniuses.

> Genetics ... teaches that humanity consists of numerous hereditary strains, good, mediocre, and bad, which are for all purposes of practical sociology unchangeable; that this principle applies alike to physical, mental, and spiritual qualities.[75]

To the eugenists many of the social reforms advocated by the environmentalists seem of very dubious value. The clearance of slums, free medical care for the poor, the granting of money to those unable to support themselves, and universal education at times may be very injurious to the community. It is, say the eugenists, impossible permanently to improve the human stock in this fashion. Inferior stock will continue to breed inferior children, however much we may improve its external surroundings. Moreover, financial and medical aid to the social misfits may well mean that many inferior strains will be artificially preserved when they ought to be allowed to perish. In addition, social reforms may well involve a waste of necessarily limited resources in favor of the weak to the neglect of and at the expense of the innately superior. To the eugenists the environment may not be completely neglected, because faulty training or meager schooling would retard the development of even superior individuals, but they insist that the only way in which mankind or the nation can be surely and lastingly improved is by increasing the number of persons hereditarily endowed with superior qualities, and decreasing the number of persons hereditarily endowed with inferior qualities.

The third basic doctrine of the eugenist school is that the innately superior persons and stocks tend to rise to the top of the social, economic, and political ladder, and the innately inferior persons and stocks tend to stay at the bottom of this ladder. In other words, in every country whatever its political or economic system may be, the higher classes are generally innately superior to the lower classes, and in a rough-and-ready way we may say that the social and economic position of any human group corresponds fairly closely to its innate qualities and capacities.

The eugenists devote much time to showing that the upper and middle classes, in spite of their inferiority in number, have produced far more men of genius and of talent than the lower classes. In Europe, the royal families have led in the production of men of genius. In a study made of royal families, amongst 800 individuals, 25 are declared to have been geniuses, an unusually high average.[76] A study of the most outstanding persons in English history shows that the upper and professional classes, though numbering only $4\frac{1}{2}$ per cent of the population, have produced 63 per cent of the men of genius, while the laboring class, numbering 84 per cent of the population, have produced only 12 per cent of the British men of genius. Especially noteworthy, so the eugenists tell us, is the fact that the common laborers, that is, the more or less unskilled laborers, numbering 74 per cent of the population, have produced only 2½ per cent of the men of genius.[77]   It is claimed that studies in France, in Germany, and in the United States have led to very similar conclusions.

The environmentalists, of course, claim that these conclusions are fallacious; that, even if the figures cited be true, they prove nothing because of the fact that the upper and middle classes have had greater educational advantages and have had greater leisure as a result of their economic independence and so could devote themselves with less difficulty to the higher things of life.   To the eugenists all such arguments are absurd.   "I believe," says Galton, "that if the eminent men of any period had been changelings when babies a very fair proportion of those who survived and retained their health up to fifty years of age, would, notwithstanding their altered circumstances, have risen to eminence." [78] In those few cases where geniuses are born among the lower classes, such persons have been able to overcome the handicaps of their unfortunate environment.

> It is a fact that numbers of men rise before they are middle aged from the humbler ranks of life to that worldly position in which it is of no importance to their future career how their youth has been passed. . . . Another argument to prove that the hindrances of English social life are not effectual in repressing high ability is that the number of eminent men in England is as great as in other countries where fewer hindrances exist.[79]

The eugenists claim that the position assumed on this point by Galton has been proved by the results of recent intelligence tests.   "It is extremely significant to observe how closely intelligence is correlated with industrial or professional occupation, social, or economic status." [80] In a series of tests upon the intelligence of children in the American schools it was found that intelligence of 110 to 120 I.Q. (the range defined as superior intelligence) is approximately five times as common among children of superior social status as among children of inferior social status, the group with "superior intelligence" being made up largely of children of fairly successful members of the mercantile or professional classes.   In a still higher intelligence group, those with an I.Q. above 120, defined as children "with very superior intelligence," the results are even more striking.   Among a series of 476 children "there was not a single one reaching 120 whose social class was described as 'below average.' . . . The 120–140 group is made up almost entirely of children whose parents belong to the professional or very successful business classes.   The child of a skilled laborer belongs here occasionally, the child of a common laborer very rarely indeed." [81]

It is claimed that very similar results were obtained from intelligence tests made up of adults. In this connection great emphasis is laid upon the tests conducted upon 1,700,000 officers and men during the World War. In the first place, it was found that there was a great difference between the native intelligence of officers, non-commissioned officers, and privates. The great majority of officers were found to have either "very superior" or "superior" intelligence. Among the sergeants and corporals more than one half were graded "average" in intelligence. With the rank and file, persons of "average" intelligence constituted the overwhelming majority with a small minority of persons with "very superior," "superior" intelligence, and with a somewhat larger minority of persons with definitely "inferior" intelligence.

> Next as to the correlation between intelligence and civilian occupations: the professions were found to contain a great majority of A and B men (i.e., persons with "very superior" and "superior" intelligence). The percentage of superior intelligence sank steadily through the skilled and semi-skilled occupations until it was least of all among the common laborers, very few of whom were found to possess intelligence grading higher than C ("average" intelligence) while most of them graded C − ("low average" intelligence) or D ("inferior" intelligence).... In other words, a given population tends to become more and more differentiated biologically, the upper social classes containing an ever larger proportion of persons of superior natural endowments, while the lower social classes contain a growing portion of inferiors.[82]

Arguing from these premises the eugenists draw some very interesting conclusions in the field of social and political theory. In the first place it seems clear to them that education must be different for the different social groups, corresponding to the differentiation in their inner ability. The old American theory of education — a state school attended by rich and poor, high and low — is assailed. The lower classes should indeed be educated, but in such a way as to prepare them for their menial position in life. It is better that the higher classes go to special schools where care can be taken in developing their superior intelligence. In the second place the eugenists claim that a rather rigid class system is advantageous socially and politically.

> Let there be a ladder from class to class and from occupation to occupation, but let it not be a very easy ladder to climb. Great ability (as Faraday) will get up and that is all that is socially advantageous. The gradation of the body social is not a mere historical anomaly; it is largely the result of long continued selection, economically differentiating the community into classes, roughly fitted to certain work.[83]

The fourth basic doctrine of the eugenists is that under present conditions the superior stocks show a tendency to die out, while the inferior
stocks are increasing in number. It is, of course, a notorious fact that
the upper classes are less fertile than the lower classes, certainly at the
present day. More often than not, the upper classes and upper middle
classes have only one or two children, while the ditch-digger or the unskilled laborer has a family of nine or ten. If the ditch-digger were
innately as capable as the professional man, or if his children were
mentally on a par with those of the professional man, there would be
nothing tragic or dangerous about this situation, but according to the
eugenists' creed, as we know, the professional man is usually a man with
superior intelligence, able to transmit this superior intelligence to his
children, while the ditch-digger is usually a man of low intelligence and
his children will, in all likelihood, also be persons of low intelligence.
According to the eugenists, it is impossible to effect any permanent
improvement in inferior stocks; they breed true to type, generation after
generation. If this be true it is obvious that with the superior stocks
constantly decreasing in number, and the inferior stocks constantly increasing in number in any given nation, that nation is inevitably
destined to degeneration.

> As civilization progresses, inborn superiority tends to drain out of the
> lower social levels up into the higher social classes. And probably never
> before in human history has this selective process gone on so rapidly and so
> thoroughly as today. But it may be asked, is this not a matter for rejoicing?
> ... Unfortunately no; not as society is now constituted. On the contrary,
> if these tendencies continue under present social conditions the concentration
> of superiority in the upper social levels will spell general racial impoverish-
> ment and hence a general decline in civilization. Let us remember that fatal
> tendency to use up and exterminate racial values, to impoverish human
> stocks by the dual process of socially sterilizing superior strains and multi-
> plying inferiors. The history of civilization is a series of racial tragedies.
> Race after race has entered civilization's portals; entered in the pink of condi-
> tion, full of superior strains, slowly selected and accumulated by the drastic
> methods of primitive life. Then, one by one, these races have been insidiously
> drained of the best until, unable to carry on, they have sunk back into im-
> potent mediocrity.[84]
> The civilization of America depends on your continuing to produce A and
> B men in fair numbers. And at present A men are 4 per cent, the B men 9
> per cent and you are breeding from the lower part of the curve. The A men
> and the B men, the college bred, do not maintain their numbers, while the
> population swells enormously. If this goes on for a few generations, will
> not the A men and even the B men become as rare as white elephants, dropping
> to a mere fraction of one per cent. It is only too probable.[85]

The older Social Darwinists, men such as Spencer, and to a certain extent even Bagehot and Gumplowicz, could look with favor upon *laissez faire* and governmental inaction in the social and economic spheres. To them the struggle for existence in this, as in all other spheres, led to the survival of the fittest, and the fittest "are, broadly speaking," the best. To them it is, therefore, unnecessary and even unwise for the state to step in and try consciously to modify the natural course of evolution. Leave things alone, and natural forces will continue to foster evolution and progress. To the eugenists, on the other hand, no such optimistic view is possible. To them the course of *natural* selection is leading to racial and hence to national degeneration. To them the only way in which this degeneration can be stopped is for the state to abandon its policy of *laissez faire* and substitute *artificial* (that is, state-controlled) selection for natural selection.

The eugenic program demands a far-reaching plan for state activity. The program demands that the state

> **(1)** see to it that the most inferior persons have no children at all. This is to be accomplished by the compulsory sterilization of the least desirable element in the population, such as lunatics, feeble-minded persons, and habitual criminals. **(2)** The state must also see that other inferior persons have fewer children than they do now. There must always be hewers of wood and drawers of water, and as a result it is neither possible nor advisable to sterilize the general run of the lower classes, who must always provide this element in the community.... It is, however, necessary that the state see to it that this section of the population does not increase out of all proportion to the other groups within the nation. This may be done in part by the inculcation of birth control principles amongst the lower orders and in part by the closing of certain charitable institutions (e.g. free maternity hospitals) which merely encourage the poorer classes to produce children with no thought of the future. **(3)** The state must also see to it that a larger number of superior persons have children than at present. By means of stringent taxation college graduates and "other superior persons" should be compelled to marry and produce children. As many members of the upper middle class are hindered by economic strain from having large families, the state should provide subsidies for each child born to persons who can prove themselves to be "of superior stock."

Many of the eugenists go even further in their advocacy of state interference. If it can be proved that the present economic setup favors the increase of the inferior and the decrease of the superior stock, the state must step in and radically change this setup and provide one which is capable of improving the racial strain.

Unless we are prepared to cast away the labors of our forefathers and to vanish with the Empires of the past, we must accept the office of *deciding who are the fittest to prosper* and to have offspring, who are the persons whose moral and intellectual worth make it right that they and their descendants should be placed in a position of pre-eminence in our midst, and which are the families on whose upbringing the time and the money of society are best bestowed. We must acquiesce in the principle that the man who has made his five talents into ten shall profit by the skill and energy he has shown, and that the man who has repeatedly failed to use his one talent shall have no further chance of wasting the corporate resources on himself and his descendants.[86]

It would perhaps be unfair to say that the eugenists are radical etatists, but it is certainly true that the eugenist creed gives strong even if indirect support to the etatist cause. It is equally true that the eugenist creed gives strong even if indirect support to authoritarianism as opposed to democracy. With the British and American eugenists, living as they do in countries with strong liberal traditions, this opposition to democracy has to be discreet lest it arouse vehement public opposition to the whole eugenist movement, but however veiled or disguised, this anti-democratic feeling is to be found in nearly all of the eugenist writings. Professor East, one of the least radical of the eugenists, says:

Our whole governmental system is out of harmony with genetic common sense. Would it not be better to revise it radically?... Is there any reason to suppose that the country would not be better off if suffrage depended upon educational qualifications *at least* as high as that which our best high schools demand in their entrance examinations? [Elsewhere we learn that this would deprive at least 40% of the populace of their voting rights].... I would even go further and suggest experimenting with the plural vote with higher qualifications as prerequisites.[87]

Lothrop Stoddard is even more vigorous in his onslaughts on democracy.

For the past half century the democratic idea has gained an unparalleled ascendancy in the world, while the aristocratic idea has been correspondingly discredited. Indeed so complete has been democracy's triumph that it has been accorded a superstitious veneration and any criticism of its fundamental perfection is widely regarded as a sort of *lèse-majesté* or even heresy. Now this is an unhealthy state of affairs.... The fact is that modern science is bringing the democratic dogma under review, and it is high time that scientists said so frankly. Nothing would be more laughable if it were not so pathetic than the way scientists interlard their writings (which clearly imply criticism of democratic philosophy) with asides like "of course this isn't really against

democracy, you know." Now these little pinches of incense upon the democratic altar may keep near heretics in good standing. But it is unworthy of
the scientific spirit and, what is more important, it seriously impedes progress.[88]

Stoddard admits that there was something wrong about aristocratic
rule in times past, because the older aristocracies were based, to a certain
extent, upon artificial inequalities; the older aristocratic classes included
both superior and inferior stocks, and those few superior persons to be
found in the lower orders were prevented from entering the ruling
groups. As opposed to the older artificial aristocracy, he pleads for a
neo-aristocracy, an aristocracy based upon genuine worth, though he
admits that his neo-aristocracy will tend to be more or less hereditary
because superior persons generally produce superior children. Even
Stoddard is cautious in some respects. He refuses to give us any detailed outline of his ideal system of government. But he is certain
that it is the superior persons, and the superior persons only, who found
and further civilizations. As for the intermediate mass of mankind, it
merely accepts the achievements of the creative pioneers, that is, the
members of the superior groups. Even lower than the intermediate
mass are the numerous inferiors. "The inferior elements are instinctively the enemies of civilization." [89] Such being the case, it seems
obvious, at least to Stoddard, that social and political agencies which
foster and control the progress of civilization should be in the hands of
the definitely superior groups.

Stoddard is especially vehement in his opposition to socialism and
communism with their demands not only for political but also for social
and economic equality. He is vociferous against communism with its
demands for a bloody revolution and the violent overthrow of the
present social and economic order. To Stoddard there was some excuse
for accepting the communist creed as long as philosophers believed in
the innate equality of men, and that differences between men were due
merely to environmental (including economic) differences. Now,
however, that the eugenists have "proved" that men are innately and
biologically unequal, communism is scientifically absurd. It is now
nothing more than the creed of the "underman," the biologically inferior person who resents the fact that other persons are inherently and
permanently superior to himself.

How does the Underman look at civilization? This civilization offers him
few benefits and fewer hopes. It usually affords him little beyond a meager
subsistence. And sooner or later he senses that he is a failure, that civilization's prizes are not for him.... The very discipline of the social order op-

presses the Underman, it thwarts and chastises him at every turn. Such is the Underman's unhappy lot. Now what is his attitude towards that civilization from which he has so little to hope? What but instinctive opposition and discontent? These feelings, of course, vary all the way from unreasoning dislike to flaming hatred and rebellion. But in the last resort they are directed not merely against imperfections in the social order but against the social order itself.... We must realize clearly that the basic attitude of the Under man is an instinctive and natural revolt against civilization.... [90]

So long as all men believed all men to be potentially equal, the underman could delude himself into thinking that changed circumstances might raise him to the top. Now that nature herself proclaims him irremediably inferior, his hatred knows no bounds. This hatred he has always instinctively. Envy and resentment have ever been the badges of base minds. Yet never have these badges been so fiercely flaunted, so defiantly worn as today This explains the seeming paradox that just when the character of superiority becomes supremely manifest, the cry for levelling "equality" rises supremely shrill.... Nature herself having decreed him uncivilizable, the Underman declares war on civilization.... Let us understand once and for all that we have among us a rebel army — the vast host of the unadaptable, the incapable, the envious, the discontented, filled with instinctive hatred of civilization and progress and ready on the instant to rise in revolt. Here are the foes that need watching. Let us watch them. [91]

To Stoddard it seems clear that if civilization is to be preserved and further progress is to be made, it is necessary for the superior groups, the bulwarks of civilization, to band together to keep the inferior groups in their place. In other words, lest chaos break out, the underman must be kept under. It is useless to try to argue with the underman, as he is a prey to passion and oblivious to reason. He is essentially "unconvertible." As he relies not upon reason or persuasion, but upon force, the superior group must likewise use force in keeping the underman in his place, in making him, willy-nilly, attend to his station and its duties.

THE DOCTRINE OF RACIAL SUPERIORITY

Differing from the eugenists' creed in many details, but agreeing with it in essentials, is the doctrine put forward by the racialists. The eugenists claim that superiority and inferiority are innate and hereditary. The racialists agree with this theory, but go even further and claim, not only that certain family stocks are better than other family stocks, but also that some human races are infinitely superior to other human races. Just as the eugenists preach that it is the duty of the better stocks to guide and control the inferior stocks, so the racialists claim that it is the

duty of the superior races to guide and control the destinies of the inferior races.

Several of the major apostles of eugenics have supported some of the
general premises of the racialist creed. Thus, for example, Karl Pearson
emphatically asserts that changes in the racial stock of a population
furnish the most important factor in the rise or fall of a nation. He
takes for granted that the white races are superior to the other races.

> What I have said about bad stock seems to me to hold for the lower races
> of man. How many centuries, how many thousands of years have the Kaffir
> or the Negro held large tribal districts in Africa undisturbed by the white
> man? Yet their inter-tribal struggles have not yet produced a civilization
> in the least comparable with the Aryan. Educate and nurture them as you
> will, I do not believe that you will succeed in modifying the stock. History
> shows me one way and one way only in which a high civilization has been
> produced, namely in the struggle of race with race, and the survival of the
> physically and mentally fitter races.[92]

Because of this position, Pearson declares that intermarriage between
widely different races is not desirable; through such intermarriage, even
if the bad stock is raised, the good is lowered. He is terrified lest the
inferior races will continue to breed more rapidly than the superior
races, thereby filling up the world with less worthy stock. This fear
leads him to advocate imperialism, an imperialism of a rather brutal
sort. Not only should the superior races guide and control the inferior
races, but in many cases the superior race "should completely drive
out the inferior race" — so as to provide additional space in which
the superior race can thrive and breed. Galton, the founder of eugenics, did not trouble to draw explicitly the far-reaching political conclusions of Pearson, but even he emphasized the great mental differences between various races. To Galton there is "a difference of not
less than two grades between the black and white races, and it may be
more. . . . The Australian type is at least one grade below that of the
African Negro." [93]

But though the eugenists thus lend considerable support to the racialist creed, they are, for the most part, far more cautious and more conservative in their treatment of racial problems than are most of the
radical, thoroughgoing racialists. To the orthodox eugenists the individual or the family stock is of more importance than the racial stock.
To them the *average* intelligence of the Negro is lower than the *average*
intelligence of the white, but they admit that many Negroes are more
intelligent than many whites, and they are more interested in preserving

the better stocks within the white races than they are in preserving all white stocks just because they happen to be white.   Thus we find Hankins saying:

> In view of the wide range of variation among members of the same race, inferiority or superiority can not be attributed to an individual on account of his race.   A short member of a tall race may be distinctly shorter than a tall member of a short race.   So with intelligence, organizing ability, or artistic sense.[94]

East, another ardent eugenist, comes to the same conclusion when he says:

> Greatness is an individual matter.   There are no uniformly great races. . . . The simpletons of the world need not plume themselves on their racial connection; they cannot hide their qualities by braying about the worth of their relatives.[95]

To the racialists, on the other hand, the race is more important than the individual or the family stock.   To them a white man is innately superior to the Negro merely because he *is* white.

The apostles of the racialist creed are far too numerous to list in detail.   But among this group are a few who are especially worth noticing because of the influence they have exerted upon political speculation. Among such persons are the Comte de Gobineau, in the middle of the nineteenth century, and Houston Stewart Chamberlain, at the close of the nineteenth century, and such recent writers as Hans Gunther, Eugen Fischer, and Fritz Lenz.

Count Arthur de Gobineau (1816–1882) may be regarded as the founder of the modern racialist school.   He was primarily a diplomat, an artist, and a poet, but he also wrote a number of books on historical and ethnological problems, of which the most important and the most influential was *The Inequality of Human Races.*   Gobineau was far more a man of letters than a scientist, and he put forth many ideas which later on even his most ardent disciples have been forced to disavow. Nevertheless in the course of his long and rather rambling work Gobineau developed a number of cardinal doctrines or theses which in some form or other have been adopted by practically all the advocates of racialism.   Among these, four are of especial importance.

The first of these cardinal doctrines is that mankind is divided into a number of separate races, each with its own physical, emotional, and mental characteristics.   The obvious differences between the black skin of the Negro, the yellow skin of the Chinese, and the white skin of the European is no greater than the invisible, but none the less real, differences between the emotional and mental characteristics of the members of these three races. These differences are, of course, considered hereditary, and are in no way affected by education or environment. Just as a Negro invariably transmits his kinky hair and his black skin to his children, so he likewise invariably transmits the emotional and mental features characteristic of the black race. All pure-blooded blacks will therefore inevitably inherit the same general emotional and mental characteristics. In the case of intermarriage between races, the children will continue to have the emotional and mental characteristics of both parents, but in a diluted form. A white father and a black mother produce children which are neither white nor black but chocolate-colored. In like manner mulatto children will inherit some but not all of the intelligence and imagination characteristic of the white races, and some but not all of the artistic and musical sense which (according to Gobineau) is especially characteristic of the Negro race.

The second cardinal doctrine of Gobineau's creed is that as races radically and innately differ from one another, it follows that some races are invariably and inevitably superior to others. Among the pure-blooded races the Negroes rank the lowest of all (at least as regards their intellectual ability), then come the members of the yellow race, and then the members of the white race. The black race represents passion, is animal-like, with highly developed senses but poor reasoning power. The Negroes are carefree, capricious, and gluttonous, yet have a strongly marked musical and artistic capacity. The Negroes tend towards extreme individualism, even anarchy, and the only way in which they can be ruled is by despotism. The yellow race, though clearly superior to the Negroes, is still not the highest, as its essential characteristic is mediocrity. The members of this race are stubborn, apathetic, and practical. They have a pronounced leaning to law and order, but are uninventive and incapable of producing great leaders or great geniuses. The whites, on the other hand, excel in most physical, mental, and moral qualities. They are neither as sensuous and passionate as the blacks nor as apathetic and unemotional as the yellows. They are rich in reason, energy, resourcefulness, and creativeness. But even among the white peoples, there are notable differences. The Semites, for example, are somewhat inferior to the other white groups, as they are really a combination of white and black races. The Slavs are also somewhat inferior, as they represent a combination of the white and yellow races

The greatest of the white races is the Aryan race, to which belonged the Germanic peoples of antiquity, but which is now to be found in greater purity among the aristocrats of France and England than in Germany proper.

The third cardinal doctrine of Gobineau's creed is that a slight mixture of races is usually productive of much good, and at times has been the cause of a great advance in civilization.   In Gobineau's opinion, mankind has produced ten great civilizations in times past.   All of these civilizations were created by the white races, more especially by the Aryans, but only after the white races had conquered and partially mixed with other peoples.   The Indian civilization was produced by the Aryan conquest of and partial mingling with the native Dravidians.   The Egyptian civilization was created by an Aryan colony from India which settled in the Nile Valley at an early period and intermarried, to a certain extent, with the non-Aryan aborigines.   Chinese civilization began with an invasion of the Yellow River Basin by different branches of the Aryan race.   To Gobineau, if the three great races had remained strictly separate, supremacy would always have remained in the hands of the pure white race, but the world would have missed certain advantages which have followed from the admixture of blood.   Thus, for example, artistic genius, which is foreign to each of the three main races, arose only after the mingling, in certain proportions, of the whites and the blacks.   In Egypt the admixture of Negro blood was too great, but Greece had the exact dosage of Negro blood to make it supreme in artistic endeavor.

The fourth cardinal doctrine in Gobineau's creed is that while a small admixture of alien blood improves races — even improves the noble Aryan race — yet a large or constant admixture of such alien blood inevitably produces racial degeneration, which in turn leads to cultural and even to political degeneration.   In other words, civilization is created by the right amount of race mixture and is destroyed by too much.   Gobineau was thoroughly pessimistic with regard to the modern world.   Everywhere he saw evidence that the noble Aryan race is becoming polluted by the lesser breeds, with the result that the future of world civilization appeared very gloomy.   To take but a single example of his reasoning along this point: Originally the Aryans in India were a small conquering and governing aristocracy.   A small admixture of Dravidian blood permitted this little group to produce the great civilization of Vedic antiquity.   As time went on, however, the Aryan aristocracy absorbed more and more Dravidian blood (in spite of would-be strict caste laws) with the result that the governing group lost its racial identity. In consequence India began to degenerate. She became a prey to new invaders. Not only did she lose her political independence, but even her artistic and literary life became stagnant. To Gobineau, the story of India is but a prototype of racial history in other parts of the world.

To Gobineau, even Europe, the modern homeland of the white races, presents us with a similar picture. The great civilizations of Greece and Rome were founded by Aryan invaders who intermarried only to a slight extent with the aboriginal populations. As time went on, however, the invaders lost their racial purity, and the more racial amalgamation progressed, the more the governing aristocracies (the creators of civilization) lost their precious qualities. As a result both Greece and Rome eventually collapsed, more from racial degeneration than from any other cause. Modern Europe shows us another vivid and tragic picture of racial amalgamation — and cultural decay. The members of the old aristocracy of France were descended in large measure from the Frankish invaders of the early Middle Ages, while the lower classes in France were the descendants of the Latinized Celts. To Gobineau there was a *racial* difference between these two groups, as the Franks were far closer to the original Aryan type than were the Celts. As long as the French aristocracy remained relatively pure, it was able to create and preserve a characteristic French civilization. But with the relaxing of the social distinctions and the consequent intermarriage between the various classes in modern times, the French aristocracy has steadily degenerated. To Gobineau, the French Revolution was especially disastrous to French civilization, as it resulted in the killing of large numbers of the upper classes (with their higher proportion of pure Aryan blood) and the political and social triumph of the lower classes in which Aryan blood was greatly diluted.

With Gobineau's glorification of the Germanic-Franks it might appear, at first sight, as if his doctrine meant the glorification of everything German. But Gobineau was too good a Frenchman to permit this interpretation of his doctrine to gain ground. He sharply distinguished between the glorious *Germains* of former times and the degenerate *Allemands* of modern times. To him, the modern Germans were racially even more mixed and hence more impure than the French, or, at least, than the French upper class. To Gobineau the purest Aryan blood in the present time is to be found in England and in America, a fact which accounts for the much talked-of Anglo-Saxon supremacy in world affairs.

But even here racial amalgamation is rapidly taking place — the English with the Celts, the Americans with Negroes and South European immigrants — with the result that both England and America are faced with inevitable decay in the not distant future.

Though Gobineau was, if anything, anti-German rather than pro-German, it was in Germany that his main doctrines awakened the most vociferous applause, and it was in Germany that he found the most eloquent and influential apostles.   It was in Germany, and not in France, that a Gobineau Club was founded with a view to popularizing and disseminating the Gobineau creed.   Among the more important members of this club was the well-known musician, Richard Wagner, and because of Wagner's activity Gobineau's doctrine, in a new and pro-German phase, found widespread acceptance in Germany's literary and musical circles.   Even more important, was the support given to Gobinism by Houston Stewart Chamberlain.   Houston Stewart Chamberlain (1855–1926) came of a brilliant but rather erratic English family.   His brother, Basil Hall Chamberlain, left England and settled in Japan.   There he married a Japanese girl, became a Japanese subject, and so thoroughly immersed himself in Japanese studies that he became the Professor of the Japanese Language at the Imperial University of Tokyo.   Houston Stewart Chamberlain, after leaving England, chose Germany rather than Japan for his permanent habitat and his spiritual home.   He became a German subject, married a German girl (the daughter of Richard Wagner), and wrote a large number of very popular books — in German.

Among the most important of these books is his *Grundzüge des Neunzehnten Jahrhunderts* (1899) translated into English (by another person) as *The Foundations of the Nineteenth Century*.   Despite the many absurdities contained in it, this work must be declared to be epoch-making, as it exerted an enormous amount of influence throughout the length and breadth of Germany.   Kaiser Wilhelm II was an enthusiastic admirer of the book, read it aloud to his sons, and subscribed to a fund which was raised to promote the spread and use of the book by placing presentation copies in all popular libraries.   Houston Stewart Chamberlain's central theme is the same as that of Gobineau, though the method of treating the subject is somewhat different.   In addition, it may be said that whereas Gobineau aimed at glorifying the Aryan race in general, Chamberlain's goal was the glorification of the Teutonic race or sub-race in particular.   Moreover, Chamberlain, unlike Gobineau, considered modern Germany to be the direct heir of the ancient Germanic tradition and the predestined cultural and political leader of the world during the centuries to come.

Chamberlain, echoing Gobineau, emphasizes the enormous differences, both physical and spiritual, between the various races. "The human races are in reality as different from one another in character, qualities, and above all in the degree of their individual capacities as a greyhound, bulldog, poodle, and Newfoundland dog."[96] Chamberlain is thoroughly convinced that there is an intimate connection between a man's ability and personality and the race to which he happens to belong. Is not all history

> there to show us how personality and race are most closely connected, how the nature of the personality is determined by the nature of its race, and the power of the personality dependent upon certain conditions of its blood? . . . Horses and especially dogs give us every chance of observing that the intellectual gifts go hand in hand with physical; this is especially true of the moral qualities.[97] [As with animals so with men.] To think that at the close of the nineteenth century a professor could still be ignorant that the form of the head and the structure of the brain exercise quite decisive influence upon the form and the structure of the thoughts so that the influence of the surroundings, however great it may be estimated to be, is yet by this initial fact of the physical tendencies confined to definite capacities and possibilities, in other words, has definite paths marked out for it to follow![98]

The racial background is always of importance, but it becomes of even greater importance when man becomes fully aware of the meaning of race and the glorious potentialities of his own racial heritage.

> Nothing is so convincing as the consciousness of the possession of race. The man who belongs to a distinct pure race never loses the sense of it. . . . The guardian angel of his lineage is ever at his side, supporting him where he loses his foothold, warning him like the Socratic Daemon where he is in danger of going astray, compelling obedience and forcing him to undertakings which, deeming them impossible, he would never have dared to attempt.[99]

It goes without saying that Chamberlain argues that some races are inferior, others superior; that the black and yellow races are far surpassed by the white races; that even among the white races some are far superior to others. Departing slightly from Gobineau, he claims that four peoples, each of which was a special sub-race or else a special racial amalgam, have laid the foundations of modern civilization. These four peoples were the Jews, the ancient Greeks, the ancient Romans, and, above all, the modern Teutonic peoples. Each of these peoples has or had, because of its racial background, its good and its bad points; each, because of its peculiar characteristics, has played a major role in the formation of world culture, such as we know it today. The Jews have directly influenced history by the Old Testament and Judaism; indirectly through Christianity. They have, moreover, for good and for bad greatly influenced the social-economic condition of modern Europe in consequence of their dispersal through all the major European countries. The Greeks of antiquity, because of their unique racial characteristics, were able to lay the foundations for modern art, poetry, and philosophy. The ancient Romans, though inferior in some respects to the Greeks, played an all-important role in forming modern ideas on law, statecraft, the duties of citizens, the sanctity of the family and of property. On the basis of these legacies from the ancient world, the Teutons, the greatest of all the peoples, have in mediaeval and in modern times been able to shape and create the Western civilization of the nineteenth century.

Though Chamberlain was willing to admit that the modern world owes an enormous debt to the Jews, the Greeks, and the Romans of antiquity, he is convinced that all these peoples possessed certain important weaknesses which made them inferior in many respects to the Teutonic peoples into whose hands has passed the task of carrying on world civilization. The ancient Jews, for all their religious fervor, were a hard, cold, materialistic people — no wonder that the Old Testament, the principal product of their culture, is characterized by rigidity and formalism, that they conceived of God as a ruthless and jealous despot.

> The Indo-Europeans, by purely religious ways, had attained to conceptions of an individual divinity that were infinitely more sublime than the painfully stunted idea which the Jews had formed of the Creator of the World.[100]

To Chamberlain it seems surprising that Christianity, with its emphasis upon "the life of the Spirit," with its opposition to materialistic and formalistic concepts, should have started as a Jewish sect. Chamberlain tried to account for this seeming paradox by claiming that in reality Jesus himself was not racially a Jew. To be sure, he was reared in the Jewish faith and absorbed many Jewish traditions, but he was a Galilean, not a Jew, by birth; and the Galileans, Chamberlain seeks to prove, were non-Jewish in origin, in all probability were Aryans. "There is not the slightest foundation for the supposition that Christ's parents were of Jewish descent." [101] St. Paul, the great apostle of Christianity shows many traits which are distinctly non-Jewish, and to Chamberlain this fact can best be accounted for by supposing that though St. Paul's father was a Jew, his mother was a Greek.[102]

To Chamberlain it is a great tragedy that Jesus, the religious teacher of the modern world, should have been brought up in a Jewish background. Though racially, and hence inwardly and emotionally, not a Jew, he was too intimately associated with the Jews and their characteristic religion to escape entirely from Jewish influence. In reality Christianity should be looked upon, not as a culmination or perfection of Judaism, but as its direct negation. But because Christianity arose in Judea, neither Christ himself nor the religion he founded was able to escape entirely from the dead hand of Jewish tradition.

> Whoever lived in the Jewish intellectual world was bound to come under the influence of Jewish ideas. And though He [Christ] brought a new message... yet the personality, the life, the message were none the less chained to the fundamental ideas of Judaism.[103]

As a result Christianity was badly Semitized. The conversion of the Greeks and the Romans to Christianity helped somewhat to Aryanize, that is, to elevate this religion. Even so the legalism of Rome and the Roman Church nearly wrecked the spiritual character of Christ's message. The true meaning, the inner essence, of Christianity only became apparent at the time of the Reformation when leadership in religious matters was taken over by the Teutonic peoples.

Chamberlain feels that the destruction of Palestine as a political entity and the dispersal of the Jewish "race" throughout Europe has proved to be a major calamity. To him, the Jew because of his racial background has always remained an alien in Western civilization — he is always at odds with the true European spirit and will wreck it unless he be kept in check, or better still, deported.

> The Indo-European moved by ideal motives opened the gates in friendship the Jews rushed in and planted the flag of his, to us, alien nature. I will not say on the ruins, but on the breaches of our genuine individuality.... The political and social influence of the Jews has been very variously judged, but the greatest politicians of all times have regarded it as pernicious.... Wherever they are admitted to power, they abuse it.... The presence of an indefinite number of Jews is so pernicious to the welfare of a European state that we dare not be influenced by general humane principles.[104]

The Jews, to Chamberlain, are characterized by cold rationalism, by calculated egotism, by crass materialism, and they generally manage to contaminate the Aryans with whom they come into contact, imbuing the latter with the same spirit. The frequent intermarriages which take place between Jews and Aryans result only in polluting the noble Aryan race. Unless we look out, all Europe will eventually be "a herd of pseudo-Hebraic mestizos. a people beyond all doubt degenerate physically, mentally, and morally." [105] Worse still, the Jew by his very pres-

ence in the country can infect the land with the Jewish spirit even without racial intermixture taking place. "Often it needs only to have
frequent intercourse with Jews, to read Jewish newspapers, to accustom
oneself to Jewish philosophy, literature and art" to Semitize the purest
blooded Aryans.[106] Unfortunately, in modern times in Europe the
Jewish element has definitely been increasing.

> We live today in a Jewish age. . . . This alien people has become precisely
> in the nineteenth century disproportionately important and in many cases
> actually a dominant constituent of our life.

If world civilization is not to decay, this Semitizing process must be
vigorously stopped.

Chamberlain is somewhat kinder in his treatment of the ancient
Greeks and Romans, but even here he is careful to show that they did not
measure up to the full stature of the Teutonic peoples. Chamberlain
tells us that because of her greatness in the past, the very soil of Greece
must be considered sacred. Greek art, Greek architecture, Greek poetry
still serve as the bases and the inspiration of modern culture. It was
Greece, moreover, which laid the foundations for modern physical
science. Chamberlain is less enthusiastic about the role played by
Greek philosophy in subsequent European history. He feels that the
metaphysical speculations of such persons as Aristotle were more of a
curse than a blessing to subsequent generations. But whether for good
or for evil, the influence of Greek philosophy upon the intellectual structure of later Europe cannot be denied. Chamberlain is insistent that
the characteristic features of Greek civilization were due almost entirely
to the racial background of the Greeks. Hellenic culture was produced,
and could only have been produced by a particular racial type.

> Everything which had given an everlasting significance to the word "Hel-
> lenic" gradually disappeared when from the north, east, and west new bands
> of unrelated peoples kept flocking to the country and kept mingling with
> genuine Hellenes.[107]

Chamberlain feels that the world lost a good deal with the passing of
the "pure" Hellenic race, but he is also careful to point out that there
was a very seamy side to the Greek national character. Great artisti-
cally and intellectually, the Greeks were very weak on the moral side.
The Greek states were

> cruel, short-sighted democracies, blinded with self-love, and based upon
> slavery and idleness. . . . I said cruel, and in fact that trait is one of the most
> characteristic of the Hellenes, common to them and the Semites. Humanity,
> generosity, pardon were as foreign to them as love of truth. . . . To spare

prisoners, to give a kingly reception to a conquered prince, to entertain and give presents to envoys of the enemy instead of killing them ... the assumption that the first duty of every man is to speak the truth, ingratitude being regarded as a crime punishable by the state — all this seems to a Herodotus, a Xenophon almost as ridiculous as the Persian custom not to spit in the presence of others. ... The whole of Greek history is filled with the mutilation not only of corpses, but of living people, torture, and every kind of cruelty, falsehood, and treachery. ... The Greeks fell, their wretched characteristics ruined them, their morality was already too old, too subtle and too corrupt to keep pace with the enlightenment of their intellect.[108]

To Chamberlain, the Romans, at least the "pure" Romans of the Roman Republic, were morally far superior to the Greeks. It was the staunchness of their moral character which enabled the Romans to establish family life, in the modern sense of the word, and to lay the foundations for all subsequent legal, political, and administrative developments.

What Rome gave and securely established was a life morally worthy of man. The Romans did not invent marriage, they did not invent law, they did not invent the constitutional freedom-loving state; all that grows out of human nature and is found everywhere in some form and to some degree; but what the Aryan races had conceived under these notions as the bases of all morality and culture had nowhere been firmly established till the Romans established it.[109]

Chamberlain also feels that the Romans performed a magnificent service to humanity by destroying the political power of the Semitic race, first at Carthage and later at Jerusalem. If the Semites, instead of the Romans, had become the masters of the ancient world, nineteenth century civilization, as we now know it, would have been impossible. The Greek destruction of the Persian Empire was of far less significance than the Roman destruction of Carthage, for the struggle between the Greeks and the Persians was between two Aryan peoples, while the struggle between the Romans and the Carthaginians was between the superior Aryan and the inferior Semitic race — and how catastrophic it would have been for the inferior race to have won.

Chamberlain claims that the Romans made a great contribution to world civilization. But he also claims that this contribution was made by the citizens of the early Roman Republic, when the Roman people were still, from the racial point of view, more or less pure. In later days, in the days of the Empire, the Romans lost most of their old moral vigor, largely because of racial mixture. The later Roman Empire was so cosmopolitan in character that it became a veritable chaos of peoples. Very few of the later Roman emperors were of Roman or even of Italian origin. The same thing was true of the senators and of the members of the governing civil and military bureaucracy. As a result, the intellectual and moral stability so characteristic of the early Roman race gradually disappeared. The granting of full citizenship rights to all the polyglot subjects of the empire was the final blow. Thereafter decay, disintegration, destruction were inevitable. Not only did the Roman Empire fall, but the Roman people, who created the Roman civilization, became a mob of useless half-breeds, incapable of further creative activity.

We must, says Chamberlain, weep for the passing of the Romans as we weep for the passing of the Greeks, but we must also remember that the Romans had a weak as well as a strong side. If the Romans were morally much stronger than the Greeks, intellectually they were much weaker.

> Has all the poetry of Greece succeeded in striking even a spark out of this sober inartistic heart? Is there among the Romans a single true poetic genius? ... What is one to say of a history which embraces more than twelve hundred years and does not show a single philosopher? ... Where is there a single creative natural scientist among the Romans? ... Where is there a mathematician of importance? Where a meteorologist, a geographer, an astronomer? [109a]

The Roman people because of their peculiar racial characteristics were capable of producing many great and important things, but these same racial characteristics made it impossible for them to produce a single intellectual or artistic genius.

To the Semites, the Greeks, and the Romans of antiquity there succeeded the Germanic or Teutonic peoples as the leaders and creators of world civilization. To Chamberlain, the Germanic peoples have proved themselves to be the greatest and noblest of all the human races. The Germanic peoples have been able to take over Christianity from the Jews; art, literature, and science from the Greeks; family, legal, and political organization from the Romans. The Germanic peoples have much of the artistic and all of the scientific ability of the Greeks, and are much superior to the Greeks in moral worth. The Germanic peoples have all of the moral worth of the Romans and far transcend them in intellectual ability.

It was the Germanic peoples who saved world civilization from extinction.

> There is no doubt about it. The raceless and nationless chaos of the later Roman Empire was a pernicious and fatal condition, a sin against Nature.

Only one ray of light shone over that degenerate world. It came from the North. *Ex septentrionale lux.*[110]

It was the destiny of the Germanic peoples not to destroy Roman civilization, but to preserve it from the decay into which it was automatically sinking. It was, moreover, the destiny of the Germanic or Teutonic peoples not merely to preserve the civilization of antiquity, but also to transform and add to it in such a way as to form the glorious civilization of the nineteenth century.

> The Teuton is the soul of our culture. Europe today with its many branches over the whole world represents the chequered result of an infinitely manifold mingling of races: what binds us together and makes an organic unity of us is Teutonic blood. If we look around we see that the importance of each nation as a living power today is dependent upon the proportion of genuinely Teutonic blood in its population.[111]
>
> It was Teutonic blood ... and Teutonic blood alone ... that formed the impelling force and the informing power [in the creation of modern culture]. It is impossible to estimate the genius and the development of our North European culture if we obstinately close our eyes to the fact that it was a definite species of mankind which constitutes its physical and moral basis. We see that clearly today, for the less Teutonic a land is, the more uncivilized it is.[112]

It is true that the Latin countries, Italy, Spain, France, have added much to modern civilization, but in all such cases it was the Germanic element, the descendants of the German conquerors of earlier times, who constituted the creative force behind such cultural achievements.

> How splendid was the glory of Italy, how it went ahead and held aloft the torch for other nations on the road to a new world, while it still contained in its midst elements outwardly Latin, but inwardly thoroughly Germanic![113]

It was the Germanic elements in the Latin countries which produced the wonderful reawakening of learning in the thirteenth century; it was the same Germanic element in Italy which brought about the later Renaissance. The subsequent decay of Italy is due to the fact that the Germanic element became more and more diluted. What is true of Italy is true of Spain and the other Latin countries.

> What a magnificent people the Spaniards were! For centuries the West Goths were strictly forbidden to marry "Romans" whereby a feeling of race nobility was developed, which long prevented mixing ... but gradually ever deeper and deeper breaches were made in the dam and after mingling with Iberians, with the numerous remnants of the Roman chaos of peoples, with Africans of the most various origins, with Arabs and Jews, they lost all that the Germanic people had brought with them, their military superiority, their

unconditional loyalty, their high religious ideal, their capacity for organizing, their rich artistic creative power; we see today what remained over when the Germanic blood as the physical substratum was destroyed.[114]

To Chamberlain, French civilization is higher and has lasted longer than that of the other Latin peoples because the Germanic element is stronger there than in the other countries with Romance languages, but it goes without saying, that to him and to his followers, the true home of modern culture is in those lands in which Germanic blood is even less diluted, namely, in England, the Scandinavian countries, and, above all, in Germany itself.

> He who at the present time travels from London to Rome passes from fog into sunshine, but at the same time from the most refined civilization and high culture into semi-barbarism, dirt, coarseness, falsehood, poverty.[115]

In Chamberlain's picture, England, Chamberlain's motherland, is thus seen to be superior to France and Italy, but it is in Germany, Chamberlain's adopted home, that we find the quintessence of the Germanic virtues, together with creative genius in the field of art, music, literature, science, and philosophy.

Chamberlain closes his book with the hope that Germany will not permit herself to be de-Germanized by intermarriage with Jews and other inferior, non-Germanic stocks, nor by the acceptance of corrupt, alien doctrines such as those which preach the equality of persons or the equality of races. Above all it is necessary, if world civilization is to be preserved, that Germany and the other Germanic peoples maintain their leadership in the world of politics as well as in the other spheres of human activity.

Neither Gobineau nor Chamberlain was an anthropologist in the scientific sense of the word, nor were they at all acquainted with technical anthropological literature. As a result they were guilty of many statements which were flagrantly contradictory to many of the accepted facts of scientific research. Early in the twentieth century, however, there arose a group of writers who were profoundly affected by the main ideas put forth by Gobineau and Chamberlain, but who attempted to transform these ideas so as to make them conform with the teachings of orthodox biology and anthropology. Among this group of writers the most important are Hans Gunther, Eugen Fischer, and Fritz Lenz. Of these, Gunther is the most influential, and in later years has become the semi-official anthropologist of the Nazi Party.

This new group of writers is much more careful and much more cautious in their use of the term "race." For all their emphasis upon race and the importance of race, Gobineau and Chamberlain were not very certain or very clear as to what they meant by it. Both were apt to confuse national, linguistic, and even religious groups with racial groups Thus Gobineau speaks of the Aryan and Semitic races, whereas properly speaking these terms apply only to languages. Semitic languages are spoken by persons belonging to many different racial types; and the same thing is true of the Aryan or Indo-European languages. It is ridiculous to speak of the Germanic or Celtic or Slavic races, because these, too, are linguistic rather than racial terms. Some Celts are short and dark, others tall and blond; the same is true of the Germans and the Slavs. Yet the short dark persons and the tall blond persons obviously belong to different races. Chamberlain is much less careless in such matters than Gobineau, yet even Chamberlain was never quite certain whether his noble "Germanic" race was blond or brunette, and even Chamberlain thought that his "Germanic" race included long-headed types and broad-headed types, persons with long aquiline noses (like Dante) and persons with short stubby noses (like Luther).

The new group of racialists are much more scientific in this respect. To them race means a group of persons possessing the same body type, irrespective of the language they speak, the country they inhabit, or the religion they profess. This body type, like most other physical characteristics, is considered to be hereditary and is therefore subject to all the laws of heredity as brought out by general biological research. Race thus becomes a concept which can only be reached after inquiring into the measurable and calculable details of the bodily structure; after measuring, for example, the height, the length of the limbs, the skull and its parts, and after determining, on a standard color scale, the color of the skin, the hair, and the eyes. The new racialists in taking this standard of race are in agreement with all orthodox anthropologists. But they disagree with most orthodox anthropologists (and agree with Gobineau and Chamberlain) by making the further assumption that each racial type has certain definite emotional and intellectual characteristics peculiar to itself. We thus come to Gunther's definition of a race as "a human group which is marked off from every other human group through its own proper combination of bodily and mental characteristics, and in turn produces only its like." [116]

The new group of racialists admit that the total number of racial types is quite large. Thus for example, there is not one Negro race but several

Negro races.   In like manner there are many different races among the so-called yellow peoples, and an equal number among the so-called white peoples.   There are thus not three main races, but rather three main groups of races.   Nevertheless all the races within each group possess certain physical, emotional, mental characteristics in common.   After studying these characteristics the new group of racialists, echoing Gobineau, come to the conclusion that the white groups as a whole are definitely superior to the black and yellow groups, physically, emotionally, and mentally.   The Negro races are declared to be composed of happy-go-lucky persons dominated by their sense impressions, having little thought for the morrow and with little self-control and with quite a low intellectual capacity.   The Negroes have little aptitude for political organization, as is witnessed by such Negro states as Haiti and Liberia. The Negroes are incapable of producing works of genius in any field. The yellow races are declared to be distinctly higher than the Negro races, but even they suffer in comparison with the whites.   They have a much greater imitative than a creative ability.   They frequently have good memories but very seldom do they possess profound critical insight. They have a keen historical sense but little interest in abstract science. They are essentially practical, little given to phantasy or imagination, which is one reason that they have never developed the European concept of romantic love.[117]

The new school of racialists spends a great deal of time distinguishing between the various European races, all of which, of course, are within the white racial group.   Most of the members of this school distinguish five major races, namely, the Nordic, the Alpine, the Mediterranean, the East Baltic, and the Dinarian races.   Of these, the Nordic, Alpine, and Mediterranean are of the greatest importance, as most of the peoples of Western Europe are descended from one or other of these human stocks. The Nordic race is found in its greatest purity in Scandinavia, northern Germany, and the British Isles, but it is also comparatively strong in northern France.   The Alpine race is found in its greatest purity in South Germany, Switzerland, northern Italy, and central France.   The home lands of the Mediterranean race are western Ireland, southern France, Spain, Portugal, and Italy south of Rome.   In a slightly different form, the Mediterranean race also extends all over Africa north of the Sahara.   The East Baltic race has its headquarters in the Baltic states, such as Finland and Latvia.   The Dinarian race is found in the Tyrol, but is strongest in the Dinarian Alps, that is, in Jugoslavia.   It is thus seen that the racial distribution of Europe in no way coincides with political or linguistic boundaries. The Germans, for example, are part Nordic, part Alpine; the Italians part Alpine, part Mediterranean; while the French are part Nordic, part Alpine, and part Mediterranean. No one region in Europe is absolutely pure racially. Because of the frequent migration of peoples, individually and collectively, one finds representatives of all the major races in the most unexpected places. There is, for example, a pronounced Mediterranean strain in portions of Norway and Denmark, and pronounced Nordic types are found even in Spain and Italy, a relic of Nordic invasions in the past.

Gunther tells us that each of these five European races has a number of strongly marked physical characteristics:

> The Nordic race: tall, long-headed, narrow-faced with prominent chin, narrow nose with high bridge; soft smooth or wavy light hair; deep-sunk light (blue or grey) eyes; rosy-white skin.
>
> The Alpine race: short, short-headed, broad-faced, with chin not prominent; flat short nose with low bridge; stiff brown or black hair; brown eyes, standing out; yellowish brownish skin.
>
> The Mediterranean race: short, long-headed, narrow-faced, with less prominent chin; narrow nose with high bridge; soft, smooth or curly brown or black hair; deep-sunk brown eyes; brownish skin.
>
> The East Baltic race: short, short-headed, broad-faced, with heavy massive under jaw ... flat, rather broad, short nose, with low bridge; stiff light hair, light eyes, standing out, light skin with grey undertone.
>
> The Dinaric race: tall, short-headed, narrow-faced, with a steep back to the head, looking as if it were cut away; very prominent nose which stands right out, with a high bridge ... curly brown or black hair, deep-sunk eyes; brownish skin.[118]

Of great importance is the fact that Gunther and his fellow thinkers are convinced that each of the five foregoing races has its own emotional and mental characteristics. In all the works written by the members of this school, we find that with respect to all these non-material characteristics the Nordics are said to be superior to all the other races.

> We may take judgment, truthfulness, and energy to be the qualities which are always found marking out the Nordic man.... He feels a strong urge towards truth and justice, and shows therefore a practical attitude, an attitude of weighing, which often makes him cool and stiff. He is distinguished by a highly developed sense of reality, which in combination with an energy that may rise to boldness urges him on to far-reaching undertakings.... Passion in the usual meaning of the rousing of the sense or the heightening of the sexual life has little meaning for him.... Just as he himself quickly grasps the idea of duty, so he is inclined to demand the fulfillment of duty from those around him as he does from himself; and in this he easily becomes hard and even ruthless, although he is never without a certain knightliness.... In his

intercourse with his fellows he is reserved and individualistic. The disinclina-
tion to show his feelings often springs in the Nordic man from a remarkable
depth of character which can not and will not express itself quickly and
vividly in word and bearing.

His imaginative powers ... lead him not so much into the boundless as
rather out of reality and back again into it. Hence comes the fitness of the
Nordic race for statesmanlike achievements.... The sense for reality, the
energy, self-reliance and boldness of the Nordic race are one reason why all
the more important statesmen in European history would seem to be predominantly Nordic.... There is always a stream of Nordic blood flowing
from the countryside into the towns whither the Nordic man always has been
and always will be led by his lust for competition, for culture, for leadership,
and for distinction.... In its highest representatives the Nordic race has ...
a yearning towards the sublime and the heroic, towards extraordinary deeds
and works calling for a life's devotion. In Nordic men there is often to be
seen too a peculiarly wide range of development in the mental life.... It is
not to be wondered at, therefore, that it is this Nordic race that has produced
so many creative men, that a quite preponderating proportion of the distinguished men in European and North American history show mainly
Nordic features, and that in those peoples with less Nordic blood the creative
men have always come from a district where there has been or is a marked
strain of this blood.... If then the Nordic race has always been especially
rich in creative men it is no wonder that the peoples with Nordic blood have
always gone down when the blood has gone dry.... The Nordic race seems
to show special aptitude in the domain of military science owing to its warlike spirit ... in the arts it inclines particularly to poetry, music, painting.

Northwest Germany, where the Nordic race shows its greatest predominance within the Germanic tribes, has the lowest criminal percentage. The
figures for crime rise as we go east and south, that is, in the direction of the
lessening of the strain of Nordic blood.... In outward appearance one is
struck in all classes by the relatively greater personal cleanliness of the
predominantly Nordic element and their delight in bodily exercise....[119]

In contrast with the glorious Nordic race, the Alpine race, in Gunther's
picture, appears much inferior.

The Alpine man may be called reflective, hard-working and narrow-minded
... together with reserve, sullenness, mistrust, slowness.... The Alpine man
is sober, practical, a hard-working small business man who patiently makes
his way by dint of economy, not of enterprise.... Since his aims are narrower
and he lacks any real boldness in thought or deed he often gets on better than
the more careless, dashing, and not seldom unselfish Nordic man. The
Alpine man ... is circumspect and likes to feel that his thoughts and ideas
are not different from those of the generality.... In predominantly Alpine
societies the class distinctions have little importance, all are equal.... [The
Alpines] have a liking for the mediocre and the ordinary and discourage
competition. This inclination towards the democratic theory of equality is
grounded on the fact that they themselves never rise above the average and

have a dislike if not a hatred for greatness, which they can not grasp. Thus everything noble or heroic — generosity, light-heartedness, broad-minded ness, are essentially un-Alpine attributes.

The Alpine man and his family make up a close, busy, selfish group. All individuality is foreign to him; in political life, too, he inclines to broad mass organization. He is far removed from any warlike inclination as also from any wish to govern or to lead. As it is his lot to be led, he is generally a quiet follower, although with a tendency to grumble and be envious. The Alpine woman is even more given than the man to plodding industry and soulless toil. The Alpines show little or no sense of humor or of jokes against themselves.... Fraud, blackmail and threats would appear to be more frequent in the predominantly Alpine parts of Germany.[120]

We need not concern ourselves with the analysis given the East Baltic and Dinarian races, but a word should be said regarding the picture painted of the Mediterraneans, because of the great part played by these Mediterraneans in West European life.

This race is painted by all observers as passionate and excitable. It has less depth of mind and is easily roused and easily reconciled; loves strong, vivid colors and vivid impressions of all kinds;... takes great joy in the spoken word and in pleasing and lively movements; and is inclined to find suppleness and craft particularly worthy of interest and praise.... The Mediterranean man is eloquent, often a skilled orator, not seldom is he [merely] talkative and somewhat superficial. His spirits are quick to rise and quick to sink.... The Mediterranean man is not very hard-working, often he is lazy.... He is not very drawn to money-making.... He has as little of the Nordic energy as he has of the industry and activity of the Alpine race.

The Mediterranean man is very strongly swayed by the sexual life.... A disposition to cruelty and sadism may perhaps stand in relation to the stronger sexuality. In public life the Mediterranean man shows but slight sense of order and law and a want of forethought. He is quickly aroused to opposition and is ever wishing for a change.... There is a tendency to lawless, anarchical conditions, to secret plotting (Camorra and Maffia in Italy, Sinn Fein in Ireland) and to an adventurous life of robbery. The predominantly Mediterranean south of Italy is characterized by a higher percentage of deeds of violence and murder; and Nicefore significantly calls a district where the Mediterranean element is markedly predominant the criminal district.[121]

While Gunther denies that there is any direct connection between race and either religion or language, he does think that there is at least an indirect connection. He does think that the emotional and mental characteristics of the Nordic race are closely allied to the spirit of Protestantism, as a result of which Protestantism has its home in those countries which are most purely Nordic, while Catholicism appeals more to the Alpine and Mediterranean races. In like manner there is a connection between race and language to the extent that the Aryan or Indo-European languages arose among the Nordic peoples and were later imposed by Nordic conquerors upon the Alpine and Mediterranean races who originally spoke non-Indo-European languages. Incidentally, whereas many of the older scholars taught that the Aryans originated in Central Asia and only migrated to Europe in comparatively modern times, Gunther and his school stoutly maintain that the Nordic race, the true creator of the Aryan languages, arose in Germany. The spread of the Aryan languages is thus seen to be the result of the spread of conquering and "civilizing" groups of Nordics migrating from Germany since very early times.

Gunther, following the tradition established by Gobineau and Chamberlain, maintains that there is also a very close connection between race and culture. He makes an elaborate survey of the great cultures of Europe and Asia, and he comes to the conclusion that most of these cultures have been produced by Nordics conquering and settling in different parts of the world. He carefully ignores the important roles played by the ancient Egyptian and Mesopotamian civilizations, which arose among representatives of the Mediterranean race, and stresses the importance of the ancient civilizations of India, Persia, Greece, and Rome. In each of these countries, it is claimed, civilization arose subsequent to and as a result of the Nordic conquest of earlier non-Nordic peoples. In each country a high state of civilization persisted as long as the governing Nordic class kept relatively pure racially; in each country civilization decayed as soon as intermarriage led to the absorption and disappearance of the Nordic stock. To Chamberlain, Gunther's master, the greatness of Greece and Rome was due to a particularly fortunate racial blend; to Gunther himself this greatness was due not to the blending of races but to the predominance of one particular race — the noble Nordic race.

> The heroic sagas of the Hellenes are a clear reflection of the Nordic race. . . . All these [invading] tribes from the first beginnings of the immigration are characterized by the Nordic house, Nordic styles and weapons. . . . Slowly there is born out of the world of the Nordic rulers and that of the Mediterranean people of the lower orders that wonderful mingling of forms we know as the "happy" Grecian world. But the upper stratum of Hellenic ideas, the religion of men such as Homer, Hellenic science and philosophy, Hellenic art, bear clear witness to the Nordic nature of the creative class of men in Greece. . . . When non-Nordic people had become more numerous among the Hellenes the use of fair dyes became more frequent. . . . Thus does an age that has become poor in Nordic blood seek an outward likeness with the early and the heroic ages. . . . In Plato's time denordicization and degeneration — the

two phenomena preparing the way for the fall — had already made much progress.... In Athens as in Sparta the decline is clearly marked by the exhaustion of the blood of the Nordic race.[122]

According to Gunther, we may indeed look with sympathy at the attempt of the modern Greeks to revive the glories of ancient Greece, but we must realize that this attempt is hopeless. The Nordic blood of ancient Greece has long since died out; the modern Greeks are a mixture of Alpine and Mediterranean, and with such a stock the revival of ancient Greece is impossible.

As with Greece, so with Rome.

> The Romans were the final inheritors of all power in the ancient world of the Mediterranean. They too were sprung from Nordic blood.... When we consider Roman history we have the feeling that in comparison with the non-Nordic people of Italy, the number of the Nordic newcomers who now prepared to found a world empire was not very great, but that the Nordic *gentes*, through the strict discipline and a stern and simple warriors' code, so fashioned and handed on the Roman type of the Nordic nature that down to late times the men of the blood of this creative race stood out as an unchanging people, filled with stern resolve.[123]

Unfortunately Rome, like Greece, became slowly denordicized and as a result was bound to decay. "Along with denordicization came a degeneration whose marks make the last days of Rome so repulsive." [124]

In one respect Rome, or rather Italy, was more fortunate than Greece, or Persia, or India. The latter countries had only one great wave of Nordic invaders. As a result when these invaders polluted their blood with non-Nordics, there was nothing which could stave off cultural decay. To Gunther, we should not be surprised that in modern times neither India, nor Persia, nor Greece has been able to contribute much to world civilization. The West Roman Empire, however, and with it Italy, was granted a kinder fate. This whole region was subjected to wave after wave of Germanic invasions. In consequence the Nordic element in the Latin-speaking countries was renewed and revivified. Small wonder then that Italy, and with Italy, Spain, Portugal, and France, was able to rekindle the fires of civilization, and actively aid in creating modern cultures.

Gunther goes on to say, however, that in all the Latin countries the Nordic element is once more dying out, with the result that little can be expected of them in the future. It is only from Scandinavia, the Anglo-Saxon countries, where the Nordic element is still predominant, and above all from Germany, the original home of the Nordic race, that we can look forward to any cultural advances in the future. Even in these countries, however, there has been a steady increase in non-Nordic elements. There is very grave danger that even Germany may be completely denordicized. This in turn means that the future of world civilization is in very grave danger.

> It is only the awakening of a racial consciousness in predominantly Nordic men that can stay the dying out of the Nordic race. . . . If the ruling classes in these peoples take to themselves the Nordic ideal as a common gift and possession, then there are grounds to hope for a new nordicizing of the Germanic peoples.[125]

The doctrine of the racialists is of great importance because it has been taken over bodily by the present-day Nazis in Germany. It is also of importance even outside Germany because racialism, wherever adopted, has served as a valuable weapon in support of authoritarianism and etatism.

The connection between racialism and authoritarianism, or at least between racialism and belief in aristocratic versus democratic control, is obvious. Democracy is usually based upon a belief in some sort of human equality. The racialists along with the eugenists insist upon the absolute and innate inequalities between man and man. The eugenists claim that it is the duty of the "superior" stock to guide and control the "inferior" stocks. The racialists claim that it is the duty of the "superior" races to guide and control the "inferior" races. This is in itself strongly opposed to the old democratic formulas. Moreover, most of the racialists tend to associate race conflict with class conflict. They believe that in all countries with a mixed population (and all countries are racially mixed), the upper classes tend to have a much larger Nordic element than have the lower classes. As a result, it seems clear to the racialists that in such instances, at least, the upper classes should have political control over the state.

Gunther, with most of the other racialists, makes a great point of sup- porting aristocratic versus democratic control throughout the whole of human history.

> Greek history might be represented as the play between the spirit of the Nordic upper class and that of the foreign lower orders.[126]

Gunther is far more friendly to aristocratic Sparta (where the non-Nordic helots were kept in their place) than to democratic Athens. As a result of democratic control in Athens, the Nordic upper classes lost their power and prestige. They began to marry with the wealthy upstarts from the lower non-Nordic orders. As a result the Athenian people soon became a mob of "degenerate, pleasure-seeking beggars, without loyalty or belief, and without hope for a better future." [127] For similar reasons Gunther sympathizes with the Roman patricians in their struggle with the plebeians, for the patricians were mostly descendants of Nordic conquerors while the plebeians "correspond to the earlier population, predominantly Mediterranean." To Gunther it was a national catastrophe when the patricians were forced to give political rights to the plebeians; it was an even greater catastrophe when the patricians were forced to legalize marriage between the members of the two orders.

As with the ancient, so with the modern world.

> Every constitutional change may disturb the class divisions. . . . The lower orders press for a shifting of power. . . . Racial mixture progresses as soon as "the people" — the Demos, the Plebeians, the lower castes — has shaken the class divisions. . . . The rule of the people now means the rule of the masses, who can not bear any men of distinction . . . who are led by agitators and above all by the money of non-Nordic upstarts.[128]

To Gunther the French Revolution brought about the ruin of France, for it was essentially the successful revolt of the non-Nordic lower orders against the Nordic aristocracy. (This idea was taken over directly from Gobineau.) Even in Germany class distinctions and race distinctions go hand in hand. In Germany there is a large element of Alpine and Dinaric stock in addition to the original Nordics. In fact even in Germany the pure-blooded Nordics constitute a comparatively small minority. Broadly speaking, however, this Nordic minority tends to gravitate towards the top of the social and economic pyramid. "Always, where the hindrances are not too great, the average higher gifts of the more Nordic men lead them into the upper classes." [129] From this fact it follows that even in Germany political control should be vested, not in the "masses," but in the "superior" social groups.

The connection between racialism and etatism is more obscure, but none the less profound. To be sure, the earlier racialists, such as Gobineau and Chamberlain, were far from being radical etatists; in fact we find in their writings a distinct tendency to defend individualism. Among the later racialists, however, there grew up the doctrine that if civilization is to be saved, the individual must completely subordinate himself to his race; and from the subordination of the individual to the race, to the subordination of the individual to the "nation," and then to the state were not difficult steps. True political science, says

Gunther, must not lay stress upon the "individuality" of a man, but upon the fact that he is

> a member of the community, the community of the passing and the coming generations....[130]
>
> Always the decay of a culture founded by the Nordic tribes has been brought about by theories of "enlightenment" and "individualism." Decadent Athens shows this with her enlightenment... with its exaggerated individualism....[131]

Buddhism is condemned because it "stressed the individual and took him out of the community,"[132] and likewise stoicism, for the Stoics by their emphasis upon individualism "overlooked the fact that by this very aim they were cutting away the last of the roots linking the individual with his people and race."[133]

> If we investigate quite empirically what is the prevailing idea among the Western peoples of the essential nature of a nation we shall find that by a nation no more is generally understood than the sum of the now living citizens of a given state. We shall find further that the purpose of the state is generally held to be no more than the satisfaction of the daily needs of the sum of individuals or else only of the sum of individuals who are banded together to make up a majority. The greatest possible amount of "happiness" for individuals is to be won by majority decisions. Racial and eugenic insight brings a different idea of the true nature of a people. A people then is looked upon as a fellowship with a common destiny of the past, the living, and the coming generations — a fellowship with one destiny rooted in responsibility towards the nation's past, and looking towards its responsibility to the nation's future, to the coming generations.... The striving that can be seen among the youth for an organic philosophy of life — that is, a philosophy sprung from the people and the native land, bound up with the laws of life and opposed to all "individualism" — must in the end bind the youth to the life of the homeland and of its people, just as the German felt himself bound in early times, to whom the clan tie was the very core of his life.[134]

NOTES TO CHAPTER TEN

1. T. N. Carver, *Essays in Social Justice*, p. 94. Reprinted by the permission of the President and Fellows of Harvard College.

2. Charles Darwin, *Origin of Species*, pp. 70, 71.

3. *Ibid.*, pp. 71, 72.

4. Herbert Spencer, *Data of Ethics*, p. 123.

5. William James, *The Will to Believe*, p. 218. By permission of Longmans, Green and Company, Inc.

6. Spencer, "The Social Organism," *Essays*, I, 272. By permission of D. Appleton Century Company, and The Rationalist Press Association.

7. Spencer, *Principles of Sociology*, I, p. 445.

8. *Ibid.*, I, p. 449.
9. Spencer, "The Social Organism," *Essays*, p. 276.
10. W. Bagehot, *The English Constitution, Works*, V, **p. 164.** By permission of Longmans, Green and Company.
11. Bagehot, *Physics and Politics, Works*, VIII, p. 58.
12. *Ibid.*, p. 65.
13. *Ibid.*, p. 16.
14. *Ibid.*, p. 40.
15. *Ibid.*, p. 36.
16. *Ibid.*, p. 100.
17. *Ibid.*, p. 16.
18. *Ibid.*, p. 33.
19. *Ibid.*, p. 138.
20. *Ibid.*, p. 34.
21. *Ibid.*, p. 138.
22. *Ibid.*, p. 17.
23. *Ibid.*, pp. 17, **18.**
24. *Ibid.*, p. 37.
25. *Ibid.*, p. 20.
26. *Ibid.*, p. 18.
27. *Ibid.*, p. 43.
28. *Ibid.*, p. 139.
29. *Ibid.*, p. 66.
30. *Ibid.*, p. 28.
31. *Ibid.*, p. 141.
32. *Ibid.*, p. 139.
33. *Ibid.*, p. 54.
34. *Ibid.*, p. 49.
35. *Ibid.*, p. 80.
36. *Ibid.*, p. 50.
37. *Ibid.*, p. 140.
38. *Ibid.*, p. 17.
39. Bagehot, *Works*, I.
40. Bagehot, *The English Constitution*, p. 330.
41. Bagehot, *Physics and Politics*, p. 115.
42. *Ibid.*, p. 117.
43. *Ibid.*, p. 124.
44. *Ibid.*, p. 120.
45. Originally Gumplowicz was a convinced polygenist, teaching that the various human stocks are descended from different animal ancestors. It was due to the influence of Lester Ward that Gumplowicz finally came around to a monogenetic explanation of human evolution. See J. P. Lichtenberger, *Development of Social Theory*, p. 453.
46. Ludwig Gumplowicz, *Outlines of Sociology*, p. 157. By permission of the American Academy of Political and Social Science.
47. *Ibid.*, p. 7.
48. *Ibid.*, p. 113.
49. Franz Oppenheimer, *The State*, p. 15. Copyright, 1914, 1922. By permission of The Viking Press, Inc., New York.
50. *Ibid.*, p. 64.
51. *Ibid.*, p. 68.
52. *Ibid.*, p. 70.

53. L. F. Ward, *Pure Sociology*, p. 206. By permission of The Macmillan Company, publishers.
54. Gumplowicz, *Outlines of Sociology*, pp. 178, 179.
55. *Ibid.*, p. 182.
56. *Ibid.*, p. 180.
57. *Ibid.*
58. *Ibid.*, pp. 152, 153.
59. *Ibid.*, pp. 180, 181.
60. Oppenheimer, *The State*, pp. 89, 90.
61. Gumplowicz, *Outlines of Sociology*, p. 133.
62. Oppenheimer, *The State*, p. 5.
63. Gumplowicz, *Outlines of Sociology*, p. 145.
64. *Ibid.*, p. 118.
65. Gumplowicz, *Rassenkampf*, p. 220.
66. Oppenheimer, *The State*, p. 272.
67. Gumplowicz, *Outlines of Sociology*, p. 116.
68. L. Stoddard, *The Revolt Against Civilization*, pp. 30, 31. By permission of Charles Scribner's Sons.
69. *Ibid.*, pp. 56, 69.
70. F. Galton, *Hereditary Genius*, p. 1. By permission of The Macmillan Company, publishers.
71. *Ibid.*, p. 58.
72. Karl Pearson, *The Scope and Importance to the State of the Science of National Eugenics*, p. 26. By permission of the Cambridge University Press and The Macmillan Company, publishers.
73. Galton, *Hereditary Genius*, p. 12.
74. W. C. D. Whetham, *Heredity and Society*, p. 4. By permission of Longmans, Green and Company.
75. Quoted from H. Parshley in H. E. Barnes, *History and Prospects of the Social Sciences*, p. 133. By permission of Alfred A. Knopf, Inc.
76. See F. A. Woods, *Mental and Moral Heredity in Royalty.*
77. See H. Ellis, *A Study of British Genius.*
78. Galton, *Hereditary Genius*, p. 34.
79. *Ibid.*, pp. 34, 35.
80. Stoddard, *The Revolt Against Civilization*, p. 60.
81. L. M. Terman, *The Measurement of Intelligence*, p. 96. By permission of Houghton Mifflin Company.
82. Stoddard, *The Revolt Against Civilization*, pp. 70, 77.
83. Pearson, *The Function of Science in the Modern State*. By permission of the Cambridge University Press and The Macmillan Company, publishers.
84. Stoddard, *The Revolt Against Civilization*, p. 83.
85. McDougall, *Is Democracy Safe for America?* p. 163. By permission of Charles Scribner's Sons.
86. Quoted from W. C. Whetham in Stoddard, *The Revolt Against Civilization*, p. 242.
87. E. M. East, *Heredity and Human Affairs*, p. 300. By permission of Charles Scribner's Sons.
88. Stoddard, *The Revolt Against Civilization*, p. 264.
89. *Ibid.*, p. 21.
90. *Ibid.*, p. 24.
91. *Ibid.*, pp. 86, 87.
92. Pearson, *National Life from the Standpoint of Science*, p. 20. By permission of the Cambridge University Press and The Macmillan Company, publishers.
93. Galton, *Hereditary Genius*, pp. 327, 328.

94. F. H. Hankins, *The Racial Basis of Civilization*, p. vii. By permission of Alfred A. Knopf, Inc.
95. East. *Heredity and Human Affairs*, pp. 178, 179.
96. H. S. Chamberlain, *The Foundations of the Nineteenth Century*, I, 261. By permission of Dodd, Mead and Company and John Lane, The Bodley Head, Limited the original publisher.
97. *Ibid.*, I, 260, 261.
98. *Ibid.*, I, 210.
99. *Ibid.*, I, 269.
100. *Ibid.*, I, 218.
101. *Ibid.*, I, 206.
102. *Ibid.*, II, 57.
103. *Ibid.*, I, 247.
104. *Ibid.*, I, 331, 344, 345.
105. *Ibid.*, I, 331.
106. *Ibid.*, I, 491.
107. *Ibid.*, I, 262.
108. *Ibid.*, I, 61, 68.
109. *Ibid.*, I, 106.
109a. *Ibid.*, I, 35.
110. *Ibid.*, I, 320.
111. *Ibid.*, I, 257.
112. *Ibid.*, II, 188.
113. *Ibid.*
114. *Ibid.*, I, 520, 521.
115. *Ibid.*, II, 188.
116. H. F. K. Gunther, *Racial Elements of European History*, p. 3. By permission of E. P. Dutton and Company, Inc.
117. See F. Lenz, "*Die Seelischen Unterschiede der grossen Rassen*," in Baur, Fischer, Lenz, *Menschliche Erblichkeitslehre*, pp. 411 ff.
118. Gunther, *Racial Elements of European History*, pp. 3, 4.
119. *Ibid.*, pp. 51–55.
120. *Ibid.*, pp. 59–61.
121. *Ibid.*, 56, 57.
122. *Ibid.*, p. 167.
123. *Ibid.*, pp. 173, 176.
124. *Ibid.*, p. 186.
125. *Ibid.*, p. 252.
126. *Ibid.*, p. 164.
127. *Ibid.*, p. 169.
128. *Ibid.*, pp. 194, 195.
129. *Ibid.*, p. 240.
130. *Ibid.*, p. 166.
131. *Ibid.*, p. 167.
132. *Ibid.*
133. *Ibid.*, p. 187.
134. *Ibid.*, pp. 263, 264.

BIBLIOGRAPHY

FOR THE GENERAL IMPLICATIONS OF SOCIAL DARWINISM

W. A. Locy, *Biology and Its Makers*, third edition, New York, 1915 (for the difference between Darwinian and other theories of evolution). C. Darwin, *Origin of Species*, fifth edition, New York, 1871. H. Spencer: *First Principles*, second edition, New York, 1873; *Principles of Biology*, 2 vols., revised edition, New York, 1900–1901; *Principles of Psychology*, 2 vols., third edition, New York, 1895; *Principles of Sociology*, 3 vols., 1877–1896; *Data of Ethics*, New York, 1879; *Essays*, 3 vols., New York, 1891. W. H. Hudson, *Introduction to the Philosophy of Herbert Spencer*, New York, 1900. D. Duncan, *Life and Letters of Herbert Spencer*, New York, 1908. J. Rumney, *Herbert Spencer's Sociology*, London, 1934. W. Bagehot, *Works*, 9 vols., London, 1915. (Vol. I contains *Letters on the French Coup d'État of 1851*; vol. V contains *The English Constitution*; vol. VIII contains *Physics and Politics*. There are numerous separate editions of the two latter works.) Mrs. R. Barrington, *Life of Walter Bagehot*, London, 1915. W. Irvine, *Walter Bagehot*, New York, 1939. L. Gumplowicz: *Outlines of Sociology*, Philadelphia, 1899; *Ausgewaehlte Werke*, 4 vols., Innsbruck, 1926–1928. (Vol. 3 contains his *Rassenkampf*.) B. Zebrowski, *Ludwig Gumplowicz*, Berlin, 1926. G. Ratzenhofer, *Wesen und Zweck der Politik*, 3 vols., Leipzig, 1893. F. Oppenheimer: *The State*, second edition, New York, 1922; *System der Sociologie*, 3 vols., Munich, 1924. H. E. Barnes, "The Struggle of Races and Social Groups," in *Journal of Race Development*, vol. IX, 1918–1919, pp. 394 ff. A. Small, *General Sociology*, Chicago, 1905. L. F. Ward, *Pure Sociology*, New York, 1903. J. P. Lichtenberger, *Development of Social Theory*, New York, 1925 (especially chapter XV).

FOR THE EUGENISTS

The best general statement of the political tendencies of the eugenists is to be found in L. Stoddard, *The Revolt Against Civilization*, New York, 1922. See also F. Galton: *Hereditary Genius*, second edition, London, 1892; *Natural Inheritance*, London, 1889; *Noteworthy Families*, London, 1906. K. Pearson: *Life, Letters and Labours of Francis Galton*, 3 vols., London, 1914–1930; *National Life from the Standpoint of Science*, second edition, London, 1905; *The Scope and Importance to the State of the Science of National Eugenics*, third edition, London, 1911; *Nature and Nurture*, London, 1911; *The Function of Science in the Modern State*, second edition, Cambridge, 1919. E. S. Pearson, *Karl Pearson*, Cambridge, 1938. F. A. Wood: *Mental and Moral Heredity in Royalty*, London, 1906; *The Influence of Monarchs*, London, 1913. H. Ellis, *A Study of British Genius*, second edition, London, 1926. L. M. Terman: *The Measurement of Intelligence*, Boston, 1916; *The Intelligence of School Children*, Boston, 1919; *Genetic Study of Genius*, 3 vols., Stanford, 1925–1930. W. C. D. Whetham, *Heredity and Society*, London, 1912. E. M. East, *Heredity and Human Affairs*, New York, 1929. H. E. Barnes, *History and Prospects of the Social Sciences*, New York, 1925.

FOR THE RACIALISTS

For a general survey of the racialist creed and its development, see F. H. Hankins, *The Racial Basis of Civilization*, New York, 1926. L. L. Snyder, *Race, a History of Ethnic Theories*, New York, 1939. A. de Gobineau: *The Inequality of Human Races*, New York, 1914; *Essai sur l'inégalité des races humaines*, 4 vols., Paris, 1853–1855. H. S. Chamberlain, *The Foundations of the Nineteenth Century*, 2 vols., London, 1910. H. F. K. Gunther: *Racial Elements of European History*, New York [1928]; *Rassenkunde des deutschen Volkes*, Munich, 1922. E. Baur, E. Fischer, F. Lenz, *Menschliche Erblichkeitslehre*, third edition, Munich, 1927. Students of racialism should also consult the following books not mentioned in the text: M. Grant, *Passing of the Great Race*, New York, 1916. L. Stoddard, *Racial Realities in Europe*, New York, 1924. O. Ammon: *Die naturliche Auslese beim Menschen*, Jena, 1893; *Die Gesellschaftsordnung*, Jena, 1900. G. V. de la Pouge: *Les Sélections sociales*, Paris, 1896; *L'Aryen*, Paris, 1899; *Race et milieu social*, Paris, 1909. It should be noted that there are a large number of books which attack the racialist creed. See especially F. O. Hertz, *Race and Civilization*, New York, 1928.

Part Four

THE TRIUMPH OF ABSOLUTISM
FASCISM AND NATIONAL SOCIALISM

CHAPTER XI

The Political Philosophy of Fascism

As WE have already seen, all through the nineteenth century, when the forces of liberalism seemed to be increasingly popular and powerful, there was, nevertheless, a strong undercurrent of feeling in favor of etatism and authoritarianism. On the surface, in the world of active politics, in the slogans of the political parties, liberalism seemed to grow stronger and stronger from decade to decade. But below the surface, in the world of philosophers and writers, and among those who were or who claimed to be scientists, there was growing up a tradition or school of thought which emphasized the doctrines that the individual must be subordinated to the state and that the government of the foolish many must give way to government by the wise few. As time went on this etatist-authoritarian tradition slowly but steadily grew in strength and in power. Eventually, in the troubled years following the first World War, this tradition came to the surface in the world of active affairs. The doctrines which had formerly been preached by closet philosophers, dreamy literary men, or academic recluses were advocated by powerful and vociferous political groups. Before long these groups, in several instances, were able to transform their abstract theories into concrete realities.

In point of time, it was the Italian Benito Mussolini and his followers, the Fascists, who were the first to transform this etatist-authoritarian tradition from idle speculation into active and vigorous reality. For this reason Mussolini and the Fascists are especially worthy of our attention. We have already seen how the etatist-authoritarian tradition in its modern form came into existence during the closing years of the eighteenth century in the minds of such thinkers as Kant, Fichte, and Hegel. We have already seen how this tradition was fostered and somewhat transformed in the course of the nineteenth century by the group of persons we have called the traditionalists, the irrationalists, and the Social Darwinians. It is now time to examine how this tradition came to maturity and received concrete embodiment in the Italian state as reconstructed by Mussolini in the twentieth century. Above all, it is of interest to observe how closely the concrete manifestation of the present day corresponds with the abstract speculation of earlier times. In point of fact, we shall see that the correspondence between the two is amazingly exact, and that many phases of the present-day concrete manifestation are only intelligible in the light of the earlier abstract speculation.

MUSSOLINI AND THE RISE OF FASCISM

The personal history of Mussolini and the story of the development of the Fascist Party which he founded are too well known to require more than casual restatement. Mussolini was born in 1883 in Central Italy of lower middle class parents. His father was an earnest, impecunious blacksmith. His mother aided the slender family income by teaching in an elementary school. Mussolini himself, after a normal school education, was at times a teacher, and at other times a day laborer, earning his living, for several months at least, as a mason. In later life he devoted himself to journalism and to political agitation. For many years he was a left-wing revolutionary Socialist; for some time he was the editor of the Socialist newspaper *Avanti* (Forward). He broke with the Socialist Party and was forced to resign his editorship of the party newspaper in 1915 as a result of his war policy. The Socialist Party remained internationalist and pacifist; Mussolini, even at this early date, advocated a nationalist and militarist policy. With money supplied by secret backers interested in war propaganda, he started a newspaper of his own, *Popolo d' Italia* (People of Italy), which has remained his personal organ ever since. For some years he insisted that in spite of his nationalism and his militarism he was still a Socialist at heart, and the early program of the Fascist Party, which he founded March 23, 1919, contained a number of rather radical semi-Socialist demands. At this time the Fascists still wanted to be "revolutionary, proletarian, a band of fighters for a new Italy, not merely defenders of the existing social order and vested interests in the face of bolshevism." [1]

As time went on, however, Mussolini and his fellow Fascists were forced by circumstances to adopt a far more conservative position. The orthodox Socialists, regarding Mussolini and his friends as renegades, if not traitors, to the Socialist cause, resolutely refused to have anything to do with them; and as the Socialists continued to get the support of the broad mass of the proletariat, it became obvious to Mussolini that he must get the support of a different element in the population if his Fascist Party was to gain strength or even to persist. In November, 1919, when Mussolini was still preaching radicalism, he and his party received a crushing blow in the elections. The Fascists failed to gain a single seat in the Chamber of Deputies, while the Socialists succeeded in electing 156 members. As a result Mussolini abandoned much of his earlier radicalism. If the Socialists, the Communists, the radicals would not cooperate with him, he would oppose them — fight them with all the means in his power. With Mussolini opposition always means violent, forceful opposition, based not upon the battle of words but upon direct action. Fascist bands broke up Socialist meetings, burned Socialist newspaper plants, and gave various Socialist leaders a very rough handling. Before long Fascism, from being "proletarian, revolutionary," came to be known as the bulwark of law and order, of discipline and of authority — even though law and order were often preserved by somewhat illegal and disorderly means. The slogan of the Fascists now became "Down with the Red Menace." Mussolini proclaimed the necessity of saving the country from the horrors of class war as preached by the Socialists. The Fascists aided in putting down strikes and insisted that the rights of private property be respected. As the result of this change in policy Mussolini gained thousands of new recruits for his party, chiefly among persons who thought that the government was too weak-kneed in putting down proletarian unrest. In the election of March, 1921, the Fascists won 34 seats in the Chamber of Deputies and definitely became a force with which to reckon.

Thereafter the growth of Fascist strength was amazingly rapid. Had Italy possessed a strong government capable of dealing with the prevalent social and industrial unrest, it is probable that the growth of Fascism would have been checked. But no party had an absolute majority in the Chamber of Deputies. The various bourgeois or anti-Socialist parties together outnumbered the Socialists and Communists, but they could not agree on a program of action, and in the absence of positive action the country seemed to be going to the dogs. Mussolini with his emphasis upon violent and direct action seemed to be the white hope of the existing social order. On the principle that it takes a thief to catch a thief, it seemed to many that it took a Socialist, or at least a renegade Socialist to put down the Socialist menace. By appealing to "national honor," and "national glory," by promises to make Italy the leader of the world, he secured the allegiance of large numbers of the working class. In this manner he diverted the animosity of the proletariat away from the capitalists and directed it towards the "foreigners," who were blamed for most of Italy's woes. Not only did Mussolini thus wean away many workers from adherence to orthodox socialism and its doctrine of class struggle, he also managed to organize several trade unions pledged to support Fascism and "class cooperation" in the interests of the nation. Impressed by these developments, the great bankers and industrialists, seeing in Mussolini a bulwark for their vested interests, hastened to give the Fascists their moral and, more to the point, their financial support. Millions of *lire* were poured into the coffers of the Fascist Party and Mussolini was thereby enabled to carry on operations on an ever larger scale.

But though Mussolini by appeals to "patriotism" was able to win over a considerable section of the working class and by appeals to "security" to win the support of a large number of the wealthy capitalists, his chief support came from the members of the lower middle class. The Italian lower middle class were frightened by the pretensions of the lower classes, with their threat of communism, and at the same time they were resentful against the power and prestige of the great capitalists with their huge, ill-distributed fortunes. To this lower middle class Mussolini seemed conservative enough to protect them against the bolshevism of the great unwashed, and yet radical enough to protect them against complete domination by the great banking institutions and the commercial and industrial trusts. Mussolini was clever enough to seduce many workers into supporting him; he was clever enough to blackmail the great industrialists into supporting him: but his real rise to power was due neither to the workers nor to the capitalists, but to the local butcher, baker, and candlestick maker, to the members of the same lower middle class from which he himself sprang.

This fact is of great significance when we remember that it was this same lower middle class in Germany which carried Hitler and the Nazi Party to power; that it is this same class which forms the chief support of the Fascist and semi-Fascist organizations in other countries. It is from among this class in the United States that Father Coughlin and others of his ilk secure their greatest following. In Father Coughlin's speeches we still hear, as we heard in Mussolini's speeches twenty years ago, alternate diatribes against communism and the "minions of Wall Street." There are some political scientists who claim that liberalism with its emphasis upon individualism and parliamentary government was developed by the upper middle and middle classes in their struggle against monarchic despotism; and that individualism and parliamentary government only work well when these same classes retain effective political control; that when political control passes into the hands of the lower middle class some kind of Fascist government is bound to arise. The history of France and America shows that this doctrine is not strictly true; that the rise of the lower middle class to a large share of political power is still compatible with the retention of individualism and democracy as governmental principles. It is, nevertheless, true that the lower middle class, especially in times of great economic stress, is peculiarly susceptible to Fascist or semi-Fascist propaganda and that if an economic condition should arise in America such as Italy witnessed in the period 1920–1922, this class is likely to produce an American version of the Fascist dictatorship.[2]

In the years following 1921 Mussolini, having won for himself a place in the political sun, set out to improve and strengthen his position. Not content with carrying on political propaganda both in newspapers and in Parliament where he was still only a minority leader, he began to prepare for the seizure of power by direct action. Taking advantage of the financial support given him by the capitalists and of the great following he found among the Italian lower middle class, Mussolini set about organizing, or rather reorganizing and expanding, the Fascist militia, groups of armed, uniformed, and disciplined young men pledged to carry out all orders given them by the party leaders, whose aims and duty it was to see that the Fascist program was carried out both locally and nationally. Although this Fascist militia constituted only a fraction of the population, it had the sympathy and occasionally the silent support of a much larger section of the community, in fact, of nearly all persons whose chief dread was of a communist revolution. Taking advantage of this fact Mussolini in 1922 prepared to strike. Late in October he ordered his Fascist "legions," the members of the Fascist militia, to march on Rome.

> Luigi Facta, who headed the shadowy government then in office, decided to oppose the advance of the Fascists. A state of siege was declared, but the order had to be countermanded, for the king refused to sign the decree. While the black shirted cohorts were closing in on Rome, Mussolini was offered an opportunity to become part of a coalition government, but declined. On the 29th the King called him to Rome and the next day, amid scenes of extraordinary enthusiasm, he formed a government.[3]

But though Mussolini thus came to power in 1922 he was very slow and cautious in imposing all the Fascist ideals upon the Italian state. His policy seems to have been "Fascism on the installment plan." At first he was content to be the Prime Minister of a coalition cabinet, several of his fellow Ministers being persons who were not members of the Fascist Party. Many officials in the bureaucracy were, to be sure, dismissed, and their places taken by Fascists, but an even larger number were permitted to retain their offices. The Chamber of Deputies was bulldozed into submission, but for some time it was permitted to remain in existence and to include within its membership the representatives of parties directly opposed to Fascism. As time went on, however, Mussolini was able to consolidate his position as the greatest and strongest force in Italian public life. In 1925 he felt strong enough to strike once more. In that year and in the years which followed he proceeded to carry out his program of making Italy a completely totalitarian state. All non-Fascist parties were forcibly dissolved. A rigid censorship was placed on the press, and any opposition to Fascism was ruthlessly punished. Local self-government was suppressed, all local officials being appointed by the Fascist-controlled central government. All government officials, including university professors, were forced to swear allegiance to the Fascist cause. Even among private persons open opposition to Fascism was punished by imprisonment or exile. Trial by jury, because of the democratic element involved, was abolished. For several years the Chamber of Deputies was permitted to maintain a shadowy existence, though after 1928 the members of this body were nominated by the Grand Council of the Fascist Party. In 1939 the process of making Italy totalitarian was completed by the suppression of the (theoretically) elective Chamber and the substitution for it of a Chamber of Fasci and Corporations, all of whose members owe their position to executive (and Fascist) appointment.

THE IDEOLOGICAL BACKGROUND

When we turn from an examination of the history of Fascism to a study of its political philosophy we meet with an initial difficulty. During its early years the Fascist Party was exceedingly opportunistic, embracing and abandoning doctrines according to the mood of the moment, or rather abandoning those doctrines which proved unpopular and embracing those which promised to draw popular support. It would, of course, be unfair to quote from the speeches made by Mussolini in his old Socialist, pre-Fascist days; but it is surprising to find that even in the years following 1919, when the Fascist Party was officially organized, Mussolini alternately attacked and defended a large number of different political propositions. In 1919 Mussolini was still in favor of a republican form of government; in 1922 he declared in favor of the existing monarchy. In 1919 Mussolini was still in favor of universal suffrage and proportional representation. A few years later he declared his opposition to parliamentary government and electoral machinery in any form. In 1919 Mussolini had a close alliance with the Futurists, who violently attacked all traditions and demanded the suppression of all institutions, customs, and beliefs which had come down from the past. A few years later Mussolini swung over completely to the principle of "historic continuity," the linking of the present with the past. In 1919 Mussolini, a former atheist, was still violently anti-clerical. A few years later he came out in support of the Catholic Church. As late as 1922 he declared in favor of economic liberalism — the principle of *laissez faire* — arguing that the economic activities of a nation must not be handed over to the control of governmental agencies. A few years later he demanded that all economic activity be controlled and regulated by the state.

During the early period (1919–1925) the Fascists were quite willing to admit their inconsistencies — in fact tended to glory in them. Fascism, they declared, was not a dead body of dogmas but a living movement, and like all living things it needed to change with the times. Fascism, they said, refused to be tied down by abstract or formal principles (*prejudiciali*). After 1925, however, a great change took place. Fascism became stabilized. By this time the Fascists had undisputed control over all the organs of the state. The days of revolutionary ardor were over. They no longer had to put forth programs merely to win popular support. On the other hand they were placed in a position of great responsibility. On them depended the present and the future of Italy. It was high time that they formulated a statement as to the general principles in accordance with which they were determined to rule the nation. In August, 1925, therefore, we find the first authoritative statement of the philosophy of Fascism in a speech (*The Political Doctrine of Fascism*) made by Alfredo Rocco, then Fascist Minister of Justice and Mussolini's intimate adviser on matters of general policy. In addition there are also available a number of Mussolini's own articles and speeches, of which the most important is *The Political and Social Doctrines of Fascism*, an article written in 1932 for the *Italian Encyclopaedia*, which is largely a restatement and expansion of the ideas expounded by Rocco. Of great interest and importance are the writings of two other men, Gentile and Palmieri. Both Gentile and Palmieri are out and out Neo-Hegelians, not only politically but also philosophically, and both these writers have expounded and defended Fascism from a Neo-Hegelian or idealist point of view. The Fascist Party has not yet adopted Neo-Hegelianism as its official philosophy, but the writings of Gentile and Palmieri have received the official approval of Mussolini and have appeared under the auspices of the Fascist Party.

Fascism, after wavering between individualism and etatism, has, in later expositions of party philosophy, declared wholeheartedly for radical, thoroughgoing etatism and, after wavering between democracy and authoritarianism has declared for thoroughgoing authoritarianism. Of great significance in this respect is the fact that the Fascists have drawn largely from the store of ideas supplied by the purely speculative philosophers of the nineteenth century. As we know, etatism and authoritarianism were defended from many widely divergent points of view, but especially by the groups which we have called the Social Darwinists, the irrationalists, the traditionalists, and the idealists. Among these different groups there were many points of dissimilarity and even of open opposition. Especially was there a deep cleavage between the irrationalists and the Social Darwinists on the one hand with their "scientific naturalism" and "realism," and the traditionalists and the idealists on the other with their emphasis upon the non-material or "spiritual" values. Despite this opposition, however, the Fascists have not hesitated to use the arguments and ideas of all four of these schools. When one peers below the surface it would seem that Mussolini himself is primarily affected by irrationalism and Social Darwinism, but that he sees the value of traditionalism and idealism as "window dressing" — as means of presenting Fascist doctrines in such a way as to appeal to large sections of the populace who would be shocked by the cold-blooded naturalism of the other two schools.

The Social Darwinists, as we have seen, start with the assumption that all life, or at least all progress, is based upon the struggle for existence, the elimination of the unfit, and the survival of the fittest. The later members of this school also emphasize that the struggle or conflict is not only between individuals but also and more especially between groups; that in all struggles between an individual and a group, the group wins; that in the struggle between groups it is the more coherent, compact, homogeneous, disciplined group which wins. There is no evidence that Mussolini ever came directly into contact with the writings of Bagehot and Gumplowicz, the chief apostles of Social Darwinism; but

from his own speeches and writings it is certain that he was deeply affected by popular second- and third-hand rehashes of the ideas formulated by these men.   It is also certain, from direct evidence, that Mussolini was deeply affected by Nietzsche, who in addition to being an
irrationalist was also an important apostle of Social Darwinism.

Again and again in Mussolini's writings and speeches we find ideas
reminiscent of the earlier Social Darwinists.

> Strife is the origin of all things. . . . Strife will always remain at the root of
> human nature, like a supreme fatality. And on the whole it is well that it is so.
> Today strife is possible in war, in economics, in ideas; but the day in which
> there would be no more strife would be a day of melancholy, of the end of
> things, of ruin.[4] Humanity is still and always an abstraction of time and
> space; men are still not brothers, do not want to be, and evidently can
> not be.   Peace is hence absurd or rather it is a pause in war.   There is some-
> thing which binds man to his destiny of struggling.   The motives of the
> struggle may change indefinitely; they may be economic, religious, political,
> sentimental, but the legend of Cain and Abel seems to be the unescapable
> reality while "brotherhood" is a fable. . . . The Christian and Socialist "men
> be brothers" is a mask for the eternal and immutable "homo homini lupus"
> . . . and man will continue to be a wolf among wolves for a bit of land, for a
> trickle of water, for a crumb of bread, for a woman's kiss, for a necessity —
> or a caprice.[5]

In consequence of this position Mussolini advocates nationalism as
opposed to internationalism and glorifies war as opposed to peace.   He
assails the socialist doctrine that international misunderstandings are
due to the machinations of the capitalist class, and the notion that were
the capitalists removed the peoples of the world would live in amity.

> At bottom internationalism is an absurd fable; the great masses do not
> escape nor can they, and it is the best of fortune that they can not escape the
> insuppressible datum of race and nation. . . . Put workers representing various
> countries around the same table — witness the Washington Conference —
> and you will hear the same unintelligible clamor of a new Babel; bring labor-
> ing masses of different races into forced contact and you will have the story
> of Upper Silesia, or of the Teschen Basin or of Trieste.[6]

To Mussolini, as to the great Social Darwinist Gumplowicz, the whole
history of mankind is a *Rassenkampf*, a conflict of races and nations;
so has it always been, so will it always be.

> Above all Fascism . . . believes neither in the possibility nor the utility of
> perpetual peace.   It thus repudiates the doctrine of Pacifism — born of a re-
> nunciation of the struggle and an act of cowardice in the face of sacrifice.
> War alone brings up to its highest tension all human energy and puts the
> stamp of nobility upon the people who have the courage to meet it.   All

other trials are substitutes, which never really put men into the position where they have to make the great decision — the alternative of life and death. Thus a doctrine which is founded upon this harmful postulate of peace is hostile to Fascism. . . . And thus hostile to the spirit of Fascism . . . are all international leagues and societies, and societies which, as history will show, can be scattered to the winds when once strong national feeling is aroused by any motive — sentimental, ideal or practical. . . . Thus the Fascist accepts life and loves it, knowing nothing of and despising suicide; he rather conceives life as duty, and struggle, and conquest.[7]

It is important to notice that Mussolini accepts Nietzsche's interpretation of Social Darwinism, rather than other versions, in that he insists that life is not merely a struggle for *existence*, but also a struggle for domination and power. To Mussolini and to Nietzsche the basic factor in human psychology is not merely the "will to live," but also and more especially the "will to power." To Mussolini, moreover, the will to power should and must motivate not only individuals but also states. "The value of Fascism lies in the fact that . . . it has a will to exist and a will to power, a firm front in face of the reality of violence. . . . The Fascist state is an embodied will to power." [8] It is this doctrine which drives Mussolini from a defense of nationalism to a defense of imperialism. The older nationalists, men such as Fichte and Mazzini, claimed that every nation had a right to its place in the sun, that every nation must fight to secure and maintain its existence, but they expressly denied that any nation has the right to conquer or dominate any other nation. To Mussolini this idea is sheer nonsense. In the uniform struggle for existence only the fit have the right to survive — and these fit not only have the right to survive but also have the right to conquer, to control, the less fit.

> The right to national independence does not arise from any merely literary and idealistic form of self-consciousness . . . but from an active self-conscious political will expressing itself in action and ready to prove its rights.[9]

In other words, no nation merely because it is a nation has the right to exist. A nation has the right to exist only if it can successfully compete with other nations in the general struggle for existence. In like manner any nation has a perfect right to dominate any other nation if it is physically able to do so.

> Imperialism is the eternal and immutable law of life. At bottom it is but the need, desire, and will for expansion which every individual and every live and virile people have inside them.[10]
>
> For Fascism the growth of empire, that is to say the expansion of the nation, is an essential manifestation of vitality, and its opposite a sign of

decadence. Peoples which are rising, or rising again after a period of decadence are always imperialist; any renunciation is a sign of decay and of death.[11]

It is Social Darwinism, the belief that human history is the story of
the eternal, inevitable conflict between groups, especially between
nations, which has driven Mussolini to advocate certain measures in
the realm of practical politics. Take for example his objection to birth
control and his ardent preaching in favor of an ever-increasing population. To his mind the fact that Italy is already overpeopled, or that
she is unable to support her present population in decency or comfort
is non-essential, or rather beside the point. To him the essential point
is that the Italians are bound to compete with the other nations of
Europe, and how can they successfully compete with their rivals if
Italy is permanently outnumbered?

> Some unintelligent persons may say: there are already too many of us....
> Intelligent persons reply: there are too few of us.... Let us speak plainly.
> What are forty million Italians to ninety million Germans and two hundred
> million Slavs.... Gentlemen, if Italy wants to count for something, it must
> appear on the threshold of the second half of the century with a population of
> not less than sixty million inhabitants.... If we fall off we can not make an
> Empire.[12]

Of even greater importance is the fact that Social Darwinism has profoundly affected Mussolini's views as to how the government should
be run. Bagehot, it will be remembered, claimed that in the early
conflicts between groups it was the coherent, compact, homogeneous
group which won over the loose, incoherent, incompact, heterogeneous
group. Groups which act alike, talk alike, think alike triumph over
groups in which the individuals act, talk, and think differently. Hence
the need for rigid discipline and for the persecution of aberrant minorities. To Mussolini this is true not only for early primitive times but
also for the present; not only for primitive tribal organizations, but also
for modern states. In times of war a nation which is undisciplined,
dominated by individualistic trends, will be defeated by a nation in
which all individuals are subordinated to and controlled by the state —
and to Mussolini all nations at all times are in a state of war, open or
secret. Hence the need of etatist principles at all times.

> Empire demands discipline, the co-ordination of all forces, and a deeply felt
> sense of duty and sacrifice. This fact explains many aspects of the practical
> working of the regime, the character of many forces in the state and the
> necessarily severe measures which must be taken against those who oppose
> this spontaneous and inevitable movement of Italy in the twentieth century.[13]

Just as Social Darwinism leads Mussolini to defend etatism, so likewise does it lead him to defend authoritarianism.   Even Macaulay,
that staunch pillar of liberalism, admitted that in times of war, democratic control was always a nuisance and at times a calamity, that no
army has ever prospered under a debating society.   Bagehot went
further and declared that "so long as war is the main business of
nations, temporary despotism is indispensable."   To Mussolini with
his belief in the constancy and universality of war, Bagehot's premises
make it necessary to conclude that permanent, not temporary, despotism
is indispensable.   "Never before has the nation stood more in need of
authority, of direction, and of order." [14]

As we have already seen, different from, but closely related to, Social
Darwinism were the doctrines preached by the eugenists and the racialists.   It is therefore noteworthy that whereas Fascism has been profoundly affected by orthodox Social Darwinism, the ideas of the eugenists and the racialists have as yet played only a minor role in the formation
of Fascist ideology.   There are indeed two points on which the eugenists
and the Fascists are in fundamental agreement.   One is that men are
innately and fundamentally unequal; the other, that political, social, and
economic control should rest not with the masses but with that small
group of elite who are clearly superior to the masses.   According to
Mussolini, "Fascism ... affirms the immutable, beneficial, and fruitful
inequality of mankind." [15]   On the basis of this inequality, "Fascism
denies that the majority, simply by the fact that it is a majority, can
direct human society; it denies that numbers alone can govern by means
of a periodical consultation." [16]   But though Fascism thus agrees with
the eugenists in two essential respects, the Fascists, unlike the eugenists, have never emphasized the idea that superiority is hereditary, that
superior stocks tend to breed superior stocks, or that inferior stocks
tend to breed inferior stocks.   This may be partly due to the fact that
the Fascists received so much support from the lower middle class; that
so many of the Fascist leaders have themselves emerged from this same
social group; and that the Italian lower middle class has long disliked
the special privileges of the old hereditary aristocracy.   At the same
time it is interesting to observe that among some of the Fascists there is
already a movement in favor of creating a new hereditary aristocracy
composed of the Fascist leaders, for the purpose of breeding "true
gentlemen." [17]   And even Mussolini tells us:

Sometimes I play with the idea of a laboratory for making generations;
that is of creating the class of warriors ever ready to die, the class of inventors

pursuing the secret of mystery, the class of judges, the class of great captains of industry, of great explorers, of great governors. It is by means of such methodical selection that the great classes are created, which in turn will create the Empire.[18]

In other words, Mussolini "sometimes plays with the idea" of turning Italy into a giant eugenic laboratory.

The connection between Fascism and racialism is even more casual, though it too is not entirely non-existent. For many years Mussolini pooh-poohed the whole of the racialist creed, the idea that one race is superior to another, that it is the task of the superior races to govern the inferior ones, and that it is the duty of the superior races to keep themselves racially pure. As late as 1932 he declared,

> Of course there are no pure races left; not even the Jews have kept their blood unmingled. Successful crossings have often promoted the energy and beauty of a nation. Race! It is a feeling, not a reality; ninety-five per cent, at least, a feeling.... National pride has no need of the delirium of race.[19]

A few years later Mussolini completely changed his tone. Events in Germany convinced him that even though race is a myth it is a very useful myth in stabilizing an authoritarian regime. Although there are only about forty thousand Jews in Italy, and although these Jews play a relatively insignificant part either in the public or the private life of the country, Mussolini also learned that the Jews could serve as a convenient scapegoat in that they could be blamed for many of the economic ills which still beset Italy after several years of Fascist control. By way of popularizing racialism most Jews holding public office lost their posts. On July 14, 1938, a group of Fascist professors, acting under the auspices of the Ministry of Popular Culture, issued a manifesto on racialism similar to pronouncements of the German Nazis. It is possible that the Italian conquest of Ethiopia had something to do with this change in Fascist ideology. The theory of black inferiority and the need for white rulership could be used to defend Italy's aggression. Of equal importance was the fact that racialism could be used as a propaganda weapon in preventing the new Italian colonists from mating with the women of Ethiopia.

Fascist racialism is still in its infancy, and as yet it is impossible to foresee how far and in what direction it will go. It is obviously impossible for the Fascists to follow Houston Stewart Chamberlain or Gunther in advocating Germanic or Nordic supremacy, as the Nordics constitute only a minor element in the racial make-up of the Italians. It is possible (in spite of the fact that northern Italy is mostly non-

Mediteranean) that the Fascists will build up a legend in favor of the Mediterranean race; but it is more probable that they will revert to the simpler theory that the Italian people do indeed form a blend of races, but an ideal blend of the best elements of the best races, and that this ideal blend, having been created, must not be corrupted by further racial mixture.

It is obvious that Social Darwinism has played a great part in the development of Fascist ideology. It soon becomes clear that irrationalism figures in an equally significant role. Again and again Mussolini tells us how much he has been influenced by such great irrationalists as William James, Bergson, Nietzsche, Sorel, and Pareto. The list of these names shows that Mussolini has been interested, not merely in the practical or political phases of irrationalism, but also in its more general or metaphysical aspects.

Again and again the Fascists tell us that Fascism is an anti-intellectual movement, a revolt against the cold reason of intellect, that Fascism supports the superior claims of instinct over reason. Mussolini has often expressed his disdain of abstract thinking and exalted Fascism by contrasting its live reality with the sterile theory of other movements. "Fascism is based on reality, Bolshevism is based on theory.... We want to be definite and real. We want to come out of the cloud of discussion and theory." "My program is action, not thought." [20] It is no wonder that the phrase "we think with our blood" has become a Fascist slogan. "My blood tells me," "I must listen to my blood" are phrases sometimes used by this statesman-gladiator. "It is no good," he will add, "I am like the animals, I *feel* when things are going to happen; some instinct warns me, and I am obliged to follow it!" [21] "Before all I trust my insight. What I call my insight — it is indefinable." [22] According to Palmieri, Fascism stresses "the supremacy in this life... of Poetry over Science, of Intuition and Inspiration over experience and method." [23] Even Gentile, the chief professional philosopher in the ranks of Fascism, declares,

> I am convinced that the true doctrine is that which is expressed in action rather than in words or books, in the personality of men and in the attitudes they assume in the face of problems, and this is a much more serious solution to problems than abstract dissertations, sermons, and theories. [24]

Rocco joins the chorus when he says,

> It is true that Fascism is above all action and sentiment, and that such it must continue to be. Were it otherwise it could not keep up that immense

driving force, that renovating power which it now possesses, and would be merely the solitary meditation of a chosen few. Only because it is feeling and sentiment, only because it is the unconscious awakening of our profound racial instinct, has it the force to stir the soul of the people, and to set free an irresistible current of national will.[25]

Rocco admits that natural intelligence is of great service in the task of governing, but adds, "Still more valuable is the intuitiveness of rare great minds." [26] Rocco is certain that Mussolini is the ideal head of the state because he possesses "infallible intuition which assists him in times of crisis." [27] To Rocco and his fellow Fascists the broad mass of the populace have very little intelligence; nevertheless,

> among people with a great history and with noble intelligence, even the lowest elements of society possess an instinctive discernment of what is necessary for the welfare of the race, which in moments of great historical crises reveals itself to be almost infallible.[28]

From these statements it is obvious that the Fascists are in accord with the older irrationalists when the latter proclaim that reason alone cannot solve the problems of social and political life, that higher than ideal theorizing and speculation is heroic, creative *action*, guided by intuition, instinct, "feeling."

Even more significant is the fact that Mussolini wholeheartedly accepts the pragmatic doctrine regarding the nature of truth and of moral standards. Mussolini, in fact, tells us that pragmatism is "one of the foundation stones" of Fascism. To the rationalist certain doctrines, certain facts, certain scientific laws are absolutely and eternally true. Further research may reveal new details regarding the old laws, may even reveal new laws, but this in no way invalidates the old laws. In like manner the rationalists claim that certain standards of right and wrong, of good and bad are absolute and eternal. In contradiction with these ideas the pragmatists, and with them Mussolini, claim that all doctrines, "facts," "laws," are merely working hypotheses — hypotheses which are not necessarily "true" but which are serviceable in aiding human *action*. From this it follows that the laws or rather the hypotheses which are serviceable to one generation are not serviceable to another generation, and hence must be discarded and replaced by new ones. To say that an idea is true is merely to say that it has proved useful to the preservation of the individual or the race, that it has enabled the individual or the race to act in such a way that it succeeds in the struggle for existence. In like manner the irrationalists, and with them Mussolini, claim that all standards of value and moral codes are merely weapons in the struggle for power.   All moral codes are merely standards created by the group to protect its own interests, and to discipline the members of the group, so that the group itself can better struggle with and dominate over other groups.   As the conditions necessary for the maintenance of the community and for the discipline of the community differ from time to time, it follows that the standard of values and the code of morals imposed by the community upon its members must also vary from century to century.   It also follows that as moral codes are merely arbitrary standards which the community imposes on its members for purposes of discipline, they do not and cannot apply between states.

It is only when we bear in mind the ideas expounded by Mussolini's teachers, James, Nietzsche, and Sorel, that we can understand the true significance of some of Mussolini's remarks.   It is because Mussolini has adopted the pragmatist attitude towards truth and moral values that he is able to assert that Fascism has no "preconceived notions, no fixed ideas." [29]   It is for this reason that he declares that Fascism "rejects the idea of a doctrine suited to all times and all peoples," that he insists that doctrines are of value only because

> all doctrines aim at directing the activities of men towards a given objective. ... A doctrine must therefore be a vital act and not a verbal display. Hence the pragmatic strain in Fascism, its will to power, its attitude towards violence, and its value.[30]

And again

> The sanctity of an -ism is not in the -ism; it has no sanctity beyond its power to do, to work, to succeed in practice.   It may have succeeded yesterday and fail tomorrow.   Failed yesterday and succeed tomorrow.   The machine first of all must run.[31]

It is because Mussolini sees in moral codes only the means whereby the community for its own advantage disciplines its members that he asserts that whereas "the state has not got a theology, it has a moral code." [32]   A moral code inculcating "a deep sense of duty and a spirit of self-sacrifice" has no eternal, absolute value, but pragmatically it is extremely valuable because it makes for "discipline and the co-ordination of efforts" and thereby permits Italy to go on with her imperialistic designs.[33]   In accepting pragmatism, Mussolini has also accepted Sorel's doctrine of "the Myth."   To Sorel, it will be remembered, a myth is a useful fiction, "a body of images capable of evoking sentiment instinctively," and of enormous value irrespective of whether or not the myth is logically sound.   Echoing Sorel, Mussolini proclaims:

We have created our myth. The myth is a faith, a passion. It is not necessary that it shall be a reality. It is a reality by the fact that it is a goad, a faith, that it is courage. Our myth is the nation, our myth is the greatness of the Nation. And to this myth, to this grandeur, that we wish to translate into a complete reality, we subordinate all the rest.[34]

Another basic doctrine common to the irrationalists and to the Fascists is that men, or at least the broad mass of men, are essentially irrational animals and that all social and political activity must be based on this assumption. To Mussolini

it is faith that moves mountains, not reason. Reason is a tool, but it can never be the motive force of the crowd. Today less than ever.... The capacity of the modern man for faith is illimitable.... Everything depends upon one's ability to control the masses like an artist.[35]

When Mussolini was asked whether a dictator can really be loved by the populace, we find him replying, "Yes, provided that the masses fear him at the same time. The crowd loves strong men. The crowd is like a woman." [36] When asked why, after many years in power, Fascism speaks of itself as a permanent revolution, Mussolini immediately replied, "We need to speak of permanent revolution because the phrase exerts a mystical influence upon the masses." [37] "For me the masses are but a herd of sheep.... If you would lead them, you must guide them by two reins, enthusiasm and interest." [38] In admitting that men are guided or partly guided by their interests, Mussolini admits that rational self-interest plays an important part in motivating human action. But he is far from admitting that rational self-interest is the chief or even the most important factor in determining human conduct. Mussolini tells us that Fascism rejects the theory of the economic man, the man who obeys the laws of supply and demand, who buys in the cheapest and sells in the dearest market. "The economic man does not exist. Man is integral, he is political, he is economic, he is religious, he is saint, he is warrior." [39] To Mussolini this is merely a polite way of saying that man, under the influence of political or religious myths, will frequently do things which are contrary to his economic or rational interests. "Fascism believes now and always in sanctity and heroism, that is to say in acts in which no economic motive, remote or immediate, is at work." [40] It is for this reason that Mussolini violently objects to Karl Marx's economic interpretation of history.

Incidentally it should be noted that Mussolini, following in the footsteps of James, Bergson, and Sorel, denies not only economic determinism but also all other forms of determinism. Mussolini follows these other irrationalists in rejecting the theological fatalism or deter-minism of Calvin, the idealistic determinism of Hegel, and the racialism and environmentalism of later thinkers. To Mussolini as to James a man may be strongly influenced by his environment, his racial or his historical background, or by economic factors, but he always remains a free agent, able to shake off these influences and control his own destiny. To Mussolini as to Bergson, evolution is the free creative activity of the mind or rather of the will which creates new and un-predictable forms as it surges upward. To both men there is a tendency towards something, but never a fixed goal. Along with James' indeter-minism, Mussolini has also accepted James' attitude towards the problem of optimism and pessimism. James, as we know, refused to admit that the world is essentially good or essentially bad. He claimed that some features of the world are good, others bad, and that it lies in our power to increase the good and decrease the bad. Not only does Mussolini accept this doctrine but he also agrees with Sorel in rejecting the theory of inevitable progress. To Mussolini as to Sorel, progress is possible, but it is not certain. It is not even probable unless man can be re-awakened to the need of irrational but heroic action. Mussolini's attitude towards such problems is summed up in his statement that Fascism is

> neither pessimistic nor supinely optimistic, as are generally the doctrines (all negative) which place the centre of life outside man, whereas by the exercise of his free will, man can and must create his own world. Fascism wants man to be active and to engage in action with all his energies; it wants him to be manfully aware of the difficulties besetting him and ready to face them.... Hence the essential values of work, by which man subjugates na-ture and creates the human world, economic, political, ethical, intellectual.[41]

The more one studies the life, the speeches, and the writings of Mus-solini, the more one becomes convinced that Social Darwinism and ir-rationalism constitute the real underlying bases of the whole of his political philosophy. In later years, however, especially since coming into power, he has found it necessary to supplement and even to cloak these two creeds by appeals to other doctrines. Social Darwinism and irrationalism do not and probably never will find widespread popular appeal, and in order to win the sympathy of the masses and rally them to the support of Fascism, Mussolini has taken over from others several additional ideological defenses of the Fascist position. As he himself has remarked, "We play on all the strings from violence to religion from art to politics." [42]

Among the most important and valuable of these additional defenses of Fascism is the appeal to tradition and to traditionalism, especially the form of traditionalism developed by such early apostles of etatism as Mazzini and Treitschke. In some ways Mussolini's acceptance of traditionalism as an integral part of the Fascist creed is startling and even amusing when one takes into consideration his earlier life and ideas. Throughout most of his life Mussolini has been a revolutionary, in violent opposition to inherited or traditional doctrines, customs, and institutions. As a disciple of Nietzsche and Sorel, Mussolini for many decades openly espoused the doctrine that we must break not only with old dogmas and old institutions, but also with old values, old standards of right and wrong. During the early stages of Fascism (1919–1921) the Fascists were intimately allied with the so-called Futurists, led by Marinetti. In view of the later traditionalism of the Fascist Party it is interesting to read some of the declamations of Marinetti, Mussolini's erstwhile friend and ally.

> The cult of the past and mercantilism in art; these are the two terrible plagues that are devastating our country.... We combat the majorities corrupted by power, and we spit on current and traditional opinion.... Our poetry is poetry essentially and totally rebelling against all used forms.... We are convinced that nothing is more easy and more despicable than public approval, soliciting popular and traditional tastes.... To youth we ascribe all rights and all authority which we deny and seek to wrest brutally from the old, the dying, and the dead.[43]

Because of his opposition to traditionalism we find that Marinetti, who in 1919 stood side by side with Mussolini as a candidate for Parliament, demanded "the abolition of museums, libraries, and academic institutions of every kind," because they express the voice of the past.

For several years Mussolini felt deep sympathy for Marinetti and for his ideas. As late as 1932 he declared,

> Every revolution creates new forms, new myths, and new rites and the would-be revolutionist, *while using old traditions*, must refashion them. He must create new festivals, new gestures, new forms which will themselves become traditional.

Nevertheless since coming into power in 1922 Mussolini's attitude towards tradition has been undergoing a slow but thoroughgoing transformation. Mussolini and with him the Fascist Party has now become the bulwark of tradition and of respect for established laws and beliefs. It has chosen to set its standards by Rome, especially by the Rome of classical antiquity; it has chosen to submit to age-old Italian institu·

tions, including even Catholicism, which was once regarded by Mussolini as the arch enemy of his ideals. The reasons for this transformation are not hard to find. To a certain extent, Mussolini's conversion to traditionalism was honest and sincere. Mussolini was always an ardent nationalist, and he now began to realize, as Mazzini and Treitschke long before him had realized, that there is a close association between nationalism and traditionalism and that if he was going to remain a nationalist he would also have to be a traditionalist. With Mazzini and Treitschke, Mussolini came to believe that a nation is what it is because of what it has been, because of the experiences it has undergone, because of the store of traditions it has accumulated. To remain an anti-traditionalist meant to wreck the cause of Italian nationalism — hence traditionalism had to be adopted, little as it suited Mussolini's character and personality.

But although Mussolini's conversion to traditionalism was, in part at least, sincere, this conversion was greatly aided by the fact that Mussolini found that tradition was a valuable ally from the practical, pragmatic point of view. If in the eternal struggle between groups the coherent, compact groups triumph over the loose, incoherent groups, it follows that the groups in which a uniform tradition is strong will normally triumph over groups in which the power of tradition and the discipline which comes from tradition is weak. As Bagehot put it, to make a group coherent and compact,

> what you want is a comprehensive rule binding men together, making them do the same thing. What this rule is, does not matter so much. A good rule is better than a bad one, but any rule is better than none.

To Bagehot this comprehensive rule binding men together was furnished in early times by customary law. To the Fascists the role of customary law is in modern times taken by tradition. To the Fascists, tradition is a strong social force giving strength and unity to the state and to the government. As a result any state or government which fails to utilize this force would render itself weak. To Mussolini many of the traditions which have grown up in Italy are irrational and even ludicrous, but that does not make them any the less valuable. It is the duty of statesmen to utilize any social dogma or social tradition, however intrinsically absurd, to give stability to their regime, for without internal stability no nation can successfully compete with other nations. Take, for example, that form of tradition called religion. For many years Mussolini was an avowed and passionate atheist. Even now it is certain that he accepts almost none of the dogmas of the Catholic Church, yet once he was in power he hastened to make friends with the Catholic Church on the ground, which he himself admits, that "beyond question power and harmony are promoted for a statesman if he adheres to the religion of the majority of his fellow countrymen." [44] In other words Mussolini has found in the Catholic tradition, absurd though it seems to him, a powerful social force which is advantageous for his own ends.

It would be ridiculous to regard Mussolini as primarily a traditionalist even in the later stages of his intellectual development. Primarily he was and still is an irrationalist and a Social Darwinist, and it is only be-cause he is that he has become converted to the use and defense of traditionalism. As an irrationalist he sees the value of absurd tradi-tions, just as Sorel saw the value of absurd myths. As a Social Dar-winist he sees that tradition gives to the Italians a strong mental and spiritual discipline, rendering them more homogeneous and compact and hence better able to struggle with and triumph over the peoples of other nations. But though Mussolini is thus only indirectly and second-arily a traditionalist, in the last few years he has paid loud lip service to the traditionalist cause. "Tradition certainly is one of the greatest spiritual forces of a people, in as much as it is a successive and constant creation of their soul." [45] . . . Hence the great value of tradition in records, in language, in customs, in rules of social life. "Outside history man is a non-entity. . . . The state . . . safeguards and transmits the spirit of the people elaborated down the ages in its language, its customs, its faith. The state is not only the present, it is also the past." [46]

> You assuredly should not forget that every nation has a history. All the peoples that have a history have an honor peculiar to themselves. It is their heritage from their forefathers which justifies their existence.[47]
> We must never disrupt the continuity of tradition. Traditions constitute a great moral force in the history of the people, and if you eliminate them you eliminate the foundations on which the history of the future is to be built, for that history is nothing more than a further achievement and a further per-fection of the past.[48]

Needless to say the traditionalism which has been accepted by Mussolini as an integral part of Fascism is reflected in the writings of the other Fascist authors. Thus we find Rocco attacking liberalism and the liberal theory of the state on the ground that to the liberals the state is merely the sum total of the individuals in the community at any one time.

> An atomic view of this kind is necessarily anti-historical in as much as it considers society in its spatial attributes and not in its temporal ones; and

because it reduces social life to the existence of a single generation. Society thus becomes a sum of determined individuals, viz. the generation living at a given moment. This doctrine, which I call atomistic and which appears to be anti-historical, reveals from under a concealing cloak a strongly materialistic nature. In its endeavors to isolate the present from the past and the future it rejects the spiritual inheritance of ideas and sentiments which each generation receives from those preceding and hands down to the following generation, thus destroying the unity and the spiritual life of human society.[49]

Fascism, on the other hand, is said to replace the old atomistic and anti-historical doctrine with an organic and historic concept.

For Liberalism society has no purposes other than those of the members living at a given moment. For Fascism society has historical and immanent ends... quite distinct from those of the individuals which at any given moment compose it, so distinct in fact that they may even be in opposition.[50]

To the Fascists the Nation is the supremely important entity to which all individuals must be sacrificed, and after all what is the nation but

an entity with a unity brought about by common traditions among the people who compose it, traditions formed in the course of time owing to the working of a variety of influences such as... community of languages, race, culture, religion, laws, customs, history feelings, and volitions.[51]

But though Fascism is thus definitely wedded to traditionalism, it should be noted that the traditionalism which it has adopted is definitely of the type which we have called Hegelian. We have already distinguished between the old traditionalism of De Maistre and the new of Hegel. The old traditionalism was opposed to all theories of progress, improvement, or evolution. To this school political action should consist of clinging resolutely to the old ways of doing things, and to old doctrines and ideas. The new traditionalism of Hegel, of Mazzini, of Treitschke, went hand in hand with a belief in progress and evolution. Traditionalism of this sort was compatible with advocating violent, bloody revolution. The new traditionalism teaches that progress in the present and future is perfectly possible, but only when such progress is made dependent upon traditions handed down from the past. To the new traditionalists each generation must create its own ideas and ideals but they must be rooted in and grow out of the ideas and ideals of past ages. Even a cursory glance at Fascist writings shows that Mussolini's traditionalism belongs to the new and not to the old school. To Mussolini, "life is in continual flux, and in process of evolution." [52] "Each age has its own doctrine." [53] Fascism "rejects the idea of a doctrine suited to all ages and all peoples." [54] Although Fascism is in favor of etatism and authoritarianism, it rejects the particular form of etatism and authoritarianism in vogue in the eighteenth century. Fascism

> should not be interpreted as implying a desire to drive the world backwards to positions occupied prior to 1789.... History does not travel backward. The Fascist doctrine has not taken De Maistre as its prophet. Monarchical absolutism is dead and so is ecclesiolatry.[55]

It is indeed surprising to find pragmatic, revolutionary Fascism becoming the defender of traditionalism. It is even more startling to see this same Fascist movement making an intimate alliance with idealism, more especially with that brand usually called Neo-Hegelianism. Mussolini is admittedly so realistic, so naturalistic, so convinced that the only reality is the will to power and the ruthless struggle for existence, that it is difficult to picture him wrapped in the mantle of idealism. And yet not only has this mantle been used, but it has proved extremely useful to the Fascist cause. There are many reasons why Mussolini has been willing to toy with Neo-Hegelianism. In the first place he has always been willing to accept support from whatever source it comes. He is far from being a Neo-scholastic, or even an orthodox Catholic, but when a person, such as Barnes,[56] writes a book in favor of Fascism using Catholic Neo-scholasticism as a base, Mussolini is always willing to give the author a smile of welcome. As we know, Hegel was a strong advocate of etatism and authoritarianism, and in pre-Fascist Italy the followers of Hegel, the Neo-Hegelians, were among the most eloquent apostles of these two principles. It is not surprising, therefore, that Giovanni Gentile, one of the most outstanding of the Neo-Hegelians, was willing to embrace Fascism at an early date, defending the Fascist state from his own Neo-Hegelian point of view. Nor is it surprising, considering that Gentile was one of the leaders of Italian intellectual life, with disciples all over the country, that Mussolini was willing to admit Gentile within the Fascist camp and to allow the philosopher to use what argument he pleased in defense of the Fascist theory of the state.

At first Mussolini himself and most other Fascist leaders maintained a position which might be called benevolent neutrality with respect to Neo-Hegelianism. They were willing to receive Neo-Hegelian support, but they were unwilling to commit themselves to aid Neo-Hegelianism in its struggles with other philosophical schools. Even today Neo-Hegelianism is far from being the official philosophy of Fascism. Nevertheless within the last few years the Neo-Hegelians have enormously strengthened their position within the Fascist Party.   Gentile himself, after serving as Minister of Education, was made editor of the semi-official *Italian Encyclopaedia* and Director of the National Fascist Institute of Culture, which is the official propaganda organization of the Fascist regime.   In these various capacities he has managed to give a Neo-Hegelian veneer to many of the official and semi-official exposi-tions of Fascist principles, both to those written by himself and to those composed by subordinates.   In recent years we find even Mussolini and Rocco, who are definitely not Neo-Hegelians in their metaphysics, using many of the terms, phrases, and arguments invented by the Hegelian school.   This, no doubt, is partly due to the fact that these terms are found to have popular appeal, that they are seen to sway the sentiments of thousands of persons who would be repelled by the frank discussion of irrationalism and Social Darwinism.   But it is also true that Mussolini has seen that his own versions of irrationalism and Social Darwinism are not necessarily incompatible with a milk and water version of Neo-Hegelianism.   We have already seen that Hegel, gen-erally regarded as the apostle of rationalism, was in reality the prophet of "creative unconscious reason," or of intuition, and that Neo-Hegeli-anism can easily be reinterpreted to make it defend irrationalism.   We also know that though Hegel lived and died before Darwin, he was a great apostle of the general principle of evolution and proclaimed that evolution can only take place through conflict — the basis of the Hegelian dialectic.   Last but not least, Mussolini has found in the Hegelian version of traditionalism the type which he can wholeheartedly accept.   In consequence of all these facts we need not be surprised that ever greater favor is being shown to idealistic interpretations of the Fascist creed.

In using idealistic weapons with which to defend Fascism and attack liberalism, frequent use is made of three different phases of the old ideal philosophy.   The first of these we may call *moralism*, an attitude found not only in Hegel, but also in Kant, Fichte, Carlyle, and Mazzini. It is the belief that in politics as in ethics the chief concern must be, not what man wants to do, but what he should do.   This attitude is re-flected in Kant's Categorical Imperative.   It is reflected in the Mazzinian creed that we must concern ourselves with the duties of man and not with the rights of man.   It is reflected in Carlyle's dictum that we must seek blessedness, not happiness.   It is reflected in the view of Green that the chief function of society and the state is to promote the moral welfare of man.   The Fascists claim to have adopted this attitude, and contrast their own position with that of liberalism, which they insist is based upon selfishness and hedonism. To Fascism the liberal position is best represented by Bentham and his fellow utilitarians. To Bentham every man is motivated by self-interest; and by self-interest Bentham means that every man spends most of his time trying to avoid pain and to secure happiness for himself. As the supreme goal of every individual is to secure the maximum of happiness for himself, so must the goal of the state consist merely in trying to secure the greatest happiness for the greatest possible number of its citizens. The Benthamites further claim that general happiness can best be achieved by allowing every person to do as he pleases, providing that he does not criminally interfere with his fellow citizens. The Fascists declare that this idea is low and materialistic. They also declare that the old liberal doctrine that every man has a natural, God-given right to "life, liberty, and the pursuit of happiness" is equally low and materialistic. To the Fascists man is primarily a creature of duties rather than of rights. Man's primary duty is to serve his community and nation, and this frequently means that it is his duty to give up his life, his liberty, and his pursuit of happiness for the benefit of the community or the nation.

Fascism starts from the proposition that man is not always motivated by self-interest, and that when dominated by some ethical, political, or religious ideal, he frequently performs actions which are directly opposite to his own self-interests.

> Fascism rejects the doctrine of materialism and any other doctrine which attempts to explain the intricate history of human societies from the narrow and exclusive stand point of the pre-eminence of material interests.[57]

On this point the idealist phase of Fascism coincides with its irrationalist phase, save that the idealists talk of man being motivated by ideals, while the irrationalists claim he is motivated by myths, fictions, traditions, and the like. Having demonstrated to its own satisfaction that man can be motivated by things other than rational self-interest, Fascism then claims that he should put duty, self-sacrifice, desire for heroic action, ahead of such considerations as self-gain or personal happiness.

> Fascism sees in the world not only those superficial material interests in which man appears as an individual, standing by himself, self-centered, subject to natural law which instinctively urges him towards a life of selfish momentary pleasure; it sees not only the individual but the nation and the country, individuals bound together by a moral law.... It builds up a higher life based on duty ... in which the individual by self-sacrifice, the renunciation

of self-interest, by death itself can achieve that purely spiritual existence in which his value as a man consists. . . . Life as conceived by the Fascists is serious, austere, religious, all its manifestations are poised in a world sustained by moral forces and subject to spiritual responsibilities. The Fascist disdains an easy life. . . . Fascism denies the materialistic conception of happiness as a possibility . . . and abandons it to the economists of the mid-eighteenth century. This means that Fascism denies the equation: well-being equals happiness, which sees in men mere animals, content when they can feed and fatten, thus reducing them to a vegetative existence pure and simple.[53]

From these statements, all of them made by Mussolini himself, it is obvious that the relativist, irrationalist, Social Darwinist founder of Fascism has learned the idealist phraseology well and knows when and how to use it. But when one reads the whole of the writings from which these statements were taken, it is also obvious that this idealistic moralism is only a dressing for a much more deep-seated Social Darwinism. Mussolini, the great prophet of morality, of duty, of self-sacrifice for the individual, holds that there is no moral code binding upon the state in its relations with other states.   The only duty the state has to consider is the duty of making war, of increasing its power and its territory.   The self-sacrifice, the abnegation which is said to be good for the individual is said to be bad for the community.   In other words, behind the mask of idealism Mussolini's true doctrine is that in the struggle for existence the group which is the best disciplined, the group whose members are most imbued with the spirit of duty and self-sacrifice, will triumph over other groups, and for this reason and for this reason only, it is necessary to use the catchwords of the older moralists.

In this connection it is advisable to point out a curious paradox in the history of political thought. Frequently the political philosophers who have talked very little about abstract morality have been the persons who have done the most to alleviate the real ills of suffering mankind, and the political philosophers who have been most insistent upon mouthing moralistic platitudes have also preached doctrines which shock the moral sense of the average intelligent person. Bentham and his followers, for example, identified goodness with happiness, and thought that all talk of abstract morality was absurd, yet they were behind all the social, political, and legal reforms which took place in England during the early part of the nineteenth century. They wished to protect the majority from the rule of the minority and yet shield minorities from all oppression by majorities. They demanded the freeing of slaves and the education of the poor. They were bitterly opposed to war and imperialism and demanded that England free the colonies which she had secured by force.   Carlyle, on the other hand, who despised the utilitarian creed as materialistic, who thought that all political problems should be settled in accord with God-given moral laws, who thought that man should seek blessedness, not happiness, was also the man who demanded that the minority should rule the majority, and force it to act, talk, think, believe in a way the minority thought proper.   He was in favor of slavery and the scourging of prisoners at home; he was in favor of endless warfare and imperialism abroad.   He began by saying that right is might; he ended by saying that might is right.   There are many analogies between the creeds of Carlyle and Mussolini, the most striking being the close union between "anti-materialistic moralism" and the belief in brute force to be applied both within and without the nation.   But between Carlyle and Mussolini there is one great difference.   We have good reason to believe that Carlyle sincerely and honestly believed in the supreme, absolute moral code which he preached.   We have equally good reason to suppose that Mussolini sincerely disbelieves in any and every supreme, absolute moral code.   To him the only absolute good is the success of the group or the state, and talk of moral virtues is merely propaganda, a means to induce men to sacrifice themselves to this end.

If moralism is the first point on which the Fascists have agreed to join hands with the idealists, the second point of agreement is in the definition and interpretation of the term liberty or freedom.   At first the Fascists were naïve enough to admit openly that they were opposed to individual liberty on the ground that the granting of any appreciable amount of liberty to the individual would make the state dangerously weak.   Before long, however, they learned from the idealists that it was possible to take away liberty in practice and yet pay lip service to it in theory.   This paradox was made possible by the use of liberty in the sense in which it had been used by such men as Kant, T. H. Green, and Hegel.   It was Kant, it will be remembered, who said that a man is truly free only if and when he is obeying the precepts of the moral law. It was T. H. Green who elaborated this idea and emphasized the idea of "positive" as opposed to "negative" liberty.   To Green a man is not free when he is a slave to alcohol, to lust, or to avarice; in other words, he is not free when he does "what he likes to do"; he is free only "when he does something worth doing."   Speaking from the same point of view, Green further says that a man is truly free only if he is able to develop his latent faculties for mental and moral improvement.   Hegel carries this idea still further and declares that a man is truly free only when he subordinates himself to the will of the state. To Hegel a man is free only if he obeys the moral code, and it is the state which tells us what the moral code should be. To Hegel a man is free only if his acts are in accord with reason, and by reason he means reason "as embodied in rational institutions such as the state." To obey the laws of the state, therefore, means merely acting in accord with reason, the inner essence of each man. Hence, in obeying or in being forced to obey these laws, man becomes free for the first time.

While Mussolini was still a revolutionary he would have been horrified at such a doctrine, but once he and his fellow Fascists had seized power and had control of the state, they embraced the idealist theory of freedom with open arms. Mussolini himself gives a milk-and-watery version of this theory when he says:

> The Fascist state... has curtailed useless or harmful liberties while pre-serving those which are essential. In such matters the individual cannot be the judge, but the state only.[59]

The Hegelian doctrine that the will of the state expresses the real will of the individual is paraphrased by Mussolini in the words, "Fascism reasserts the rights of the state as expressing the real essence of the individual." The Hegelian notion that freedom consists in the development of the higher faculties and capacities of man is paraphrased by Rocco as follows:

> There is a Liberal theory of freedom, and there is a Fascist concept of Liberty. We, too, maintain the necessity of safeguarding the conditions which make for the free development of the individual.... We do not, however, accept a bill of rights which tends to make the individual superior to the state and empower him to act in opposition to society. Our concept of liberty is that the individual must be allowed to develop his personality in behalf of the state.[60]

Needless to say, this general idea receives even clearer expression in the writings of Gentile and his disciples who are admittedly Neo-Hegelians in addition to being ardent Fascists. To Gentile,

> Liberty is, to be sure, the supreme end and aim of every human life, but in so far as personal and social education realizes it by evoking this common will [i.e., the true moral will] it presents itself as law and hence as the state. The maximum of liberty coincides with the maximum strength of the state.... The state is liberal in fact and not merely verbally if it promotes the development of liberty considered as an ideal to be attained and not as a natural right to be guaranteed.[61]

The clearest exposition of this whole theory is to be found in the writings of Palmieri.

> Fascism holds that personal liberty is simply a means to the realization of a much greater end, namely, the liberty of the Spirit, the last meaning the faculty of the human soul of rising above the power of outward circumstances and inward needs to devote itself to the cult of those ideas which form the true goal of life. ... In the Fascist conception to be free means to be no more a slave to one's own passions, ambitions or desires; means to be free to will what is true and good and just...; means, in other words, to realize here in this world the true mission of man.[62]

The third point of agreement between the Neo-Hegelians and the Fascists is the emphasis laid upon and the interpretation given to the terms spirit and spiritual. Almost all the Fascists proclaim that liberalism has a materialistic basis, while Fascism has a spiritual basis. Mussolini tells us that the Fascist concept of life "is a spiritual one, arising from the general reaction of the century against the flaccid materialistic positivism of the nineteenth century." [63]   Rocco thinks that Fascism is unique because alone among political creeds it recognizes the fact that

> man is not solely matter and the ends of the human species, far from being the materialistic ones we have in common with other animals, are rather and predominantly the spiritual finalities which are peculiar to man.[64]

As usual Palmieri is even more explicit.

> Man is above, outside and against nature. Man is part and product of nature. These two visions of man, like the two poles of Being, set in antithesis to each other and, separated by an unbridgeable chasm, represent the two contrasting philosophies of our time, Fascist idealism and modern materialism.[65]

In reality this talk of spirit and spiritual is based upon the fact that so many of the expounders of Fascism are steeped in the metaphysics of Hegel and that those Fascists who are not Hegelians have been willing to take over many of the phrases and, in a more or less unconscious way, many of the basic doctrines of the Hegelian school. To Hegel, it will be remembered, the only ultimate reality in the universe is *Geist*, that is, mind or spirit. Far from mind being a product of matter, in reality matter is a product of or at least a partial and one-sided embodiment or manifestation of mind. The Hegelian philosophy does not deny the existence of the external objective world, but it insists that this world is essentially mental or spiritual or ideal in character and is merely one phase of a greater reality. In like manner, all human souls or minds are really parts of one great mind or soul, the Universal Spirit — the individual mind being only a transient modification of the Absolute, "as evanescent and unsubstantial as the passing waves of the ocean."

Going still further Hegel asserted that there is an everlasting evolution or development taking place within this one ultimate reality, the Universal Spirit, and that the universe, visible and invisible, is but a part of the eternal self-unfolding of this spirit. At a very early stage spirit embodies or reveals itself in the form of seemingly inert matter, then in the form of organic life, and finally as man. But though physical evolution reached its goal in the emergence of mankind, the process of spiritual evolution, the continued "unfolding of spirit," is not yet completed. The further development or manifestation of spirit is seen in the creation of human institutions, the family, society, and finally the state. Each of these institutions must be regarded as ever more perfect embodiments or incarnations of the spirit. Each nation has a *Volksgeist*, a spirit of its own, which is a concrete reality and not merely a metaphor, although, of course, all these national spirits are merely facets of the one Universal Spirit. The state is "the Divine Idea as it exists on earth." The ultimate actualization or realization of the spirit "is to be found in the state, in its laws, in its universal and rational arrangements." "The state is the march of God [i.e., the Spirit] in the world." "The state is the divine will as a present spirit, which unfoldr itself in the actual shape of an organized world."

It is highly doubtful if Mussolini really believes in the absolute truth or validity of the Hegelian philosophy. It is possible that he accepts some form of it as a useful working hypothesis. It is certain that he believes it to be a valuable weapon in converting the Italian people to devote themselves to the service of the Fascist state. For this reason it is not surprising to find him making use of terms which are borrowed directly from the Hegelian jargon, as when he says:

> The state as conceived and realized by Fascism is a spiritual and ethical entity... an organization which in its origin and growth is a manifestation of the Spirit. The state... transmits the Spirit of the People etc.[66]

But if Mussolini is only a pragmatist who occasionally likes to pose as an idealist, there can be no doubt that Neo-Hegelianism finds sincere and ardent support among many of his followers and has become at least the semi-official basis for the Fascist theory of the state. Palmieri tells us that in "the philosophy of Fascist thinkers... Reality cannot be apprehended until it is transformed into pure Thought.... No aspect of Reality can partake of the truth which is outside of Thought." [67] In other words, with the Fascists, as with Hegel, the only ultimate reality is thought, or mind, or spirit. Nature, as distinguished from spirit, is a mere figment of the mind. With the Fascists, as with Hegel, the spirit, the only ultimate reality, is not something eternally quiescent or changeless, but constantly develops, unfolds itself; the history of the world is the story of this unfoldment or self-realization of the spirit. As Gentile puts it:

> Reality is Spirit, and Spirit never *is*, but is always coming to be; not something given, but a free activity. That is what distinguishes it from nature, and such being its essence, Spirit, which is identical with Reality, is history or the process of self-realization. [68]

With the Fascist Gentile, as with Hegel, spirit is not to be identified with the separate, individual human minds, for these are unreal abstractions or rather momentary phases in the development of the Universal Spirit, which we may also call the "one Universal Person ... the one man in which all individuals are united and with whom they are all identified." With the Fascists, as with Hegel, spirit, the one Universal Person, is identified with the state, or at least the state is regarded as the final, most perfect embodiment of the spirit. The state is declared to be "a soul, a person, a potent will conscious of its ends and vastly superior to individuals." [69] With Gentile, as with Hegel, the real will of the individual is identified with the will of the state.

> In the way of conclusions, then, it may be said that I, as a citizen, have a will of my own, but that upon further investigation my will is found to coincide exactly with the will of the state, and I want anything only in so far as the state wants me to want it. [70]

Palmieri is trying to express the same general idea when he says,

> Fascism maintains that the meaning of life is found only in the realization of a full life of the Spirit; that this realization, in turn, is achieved only when the individual's spiritual needs, aspirations and longings are rooted, integrated and nurtured in the family, the church, the nation, and the state; that these institutions, forming the framework of all life of the Spirit, enjoy in turn an existence of their own; timeless and absolute, whose essence partakes of the Spirit itself, and is not contingent upon the will and the actions of man. [71]

The doctrines of the idealist wing of the Fascist Party are obviously only a paraphrase of the doctrines of Hegel. It is equally obvious that they are in opposition to the doctrines, both philosophical and theological, of the Roman Catholic Church. For this reason it is surprising that it was the idealists who were most active in bringing about the liaison between the Italian state and the papacy.   It was in fact **Gentile, the** high spirit of idealism, who introduced the compulsory teaching of Catholicism in the public schools.   This seeming paradox is accounted for by the fact that the idealists have their own way of dealing with Catholic dogmas.   This way is well expressed by Giuliano, **one** of Gentile's close associates:

> If we want to teach children religion, we must teach them a real and genuine religion, with its mythology, with its mythical personifications, and with its dogmatic commandments.... To restore to the people a sense of the sacredness of life, we must have patience and return to our Christian tradition.... Though Christianity at a particular state in its development has wrapped itself in a rigid theology, it does not cease to represent, to be sure in the form of myths, the essential revelation of the reality of the spirit.... We can and must go beyond the limits of Catholic orthodoxy, but we can not remain absolutely indifferent to a faith and an institution that represents the central nucleus of our national tradition.[72]

FASCISM AND ETATISM

After our long survey of the intellectual background of Fascism, the connection between Fascism and such doctrines as Social Darwinism, irrationalism, traditionalism, and idealism, we are now in a position to examine more closely the more concrete evidences of Fascist thought, more especially what Fascism has to say regarding etatism and authoritarianism.

There can be no doubt that Fascism is now thoroughly and absolutely etatist, but there can also be no doubt that Fascism adopted radical etatism only after having played for some little time with individualism.   Mussolini started in life as a syndicalist, whose creed was that economic and political power should rest with the local syndicates or trade unions rather than with a strong central government.   For many years Mussolini maintained this general attitude even after he had finally abandoned syndicalism and had founded the Fascist Party.   In 1920 we find him writing in his newspaper an article attacking the daylight-saving bill and making this bill an issue on which to attack the whole principle of etatism.

> I, too, am against the daylight saving bill because it represents another form of state intervention and coercion.   The state with its enormous bureaucracy induces a feeling of suffocation.   The state was tolerable to the individual as long as it contented itself with being soldier and policeman, but today the state is everything; banker, money lender, gambler, sailor, procurer, insurance agent, postman, railway official, impressario, manufacturer, school master

professor, tobacconist, and a great number of other things, besides being as always policeman, judge, jailer, and tax collector. The state — this Moloch of fearsome aspect — does everything, controls everything, and sends everything to perdition. Every state undertaking is a calamity. State art, state schools, state postal services, state shipping, state trading, alike are disastrous — the litany could go on to infinity. The future prospects are terrifying.... We are approaching the complete destruction of human personality. The state is the gigantic machine which swallows living men and casts them forth as dead ciphers.... The great curse which fell on the human race in the misty beginnings of its history and has pursued it through the centuries has been to build up the state and to be perpetually crushed by the state.[73]

As the months went by Mussolini lost much of his hatred of the state. He began to preach that law, order, discipline, must be maintained, and he became convinced that law, order, and discipline could be based only upon a strong authoritarian state. Even so his conversion to thoroughgoing etatism was slow and gradual. For some years after 1920 he was much influenced in his political theorizing by Alberto de Stefani, a professor of economics, and later Mussolini's first Minister of Finance. De Stefani grew up steeped in the economic individualism, the doctrine of *laissez faire*, preached by Adam Smith and Ricardo. In later life he was deeply impressed by Pareto. Guided by Pareto, De Stefani accepted authoritarianism as opposed to democracy and taught that governmental control should rest in the hands of a strong, vigorous aristocracy, which should be ruthless in putting down disorders caused by the turbulent masses. But De Stefani, like Pareto, retained a large portion of the old individualist creed. He believed that whereas the government should be strong, forceful, and if necessary, brutal, yet the functions of government should be comparatively few in number. De Stefani was opposed to governmental control or operation of any commercial or industrial enterprise (such as the railroads). He was in favor of free trade in theory and a low tariff in practice. He was opposed to any governmental attempt to control or regulate private industry. He was opposed to any elaborate program of public works; he was in favor of a frugal government and a balanced budget. He was opposed to the heavy taxation of private wealth on the ground that such taxation was motivated by socialist prejudices and was basically unsound from the point of view of pure economics.

The basic individualism of De Stefani's political creed is clear from his numerous speeches in Parliament and from his official acts during the period (1922–1925) he served as Minister of Finance. In one of his speeches he tells us:

> There have always existed two opposed conceptions of history: the individu-
> alistic and heroic conception of our Latin race, and the socialistic gregarian
> conception which is Teutonic and characteristic of current socialism.…
> Solidly opposed to socialism stands the individualistic conception that we
> have inherited from liberalism, from our forefathers of the *Risorgimento.*…
> The historical function of Fascism is very clear today and does not lend it-
> self to equivocation: Fascism is an aristocratic and individualist movement.[74]

De Stefani's official acts, in which he was supported by Mussolini, were consistent with this philosophy. He dismissed thousands of unnecessary governmental employees. By rigid economies he balanced the budget and reduced the national debt. Protective tariffs were lowered in some instances and abolished in several others. Government protection and subsidies for cooperatives were withdrawn. Instead of undertaking extensive public works, De Stefani turned over the funds available for such purposes to private concerns. An attempt was made to eliminate government monopolies. Telephones were actually turned over to private companies, and schemes were drawn up whereby telegraph, railroads, and even the post offices were eventually to undergo a similar fate. De Stefani did, indeed, officially encourage private capitalists to undertake certain industrial and agricultural enterprises, but as far as possible such enterprises were free from all governmental control and regulation.

Needless to say, De Stefani's economic policies met with warm approval among most successful business men and industrialists both in Italy and abroad. While his policies were still in operation many good citizens of the United States were heard to say, "What this country needs is a Mussolini," unaware that what they should have said was, "What this country needs is a De Stefani." In 1925, however, and in the years which followed, the industrialists, especially the Italian industrialists, met with a rude shock. The Fascist Party, as we know, derived a good deal of its support from the lower middle classes, and persons of this ilk were as frightened of capitalistic and industrial dictatorship as they were of the dictatorship of the great unwashed. To this group economic liberalism, the unfettered, uncontrolled march of capitalism, seemed to spell the ruin of "the little man" in business. As a result many of the Fascist leaders were opposed to De Stefani and to the whole of his political and economic philosophy. Just at the time when opposition from this source was coming to a head, some of the leading bankers were unwise enough to quarrel with De Stefani over certain details of financial administration. In 1925 De Stefani was forced to resign. His successors were far less wedded to the principles of individualism and *laissez faire*, and as time went on economic conditions forced them gradually to embark upon a vigorous policy of state interference in and control of all manner of commercial and industrial enterprises. The economic turmoil following the stabilization of the lira in the later twenties, the consequences of the world-wide depression which began to be felt in Italy in the early thirties, the financial and industrial adjustments made necessary because of the sanctions imposed by the League of Nations in 1935, all served as excuses justifying the increased state interference with the normal workings of Italian economic life.

What began as pure opportunism — the manifest need for the state interference in one or two specific cases — soon led to the development of an elaborate political dogma, the sum and substance of which was that it is always necessary for the state to guide and control the economic activity of all of its citizens. Before long, Mussolini, who had supported De Stefani for many years, was saying, "Fascism is definitely and absolutely opposed to the doctrines of Liberalism both in the political and economic sphere." [75] We now find that Fascism is opposed both to socialism and to *laissez faire* individualism. In opposition to socialism, Fascism stresses the need for private property and individual initiative. The Charter of Labor (composed in 1927, and regarded as the Magna Charta of Fascism) proclaims that Fascism "considers private enterprise in the domain of production to be the most efficient method and the most advantageous to the interests of the nation." [76] Rocco tells us that socialism is and always will be a failure because

it does not take into account human nature.... It will not recognize that the most powerful spring of human activities lies in individual self-interest and that therefore the elimination from the economic field of this interest results in complete paralysis.... Socialism committed an irreparable error when it made of private property a matter of justice while in truth it is a problem of social utility. [77]

But while Fascism thus dismisses socialism as an idle and catastrophic dream, it also dismisses as absurd the old liberal dogma expounded by Locke that man has a natural, innate right to property, that property rights existed prior to and independently of the state, that the state has no right to control or regulate what a man does with his property, but merely has the duty of protecting existing property rights against criminal attacks. According to the Fascists, men have no "natural" rights whatsoever, certainly no natural rights to property. Any property rights which exist are derived from and granted by the state. What the state grants, it may also take away. The state has a perfect right to confiscate all property and inaugurate a communist regime. But it does not, and should not do so, for purely pragmatic reasons. Normally people work better and produce more when they are stimulated by the profit motive. The state is better off when its inhabitants thus work better and produce more. Hence under normal conditions the state, looking to its own advantage, should maintain private enterprise. Under certain conditions, however, when the state sees that its own advantage lies in interference with private property, it should not hesitate to intervene. As Rocco remarks, "the recognition of individual property rights, then, is a part of Fascist doctrine, not because of its individual bearing, but because of its social utility." [78]

> In other terms, Fascists make of the individual an economic instrument for the advancement of society, an instrument which they use as it functions and which they subordinate when no longer serviceable. In this guise Fascism solves the eternal problem of economic freedom and of state interference, considering both as mere methods which may or may not be employed in accordance with the needs of the moment. [79]

For this reason the Fascists proclaim that the state must intervene in economic production

> when private enterprise fails or is insufficient or when the political interests of the state are involved. Such intervention may take the form of control, encouragement, or direct management. [80] [A state so conceived] introduces order in the economic field. If there be one phenomenon which requires regulating and which should be directed towards certain fixed objectives, it is precisely the economic phenomena, for they concern the whole nation. Not only must industrial economy be regulated, but agricultural economy, commercial economy, banking and even artisan activities. [81] Work in all its forms — intellectual, technical, or manual — whether organization or execution, is a social duty. And for this reason ... it is regulated by the state. [82]

The notion that the state should supervise all phases of economic life is no idle theory. Since the fall of De Stefani it has been increasingly witnessed in Fascist practice. Strikes and lockouts have been prohibited by law; in cases of industrial disputes both employers and employees are forced to accept the decisions of a state-controlled labor court. Again and again the state has arbitrarily stepped in and determined how many hours a man shall work in a certain industry and how much he shall be paid for his work. On several occasions the state has arbitrarily fixed prices, both wholesale and retail. On several occasions the state has told private enterprise what it may and may not import and export. On several occasions it has told farmers what they may and may not grow on their land. In most cases private industrialists may not enlarge their plants or materially increase or decrease their yearly output without the permission of a government-controlled organ. In several instances competing firms have been forced to amalgamate on the ground that in this way the national interests can be better served. Small wonder that Mussolini, for all his opposition to orthodox socialism, openly boasts that "we have bitted and bridled capitalism," and not capitalism only, but also the economic activity of the whole mass of the proletariat.

Having thrown economic individualism to the winds, Fascism, determined to go on with the good work, crushes all other forms of individualism and individualistic activity. Not only the economic but also the social, cultural, intellectual, and even the athletic activity of its citizens were in the course of a few years subjected to the control and regulation of the Fascist state. In liberal countries we are accustomed to think that the state and politics represent only one phase and not an all-important phase in the total life of the average citizen. To the liberals, at least to the old-fashioned liberals, the chief purpose of the state is to keep out alien invaders and to maintain law and order inside its territory. As long as a citizen refrains from committing a crime and pays sufficient taxes to pay his share for the upkeep of the army, the police force, and a few administrative officials, he need not concern himself with purely political matters. He may be interested in culture and go to museums, art institutes, and operas, but this does not bring him into contact with the state, as in America most such institutions are privately endowed and privately run. He may be interested in sport and go to baseball games or football matches, join an athletic or a golf club, but with such matters the state has nothing to do. He may be interested in the drama and go to the movies or to plays, or he may join an amateur dramatic society, but with these activities, again, the state has nothing to do. He may be interested in social welfare work and take an active part in the Boy Scouts, the Y.M.C.A., social settlements, adult education movements without coming into contact with state officials. If he is interested in social intercourse with his fellow citizens, he may join one of a hundred clubs or fraternal organizations; he may become a Rotarian, an Elk, or a Freemason without asking permission of the state. The newspapers, the magazines, the books he reads fall under government censorship only if they are criminally libelous or obscene. In America, at least, the great news agencies, such as the Associated Press and the United Press, the radio chains, such as the N.B.C. and the

C.B.S., are private enterprises.   In America the vast majority of the colleges and universities are private institutions; the numerous scientific and learned institutions have no connection with the government.

To the Fascists since 1925, such a condition is appalling.   It is evidence that our civilization is "atomistic" and "materialistic." According to the Fascist creed the state "is an organic whole, having life, purposes, and means of action superior in power and duration to those of the individual citizens, single or associated, of which it is composed." [83] As Rocco remarks:

> since the state must realize its own ends, which are superior to those of the individual, it must also have superior and more powerful resources.   The force of the state must exceed every other force; that is to say, the state must be absolutely sovereign and must dominate all the existing forces in the country, co-ordinate them, solidify them and direct them to the ends of national life.... Unlike the Liberal-democratic state, the Fascist state can never consent that social forces should be left to themselves.... It is not only in the economic field that this state action operates.   According to Fascism's all-embracing ideal the state must preside over and direct national activity in every field.   No organization... can remain outside the state.   Fascism is therefore near the people; it has educated them politically and morally and has organized them not only from the professional and economic point of view but also from the military, cultural, educational and recreative point of view.[84]

Mussolini gives support to this position when he says:

> Anti-individualistic, the Fascist conception of life stresses the importance of the state and accepts the individual only in so far as his interests coincide with the state, which stands for the conscience and the Universal Will of man as an historic entity.... The Fascist conception of the state is all-embracing; outside of it no human or spiritual values can exist, much less have value.   Thus understood, Fascism is totalitarian and the Fascist state ...interprets, develops, and potentiates the whole life of a people.   No individuals or groups (political parties, cultural associations, economic unions, social classes) exist outside the state.... The Fascist state... sums up the manifestations of the moral and intellectual life of man.[85]

This whole attitude is expressed in the Fascist war cry, "All is in the state and for the state; nothing outside the state, nothing against the state."

Fascism has already gone a long way toward transforming its theoretical totalitarianism into concrete reality.   The *Balilla* (or Cub Scouts), the *Avanguardisti* (or Boy Scouts) have been formed and are still rigidly controlled by the Fascist Party acting in the name of the state. The state has always played an important role in Italian educational life, but state regulation in this field has become even more stringent since the rise of the Fascist regime. The vast majority of the schools of all grades are directly operated by the state; the private schools which still exist are subject to minute control both as to organization and curriculum. In all schools, whether public or private, all pupils must be taught that the supreme object in life is devotion and submission to the state. All primary schools are forced to use textbooks which are especially prepared and published by the state. Secondary schools are somewhat more free in this respect, but even they must choose their texts from a limited list especially approved by the Ministry of National Education. Mussolini has also seen to it that the universities are completely dominated by the Fascist ideology, including its worship of the state. In order to receive an appointment in any of the universities it is necessary to be a member of the Fascist Party and in addition to swear "to exercise the office of teacher . . . with the purpose of forming citizens industrious, honest, and devoted to the Fatherland and the Fascist regime." Professors are state servants and are appointed and dismissed by the Minister of Education; this official sees to it that all professorial lectures lead to the glorification of the state. A professor, writing on the principles of economics, is required to show that the old individualistic economics has been rightfully supplanted by the new "corporative," i.e., state-controlled economics. Much of the social life of the students in the universities is centered around the Union of University Fascists, a government-controlled organization.

Practically all scientific and art museums are operated by the state, and in such institutions great emphasis is given to those exhibits which display the national glories of Italy, especially of Fascist Italy. In order that the cultural and intellectual life of the country may be more completely moulded and guided, the Fascists have established two new institutions, the Italian Royal Academy and the National Fascist Institute of Culture. The Academy has as its purpose to promote and to control scholarship and scientific research throughout Italy. It was founded in response to the

> need for an organ fit to represent all the intellectual activities of the country and to co-ordinate them all. . . . The concept took root and gained in consistency that the state, just as it has intervened in economic life and in the relations between the various categories of producers, could and should intervene more effectively in the field of culture. . . . In promoting its foundation the Head of the Government (i.e. Mussolini) was fully conscious of the necessity of . . . giving, through the medium of the high council of scientists, men of letters, and artists, some guidance to the spiritual forces of the nation . . . of preserving the national character in its purity and favoring its expansion and influence beyond the national boundaries.[86]

The motto of the Academy is "not science for the sake of science and art for art's sake; but science and art together consciously, intentionally and directly working for the progress of the nation." [87]   With this end in view the Royal Academy affords official recognition, gives prizes, and grants subsidies to those enterprises which tend to promote the intellectual development of the Fascist state.   In point of fact the Royal Academy has frequently served to aid in the spread of Fascist propaganda.

Even more important in this respect is the National Fascist Institute of Culture, which controls and coordinates the activities of the numerous local institutes of culture scattered throughout the country.   While the Royal Academy supposedly specializes in the higher realm of scientific research, the National Fascist Institute of Culture aims at the promotion and spread of Fascist culture among the people of Italy.   Its purpose, therefore, is to foster an interest in "culture" among the masses and to see to it that in acquiring culture the masses also acquire a Fascist culture.   With this end in view the Institute publishes a magazine and numerous books and arranges for a large number of lectures on art, music, etc., before various types of audiences.   In reality, as Finer points out, these books and lectures

> represent one more stage in the inculcation of a uniform set of values in citizens throughout the kingdom.... In some of the meetings there is simply a regurgitation of the Duce's latest speech, together with a tame commentary by a tamed lecturer.[88]

The control of the state over the intellectual life of its citizens is enormously aided by the laws governing the publication of newspapers, magazines, and books.   Censorship laws, rigidly and ruthlessly carried out, have suppressed all newspapers and magazines which were antagonistic to Fascism and the Fascist attitude towards the state.   A large number of the still-existing periodicals are either directly owned by various Fascist institutions or by prominent Fascist leaders.   Those which are still "independent" are made subservient to the state in a number of different ways.   One such method is the law whereby no one may practice journalism unless he is a member of the Professional Roll of Journalists, admission to which requires certain educational requirements and proof of "good moral and *political*" standing.   In point of fact the state control over the press is not only negative, but also positive; not only does the state prevent the publication of news or opinions which are considered deleterious; it can also force the publications of news items or editorials which it considers useful.   Thus, for example, on one occasion the press was ordered to "make sympathetic comment on the rebirth of the military spirit in Germany," and on another "publish the news about the increase in unemployment in England in striking style." Government control of the press is aided by the fact that the Stefani News Agency, corresponding to the Associated Press and United Press in America, is immediately subject to the orders of state officials. What is true of newspapers and magazines is also true of books. No books are permitted to be published which are considered "contrary to the national interest" and at the same time the state directly or indirectly sponsors the publication of a large number of books expressing ideas which the government wishes to have expressed. Of great importance is the fact that the state has established complete control over the radio and cinema industries. Only those radio programs and those moving pictures are permitted which fit in with the state's cultural program, and in addition there are numerous radio addresses and "news" reels prepared by and on behalf of the state.

Even the social life of the Italians is carefully supervised. Masonic lodges and other secret or semi-secret societies are prohibited by law. No economic association can exist except under official recognition and control. All other associations and institutions, including those purely social in character, must furnish the government full information regarding themselves, their objects, and their members, and at any moment they may be dissolved by government decree. All public meetings, including those devoted to charity, to sports, to science, or to the commemoration of some person or event, can be held only after obtaining the permission of the government. Not content with these negative measures the state is trying, very successfully, to direct most Italian social life into channels which are directly controlled and supervised by governmental agencies. The most important unit created with this end in view is the *Opera nazionale Dopolavoro*, or the National Leisure Time Organization, which is a state-controlled federation of thousands of sporting, educational, and artistic groups. It is the purpose of this organization to promote athletic events of all sorts, to foster amateur dramatic and musical enterprises, to arrange educational and recreational tours, all under the direct supervision of the government or its agent the Fascist Party. It is indeed the announced intention of the Fascist government to keep its subjects so busy with social enterprises instituted and operated by the state that they have no time for privately established organizations.

One of the most important features in the totalitarian state envisioned by Mussolini is its attempt to dominate, not only the outward and physical, but also the inward or moral, life of its citizens. In the old liberal state it was thought that the formulation of a moral code and its enforcement upon the citizenry lay outside the functions of the government. To the liberal, the state had, indeed, the duty of maintaining law and of punishing crime; but as long as a man committed no crime and as long as he did not interfere with the rights of, or inflict damage upon, others, the state should not be concerned with his private morals, or even with the moral code upon which his actions were based. In marked contrast with this liberal attitude is the Fascist declaration that control over morals, as well as over law, lies within the domain of the state. To the Fascists it is not for the individuals or for the church to lay down the standard of what is right and what is wrong; it is the state which must make this standard, and making due allowance for the frailties of human nature, it is the duty of the state to see that this standard is carried out in everyday life. In accordance with this attitude we find Mussolini stating that though the state has no theology, it does possess a moral code.[89] This same attitude is voiced by Rocco when he says that the Fascist state has its own morality, which it must defend and which it must instill into the people.[90]

It is this attitude towards morals which has brought the Fascist movement into sharp opposition with the pope and the Catholic Church. Orthodox Catholicism teaches that the church must be supreme not only in matters of faith but also in matters of morals. According to Catholic belief it is for the church to reveal the eternal laws of right and wrong, which are the same for all peoples and for all nations. Mussolini and his fellow Fascists have been willing to grant the Catholic Church many favors. They have given the pope juridical independence. They have had the Fascist banners blessed by bishops and have placed crucifixes in every school room, but on the all-important question of morals they have remained adamant. Mussolini's feelings on this matter are very clear when he proclaims:

> Let no one think of denying the moral character of Fascism. . . . What would the state be if it did not possess a spirit of its own and a morality of its own? . . . The Fascist state claims its ethical character. It is Catholic, but above all it is Fascist, in fact it is exclusively and essentially Fascist. Catholicism completes Fascism, and this we openly declare, but let no one think that they [i.e. the Catholics] can turn the tables on us under cover of metaphysics or philosophy.[91]

By way of summary we may say that after some preliminary hesitation between individualism and etatism, the Fascists have definitely committed themselves to wholehearted support of etatism in a form so radical that we may call it totalitarian etatism. As the Fascists themselves point out, it is this phase of their political philosophy which distinguishes Fascism most sharply from liberalism.

> For Liberalism, society has no life distinct from the life of the individuals. For Fascism the life of society overlaps the existence of individuals and projects itself into the succeeding generations for centuries and millennia. . . . For Liberalism the individual is the end and society the means. . . . For Fascism, society is the end, individuals the means, and its whole life consists of using individuals as instruments for its social ends.[92]

Curiously enough, the Fascists also insist that it is their fundamental etatism which distinguishes Fascism from classical socialism. To the Fascist, orthodox socialism is really based upon an individualistic philosophy. The socialist state is essentially interested in the comfort and welfare of its individual citizens. To secure this welfare, and for this reason only, it takes over and operates the means of production. To the Fascist, the welfare of the state is of greater importance than the welfare of the individual citizens; and if the state is benefited by having some of its citizens rich, some poor, some employers, others employees, it is the sacred duty of these citizens to give up their demands for economic equality and accept economic inequality and state-regulated capitalism, or whatever form of economic operation the state, for its own benefit, finds it useful to establish.

FASCISM AND AUTHORITARIANISM

Having examined the etatist phase of Fascism, we may now turn to a discussion of its other principal feature, authoritarianism. Here too we find that Fascism in its earlier stages pursued a rather vacillating course, sometimes appearing to favor democracy, and at other times authoritarianism. The original (1919) program of the Fascist Party was decidedly democratic in tone. At this time the Fascists were in favor of a republic as opposed to a monarchy. They wished to abolish the Senate, membership in which was appointive, and concentrate power in the Chamber of Deputies, to be elected by universal manhood suffrage. It is highly probable, however, that much of this program was put forward for propaganda purposes and was not wholeheartedly accepted by the Fascist leaders. A year or two later, even before the march on Rome, Mussolini had departed from this position, and openly

declared himself to be "anti-democratic and anti-parliamentary."
After coming to power he has preserved the monarchy and the Senate,
which he formerly attacked, has abolished the Chamber of Deputies,
which he formerly defended, and far from extending the suffrage, has
completely done away with the electoral machinery.

The shift from democracy to authoritarianism is, however, intelligible
in view of Mussolini's early background and subsequent career. Even
in the early days, when Mussolini was a socialist and claimed to be a
spokesman for the masses, he was skeptical both of democracy in general
and of parliamentary government in particular, though he was usually
careful to guard his statements on such matters lest he make too many
enemies among his own followers. At this time Mussolini's political
philosophy was essentially that of Sorel: everything for the masses, for
the proletariat, but the masses must be led, nay rigidly controlled, by a
small group of elite from their midst. Moreover, what is wanted is
action and not talk, and as parliamentary government is essentially
government by talk — down with parliament! For all his vacillations
on matters of detail Mussolini's fundamental philosophy has not greatly
changed since this early period save that now his motto is, Everything
for the nation as a whole, rather than, Everything for the proletariat.

In arguing against democracy the Fascists make use of two main
theses. One is that authoritarianism is better than democracy; that
it is better for the wise few to govern than for the foolish many to attempt to do so — essentially the same type of argument as that used by
Carlyle. The other thesis is that really democratic rule is impossible,
that even in so-called democratic states effective control lies with a
small minority of wire-pullers, plutocrats, and demagogues. Such
being the case, minority rule is inevitable, and it is better that the state
be openly ruled by a good minority, such as the Fascist leaders, rather
than by a bad minority, such as every pseudo-democratic regime en-
genders. This thesis is only a variation of the ideas put forward by
Pareto.

It is this second thesis, the idea that democracy is impossible of
achievement, which dominates Mussolini's mind when he says that
Fascism

> trains its guns on the whole block of democratic ideologies and rejects both
> their premises and their practical applications.... Fascism denies that
> numbers as such can be the determining factor in human society, it denies the
> right of numbers to govern by means of periodic consultations; it asserts the
> irremediable and fertile and beneficent inequality of man, who can not be

levelled by any such mechanical and extrinsic device as universal suffrage. Democratic regimes may be described as those under which the people are, from time to time, deluded into the belief that they exercise sovereignty, while all the time real sovereignty resides in and is exercised by other and sometimes irresponsible and secret forces. Democracy is a kingless regime infested by many kings, who are sometimes more exclusive, tyrannical, and destructive than one, even though he be a tyrant.[93]

The other thesis, the idea that authoritarianism should be adopted because it is better than democracy, is voiced by Mussolini when he says:

All is the principal adjective of democracy.... It is time to say: A few and chosen. Democratic equalitarianism, anonymous and grey, which forbad all color and flattened every personality, is about to die.... Once there were courtiers who burned incense before the kings and the popes; now there is a new breed which burns incense, without sincerity, before the proletariat.... These [members of the proletariat] do not know even how to control their own families. We are different.... We do not exclude the possibility that the proletariat may be capable of using its present forces for other ends, but we say that before it tries to govern the nation it must learn to govern itself, must make itself worthy, technically, and still more, morally, because government is a tremendously difficult and complicated task.[94]

This idea is expressed even more clearly by Rocco:

Democracy turns over the government of the state to the multitudes of living men that they may use it to further their own ends. Fascism insists that the government be entrusted to men capable of rising above their own private interests and of realizing the aspirations of the social collectivity, considered in its unity and in its relation to the past and the future. Fascism therefore ... proclaims that the great mass of citizens is not a suitable advocate of social interests for the reason that the capacity to ignore private individual interests in favor of the higher demands of society and of history is a very rare gift and the privilege of a chosen few.[95]

In rejecting democracy and accepting authoritarianism the Fascists have thrown overboard many of the old ideas and postulates which were so dear to the classical liberals. Thus, for example, the liberals asserted that "government must rest upon the consent of the governed." With Gumplowicz, the Fascists declare that state and government have nearly always originated in conquest and not in voluntary compact and that in their maintenance force is even more important than consent. Thus we find Mussolini saying:

A government that was based exclusively on the consent of the people and renounced any and every use of force ... never was and never will be; consent is as changeable as the formations in the sands of the seashore. We can not have it always. Nor can it ever be total.... Whatever solution you happen to give to any problem whatsoever, even though you share the Divine wisdom, you would inevitably create a class of malcontents.... How are you going to avoid that this discontent spread and constitute a danger for the solidarity of the State? You avoid it with force: by bringing a maximum of force to bear, by employing this force inexorably whenever it is rendered necessary. Rob any government of force and leave it only with its immortal principles, and that government will be at the mercy of the first group that is organized and intent on overthrowing it. Now Fascism throws these lifeless theories on the dump heap. When a group or a party is in power it has the obligation of fortifying itself and defending itself against all.[96]

Palmieri expresses the same doctrine in somewhat more idealistic terms.

Gone forever is the time when it was possible to find a way to the heart of man through his devotion to higher things than his personal affairs; gone is the time when it was possible to appeal to the mystic side of his nature through a religious commandment.... All that remains is an appeal to force, to compulsion, intellectual as well as physical; an appeal to what lies outside of man, to what he fears and with what he must of necessity abide. Such a forceful appeal is made at present by Fascism, which, compelling the elder and educating the younger, is slowly but surely bringing the Italian people to a comprehension of the worth, the beauty, and the significance of the National Ideal.[97]

Another liberal slogan that has been swept aside by the Fascists is that "ultimate sovereignty must rest with the people; and that all rulers and magistrates derive their authority by delegation from the people." According to the Fascists, sovereignty, or ultimate control over the life and fortunes of the citizens of the state, rests not with the mass of citizens but with the state itself, or as Rocco puts it:

Democracy vests sovereignty in the people, that is to say in the mass of human beings. Fascism discovers sovereignty to be inherent in society when it is juridically organized as a state.... Fascism rejects the dogma of popular sovereignty and substitutes for it that of state sovereignty.[98]

According to the Fascist theory ultimate power resides in the state itself, and is represented and embodied in the king (in name) or in Mussolini as "head of the government" (in reality). All other magistrates and officials acquire their power, by delegation to be sure, but by delegation not from the people but from the king and from the head of the government. As Palmieri puts it:

We find that the highest achievement of the Fascist reform consists in having shorn the People of all power, and in having conferred this upon a central organ which in turn delegates its authority to secondary and derivative organs of control and direction of the national life. The true essence of the

Fascist constitution of the state lies thus with the derivation of authority from above rather than from below, from the king rather than from the people.[99]

It is on the basis that "all power must be delegated from above and not from below" that Fascism has abolished even the pretense of local self-government. Not only are all the prefects, or governors of the provinces, appointed and dismissed by the head of the government, speaking for the king, but the same is true of all the *podeste*, or mayors of the communes, the basic units of local government. In fact every single official in the Italian administrative hierarchy from the highest to the lowest is either directly or indirectly appointed by and is responsible to the head of the government.

> Having brought about its momentous reform of government, Fascism assumes the other arduous task of renewing the whole administrative structure of the state. This renewal is accomplished by destroying once and forever the notion of the Liberal-democratic doctrine that local authority depends on the local expression of the numerical majority of the sovereign people, and substituting for it the conception that local authority as well as all authority derives from a common source, the [central] executive power which is above all local prejudice, ambition, or interests.[100]

It is interesting to note that the principle of centralized authoritarianism is applied, not merely to the administrative hierarchy of the state, but also to the organization of the Fascist Party. Originally each *Fascio*, or local branch of the Fascist Party, was self-governing, making its own rules and regulations and electing its own officials. In each province there was a federation of the local *Fasci*, governed by a provincial congress consisting of representatives elected by the local branches. This provincial congress also made its own rules and regulations and elected its own provincial secretary and its own board of directors. Finally, there was the national organization, with a national congress consisting of elected representatives of the local organizations. This national congress had control over the general policies of the party and also elected a central committee and a directorate to look after all matters of detail. The important post of secretary general of the Fascist Party was filled by the directorate, which nominated and the central committee which appointed this official. At this time the Fascist Party, for all its talk of authoritarianism, was essentially democratic in organization, at least on paper. Later "reforms," however, have completely wiped out all traces of this early democracy.

Especially since the reorganization of 1932, the Fascist Party, like the Fascist state, has been based upon the principle of centralization and the delegation of authority downward.   Supreme control over the party now rests in the hand of the leader (*Duce*) of the party, Mussolini, who holds this position for life.   On all important points the leader is supposed to consult the Fascist Grand Council, but he is not necessarily bound by its decisions, and most of its members, moreover, are appointed and dismissed by the leader.   The leader also appoints and dismisses the secretary general of the party, the chief executive officer in charge of all matters of detail.   Again the leader appoints and dismisses the provincial secretaries and the members of the provincial directorates.   All such persons are merely the agents of the national leaders.   Finally the provincial secretaries appoint the secretary and the directorate of the local *Fasci* and have complete charge over all of their activities.   As things are at present all party officials are appointed, not elected.   The members of the local *Fasci* do as they are told by their local secretary, who has autocratic powers.   No longer are there provincial congresses nor is there even a national congress, though from time to time the party stages a mass rally in Rome of the members of the party hierarchy.   This rally is given the name of the Grand Report, as its principal function is to hear (and to cheer) a speech made by the leader on the state of the nation.

Among the many other liberal doctrines which have been discarded by the Fascists are the old notions of check and balance and the separation of powers, both of which were defended so stoutly by Montesquieu and both of which in a slightly different form play such an important role in the American Constitution.   As the Fascists are fond of pointing out, both these doctrines were developed with the idea of protecting the individual and individual rights from complete domination either by the state as a whole or by any one group within the state.   Both doctrines are closely associated with the ideas that government is only a necessary evil, that all governments tend to be tyrannical, and hence that a weak government is better than a strong government.   According to Montesquieu, if control over the state be divided between the king, the aristocracy, and the common people, these three groups will so check and balance one another that the individual citizen will be protected from despotic misrule.   In America, which has neither king nor hereditary aristocracy, the principle of check and balance was applied in several other ways, chiefly by dividing governmental powers between the states and the federal union.   The doctrine of the separation of powers, accepted both by Montesquieu and the Americans, is of course merely another special form of check and balance. By separating the executive, the judicial, and the legislative function, by placing them in the hands of separate independent bodies, it was felt that the private citizen received additional support against the possible attempts at tyranny on the part of those in authority.

With the Fascist demand for a strong state guiding and controlling every phase of individual activity it is obviously impossible for the Fascists to accept either check and balance or the separation of powers. For the state to be strong it must be unitary, with all power concentrated in a single group, or preferably in the hands of a single individual. Control over the state cannot be divided between the monarchy, the nobility, and the masses, but must be placed nominally in the hands of the king, actually in the hands of the head of the government. Control over the state cannot be divided between the national and the local agencies, but must rest completely and absolutely with the national government. Finally, this national government must be completely unitary. The head of the government must have control, not only over the executive functions, but also over the judicial and legislative functions. In claiming that it is impossible to distinguish between the executive and the judicial functions the Fascists can claim that they stand in comparatively good company. Even liberals, such as Locke, Rousseau, and Paine, to say nothing of such etatists as Hegel, thought that the executive and judicial functions are identical in that both merely aim at carrying out or applying the laws laid down by the legislative body. Even so it is certain that Locke and Rousseau and Paine would have been appalled at the extent to which the judicial hierarchy has in Italy been completely subjected to control by the purely executive and administrative hierarchy. Jury trials have been abolished as a relic of the barbarous democratic days; and in law cases all points both of law and of fact are decided by judges who are not only appointed by the head of the government, but who may also be dismissed by him at any time. In point of fact the Fascist judges have consistently shown in making their decisions that they are influenced, not merely by the letter or the spirit of the law, but also by the purely political policies of the Fascist Party and its leader.

In refusing to distinguish between the executive and the legislative function, Fascism made a sharp break with the liberal philosophers and turned the clock back to where it stood in the seventeenth century. As the Fascists themselves put it,

Having denied the sovereignty of the people, Fascism holds that the branch of the legislative elected by popular vote..., which represented both the symbol and the repository of this sovereignty in the Liberal state, loses practically all its previous importance and becomes simply a consultive organ, whose proper function is collaboration with the other powers of the state.[101]

Until 1939, Italy possessed a so-called Chamber of Deputies, and though the members of this body were nominated by and completely subservient to the Fascist Grand Council — and that means to Mussolini — yet in theory, at least, these persons were elected by popular vote. In 1939, however, this chamber was abolished and its place taken by the Chamber of Fasci and Corporations, all of whose members hold office *ex officio*, owing their legislative positions to appointments which they hold from the *Duce* to other administrative organs of the regime. As things are at present, the members of this body are not representatives of the people whose permission must be secured before legislation may be passed, but merely government-chosen experts in various fields of politics and economics whose advice may be taken before the government embarks upon the business of making general laws. The purely consultive character of this chamber is emphasized by the fact that many bills do not need to be passed by the chamber as a whole, but merely by one or other of the various committees into which the chamber is broken up; each committee consisting of a certain number of persons who are considered experts in a particular field.

The control of the government is made absolute by the fact that each national councilor (as the members of the new chamber are called) owes his membership to an executive appointment, which the head of the government may at any time cancel. Incidentally there is no fixed legislative term. All members of the new chamber hold office indefinitely until dismissed by the executive. Executive control over the Senate, the other legislative chamber, is equally absolute. Senators hold their office for life, but the number of senators is unlimited, and Mussolini could at any moment swamp the upper house with new appointees should the existing senators try to act in any way contrary to his wishes. As the Fascists openly proclaim, the new law regarding the legislative process

reaffirms that the government is the central power in the legislative function to which the Senate and the Chamber only lend their complementary support, and that the *Duce* of Fascism, the Head of the Government, there, as in every other field of activity, is the supreme stimulus. [And again] the Fascist reform brings the legislative function within the scope of the government and puts an end to the outworn myth of the separation of powers.[102]

From the foregoing passages it is obvious that the Fascists are advocates of radical authoritarianism, both in theory and in practice. At the same time it must not be forgotten that there is a curious strain of semi-democracy running through the whole fabric of Fascism. Authoritarianism, or even dictatorship and despotism, is perfectly compatible with democracy, at least in the sense that dictatorship has frequently won the admiration of the bulk of the populace — who have often willingly transferred their political rights to a single all-powerful ruler. Julius Caesar and Augustus Caesar were the leaders of the "popular" party against the "aristocratic" party; the majority of the citizens supported the Caesars in their substitution of imperial rule for the semi-parliamentary institutions of republican Rome. Napoleon I had the overwhelming support of the French people when he overthrew the Directory with its semi-parliamentary institutions and made himself the dictator of France. In like manner, his nephew Napoleon III had the masses of France behind him when he established the Second Empire.

The case of Andrew Jackson is also of interest in this respect. Jackson made no attempt to overthrow the Constitution or to become a dictator, but during his term the power and the prestige of the presidency enormously increased. For the first time the President came to be regarded as the supreme representative of the people. Jackson's election to the presidency was a triumph for the mob; he had little patience for his opponents who still commanded a considerable section of the Senate and the House of Representatives. Time after time he vetoed acts of Congress on the ground that surely he, as the representative of the people, ought to know what the people wanted. To Jackson the members of Congress represented the sectional interests while he represented the people as a whole, and hence he demanded an active share in legislation. It is no accident that the participation of the mob in American politics always coincides with the rise in importance of the executive. American as well as European history shows that where the upper middle and middle classes have a predominant interest in the state, they tend to delegate their powers to a legislative assembly, but that where the rank and file secure political control, they tend to delegate their authority to a single individual.

The rise of Mussolini must be understood in the light of these historical precedents. Fascism was and still is essentially a mass movement. The Fascists received support and financial aid from occasional aristocrats and from several wealthy capitalists, but their principal support and the personnel of their leaders came from the lower middle class. Originally, no doubt, the Fascists constituted only a minority of the Italian populace, but it was a large as well as a compact minority, and in the course of time the Fascists have been able to win the whole-hearted support of the majority of the populace.   It is true that there are many persons and many groups in Italy who detest Fascist rule; it is true that the "plebiscites" which the Fascists have occasionally held can in no way be trusted as real indications of Italian popular feeling — but it is also true that all competent observers agree that the Fascist regime is now definitely supported by at least sixty per cent of the populace.   Fascism is undoubtedly a tyranny, but for all its authoritarianism, it is the tyranny of a majority over a minority rather than a tyranny of a minority over a majority.   The absolutism of Mussolini is not the absolutism of Louis XIV, who claimed to rule his subjects by divine right; rather it is the absolutism of a Caesar or a Napoleon who claimed to rule as the supreme representative of the populace.   The absolutism of Louis XIV we may call a transcendental absolutism; that of a Caesar we may call immanent.   If our use of the terms be correct, the absolutism of Mussolini is definitely immanent rather than transcendental.

The doctrine of the Fascists on this point is little more than an expansion of the ideas first laid down by Rousseau.   To Rousseau and the Fascists the state is a real entity with a soul, a mind, and a will of its own, and this collective will must have control over the destinies of all the individual citizens.   To Rousseau, as to the Fascists, the collective will invariably seeks the interests of the community as a whole, or, as Rousseau puts it, "the general will is always right and always tends to the public advantage."   Rousseau himself believed that in the long run the decisions of the majority of the people tend to accord with the true general will, but he was willing to admit that in some cases a small group of men or even a single man could better discern the common good and hence the general will than a vast ignorant majority. At this point the Fascists step in and claim that the wise few, or the all-wise one, are invariably better judges of the collective will than the majority.   According to this theory when the few or the one command they are not to be regarded as expressing their own wills, but the will of the whole nation.

According to Fascist theory the state should not be a government of the people by the king for the benefit of the king and his courtiers. Rather should it be a government of the people, for the people, by those few rare minds who are able to discern the true interests of the people. It is this notion which Mussolini has in mind when he says,

> In rejecting democracy Fascism rejects the political lie of political equalitarianism. . . . But if democracy be understood as meaning a regime in which the masses are not driven back to the margin of the state, then the writer of these pages has already defined Fascism as an organized, centralized, authoritarian democracy.[103]

It is this same notion, from a different point of view, which Mussolini expresses when he says that Fascism

> is the purest form of democracy if the nation be conceived . . . as the most powerful idea which acts within the nation as the conscience and the will of a few, even of one, which ideal tends to become active within the conscience and the will of all — that is to say of all those who rightly constitute a nation . . . and have set out upon the same line of development and spiritual formation as one conscience and one sole will.[104]

In spite of its authoritarianism, Fascism not only was but still is a mass movement. This can be seen by the recent developments within the party itself. If Mussolini and the other Fascist leaders had been absolutists in the seventeenth century sense, they would have been willing to disband their party once they had secured control over the machinery and armed forces of the state. Thereafter, with or without a party, their will would have been the law, and they could easily have enforced these laws without any great popular hullabaloo. As we know, however, the party was not disbanded; it was carefully kept intact and allowed to grow in strength. It now numbers nearly two million, with provisions for the gradual recruitment of new members from the rising generation as they reach maturity. The reason for this policy is undoubtedly to keep the regime in touch with the masses and the masses in touch with the regime. For all their talk about authority, hierarchy, and discipline, the Fascist leaders feel the need for widespread popular support, and such a support is given by the continued activity of the Fascist Party. The party, moreover, serves the useful purpose of acting as a propaganda agent in instilling Fascist ideas and ideology among the mass of Italians, including those who are outside the party organization. The Fascist leaders are perfectly willing to use brutal, ruthless force to keep themselves in power, but at the same time they are desperately anxious to have the Fascist ideal of an authoritarian, totalitarian state voluntarily, enthusiastically, and wholeheartedly accepted by the citizenry. The totalitarian state cannot become truly totalitarian, embracing the whole social and emotional life of the community until the

masses by education and propaganda come to a point where they instinctively and unconsciously think of all phases of life as so many
phases of the state's activity.   It is this aspect of Fascism which permits Mussolini to call Fascism "an organized, centralized, authoritarian
democracy."

Gentile, the official Fascist philosopher, as usual gives a Neo-Hegelian
interpretation of this when he says:

> For Fascism the state is a wholly spiritual creation.   It is a national state,
> because from the Fascist point of view the nation itself is a creation of the
> mind. ... This state of the Fascists is created by the consciousness and the
> will of the citizen, and is not a force descending on the citizen from above or
> without. ... The Fascist state is a people's state, and as such the democratic
> state *par excellence*.   The relationship between the state and the citizen is
> accordingly so intimate that the state exists only in so far as the citizen causes
> it to exist.   Its formation, therefore, is the formation of a consciousness of it
> in individuals, in the masses.   Hence the need of a party and of all the instru-
> ments of propaganda and education which Fascism uses *to make the thought
> and will of the Duce the thought and will of the masses*.   Hence the enormous
> task which Fascism sets itself in trying to bring the whole mass of the people,
> beginning with the little children, inside the fold of the party.[105]

Palmieri follows his master, Gentile, in identifying Fascism with "New
Idealism" and adds:

> The New Idealism must not remain the intellectual pastime of the elite
> but must leaven the life of the masses.   It is to the masses and not to the few
> that the New Idealism must bring its message of salvation and bring it in
> such a form as to make it easily intelligible and readily accepted.[106]

FASCISM AND THE CORPORATE STATE

We cannot conclude our survey of Fascism without a brief discussion
of the theory of corporations and corporatism upon which so many
Fascist writers lay great stress.   So much emphasis, in fact, has been
laid upon the corporative idea that it is sometimes thought that corporatism and Fascism are one and the same thing.   This is certainly an
exaggeration, to say the least.   To the orthodox Fascist, corporatism is
a means rather than an end.   Fascism, in its essence, is a combination of
etatism and authoritarianism.   By the corporate system, or corporatism,
on the other hand, is meant the set of institutions through which the
state attempts to control the economic life of the nation on a more or
less authoritarian basis.   To the Fascists the basic principles of Fascism
are eternal, while the corporative idea is merely an expedient, possibly

only a tentative expedient, whereby these principles can be carried into effect. As Palmieri remarks,

> If today the Corporative principle seems to answer exactly to the need of the hour, it may also happen tomorrow that another system may better answer the same purpose.[107]

But though corporatism is thus clearly stated to be a means to an end rather than an end in itself, the corporative idea has undoubtedly struck deep roots within the body of Fascist ideology, and more and more we find the Fascists proclaiming that after all it is corporatism which is Fascism's great contribution to the political and economic thought of the twentieth century, and that corporatism in some form or another is destined to take the place both of old-fashioned liberalism or individualism and of socialism in all countries in the course of the next few decades.

For all their talk of the corporative idea, the Fascists are curiously vague in their definition of this principle. But from their numerous utterances on the subject it becomes clear that corporatism is a combination of two basic doctrines; one is that man is essentially not an isolated but a group-forming animal; the other is that all groups must be subordinated to and controlled by the supreme group, the state. Neither of these doctrines is in any way new; in fact both were preached by many if not all of the spiritual ancestors of Fascism in the nineteenth century, but it is the Fascists who have most strongly emphasized both doctrines and directed the searchlight of publicity and propaganda upon them.

The idea that man is a group-forming animal, that an individual has importance and significance only as a member of a group, was talked about by Hegel, by Mazzini, by Durkheim, by Gumplowicz, to mention only those whose political and social theories we have considered in this book. To Hegel (writing in 1821) men take a great step forward when they cease to regard themselves as isolated individuals and group themselves together in voluntary associations which he, like the later Fascists, calls corporations. To Hegel the tendency of mankind to form such groups was the sign of a "spiritual" nature or blind groping toward the perfect union of mankind in the form of the state. In the corporation "the particular and self-seeking end" of human beings is transformed into something "actively universal." Speaking of the decay of the mediaeval guilds, he says:

> In modern times the Corporation has been superseded with the intention that the individual should care for himself.... It is, however, needful to

provide the ethical man with a universal activity, one above his private ends
This universal with which the state does not always supply him, is given by
the Corporation.

Mazzini, like Hegel, was an advocate of group or corporate action.
There should exist inside each state a large number of smaller but active
groups in which the citizens might practice the divine principle of association.   Mazzini, like the modern Fascists, was hopeful that the
development of group or corporate life would solve the economic problem.
Private property and enterprise were not to be abolished, but in place
of cut-throat individualism, he hoped to substitute the voluntary grouping of workers and producers into guilds and corporations.   Cooperation
as opposed to competition was to be the motto of the new age.

Durkheim and Gumplowicz in the latter part of the nineteenth century
were even more insistent upon the importance of group life.   To Durkheim most of a man's thought and acts are of non-rational origin and are
imposed on him by the group to which he belongs.   When we reason,
or think that we reason, we use concepts which are not the creation of
the individual mind, but are thought patterns which have been imposed
on us by the group.   Durkheim was a believer in the supremacy of the
state, but he believed that economic life was too complicated for it to
be controlled directly by the state with any chance of success.   The
activities of any given profession should be regulated by special guilds
or corporations consisting of persons intimately acquainted with its
functions and needs.   Gumplowicz was just as insistent as Durkheim
that it was not individual but group activity which counts.   "It is not
man who thinks, but his social community, the source of his thoughts
is in the social medium in which he lives."   The chief difference between
Durkheim and Gumplowicz is that whereas the former stresses the importance of the narrower occupational group, the latter emphasizes the
supreme importance of the various classes into which the state is divided.
To Gumplowicz each class is like a more or less separate race and the
whole of the political history of any country is the story of the struggle
between the classes.

The Fascists accept all that Hegel and Mazzini have to say on the
matter of group life, and much of what Durkheim and Gumplowicz
say, but they strenuously object when some writers, wishing to emphasize the group, lessen the importance of the state or claim that group
life is in competition with national life.   Thus they object to the ideas
of the great German jurist Von Gierke when he says:

The ethical, social, the religious, the artistic and literary, the economic communal experience, all create at different levels their own special organisms which have an independent existence, as opposed to the state. . . . The state is by no means simply human society; it is only one among the associational organisms of mankind, and only one definite side of human social life is represented by it.[108]

To the Fascists, as to Hegel and Mazzini, the state is the one supreme group, including and embracing all lesser groups. All such lesser groups must be subject to state control and regulation; or as Mussolini puts it, behind all lesser groups must be "the totalitarian state, that is to say, the state which absorbs all the energies, all the interests, all the hopes of a people in order to transform and potentiate them." [109] The Fascists agree with Gumplowicz concerning the importance of classes and class struggles, but they insist that classes are less important than the nation, and that class struggles may not be permitted when they interfere with the welfare of the state. Mussolini summarizes the Fascist position when he says:

> Fascism is opposed to Socialism to which unity within the state (which amalgamates classes into a single economic and ethical reality) is unknown, and which sees in history nothing but the class struggle. Fascism is likewise opposed to trade-unionism as a class weapon. But when brought within the orbit of the state, Fascism recognizes the real needs which gave rise to Socialism and trade-unionism, giving them due weight in the guild or Corporative system, in which divergent interests are coordinated and harmonized in the unity of the state.[110]

Having in mind this theoretical background we may say more specifically that corporatism to the Fascists means that control over the economic and social life of the nation shall lie in the hands of a number of occupational groups, each of which in turn is under governmental supervision and control. This system is thus opposed to strict individualism on the one hand and to direct governmental operation or even regulation on the other. Let us take a specific instance. It is unwise, say the Fascists, to allow every doctor to do as he pleases, have his own ethical code, or even his own medical and financial code. On the other hand it is, generally speaking, unwise for the state to step in directly and tell the doctors what medicine they may and may not use, what prices they should charge. Far better is it that such matters should be regulated by a doctors' guild or a national medical association composed of medical men. At the same time such a guild or association should be subject to the general control of the state, lest the regulations drawn up by the guild interfere with the welfare of the community as a whole.   As with the doctors, so with the other occupational groups. It is interesting to note that Mussolini, the great exponent of the totalitarian state, criticizes not only old-fashioned individualism, but also the N.R.A. of the American New Deal on the ground that in America governmental intervention in business is too direct and too peremptory. According to Mussolini the government should not, in most cases, hand out arbitrary codes which must be blindly followed by employers and employees, but should aid groups of employers and employees in working out codes which will be acceptable to both parties.

In attempting to give concrete form to the general principle of corporatism the Fascists have made use of two completely separate sets of institutions, which must not be confused with one another.   The one is a series of syndicates, the other a series of corporations proper.   The syndicates have been in operation since 1926, while the corporations were not established until 1934 and are still in a more or less experimental stage.   The syndicates are merely Fascist versions of the old trade unions and employers' associations, and their operation is supposed to take the place of the ruthless struggle between the classes.   In every district there is a workers' syndicate and an employers' syndicate for each of the main occupational categories.   These local syndicates are grouped to form national federations, each being considered the legal representative of all the workers or of all the employers in each major industry.   Finally, these national federations are linked to form national confederations, which represent no one industry but several closely related industries.   As things are at present, there are nine national confederations.   There is one national confederation of workers and one of employers in each of the four chief fields of economic activity: industry proper, agriculture, commerce, and banking.   The ninth national confederation consists of organizations of artists and members of the liberal professions in which no distinction is made between workers and employers.

The principal object of each syndicate, national federation, and national confederation is the settlement of labor disputes and the conclusion of collective labor agreements or contracts.   In addition they also aid in educational and social welfare work among their own members.   In case the workers in a local factory wish to have higher wages or shorter hours the local syndicate acts as their spokesman and puts the case before the local syndicate of employers.   In those cases involving workers in the same industry but living in different parts of the country the matter comes up for negotiation between one of the national federa·

tions of workers and the corresponding national federation of employers. In case of a dispute involving workers in several different occupational groups the matter is taken up by the two appropriate national confederations, the one acting for the workers, the other for the employers. As part of this new era of syndicalism the government has decreed that both strikes and lockouts are prohibited by law. All cases of industrial disputes in which the workers make demands which the employers are unwilling to accept must be referred to arbitration; and if ordinary arbitration fails the matter is placed before a state-appointed labor court whose decision is final and binding upon both parties. The Fascists claim that their syndical organization adequately protects the workers, but they make no bones about stating that ultimate control of each industry rests with the employers and not with the employees, or as the Charter of Labor puts it,

> The wage earner, artisan, employee, or laborer is an active collaborator in the economic enterprise, the direction of which belongs to the employer, who also carries the responsibility.[111]

The Fascists emphasize that membership in all of the syndicates is entirely voluntary. At the same time,

> only the juridically recognized Syndicate which submits to the control of the state has the right to represent legally the entire category of employers or workers for which it is constituted, in safeguarding its interests vis-à-vis the state and other occupational associations, in making collective contracts of working, binding on all members of the category.[112]

In other words, in each "category," that is, in each industry, the state recognizes only one syndicate, and it has the right to represent all the persons who belong to this category, whether or not they are members of the syndicate. Needless to say, the state gives legal recognition only to those syndicates which are willing to work hand in glove with the Fascist regime and which have accepted the Fascist ideology. A special law provides that each syndicate, to secure legal recognition, must "promote ... the moral and patriotic education" of its members. Moreover, this law provides that the officers of each legally recognized syndicate must "afford guarantees of ability, morality, and sound national loyalty." [113] In other words, officers must subordinate their ideas of class struggle to the promotion of the nation as a whole according to the program laid down by the Fascist Party. In point of fact, the officers of all the syndicates, local, provincial, and national, are little more than hand-picked appointees of the Fascist hierarchy.

Quite separate from, but complementary to, the syndicates are the corporations.   The syndicates are, theoretically, privately organized groups which are "recognized" (and in practice, regulated) by the state. Corporations, on the other hand, are organs of the state, that is, organized and maintained by the state and immediately subject to centralized control.   More specifically, the Fascists define the corporations as

> the organs which under the aegis of the state carry out the integral, organic, and unitarian regulation of production with a view to the expansion of the wealth, political power, and well-being of the Italian people.[114]

In reality, the chief difference between the syndicates and the corporations is that, while each syndicate represents either employers or employees, the corporations include representatives of both employers and employees, and in addition a certain number of state-appointed officials who are supposed to look after the interests of the nation as a whole — or more especially to look after the interests of the consumers, as opposed to the employers and employees, both of whom are regarded as producers in any given industry.

At present there are twenty-two corporations arranged in three main groups.   Of greater importance than the details of this organization are the general aims of all corporations.   According to Mussolini, the establishment of the corporations

> means the end of liberal capitalism, the economic system which emphasizes the individual profit motive, and marks the beginning of a new economy which stresses collective interests.   These collective interests will be achieved through the Corporate system which is based on the self-regulation of production, under the aegis of the producers. . . . When I say producers, I do not mean only employers, I mean workers as well.[115]

Each corporation is supposed to have conciliatory, advisory, and regulative powers.   In the field of conciliation, each corporation is supposed to try to maintain good feelings between the workers' syndicates and the employers' syndicates in its own category.   Collective labor disputes which cannot be settled by special bargaining are brought before a corporation conciliation board for a further attempt at amicable settlement before being carried to a labor court for final decision.   In the field of advice each corporation is supposed to be willing and ready to offer suggestions to the government when called upon to do so, with special reference to economic problems which fall within the sphere of its own interests.   Thus the government, before issuing a law or decree affecting the economic life of its citizens, usually finds it advisable to consult with one or more of the corporations, sometimes with all. In the field of regulation each corporation has the right to enact certain rules for "the collective regulation of economic relations and the unitary discipline of national production." This includes not only the power to devise regulations for the control of production and the determination of fair competition, but also "the fixing of rates for services rendered and of articles of consumption sold to the public, under non-competitive conditions." [116] In addition, representatives from the corporations constitute the majority of the members of the new National Chamber of Fasci and Corporations, and as such take an active part in general legislation for the whole country.

The corporations are still in the experimental stage, and no one is as yet certain how they will work out in practice. They have, however, been able to register several signal successes. In the field of conciliation, one of the corporations, that of Metal Workers and Machinery, was able to settle a serious dispute which broke out between the workers and the owners of the great Fiat automobile works at Turin. In the field of advice, it is known that on several occasions the government has consulted the corporations before issuing decrees or laws, and that the advice tendered by the corporations has been listened to seriously. In addition each corporation has passed a number of resolutions, many of which have led to administrative or legislative action. In the field of regulation, action has been somewhat slower, but has nevertheless led to significant results. The corporations have prepared a number of codes of fair practice, very similar to the codes formulated in the United States, under the N.R.A. — but whereas the N.R.A. is now defunct, the Italian codes are still in full force. These codes have defined and prohibited certain unfair trade practices and have fixed price scales and minimum prices for the commodities or services in question.[117]

But though the corporations are thus playing an important part in shaping the economic life of Italy, it must not be forgotten that corporations are completely subject to the state and the will of the Fascist Party. Though the majority of the members of each corporation are nominated by the various employers' and workers' syndicates, appointment to membership in a corporation is made by the government, and it is known that on several occasions the original nominees have been rejected on the ground that the persons concerned were unreliable. Moreover, by law the president of each corporation is the Minister of Corporations, who has the power to determine what is to be discussed and what is not to be discussed. Moreover, the decisions and recommendations of the corporations must be approved by the central government before they become effective.   As a result

> there is ample certainty that no discussion will ever arise within a corporation that is not welcomed by the party and government, and that no decision will ever be taken which the government does not approve.[118]

NOTES TO CHAPTER ELEVEN

1. H. W. Schneider, *Making the Fascist State*, p. 56. By permission of the Oxford University Press.
2. In this connection it is interesting to see how wrong Karl Marx was in some of his political prophecies. According to Marx, as capitalism develops, the rich will get richer and the poor poorer. At the same time the number of wealthy persons will decrease, and the number of the poor increase. Eventually the members of the middle and lower middle classes will sink to the level of the wage-earning proletariat. When such a condition arises, the members of the middle and lower middle classes will unite with the workers to overthrow the capitalist system. It is an interesting theory, but, as we have seen, the lower middle classes, when hard hit economically, instead of joining the proletariat, arise and smite the workers with all their might. Even in America the sit-down-strike and other similar phases of proletarian activity caused a wave of anti-labor feeling to sweep over the members of the American lower middle class.
3. M. T. Florinsky, *Fascism and National Socialism*, p. 18. By permission of The Macmillan Company, publishers.
4. Quoted in Schneider, *Making the Fascist State*, p. 276.
5. *Ibid.*, pp. 274, 275.
6. *Ibid.*, p. 275.
7. Benito Mussolini, *Fascism*, translation in *International Conciliation*, pp. 7, 8. By permission of the Carnegie Endowment for International Peace.
8. *Ibid.*, pp. 13, 16.
9. Mussolini, *Fascism*, translation in *Fascism, Doctrine and Institutions*, p. 12.
10. Quoted in Schneider, *Making the Fascist State*, p. 18.
11. Mussolini, *Fascism*, translation in *International Conciliation*, p. 16.
12. Quoted in Schneider, *Making the Fascist State*, p. 40.
13. Mussolini, *Fascism*, translation in *International Conciliation*, p. 16.
14. *Ibid.*
15. *Ibid.*, p. 9.
16. *Ibid.*
17. Schneider, *Making the Fascist State*, p. 252.
18. Quoted in *Ibid.*, p. 253.
19. Quoted in Emil Ludwig, *Conversations with Mussolini*, pp. 69, 70. By permission of Little, Brown and Company
20. Quoted in Coker, *Recent Political Thought*, p. 473. By permission of D. Appleton-Century Company.
21. M. Sarfatti, *Life of Mussolini*, p. 60.
22. Ludwig, *Conversations with Mussolini*, p. 109.
23. M. Palmieri, *The Philosophy of Fascism*, p. 32. By permission of author.
24. Quoted in Schneider, *Making the Fascist State*, p. 346.
25. Mussolini, *Fascism*, translation in *International Conciliation*, p. 394.
26. *Ibid.*, p. 405.
27. T. Sillani, *What is Fascism and Why?* p. 16. By permission of The Macmillan Company, publishers.

28. Mussolini, *Fascism*, translation in *International Conciliation*, p. 405.
29. B. San Severino, *Mussolini as Revealed in His Political Speeches*, p. 114.
30. Mussolini, *Fascism*, translation in *Fascism, Doctrine and Institutions*, p. 26.
31. Mussolini, *My Autobiography*, p. xiii. By permission of Charles Scribner's Sons
32. Mussolini, *Fascism*, translation in *Fascism, Doctrine and Institutions*, p. 30.
33. *Ibid.*, p. 31.
34. Quoted in H. Finer, *Mussolini's Italy*, p. 218.
35. Quoted in Ludwig, *Conversations with Mussolini*, pp. 126, 127.
36. *Ibid.*, p. 62.
37. *Ibid.*, p. 103.
38. *Ibid.*, p. 120.
39. Mussolini, *Fascism*, translation in *Fascism, Doctrine and Institutions*, p. 59.
40. *Ibid.*, p. 20.
41. *Ibid.*, pp. 8, 9.
42. Quoted in G. Volpe, *History of the Fascist Movement*, p. 105.
43. Quoted in Schneider, *Making the Fascist State*, pp. 260–264.
44. Quoted in Ludwig, *Conversations with Mussolini*, p. 178.
45. Mussolini, *Fascism*, translation in *Fascism, Doctrine and Institutions*, p. 37.
46. *Ibid.*, pp. 10, 27.
47. Ludwig, *Conversations with Mussolini*, p. 203.
48. Quoted in Palmieri, *The Philosophy of Fascism*, p. 211.
49. Mussolini, *Fascism*, translation in *International Conciliation*, pp. 395, 396.
50. *Ibid.*, p. 402.
51. Quoted in Palmieri, *The Philosophy of Fascism*, pp. 123, 124.
52. Mussolini, *Fascism*, translation in *Fascism, Doctrine and Institutions*, p. 10.
53. *Ibid.*, p. 31.
54. *Ibid.*, p. 26.
55. *Ibid.*, p. 25.
56. In his *Universal Aspects of Fascism*.
57. Mussolini, quoted in Palmieri, *The Philosophy of Fascism*, p. 77.
58. Mussolini, *Fascism*, translation in *Fascism, Doctrine and Institutions*, pp. 8, 9, 21
59. *Ibid.*, p. 30.
60. Mussolini, *Fascism*, translation in *International Conciliation*, p. 403.
61. Quoted in Palmieri, *The Philosophy of Fascism*, pp. 99, 100.
62. *Ibid.*, p. 90.
63. Mussolini, *Fascism*, translation in *Fascism, Doctrine and Institutions*, p. 8.
64. Mussolini, *Fascism*, translation in *International Conciliation*, p. 401.
65. Palmieri, *The Philosophy of Fascism*, p. 41.
66. Mussolini, *Fascism*, translation in *Fascism, Doctrine and Institutions*, p. 27.
67. *Ibid.*, p. 78.
68. Quoted in M. Rader, *No Compromise*, p. 260.
69. *Ibid.*, p. 261.
70. *Ibid.*, pp. 260, 261.
71. Palmieri, *The Philosophy of Fascism*, p. 62.
72. Quoted in Schneider, *Making the Fascist State*, p. 222.
73. Quoted in Davis, *Contemporary Social Movements*, pp. 510, 511. By permission
of D. Appleton-Century Company.
74. Quoted in Schneider, *Making the Fascist State*, p. 299.
75. Mussolini, *Fascism*, translation in *Fascism, Doctrine and Institutions*, p. 23.
76. Art. 7.
77. Mussolini, *Fascism*, translation in *International Conciliation*, pp. 405, 406.
78. *Ibid.*, p. 406.
79. *Ibid.*, pp. 404, 406.

80. *Charter of Labor*, art. 9.
81. Mussolini, *Fascism*, translation in *Fascism, Doctrine and Institutions*, p. 70.
82. *Charter of Labor*, art. 2.
83. *Ibid.*, art. 1.
84. Sillani, *What is Fascism and Why?* pp. 18, 24, 25.
85. Mussolini, *Fascism*, translation in *Fascism, Doctrine and Institutions*, pp. 10, 11, 13.
86. Volpe quoted in Sillani, *What is Fascism and Why?* pp. 163, 164.
87. *Ibid.*
88. Finer, *Mussolini's Italy*, p. 422.
89. Mussolini, *Fascism*, translation in *Fascism, Doctrine and Institutions*, p. 30.
90. Sillani, *What is Fascism and Why?* p. 18.
91. Mussolini, *Fascism*, translation in *Fascism, Doctrine and Institutions*, p. 39.
92. A. Rocco, *The Political Doctrine of Fascism*, p. 403. By permission of the Carnegie Endowment for International Peace.
93. Mussolini, *Fascism*, translation in *Fascism, Doctrine and Institutions*, p. 21.
94. Quoted in Finer, *Mussolini's Italy*, p. 208.
95. Rocco, *The Political Doctrine of Fascism*, p. 405.
96. Quoted in Finer, *Mussolini's Italy*, p. 223.
97. Palmieri, *The Philosophy of Fascism*, p. 126.
98. Rocco, *The Political Doctrine of Fascism*, p. 405.
99. Palmieri, *The Philosophy of Fascism*, pp. 140, 141.
100. *Ibid.*, pp. 139, 140.
101. *Ibid.*, p. 134.
102. Quoted in Steiner, "Fascist Italy's New Legislative System," *American Political Science Review*, June, 1939, p. 462. By permission of the *American Political Science Review*.
103. Mussolini, *Fascism*, translation in *Fascism, Doctrine and Institutions*, p. 23.
104. *Ibid.*, p. 12.
105. Giovanni Gentile, "The Philosophic Basis of Fascism," *Foreign Affairs*, January, 1928, pp. 302–303.
106. Palmieri, *The Philosophy of Fascism*, p. 47.
107. *Ibid.*, p. 156.
108. Quoted in Lewis, *The Genossenschaft Theory of Otto von Gierke*, pp. 61–63. By permission of the University of Wisconsin Press.
109. Mussolini, *Fascism*, translation in *Fascism, Doctrine and Institutions*, p. 60.
110. *Ibid.*, p. 11.
111. *Charter of Labor*, art. 7.
112. *Ibid.*, art. 3.
113. Mussolini, *Fascism*, translation in *Fascism, Doctrine and Institutions*, p. 76.
114. Palmieri, *The Philosophy of Fascism*, p. 168.
115. Quoted in W. G. Welk, *Fascist Economic Policy*, p. 117. Reprinted by permission of the President and Fellows of Harvard College.
116. *Ibid.*, p. 107.
117. For details see Welk, *op. cit.*, pp. 146 ff.
118. Welk, *op. cit.*, p. 145.

BIBLIOGRAPHY

PRIMARY.   B. Mussolini, *Fascism*.   There are several English translations. See especially one published in *International Conciliation*, 1935; and another in

Fascism, Doctrine and Institutions, Rome, 1935. In the text, I have used the version which gives the clearest interpretation of the passage in question. E. Ludwig, *Talks with Mussolini*, Boston, 1933. B. San Severino, *Mussolini as Revealed in His Political Speeches*, New York, 1923. A. Rocco: *The Political Doctrine of Fascism*, translated in *International Conciliation*, 1926; *The Transformation of the State*, translated in Sillani, *What is Fascism and Why?* London, 1931. G. Gentile: *The Philosophical Basis of Fascism*, translated in *Foreign Affairs*, 1928 (pp. 290 ff.). *What is Fascism?* Lengthy selections from this work are translated in Schneider, *Making the Fascist State* (pp. 344 ff.). M. Palmieri, *The Philosophy of Fascism*, New York, 1936 (semi-official).

SECONDARY. B. Mussolini, *My Autobiography*, New York, 1928 (largely ghost-written by R. W. Child). M. Sarfatti, *Life of Benito Mussolini*, New York, 1925. G. Seldes, *Sawdust Caesar*, New York, 1935. G. Megaro, *Mussolini in the Making*, London, 1938. E. B. Ashton, *The Fascist, His State and His Mind*, New York, 1937. G. A. Borgese, *Goliath, the March of Fascism*, New York, 1937. W. Y. Elliott, *The Pragmatic Revolt in Politics*, New York, 1928. H. Finer, *Mussolini's Italy*, New York, 1935. M. T. Florinsky, *Fascism and National Socialism*, New York, 1936. A. Lion, *The Pedigree of Fascism*, London, 1927. G. Salvemini: *The Fascist Dictatorship in Italy*, New York, 1927; *Under the Axe of Fascism*, New York, 1936. H. W. Schneider: *Making the Fascist State*, New York, 1928; *Making Fascists*, Chicago, 1929; *The Fascist Government of Italy*, New York, 1936. T. Sillani, *What is Fascism and Why?* London, 1931. G. Prezzolini, *Fascism*, London, 1926. O. Por, *Fascism*, New York, 1923. M. Rader, *No Compromise*, New York, 1939. L. Villari, *The Fascist Experiment*, London, 1926. G. Volpe, *History of the Fascist Movement*, Rome, 1934. H. A. Steiner, *Government in Fascist Italy*, New York, 1938.

SECONDARY — ECONOMIC. C. Haider, *Capital and Labor under Fascism*, New York, 1930. G. L. Field, *The Syndical and Corporative Institutions of Italian Fascism*, New York, 1938. A. Pennachio, *The Corporative State*, London, 1933. P. Einzig, *Economic Foundations of Fascism*, London, 1933. H. E. Goad, *The Making of the Corporate State*, London, 1932. F. Pitigliani, *The Italian Corporative State*, London, 1933. W. G. Welk, *Fascist Economic Policy*, Cambridge, Massachusetts, 1938 (especially valuable).

CHAPTER XII

THE POLITICAL PHILOSOPHY OF NATIONAL SOCIALISM

THE rise of Fascism in Italy is interesting, but most students of political science find the rise of National Socialism in Germany even more interesting and even more significant.

We must regard National Socialism as more important than Fascism if only because it was the Nazi triumph in Germany, far more than the Fascist triumph in Italy, which made the etatist-authoritarian creed the object of world attention, and because this attention has resulted in the springing-up of etatist-authoritarian movements in nearly all the countries of the world. For many years after the Fascists came to power in Italy, Fascism was chiefly regarded as a local and ephemeral movement. Even Mussolini for some time declared that Fascism was "not for export," that it was a purely Italian movement, little liable to lead to violent repercussions in alien lands. The average Englishman and American regarded the Italian dictatorship, not as the precursor of a new movement threatening to sweep the world, but merely as another example of the chronic inability of the backward Latin peoples to govern themselves constitutionally. To many persons the creation of a dictatorship in Italy meant little more than the oft-recurring revolutions and new dictatorships in such countries as Venezuela, Ecuador, or Peru. When, however, Germany — cultured, educated, industrial, powerful Germany — declared that the era of liberalism was over, that in the new order of things individualism and democracy must give way to etatism and authoritarianism — then, and only then, did the present and future of liberalism seem seriously threatened.

Of equal significance is the fact that German National Socialism in many ways is far more logical, consistent, and thoroughgoing than Italian Fascism in its application of many of the principles underlying the modern etatist-authoritarian ideology. This is especially true with reference to irrationalism and Social Darwinism which represent two of the outstanding features of modern etatist-authoritarian beliefs. The Fascists, as well as the Nazis, proclaim that man is irrational, that truth and falsehood, good and bad, are to be known more by intuition than by reason, but the fact that Italy is a Catholic country and that the vast majority of the Fascists are at least nominal Catholics makes it impossible for the Fascists openly and officially to draw all the logical conclusions from the irrationalist position. The Nazis, because of their greater freedom from ecclesiastical control, are thus able to proclaim from the housetops what the Fascists are only able to hint — that there is no absolute standard of true and false or good and bad; that an idea is to be considered true and an action is to be considered good only if they work for the benefit of the community.

The Fascists, as well as the Nazis, are Social Darwinists in that they preach the doctrine of the struggle for existence and the survival of the fittest, but it must not be forgotten that the eugenists' creed and the racialist creed are integral parts of Social Darwinism in the broader sense of the word, and on these points the Nazis go far ahead of the Fascists in making practical applications of these theoretical principles. Mussolini, to be sure, "sometimes dreams of making Italy a vast eugenic laboratory," but so far this dream has remained a dream. The Nazis, on the other hand, have taken the doctrines of the eugenists very seriously. It is in the sacred name of eugenics that the Nazi government has sterilized hundreds of thousands of German citizens. It is in the name of eugenics that the Nazi government is deliberately trying to increase the fecundity of certain supposedly superior stocks. In like manner the Fascists are now willing to pay lip service to the racialist creed, but so far racialism has played only an insignificant role in Fascist ideology. Among the Nazis, on the other hand, racialism is regarded as the essential basis of all true political action.

Finally we may say that National Socialism is even more important than Fascism, because both historically and geographically National Socialism is far closer to the general stock of ideas from which both Fascism and National Socialism draw their inspiration. Many persons, especially in England and America, were amazed when Hitler and his fellow Nazis were able to assume dictatorial control over Germany. Those, however, who have followed the development of the etatist-authoritarian tradition as sketched in this book should find nothing startling or surprising in the Nazi triumph in Germany. The Nazi triumph in that country is little more than "seeing the chickens come home to roost." Etatism and authoritarianism in some form or another have been preached by a large number of political philosophers in many different countries, but throughout the whole of the nineteenth century it was the German writers or their immediate disciples who made the most outstanding contributions to the development of the etatist-authoritarian ideology — and National Socialism is only the concrete embodiment of this ideology.

When all these facts are borne in mind, we should not be surprised at the present-day German acceptance of etatism and authoritarianism in their National Socialist dress; we should be surprised merely that a non-German state, such as Italy, was eleven years in advance of Germany itself in adopting a thoroughgoing etatist and authoritarian regime.

HITLER AND THE RISE OF THE NAZI PARTY

The life of Adolf Hitler and his rise to power in 1933 is too well known to require more than a brief summary. He was born in 1889, the son of a minor Austrian customs official. The fact that Hitler was born an Austrian and not a subject of the German Empire proper is a matter of some importance, at least psychologically. There were many Austrians of his generation who were wholeheartedly devoted to the Austro-Hungarian Empire and to the Habsburg dynasty. Such persons were apt to look with dislike upon the North Germans in general and upon the Prussians in particular. They were glad, as they put it, that they were not under the iron hand of the Hohenzollerns or the autocratic Prussian army officers and bureaucrats. But there were other Austrians, usually called followers of Pan-Germanism, more pro-German than the Germans themselves. They thought it horrible that the German-speaking Austrians should be linked, not with their fellow Germans to the north, but with "aliens" such as the Slavic-speaking Czechs and the Hungarian-speaking Magyars. To them it seemed dastardly that the Habsburgs thought more of their own dynastic interests than of advancing the interests of the German nation as a whole, and by the German "nation" they meant all persons who spoke German, whatever their political affiliation.

From his early boyhood Adolf Hitler belonged to this latter group, and the ideas which he acquired at this time have influenced his subsequent thought and action. To some it may seem surprising that the most passionate devotion to German nationalism was found among the German-speaking Austrians rather than among the Germans proper, but to a student of history or psychology such a situation seems perfectly natural. We all know that a convert is apt to be far more devout and zealous than his fellow religionists who are born and brought up in a particular creed. This is true in politics as well as in religion. Tom Paine, who came to America in 1774, was in 1776 far more passionate in his attacks upon England and the English king than the vast majority of persons born on this side of the ocean. The Frenchman, Gobineau, and the Englishman, H. S. Chamberlain, were more laudatory regarding the historic role of the Germans than were the bulk of the German historians. In like manner, the most fervent patriotism is frequently found among persons who are forced to spend all or a great part of their lives away from what they consider their homeland. The most zealous advocates of British imperialism were such persons as Cecil Rhodes, who spent most of his life in South Africa, and Rudyard Kipling, who spent much of his early life in India.

The social and economic position of Hitler's family is also of importance in trying to understand Hitler's psychological background. A generation or two back all his ancestors were peasants, many of them rather happy-go-lucky, down-at-the-heel peasants. Illegitimacy was far from being rare. Hitler's father was born out of wedlock and for many years used his mother's name of Schicklgruber. Few Germans realize how close they came to having to say "Heil Schicklgruber" in place of "Heil Hitler." In middle life, however, Adolf's father took the paternal name of Hitler, so that Adolf himself received his present name legally. Incidentally Adolf's father seems to have had a fair amount of push. In early life he was a cobbler, but in later years he secured an appointment in the Austrian civil service. He was in the lower ranks of this service, to be sure, but he felt immensely proud of his social advancement. He was no longer a manual laborer, but a "white-collar worker." He was no longer a member of the proletariat, but of the lower middle class. He was terrified lest his children sink back to the ranks from which he had come himself. He was especially anxious that Adolf should prove his superiority by also becoming an official.

We know from his autobiography that Adolf Hitler resolutely rejected his father's advice in so far as entering the ranks of officialdom was concerned. But this same autobiography shows how Adolf did take over from his father the typical German lower middle class attitude towards life — and politics. Hitler's book, *Mein Kampf*, is full of expressions in which he pours scorn upon the mob, the common herd, the rank and file of the workers. It is equally full of expressions showing his early envy and dislike of the upper middle and upper classes. Marxist socialism, with its program of class war and its appeals for the proletariat to unite and overthrow their economic superiors, threatened the very existence of the class to which he himself belonged. At the same time he regarded the aristocracy, the great financiers, and industrialists with a jaundiced eye. His attitude towards such persons resembled the attitude of the average American farmer or small shopkeeper towards "the snooty smart set," "the economic royalists," and "the minions of Wall Street." Hitler was always interested in preserving and strengthening the German *Volk* or nation, but to Hitler the kernel, the backbone, the essence of this *Volk* was centered in persons of his own class. To him a *Volk* was like a barrel of beer with its dregs at the bottom, its froth at the top, and its goodness in the middle portion.

Hitler's lower middle class attitude towards life is reflected not only in his views on politics but also in his attitude towards art and literature and domestic life. In Germany, as elsewhere, the lower middle class is the bulwark of conventional morality. The members of the upper and lower classes are far more willing to condone breaches of the moral code than are the members of the petty bourgeoisie. The movies, which appeal to the lower middle class, have to be far more cautious in dealing with sex problems and in using risqué language than legitimate drama, which appeals to persons on a somewhat higher social and economic scale. To the members of the lower middle class, women should not go "gadding around after fads"; they should devote themselves to *Kirche, Kinder, und Küche* (church, children, kitchen). The members of the lower middle class have always disliked cubism, expressionism, impressionism in art. To them the picture of a pretty girl on a magazine cover is greater "art" than the paintings of a Matisse or a Picasso. The members of the lower middle class have always been bored or repelled by *vers libre*, problem novels, "realistic" plays. To their minds the works of Kathleen Norris or the Elsie Dinsmore series are truer and finer literature than *Tobacco Road* or the *Grapes of Wrath*. On all such points, Hitler reflects the prejudices and beliefs of the class from which he sprang, and his political triumphs have meant the rigid suppression of all social, artistic, and literary activities which run counter to the old lower middle class preferences.

As a boy Hitler led a comparatively easy and carefree life, but after the death of his father and subsequently of his mother, his troubles began. At the age of nineteen he went to Vienna, confidently expecting to get a scholarship at the Academy of Art. To his astonishment, he failed in his entrance examinations and found himself with no funds.

no resources, and the urgent necessity of earning a living. In the years which followed he suffered incredible hardships and humiliations. For several months he was forced to work as a casual, unskilled day laborer, gaining and losing employment every week or so. Later he managed to gain a precarious livelihood as an artist, working he tells us as "a minor draughtsman and aquarellist." Actually he seems to have spent most of his time painting picture postcards and greeting cards, which were hawked around by some of his companions in misery. Many a night was spent in the Asylum for the Poor and Homeless; many a meal was secured in the charity soup kitchens maintained in monastery courtyards.

The four or five years spent in Vienna were years of bitterness and disappointment. They have left an indelible imprint upon Hitler's mind. Many of Hitler's present-day preferences and aversions can be traced to the feelings aroused in him during the Vienna period. It was in Vienna that he first became violently anti-Semitic. At this time much of the finance and industry of Vienna was in Jewish hands. An abnormally large proportion of the most prominent lawyers, doctors, writers, and theatrical producers were Jews. To Hitler this showed that the Jews already dominated Vienna and through Vienna the whole of Austria. Suffering from an acute inferiority complex, Hitler argued that his own failure, and the failure of others of his type, was due to the Jewish control of Austria's economic and cultural life. For success to be achieved, the Jews, or at least Jewish influence, must be destroyed.

In like manner, Hitler also conceived at this time a violent dislike of the then existent type of trade union, partly because the trade unions were strongly influenced by Marxian principles and stressed class interest rather than the national interest. To Hitler with his strong nationalist sentiment such ideas were horrible. There was also another more personal reason for Hitler's aversion to the trade-union movement. During the period when Hitler was securing odd jobs as a manual laborer, some of his fellow workers tried to get him to join a union. Hitler's soul revolted at the thought. It was bad enough to be forced to work temporarily as a common laborer; to join a trade union would seem to indicate that he had permanently sunk to the level of the laboring class.

> The feeling that he had lost caste... weighed heavily on the official's son. He detested the "moral coarseness" of his fellow workers and the "low level of their spiritual culture." The miserable existence of the working-class family filled him with horror. The very thought of having to spend his life in these depths was unbearable to him.[1]

By refusing to join the union, Hitler lost his job and was greatly handi-
capped in securing other employment.   Instead of blaming his social
pride and his own pig-headedness for the resultant misery, Hitler
blamed the trade-union organization.   Thereafter he was bitter in his
hatred of orthodox trade-unionism and of the political philosophy which
he associated with this movement.

In 1912 or 1913 Hitler moved from Vienna to Munich.   In his new
home he was somewhat happier.   At last he was in imperial Germany,
his spiritual fatherland.   Economically he was also somewhat better off.
No longer was he forced to eat in charity soup kitchens.   Nevertheless
he was still desperately poor, and though he was able to eke out a day-
by-day existence, there still seemed no prospects of a brilliant career
ahead of him.   And then, in 1914, came the World War.   To him the
war seemed a veritable godsend.   The war at least meant the end of the
old era in which he had been miserable; possibly it meant the beginning
of a new era in which he would gain name and fame and success.   Hitler
was determined to give up his career as an artist and become a soldier.
But instead of returning to his native Austria, he enlisted as a private
in the Bavarian army and was in active service throughout the whole
of the war.   From all accounts Hitler was a loyal and courageous soldier.
He was cited several times for bravery and was awarded the Iron Cross.
At the same time he was never popular with his fellow soldiers or with
the officers.   To both groups he always seemed cold, morose, brooding,
unsociable.   This is one reason why, in a period of rapid promotion, he
rose only to be a sub-corporal.   Needless to say Germany's defeat in
1918 came to him as a bitter and unexpected blow.   More than ever he
hated the foreigners who had brought about Germany's humiliation.
Even more intense was his hatred for the Jews and the Marxian socialists within Germany's own ranks because, very unfairly, he blamed
Germany's defeat upon the activities of these groups.

For more than two years after the war was over, Hitler made his
living by serving as a more or less secret agent for the military authorities in Munich.   These authorities were terrified lest the communists
secure permanent control over the political machinery of Bavaria.   It
was Hitler's task to keep in touch with the soldiers, workers, and professional agitators and report any signs of "subversive" activities.   In
some cases Hitler served as a political stool pigeon, and on the basis of
his secret reports several of his comrades were seized and shot.   In
other cases, Hitler had the more respectable role of roving political re-
porter.   In this role it was his task to attend various political meetings

and to keep tab on what was done and said. It was while carrying on this type of work that Hitler first (1919) came into contact with a small and obscure group known as the *Deutsche Arbeiter Partei* or the German Workers Party. The importance of this so-called party can be gauged by the fact that at this time its meetings were attended by only twenty-five to thirty persons and that it numbered only six full-fledged members.

But though in the beginning Hitler attended the meetings of the German Workers Party as a spy for the military authorities, he soon became deeply interested in the discussions which he heard there. On one occasion Hitler joined in the discussion which followed the formal speech. His remarks must have awakened general interest, for a day or two later he received a notice that he had been accepted as a member of the party. He had never applied for membership and for a time was both amused and angry at this method of recruiting members; but before long he changed his mind and joined the small party, becoming its Member No. 7. As time went on he threw himself ever more passionately into the work of the party, resigning his post as political spy for the army to devote his whole life to party activities. From a very early time he was able to guide and control the program and policy of the little group with which he had become associated almost by accident. In 1920, largely at his suggestion, the name of the party was changed from the German Workers Party to the National Socialist German Workers Party on the ground that the words National and Socialist had great popular appeal. In 1921 he was formally made the leader of the party. Thereafter he was able to rule the group with almost dictatorial powers.

Under Hitler's leadership and largely because of his genius for organization and because of his ability to sway mass meetings with his peculiar form of oratory, the party rapidly grew in numbers and influence. Party meetings, which formerly were attended by a handful of curiosity-seekers, soon attracted hundreds and later thousands of persons, ready to applaud when Hitler or one of his lieutenants made a speech. More to the point, such persons were also willing to pay substantial sums into the party's exchequer. Permanent headquarters were secured, a daily paper, the *Völkischer Beobachter* (the National Observer), was established, and active agents were sent to all portions of the country to stir up national interest in the party's activities. Of great importance was the creation of a uniformed and disciplined group, the brown-shirted Storm Troopers (*Sturmabteilung*). Originally the chief duty of the members of this group was to maintain order at party rallies by ejecting hecklers, but before long they were also busy breaking up communist meetings and beating up various opposition leaders. By 1923 the National Socialists, though still numbering only a fraction of the German population, were so well-organized and disciplined as to make them worthy of serious consideration.

In November, 1923, Hitler, emboldened by his success, committed what many observers think to be his most serious political mistake. Inspired by Mussolini's march on Rome, Hitler and the Nazis attempted an armed revolution, or at least a political *coup d'état* supported by armed bands. In trying to carry out this plan the Nazis tried to seize control of the city of Munich with the idea of using it as a base from which to march on Berlin. Hitler counted on having to face but little forcible resistance to his scheme, but on this point he was sadly disillusioned. As he and his followers marched festively down the street, they were met with a salvo of bullets. Eighteen of the Nazis were killed. Hitler himself, in order to get out of the line of fire, threw himself to the ground so violently that he dislocated his shoulder. The remaining Nazis broke and fled. The revolt was thus a complete failure. Hitler and several of his closest followers were placed on trial for treason, were convicted, and given long prison sentences. The party and the Storm Troopers were officially dissolved; the party's funds and property were confiscated; the party's newspaper was suppressed. To the casual observer the National Socialist movement seemed completely dead.

It soon developed, however, that the movement was not dead but only dormant, and the period of dormancy lasted a very short time. Hitler spent his enforced idleness in prison writing the first volume of his work *Mein Kampf*, a book later destined to become the Bible of the Nazi cause. Although he had been sentenced to five years' imprisonment, he was released at the end of 1924 after being incarcerated for only nine months. On Hitler's leaving prison his jailer confessed that he had been converted to the National Socialist cause. This in itself seemed an omen of what was going to happen in the future. While Hitler was under lock and key, many of his lieutenants had kept up their political activity. Their efforts had been so successful that already there were in the Reichstag fourteen members in sympathy with and more or less pledged to the Nazi movement. All that Hitler had to do, therefore, was to refound or rather to reorganize his party, and to prepare more strenuously than ever for his eventual triumph. The failure of 1923 had taught Hitler one thing, namely, the futility of armed rebellion or other openly illegal action. Thereafter he was determined to keep at least within the letter of the law. This meant that for his cause to meet with success it was necessary, by constant propaganda, to secure the support of the majority of the German people. After 1925 every effort was directed at this goal.

Hitler's own newspaper, the *Völkischer Beobachter*, was re-established, and in addition a large number of other newspapers, magazines, pamphlets, and books were published. Brass bands and monster processions were organized to secure publicity. In fact every form of theatricality was employed to secure popular attention. Fiery orators were sent out to arouse the masses to blind hate of the existing regime. Other more secret agents were placed in factories and even inside trade unions with the duty of spreading, half surreptitiously, the Nazi gospel among the workers. By exploiting the communist threat, the Nazis were able to secure immense sums of money from the wealthy industrialists, so that the party exchequer was never empty. But though Hitler gave up armed revolt and open illegality, he did not give up the idea of using force. The brown-shirted Storm Troop brigade was re-established, enormously enlarged, and its discipline improved. In addition a special, new, and more rigidly selected group, the black-shirted Elite Guards (*Schutzstaffel*), was created, which soon became a sort of private standing army. By breaking up communist meetings and street processions, by engaging in street brawls with communistically inclined groups, the Brown Shirts and the Black Shirts were able to impress and terrorize the electorate. In this way they both directly and indirectly aided the party enormously in its march to triumph.

At the same time it must not be forgotten that it took several years for the Nazi Party to achieve any success in the arena of active politics and that its final triumph was due in large measure to extraneous causes with which the Nazi high command, for all its genius in organization and propaganda, had nothing whatever to do. From 1925 to 1930 Germany was comparatively prosperous, and as long as business was good and jobs were plentiful the majority of the German electorate were content to retain the liberal-democratic republic established in 1919. In the elections held in 1928 the Nazis polled only eight hundred thousand votes, and the party members elected to the Reichstag constituted only a small and relatively insignificant group. The first real success of Hitler and his followers came in 1930 at a time when Germany was already badly hit by the great depression and the whole financial structure of the nation seemed to be on the rocks. A severe financial crisis always leads to the piling-up of protest votes against the regime or the party in power. The Nazis were able to take advantage of this fact and thus secured six and a half million votes which increased their delegation to the Reichstag to 107 persons. In the years which followed, the financial situation, instead of improving, grew steadily worse. Many business houses failed, many factories shut down, and the number of unemployed was greatly increased. This condition was the same in the elections which took place in July, 1932, at which time the Nazis secured nearly fourteen million votes and their delegation to the Reichstag was increased to 230 persons. Though still a minority, the Nazis now constituted the largest single party group within the German Reichstag. To Hitler it seemed the hour of destiny was near at hand.

In point of fact, however, the Nazis at this time were unable to take advantage of their favorable situation, and in the months which followed it looked as if they were fated to lose rather than gain in numbers and influence. A rift developed between Hitler and many of the wealthy industrialists who had been backing him. There was a marked diminution in the contributions to the party treasury, and with smaller funds there had to be a curtailment in propaganda activity. Just at this time the Reichstag was suddenly dissolved and new elections were held. With their funds depleted and their morale shaken, the Nazis were unable to make the same good showing as in the earlier campaign. Two million fewer persons voted the Nazi ticket and only one hundred and ninety-six Nazi members were elected to the Reichstag. Many observers, both in Germany and abroad, believed that the tidal wave of Hitlerism had lost its force and was destined rapidly to recede. Many prophesied that within two or three years the very name of Hitler would almost be forgotten. Even the Nazi leaders were filled with gloom. In the diary of Goebbels, one of the most important of the Nazi leaders, we read:

> Deep depression throughout the organization.... The situation in the party is getting worse from hour to hour.... All chances and hopes have disappeared.... For hours the Leader [Hitler] paces up and down the room in the hotel.... Suddenly he stops and says, "If the party once falls to pieces, I shall shoot myself without more ado."[2]

If all the political groups which supported the liberal republic, as opposed to Nazi dictatorship, had stuck together and formed a strong national government, there is little doubt that the triumph of Hitler could have been averted. But the supporters of liberalism (in the broader sense of the word) were split into numerous parties, each of which fought with all the others. It was found impossible to form a cabinet which enjoyed the support of the majority of the Reichstag. For a while an attempt was made to govern through a group of bureaucrats and army officers who were supposed to have no party affiliations and who might therefore enjoy the support of several of the parties. Even this attempt ended in failure. The liberal or semi-liberal parties could neither form a government themselves nor agree to support a government formed by outsiders. Germany seemed to have entered a political blind alley. To make things worse, several of the highest ranking bureaucrats began intriguing against one another, with the result that some of them decided to sell out to Hitler. Just at this time many of the wealthy industrialists, once more frightened by the menace of communism, decided to renew their alliance with the Nazis. They were followed by large numbers of the Junkers or aristocratic landowners in northeastern Germany. Even the Nationalist Party, which was normally the official mouthpiece of the industrial magnates and the semi-feudal nobility, decided that it was to their advantage to join hands with the National Socialists. The conditions by this time were all set for a grand coup. It came January 30, 1933. Some of the intimate advisers of President von Hindenburg, who were in secret alliance with Hitler, persuaded Hindenburg to dismiss the existing government and to call Hitler to form a ministry. The hour of triumph had come at last.

There is a curious parallel between the developments in Fascist Italy in the years 1922–1925 and those in Nazi Germany in the period 1933–1934, save for the fact that the developments in Germany took place at a much faster tempo. When Mussolini first came to power in 1922, it will be remembered, he did not immediately create a personal nor even a party dictatorship. His first cabinet was essentially a coalition cabinet in which there were as many non-Fascists as Fascist members. The popularly elected Chamber of Deputies was permitted to continue in existence and to take an active part in legislation. For over a year parliamentary government survived, in theory at least, and during this time Mussolini was technically bound to resign if the Chamber of Deputies had voted a resolution of non-confidence. It was not until 1925 that all the non-Fascist parties were suppressed and the machinery of government changed to give Mussolini and the Fascist Party theoretical as well as practical control over all phases of the national life. In like manner Hitler's first cabinet was a coalition cabinet. In fact, of its eleven members only three were National Socialists. Six were members of or sympathizers with the Nationalist Party. The defense ministry was placed in the hands of a professional soldier, the foreign office in the hands of a professional diplomat. The big industrialists, the wealthy landowners, the upper members of the bureaucracy, with whose aid the Nazis came to power, were foolish enough to think that they had Hitler encircled and completely in their power. In their blindness they thought that they would be able to use Hitler for their own purposes. They obviously forgot or ignored the developments which took place a decade earlier in Italy.

In the early stages of his rule Hitler seemed determined to make use of parliamentary institutions. Even after his accession to power the Nazis with their new allies, the Nationalists, were unable to secure a majority in the Reichstag; but instead of suppressing or ignoring this institution Hitler decided to dissolve the existing chamber and call for new elections in the hope of securing a Reichstag which would support his administration. Hitler thus maintained the theory of democracy and of a free election. But by this time he could rely, not only on the huge party organization, but also upon control of the police and the electoral machinery, both of which were freely used in support of his bid for power. In addition, during the early stages of the campaign the government issued a special emergency decree which subjected freedom of assembly and press to severe restrictions, and in practice these restrictions were enforced only upon the opposition parties. From the outset the non-Nazis were severely curbed in the use of the press and the radio and in their right of holding political meetings. Such meetings as were held were frequently broken up by the Nazi Storm Troopers while the police passively stood by.

But all this was not enough. The Nazis to insure success felt it was necessary to find or create a new and startling campaign issue — a last-minute bolt from the blue. This was found in the burning of the Reichstag building a week before the polling took place. There now seems to be ample evidence that this act of arson was accomplished with the connivance and even with the aid of the Nazi Party itself, but at the time all the blame could be and was thrown upon the communists. The Nazis asserted that the burning of this one building was evidence of a widespread communist plot; that the one way to keep the communists at bay was by voting the National Socialist ticket. The argument was especially effective among the inhabitants of the rural communities. In addition, the supposed communist plot was made the excuse for imprisoning nearly all the communist and many of the Social Democratic candidates, thus preventing them from making last-minute campaign speeches. Finally the scare over the "communist menace" permitted the government to issue an emergency decree indefinitely suspending freedom of speech, of person, of press, of assembly, of privacy of the mails, and authorizing confiscation of property without compensation and for undetermined purposes. This decree was of immense value to the National Socialists both during the campaign and during the years which followed; it has never been rescinded.

As the result of all these tactics the National Socialists had no difficulty in securing millions of voters for their electoral ticket. The final returns showed that over seventeen million had voted for them and an additional three million for their allies, the Nationalists. At the same time, it should be noted that the Nazis, in spite of all their efforts, polled only 44 per cent of the total vote, and even with the Nationalists they secured only 52 per cent, little more than a bare majority. If Hitler was going to carry through his elaborate program of "reforms" without having continual trouble from the Reichstag, it was obvious that he had to do something drastic. He decided that he would force the Reichstag to delegate to the government all its legislative powers for a period of four years. For this delegation of authority to be accomplished legally it was necessary to carry through a constitutional amendment, and this in turn required the consent of a two-thirds majority in the Reichstag. With a majority of only 52 per cent, how was this to be effected? Hitler got rid of a certain amount of opposition by keeping all the communist and many of the Social Democratic members in jail. He then succeeded in terrorizing a sufficient number of the remaining opposition into submission for him to carry through the constitutional amendment (which was called the Enabling Act). While debates on this act were going on in the Reichstag, the streets of the capital were full of marching Storm Troopers. Other such troopers filled the halls of the Reichstag itself and the final vote was taken in an indescribable atmosphere of terrorization. Nearly everyone believed the recalcitrant members would be shot if the bill failed to pass. In the end 441 members voted for the act and only 94 against it. Having delegated its powers to the government and having no further duties to perform, the Reichstag immediately adjourned, leaving the cabinet or rather Hitler himself with an absolutely free hand. Incidentally, the original Enabling Act has subsequently twice been renewed and is still in operation.

Once Hitler secured absolute power he did not hesitate to use it. The transformation of the government into a totalitarian dictatorship, which Mussolini took over two years to accomplish, was carried out by Hitler in little over a year.   Since 1933 practically all legislation has been by governmental decree.   All persons in the civil service who were not favorable to the Nazi regime were dismissed on the ground that they were "inimical to the state" or "politically undesirable."   The press, radio, and cinema were placed under the rigid control of the Minister of Enlightenment and Propaganda.   The universities and schools were handed over for regulation by the Minister of Education.   The non-Nazi parties were rapidly "liquidated."   The Communist and Social Democratic Parties were dissolved by governmental decree.   The other parties, under pressure from the secret police, "voluntarily" disbanded a short time thereafter.   The same fate soon befell the Nationalist Party, the partner of the Nazis in the government coalition; for having secured supreme power, Hitler no longer had need of his former allies. In the course of a few months not only did the coalition cabinet become a one-party government, but Germany itself became a one-party state. A law of 1933 proclaimed that the National Socialist Party was the only one in the realm and made it a criminal offense to attempt to establish a new party.   Not only were the political groups thus liquidated; the same fate befell such economic groups as the trade unions.   Their leaders were arrested and their funds, their offices, and their newspapers passed into the hands of the Nazi Party officials.   By September, 1933, Hitler could openly declare, "The National Socialist movement is the German Reich.   It *is* the state."

Prior to Hitler's advent, Germany was a federal, as opposed to a unitary, state.   Each constituent "land," or separate state, elected or appointed its own officials; each of these units, like an American state, was supposed to possess certain innate sovereign powers.   This condition was considered inconsistent with the carrying-out of the Nazi program. Early in 1934 by governmental decree all the sovereign rights of the "lands" were transferred to the central government.   Thereafter each constituent "land" was to be ruled over by a *Statthalter* or governor appointed by the central government and regarded as the personal representative of Hitler.   Within each "land" the *Statthalter* was vested with dictatorial powers.   He was granted the right to issue all necessary governmental decrees, having the validity of law, and also the right of appointing and dismissing all local officials.   Moreover, Hitler's attempt to secure complete control over every phase of government did not stop with the "lands" or larger political units.   The authoritarian principle was soon applied to the local communes or townships, the principal units of local government.   A new law required that the head of each such commune must "enjoy the confidence of the party and of the state" and made it his duty to keep in close touch with the local representative of the party.

The year 1934 was marked by the removal of every obstacle which might have impeded the exercise of Hitler's personal and absolute rule. June 30, 1934, witnessed the famous "bloody purge" during the course of which a large number of prominent political personages were shot. Some of these personages, like Von Schleicher, a former chancellor, were outside the ranks of the Nazi Party. Others, like the notorious Captain Röhm, were themselves prominent National Socialists, but were suspected of being out of sympathy with some of the policies laid down by Hitler. After the successful termination of this purge, the people of Germany were so terrified that scarcely a soul dared to whisper any objection to whatever action Hitler chose to take. Hitler's position was further aided by the death of President von Hindenburg in August, 1934. For many months Hindenburg had been little more than a puppet in Hitler's hands. Technically, however, the President of the Republic was still Hitler's superior, and theoretically his consent was required for all important governmental decisions. To remove any possible source of friction in the future, a governmental decree declared Hitler to be both Chancellor and President. Thereafter Hitler, the ex-corporal, was both theoretically and practically the supreme and absolute lord of Germany.

Everyone agrees that Hitler rules dictatorially. Most observers also agree that he rules ruthlessly and arbitrarily. Yet there can be no doubt that his actions have won the admiration of the majority of the German people. At the first election after his appointment to the chancellorship he and his fellow Nazis received only 44 per cent of the total vote. A few months later, when another election was called, the National Socialist ticket obtained the endorsement of over forty million voters or 92 per cent of the total vote. Since then several elections or plebiscites have been held and in each case the Nazis have won an overwhelming victory. Participation in the elections is exceedingly high, coming close to 100 per cent of those entitled to vote, and yet in each case the Nazis have polled well over 90 per cent of the votes, in some cases as high as 98 or 99 per cent. It is true that the Nazi list is the only one permitted to come before the electorate, that all rival groups and parties have been abolished. It is true that many hundreds of thousands, possibly several millions, vote for Hitler only because they are intimidated or terrorized. It is nevertheless certain that Hitler and the National Socialists have won the confidence of the great majority of the German people. It is highly probable that he will retain this confidence unless and until he is defeated in a foreign war.

Most competent observers are agreed that the popularity in Germany of the National Socialist cause is due to many reasons, chief among which was the disillusionment, disappointment, and despair which characterized Germany during the republican era and the fact that National Socialism seemed a magical antidote to this situation. There were many millions of Germans, especially among the liberal and Social Democratic groups, who were inclined to take seriously the propaganda stories put out by the Allies during the first World War to the effect that they were not fighting against Germany or the German people, but only against the Kaiser and kaiserism. Such persons were willing to believe that were Germany to become a democracy the Allies would gladly aid her in becoming a strong free nation. Such arguments enormously helped the German liberals in establishing the Weimar Republic of 1919. The subsequent rather harsh treatment of Germany by England and more especially by France rudely shattered these illusions and incidentally caused a large portion of the German public to turn against the whole notion of a liberal-democratic republic.

The German liberals themselves felt bitterly hurt by the treatment meted out to their country, but they persisted in the policy of appeasement and reconciliation with the foreign powers and of fulfillment of all the obligations which Germany assumed as the result of her defeat. They protested against some of the terms of the Versailles Peace Treaty, but they signed this document and tried to carry out its conditions. They protested against the French occupation of the Ruhr, but refused even to attempt armed resistance. They protested Germany's inability to pay any large sums in the way of reparations, but accepted the responsibilities thrust upon them by the Dawes Plan and the Young Plan. In each such case there was widespread ill-will aroused, not only against the foreign powers, but also against the whole liberal-democratic system which came to be associated with ever increasing national humiliation. In 1919 the parties which supported the liberal-democratic system (namely, the Social Democrats, the Democrats, and the members of the Center Party) polled the impressive total of twenty-three million out of thirty million votes. In the elections following the acceptance of the Treaty of Versailles, the same parties lost a total of eleven million votes, three million of which went to the Communists and another three million to the Nationalists, both of which groups had voted against the treaty. In this way important support was withdrawn from the parties which accepted the liberal theory of government, and this support was lost permanently. The government parties never regained a sufficient majority to rule effectively.

Careful and objective students of politics are inclined to believe that the Allies made a great mistake in their treatment of Germany. Either they should have been more conciliatory to the new liberal republic, or they should have been much harsher, harsh enough to crush the German nation and prevent its rising again as a single unit. Germany was piqued, she was hurt, she was humiliated, but she was not crushed, with the result that the desire to restore Germany's international prestige became a burning flame among the German masses, rendering them peculiarly susceptible to the type of propaganda handed out by the National Socialists.

It was by appealing to nationalist sentiment that Hitler secured millions of votes, but it must not be forgotten that the real rise of Hitlerism was due to its appeal to a certain type of class consciousness rather than to a national consciousness. In their burning desire to secure power, the Nazis zealously wooed all classes in the population. The laboring classes were wooed by appeals to their patriotism and by promises of "socialism." The peasants were promised an end of "interest slavery," and the partition of the great estates. The upper bourgeoisie were promised salvation from Marxism and the destruction of the trade unions. All these promises aided Hitler, but they were relatively unimportant compared with the appeal he made to, and the support he got from, the members of the lower middle class, or, as the Germans put it, the *Kleinbürgertum*. German National Socialism, like Italian Fascism, is essentially the political embodiment of a lower middle class ideology, an ideology which came into being because of the economic sufferings which the members of this class had to undergo.

In the turbulent, troubled years following the World War it was the German lower middle class which suffered more severely than any other section of the community. This class was particularly hard hit during the period of inflation (1921–1923). The upper classes, the industrialists, and the owners of landed estates were still able to live well. In many cases inflation aided rather than hurt them. They were able to pay off mortgages for a song and could always demand real value for their products. The organized proletariat also fared comparatively well, as jobs were plentiful and they were able to force up wages to meet rising prices. The middle and lower middle classes, however, found themselves on the verge of ruin. Their accumulated savings were wiped out, and the salaries and fees of the members of this group rose so slowly that hundreds of thousands of middle class families were reduced to dire poverty. From the very beginning the National Socialist Party championed the interests of this section of the community, and it is significant that its early initial successes took place during this period.

From 1924 to 1930, Germany was reasonably prosperous, and the middle classes shared in this prosperity. They no longer felt desperate, and as a result, the National Socialist Party, though continuing to hold its own, showed no widespread increase in membership. The impact of the great depression and of the huge unemployment which accompanied the depression completely changed the situation. The upper classes, though talking about ruin, still had resources from which to draw. Most manual workers had unemployment insurance which kept them from starvation. It was again the lower middle class, the *petite bourgeoisie*, which was hardest hit. Many of its members were to be found among the ever growing ranks of the unemployed, and such persons had neither financial resources nor unemployment insurance to fall back on. As Schuman remarks:

> Material deprivation was less galling than the ubiquitous sense of social degradation. Millions of middle class families felt themselves being pushed down to the level of the proletariat. A class occupying a middle position in the social hierarchy usually develops more resentments and aggressions as a result of being depressed to an inferior status than a class which is already at the bottom of the social scale and is further impoverished by economic adversity.[3]

Of great importance in this connection is the fact that just as Germany was humiliated but not crushed, so the lower middle class inside Germany was humiliated but not crushed. It was humiliated enough to feel deep resentment, yet it was still strong enough to rise and smite its enemies, real or imaginary.

> People who are desperately impoverished do not ordinarily rebel or protest effectively. They are too demoralized and disintegrated as individuals and as a group to possess the capacity for collective action. The German *Kleinbürgertum* was not in this position.... It is arguable that had the *Kleinbürgertum* been more impoverished or less impoverished it would have acquiesced in its new status. But it was sufficiently impoverished to become acutely resentful and not sufficiently impoverished to prevent it from resisting and giving effective expression to its bitterness.[4]

From a study of developments in Italy and in Germany, we may well come to the conclusion that whenever we find a situation where a nation is hurt but not crushed and its lower middle class is hurt but not crushed, we are liable to see the rise of a movement similar to Italian Fascism and German National Socialism.

Observers are agreed that the rise of National Socialism is due in large measure to its appeal to the German lower middle class. The early speeches of Hitler and the early program of the Nazi Party all included special appeals to this element in the community. The lower middle class was soothed by attacks on the "Marxist" trade unions; it was soothed by the statement that "National Socialism recognizes private property in principle and gives it the protection of the state." This phase of the Nazi program was to protect the lower middle class from the ideology common among the proletariat. At the same time the National Socialist program also contained a number of doctrines aimed at big business and the wealthy industrialists. Lower middle class un-employment was to be done away with, because "the state shall make it one of its chief duties to provide work and the means of livelihood for the citizens of the state." Other radical demands included the demand for "the abolition of incomes unearned by work and emancipation from the slavery of interest charges." War profits were to be confiscated. Business combines and trusts were to be nationalized (but not small businesses).

> We demand an extensive development of provision for old age....[5] We demand... the immediate communalization of the big department stores and the lease of the various departments at a low rate to small traders; and the greatest consideration shall be shown to all small traders supplying goods to the state.

With such a program it is not surprising that the Nazis were able to win the support of the great bulk of the lower middle class. What is surprising, and what shows the real propagandistic genius of the Nazi leaders, is the fact that they were able to identify the interests of the lower middle class with the interests of the nation as a whole. As Roberts very justly remarks, Hitler

> made his success possible by the happy fluke or unconscious inspiration (who can say which?) of organizing them [the members of the lower middle class], not on a class basis against the workers and the aristocrats, but on a broadly national basis which could be indefinitely enlarged to include all elements within the community.... He saw the *petite bourgeoisie* — the salaried classes, the small shopkeepers, the farmers and the peasants — were crying for organization just as much as the factory proletariat were. He offered them *Folkic* [i.e. national] as opposed to trade union organization, and later enwid-ened his organization to take in all sections — whether proletarian or even

aristocratic — who were ready to place patriotic over class interests. This benevolent inclusiveness — like the amorphous pantheism of some Asiatic religion — gained him more and more adherents, so that at last his rally of the *Kleinbürgertum* could be reinterpreted as the rise of a nation. . . . He solved the neurosis of a single class by invoking the idea of renascent Nationalism and discovered that the panacea he had hit upon could be indefinitely expanded. From being the lord of the *Kleinbürgertum* he became the *Führer* of the nation as a whole.[6]

THE IDEOLOGICAL BACKGROUND

After this digression on the life of Hitler and the rise of the National Socialist Party, we can return to our main task and examine the basic philosophy upon which the Nazi political ideology rests. The Nazis have been in power too short a time for them to give a final and definitive exposition of their political creed. The three most important sources for the study of National Socialist ideology are *The Political and Economic Program of the National Socialist German Workers Party*, drawn up by Gottfried Feder in 1920; *Mein Kampf*, written by Hitler in the years 1924–1927; and *The Myth of the Twentieth Century*, composed by Alfred Rosenberg, the semi-official philosopher of the party, in 1930. All three of these documents were written prior to the triumph of 1933. It must be remembered, however, that the Nazis have been far more consistent in their doctrines than have the Italian Fascists. It is true that some of the specific demands incorporated in the original *Political and Economic Program* have never been carried out, nor is it likely that they ever will be. Nevertheless there has never been any great deviation in basic attitudes since the Nazi Party first appeared on the political horizon. The Nazi intellectuals have written many philosophical interpretations of the Nazi movement since Hitler's triumph, but nearly all their doctrines are merely developments of ideas to be found in Rosenberg's *Myth of the Twentieth Century*. Such being the case, a study of the National Socialist political philosophy should not constitute too complicated a problem.

As we have already seen, idealism, traditionalism, irrationalism, and Social Darwinism constitute the four basic pillars in the construction of nineteenth century etatism and authoritarianism. As National Socialism is clearly etatist and authoritarian, it is interesting to see the attitude which the Nazis assume toward these four great schools of thought and how far they have made use of the arguments which were developed by the leaders of each school. In a general way it may be said that the

German Nazis, like the Italian Fascists, have been strongly influenced by these schools, but that there is a marked difference in emphasis between the Germans and the Italians. As we have already had occasion to observe, it seems certain that the basic philosophy of Mussolini himself is a combination (taken over from Nietzsche) of irrationalism and Social Darwinism, but because of the peculiar nature of the Italian political situation, he and his followers have found it advisable to lay comparatively little stress upon the doctrines of these two schools and to proclaim their allegiance to traditionalism and idealism. In Germany, on the contrary, we find the Nazis quietly taking over the basic assumptions of the traditionalists and the idealists, but without laying any great emphasis upon them. It is irrationalism and Social Darwinism which are made the bases of all major Nazi philosophizing and it is upon the teachings of these two schools that the greatest stress is laid.

Take, for example, the question of traditionalism. In Italy the Fascists found an enormous amount of traditional feeling centered in the monarchy and in the Roman Catholic Church. When the Fascists found that they could cooperate with, or rather make good use of, these two institutions and the traditional reverence they inspired, they forgot all about their futurist background and became zealous advocates of traditionalism as a basic political creed. In Germany, on the other hand, the situation was very different. From childhood Hitler despised the Habsburgs and in later life came to have very little use for the Hohenzollerns. Moreover, there was no question of preserving an existing monarchy. The ancient monarchy had very definitely been overthrown, and Hitler had no intention of re-establishing a dynastic house which might interfere with his own exercise of power. Hence he found it impossible to make use of the monarchic traditionalism which still existed in some parts of Germany. In like manner Hitler found it impossible to utilize any traditional reverence for the church. In Italy the Catholic Church was a symbol of national unity. In Germany the various churches were symbols and memorials of national discord. If Germany were to become strong and unified, the Germans must learn to forget the religious dissensions of the past and concentrate upon purely national ideals. Finally Hitler strongly disliked the traditional loyalty which centered in the petty states into which Germany had long been divided. If traditionalism meant separatism, he was strongly against it.

As there were so few existing traditions of which use could be made, it is not surprising that the Nazis have skipped lightly over the subject of traditionalism in expounding their political creed. At the same time

they are far from being anti-traditionalists as were so many of the clas·
sical liberals, such as Locke, Rousseau, and Jefferson.   No Nazi would
ever say with the liberals that history is the story of past abuses, or
that we must be ruled by the living rather than by the dead.   Not infrequently passages in Nazi speeches and in Nazi books pay lip service
and even more to the cause of traditionalism.

> More than fourteen years have passed since the unhallowed day when the
> German people forgot the most precious heritages of the past, its honor and
> freedom.... The national government... will shield and protect the founda-
> tions on which the strength of our nation rests.... It will make respect for
> our great past, pride in our old traditions, the bases of education of German
> youth.[7]   [And again:] Awake to a realization of your own importance.   Re-
> member your past and the achievements of your fathers.... Forget the four-
> teen years of decay and think of the two thousand years of German history.[8]

In *Mein Kampf* we find Hitler giving a somewhat more philosophical
exposition of the traditionalist position.

> If any new idea, a new doctrine, a view of life, or also a political as well
> as an economic movement tries to deny the entire past, or wants to deride it
> and to make it valueless, for this reason alone one has to be extremely cautious
> and mistrusting.   In most cases the reason for such hatred is either one's own
> inferiority or even an evil intention in itself.   A genuinely blissful renovation
> of mankind would always and forever have to continue to build in that place
> where the last foundation ends.   It will not have to be ashamed of using
> existing truths.   The entire human culture, as well as man himself, is only
> the result of one long single development, during which every generation
> added to and built in its building stones.   The meaning and the aim of revo-
> lutions is not to wreck the entire building, but rather to take away unsuitable
> stuff which had been badly fitted in and to continue to build on and add to
> the healthy spot that has been made free.[9]

Rosenberg expresses the same basic concept when he says:

> We must act in accordance with the conditions to be found in our own time.
> This means that we must reject the teachings of the false pseudo-nationalist
> philosophers who, incapable of adjusting themselves to modern times, try to
> find satisfaction in the imitation of the outward forms of antiquity.... We
> National Socialists accept with our whole hearts the present epoch, for we
> feel ourselves as vital elements in the renaissance which is now taking place.
> [At the same time we must remember that] a revolution which tries to preach
> "absolutely new ideas" to a nation which has been in existence for thousands
> of years shows that it is necessarily unorganic and anti-national in charac·
> ter.   For when we find that a nation in the course of its history has never
> accepted certain ideas or certain standards of value, it is evidence that such
> ideas and such standards are essentially alien to its nature.   A revolution or
> **an** *evolution* is sound only if it aids in restoring to a nation. in our case to Ger·

many, some of its everlasting values which have temporarily been neglected. ... The real greatness of the National Socialist movement lies in the fact that it is the embodiment of the German National Consciousness in a modern form. For this reason we feel closely akin to all the greatness which made Germany justifiably proud in the past; for this reason we are the enemies of all those who seek to pollute the essence of Germany.[10]

When we try to analyze the various statements which the Nazi leaders have made regarding traditionalism, we find that they believe in progress, in evolution, and, if necessary, in revolution. They are perfectly willing to destroy the outmoded institutions which have been inherited from their ancestors. They do, however, insist that each nation has or builds for itself a national mind or consciousness and also a national conscience, and that all changes and reforms must be made in accordance with the ideas and standards laid down by this national consciousness. What these ideas and standards are can only be known by a study of the nation's past. In other words, the Nazi version of traditionalism is essentially that espoused by Hegel, by Mazzini, and by Treitschke.

As with traditionalism so with idealism. On the surface it would appear that little stress is laid upon the classical idealist philosophy, and yet underneath the surface we find that idealism in a new and rather peculiar form is a basic element in Nazi ideology. It is certainly true that the direct influence of that form of the idealist philosophy which we call Hegelianism is comparatively small. Hegel is seldom mentioned by the official Nazi spokesmen and when mentioned is usually referred to with a sneer.[11] This is rather surprising when we remember the important part that Hegel had in shaping the etatist and authoritarian creed in the nineteenth century. This neglect of Hegel is partly due to the fact that orthodox Hegelianism was far more popular in the universities outside of Germany than in Germany itself at the beginning of the twentieth century. It was in England (with the Oxford school), and more especially in Italy, that we find the most forceful exponents of the Hegelian philosophy. In Germany, to be sure, there were and still are numerous and powerful followers of Hegel in some form or other, but in most academic circles it was popular to cry "Back to Fichte" or "Back to Kant," at least in the field of metaphysics. As a result of this shift in popularity, none of the Nazi ideologists came under the influence of orthodox Hegelian professors during their formative student years.

The neglect of Hegel is also due to the fact that there are some features of the official Nazi creed which are apparently in direct opposition to the teachings of metaphysical idealism as expounded by Hegel. To Hegel, mind is everything, matter is nothing, or at least nothing but the embodiment or the product of mind. Mind creates the brain, not the brain the mind; it is the soul (or *Geist*) which creates and shapes the body, not the body the soul. This doctrine has found great favor with the Italian Fascists, but the Nazis, having accepted the doctrine of racialism, are forced to reject this whole philosophical position. The Nazis prefer to follow H. S. Chamberlain in proclaiming that "the form of the head and the structure of the brain exercise quite decisive influence upon the form and structure of the thoughts." To them the mind and the soul of the Negro must be different from and inferior to the mind and the soul of the Nordic because of the differences in their physical structure. In like manner the Nazis are too realistic and too naturalistic to accept the purely ideological and "idealistic" interpretation of the processes of history advanced by Hegel. To Hegel, the evolution of the world and of man is caused by the unfoldment of the mind according to a logical pattern. To the Nazis the evolution of the world and of man is due to the operation of purely natural laws and natural processes, such as the struggle for existence and the survival of the fittest. Even in the purely political field there is a sharp contrast between orthodox Hegelianism with its glorification of the state, and National Socialism with its glorification of the *Volk* or nation.

At the same time it is true that indirectly, and to a certain extent unconsciously, Hegelianism has played an important role in shaping Nazi ideology. If the Nazi theorists have read very few of Hegel's own works, they have read and accepted the views of many persons who themselves were influenced by Hegel. Quite naturally, the Nazis, though not agreeing entirely with it, have been deeply affected by the political philosophy of the Italian Fascists, and the Fascists have a strong dose of Hegelianism in their creed. Moreover, when we read any of the major works composed by Nazi leaders, we constantly come across phrases and arguments taken over bodily from one or other of the numerous second-hand popularizers of Hegelianism who lived during the latter part of the nineteenth century. When we read that the *Volk* or nation is "a permanent, supernatural, mystical entity, real beyond the existing totality of all inhabitants," we are certain that National Socialism has incorporated within its creed much of the Hegelian system. This belief is strengthened when we hear the Nazis say that the *Volk* has a soul, a mind, a real or "objective" will of its own which is different from the subjective caprices and desires of the individual citizens, and that the Fuehrer (Hitler) in making his arbitrary decrees is only expressing or revealing the real will of the *Volk*. This whole doctrine is obviously a mild transformation of the old Hegelian principles.

It is true that Hegel in his old age, when he was the official philosopher of the Prussian court, glorified the state at the expense of the *Volk* or nation, but in his younger days, when Hegel was still struggling for official recognition, he glorified the *Volk* at the expense of the state. All that the Nazis have done in this respect is to follow the young rather than the old Hegel. Moreover, it is quite possible that the Nazis themselves, in the near future, will follow the same line of development as did Hegel himself. Before the Nazis acquired power, when they frequently came into conflict with the state authorities, they were vociferous in glorifying the *Volk*, of which they claimed to be the true representatives, as opposed to the state, which was still in the hands of their enemies. Since their political triumph, the Nazis have been far less loud in their deprecation of the state. More and more in their writings and in their speeches we find the state being identified with the *Volk* and the *Volk* with the state. In view of this development it seems not at all unlikely that eventually the state will receive the same deification from the Nazis as it did from Hegel a century earlier.

The National Socialists have also been profoundly influenced by Hegel's doctrine regarding the relativity of morals, the idea that there is no one absolute moral code suitable for all times and all places, but only a whole series of regional and temporary moral codes which have been created and developed by the different "communities" or nations into which humanity is divided. With the Nazis, as with Hegel, this doctrine has led to the rejection, not only of international morality, but also of international law. Even in the realm of metaphysics, we may say that the Nazi attitude on such subjects, as revealed in the works of their chief thinkers, is not so much a vehement denial of the Hegelian position as a realistic and naturalistic reinterpretation of the Hegelian philosophy. Though denying the Hegelian proposition that thought, or mind, or spirit is the only reality, they just as adamantly reject materialism or the idea that matter is the only ultimate reality. In order to avoid the charge of materialism, most of the Nazi writers bring forth the idea that matter and spirit are not antithetical, but are two aspects of the same reality. Physical characteristics (a certain shape of head, etc.) are thus not the *causes* of corresponding mental character-

istics, but are rather the external manifestation of these mental char
acteristics.   In like manner, nature and God are considered two different aspects of the same ultimate substance, so that the laws of nature,
including the law of the survival of the fittest, are also the laws of God.
It may be noted that this doctrine, though opposed to orthodox Hegelianism, is identical with the teachings of many of the so-called left-wing
Hegelians during the nineteenth century.

Even more important than Hegelianism proper is the idealistic
moralism common to Hegel, Fichte, and Kant, as well as to such thinkers
as Green, Carlyle, and Mazzini.   This is the notion that man must seek
virtue, not pleasure; that he must seek to perform his duty rather than
secure his rights; that self-sacrifice must take the place of egoistic self-
interest.   The Nazis, like the Fascists, insist that liberalism is intimately tied up with materialism, hedonism, utilitarianism, the selfish
pursuit of material comforts, and with the doctrine of the economic man
who buys in the cheapest and sells in the dearest market irrespective
of the moral or spiritual problems involved.   The Nazis, like the Fascists, claim that their creed is the expression of a demand for higher
spiritual values, of political ideals rooted, not in selfish commercialism,
but in honor, devotion, and loyalty.   But though the Nazis and the
Fascists agree in labeling liberalism as low, selfish, and materialistic,
there is a notable difference between the idealistic moralism of Italy and
that of Germany.

The Nazi writers, unlike the Fascists, attack, not only the selfish
materialism (identified with the liberal creed), but also the old or false
type of idealism and favor what they call the new or true type of idealism.   The Nazis claim that the old, false type of moral idealism is best
represented by the dogmas of the Catholic Church.   The new, true type
of idealism is the natural product of the Nordic soul, and is, of course,
the idealism of National Socialism.   The old idealism preached remorse
for sin, humility, forgiveness of injury, love for all mankind.   Such an
idealism is merely the product of the debased Semitic mind.   The new
or true idealism is based upon honor, courage, loyalty, justice (as opposed to forgiveness).   The older type of idealism is essentially a morality prepared by and for slaves and other oppressed peoples and classes.
The new type of idealism is based upon a morality fitted to leaders,
masters, a people proud of their position, and with a delicate sense of
honor to uphold.   The older type of idealism and of morality is based
upon a dogmatic code such as the table of the Ten Commandments,
supposedly revealed on Mount Sinai, and enforced by threats of hell fire.

The new type of morality is based on "the code of a gentleman," which every person who feels himself to be a gentleman willingly and gladly obeys.[12]

According to the Nazi ideology the materialism of the liberals is concerned only with the individual and the happiness and the rights of the individual. The old, false type of idealism was concerned with the universal, or what was supposedly universal, such as humanity as a whole. It formulated abstract, rational dogmas which were supposed to be true at all places and times. It formulated a supposedly universal and absolute code of ethics applicable to all peoples and all races. In contrast to all this, the new idealism is devoted neither to the service of the individual nor to the service of the universal (i.e., humanity) but to the group, that is, to the nation or to the race to which one happens to belong. The new idealism rejects the idea that any doctrine is universally and absolutely true; it insists that every doctrine is a working hypothesis which has been created by and is valid for a particular group. It rejects the notion that any moral code can be absolutely and universally applicable; it insists that all moral codes are and must be the creations of a particular group or :ace. Every person must render blind obedience to *some* moral code, but it must be to the code which his particular group has established. The Nazis try to summarize this position by saying that liberalism stands for the "I," the Catholic Church for the "All," and National Socialism for the "We."

Hitler himself repeatedly speaks of the need for and the value of idealism.

> How necessary it is to recognize again and again that idealism is not a super-fluous or even a dispensable expression of feeling, but that in truth it was, is, and will be the prerequisite for what we call human culture.... When the ideal attitude threatens to disappear, we can at once recognize a reduction of that force which forms the community and thus gives culture a presumption. As soon as egoism becomes the ruler of the nation, the ties of order loosen and in the hunt for their own happiness people fall all the more out of heaven into hell. Even posterity forgets those men who only serve their own advantage and praises as heroes those who renounce their own advantage.[13]

But when we ask what is meant by "idealism," we find that in Hitler's opinion *"True idealism is nothing but subjecting the individual's interest and life to the community"* — to the community, be it noted, and not to humanity as a whole or to some abstract ideal. Idealism, to Hitler, is thus seen to be identified with patriotism. Any ideal other than a patriotic (devotion to the group) ideal is false. "The healthy boy who is nauseated by the drivel of an 'ideal' pacifist, is ready to throw away his young life for the ideal of his nationality." [14] With this conception of what is meant by idealism, we are not surprised that Hitler adds, "Idealism alone leads men to voluntary acknowledgment of the privilege of force and strength."

Even to a casual observer it is obvious that the Nazi brand of idealism differs from all the older theories of idealism and is an idealism which is closely and intimately connected with irrationalism and Social Darwinism, two fundamental bases of the Nazi ideology; and it is to these two principles that we now turn our attention. A close survey of the National Socialist literature shows us that the Nazis have accepted practically all the irrationalist doctrines and presuppositions. In the first place we find it taken for granted that the vast majority of the population, or what we call the masses, are thoroughly stupid and irrational, being guided principally by sentiment, passion, and prejudice. Hitler tells us that

> the great masses, out of stupidity or simplicity, usually believe everything.[15] All propaganda has to be popular.... Therefore its spiritual level has to be screwed the lower, the greater the mass of people which one wants to at-tract.... The more modest, then, its scientific ballast is, and the more exclusively it considers the feelings of the masses, the more striking will be its success.... The great masses' receptive ability is only very limited, their understanding is small, but their forgetfulness is great.... The people in an overwhelming majority are so feminine in their nature and attitude that their activities and thoughts are motivated less by sober consideration than by feeling and sentiment.[16]

The Nazis are thoroughly convinced that neither in the political nor in the economic sphere is the average man always or even generally motivated by rational self-interest. He is apt to buy certain material, not because it is the cheapest and the best, but because of habit or prevailing fashion or as the result of advertising which has appealed to some sentiment or emotion. The Nazis thus reject economic determinism and regard all doctrines which are based on economic determinism, such as Marx's dialectic materialism, as scientifically unsound. The Nazis go even further and claim that in many cases it is easier to sway the masses by appealing to what seems to be an unselfish ideal rather than by an appeal to rational self-interest.

> One does not die for business, but for ideals. Nothing proved the English-man's psychological superiority in knowledge better than the motivation with which he cloaked his fight. While we fought for bread, England fought for "liberty," and not even for her own, nor for that of the smaller nations. We laughed at this impudence or we were annoyed by it, thus only proving

how thoughtless and stupid Germany's so-called statesmanship had become even before the World War.[17]

Not only are men irrational, but, according to the Nazi ideology, it is well that they should be so.   In fact the state should see to it that the bulk of the population does not seek to become too rational.   The increase of rationalism may well strengthen the principle of rational self-interest, and with the strengthening of this principle the power and strength of the community is apt to decrease.

> With this end in view the national state must direct its educational work, in the first place, not so much towards pumping in mere knowledge as towards cultivating thoroughly healthy bodies.   After that comes development of mental capability.   Here again the formation of character comes first, especially encouragement of will power and determination... and last of all comes schooling in pure knowledge.   The national state must act on the presumption that a man moderately educated but sound in body, firm in character and filled with joyous self-consciousness and power of will, is of more value to the community than a highly educated weakling.[18]

This same principle applies, not merely to the bulk of the population, but also to the leaders or rulers of the state.   The leaders must, of course, be rational enough to recognize the essential irrationality of the mob and make use of it; they must be rational enough to lay down definite plans and programs and see that they are carried out; but too much learning, too much reasoning is apt to ruin the success and the efficiency of such leaders.   Successful leadership demands fire, zeal, fanaticism, and such attitudes are incompatible with a cold-blooded, rational approach to the problems of life.

> The more intellectual our statesmen were, the weaker most of them were in real accomplishment.   Our political preparation for war and our technical armaments were insufficient, not because the brains governing our nation were too little educated, but rather because our rulers were too highly educated, stuffed with knowledge and intellect, but empty of sound instinct and utterly wanting in energy and boldness.[19]

The Nazis insist that, for a nation to be great and powerful, its citizens, both the governors and the governed, must be motivated by passionate faith, not by cold reason, or, as they put it, what is needed is not *Erkenntnis*, but *Bekenntnis*.   It is in this connection that they emphasize the value of myths.   To the Nazis, as to Sorel, a myth is a religious, political, or social doctrine which may or may not be true, and which is frequently absurd, but which is able to stir the masses to action.   The Nazis agree with Sorel, moreover, in claiming that unless a nation is dominated by one or more of these myths, it is bound to degenerate.   Germany lost her power and prestige, we are told, because

> bourgeois and Marxist Germany had become a nation without a myth, it had no highest standard of value in which it believed and for which it was ready to fight.   It was content to fill its gold sacks and try to dominate the world by economic and "peaceful" methods. . . .[20]   The task of the much-longed-for Germany of the future is to preach to the agonized and misled masses a new attitude towards life, to create for them by means of a new myth a new standard of value by which all things are to be judged.[21]

It is largely for this reason that the Nazi leaders insist upon maintaining a strong and active party organization, even after they have secured autocratic control over the state.   The state, as such, with its purely legalistic machinery can suppress communist or pacifist groups, and can, by the threat of imprisonment, restrain its citizens from saying or doing certain prohibited things; but all this is negative.   Germany can be strong only if its citizens can be imbued with passionate devotion to the new myth, the myth of the nation and of race which the Nazis have created, and it is for the party rather than for the state to see to it that the citizens are won over to belief in this myth.   In the older liberal countries we had the saying, "Where there is no vision the people perish," but it was generally felt that it was for the church rather than for the state to give the people this vision.   In Germany this saying has been changed to "Where there is no myth the nation perishes," and it is felt that it is for the party rather than for the state, or rather for the party working hand in glove with the state, to inculcate this myth in the citizenry.

From the foregoing citations it is obvious that the Nazis accept wholeheartedly all the practical implications of the irrationalist creed.   But it is of equal importance to discover that the Nazis also lay great stress upon the more theoretical and metaphysical phases of irrationalism. They are, for example, convinced that reason or logic alone can never enable us to find out what is good and bad or what is true and false. Hitler himself is in no way a metaphysician and is content to sum up this phase of the Nazi ideology by remarking, "Feeling often decides more accurately than reason." [22]   Rosenberg, however, the philosopher of the Nazi Party, goes into this problem more seriously.

> According to Hegel, Logic is a God-given science.   Such a phrase is a slap in the face directed at every true Nordic religion, and at every true form of German and Greek science.[23] . . .
>
> Just as nature and its happenings have nothing to do with reason or logical requirements, so during great historical movements the same forces of nature,

operating in the human soul, overleap the confining wall of logic.[24] The understanding, as we have seen, is a purely formal and therefore an empty tool. Its only task is the clarification of causal relationships. As soon as one enthrones this understanding as a law-giving sovereign, it means the end of all culture.[25] ... The life of a race or nation is not a logically developing system, nor yet a process which takes place in strict accord with natural laws. It is rather the unfolding of a mythical synthesis, an activity of the soul, which cannot be explained by logical formulae nor yet by merely applying the laws of cause and effect.[26]

The Nazis not only reject the theory that reason or logic can lead us to a solution of life's problem, but they also go further and, in agreement with such famed irrationalists as James, Bergson, and Nietzsche, they assert that there are no such things as eternal objective laws or eternal objective truths. The eternal truths postulated by the philosophers, the eternal laws of nature postulated by the scientists, are merely subjective creations of the intellect. Such truths and such laws are always inaccurate, are always distortions of reality, but they have served a very useful purpose in allowing man to act and have thus aided in the preservation of the race. To the Nazis, as to William James, all scientific laws are merely working hypotheses, not necessarily true, but valuable aids to further experimentation or in controlling material objects. To the Nazis, as to Nietzsche, there are no eternal or absolute moral codes, all moral codes being merely codes of discipline which a group or community has drawn up as an aid in its struggle with other groups and other communities. Each moral code is, therefore, but a weapon in the community's struggle for power.

In taking this position the Nazis are in close accord with many of the distinguished irrationalist philosophers who preceded them. On one important point, however, the Nazis have departed from their predecessors and have added a new and very characteristic doctrine of their own. This is the doctrine that every nation, and more especially that every race, is bound to have an intellectual and a moral standard peculiar to itself. What seems true to the mind of a German does and must seem false to the mind of a Chinese. What seems good to the conscience of a Nordic does and must seem bad to the conscience of a Negro. The divergence in intellectual and moral standards is not due to differences of environment or education or tradition, but to the fundamental differences in racial characteristics. To the Nazis there is not and never will be international morality, or international philosophy, or even international science.

The Nazis arrive at this extraordinary conclusion by claiming that there is no pure abstract reasoning or pure abstract science. "There is no such thing as science without certain presuppositions." [27] Even when we argue logically, we start from a few basic axioms, and these axioms are not logical in character; they are taken for granted, they are "felt" to be true, and such "feelings" differ from nation to nation and from race to race. In the case of science, the non-logical presuppositions which are always present

> are the ideas and the theories, the hypotheses which guide the various research activities along certain lines. ... These ideas are as much conditioned by race as are the evaluations placed upon things by the will. A definite type of soul, or race, approaches the problems of the universe in a very different way than does another type. Problems which perplex a Nordic nation appear to the Jews or the Chinese to constitute no problem at all. Things which become problems to an Occidental seem to other races as riddles which have already been solved. [28]

The Nazis do not hesitate to assert that even in such abstract fields as mathematics and physics there are and must be national and racial standards of true and false. The Nazi mathematicians inform us:

> We serve the German way in mathematics and wish to cultivate it. ... Creative mathematics develops the stronger and achieves the greater importance for the world, the deeper it is rooted in the national spirit. [29]

In like manner we find a Nazi who is also a distinguished scientist writing a book on *German Physics* which begins with the words:

> German Physics? one asks. I might rather have said Aryan Physics, or the Physics of the Nordic species of man. ... But I shall be answered "Science is and remains international." It is false. Science, like every other human product, is racial and conditioned by the blood.

This new concept of national as opposed to international science permits the Nazi physicists to attack Einstein's theory of relativity as a product of the Semitic mode of thought, and unworthy of acceptance by the German people. "To the abstract mathematical junk of the Jewish physicists," they oppose "the living conception of high and holy laws of nature, such as the Nordic investigator wins for himself." [30]

If the Nazis regard mathematics and physics as essentially national and racial in character, it goes without saying that these same principles apply in even greater measure to the other less exact sciences. The German approach to the problems of the living organism, of society, of finance, must necessarily differ from that of other people; hence there must be a specifically German sociology, a German biology, a German economics. Nietzsche's conception that all knowledge, all science, is merely a weapon, an efficient even though inaccurate weapon wherewith an individual or a group struggles for power over nature and over other individuals and groups, is clearly reflected in many of the Nazi writings. Thus we find a leading Nazi scholar declaring:

> We renounce international science. We renounce the international republic of learning. We renounce research for its own sake. We teach and learn medicine, not to increase the number of known microbes, but to keep the German people strong and healthy. We teach and learn history, not to say how things actually happened, but to instruct the German people from the past. We teach and learn the sciences, not to discover abstract laws, but to sharpen the implements of the German people in competition with other peoples.[31]

If the Nazis have convinced themselves that there is a national as opposed to an international standard as to what is true and false, it goes without saying that they find no difficulty in persuading themselves that there is only a national as opposed to an international standard of what is good and bad. We get a mild foretaste of this idea in the twenty-five-point program which the Nazi Party put forward in 1920. The twenty-fourth point in this program declares, "We demand liberty for all religious denominations in the state in so far as they are not a danger to it and do not militate *against the moral sense of the German race."* In the official interpretation of this program it is again stated that the Nazis demand "suppression and discouragement of dogmas which are opposed to the German moral sense." [32] The later ideologists have expanded and crystallized the dogma behind this statement, until it now reads that each race and nation has its own instinctive moral sense and its own instinctive moral code and that the individual citizen owes obedience to this code and to no other.

Rosenberg expounds this position clearly by saying that when some thinkers

> declare that God is the measure of all things... it is soon evident that what they really mean is that the priests constitute the measure of all things. In contrast to such notions the new-born [i.e., Nazi] philosophy declares that the racially determined national soul is the measure of all of our thoughts, of our aspirations and actions, the final standard wherewith to judge all values.[33]

To Rosenberg it seems obvious that the Jews have a moral sense peculiar to themselves, a moral sense that is embodied in the commandments of the Old Testament and in the Talmud. This moral sense is all very well — for the Jews; but it is inconsistent with the moral sense which

the Germans have inherited from their ancestors. The moral commandments of the New Testament and of the Catholic Church are, according
to the Nazi theory, very largely the product of the Graeco-Roman moral
sense, and hence are much higher than those produced by the Jews.
Nevertheless, even these commandments are not quite consistent with
the moral ideas which are the unconscious product of the German
national soul, and on every important moral issue the German citizen is
obliged to follow the dictates of this soul rather than the dictates of Rome.

The denial of any objective, universal, absolute standard of morality
— the idea that the moral code which the individual must obey is the
one created by the nation in which one lives — puts the Nazis in close
accord with Hegel, save that the Nazis introduce the non-Hegelian concept of race. As we read further in the Nazi books, however, we find
that the Nazis go far beyond Hegel and approach the attitude toward
morals assumed by Nietzsche. Nietzsche, it will be remembered, taught
that every moral code is but a weapon created by a group to aid it in its
struggle for power; that each group develops a standard of action based
primarily on its desire to preserve and universalize its own type; that all
moral valuations are nothing more than the expressions of the needs of
the particular community of that which is to its own advantage. It is
only when we bear Nietzsche's philosophy in mind that we can understand the true meaning of the official statement of the Nazis that *"right
is whatever profits the National Socialist movement and therewith Germany"*
and that wrong is whatever hinders or handicaps this movement.

Even a casual survey of the Nazi literature shows us that irrationalism
with all its ramifications is an integral and essential part of the National
Socialist philosophy. Such a survey also shows us that the Nazi creed is
equally dependent upon the teachings of Social Darwinism. Social
Darwinism, as we know, starts with the proposition that all progress, all
evolution is the result of the struggle for existence and the survival of the
fittest. To the Nazis this process is not merely a part of the laws of
nature; it is also a part of the laws of God.

> Nature's will is the continuous improvement of all life and consequently
> her law is the continuous victory of the stronger over the weaker species,
> the stronger elements of a stock over the weaker, the stronger race over the
> weaker race.[34]

Both Hitler and Rosenberg tell us that humanitarianism, pacifism,
democracy, egalitarianism are basically wrong because they are con
trary to "the aristocratic principle in Nature; instead of the eternal
privilege of force and strength [they] set up the mass and dead weight of

numbers." [35]   In the end, all-powerful Nature is bound to win.   As all
these principles (democracy, etc.) are contrary to Nature's laws, Nature,
sooner or later, will revenge herself by completely destroying all the institutions based on these principles.[36]   Moreover, the laws of Nature are
the laws of God.   In struggling to restore the principle of natural selection, the Nazis are thus, we are told, working on behalf of the Deity.   In
fact Hitler expressly tells us that in advocating Social Darwinism "I . . .
act in the sense of the Almighty Creator . . . I am fighting for the
Lord's work." [37]

In stressing the importance of Social Darwinism, Rosenberg declares,
"We acknowledge the old saying that combat is the father of all things,
not only as an empty formula but as the content of our lives." [38]   It is
because of his profound belief in Social Darwinism that Hitler is so violent in his opposition to birth control.

> Once propagation as such has been limited and the number of births re-
> duced, the natural struggle for existence, that allows only the very strongest
> and healthiest to survive, is replaced by the natural urge to "save" at any
> price also the weakest and even sickest, thus planting the germ for a succession
> that is bound to become the more miserable the longer this derision of Nature
> and her will is continued.   The result will be that one day existence in this
> world will be denied such a people. . . . A stronger generation will drive out
> the weaklings, because in its ultimate form the urge to live will again and
> again break the ridiculous fetters of a so-called "humanity" of the individual,
> so that its place will be taken by the "humanity" of Nature which destroys
> weakness in order to give its place to strength.[39]

The Nazis are thus seen to be passionate apostles of Social Darwinism,
but it is important to note that the Nazis have accepted, not the version
of this creed preached by Herbert Spencer, but rather the version
preached by Walter Bagehot.   Spencer, it will be remembered, thought
of the struggle for existence as a struggle between individuals — "each
man for himself and the devil take the hindmost."   Bagehot, on the
other hand, gave a collectivist or group interpretation of the doctrine of
natural selection.   Bagehot's first basic doctrine was that those individuals who are willing and able to band together to form a group invariably
win in the struggle against those individuals who remain isolated.

> An aggregate of families owing obedience to a single head would be sure to
> have the better of a set of families acknowledging no obedience to anyone. . .
> Homer's Cyclops would be powerless against the feeblest band.

Bagehot's second basic doctrine is that, in the struggle between groups,
those groups survive and prosper which are most compact, are best
disciplined, and are the most homogeneous in character.

> Unless you can make a strong co-operative bond your society will be con-
> quered and killed out by some other society which has such a bond.... What
> makes one tribe differ from another is their relative faculty of coherence.
> ... The compact tribes win.

For a tribe to secure the maximum amount of coherence and compactness
it is necessary for its members to hate all aliens and to persecute and suppress all aberrant minorities.

From their numerous writings it is clear that the Nazis give wholehearted support to both of Bagehot's basic doctrines.   As the individual
who fights alone is bound to be overcome,

> the instinct of preserving the species is the first cause of the formation of
> human communities.... The preservation of the existence of a species presup-
> poses the individual's willingness to sacrifice himself.... The most essential
> support for the formation and preservation of a state is the presence of a
> certain feeling of homogeneity... as well as the readiness to risk one's life
> for this with all means....[40] [And again:] The greater the individual's readi-
> ness to subordinate his purely personal interests, the more increases also the
> ability for the establishment of extensive communities.   This will to sacrifice
> in staking his personal labor and, if necessary, his own life for others is most
> powerfully developed in the Aryan.   He is greatest not in his mental capaci-
> ties but in the extent to which he is ready to put all his abilities at the service
> of the community.[41]

It is, we are told, because of the coherence, the compactness of the
Aryans that they have been able to dominate the rest of the world.   It is
because the Germans were less coherent, compact, homogeneous than
the surrounding peoples that they have so frequently met with defeat.

> The German people lack that sure herd-instinct which... saves nations
> from their downfall.... Had the German people in their historical develop-
> ment possessed that herd-like unity which other nations had, the German
> Reich today would probably dominate the whole world.[42]

The Nazis believe that the major task of their movement is to imbue
the Germans with this herd instinct and thereby permit the German
domination of the world.   They are convinced that if Germany is made,
by force if necessary, compact, coherent, homogeneous — herd-like — she
is bound to triumph over the liberal countries with their "absurd"
doctrine of individualism.   Individualism to the Nazis means selfishness,
egoism, the unwillingness of the individual to sacrifice himself for the
welfare of the group.   The freedom of thought and speech permitted
in the liberal countries is, according to Nazi ideology, a sign of weakness, as this freedom destroys the compact, coherent nature of the country concerned.   By whipping up hatred for the foreigner and for the

Jew, by the ruthless suppression of all minorities who dare openly to say or do anything contrary to the dominant culture pattern, the Nazis feel that they have placed Germany in a position where she is invincible to any attack directed against her by countries in which liberal principles still hold their vogue.

The Nazis have taken over Bagehot's version of Social Darwinism almost in its entirety. They have also been influenced, but to a lesser extent, by the interpretation given Social Darwinism by Gumplowicz and the members of his school. Gumplowicz, it will be remembered, thought that all social progress, the development of all early culture, takes place not merely through the struggle between groups, but more especially as the result of the domination of one group (or race) by another. Hitler makes a special application of this principle by claiming that all culture originated when members of the Aryan race conquered members of the inferior races.

> Without this possibility of utilizing inferior men, the Aryan would never have been able to take the first step towards his later culture.... For the formation of higher cultures the existence of inferior men was one of the most essential presumptions because they alone were able to replace the lack of technical means without which a higher development is unthinkable. The first culture of mankind certainly depended less on the tamed animal, but rather on the use of inferior people.... It is no accident that the first cultures originated in those places where the Aryan, by meeting lower peoples, subdued them and made them subject to his will.[43]

The Nazis have also taken over the notion, so dear to Gumplowicz, that political institutions proper, that is, the true state and its organization, as opposed to mere tribal organization, originated through conquest, the subjugation and domination of one group by another. The Nazis dismiss with a sneer the old notion that the state originated with a social contract, voluntarily entered into by persons previously living in a state of isolation. They also attack the doctrine, preached by Aristotle, that the first unit was the family and that the family slowly and spontaneously developed into the tribe, and the tribe into the state. Rosenberg tells us:

> The family has sometimes shown itself a strong, at other times a weak, basis for political and national organization. Quite often the family has consciously been made to serve such organizations, but it was never the cause or even the most important support of a state, that is to say, of a real political or social community.[44]

Political organization, Rosenberg goes on to say, is always the result of the activities of a *Männerbund*, a group or band of *men*, united by a common discipline and aiming after a common goal.   In most cases this group of men consisted of warriors belonging to a single clan, tribe, or horde who united in an effort to ward off attacks from alien groups.   By the complete conquest of one tribe by another, the men of this warrior group became the members of a governing class of a new political unit, the germ of what we now call the state.[45]

All this is in close accord with the teachings of Gumplowicz.   The Nazis differ from Gumplowicz on only one important point.   Gumplowicz taught that though the state originates by conquest, the various elements within the state, that is, the conquerors and the various conquered groups, must and should eventually amalgamate for further progress to take place.   The Nazis, on the other hand, because of their racialist doctrine, are insistent that for the conquerors to intermingle with the conquered means cultural and social decay.

> As soon as the subjected peoples began to rise and approached the conquerors linguistically, the sharp separating wall between master and slave fell.   He became submerged in the race mixture till at last... he began to resemble more the subjected and the aborigines than his ancestors.   For some time he may still live on the existing cultural goods but then petrifaction sets in, and finally oblivion.[46]

The Nazis not only give wholehearted support to the doctrines of Social Darwinism proper, they are also enthusiastic in their support of the eugenic creed, which, though separate from, is closely related to Social Darwinism.   It will be remembered that the orthodox eugenists have several basic doctrines.   (1) Men are naturally and innately unequal.   (2) These innate differences tend to be hereditary.   (3) The innately superior persons and stocks tend to rise to the top of the social ladder.   Closely associated with this doctrine is the idea that it is the duty of the state to strengthen this tendency; to make sure by legislation that control over the state rests with the superior stocks and with these alone.   (4) Under present conditions superior stocks show a tendency to die out while the inferior stocks are increasing in number.   A corollary to this doctrine is the notion that it is the duty of the state to see that this tendency is reversed, if necessary by the use of force.

The Nazi leaders have embraced all these doctrines with wholehearted delight, as is evidenced not only in their writings, but also in the decrees and laws they have imposed on Germany since their accession to power. The so-called *Nazi Primer*, an official textbook issued by the Nazi Party for educational purposes, is full of references to all of the basic tenets of the eugenist creed. **The doctrine of the innate inequality of men** is stated in the following words:

> The foundation of the National Socialist outlook on life is the perception of the unlikeness of men. . . . Every attentive observer can recognize distinctions among men in physical size and shape . . . but there are also distinctions among men with respect to mental and spiritual traits. . . . To one person work is a curse from heaven . . . for another it is a necessity of life. . . . For some courage and loyalty are the very marks by which they treasure and value a man. . . . For some courage and loyalty are nothing but great stupidities. . . . Men must therefore be considered with respect to their inner make-up.[47]

The Nazis, like the eugenists, are insistent that these inequalities are not the result of education or environment, but of heredity. "Inheritance is in the long run always victorious over environmental influences. All arguments and political demands which are based on the belief in the power of environment are therefore false and weak."[48] The Nazis, like the eugenists, also deny the inheritance of acquired characteristics.

The eugenist doctrine that the superior stocks tend to rise above the inferior stocks in the social and economic sphere is paraphrased by the Nazis to read that in the long run Nature sees to it that the strong triumph over the weak and the clever over the stupid. We are told that

> the basic idea of Nature is aristocratic.[49] The stronger has to rule . . . only the born weakling can consider this as cruel. . . . The fight for daily bread makes all those succumb who are weak, sickly and less determined. The fight . . . is thus a cause for its development towards a higher goal.[50]

But though the Nazis agree that the control of the inferior stocks by the superior stocks is right and in accordance with the eternal laws of Nature, they are less convinced than the eugenists that the present social, economic, and political set-up aids the triumph of the better stocks. To their minds a democratic constitution usually means control by a few demagogues who are frequently very inferior persons. The present economic organization often means that financial success comes to the unscrupulous speculator, another inferior sort of person. The Nazis claim that in their new state they will be able to put a stop to such a condition of affairs and restore the "natural" order of things by placing the true aristocrats at the top of the social, political, and economic ladder.

In claiming that political and economic control should rest in the hands of the "true" aristocrats, the Nazis emphasize that they have little use for the upper classes of old Imperial Germany. They believe that supreme power should lie with one man (the principle of leadership), but they are certain that this man should be neither a Habsburg nor a Hohenzollern.   It must not be forgotten that most of the Nazi leaders come from the lower middle class, and this class looked upon the old hereditary aristocracy with envy and dislike, feelings voiced by Hitler when he speaks of "the present-day decadence of our upper ten thousand." [51]   The Nazis claim that many of the old aristocrats are descended from men who secured their titles merely because they were fawning courtiers.   Moreover, the old aristocracy had no regard for eugenics and eugenic laws, married heiresses of biologically inferior stock and hence have degenerated.   In place of this old aristocracy, the Nazis are vociferous in demanding the creation of a new aristocracy, and Darre, one of the major figures in the Nazi movement, has written a special book on the subject, *Neuadel aus Blut und Boden*.   The new aristocracy is to be composed of the finest stock in the country irrespective of former social or economic position.   Normally this new aristocracy is to be hereditary, but titles are to be transmitted to children only if these children are bred in strict accord with eugenic laws.

The Nazis lay great emphasis upon the fourth doctrine in the eugenist creed, namely, that under present conditions the superior stocks are relatively infertile, and the inferior stocks relatively prolific.

> The less worthy multiply without restraint and are continually spreading their hereditary sufferings abroad. We see that from the fact that in Germany the average number of children amounts to 2.2 in the case of sound families; 3.5 in the case of weak-minded families; 4.9 in the case of criminal families. Thus the number of less worthy rose from 10 per 1,000 inhabitants in 1880 to 40 in 1930.   While the increase of the total population during this period ran to about 50 per cent, during this same period the less worthy increased by about 300 per cent, that is, six times faster than the whole population.[52]

The Nazis insist that there is a grave national peril in such a situation and that the state must use forceful measures to see that this process is reversed.   Hitler himself tells us that the state

> has to take care that only the healthy beget children. . . . The state has to appear as the guardian of a thousand years' future in the face of which the wish and the egoism of the individual appears as nothing and has to submit. . . . It has to declare unfit for propagation everybody who is visibly ill and has inherited a disease and it has to carry this out in practice.   On the other hand, it has to care that the fertility of the healthy woman is not limited by the financial mismanagement of a State régime which makes children a curse for the parents.   It has to do away with that foul, nay criminal, indifference with which today the social presumptions of a family with many children is treated. . . .[53]

The actions of the Nazis since they came into power show that to them eugenics is not a mere idle theory, but a fundamental principle which must be applied at all costs. It is certainly true that Nazi Germany has done more to carry out the program demanded by the eugenists than any other country. Among persons of sound stock, early marriage and large families are encouraged by direct financial support through government loans and through release from taxation. On the other hand, all couples intending to marry must submit to the registrar a certificate from a public health officer showing that they are not infected with any mental or bodily disease which would prevent their having healthy offspring. All doctors are bound to report cases of hereditary disease to the government and all persons who are found to be afflicted with such congenital ailments are prevented from reproducing themselves, either by being sterilized or by being castrated. Mental diseases as well as physical defects and deformities entail sterilization because of their hereditary character. The exact number of sterilizations already performed is not known; it is estimated at more than half a million and nearly three million additional persons are said to be earmarked for treatment.[54]

The Nazis have made the teachings of the Social Darwinists and of the eugenists an integral part of their ideology. Even so, both these creeds sink into insignificance compared with the emphasis laid upon the doctrines taken over from the racialist school. As Hitler himself says, "All that is not race in this world is trash." [55] In like manner Rosenberg informs us, "The idea of the genuine national state was born out of the concept of race. This idea is the final criterion of our judgment of all we do on earth." In other words, to the Nazis the teachings of Social Darwinism and eugenics are true, but they are of importance only because of the light they throw upon the important problem of race.

The Nazi theories regarding race have been taken over bodily from the teachings of such men as Gobineau, H. S. Chamberlain, and Hans Gunther, and as we are already familiar with these teachings it is unnecessary to give more than casual attention to the Nazi statements on the subject. The Nazis, like the earlier racialists, are thoroughly convinced that just as certain family stocks are innately superior to certain other family stocks, so are certain races innately and eternally superior to the other races. They are equally convinced that each race has not only its own physical characteristics, but also certain mental, emotional, and spiritual traits which are peculiar to itself. These two doctrines are the two foundation stones upon which the whole Nazi racial ideology has been erected. Rosenberg summarizes these two positions when he says:

The belief in the worth of Blood is the basic presupposition in the National Socialist philosophy of life. The essential meaning of this belief is that a definite creative soul, a definite type of character, a definite type of mentation is always associated with a definite racial type. It is not accident that the heroic figure of Siegfried is both a creation *of* German minds and a model *for* German minds, while the unscrupulous and deceiving Jacob is the ideal character of the Jews. . . . It is no accident that those who hold fast to honor are slender, tall, light-eyed, powerful men, while the descendants of Father Jacob are bent, flat-footed, dark, curly-locked figures.[56]

Hitler sums up his racial creed by saying:

In the blood alone there rests the strength as well as the weakness of man. As long as people do not recognize and pay attention to the importance of their racial foundations, they resemble people who would like to teach the greyhound qualities to poodles without realizing that the greyhound's speed and the poodle's docility are qualities which are not taught but are peculiar to the race. . . . Without the clearest recognition of the race problem there will be no rise of the German nation.[57]

Hitler is violently opposed to the idea that the mental and emotional characteristics of a race are the result of environment.

No matter how much the soil is able to influence the people, the result will always be a different one, according to the races under consideration. The scanty fertility of a living space may instigate one race towards the highest achievements, while with another race this may only become the cause for the most dire poverty. . . . The inner disposition of the peoples is always decisive for the way in which outward influences work themselves out. What leads one people to starvation, trains the other for hard work.[58]

Hitler, like the earlier racialists, is convinced that all culture and civilization is the product of a small number of gifted races, perhaps of a single race.

Everything that we admire on this earth — science and art, techniques and invention, is only the creative product of a few peoples, and perhaps originally of *one* race. On them now depends also the existence of this entire culture. If they perish, then the beauty of this earth sinks into the grave with them.[59]

Hitler then proceeds to show, to his own satisfaction, that neither the black nor the yellow races can be considered the creators of culture. In fact, to his mind the members of the black races can scarcely be considered human.

From time to time it is demonstrated to the German petty *bourgeois* in illustrated periodicals that for the first time here or there a negro has become a lawyer, teacher, even clergyman, or even a leading opera tenor. . . . While the stupid *bourgeoisie*, marvelling, takes cognizance of this miraculous training . . . the Jew knows very slyly how to construe from this a new proof of the correctness of his theory of the *equality of men* which he means to instill into the nations. It does not dawn upon this depraved *bourgeois* world that here one actually has to do with a sin against all reason; that it is a criminal absurdity to train a born half-ape until one believes a lawyer has been made of him, while millions of members of the highest culture race have to remain in entirely unworthy positions; that it is a sin against the will of the eternal Creator to let hundreds and hundreds of thousands of His most talented beings degenerate in the proletarian swamp of today while Hottentots and Zulu Kafirs are trained for intellectual vocations.... The same trouble and care, applied to the intelligent races, would fit each individual a thousand times better for the same achievements.[60]

The Nazis are all agreed that the yellow races (and their cousins, the members of the brown and red races) are considerably higher than the Negroes, for, whereas the Negroes are normally culture-destroying, the Asiatics are capable of adopting and preserving many phases of the highest culture. Nevertheless these Asiatics must be regarded as distinctly mediocre, as they seldom if ever display any genuine creative ability.

In a few decades the entire east of Asia will call a culture its own, the ultimate bases of which will be Hellenic spirit and German technique.... It is not the case, as some people claim, that Japan adds European techniques to her culture, but European science and techniques are trimmed with Japanese characteristics.... If, starting today, all further Aryan influence upon Japan should stop ... then a further development of Japan's present rise in science and technology could take place for a little while longer; but in the time of a few years the source would dry out. Japanese life would gain, but its culture would stiffen and fall back into the sleep out of which it was startled seven decades ago....[61]

Having surveyed the world, Hitler comes to the conclusion that it is only the white races which can be considered really superior or culture-creative groups. But even among the white races there are wide divergences. More especially, according to Hitler, is there fundamental distinction between the Semites, especially the Jews, and the Aryans. Hitler is insistent that the Jews constitute, not a religious or a cultural group, but a distinct race with mental and emotional characteristics peculiar to itself. The Jew, like the Asiatic, "was never in possession of a culture of his own, the bases for his spiritual activity having been furnished by others." [62] The Jew, moreover, because of his racial background, is thoroughly egoistic and materialistic. All these qualities are innate, and it is useless to try to change them through education or religious conversion. The Semites being thus eliminated from the ranks of

the culture-creative peoples, it follows that the race which is really important and really superior is the so-called Aryan race.

> What we see before us of human culture today, the results of art, science,
> and techniques, is almost exclusively the creative product of the Aryan.   But
> just this fact admits of the not unfounded conclusion that he alone was the
> founder of higher humanity as a whole. . . . He is the Prometheus of mankind,
> out of whose bright forehead springs the divine spark of genius at all times. . . .
> Exclude him, and deep darkness will again fall upon the earth, perhaps even,
> after a few thousand years, human culture would perish and the world would
> turn into a desert.[63]

While willing to admit that all branches of the Aryan race constitute a
superior group, Hitler is nevertheless insistent that the purest Aryan
stock is to be found in Germany; hence the Germans are, racially speaking, the finest group anywhere in the world.   The Latin peoples to him
are indeed Aryan, but their Aryanism has been corrupted by intermixture with Semitic and Negro stocks.   In like manner the Slavs, originally
an Aryan people, have been polluted by intermarriage with Asiatics.

It is typical of Hitler, with his educational background, that he, like
some of the earlier racialists, persists in confusing racial and linguistic
terms.   As we know, the words Semitic and Aryan, properly speaking,
apply only to certain language families, and it is a great pity that Hitler
constantly makes use of such words in a racial sense.   It must be admitted, however, that the Nazi racial ideology is not entirely dependent upon
this confusion of racial and linguistic terms, for if Hitler himself is rather
vague about the meaning of the word "race," some of his co-leaders are
much more precise about such matters.   Rosenberg, for example, and
the authors of the semi-official *Nazi Primer* are well acquainted with all
the jargon of modern anthropology, and such persons are much more
careful in their use of terms.   In place of ambiguous words, as Semites
and Aryans, they use such justifiable words as Nordic, Alpine, Mediterranean, Dinarian, Armenoid, etc.   It seems highly probable that such
racial types do really exist.   The only point on which orthodox anthropologists disagree with the Nazis is whether or not these various body
types are associated with peculiar mental or emotional characteristics.

Whereas Hitler, like Count Gobineau, glorifies the Aryan race without
telling us what this race looks like, Rosenberg, as most of the later
racialists, glorifies the Nordic race, the members of which are tall, slender, long-headed, blond, blue-eyed.   Rosenberg would, of course, justify
the Fuehrer's use of the word Aryan on the grounds that whereas many
different races have learned to speak Aryan languages, the original

Aryan tongue was developed among the members of the Nordic race, and that it was Nordic conquests which resulted in the Aryanization of the rest of the world. There is, incidentally, one phase of Rosenberg's Nordic doctrine that appears to be peculiar to himself. Most racialists admit ignorance as to where the Nordic race originally evolved, but Rosenberg tells us that it probably came from the now submerged continent of Atlantis.

Even the most violent Nazis are willing to admit that racial mixture has taken place for so long that pure races scarcely exist today. Even Germany has many different races within its boundaries. They soon add, however:

> One thing does distinguish peoples from each other...: the proportion of the races is different. Many peoples in Europe have preserved above all the Nordic character, others the Western [i.e., Mediterranean] or Eastern [i.e., Alpine] or East Baltic, and so forth.[64]

According to this view Germany is great because "the principal ingredient of our people is the Nordic race," [65] and the Nordic race is

> uncommonly gifted mentally...is outstanding for truthfulness and energy....Nordic men possess a great power of judgment....They are persistent and stick to a purpose....They are predisposed to leadership by nature.[66]

France, on the other hand, is to be regarded as decadent because the Nordic element so prominent in earlier times has now largely died out. Present-day France is now predominantly Alpine, and the members of the Alpine or Eastern race

> are unwarlike. They incline to craftiness. They lack the spirit of rulers. ... They are compliant and submissive subjects. The Eastern race is always the led, never the leader. Its capacity for holding together seldom stands out.[67] [Small wonder that] petty shop keepers, lawyers, speculators have become the leaders of public life. Democracy prevails; that means, not the rulership of character, but the rulership of gold.... For this reason the Jewish banker is able to push himself into the foreground, then the Jewish journalist and Marxist.... In the south of France large areas have become depopulated and are being replenished by Africans.... Toulon and Marseilles are constantly sending germs of bastardization into the heart of the country. Even around Notre Dame in Paris there flows a population which is ever more degenerate. Negroes and mulattoes go arm in arm with white women, a new Jewish suburb arises.... [In France] we experience at the present time the same development which once took place in Athens and Rome.[68]

According to the Nazis, the future of Russia is equally hopeless because of its racial composition. At one time Russia possessed a considerable

Nordic element and thus was able to accomplish great things. But this element has now greatly diminished. The East Baltic race is now predominant, and the East Baltic men

> are no leaders by nature, but need leadership. They, in contrast to the Nordic man, are without a real power of decision in conflicts of conscience, and so they are always cautious, never resolute. Their power of imagination is roving, unsteady.[69]

Worse still, there is now a large Mongoloid element in the Russian population, and this element has profoundly affected the character of the whole Russian people.

> Bolshevism is the revolt of the Mongoloid against Nordic culture forms, it is a longing for the steppe; it is the hate of the nomad against the roots of personality; it is the attempt to shake off Europe completely.[70]

There is one phase of Nazi racial ideology which is likely to have important political consequences in the near future, more especially if Germany is able to win a sweeping victory in the present world war. This phase is the violent diatribe against all forms of racial mixture. On this point the Nazis go far beyond the earlier racialists. Gobineau, the founder of modern racialism, did indeed preach that a large or constant admixture of alien blood produces racial degeneration, but he also taught that a slight mixture of races is usually productive of much good. In like manner, H. S. Chamberlain, another high priest of racialism, taught that a certain amount of racial blending — at least between "superior races" — is helpful rather than harmful. Hitler, on the other hand, believes in complete and absolute "racial purity." To his mind, for one race to breed with another race is contrary to the laws of Nature and the laws of God.

> ... peoples which bastardize themselves or permit themselves to be bastardized sin against the will of eternal Providence, and their ruin by the hand of a stronger nation is consequently not an injustice that is done them, but only the restoration of right.[71]

Hitler bitterly regrets the fact that even in Germany there are representatives of various racial types. Because "our basic racial types remain unblended ... the German people lacks that sure herd instinct which is rooted in the unity of the blood." [72]

This doctrine has very important consequences for the millions of German citizens who do not happen to belong to the so-called Nordic stock. Up to the present time the Nazi government has been so busy eliminating the Jewish element inside Germany that it has had no time to deal with the problem of the other "inferior," i.e., non-Nordic races. But the Nazis are definitely pledged to a program which calls for the "re-Nordicizing" of Germany, and it may well be that in the future some of the minor racial groups in Germany, such as the Alpines, will be subjected to some of the same discriminatory legislation which has been meted out to the Jews in the past few years. It is interesting to note here that Hitler himself appears to be a very typical representative of the Alpine race.

Even more important is the effect which the doctrine of racial purity is likely to have upon the territories and populations which are conquered by the Nazi sword. It is almost certain that the Nazis will try to establish a sort of caste system between the German rulers and the conquered peoples. "The stronger has to rule and he is not to amalgamate with the weaker one lest he sacrifice his own greatness." [73] Even more startling is the definite possibility that the Nazis may embark upon a program calling for the wholesale slaughter of populations dwelling in lands needed for German colonization. Some of the old pre-war Nationalists were in favor of the forcible Germanization of the non-German minorities within the empire, a policy which would have imposed the German language and culture upon such groups as the Czechs and Poles. Hitler tells us that he is violently opposed to this policy. He is certain that

> Germanization can only be carried out with the *soil* and never with *men*. For what one generally understood [by Germanization] was only the enforced outward acceptance of the German language. But it is a hardly conceivable mistake in thinking to believe that... a negro or a Chinese would become a German because he learns German and is prepared to speak the German language in the future and perhaps to give his vote to a German political party.... As the nationality, or rather the race, is not rooted in the language but in the blood, one could be permitted to speak of a Germanization only if one could succeed in changing, by such a procedure, the blood of the subjugated. But this is impossible.... What in history has been profitably Germanized was the soil which our forefathers acquired through the sword and settled with German peasants. [74]

Again and again Hitler tells us that Germany is too small; that she needs territorial expansion, more especially territorial expansion on the continent of Europe. Needless to say, the territory to be acquired must be "Germanized." We now know what the process of Germanization requires.

THE NAZIS AND ETATISM

After our survey of the more theoretical aspects of the Nazi ideology, we can now turn to a discussion of its more practical phases, especially tc its treatment of governmental matters.

In the first place, it must be noted that, though there is a close similarity on most points between the doctrines of Italian Fascism and German National Socialism, there is a profound and fundamental cleavage between the two schools of thought on the nature and the function of the state. To the Fascists the state is directly and of itself the supreme unit in human existence. To them the state is an end in itself and not the means to an end. To them the state is not only more important than the individual, it is also more important than the so-called nation, for in Fascist ideology it is not the nation which creates the state, but rather the state which creates the nation. As Mussolini himself tells us:

> It is not the nation which generates the state; that is an antiquated naturalistic concept which affords a basis for nineteenth century publicity in favor of national governments. Rather it is the state which creates the nation, conferring volition and therefore real life on a people made aware of their moral unity.[75]

To the Nazis, on the other hand, the supreme unit is the *Volk*, a term which we must translate "nation," though it implies a certain racial homogeneity, which is usually absent in the English or American use of the word. To the Nazis the *Volk*, or nation, is not only more important than the individual, it is also more important than the state. At its best the state is only an organ or legal agent of the nation, but not infrequently the state betrays its trust and looks after its own interests or after the interests of some particular class within the state rather than after the welfare of the nation as a whole. In such a circumstance it is the duty of the citizens to arise and destroy the state. As Rosenberg tells us, National Socialism

> places nation or race higher than the state in its various forms. It declares that the protection of the nation is more important than the protection of a religious creed, a class, a monarchy or a republic. It sees in the betrayal of a nation a more serious crime than so-called treason against the state.[76]

Hitler expresses the same idea when he says:

> It should never be forgotten that not the preservation of a state or a government is the highest aim of human existence, but the preservation of its kind [i.e., of its own species]. . . . The state represents not an end but a means. . .

We must sharply distinguish between the state as a vessel and the race as the content. This vessel has meaning only if it is able to preserve and protect the contents.[77]

But great as is the difference between the Fascist and the Nazi ideas regarding the importance of the state, this difference is soon seen to be more on the surface than underneath. The Nazi attack of the state is directed against the "false" state, the legalistic state, the state which is separate from and in opposition to the *Volk* or nation. Once a "true" state has been founded, a state which is a *Volksstaat* or nation-state, a state which is merely the executive organ of the nation, it must not only be obeyed but worshiped. Nazi attacks on the state all date back to the period when the Nazi Party was in violent opposition to the government set up by the Weimar Constitution. Once they came into power they asserted that the true nation-state had been inaugurated and hence was to have supreme and absolute power over all its citizens. In point of fact, in all the Nazi writings which have appeared since 1933, the state has been eulogized almost as much as in Fascist utterances. We must not forget that Mussolini's conversion to state-worship also took place after the triumphal march on Rome.

In any case the Nazis, both before and after their accession to power, are unanimously agreed that the individual counts for nothing, that the individual must always be subordinated to and sacrificed for the community, the nation, and the nation-state, should such an entity be in existence. The chief motto or slogan of the Nazis, a slogan which is repeated in nearly every article and speech, is "*Gemeinnutz vor Eigennutz*," which can be translated either "common interest before self-interest," or, "the welfare of the community is more important than the welfare of the individual." In this connection we must not forget that the basis of all virtue, of all idealism, is said by the Nazis to consist in the willingness of the individual to sacrifice himself for the group of which he forms a part, that goodness itself is defined as that which serves the interest of Germany and the German people as a whole. In case the individual does not subordinate himself voluntarily, he must be compelled to do so. "There is no liberty to sin at the expense of posterity, and with it the race.... The right of personal freedom steps back in the face of the duty of the preservation of the race." [78]

It is not surprising to find the Nazis teaching that the welfare of the individual must be subordinated to the welfare of the nation. What is surprising is that the Nazi ideologists teach, and the German citizens believe, that if and when the individual subordinates himself to the nation, he becomes really "free" for the first time.   The Nazis use a large number of arguments to prove this point.   In the first place, they say that a man can be free only if he is the citizen of a nation which is free, that is, not in bondage to other states.   Thus a German citizen can be really free only if Germany is not held down by other nations But a nation (for example, Germany) can only secure and preserve its freedom if the individual citizens subordinate their selfish interests to the national interest.   Another argument used is that based upon the definition of freedom given by Kant: a man is really free only if and when he is able to do and does the *right* thing, the thing which he ought to do; he is free only when he follows the dictates of his "free moral will" and not the dictates of his whims, caprices, and desires.   The Nazis use this type of argument when they claim that their rigorous press laws are merely means to "free" the press from the pollutions and corruptions brought in by Jews, Marxists, and other degenerate persons. Finally, we may note that the Nazis make frequent use of the type of argument first brought in by Hegel and his followers.   The Hegelians, it will be remembered, not only distinguished between the "apparent," the "actual," and the "subjective" will, on the one hand (i.e., the dictates of the wishes and desires), and the "real" or "objective" will, on the other (i.e., the dictates of the "free moral will"), but they also claimed that the commands of the state are really the commands of the "real, objective" will of each individual.   Thus the individual is truly free only when he disregards his private whims and passions and blindly obeys the dictates of his own "objective" will as embodied in the commands of the nation-state.

Not only are the Nazis radical, thoroughgoing etatists (even though the state they worship is the nation-state); but they, like the Fascists, are firm believers in totalitarianism — the doctrine that the state should dominate each and every phase of the citizen's activity and not merely the phase which is ordinarily called political.   If we bear in mind Mussolini's statement of the totalitarian principle, "All is in the state and for the state; nothing outside the state, nothing against the state," we may say that this same principle applies equally to the Nazi theory of government, once we change the term state to nation-state. We may even say that Nazi Germany is more zealous in its acceptance of totalitarianism than Fascist Italy.   This is partly because of the fact that the Nazis are more thoroughgoing in their acceptance of irrationalism than are the Fascists.

By the official acceptance of Roman Catholicism, the Fascists have been forced into an alliance with an organization which is essentially international in character. To the Catholic Church certain religious dogmas, certain philosophical doctrines, certain scientific laws, certain moral commandments are universally and absolutely true, applying to all nations and to all persons irrespective of their race or their nationality. In like manner the Catholic theologians insist that there is a body of "natural law" separate from and higher than the positive laws enforced in any one state; these same theologians insist, moreover, that for state-made laws to be valid or binding upon the citizens, they must be in general accord with the higher natural laws. All these ideas are in direct opposition to totalitarian principles and hence are very irritating to the Fascists, but as long as the vast majority of the Italians are pious and orthodox Catholics, and as long as the Fascist regime officially supports the Catholic Church and Catholic dogma, it is impossible for the Fascist leaders openly to deny such concepts and insist that the state must be supreme in these as in other fields.

On this point the Nazis have the advantage. Although Hitler himself is a nominal Catholic, and although Catholicism is accepted by a considerable portion of the German population, Catholicism has not the same hold upon Germany that it has upon Italy. For this reason the Nazis have been able to direct open attacks upon absolutism and internationalism in all fields, including the fields of ethics, of law, of science, and even of religion itself. If Nazi irrationalism is right and there is no universal science but only a group of sciences, each one rooted in a particular race or nation, then it follows that the nation-state has the right to determine what the content of its own national science shall be and also how the science can best be cultivated. As there are no eternal, objective truths but only a series of subjective truths, or rather national approximations to truth, it follows that it is the duty of the German nation-state to determine whether such Jewish formulations of truth as Einstein's theory of relativity shall or shall not form part of the German scientific outlook. As with the so-called facts and laws of science, so is it with the concepts of philosophy and the doctrines of religion.

If Nazi irrationalism is right and there is no eternal objective standard of what is morally right or wrong but only a series of racial or national codes, then it is obviously the duty of the German nation-state to determine what the German code of morality shall be, and it is the duty of the German nation-state to see that the German citizens follow the precepts of this code and not the dictates of individual caprice (the so-called individual conscience) or of some would-be international code,

such as that laid down by the Catholic Church.   What is true in the
field of ethics must be equally if not more true in the field of law.   If
Nazi irrationalism is true, it is obvious that there can be no such thing
as natural law or a law of reason applicable to all peoples and all nations.   To say that the civil law or statutes of any one state must conform with the dictates of the universal rational law is ridiculous.   The
concept of what is legally right and wrong is just as subjective and as
national in character as the concept of what is morally right and wrong.
"Law is as little a bloodless scheme as Religion, or Art; it is always intimately linked with a certain type of Blood [i.e., Race]." [79]   If law, like
morals, is only an expression of the soul of a nation, then it is for the
nation-state, the concrete embodiment of this soul, to determine the
content of this law without reference to any outside authority.

The Nazis believe that it is necessary to apply the totalitarian principle to the fields of art, literature, drama, music, and architecture.   To
the liberals, art and literature have, for the most part, nothing to do
with politics, and as long as artists and writers are neither criminally
libelous nor criminally obscene, it is the duty of the state and of the
government to leave them strictly alone.   To the liberals, it is certainly
not the duty of the state to tell artists whether they shall be classicists
or modernists, to tell writers that they must, under pain of punishment,
be realists or romanticists.   To the Nazis all these liberal notions are
ridiculous.   According to the Nazi philosophy, there is not only a national standard of what is good and bad, but also a national standard of
what is beautiful and ugly.   It is the duty, therefore, of the nation-state
to make clear to the individual citizens just what this national standard
is and to force these citizens to follow this standard in all their attempts
at artistic creation.

The Nazis tell us that in the new German state there must be a

> strong internal unity between state and culture.   This condition finds its
> outer expression in the fact that the spiritual life of the people, as it reveals
> itself in cults, myths, and art, must in a certain definite way receive, as its
> highest guiding laws, directive ideas, the right of formulation of which has
> been transferred to political bodies and the leaders.... For the National
> Socialist state, culture is an affair of the nation, it is a means for spiritual
> leadership and required to be positively manipulated in order that all may
> be educated to a sense of responsibility, which promotes the shaping of the
> nation.... [80]   Art and civilization are implanted in the mother soil of the
> nation.   They are consequently forever dependent on the moral, social, and
> national principles of the state. [81]

On the ground that the German soul must not be polluted by contacts with the product of Jewish culture, the Nazis demand that the poems of Heinrich Heine be consigned to the flames and that performances of Mendelssohn's "Jewish" music be prohibited. In like manner Hitler proclaims that modern art must be abolished on the ground that it is alien to the German national consciousness, that it has been invented by Jews for the exploiting of stupid people. "It is an affair of the state — that means of the government — to prevent a people from being driven into the arms of spiritual lunacy." [82] As a result of this policy the Nazis demand that all modernistic paintings be withdrawn from public exhibition. As with art, so with literature. The state must especially concern itself with newspapers and magazines, as it is these, more than books, which influence the broad mass of the people. The state, Hitler tells us, must not be led astray by the will-of-the-wisp of "so-called freedom of the press. What the liberal press did was to dig a grave for the German Nation and the German Reich." It is the duty of the state, by using the press, "to put before the nation the food that it needs and is good for it." [83] This whole position is summarized in the original program of the Nazi Party, "We demand the legal prosecution of all tendencies in art and literature of a kind calculated to disintegrate our national life."

In short, the totalitarian principle inherent in the Nazi ideology demands that all phases of cultural life, whether scientific or religious, whether literary, artistic, or musical, must be inspired and guided by the nation-state. Since coming into power the Nazis have exerted every effort to apply this principle throughout the length and breadth of Germany. Lack of space prevents our mentioning more than two or three outstanding developments along this line, but our understanding of National Socialism would be woefully incomplete without brief mention of the Nazi effort to curb and control the churches, its institution of the National Chamber of Culture, and its radical reorganization of the German system of education.

In its attempt to bring the churches within the scope of the totalitarian state, the Nazis have been forced to treat the Catholics and the Protestants in quite different fashions. Although Catholics constitute only a minority of the German-speaking population, the Catholic Church is very strong and well-organized, and has a very firm hold over most of its laity (even though this hold is weaker than over the Italian laity). It has, moreover, a long and jealously guarded tradition of independence from secular control. As a result the Nazis have felt it necessary to treat the Catholic Church with comparative caution. In

1933 Hitler even signed a concordat with the pope, whereby the pope promised to stop the political activity of all priests and members of religious orders, and in return the Nazis promised freedom of private and public worship, guaranteed religious instruction in all schools, and the establishment of confessional Catholic schools when demanded by the parents.   Finally, it was agreed that the Catholic organizations for purely religious and cultural purposes should function without hindrance.   In the years which followed, however, the Nazi regime has spared no effort to undermine the position of the Catholic Church as an independent institution.

> There is scarcely any provision in favor of the church as laid down in the Concordat which the regime has not violated by its subsequent policies. Catholic Youth organizations, even of non-political character, were suppressed. By the law on the Hitler Youth the state and the party usurped the educational monopoly. In 1937 the regime began to wage a "white" war against Catholicism by the persecution of individual priests and wholesale judicial terror. Scandalous trials were staged against scores of priests, lay officers and members of the congregations for currency violations and moral turpitude. These trials, widely exploited by the regime in order to stir up resentment against the Church, sent hundreds of priests to prison and concentration camps. . . . Lately restrictive measures of the regime have been intensified and an inventory of the entire Church property ordered — an ominous sign after the anti-Semitic precedent.[84]

The Nazi attempt to subordinate and control the various Protestant bodies has been even more vigorous and more direct.   Incidentally it has also been more successful because of the peculiar nature of Protestantism in Germany.   Most German Protestants are followers of Luther, and Luther, it will be remembered, was a firm believer in the sanctity of the secular authority and in the supremacy of the secular authority over all religious organizations.   To Luther, the head of the temporal state should also be head of "the church visible" and should have control over all its activities.   Equally important is the fact that the Protestant bodies lost much of their hold over the laity in the century before the coming of National Socialism.   While the Catholics continued to believe in all their dogmas and in the infallibility of both the Bible and the church, many of the Lutherans, influenced by the "higher criticism," rejected the infallibility even of the Bible and were distinctly skeptical of many of the old, traditional church doctrines.   For all these reasons the Protestant churches in Germany were far weaker than was the Catholic Church and were far more susceptible to a frontal attack.   Under the auspices of the National Socialists the twenty-eight Protestant church organizations, which formerly had been grouped together in the form of a loose federation, were united to form a single German Evangelical Church, governed by a single Reichs bishop. The new bishop, Ludwig Mueller, was an intimate friend of Hitler's, and proved himself more than willing to carry out the Nazi program of subordinating the church to the state and to the Nazi Party. Moreover, by clever manipulation, the pro-Nazi group within the church managed to secure a majority in the National Church Synod, with the result that the Nazification of the united Protestant Church could go forward without encountering serious obstacles. There was indeed a small minority of pastors who protested against the policies and the aims of the Nazi regime on the ground that Nazi racialism was contrary to Christian humanitarianism, but this minority was never able to cause the new regime any serious trouble. The more vociferous opponents of the Nazi creed have been placed in concentration camps. In other cases dissident pastors have been deprived of their salaries, forbidden to preach, to use church property, or to publish their opinions. At present only a handful of the ministers continue to fight against the totalitarian state.

In this connection it is important to bear in mind that the Nazi state has been able to win complete control over the spiritual activities of many of its citizens not merely by the legal shackling of the ecclesiastical organizations, but also by the subtler means of undermining the popular acceptance of old forms of religion. As the result of incessant propaganda, the majority of German youth today is growing up in the belief that the state is more important than any church, that devotion to the nation is more essential than devotion to any creed. Hitler himself has been very cautious in his statements on the subject of religion, but he has given free rein to his followers to confess the anti-ecclesiastical bias of the Nazi Party. Thus, in an official publication of the National Socialist Movement,[85] we find it stated: "It is said that the body belongs to the state and the soul to the church or to God. This is no longer the case. The whole man belongs body and soul to the German nation and to the German state. The latter has taken also matters of faith under its own control." Rosenberg in a radio speech [86] tells us:

> Only those religions which do not contradict Teutonic values can be recognized and defended. When a National Socialist dons his brown shirt and becomes a soldier of Hitler, his religion is his faith in his Leader. We National Socialists must refuse to allow German history and Teutonic majesty to be subordinated to so-called religion.

Some of the minor Nazi leaders are even more outspoken in their attacks on orthodox religion. Thus Spaniol [87] declares:

I do not believe that the churches will continue to exist in their present form. In the future religion will be called National Socialism. Its prophet, its pope, its Jesus Christ will be called Adolf Hitler.

Knauth [88] informs us:

Christianity is the remnant of an outdated and dying culture and it is therefore a major obstacle in the evolution of the new millennium. It must be eliminated and in its place must come a belief in a non-confessional God, whose essence lies in the state.   Christianity as the first international doctrine must be held responsible for Bolshevism, the caretaker of a dying millennium. Its task has been to equalize all human beings without regard to race or blood When the whole national life has been reconstructed, when politics, economics culture, have been developed anew, the religious life in Germany can no longer be dominated by a Jewish Bible.

It was comparatively easy for the Nazis to secure complete control of all scientific activity in Germany through manipulation and "reform" of the various educational and learned institutions scattered throughout the country.   The number of privately run schools and museums in Germany has always been very small.   But prior to the Nazi regime most such institutions were controlled by the "lands" or separate states, thus securing a fair amount of decentralization in administrative control. Under the Nazi regime all this has been changed.   Those few private schools which existed have been abolished, thus getting rid of the confessional private institutions in which the teaching of devotion to the state was not made the center of educational activity.   Equally important is the fact that local jurisdiction in school affairs has been done away with; all schools and other learned institutions are placed directly and completely under the central government.   Needless to say that the Nazi Minister of Education is a fanatical party member whose main mission in life is to imbue all students, teachers, and even research men with the Nazi ideology.

We are officially told that "the chief task of all schools is the education of youth to the service of the nation and the state in the spirit of National Socialism." [89]   In contrast with the old liberal theory of education, which, it is claimed, was concerned only with the training of the mind. the Nazi educational system lays especial emphasis upon the development of the body and of character.   "The whole man must be so formed as to create the type which the Leader demands as a guarantee for the future of his work." [90]   In order to carry out this program, thousands of students and teachers, who were Jews or who seemed to be tinged with pacifist, socialist, or even liberal views, were driven from their posts. Those who remain are repeatedly warned that academic freedom is at an end and that they must embrace and inculcate the Nazi philosophy with its theory of the totalitarian state.

> All education must today be political education, in order to safeguard the life of the community and therewith the life of the individual. And all learning must fulfil the unqualified goal of education in co-operation with the political function.

And again:

> Absolute academic freedom in universities is absolute nonsense. . . . The university is itself an organ of the whole and therefore has its being, like every other organ, directly in the name of and by right of the whole. Consequently, the whole, represented in the State, must see to it that no self-governing member separates itself from the totality, from the sworn goal of racial unity and *Weltanschauung* [outlook on life].[91]

Although the Nazis speak of the universities as being "self-governing bodies," we must remember that the appointment, promotion, and dismissal of all faculty members rests, not with the universities themselves, but with the Ministry of Education in Berlin. In the old days the "rector" or president of each university was elected by the members of its own faculty. Under the Nazi regime the rector is appointed by the Minister of Education "and is responsible to him alone" for all his actions. In the old days it was the faculty which decided most points of academic policy and procedure. Today all such matters are decided by the rector himself, acting on orders from Berlin. Immediately under the rector in each university are two newly created posts, the leader of the faculty and the leader of the students. Both these posts are filled by the Minister of Education on the joint recommendation of the rector and of the leader of the local National Socialist Faculty League and of the local National Socialist Student League, respectively. In other words, the universities are subordinated not only to the state but also to the party organization. The Nazis have deliberately restricted the number of persons permitted to enter the universities and other higher educational institutions, in order not to create "an academic pro letariat." In practice this means that only boys who are strongly pro-Nazi in their sympathies are allowed to matriculate. There are numerous scholarships for the benefit of poor students, but the vast majority of such scholarships are reserved for children who have been active members of some party organization. For those persons who are unfortunate enough to be Jews in "race" or liberals in politics, education necessarily ends at high-school age. The professions are closed to them.

Needless to say, the curriculum in all German schools, from the lowest to the highest grades, has undergone complete transformation. All schools have been ordered to lay especial emphasis upon the "science of heredity" and of "race," that is, to the teachings of the eugenists and the racialists, so that the detailed study of such subjects has been made obligatory in practically all academic institutions. By governmental decree, all schools are required to make constant and frequent use of such works as Hitler's *Mein Kampf*, Rosenberg's *Myth of the Twentieth Century*, and Gunther's *Anthropology of the German Nation*. In addition, the higher schools have been forced to institute a number of courses dealing with military science and with "geo-politics," a Nazified version of political and economic geography. Even the courses and the textbooks dealing with the ordinary subjects have been completely transformed to make them serviceable to Nazi propaganda. History, for example, is no longer regarded as a matter of objective fact, but merely a means for instilling German patriotism. A similar twist is given to the teachings of the other social sciences, and even the physical sciences are so taught as to permit of frequent reference to Nazi principles.

In addition to the formal school system, the Nazis make use of the various youth organizations to instill Nazi propaganda among the rising generation. Strong pressure is placed upon all boys and girls to join strongly nationalized and strongly militarized versions of what we should call the Boy and Girl Scout movement. At the age of ten little boys are drafted into the Young Folk, at the age of fourteen into the Hitler Youth, and there are corresponding organizations for girls. In both the Young Folk and the Hitler Youth the boys are taught gymnastic and military drill, are educated to lead a Spartan life of discipline, obedience, and self-sacrifice, so that they may prove worthy soldiers in after life. They are drilled by party officials in the slogans and tenets of National Socialism, are taught adulation of the leader and other party heroes, and urged to place "service to the nation" above all individual or even family considerations. In this connection it is interesting to note that one outstanding result of the Hitler Youth movement has been the weakening of the old family ties which were once so strong in Germany. "The lives of all German youths belong solely to Hitler," shouts Von Shirach, the leader of the Hitler Youth, and more and more this slogan is being applied in everyday life. The average boy has so much of his time, his interest, and his attention directed towards the activities of the state-controlled youth organization that he has no time and no energy left for activities which center in the home.

It should be added that the state and party controls extend, not only over the schools and the youth organizations which aim at shaping the minds of persons of student age, but also over the various academies, learned institutes, and learned societies which serve to coordinate the intellectual activities of professional scholars. The German Archaeological Institute sees to it that research in archaeology is made to serve Nazi ends. The German Historical Commission sees to it that only those learned monographs on historical problems are published which fit in with what the Nazi regime thinks history should be. In a word, no phase of German intellectual life is left which has not been commandeered into service for the state.

As with the intellectual, so with the literary and artistic phases of German life. As the official Nazi sources put it:

> The totalitarian state does not recognize the separate existence of art — it rejects the idea of art for art's sake. It demands that artists take a positive position towards the state, towards the German nation. towards the German cultural heritage.[92]

A Nazi law specifically states that

> it is the business of the State to combat injurious influences and encourage those that are valuable, actuated by a sense of responsibility for the wellbeing of the community.... All creative forces in all spheres must be assembled under Reich leadership with a view to the uniform moulding of the will.[93]

In order to secure this object, the Nazis have set about the complete suppression of books, newspapers, works of art, and musical compositions which do not meet with their approval, even when such books, newspapers, works of art, or musical compositions have nothing whatever to do with politics. Incidentally this suppression applies, not merely to contemporary creations, but also to earlier works. Thus, in 1933, shortly after coming to power, the Nazis instituted a series of public bonfires in which the writings of authors displeasing to the party leaders were consigned to the flames. In Berlin alone twenty thousand books were burned, including the works of such popular German authors as Sigmund Freud, Emil Ludwig, Eric Remarque, and Thomas Mann. Nor were the works of foreign authors spared. The works of such French writers as Émile Zola, André Gide, and Marcel Proust; of such English authors as Havelock Ellis and H. G. Wells; of such American authors as Helen Keller and Jack London were among those committed to the flames. The copies of all such works which were not burned are kept under lock and key in a few special libraries and are not available to the ordinary citizen. Needless to say, any bookseller who attempts to sell such books is instantly punished.

The Nazis are even more rigid in the control they exercise over contemporary creations in the literary, artistic, and musical worlds. Special efforts are made to control and regiment the press, the theater, the cinema, and the radio because of their wide popular appeal. In order to carry through their program of "totalitarian coordination" in all fields of cultural activity, the Nazis have created what is called the national chamber of culture. This in turn is divided into seven subordinate chambers, namely, literature, press, radio, cinema, theater, music, art, all of them subject to the Minister of Propaganda and Public Enlightenment. A special statute provides that any person who participates in the production, reproduction, or the distribution of cultural goods must be a member in good standing of one or other of the seven branches of the national chamber of culture, and if any person loses his membership through "professional misconduct," which means any activity displeasing to the Nazi regime, he is barred from his profession and is exposed to what is very appropriately called "professional death," because in most cases expulsion means starvation.

In each of the seven divisions there has been a ruthless "purge of undesirables" and a rigid "unification of outlook." Let us take, for example, the newspaper world. No person may serve either as an editor or a journalist unless he is a member of the press division of the chamber of culture. For a person to be entered on the official list of eligible persons he must be an "Aryan," nor can he be married to any person of non-Aryan descent. Moreover, all editors and journalists, because of the influence which they exert upon public opinion, must be regarded as public officials and their functions as a public task. Hence it is necessary that they possess "special spiritual qualities," lest they be unable to live up to their heavy duties and responsibilities. For this reason the press division must be extremely careful whom it admits to official membership. If any person offends the honor and dignity of the German nation, if he is guilty of "weakening the strength of Germany internally or externally," if he "confuses selfish private interests with the common interest," in other words, if he says or writes or publishes anything contrary to the tenets of Nazidom, he must be struck off the rolls. Normally offenders are tried before a professional court whose members are nominated by the Minister of Propaganda, but to obviate any trouble which might arise in dependence on this routine, both the Minister of Propaganda and his subordinate, the head of the press division, are given the right to dismiss any editor or journalist at any time and without assigning any reason. Because of these regulations it is small wonder that

German newspaper editors quickly suppress any news or the expression of any views which might be displeasing to the government. Nor is it in any way surprising that all the key positions in the daily press are now held by trusted party members.

As with the editors and journalists, so with the authors and publishers of books, actors and theatrical directors and producers both of the legitimate stage and of the cinema, composers and musicians, painters and sculptors, the writers of radio scripts and radio announcers. Such persons have to be registered with the chamber of culture and are liable to have their registration cancelled if at any time they do anything either publicly or privately which meets with the disapproval of the state and party officials.

The Nazi state is certainly totalitarian in the sense that it controls the religious, the intellectual, and the cultural life of its citizens. It is also totalitarian in the sense that it demands and secures complete control over every phase of economic activity. In this connection it must be emphasized that one of the most fundamental and most important features of the Nazi creed is the doctrine that economic considerations are inferior to and must be subordinated to political considerations; that most so-called economic laws are completely false, and that even when such laws have relative validity, they may at any time be superseded by political laws, made and enforced by the state. This doctrine is, of course, in marked contrast to the old liberal creed. To the liberals, economic laws, such as the law of supply and demand, have an eternal objective existence, and any attempt on the part of the state, with its man-made statutes, to interfere with these laws is bound to end in disaster. To the liberals, at least to the old-school liberals, it is the law of supply and demand which really regulates the price of commodities and the wages of laborers, and any effort on the part of the state to regulate prices or wages is foolish, because it is bound to be ineffective. To the Nazis all such notions are anathema. According to them it is possible for the state not only to increase and decrease supply, but also by force and by propaganda to increase or decrease demand for a certain article or for a certain type of labor, and it is the duty of the state to see to it that both supply and demand be so regulated as to conform with the best interests of the nation (*das Volk*).

The Nazis do, indeed, tell us that they are firm believers in the principle and sanctity of private property. They are violent in their opposition to communism and to all those forms of socialism which advocate state ownership and operation of the means of distribution or of production. But in marked contrast with the old liberal creed, they insist that property can only be acquired and held subject to certain definite conditions, and it is for the state to say just what these conditions shall be. The Nazis have, in fact, taken over almost in its entirety Fichte's theory of the nature and function of property. Both Fichte and the Nazis claim that the ownership of property is really the stewardship or the trusteeship of property. According to this theory, ownership means the right to the exclusive use of a certain object, but as soon as a person abuses or misuses this object, his trusteeship over it may and should be taken away. The Nazis, like Fichte, declare that it is the duty of the state to provide employment and a subsistence wage to all persons able and willing to work, and the Nazis, like Fichte, claim that this can be done only if the state supervises and regulates all possible forms of economic activity. The Nazi economic policy, like that of Fichte, is based upon the private ownership (i.e., trusteeship) and the private operation of all trade and industry, but on the condition that this private ownership and operation shall, at all times, be subject to state guidance and control.

In order to facilitate political control over the economic forces and economic activities inside Germany, the Nazi regime has created a number of so-called "estates." These estates appear, in some respects, to be a revival of the old mediaeval guilds. Even closer is the resemblance between these estates and the syndicates and corporations of Fascist Italy. There are, however, several important distinctions between the Italian and the German systems. The Italian system, at least in theory, aims to provide for economic autonomy and the administrative self-government of the various economic groups; hence the title of the corporative state given to the Italian system. In the German system, on the other hand, the estates are openly and admittedly mere organs of the state, or rather agencies for the control of all phases of economic life by the state and party. In Italy the corporations, in theory at least, participate in the formation of national economic policies. In Germany the estates merely seek to apply and carry out the policies laid down by the government.

Another important distinction between the German and the Italian systems is that the Italian system makes at least a pretense at preserving democratic self-government, inasmuch as the officers of each syndicate are "nominated" by the members of the syndicate itself, even though their appointment has to be confirmed by the government. In Germany, on the other hand, in strict conformity with the "leadership principle" (authority from above rather than from below), the administrative hierarchy of each estate is selected by the government entirely on its own initiative. Another very important difference between the two systems is that the Italian system preserves certain class distinctions, while in Germany such distinctions are theoretically wiped out. The Italian Fascists tell us that the nation is more important than any class and that the welfare of each class must be subordinated to national interests, but class organization is still permitted to exist. There is a syndicate for employers and a syndicate for employees in each field of economic enterprise. In Germany, on the other hand, class distinctions are supposedly ignored. The food estate includes both landlords, tenant farmers, and agricultural workers. The labor front includes both the owners of factories, executive officers, and the rank and file of the skilled and unskilled workers. In all points the German system is both more authoritarian and more totalitarian than its Italian counterpart.

A word should be said about the operation of each of the three major estates — the food or nutrition estate, the estate of trade and industry, and the labor front. It should be noted that the food estate is certainly as important as either of the others. This is partly due to the great emphasis which the Nazis lay upon agriculture and the agricultural section of the population. The Nazis are convinced that the real strength of a nation lies in its soil and with the persons who live on and from the soil. The Nazis tell us:

> The Germany of the future can only be a peasant state or it will disappear like the empires of the Hohenstaufens and Hohenzollerns.... All the blows of fate, all crises can be overcome if a healthy and strong peasantry forms the living foundations of a people. Nations which sacrificed their peasantry to a mammonism not rooted in the people vanished forever from the stage of history.[94]

Because of this attitude the Nazis preach the superiority of rural to urban life. They bemoan the too rapid industrialization and urbanization which took place during the nineteenth century. They are convinced that the state must check the constant flow of population from the farms to the factories and the growth of huge municipal communities.

The Nazis are also convinced that for agriculture to be protected from internal decay it is necessary first to improve the social status of the farmer, especially the small farmer, and secondly, to give him increased economic security, especially by preventing the loss of his lands through foreclosure on mortgages. With this end in view the Nazis passed the Hereditary Farm Law in 1933. According to this act, all small farmers owning their own land were to be made members of a petty "nobility," with a title which we may translate as "hereditary yeoman." In this manner the farmers were at once made into a specially privileged class, with a number of duties and rights peculiarly their own. All estates up to about three hundred acres were converted into hereditary home-steads. Upon the yeoman's death the estate passes undivided to his oldest (sometimes to his youngest) son or to the nearest male relative. The other children do not share in the inheritance of the land, though they are entitled to claim support from the farm and in turn are liable to service on the farm. The yeoman, moreover, has no right to sell or to mortgage his estate or any part thereof without permission of the local hereditary farm tribunal. The soil is thus made sacred and inalien-able. Further additional laws and decrees prohibit surplus imports from abroad and arrange for certain special marketing facilities, with the result that the farmer is no longer exposed to the vicissitudes of ordinary market fluctuations. In practice, whatever the farmer pro-duces is sold in advance and at a "fair price" determined by the state.

But important as are the hereditary yeomen and their hereditary estates, they constitute only one element in the huge food estate, for this estate includes all persons and all groups of persons who are directly concerned with the production, processing, and distribution of food-stuffs. It thus includes both farmers and landless agricultural workers, and also the manufacturers of foodstuffs, such as cheese, sugar, and beer. The food estate has also absorbed the numerous farmers' cooperatives and other similar organizations which existed prior to the advent of the Nazi regime. The food estate, as all the other estates, is organized on the leadership principle. Its head, the national peasant leader, appoints the chief officers of the organization, who again appoint their subordinates and so on all down the line. We are expressly told that it is the duty of the state to lay down the general lines of policy and that it is the duty of the food estate, with its huge complex organization, to see that this policy is duly carried out.

The ultimate goal of the food estate is to create in Germany a bal-anced economy whereby the supply of and the demand for foodstuffs will be in a state of equilibrium. In order to realize this aim, all the members of the estate are subjected to very severe regimentation. The farmer is no longer free to plant and grow whatever he sees fit. If the government so orders, he must let his land lie fallow, and if he is permitted to plant crops he must plant those crops and in those quanti-ties which the state authorities consider best in accord with "the national welfare." Farmers are required to deliver at specific dates specified amounts of grain. In like manner millers receive definite orders as to how much, and what kind of grain they are to mill. Finally, the food estate, acting for the government, has the power to fix all prices, both of raw and of finished articles. It has also the power to close temporarily or permanently any grocery store, mill, or bakery which it considers economically unsound or otherwise undesirable.

Membership in the estate of trade and industry is compulsory for all firms engaging in any industrial or commercial enterprise, except for those directly concerned with agriculture. This estate also embraces a large number of professional organizations, as well as numerous local and provincial chambers of commerce and industry. Control over the whole estate is centered in a national economic chamber. This chamber, like the other Nazi institutions, is also based on the leadership principle. The leader or president of the chamber is appointed by the Minister of Economics and can be removed by him at any time and for any reason whatsoever. All other officials of this estate and of all its ramifications are appointed from above and not elected from below, as was formerly the case with the old trade associations. In this way the state, directly or indirectly, has practically unlimited power over the entire business of the country and unlimited possibilities for influencing it. When we remember that industry and big business helped Hitler secure power in order to get rid of the threat of communism, it is interesting to find that they have found in the Nazi regime a master which is almost as stern. In Germany, even more than in Italy, the rights of private ownership and private initiative have been subjected to many serious limitations.

In the first place, the state has complete control over the currency, which has no gold backing, but is a "managed" currency, the management of which lies in the hands of government officials. Even more important is the fact that the state exercises complete control over credit and credit expansion. The Reichsbank, or National Bank, which was formerly run by an elected board and an elected president, is now entirely controlled by a president appointed by the government. A bank supervision board, another state-appointed organ, possesses and exercises wide powers over all other banking institutions. A bank reform law prohibits the opening of new credit institutions or new branches of existing credit institutions without special governmental permissions. As a result of these measures, credit is cut off from those business enterprises which fail to cooperate wholeheartedly with the Nazi regime and ample credit is available to those enterprises which the regime considers useful or desirable.

Moreover, the state, through the national economic chamber, has the power to interfere directly with any industrial or commercial firm. The state can demand the creation of new establishments or the closing of existing ones. No firm can even expand its existing plant if in the opinion of the authorities its present capacity is adequate to meet the need. The "one-price" stores and the chain stores (the German equivalent of our A. and P. or National Tea Stores) have always been unpopular with the Nazi leaders. Those already in existence are permitted to continue in operation, but the opening of more such concerns is altogether prohibited. In the future, moreover, no new retail shop can be opened without a license, and the issuance of such a license is made dependent, not only on the need of a new shop in the locality, but also on the "moral and professional standing" of the applicant. The government, too, has extensive powers over the creation, transformation, and dissolution of trusts and combines (which in Germany are called "cartels"). The government may at any time force an individual firm to enter a cartel. In many cases the mere threat of compulsory cartelization is sufficient to prevent a firm from underselling or otherwise engaging in "unfair" competition with its rivals.

Even inside the individual firm the state may and frequently does prescribe types, quality, and quantity of production. It may and frequently does lay down the number of hours the laborer must work, the wages he must be paid, the wholesale and retail price of the finished article. By way of carrying out the principle that the ownership of property is merely trusteeship, a special law was passed which provides that the owner of a business may be removed if he abuses his authority by maliciously exploiting the labor of any of his employees or "wounding their sense of honor."

> Instances of the removal of owners are rare, but have, nevertheless, occurred, usually on the ground of "anti-social conduct." For example, a baker in the Rheinland had trouble with his employees. His establishment was inspected and declared unsanitary. The owner was removed and replaced by a trustee appointed by local authorities. The salary of the trustee was paid from the profits of the enterprise and the owner was entitled to whatever was left over.[95]

Instances of this sort are comparatively rare, but they are still numerous enough to have made most German business men completely subservient to governmental prompting.

The last, the largest, and the most comprehensive of the estates into which the German populace is divided is the labor front. The labor front is defined as "the organization of Germans engaged in productive work, whether of brain or hand." This means that the labor front includes, not only laborers in the ordinary sense of the word (employees and factory hands), but also independent artisans and employers, both great and small, as well as members of the liberal professions, on the ground that all such persons are engaged in "productive work." In practice the labor front includes the members of the food estate, the estate of trade and industry, and in addition all other persons who earn their living and who are not otherwise organized. Small wonder that whereas the old pre-Nazi trade unions numbered altogether only about five million persons, the new labor front (which has supposedly taken the place of the trade unions) has a membership of over thirty millions. This huge number is due to the fact that membership, for all practical purposes, is compulsory, as no one is allowed to secure any gainful occupation unless he is possessed of a membership card.

The organization of the labor front shows clearly one of the principal differences between Fascism and National Socialism. Fascism still believes in a conflict, even though a controlled and regulated conflict, between capital and labor, and has built up its corporate state on the basis of two separate but parallel sets of organizations, one for the employers, the other for employees. According to the Nazi ideology, however, the employer is not an hereditary enemy of labor, but is merely a co-worker in a common enterprise, and both employers and employees must "work together for the furtherance of the purposes of the enterprise and for the benefit of the nation and the state in general." More specifically, it is said that in any well-conducted business enterprise the employer must be regarded as the leader and the employees are the leader's loyal followers. From this point of view it seems to the Nazis only natural that both the leaders and the followers should be members of the same labor front, and also that the labor front must, by appropriate regulations, see to it that the relations between leaders and followers be kept on an ideal basis. In other words, the labor front is not a representation of labor interests, but is an organ of the totalitarian state for the regimentation of labor.

According to the Nazi creed, it is the function of the state and of its organ, the labor front, to teach "the nobility of creative labor." As part of this educational program the state has passed a law requiring all young men, irrespective of their social or economic background, to spend six months in a labor camp doing physical labor for the state by way of preliminary training for a life of labor later. In addition to providing this initial training, the state, through the labor front, must also tell its citizens how much labor shall be done and under what conditions. In a liberal state each youth has the right to choose what occupation he would like to enter. In Nazi Germany, on the other hand, all youngsters when first seeking employment are registered with an official employment agency and are given jobs in accordance with the needs of industry, quite irrespective of their preferences. In a liberal state, if a worker is dissatisfied with his present post he is free to seek another one or even to choose an entirely different occupation. In Nazi Germany no worker or employee may leave a job without the permission of the leader of the local labor office.

Under a law passed in 1938 this same official was given the power to assign to anyone, no matter what his present occupation, any kind of employment which the state deems advisable and for an indefinite period. Lack of training is not considered an excuse for refusal to take an assigned post, as whoever is called must undergo training to fit him for whatever labor may be assigned to him. In many cases small unremunerative shops have been closed and the owners and employees drafted for work in the factories. Thousands of workers from relatively unimportant factories have been involuntarily transferred to do work on "nationally important" undertakings, such as the making of munitions or fortifications.

The conditions of labor are controlled by the state through its numerous regulations affecting wages and the number of hours a week each employee shall work. General control over labor conditions is placed in the hands of a so-called trustee of labor (there are fourteen such persons, one for each industrial subdivision of the country), who is, of course, appointed by the state and is always a staunch National Socialist. It is the duty of the local labor trustee to fix a general norm for wages and working conditions in his district, to which norm all local leaders or employers are expected to adhere. The labor trustee, moreover, has the right to order wage changes in any individual plant, and employers are prohibited from making any alteration in wages or living conditions without first securing the consent of this official.

The Nazi regime, like the Italian, strictly prohibits both strikes and lockouts, but in Italy collective bargaining between the employer and the employee groups is still permitted. In Germany, owing to the peculiar organization of the labor front, even this procedure is ruled out. Normally in every industrial or commercial firm the owner or employer, as the leader of the "common enterprise," must make the decisions "in all matters that affect the establishment." In enterprises employing twenty or more workers, however, the employer is forced to consult with, but is not bound to follow the advice of, an advisory council, consisting of from two to twenty persons who are elected by the employees from a list drawn up by the employer and the head of the Nazi Party organization in the plant. In case the workers reject this and other lists presented to them, the council is appointed by the labor trustee. All disputes which arise between the employers and his advisory council or any employee is brought in the first instance before the labor trustee for arbitration. For more serious disputes there is provision for settlement by more elaborate labor courts, and social honor courts.

The Nazi regime, through the labor front, has been amazingly successful in what we may call the commercial exploitation of non-commercial incentives.

> Social philosophers ... have long held that "man does not live by bread alone." But only recently has industry learned that significant as hours and wages and other conditions of employment may be, they do not themselves call out the highest levels of labor productivity. ... Interest and emotional drives lead to higher and better sustained levels of output than can be provided by mere wage and hour considerations. With non-commercial incentives, fatigue is lowered, improvements in processes and methods are more easily introduced and friction between management and men is reduced to a minimum.[96]

The Nazis were not the first to make this discovery, but they have applied it more consistently and on a larger scale than anyone else. The Nazis felt that it is necessary for the German laborers to work for long hours and at low wages, but argued that these long hours and low wages could be compensated for by stimulating surroundings. Labor front officials are constantly and successfully urging factory owners to build clean bright plants and maintain strict sanitary conditions, so that the laborers can more readily come to believe in the "dignity of labor." Moreover, under labor front pressure much is done to beautify the plants, both by employers and employees, on the ground that the more beautiful the surroundings the better the quality of work.

The most important development in the use of non-commercial incentives throughout the labor world is the so-called "strength through joy" division of the labor front. Copied from the *dopolavoro* organization of the Italian Fascists, though considerably improved upon, it provides, in times of peace at least, a vast number of individuals with low·cost tours throughout Germany, a smaller number with ocean trips and aims to provide every German worker with one vacation trip a year. It also makes provision for all kinds of sports, encourages the development of folk customs and traditions, provides travelling and stationary theaters and cinemas, and engages in various forms of culture work.[97]

Incidentally it may be said that the "strength through joy" movement serves a twofold purpose. On the principle that better vacations make for better work, it aids in improving the quantity and quality of industrial output. At the same time this same organization aids the Nazis in establishing a completely totalitarian regime. As a result of the "strength through joy" movement so many activities are carried out under the auspices of the state that the worker is never left alone, even after work, but is made to feel conscious of the omnipresent solicitude of the Nazi state.

THE NAZIS AND AUTHORITARIANISM

The Nazi regime, both in theory and in practice, is as wholehearted in its acceptance of authoritarianism as in its acceptance of etatism. In fact, the Nazi theory of the ideal form of government is little more than an echo of the statement made by Carlyle in 1840 when he said:

Find in any country the ablest man that exists there; raise him to the supreme place and loyally reverence him: you have a perfect government for that country; no ballot box, parliamentary eloquence, voting, constitution building or other machinery can improve it a whit. It is the perfect state, the ideal community.[98]

The Nazis, like Carlyle, are violent in their attacks upon any and every form of democratic or parliamentary government. According to Hitler:

Democracy of the West today is the forerunner of Marxism, which would be inconceivable without it. It is democracy alone which furnishes this universal plague with the soil in which it spreads. In parliamentarism, its outward form of expression, democracy created a "monstrosity of filth and fire." ... Is it at all possible to make a wavering majority of people ever responsible? Is not the very idea of all responsibility closely connected with the individual? ... Must not the task of the leading statesman be seen in the birth of a creative idea or plan in itself, rather than in the ability to make the ingenuity of his plans understandable to a flock of sheep and empty-heads for the purpose of begging for their gracious consent? Is the inability of a leader proved by the fact that he does not succeed in winning the majority of a crowd of people for a certain idea? ... Is not every ingenious deed in this world the

visible protest of genius against the inertia of the masses? . . . The parliamentary principle of decision by majority, by denying the authority of the person and placing in its stead the number of the crowd in question, sins against the aristocratic basic idea of Nature. . . .[99]

Hitler assails democracy on the ground that in most so-called democracies, real authority rests, not with the elected representatives of the people, but with a few wire-pullers who work behind the scenes.

It is not the object of our present-day democratic parliamentarism to form an assembly of wise men, but rather to gather a crowd of mentally dependent ciphers. . . . Only thus is it possible that the actual wire-puller is able to remain cautiously in the background without ever being called to account.[100]

With his passionate hatred of the Jews, Hitler believes that democracy is a product of the Jewish spirit. To his mind the Jew seeks

the victory of "democracy" as he understands it because it eliminates the personality — and in its place it puts the majority of stupidity, incapacity, and last, but not least, cowardice.[101]

Hitler rejoices that the army served as a bulwark of the aristocratic tradition even during the time when the democratic principle was sweeping the political world.

The greatest service of the army of the old Reich was that, in a time of the general "counting by majority" of the heads, it put the heads above the majority. In the face of the Jewish democratic idea of a blind worship of numbers, the army upheld the faith in personality.[102]

Hitler attacks democracy from many different angles, but it soon becomes obvious that he lays greatest stress on the arguments taken over from the racialists and the eugenists, which may be summarized as follows: Just as some races are superior and others inferior, and the superior races have the natural God-given right to rule over the inferior races, so in like manner, within any one race certain individuals are vastly superior to the general average, and these individuals have a natural God-given right to rule over all the others. Or, to use Hitler's words:

Just as in general I have to evaluate the nations differently on the basis of the race to which they belong, thus also the individuals within a national community. . . . A view of life which, by rejecting the democratic mass idea, endeavors to give this world to the best people [i.e. race], that means to the most superior men, has logically to obey the same aristocratic principle also within this people and has to guarantee leadership and highest influence within the respective people to the best heads. With this it does not build up on the idea of the majority, but on that of the personality. . . . Organization has to start from the principle that for humanity blessing has never lain in the masses, but in its creative heads. . . . It is in the interest of all to safeguard their most decisive influence and to facilitate their activity. Certainly, this interest is not satisfied and is not served by the rule of the masses who are either unable to think or are inefficient, in any case not inspired, but solely by the leadership of those whom Nature has endowed with special gifts.[103]

Arguing from these premises, Hitler comes to the conclusion that

the best State constitution and State form is that which, with the most nat-ural certainty, brings the best heads of the national community to leading importance and to leading influence. . . . The State in its organization, be-ginning with the smallest cell of the community up to the highest leadership of the entire Reich, must be built upon the principle of personality. There must be no decisions by majority, but only responsible persons, and the word "council" is once more reduced to its original meaning. At every man's side there stand councillors, but *one man decides.* The principle which once made the Prussian army the most marvellous instrument of the German people has to be some day in a transformed meaning the principle of the construc-tion of our whole State constitution: *Authority of every leader towards be-low, and responsibility towards above.* Even then one will not be able to do without those corporations which today we call parliaments. The coun-cillors will then actually give counsel, but responsibility can and must be borne always by *one* man and thus he alone can and must have the authority and right of command. . . . No voting ever takes place in any chamber. . . . They are working institutions and not voting machines. The individual member has an advisory vote but never a deciding one. The latter is the exclusive privilege of the respective responsible chairman.[104]

All the Nazis are in agreement that the foolish many shall be con-trolled by the wise few and that the wise few, in their turn, must be guided by a single leader. In practical politics this means that the state should be ruled over by an absolute dictator who has the right to make and unmake any law he pleases and who directly or indirectly appoints and dismisses, on his own responsibility, all lesser members of the government. There seems, however, to be some difference of opinion among the Nazi ideologists as to how this absolute dictator should be chosen. Even Hitler, himself, is far from being consistent upon this point. In some passages he tells us that the supreme ruler should be elected by the people. "The [Nazi] movement in small things as well as in big things represents the principle of Germanic democracy: choice of the leader, but absolute authority of the latter." [105] At other times he is extremely skeptical of all forms of electoral machinery.

One cannot contradict too sharply the absurd opinion that men of genius are born out of general elections. . . . The masses' aversion to every superior genius is an instinctive one. It is easier for a camel to go through the eye of a needle than that a great man is "discovered" in an election.[106]

Rosenberg agrees with his chief in denying the virtues of the electoral process.

> As things are today the nation is very seldom able directly to recognize a great man. . . . In ordinary life the election of a President or of an Emperor is only a question of gold bags. As a result in ninety-nine out of a hundred cases it is an agent of the Stock Market, of High Finance rather than a true national leader who comes to the top. For this reason the future German Nation-state must completely break with this aspect of a deceitful democracy.[107]

In view of these statements it seems that true Nazi ideology demands that the wise few should *impose* a leader upon the sheep-like multitude. In practice, moreover, we know that Hitler has already nominated his successor with no attempt made at finding out whom the German populace would prefer to have.

The National Socialists, like the Fascists, are also thoroughgoing authoritarians in that they attack the theory of check and balance and of the separation of powers. To them the one all-powerful leader must have control over both the executive and the legislative functions, and at least indirectly over the judicial functions as well. As yet the Reichstag has not been abolished, but it now serves merely as a sounding board for the Fuehrer whenever the latter wishes to direct public attention to some important new policy. The Reichstag has formally delegated to the government, i.e., to Hitler, practically all its legislative functions, and the vast majority of the new laws in Nazi Germany are, technically speaking, not laws at all but executive decrees. The raising and spending of money are matters resting entirely with the government, the Reichstag no longer being even consulted on such matters. It goes without saying that the government has complete control over the conduct of foreign affairs, the making of war, and the signing of treaties.

In like manner Hitler completely dominates the judicial branch of the state and there is no longer even a pretense of maintaining an independent judiciary. The Fuehrer has not only the privilege of mercy, but also the power of quashing pending criminal proceedings. More important still, when, in the early stages of the regime, some of the courts were bold enough to question the validity of certain governmental acts, the government promptly withdrew consideration of such cases from the ordinary courts and placed them under special new courts dominated by Nazi partisans. Bit by bit "politically unreliable" members of the judicial profession have been weeded out by outright dismissal and their places taken by persons devoted to the Nazi cause, who openly subscribe to the doctrine that whatever the Fuehrer wills to be law is law and therefore binding upon all judges and courts.

The very fact that the Nazis, like the Fascists, have abolished all minority or opposition parties is another sign of the Nazi acceptance of the authoritarian principle. Equally significant is the fact that the Nazis vehemently deny that the government must rest upon the consent of the governed and that all the powers which the government possesses are those delegated by the people. The denial of both these doctrines is very clearly summarized in the famous Nazi slogan, "The laws of Nature demand that authority shall be exercised from above downward, and responsibility from below upward." From this it follows that at all times the government must be willing to use force against any subjects who dare to rebel or even to protest against it. As Hitler tells us:

> An institution which is no longer determined to defend itself with all weapons practically gives itself up. Every half measure is then the visible symptom of internal decay which will and must be followed, sooner or later, by external collapse.[108]

Hitler further tells us that force to be successful must be used ruthlessly, relentlessly, and persistently.

> The very first condition for such a manner of fight with the weapons of pure force is, and always will be, perseverance. That means that only the continued and regular use of the methods applied for suppressing a doctrine permits of the possibility of success. As soon as intermittent force alternates with indulgence, the doctrine to be suppressed will not only recover again and again, but it will be able to draw new values from every persecution. ... Only in the eternally regular use of force lies the preliminary condition for success.[109]

The Nazis proceed to assure us that a government is willing to embark upon the "eternally regular use of force" only if its members and their immediate aids are imbued with fanatical zeal. Hence fanaticism and fiery zeal are the essential features of a successful and stable administration.

> The greatness of every powerful organization ... is rooted in the religious fanaticism with which it intolerably enforces itself against everything else, fanatically convinced of its own right.[110]
> The nationalization of the great masses can never take place by way of half measures, by a weak emphasis upon a so-called objective viewpoint, but by a ruthless and fanatically one-sided orientation as to the goal to be aimed at. ... The driving force of the most important changes in this world has

been found less in a scientific knowledge animating the masses, but rather in a fanaticism dominating them and in a hysteria which drove them forward. ... One can only succeed in winning the soul of a people if, apart from a position of positive fighting of one's own for one's own aims, one also destroys at the same time the supporter of the contrary.[111]

The foregoing quotations alone are enough to convince us that the Nazis are thoroughgoing authoritarians, and that being authoritarians they are vehemently opposed to democratic control over the machinery of government. At the same time it must be noted that in National Socialism, as in Fascism, there are a number of ideas which can only be described as being democratic in character. In the first place the Nazis, like the Fascists, but to a far greater degree, insist upon equality of opportunity for promotion to leadership, irrespective of a person's social or economic background. In other words, they insist upon "a career open to talent," or, to use Carlyle's phrase, "the tools to him who can best use them." On this point Nazi authoritarianism differs markedly from the type of authoritarianism dominant in the sixteenth and seventeenth centuries. This earlier type of authoritarianism was largely centered in a belief that special powers and privileges should be accorded to an hereditary aristocracy and more especially to an hereditary monarchy. As we have already seen, the Nazis have no use whatsoever for an hereditary aristocracy or at least for the sort of hereditary aristocracy which existed in pre-war Germany. They are equally skeptical of the virtues of hereditary monarchy. As Hitler tells us

only in the rarest cases are the monarchs the elite of wisdom and reason, or even of character. ... The fortune to possess a great monarch in the person of a great man falls only so rarely to the share of the people that they have to be content if the malice of Fate at least abstains from making the very worst mistake.[112]

The state must indeed be run by an aristocracy, and the aristocracy must be headed by an all-powerful leader, but according to Nazi theory, this aristocracy shall be an aristocracy of talent and not of birth. Or, as Hitler puts it, "The best state constitution ... is that which brings the best heads of the national community to leading importance and to leading influence." [113] For this reason Hitler dislikes the rigid class distinctions which were so characteristic of old Germany. He assails the old army system according to which the members of the upper and upper middle classes were given special privileges and served for a shorter period of time in the ranks than the masses.[114] Above all, Hitler is insistent that the higher educational institutions, from which the leaders of the future are to be chosen, must be open to boys of genuine talent from all classes and not merely to the scions of well-to-do families.[115] Hitler declares that Germany and other secular states can well learn something from the Catholic Church in this respect.

> In the celibacy of its priests roots the compulsion to draw the future generation of the clergy, instead of from its own ranks, again and again from the broad masses of the people. . . . It is the origin of the incredibly vigorous power that inhabits this age-old institution. This gigantic host of clerical dignitaries, by uninterruptedly supplementing itself from the lowest layers of the nations, preserves not only its instinctive bond with the people's world of sentiment, but it also assures itself of a sum of energy and active force which in such a form will forever be present only in the broad masses of the people. . . . It will be the task of the folkish State to take care by its educational arrangements that, by fresh infusion of blood from below, a perpetual renovation of the existing intellectual layers takes place.[116]

National Socialism, like Fascism, may also claim to be democratic in that it makes a tremendous effort to secure popular support for its ideas and its policies. For all its authoritarianism the Nazi movement, like its Italian prototype, is essentially a mass movement. The Nazi regime is not the dictatorship of a select few who are far removed from the madding crowd; it is rather the dictatorship of a mob which has been stampeded into action and then guided and controlled by a few master manipulators, who in turn are led by a man whose chief claim to genius is his superb insight into mob psychology. To secure mass support it is sometimes necessary to use only coaxing or theatrical effects in speaking or writing. It is sometimes necessary to use force, for when it will not be coaxed the mob can frequently be terrorized into rendering blind obedience. But in any event the Nazis are convinced that it is necessary at all costs to win the support of the masses, whatever the means employed. "A view of life may in general only hope for victory if the broad masses, as the bearers of the new doctrine, declare themselves ready to take upon themselves the necessary fight." [117] To be permanently successful a political movement must above all "devote itself to winning over the masses. . . . One needs the children from the great masses of the nation. They alone are determined and tough enough to fight this struggle to the bloody end." [118]

NOTES TO CHAPTER TWELVE

1. H. Billinger, *Hitler Is No Fool*, p. 10.
2. Goebbels, *My Part in Germany's Fight*, pp. 205 ff.
3. F. L. Schuman, *The Nazi Dictatorship*, p. 105. By permission of Alfred A. Knopf, Inc.
4. *Ibid.*
5. Compare the American Townsend Movement, which has also drawn its strength from the lower middle classes.
6. S. H. Roberts, *The House that Hitler Built*, p. 44. By permission of Harper and Brothers.
7. Schuman, *op. cit.*, p. 195.
8. *Ibid.*, p. 232.
9. Adolf Hitler, *Mein Kampf*, p. 358. By permission of Houghton Mifflin Company.
10. A. Rosenberg, *Wesensgefüge des Nationalsozialismus*, p. 9.
11. Rosenberg, *Der Mythus des 20ten Jahrhunderts*, p. 525.
12. *Ibid.*, pp. 119, 146.
13. Hitler, *Mein Kampf*, pp. 410, 412.
14. *Ibid.*, p. 411.
15. *Ibid.*, p. 447.
16. *Ibid.*, pp. 230–237.
17. *Ibid.*, p. 200.
18. Hitler, *My Battle*, p. 166; *Mein Kampf*, p. 613. By permission of Houghton Mifflin Company.
19. Hitler, *My Battle*, p. 178; *Mein Kampf*, p. 642.
20. Rosenberg, *Der Mythus des 20ten Jahrhunderts*, p. 520.
21. *Ibid.*, p. 545.
22. Hitler, *Mein Kampf*, p. 224.
23. Rosenberg, *Der Mythus des 20ten Jahrhunderts*, p. 287.
24. Quoted in M. Rader, *No Compromise*, p. 22.
25. Rosenberg, *Der Mythus des 20ten Jahrhunderts*, p. 137.
26. *Ibid.*, p. 117.
27. *Ibid.*, p. 119.
28. *Ibid.*, p. 120.
29. Quoted in Rader, *op. cit.*, p. 31.
30. *Ibid.*, p. 30.
31. *Ibid.*, p. 29.
32. Point 29.
33. Rosenberg, *Der Mythus des 20ten Jahrhunderts*, p. 697.
34. M. Oakeshott, *Social and Political Doctrines of Contemporary Europe*, p 198 By permission of the Cambridge University Press and The Macmillan Company publishers.
35. Hitler, *My Battle*, p. 25.
36. Rosenberg, *Der Mythus des 20ten Jahrhunderts*, p. 560.
37. *Ibid.*, p. 25.
38. Quoted in Rader, *op. cit.*, p. 164.
39. Hitler, *Mein Kampf*, p. 171.
40. *Ibid.*, pp. 197–198.
41. *Ibid.*, p. 407.
42. *Ibid.*, p. 598.
43. *Ibid.*, pp. 404, 405.
44. Rosenberg, *Der Mythus des 20ten Jahrhunderts*, p. 485.
45. *Ibid.*, p. 486.

46. Hitler, *Mein Kampf*, p. 406.
47. H. L. Childs, *The Nazi Primer*, pp. 5–7. By permission of Harper and Brothers.
48. *Ibid.*, p. 59.
49. Hitler, *Mein Kampf*, p. 103.
50. *Ibid.*, pp. 390, 391.
51. *Ibid.*, p. 103.
52. Childs, *The Nazi Primer*, p. 68.
53. Hitler, *Mein Kampf*, p. 608.
54. L. Loewenstein, *Hitler's Germany*, p. 106. By permission of The Macmillan Company, publishers.
55. Hitler, *Mein Kampf*, p. 406.
56. Rosenberg, *Wesensgefüge des Nationalsozialismus*, pp. 12, 13.
57. Hitler, *Mein Kampf*, p. 469.
58. *Ibid.*, p. 396.
59. *Ibid.*
60. *Ibid.*, p. 640
61. *Ibid.*, pp. 398, 399.
62. *Ibid.*, p. 414.
63. *Ibid.*, p. 398.
64. Childs, *The Nazi Primer*, p. 15.
65. *Ibid.*, p. 34.
66. *Ibid.*, p. 20.
67. *Ibid.*, p. 31.
68. Rosenberg, *Der Mythus des 20ten Jahrhunderts*, pp. 102–104.
69. Childs, *The Nazi Primer*, p. 33.
70. Rosenberg, *Der Mythus des 20ten Jahrhunderts*, p. 113.
71. Hitler, *Mein Kampf*, p. 452.
72. *Ibid.*, p. 598.
73. *Ibid.*, p. 390.
74. *Ibid.*, pp. 588–591.
75. Mussolini, in *Fascism, Doctrine and Institutions*, p. 12.
76. Rosenberg, *Der Mythus des 20ten Jahrhunderts*, p. 542.
77. Hitler, *Mein Kampf*, pp. 122, 592, 595.
78. *Ibid.*, pp. 346, 348.
79. Rosenberg, *Der Mythus des 20ten Jahrhunderts*, p. 572.
80. Quoted in Robert A. Brady, *The Spirit and Structure of German Fascism*, p. 79. Copyright, 1937, by Robert A. Brady. By permission of The Viking Press, Inc., New York.
81. *Ibid.*, p. 99.
82. Hitler, *Mein Kampf*, p. 354.
83. *Ibid.*, p. 330.
84. Loewenstein, *Hitler's Germany*, pp. 164, 165.
85. *National Socialistische Monatshefte*, ed. by Rosenberg, September, 1933.
86. Delivered February 22, 1936.
87. In a speech delivered in Saarbruecken, January, 1935.
88. In his book *Gottglauebiges Volk*.
89. Meissner and Kaiserberg, *Staats und Verwaltungsrecht im dritten Reich*, p. 172
90. *Ibid.*
91. Quoted in Schuman, *The Nazi Dictatorship*, p. 370.
92. Meissner and Kaiserberg, *op. cit.*, p. 180.
93. Quoted in Roberts, *The House that Hitler Built*, p. 242.
94. Quoted in Brady, *The Spirit and Structure of German Fascism*, p. 231.

NATIONAL SOCIALISM 675

95. M. T. Florinsky, *Fascism and National Socialism*, p. 108. By permission of
The Macmillan Company, publishers.
96. Brady, *op. cit.*, p. 122.
97. R. E. Westmeyer, *Modern Economic and Social Systems*, p. 483. By permission
of Farrar and Rinehart.
98. Carlyle, *Heroes and Hero Worship*, p. 197.
99. Hitler, *Mein Kampf*, pp. 99–103.
100. *Ibid.*, p. 116.
101. *Ibid.*, p. 436.
102. *Ibid.*, p. 386.
103. *Ibid.*, pp. 660, 661, 665.
104. *Ibid.*, pp. 669–671.
105. *Ibid.*, p. 478.
106. *Ibid.*, p. 113.
107. Rosenberg, *Der Mythus des 20ten Jahrhunderts*, p. 547.
108. Hitler, *Mein Kampf*, p. 336.
109. *Ibid.*, p. 222.
110. *Ibid.*, p. 487.
111. *Ibid.*, p. 468.
112. *Ibid.*, p. 324.
113. *Ibid.*, p. 669.
114. *Ibid.*, p. 385.
115. *Ibid.*, pp. 637, 641.
116. *Ibid.*, p. 644.
117. *Ibid.*, p. 127.
118. *Ibid.*, pp. 132, 136.

BIBLIOGRAPHY

PRIMARY. G. Feder, *Hitler's Official Programme and Its Fundamental Ideas*,
London, 1934. A. Hitler, *Mein Kampf* (complete English translation with
notes), New York, 1939. See also the earlier, incomplete, but much smoother
translation entitled *My Battle*, Boston, 1933. A. Rosenberg: *Der Mythus des
20ten Jahrhunderts*, twentieth edition, Munich, 1934; *Wesensgefüge des Na-
tionalsozialismus*, Munich, 1933; *Blut und Ehre*, seventeenth edition, Munich, 1938;
Gestaltung der Idee, Munich, 1938. H. Göring, *Germany Reborn*, London, 1934.
R. W. Darré: *Das Bauerntum als Lebensquell der Nordischen Rasse*, Munich, 1934;
Neuadel aus Blut und Boden, Munich, 1935. H. L. Childs, editor, *The Nazi
Primer*, New York, 1938.
SEMI-OFFICIAL. There are a number of books published under the auspices of
the Nazi Party for propaganda purposes. These are of some importance in trying
to understand the aims and purposes of the Nazi leaders. See especially P.
Bouhler, *Adolf Hitler*, Berlin, 1938. E. Schinnerer, *German Law and Legislation*,
Berlin, 1938. R. Frercks, *German Population Policy*, Berlin, 1938. T. Wilhelm
and G. Graefe, *German Education Today*, Berlin, 1937. F. Edel, *German Labour
Service*, Berlin, 1937. B. Rauecker, *Social Policy in the New Germany*, Leipzig,
1936. C. Santoro, *Hitler Germany as Seen by a Foreigner*, Berlin, 1938. O. Meiss-
ner and G. Kaiserberg, *Staats und Verwaltungsrecht im dritten Reich*, Berlin, 1935.
SECONDARY. K. Heiden, *Hitler, a Biography*, New York, 1936. H. A. Heinz,
Germany's Hitler, New York, 1934. E. Lengyel, *Hitler*, New York, 1932. R

Olden, *Hitler*, New York, 1936. T. Abel, *Why Hitler Came into Power*, New York, 1938. H. F. Armstrong, *Hitler's Reich, The First Phase*, New York, 1933. H. Billinger, *Hitler Is No Fool*, London, 1940. R. Brady, *The Spirit and Structure of German Fascism*, New York, 1937. O. Dutch, *Hitler's Twelve Apostles*, London, 1939. F. Ermarth, *The New Germany*, Washington, 1936. M. T. Florinsky, *Fascism and National Socialism*, New York, 1936. M. Fry, *Hitler's Wonderland*, London, 1934. K. Heiden, *History of National Socialism*, London, 1934. C. B. Hoover, *Germany Enters the Third Reich*, New York, 1933. A. Kolnai, *War Against the West*, New York, 1938. H. Lichtenberger, *The Third Reich*, New York, 1937. L. Loewenstein, *Hitler's Germany*, New York, 1939. F. M. Marx, *Government in the Third Reich*, New York, 1937. E. A. Mowrer, *Germany Puts the Clock Back*, second edition, New York, 1937. M. P. Nicolai, *From Nietzsche Down to Hitler*, London, 1938. M. Oakeshott, *The Social and Political Doctrines of Contemporary Europe*, Cambridge, 1939 (pp. 190 ff.). M. Rader, *No Compromise*, New York, 1939. H. Rauschning: *The Revolution of Nihilism*, New York, 1939; *The Voice of Destruction*, New York, 1940. S. H. Roberts, *The House that Hitler Built*, New York, 1938. F. L. Schuman, *The Nazi Dictatorship*, New York, 1935. L. L. Snyder, *From Bismarck to Hitler*, Williamsport, 1935. R. E. Westmeyer, *Modern Economic and Social Systems*, New York, 1940.

INDEX

678

INDEX